enigma
books

Colonel Paul Paillole

Fighting the Nazis

French Military Intelligence
and
Counterintelligence

1935-1945

enigma books

Enigma Books
580 Eighth Avenue, New York, NY 10018
www.enigmabooks.com

Originally published in French under the title:
SERVICES SPÉCIAUX 1935-1945

Translated by Robert L. Miller

First English-language Edition
Printed in the United States of America
ISBN 1-929631-13-8

Library of Congress Cataloging-in-Publication Data

Paillole, Paul.
[Services speciaux, 1935-1945.]
Fighting the Nazis : French military intelligence and counterintelligence, 1935-1945 / Paul Paillole ; translated by Robert L. Miller. — 1st English-language ed.

p. : ill. ; cm.

Includes index.

ISBN: 1-929631-13-8

1. Paillole, Paul. 2. World War, 1939-1945—Secret service—France. 3. World War, 1939-1945—Secret service—Germany. 4. World War, 1939-1945—Personal narratives, French. 5. Intelligence service—France. I. Miller, Robert L. (Robert Lawrence), 1945- II. Title. III. Title: Services spéciaux, 1935-1945.

D810.S7 P34 2003
940.54/85

Fighting the Nazis

French Military Intelligence
and
Counterintelligence

1935-1945

Table of Contents

PART III

DELIVERANCE
November 1942–November 1944

Main Abbreviations and Acronyms

Abwehr	German military intelligence
AFN	*Afrique du Nord*—French North Africa
AMGOT	Allied Military Government in Occupied Territories
AOF	*Afrique Occidentale Française*—French West Africa
AS	*Armée Secrète*—Secret Army
Ast	*Abwehrstelle* or Abwehr substation
BBC	British Broadcasting Corporation
BCRA	*Bureau Central de Renseignement et d'Action*—Gaullist intelligence service in London headed by André Dewawrin, alias "Passy"
BMA	*Bureau des Menées Anti-Nationales*—Vichy military counterintelligence
BSM	*Bureau de Sécurité Militaire*—military security
Cagoule	literally, "the hood"; secret fascist group dedicated to violent action headed by Eugène Deloncle; uncovered in 1937. See CSAR, below
Cambronne	covert name for the headquarters of *Travaux Ruraux* in the Villa Eole in Marseille
Carabinieri	Italian military police with peacetime civilian assignments
CE	*Contre Espionnage*—Counterespionage
CFLN	*Comité Français de Libération Nationale*—French Committee of National Liberation
Chistelle	short for Chifferstelle, encryption section of the Reich Defense Ministry
Cinquième Bureau	5th Bureau created in wartime combining all military intelligence units
CNR	*Comité National de la Résistance*—main resistance committee inside France headed by Jean Moulin, then by Georges Bidault
CSAR	*Comité Secret d'Action Révolutionnaire*, the official name of the "Cagoule"

Deuxième Bureau	2nd Bureau—equivalent of U.S. Army G2—as overall military intelligence directorate
DGER	*Direction Générale des Etudes et Recherches*, replaced the DGSS and was headed first by Jacques Soustelle, then by Passy in 1944-1945
DGSS	*Direction Générale des Services Spéciaux*—new unit replacing both the London-based BCRA and the traditional service in 1944; headed by Jacques Soustelle
DST	*Direction de la Surveillance du Territoire*—replaced the *Surveillance du Territoire* in 1944
Ecole de guerre	French war college
EMA	*Etat Major des Armées*—French army general staff
FFC	*Forces Françaises Combattantes* (Resistance networks, intelligence and action)
FFI	*Forces Françaises de l'Intérieur*—resistance movement inside France having military status
FFL	*Forces Françaises Libres*—de Gaulle's Free French in England
Force A	Allied counterintelligence and subversive action group acting behind enemy lines
Forschungsamt	Signals intelligence service created and controlled by Hermann Göring
GAD	*Groupes d'Autodéfense*—became the ORA
Gendarmerie Nationale	Local police force covering all French territory
GESTAPO	*Geheimstaatspolizei*—German secret police
GFP	*Gehiemfeldpolizei*—German secret military police force during wartime
GPRF	*Gouvernement Provisoire de la République Française*—French provisional government first set up by de Gaulle in Algiers
GQG	*Grand Quartier Général*—Supreme Army Headquarters
HC	*Honorable Correspondant*—secret agent in place of French intelligence
IRA	Irish Republican Army
IS	Intelligence Service alternate name used for British intelligence—MI6

KO	*Kriegsorganisation*—Abwehr station in a neutral or friendly country
KRIPO	*Kriminalpolizei*, the detective police force
LVF	*Légion des Volontaires Français Contre le Bolchevisme*—Vichy-sponsored French volunteers in the Waffen SS
Mesure D	Order to terminate immediately (summary execution)
Mesure F	Order to terminate at a later date (place on special list)
MI5	British Military Intelligence—counterintelligence
MI6	British Military Intelligence—foreign intelligence, also known as SIS or IS
Milice	*Milice Française*—Fascist-type police force organized in 1943 by Joseph Darnand under Vichy
MSR	*Mouvement Social Révolutionnaire*—collaborationist party headed by Eugène Deloncle (see "Cagoule")
ND	*Nachrichtendienst,* the secret intelligence service of Imperial Germany until 1918
NSDAP	*National Sozialsitische Deutsche Arbeiter Partei*—National Socialist Worker's Party, the official name of the Nazi Party
OKW	*Oberkommando der Wehrmacht*—German High Command
ORA	*Organisation de Résistance Armée*—French army resistance organization
OSS	Office of Strategic Services—U.S. intelligence service headed by William J. Donovan, 1942-1946
OVRA	*Organizzazione Volontaria Repressione Antifascismo*—Mussolini's secret police
PC	*Poste de Commandement*—command post
PCF	*Parti Communiste Français*—French Communist Party
Phalange Africaine	Collaborationist fighting group operating in Tunisia in 1943
PJ	*Police Judiciaire*—French police detectives
PPF	*Parti Populaire Français*—collaborationist party headed by Jacques Doriot
PTT	*Postes Téléphone et Télégraphe*—postal, telephone, and telegraph a government service in France
QG	*Quartier Général*—headquarters HQ
Quai d'Orsay	location and name of the French ministry of foreign affairs

RAF   Royal Air Force

RG   *Renseignements Généraux*—intelligence bureau of the police forces

RGPP   *Renseignements Généraux de la Préfecture de Paris* intelligence bureau of the Paris police prefecture

RNP   *Rassemblement National Populaire*—collaborationist party headed by Marcel Déat

RSHA   *Reichssicherheits Haupt Amt*—Nazi party main security office; included all SS and Gestapo security functions, headed by Reinhard Heydrich until 1942, then by Ernst Kaltenbrunner

SA   *Sûreté aux Armées*—militarized police force

SCR   *Section de Centralisation des Renseignements*—French military counterintelligence up to September 1939

SD   *Sicherheitsdienst*—Nazi party security force inside the RSHA

SDECE   *Service de Documentation Extérieure et de Contre-Espionnage*—successor to the DGER in 1945

Services Spéciaux   general name of the French intelligence services

SIM   *Servizio Informazioni Militari*—Italian military intelligence

SIPO   *Sicherheitspolizei* security police forces

SIS   Secret Intelligence Service: British foreign intelligence, also known as MI6

SM   *Sécurité Militaire*—Military Security protection of the French armed forces; until the end of 1944 it covered both military security proper and counterespionage

SN   *Sûreté Nationale*—French national police force

SNCF   *Société Nationale des Chemins de Fer Français*—French national railroads

SOE   British Special Operations Executive—operating behind enemy lines mainly for sabotage and providing help to the resistance

SOL   *Service d'Ordre Légionnaire*—action group of the Vichy *Légion Française des Combattants*

SR   *Service de Renseignements*—French foreign intelligence service part of the *Deuxième Bureau*

SS   *Schutzstaffeln*—Nazi Party elite formations originally intended to protect the leadership; later became large military units, such as the Waffen SS

SSM		*Service de Sécurité Militaire*—military security service
TR		*Travaux Ruraux*—literally "Rural Works"; organization used to camouflage French covert counterespionage from 1940 to 1944
	TR 112	Limoges headed by Rigaud
	TR 112 *bis*	Paris annex headed by Martineau
	TR 113	Clermont-Ferrand headed by Johanès
	TR 113 *bis*	Paris annex headed by Garder
	TR 114	Lyon headed by Hugon
	TR 115	Marseille headed by Guiraud
	TR 117	Toulouse headed by d'Hoffelize
	TR 119	Algiers headed by Doudot and later Allemand
	TR 120	Rabat headed by Breteil
	TR 121	Tunis headed by Fontès
	TR 125	Barcelona headed by Larquier
V. Mann		*Vertrauensmann*—"trustworthy man"; Abwehr agent
W.		French counterespionage penetration agent inside enemy services (not to be confused with a "double agent")
W. 2		Enemy penetration agent known to French counterespionage
ZL		*Zone Libre*—Free Zone under Vichy control; not occupied by the enemy until November 8, 1942
ZO		*Zone Occupée*—Occupied Zone under German occupation
Zone Interdite		"forbidden zone"—restricted occupation area located in northern France along the Belgian border

Publisher's Introduction

Few careers can match that of Colonel Paul Paillole of the French intelligence service. He entered the old offices of the *Service de Renseignement* at 2 *bis* Avenue de Tourville at the end of 1935 and served his country in his specialty of counterintelligence until November 1944, after ten epic years in the history of France and indeed the world. The traumas of 1940, defeat, Vichy and the occupation, collaboration, resistance and finally liberation swept so many men and women away in the world war that lasted for 5 years. Paul Paillole was actively involved in that struggle. This remarkable memoir is his legacy to the many French patriots who lost their lives in the cause of freedom from tyranny and chose to do their duty in ways that were to remain forever secret. Paillole was in the thick of the fight, as a staff officer in charge of counterespionage. Working closely with his commanding officer, Colonel Louis Rivet, he steered a mass of men and women in the silent fight against the Nazis, at war, in resistance, and later to victory.

Born in 1905, Paul Paillole was a graduate of Saint-Cyr, France's top military academy, which has traditionally filled the ranks of the officer corps. To his surprise, after a short period of service he was assigned for duty to the *Deuxième Bureau*, specializing in counterintelligence and analysis. These duties entailed both the responsibility for the proper use and management of the massive archives and files of French army intelligence located in the famous offices near the Invalides, and acting as case officer for a long list of informants and agents. His description of the atmosphere of those "darkened hallways" and the brilliant and quirky professionals who worked there in the 1930s (for example, the famous Colonel Bertrand, who broke the Enigma machine code, making it available to the British) and the work methods used are probably among the most vivid of any memoir by an intelligence officer. His devotion to his country and to his mission was nothing less than total. Paillole's discovery of intelligence and counterintelligence came as a real "coup de foudre" which, after the first few weeks, became the beacon for his entire military career, along with those other officers who shared his enthusiastic commitment. Paul Paillole died on October 15, 2002, at his home near Paris.

This book is filled with precious operational and organizational detail with references to and descriptions of literally hundreds of espionage and counterespionage cases taking place before and during the Second World War. In the interwar years the effectiveness of French counterespionage was greatly hampered by extremely lax peacetime laws that failed to effectively protect France from foreign spies. In fact, the reinforcement of the French legal system in peacetime and the new laws Paillole and his superiors were requesting were finally enacted in 1939, just a few months before the war began. By then German and Italian espionage operatives had done their damage, not so much in stealing French military secrets, but by sapping the morale of the French people and leadership and sowing doubt and fear in the minds of many.

France was riddled with subversive Nazi-leaning and deceptively neutralist and pacifist propaganda that ended up benefiting Germany in the late 1930s. A clearly defeatist atmosphere was pervasive leading up to 1939, and continuing even during the phony war when strict censorship controls were being enforced. Many of those pro-German organizations headed by extremists before 1939 slipped quite naturally into their role as collaborators once France was defeated in June 1940: de Brinon, Doriot, Déat, Paquis, Brasillach, Rebatet, and many others were ready and willing to work for the *propagandastaffel* and some of them later even volunteered to fight in Russia wearing Waffen SS uniforms. Paillole's counterespionage held a close watch over all these individuals, closer than the Gaullist BCRA in London, keeping a detailed list of traitors and collaborators of all kinds. In November 1944 Paillole estimated that there were some 20,000 dangerous and armed French traitors who had followed the retreating German armies back to Germany, Doriot and Laval among them.

Paillole's book raises a number of important issues about the intelligence function in France in 1935-1945; the main problem being the way intelligence was used by the military and political leadership. The German offensive of May 10, 1940, with its two-pronged attack into Holland and Belgium and main thrust through the Ardennes, which is still the subject of much debate among historians, was an event Paillole witnessed from the vantage point of counterintelligence. The Ardennes plan was known to French intelligence by April 1940 and Paillole was able to personally brief General Georges, second in command to Generalissimo Maurice Gamelin who was attending a conference in London at the time.[1] Apparently no special action was taken nor was it clear that the warning had been duly noted and passed along since it came among a flood of many other plausible and implausible warnings. The German attack on May 10, 1940 toward Sedan came as a surprise to the local commanders caught uninformed and unprepared.

On many occasions French intelligence clearly had to overcome as many obstacles to its effectiveness inside France's administrative and political sphere as it did in facing the enemy. A telling detail surfaces when, before the war, Paillole found out that there were many files and archives containing vitally important information on individuals engaged or suspected of engaging in espionage that were not accessible to military counterintelligence—in particular the files of the Paris police intelligence unit, the *Renseignements Généraux de la Préfecture de Paris* (RGPP). Gaining access to those files and collating the information they contained opened up new opportunities for military counterespionage. The firewall of administrative inertia and territorial behavior was possibly one of the main obstacles to effective counterintelligence in France (as in many other western countries) not just in the 1930s but also throughout most of its recent history. Information existed but it was buried among many organizations that failed to share it among themselves thereby endangering the necessary protection effort. The second obstacle was the evaluation of the information received and the task of convincing its potential users of its value. Many French politicians, for example Edouard Daladier, as prime minister and minister of war, relied more on their own "private" intelligence sources rather than on what Rivet and Paillole were providing, even though competent counterintelligence professionals had never vetted those mysterious private sources, an extremely dangerous practice for the political leadership.

The catastrophic defeat of 1940 was a defining moment for most French officers and soldiers. For the professionals, what almost all military experts had considered unthinkable as late as May 9, 1940, suddenly turned into the awful reality of the battles that cost France the war. Some sixty years after those momentous events, historians are still arguing whether or not that defeat was indeed inevitable or whether a set of incredibly favorable circumstances conspired in handing Hitler a victory he never dreamed could be so easy.[2] After the defeat and the armistice of 1940 only a handful of French officers and servicemen answered the call of General Charles de Gaulle in his London broadcast on June 18, 1940. The vast majority took a "wait and see" attitude and tried, for a time, to rationalize the policy of collaboration that followed the meeting bewteen Hitler and Pétain at Montoire on October 24, 1940. Most of the officers were not taken in by the collaborationist policies and other extreme measures, such as the anti-Semitic laws imposed by the Vichy regime. Only a very small minority of professional soldiers gave active support to those extremist views, going so far as to join the LVF to fight on the Russian front or working hand in hand with German intelligence and the Gestapo against other Frenchmen, as Paillole and his unit discovered.

Paillole and his men remained uncomfortably under Vichy rule until the Operation *Torch* landings in North Africa on November 8, 1942. The period of mounting frustration and fear from June 1940 to November 1942, when the Germans respected the terms of the armistice, permitted French counterintelligence to reorganize and fight the German presence at close range inside France. Paillole set up the covert *Travaux Ruraux*, the famous "*TR*" networks, that gathered massive information on German espionage networks, plans and capabilities, not just in France but also in North Africa and elsewhere in Europe. Quietly resisting an increasingly collaborationist government headed first by Pierre Laval, followed by Admiral Darlan, who oddly enough went even further down the path of military collaboration with Nazi Germany, French intelligence built its networks and worked actively with military resistance groups, such as *Combat*, created by Henri Frenay. By the time France was liberated in the summer of 1944 military counterespionage had a wealth of intelligence on the Nazis and their collaborators and was able to pinpoint the key individuals to be arrested or summarily executed. While Germany began its fateful string of losses after Stalingrad and the defeat in Tunisia, the effectiveness of the Abwehr also started to sink. French counterespionage was in place and organized to take advantage of the massive German intelligence failure.

In the complicated political triangle of Vichy and Generals Giraud and de Gaulle, Paillole points out two instances where his own career may have been affected by a simple decision. On both occasions, during his first trip to London in December 1942, immediately following his narrow escape from Vichy-controlled France and again when Paillole returned to London to prepare for counterespionage inside occupied France with Allied intelligence services, Passy—head of de Gaulle's intelligence service, the BCRA—asked Paillole whether he wished to meet with General de Gaulle. It was awkward enough in December 1942, since Paillole was not alone during his meeting with Passy and Colonel Ronin, who was also present, had made him promise that they would both refuse to see de Gaulle out of loyalty to Rivet, their chief in Algiers. On the second occasion while the de Gaulle-Giraud struggle was raging and Paillole still felt he owed his loyalty to Giraud, he again avoided a meeting with de Gaulle. Soon after, in 1943, the Gaullists gradually eased Giraud out of the leadership of the Free French government. De Gaulle took over both the French provisional government and the French army with Algiers as France's temporary capital. Paillole did eventually meet with de Gaulle in Algiers at that time and the meeting had a very positive outcome. But perhaps an old grudge lingered in de Gaulle's mind, affecting his attitude toward Paillole later in 1944 when, upon being asked to leave the Special Services, Paillole was refused a command in the field. The general's memory was known to run deep and he kept his own counsel.

Even though clearly a painful chapter for Paillole, the bitter rivalry that opposed Giraud and de Gaulle, the two French generals of the resistance, played an important part in the intelligence structure. There is no question that Paillole's preference went to the man with whom he identified the most, Henri Giraud, who had made a daring escape from a German military prison while his family suffered greatly at the hands of the Nazis. Giraud the military leader was not as politically savvy as de Gaulle who eventually became the sole head of the provisional government in Algiers in 1944. From that moment on the traditionalists' hold over French military intelligence was compromised and eventually terminated by de Gaulle's decision to split espionage from counterespionage. New men and a new organization emerged from the vast rearrangement in a liberated France, leading eventually to the creation of the SDECE in 1945. But it would be an oversimplification to say that Paillole and Rivet represented a "traditional" point of view that held to the concept of unity of the Special Services under one roof, namely intelligence gathering and counterespionage, while the "newcomers" such as Passy and Soustelle favored a radically different approach. Could it be that by splitting the intelligence services de Gaulle was responding to political requirements that were inevitably tied to the liberation of France? Keeping espionage separate from counterespionage must have contributed to many other problems that hampered the effectiveness of the French Special Services soon after by, among other things, reducing the degree of professionalism of its officers. The restructured French espionage establishment in 1944 had an impact on French intelligence during the cold war and the crises of the 1950s and 60s in Indochina and North Africa.

Clearly, excessive compartmentalization between intelligence and counterintelligence information and the obstacles to the flow of intelligence among competing and overlapping agencies as described here are disturbingly reminiscent of the explanation widely offered for what is called the American intelligence failure before the terrorist attacks of September 2001. The information existed but was scattered in such a way that couldn't help the officials in charge understand the true nature of the threat. Regarding the intelligence failure issue relating secret information to decision-making, Ernest May draws a rather troubling parallel: "And it must be added that in these respects the United States and most other democracies today resemble France and Britain of 1940, not Germany." [3]

These closing comments give an added sense of relevance to this remarkable memoir.

—Robert L. Miller

1. See Douglas Porch, *The French Secret Services* (Farrar Straus & Giroux 1995), p.171
2. See Ernest R. May, *Strange Victory: Hitler's Conquest of France* (Hill and Wang 2000). Professor May argues that even though the French High Command had made huge strategic mistakes, France's armed forces were better equipped, more numerous that those of the Wehrmacht in 1940. The contention that the French army was weaker than Germany's does not hold up to analysis, according to May. France's defeat should be attributed more to the fact that Hitler's military planners showed much more daring and imagination in taking advantage of strategic opportunities in using intelligence. Also, the issue of the relative strength of the opposing armies is laid to rest in the following note in *Hitler and His Generals*, Helmut Heiber and David M. Glantz, Eds. (Enigma Books, New York 2003): "In May 1940 Hitler had 136 divisions deployed along the western borders of Germany facing 137 enemy divisions including 91 French, 12 British, 23 Belgian, and 11 Dutch."
3. Ernest R. May, op.cit. pp. 348-349

The greatest insult one could inflict upon the
TRUTH
would be to know where it is and at the same time
to turn one's back on it or to forget it.

BOSSUET

Author's Introduction

Why I decided to write this book

O nce I retired from active military service on December 26, 1945, I had written, in the customary style of military reports, an account of the activities of French counterespionage between 1940 and 1944. That report, of which about one hundred copies were printed, was addressed to my fellow comrades in arms, the historical services, government officials and my commanding officers. The first among them, having a personal interest in this matter, was General Louis Rivet, former Head of the Special Services of National Defense from 1936 to 1944. He acknowledged receipt with the following letter:

Paris, December 18, 1946

My Dear Friend,

As I arrived home last night I found your "Report." I immediately began reading it. I read and read again, and plunged into that incredible past you have brought back to life. I was completely swept into it. It was past midnight when, having reached the final section, I realized how late it was. This morning I could not resist the need to join you once again in battle, that stupid and splendid struggle, which was both yours and mine.

Thank you my dear comrade in arms.

Because of you, because of the proud recounting of your sorrows and your glories, I find my past service avenged of stupidity and crime. Through the detailed precision and the scrupulous truth of the facts, the history of the best period of our counterespionage has finally been written. Because of the magnificent spirit you project onto this picture you offer those who shall come after you not just a vast fresco, but also a timeless example that must be followed if patriotism is still to have any meaning.

You have decided, because of your great heart, to speak primarily of your leaders (those who deserved it), your fellow soldiers, and your men. I feel a bit uneasy. But you write such an effective account of the French intelligence service, in such a realistic way, that my renewed passion reappears and I must therefore forgive you for churning up all those old, forgotten feelings! And tears welled up in my eyes as I read the list of those of us who died, whose many faces come back to memory, I can only embrace you in front of the blood-soaked Calvary where our duty one day ordered us to lead our great and dear comrades in arms.

Thank you again, my very dear friend! You have awakened certain feelings that I hold very deeply in sorrow and grandeur. I read your "Report" two days after what I experienced in Liège, where our Belgian friends, the survivors of the intelligence services in that border area, honored the dead who had sacrificed themselves for the freedom of our two countries (24 executed by firing squad, 160 sent to concentration camps).

I discovered after a few days, having experienced the pride of success, the painful cost of the oath we took when we swore to CONTINUE and to UPHOLD.

I shall see you soon, dear friend; I embrace you for the good you do to me; and the magnificent tribute you offer to the entire old French intelligence service.

L. RIVET

Thirty years later, my fellow officers and myself never shunned inquiries by serious writers. I still have found too few works—both written and audio-visual—offering the complete and truthful account of what our task was all about. On the contrary, I read and hear, regarding the mission and the organization of the Special Services of National Defense, before and after the Second World War, comments and opinions, which consciously or not offend the TRUTH and border on the ABSURD. Without breaking the rules of that SECRECY that I have so passionately defended, I find that the time has come to break a silence imposed upon me by the often too rigid traditions of our old organization.

I feel that I am true to the feelings expressed by Louis Rivet in his letter in giving to those who follow in our footsteps and to history this memoir, no doubt more detailed and complete than the one he thanked me for, since he had dedicated 25 years of his life to our work.

In doing this I am also aware that I am paying my respects in his name as well to the many comrades we knew and to those who still remain unnamed, along the path we followed long before 1940, who dedicated, and many times sacrificed, themselves with no other ambition than to do their Duty.

P.P.

PART ONE

THE COLLAPSE

November 1935–June 1940

1

One Against Ten

In November 1935 Europe was swept by violence. Fascism had taken root in Italy; following its brutal colonization of Libya came the conquest of Ethiopia. The world looked on with no other reaction than lending a pitiful ear to the complaints of the Negus, Haile Selassie, and a platonic condemnation of aggression. Germany did not join in: Hitler was now in power. Since January 30, 1933, a police state had been imposed by the national socialist dictatorship. Racism, anti-Semitism, pan-Germanism were the subspecies of a doctrine that, as it extolled the superiority of the German race, flattered a nation humiliated by its defeat in 1918, fulfilling the wishes of an army that fed on the spirit of revenge, believing only in strength and in the Greater German Reich. The Reichstag fire, the Night of the Long Knives, which witnessed the bloody purge of the Nazi Party on June 30, 1934, were the forerunners of more sinister methods and of Hitler's implacable determination. Some 88% of German voters approved these policies in August 1934 and made Hitler the Führer of the German Reich.

Just as in Italy, industry gave the German economy a second wind, since it had recently recovered the Saar and its industrial resources. Faced with the growing strength of National Socialism, the USSR joined the League of Nations, drew closer to England, and had just signed a mutual assistance pact with France on May 2, 1935. At the same time Russia was helping train the Reichswehr by opening its vast military training grounds to German air force pilots and tank commanders. Inside the Soviet Union, Stalin pursued a Machiavellian policy similar to his foreign policy. Some very real social and economic improvements had strengthened his personal position. The murder of Sergei Kirov, the Leningrad party secretary, was used to justify an implacable purge. About one hundred members of the opposition were quickly executed. The Party's dictatorship of the proletariat was now in the hands of a man whose personality was being extolled by wild propaganda efforts.

Republican Spain was rocked and weakened by endless separatist, religious and social conflicts. The miners' revolt in the Asturias region, those killed in Oviedo, cast a long shadow over Spain's political life. The right-wing parties (the Falange, the Carlists, etc.) began organizing themselves as the opposition. Between June and August 1935, the left had regrouped under the umbrella of the *Frente Popular* in order to come to power. Democratic England was more interested in its improved economy and in King George V's jubilee than in Hitler's rise to power and the misfortunes of Haile Selassie, the King of Kings.

France, still under the shock of the February 1934 riots and the financial scandals that sparked them, such as the Stavisky affair, was in a state of political turmoil. The Leagues and other right-wing groups that the left wanted to stop appeared to be more turbulent than they were effective. The left was also preparing the coming of the Popular Front and strikes were upsetting the social environment. Within twenty months, Daladier, Doumergue, Flandin, Bouisson, and Laval all followed each other as prime ministers under the tearful eyes of president Albert Lebrun. Laval, Prime Minister since June 1935 after having served as foreign minister, pursued his conciliatory policy with the totalitarian countries. No pro-French propaganda could be seen anywhere in the Saar during the referendum that approved its return to Germany. Inside France, legal decrees were unable to solve the economic crisis; while Nazi propaganda and the increasing number of espionage trials were proof enough of the moral and material rearmament of Germany as well as the danger it represented to peace.

I felt that my fellow citizens were unaware of all these facts. In my circle of officers in Lyon an easy going attitude prevailed, no one higher up took the trouble to keep us informed and draw the obvious conclusions for our national defense. We were much more aware of the troubles inside the army and the rather unpleasant anti-militarist propaganda spreading around unchecked.

I was about to turn thirty. I had completed my assignment as a lieutenant and I was expecting my next orders with curiosity and impatience. Normally following the rank class that I had just completed at Mourmelon, I should have been appointed as an instructor at one of the top military schools. Finally my orders arrived! I read those orders ten times over, directing me to join as of December 1, 1935, the *Deuxième Bureau* of the Army General Staff. I couldn't understand. Why the Army General Staff and the *Deuxième Bureau*? To do what? I was bold enough to place a phone call to Paris as I became increasingly puzzled. I was told that I was to replace Gendarmerie Commander Sérignan at the Special Services of the *Deuxième Bureau*. But rather than report to the Ministry of War on the Boulevard Saint-Germain, I was to proceed to number 2 *bis* Avenue de Tourville, one of the military buildings surrounding the Invalides.

Since graduating from Saint-Cyr, my only contact had been at the troop level and I was quite pleased about that. An internship at the Gendarmerie School at Versailles made me appreciate the intricacies of legal and procedural problems. My knowledge of foreign languages was rudimentary…such a background appeared somewhat thin for a "special" assignment even though it was very attractive. I was very much interested in espionage and counterespionage. I had taken real pleasure in reading the novels by Robert Dumas and the more popular ones by Pierre Nord. The adventures of the handsome Captain Benoît appealed to my imagination while I harbored few illusions as to the distance separating fiction from reality. I was after all a "sportsman," and my company commander, the excellent Captain Barriot, boosted my confidence when he said that they "could easily hand me the command of an entire fleet!" So I decided to accept the *Deuxième Bureau*. I would find out soon enough!

In Paris on Monday, December 1, 1935, I listened to the welcome given me by Commander de Robien. When I first met the man who would be my boss at the German counterespionage section he appeared to be a bit aloof. While Commander Sérignan was introducing me around he told me about de Robien's career, his passion for very neat work and his elegant way of sidestepping the daily drudgery. One of his brothers was a minister plenipotentiary at the Quai d'Orsay and he was quite impressive himself. He was about fifty years old, with graying hair and a distinguished looking, somewhat chiseled face, his eyes hidden behind thick and slightly dark eyeglasses seemed to look at you playfully. His tapered fingers were stroking a long black cigarette holder. The aroma of English tobacco permeated the large and rather dull half-attic he used as his office.

To the left of de Robien, facing the window, a young thirty-year-old man saluted me courteously before returning to the papers that littered his desk. His name was M. Darbou. I was told that his brother, nick-named "the lion," headed a branch of the intelligence and counterintelligence section in Lille very effectively and somewhat roughly. The empty and austere worktable facing de Robien was assigned to me. There was no other furniture in the room except for some shelves that were filled with files. De Robien was chatting with Sérignan about something called the Frogé affair, which was being trumpeted by the yellow press, apparently for political reasons. This Frogé character was the deputy military supplies officer at Belfort and had just been sentenced to five years in prison for treason by the civilian courts, the maximum sentence provided by law. For such a crime it was really a rather cheap price to pay! Frogé kept on repeating that he was innocent and his defenders were talking about an alleged police conspiracy set up with the complicity of my unit, the *Deuxième Bureau*! I was beginning to feel uneasy. Could this be a new Dreyfus Case?

The conversation stopped because Sérignan had to leave urgently for the headquarters of the Gendarmerie where he was starting a new important position and promised to a very bright future. Counterespionage was clearly not to his liking and the Frogé matter didn't inspire him at all. On the other hand de Robien wanted to finish dictating his mail. It was ten o'clock and I sensed him getting impatient, chilly as he was wearing his long coat with an astrakhan fur collar, which he had not even bothered to take off. Sérignan urged me on to the next office: a large room with shelving all the way to the ceiling, bursting with files. In front of a long and narrow central cabinet, two archivists in white smocks glanced up at us quickly then went back to their work in the files. A sour taste was bothering me, a mixture of cheap tobacco, dust, and paper.

A man about forty smiling broadly and wearing civilian clothes emerged from a tiny office near a narrow window. M. Garnier was obviously pleased to see that Sérignan's replacement had arrived.

"What we have here are about 100,000 card files and 25,000 general and specific files. Once a document reaches our section it first comes to the archives. We examine it and look for everything that might relate to it. Then we return the document to the case officer and file it once he's finished."

What Garnier hadn't told me was that he saw everything, read everything, and never forgot anything. He was the enlightened despot of this inner sanctum where he supervised six or seven archivists. Within this huge accumulation of papers coming from innumerable sources no one could match Garnier in discovering the one item that would explain a situation or define a person.

"He spends his Sundays here and never leaves before 8 p.m.," Sérignan whispered to me as we walked to the door.

I reported at 9 a.m. to 2 *bis* Avenue de Tourville. I was entering the unknown. Fortunately I was happy to see Commander Sérignan at the great iron door opening onto the courtyard. Two suspicious ushers, Nicolas and Douarin, led us to the waiting room on the ground floor, which also included the offices of the chief of staff of the Special Services, the administrative staff and the intelligence service.

"Colonel Roux, the big boss, is quite pleasant and affable," Sérignan had told me.

A rather round man wearing civilian clothes, the colonel gave us a friendly reception, with only one comment that sounded sincere regarding my "excellent reputation" and my future rise in the ranks, whatever the case may be.

"I shall introduce you to my deputy and future replacement Lieutenant Colonel Louis Rivet, he will give you your assignment."

The man I met and who was to have a profound influence on my training and my career was amazingly unassuming: a fine distinguished face, still young looking despite early baldness and a deep, peaceful sounding voice:

"Would you like to try out the German counterespionage section on the second floor? Commander Sérignan is unfortunately leaving us. I shall be here to help you along with your commanding officers: commander de Robien and Lieutenant Colonel Grosjean, who is in command of our entire counterespionage."

I left Rivet feeling reassured and convinced that he would help me given the friendliness of his welcome. We quickly went up one floor and Sérignan introduced me to de Robien; then we knocked on the door opposite my future office. The officer of the engineer corps who opened was Captain Bertrand. He had strangely piercing eyes and his manner of speech was very precise; in a few words he explained his duties to me: ciphers and decryption. I knew how important this specialty was and I could easily imagine its positive contribution to the Special Services. I didn't dare ask too many questions since these functions were so new to me that they appeared complicated and mysterious.

I quietly returned to my office after thanking Bertrand. Sérignan had disappeared and de Robien with a smile and a wave of the hand made me understand that he had to finish his mail. He was dictating a letter to the minister of foreign affairs, discreetly drawing his attention to the suspicion surrounding personnel at a French embassy in a Balkan country. Then there was a note to an office that appeared to be under his command. The style had changed: he was issuing orders to begin an investigation. Slowly I moved near the window. Two magnificent police dogs at play in the courtyard in front of me, surrounded by austere looking buildings similar to our own. Far away in the distance, the golden dome of the Invalides glittered under a pale sunlight. I was listening. De Robien was now dictating a letter to the 5th section of the general information division at police headquarters because an informer had revealed the suspicious connections of a newsman in Paris.

From time to time Garnier limped in with another relevant file and the dictation would begin again:

"Memo to the Police Department…"

"Memo to the B.S.L.E. (Special Office of the Foreign Legion) in Marseille: a suspicious legionnaire has arrived at Fort Saint-Nicolas."

"Letter to the government commissioner at the military court in Nancy, with expert opinion on the secret classification of information sought by a soldier indicted for espionage. I found it odd, this time it's the military court that has jurisdiction, while in the case of Frogé, a regular army officer, the matter was handed to the civilian courts… None of this was either clear or simple!"

De Robien had finished and was now able to give me his full attention. I told him about my background, how surprised I was to be stationed in such a specialized service and my fear of not being productive immediately. That broke the ice. A fellow soldier, charming and considerate, replaced the tough and somewhat formal department head. He was obviously impressed by my concern and my reserved attitude. In a friendly and informal way he accompanied me to the office of Lieutenant Colonel Grosjean, the head of counterespionage; a courteous cavalry officer with bushy eyebrows. He paid little attention to me and started a conversation with de Robien regarding their coming rotation to troop command. Both were complaining that they had not yet "seen" their replacements. Things sounded very strange to me! I had just stepped into this unit and my commanding officers were getting ready to leave! We quickly saluted our three fellow officers in the section dedicated to non-German foreign activity. They were also moving on to new assignments!

It was noon. I sidestepped an invitation to have lunch with de Robien; I felt the need to be alone and think. I could see that my assignment was at a different level than what I had been until then accustomed to. I was amazed at the ease with which de Robien unraveled the issues, and handled files, and wrote letters to the ministries, the administrators, the offices of the special services in France and abroad. Whether he was requesting something or writing as a commander, he was able to fulfill his task so effortlessly, with such technical expertise and authority, something I had not been trained for. Yet that initial contact didn't disappoint me. Both de Robien and Rivet were to be the officers with whom I was to have the most frequent contact. They had different but equally attractive personalities and from what I could gather my work promised to be intriguing and interesting. The most important thing was that de Robien not move on before I had been able to learn the ropes. I quickly returned to my office and Darbou was already there.

He was quite talkative and painted a vivid picture of the unit: under Colonel Roux, who was to be replaced by his deputy Rivet, the *Deuxième Bureau* (S.R.-S.C.R.) at its headquarters at 2 *bis,* Avenue de Tourville included a general staff, several technical services, and above all the research information section (S.R.) and an information centralization section (S.C.R.), which was actually counterespionage (C.E.). The information gathered, covertly for the most part, by the S.R. was then transmitted for analysis to the *Deuxième Bureau* of the army general staff (E.M.A.) on the Boulevard Saint-Germain. After having "digested" or compared the information to other generally open sources (the military attachés' reports, for example), the army general staff would pass them on in abridged form with its comments to the High Command or to the relevant ministries. This way of transmitting S.R. information was necessary to protect the secrecy of its sources, while ensuring that the importance of the item was underscored.

Our section, the S.C.R., in liaison with the Ministry of the Interior and in particular the *Sûreté Nationale* (S.N.) and the *Préfecture de Police* (P.P.) was dedicated to fighting foreign activities that could be harmful to our national defense and to the army. We gathered counterespionage information beyond our borders and ensured the protection of the S.R. The central service included about twenty officers, recruited for the most part through cooptation from the army and the air force (the Navy has its own S.R. but no counterespionage), as many non-commissioned officers and some thirty civilian employees: technicians (communications, photography, etc.) archivists, secretaries, typists, guards and drivers.

A section called P.R. *(Propagande Révolutionnaire)* handled cases of political infiltration within the army and reported directly to the minister's office. Commander Serre headed the service before being replaced by Commander Jacquot, an extremely well-educated and brilliant officer.* He would often visit and ask for our input, research the archives and inquire about our problems. Jacquot was to help us solve many problems thanks to his sharp intellect and his entrée to Daladier and his top aides, Clapier and Genébrier.

A very small budget, culled from the secret funds of the Ministry of War, kept the service going on a shoestring. Five or six automobiles were assigned to our sections, as well as some free passes on the S.N.C.F. (the French national railroads). Darbou, who had no qualms in considering himself equivalent to officers' rank, kept telling me that everyone here was of top quality, carefully selected and totally trustworthy as far as security was concerned and I was absolutely convinced this was true.

Reporting directly to the central service was a chain of field offices located near the borders (Lille, Metz, Belfort, Marseille, Algiers, Tunis),** along with a number of camouflaged observation posts abroad, called "specific productive elements," of our Special Services. Apart from Metz and Belfort, these listening posts did not use trained counterespionage personnel and included five to ten officers, highly praised by Darbou for their technical expertise.

De Robien just walked in and confirmed this opinion. He sometimes poked fun at the low esteem displayed too often by some listening post commanders towards counterespionage, which they considered a police function and he added, this time very seriously:

"To tell you the truth, we have not yet recovered from the Dreyfus Affair and the mistakes of our elders. Despite the remarkable work done by our services during the Great War, despite the proof they gave of their loyalty, the return to peacetime in 1918 also created some confusion as to

---

* After leading, with André Malraux, several *maquis* in 1943 and 1944, Jacquot will join the 1st French Army. General of the Army Jacquot was to hold important positions within NATO later on.

** Toulouse was added to these offices as of 1937.

the limits of the areas of responsibility in counterespionage. The civilian authorities had been the main beneficiaries."

He concluded:

"The army senses that it's no longer as popular as it used to be. Our leaders fear any complications that might arise from our activity: they keep silent when they have to defend us. In order to fulfill our mission of protection and security we need a lot of patience and diplomatic skill. My good friend, if you want to understand what we are up against, take peek at the files on the Frogé case and the Abwehr."

I immediately took the hint and went into the archives. With the help of the excellent Garnier I was deep into the Frogé case for most of the night. The majority of the documents consisted of police reports and notes produced by our branch at Belfort. The case began in 1932 when Daladier was Minister of War and Chéron was Minister of Justice and Chancellor. There was an incredible mess in the quartermaster's office at Belfort. People were coming and going without being checked. Important and confidential documents—some of them dealing with mobilization—were strewn on top of the desks day and night, disappearing and sometimes reappearing. No one seemed to know about it or at least that's what they claimed.

One day in October 1932, an Austrian named Gessmann told Police Commissioner M. Osvald of the counterespionage division of the *Sûreté Nationale* in Paris, that he was working for the German espionage unit at Lindau under the command of Major Gombart. He claimed, because he had personally mailed him a letter, that a French officer named Frogé was in contact with the German unit. He offered to help entrap Frogé. With de Robien's approval, Gessmann became a double agent under police supervision. Suspicion regarding Frogé was so strong that he was subjected to initial questioning on January 11, 1933 and denied everything. On May 6, 1933 he was indicted for disseminating documents belonging to National Defense but was not placed under arrest. He hired a prominent defense attorney, J. C. Legrand, and the case then began to look more and more like a scandal. It was indeed a scandal for those who believed in Frogé's innocence, for those who thought he was guilty and those who were upset by the incredible negligence of the agencies responsible for the protection of national defense secrets. After several months of investigation and only after the German agent Krauss* was

---

* A Polish officer recruited by the Abwehr in 1932.

arrested and admitted to being Frogé's accomplice. The French officer arrested on May 2, 1934 provided proof to back up that statement. Frogé was first sentenced by the civil court in Belfort, then by the court of appeals in Besançon on May 15, 1935 to the maximum punishment provided by law for treason: five years in jail and a 5,000 franc fine.

A delegation of veterans from the Belfort area, led by the author and journalist René Naegelen, was able to sit in on the secret proceedings and attest to their regularity. Since his incarceration Frogé's family and friends were attempting to attract the attention of public opinion. He was said to be the victim of criminal negligence, of incompetent or degenerate officers, of the Machiavellian intrigues of the police, of the justice system and of the *Deuxième Bureau*. Some circles, with the support of dailies such as *L'Oeuvre*, took up his defense and used the matter to attack the regime. The political unrest that preceded the 1936 elections was also getting under way.

This file, as well as the files connected to it that I was working on day after day, proved that de Robien in his candor was closest to the truth. Double agents Gessmann and Krauss were, at different levels, very clever spies. Their testimony demonstrated the depth and widespread nature of the Abwehr's work; it was only too obvious that they were not the only ones. These gentlemen were quite capable of pilfering our secrets without too much difficulty. A non-commissioned officer was given three years in prison for selling a new automatic rifle to the Germans. Frogé, a French officer condemned for treason was sentenced to a mere five years. The same kind of punishment was handed down to Lydia Stahl and twenty of her accomplices who were unmasked in 1934, thanks to the perseverance of police detectives and because of the bold and brazen way they went about their research of industrial offices in Paris. It was Gessmann once again who drew the attention of our services to the beautiful Swiss woman Lydia Oswald, having seen her in conversation with Gombart several times in Lindau.

Inspector Danger of the *Surveillance du Territoire*, right-hand man of Superintendent Osvald, was able to catch the spy queen in a Brest hotel, in the act of transmitting to Gombart several pages of information regarding underground fuel reserves and the latest models of our submarines. This message was relatively risk free, since it went through the German embassy in Paris, contrary to diplomatic rules and under the very noses of our disbelieving diplomatic personnel at the Ministry of Foreign Affairs. "The bitch" as Danger referred to her, was bold enough (or lucky enough) to be living at the embassy, thus avoiding the police check of hotel guest cards.

The captivating lady had managed to seduce a French navy lieutenant whom she had picked up at the Navy ball at the Paris Opéra, where the German naval attaché in full dress uniform guided her charms toward the right target. The navy court at Brest let her accomplice go free and sentenced her to nine months in prison on September 13, 1935. We were informed that she was now actively carrying on in the Middle East. The press would get very excited about such cases, weaving complicated plots around them, idealizing the characters involved, publishing many pictures of those society affairs that espionage trials were becoming, where the best known lawyers of the Paris bar took the floor, such as J. C. Legrand, César Campinchi, de Moro-Giafferi, Maurice Garçon, Le Coq de Kerland.

At very little cost and amid general indifference, German intelligence was infiltrating France and providing Hitler and the Reichswehr with the tools their policies required. At the same time in Berlin, two young high society women, Benita von Falkenhayn and Renate von Natzmer, were beheaded with an ax at Blossenfee Prison for having taken part in the espionage mission of the dashing Polish Captain George Sosnowski.[*]

Military authorities entrusted with national defense appeared powerless to fulfill their mission to protect the country; they no longer had the assurance of being able to pass judgment on their own men! All the army could do while the national police force and the justice system were absorbed with other "more newsworthy matters" was to maintain some rather good personal contacts between officers of the *Deuxième Bureau* and the civil servants. Some vague and confusing laws were unable to provide a satisfactory definition of what was secret, something no one believed in anymore since there were innumerable leaks at every level. The lack of discipline came from higher up and the enemy could simply read the *Journal Officiel*[**] to secure important information about our defense and our political aims. To betray one's country in exchange for five years in jail at the most, was only due to bad luck or because one wasn't clever enough. I saw the strange and costly weakness of the tools at our disposal.

---

[*] Sosnowski was sentenced to hard labor for life, along with another of his German accomplices, Irene von Iena.

[**] *Le Journal Officiel* is the equivalent of the *Congressional Record* in the U.S.

In the Frogé matter, the army's Special Services limited themselves to informing the High Command, helping the police in their task by giving them a few "confidential" military pieces of information to feed Gessmann's double dealing. And what was that double dealing worth? I found many instances of blunders, lack of caution and blatant provocations, leading me to wonder whether the Austrian's intentions were that pure after all. How much can one trust someone who is ready to betray his own commander?

I shared my doubts with de Robien, who toned down their harshness somewhat by vouching for the high professionalism of the Paris policemen and of Osvald in particular. But what if they had been themselves the targets of the clever dealing of the double agent? I decided to get to the bottom of it all, and meet with the policemen and Gessmann. I wanted to make up my own mind about such agents, the technique of penetrating the enemy and how this could be done efficiently. My study of the Frogé matter lifted a corner of the veil on the dangerous activities of German intelligence.

At that point I asked for the files on the Abwehr. The notes and reports in the files came from various sources, the oldest being those produced by the control commissions and the observation posts established in Germany, beginning in 1918. Colonel Rivet wrote a few of those reports when he was in Berlin. Other more recent reports came from our military attachés, our Special Services, and from agents reporting directly to us because of their paramount importance. This included Asché, an employee at the German Ministry of War, whose information on the secret encryption methods and procedures, as well as the results achieved by Göring's *Forschungsamt*,[*] were very accurate and extremely important and thanks to Maurice Dejean,[**] an attaché at the French embassy in Berlin, who was clever enough to penetrate the most difficult sources. The bulk of our most valuable information was actually produced by a small number of our agents who succeeded in penetrating the Abwehr. The greatest credit went to Doudot, our top counterespionage technician stationed in Metz. Other information was obtained by interrogating spies or double agents.

On January 1, 1935, Wilhelm Canaris replaced Captain Patzig as head of the Abwehr. He had just been promoted to the rank of admiral and was

---

[*] Signals intelligence service.

[**] Dejean would later become an ambassador.

the commanding officer of the fortress of Swinemünde at the mouth of the river Oder. Canaris led a quiet family life, with his wife, who was said to be extremely intelligent, and their two charming daughters. He was expecting to retire and spend most of his time reading and riding his horses, followed by his dogs along the endless sandy beaches leading far to the east. The Minister of War, General von Blomberg, had to dismiss Patzig because of his endless quarrels with the invasive leaders of the SS * at the ministry of the interior, namely Heinrich Himmler and Reinhard Heydrich. Patzig's replacement had to be a clever and versatile officer, preferably a sailor, who had traveled and was knowledgeable about foreign countries; he also had to have the trust of his military leaders and above all that of the Nazis.

Canaris did have some friends among them. Heydrich, as a lieutenant in the reserves, had served under Canaris in 1923 aboard the training cruiser *Berlin*. The two men respected one another, despite the fact that the Admiralty had discharged Heydrich rather brutally for disciplinary reasons. When Grand Admiral Raeder put Canaris' name forth as a candidate, both Himmler and Heydrich approved, which meant that Hitler also agreed. Blomberg therefore signed the transfer orders.

A rather short man physically, with snow white hair, Canaris appeared older than his 47 years despite his excellent physical shape and his piercing blue eyes. Distinguished looking, with great intuition, his superiors agreed that he displayed an exceptional ability to adapt to situations, and was extremely well educated: he was fluent in English and Spanish and conversant in French and Italian. His personal charm, his way of getting along easily with people and his versatility made him an excellent candidate to run the Abwehr under Hitler's regime. Up to that time German intelligence had fulfilled, at least officially, a defensive function and was about to become, like every other state agency, the active instrument of a new policy. The Abwehr under Canaris' leadership was at the focal point where a resurgent army whose ancient traditions he respected, and a new regime whose national objectives and effectiveness he appreciated and approved of converged. Canaris demonstrated his talent for organization in just a few short months by turning the Abwehr into a dynamic instrument able to fulfill the ambitions of the Führer with a firm commitment to serve the Reichswehr.

He would be given every tool he required and the new order demanded that every German, wherever he may be, provide full support to

---

* H. Himmler became head of the SS on January 6, 1929.

the information-gathering efforts. This defensive shield, broadened and strengthened by the Gestapo, was extremely rigorous and amazingly effective. Canaris and his staff operated out of five rickety-looking floors of the Tirpitzstufer, a building at the corner of the Bendler-strasse, which out of personal preference and respect for tradition, as well as to save money, he deliberately refused to renovate. He moved with his family into a house he bought at Schlachtensee, a few kilometers outside Berlin.

His reunion with Heydrich after some years was friendly enough and Canaris was impressed by the towering height as well as the keen intelligence of the head of the S.D.*: he would repeat to his deputy Colonel Oster, "He's the smartest among the wild animals," as they both attempted to find the best ways to avoid the penetration by the Nazis of the innermost offices of the Army and the Abwehr. Heydrich was happy to have close social relations with the head of the Abwehr, and he often spent time with the Canaris family, expressing his thoughts by simply saying: "He's an old fox."

I was now getting closer to the core of my mission. For several days I plowed through the files, where I also stumbled upon a 1925 report sent by Captain Louis Rivet, then stationed in Berlin, sounding the alarm with an impressive description of the German intelligence service since the armistice of 1918. The Treaty of Versailles stated that the intelligence service was to be disbanded and for a long time Rivet and his fellow officers had been investigating what had happened to the old imperial intelligence service and its head, Colonel Nicolaï. Later on they found Nicolaï in Brazil, where he was on a "cruise" to South American countries before traveling on to China and Japan. Without a doubt this was a reward for his excellent past service but also a valuable mission for the future German intelligence service. Throughout his world travels Nicolaï went preaching the gospel of Germany as the victim of a temporary collapse but that she would soon reemerge in the certainty of her invincibility.

The French Special Services succeeded little by little in ferreting out most of the former members of the old *Nachrichtendienst* (*N.D.*) hidden within military or paramilitary organizations or inside companies with foreign operations, such as Uberseedienst and its subsidiary, Nuntia. True to their original missions they used these covers to fulfill the secret orders coming from Berlin as they prepared for the future. Rivet called me in several times wanting to check on my progress in my new assignment, chatting in his easy and friendly way as he tried to gauge my reactions.

That day I discussed what I had found relating to the Abwehr and I hit the jackpot!

A great and prolific raconteur with a fantastic memory for detail, Rivet didn't hold back his excitement as he reminisced:

"At the end of 1925 in Berlin, I met a few officers who had belonged to the old *Nachrichtendienst*. They made no mystery of their former activities nor did they hide the fact that they had never really interrupted them at all. Some were part of the clandestine headquarters while others had secured jobs commensurate with their qualifications within the staff at the ministries of the interior, foreign affairs, and so on.

"At the beginning of 1926 I discovered, much to my surprise, next to the names of officers listed in the *Statistiche Abteilung*, a small entry "Abwehr," meaning *defense*. Three or four officers I knew were grouped under this innocent sounding sub-head under the command of a Colonel Gempp. We were already aware back then, my dear Paillole, that, despite the still functioning (armistice) control commissions, German intelligence had proudly and officially started to operate once again.

"Despite our warnings, and believe me there were many warnings, neither our Allies nor our own leaders paid any attention. We were told that this new name could only refer to a regular service whose mission it was to protect the young German army from anti-national agitators. The defeated Germany of 1918 never blamed its own soldiers for having lost the war. The German army had kept its prestige and the German intelligence service, protected by an apparently defensive official function, was pursuing its own mission. *Nachrichtendienst ist Heerendienst*, meaning "the intelligence service is the noblest service."

The service Canaris had just taken over with the mission to improve it appeared powerful enough to me since it had at least ten times more personnel than our own. It was divided into three sections: espionage, sabotage, and counterespionage. I noted the existence of Section II dedicated to sabotage, which had no counterpart within our own service. The counterespionage section included several groups sharing various tasks. The most important was Group III, with the mission of counterintelligence gathering abroad and the struggle against enemy intelligence and counterintelligence in close collaboration with the S.D. and the Gestapo. Colonel Oster, Canaris' second in overall command, was

---

* *Sichereitsdienst*, or Security Service, was the main intelligence service of the Nazi party and later of the German government.

a very energetic officer from Saxony who had been strongly influenced by imperial Germany and was opposed to the Nazi regime. He had a lot of sway with his boss due to his personality and his constant contact, inside the High Command, with the military administration and the rest of the government.

There was an Abwehr main office—*Abwehrstelle*, abbreviated *Ast*—within each one of the seven military districts known as *Wehrkreis*, which generally had listening posts along the borders. Two of these main offices were concentrating on France: Münster with its listening post at Cologne was headed by Major Rudolf, who later became commander of the Abwehr in France; and Stuttgart, which controlled the listening post at Lindau that we had discovered through the Frogé affair. Two more main offices were active against us: Hamburg for the navy and Berlin for the air force. In fact we knew very little about these offices. Our penetration was neither deep nor sophisticated enough, had no directives, no coordination and lacked additional top-level agents. Recruiting agents was no easy task and it was even less easy to handle them, follow up, and check on their penetration of German intelligence.

The Abwehr was not the only organization dedicated to intelligence gathering and the security of the German Reich. The Nazi Party had no intention of giving the Army, where many were unwilling to accept the regime, an exclusive hold on such vitally important areas even though Canaris was heading the Abwehr. Both the Gestapo and the S.D. were also entrusted with the internal security of the Reich against foreign espionage. Göring's Forschungsamt was listening in, decrypting, and analyzing every kind of message intercepted inside and outside Germany. Propaganda organizations led by Goebbels were set up in Germany and abroad, while at the same time the Ministry of Foreign Affairs was pressuring all Germans living in foreign countries to become Nazis, propagandists, and spies.

Within three weeks I was able to understand the amazing dimensions of the broadly aggressive efforts undertaken by Germany. De Robien gave me a few minor cases to look into. I met with Police Superintendent Osvald, who was greatly respected by our entire service for his dedication and professionalism and because he was a decorated combat veteran of the First World War. The working relationship with him was to be transparent and loyal. Grosjean introduced me to Mr. Jeffes, head of the British passport control section who was actually working for the MI6. Jeffes lived in luxury at the hotel Continental in the rue de Rivoli.

He reminded me of a polite businessman from the French provinces who had come to Paris to attend some meetings. He was also on the verge of being replaced.

Commander Perruche, who headed the German section within our S.R. (foreign intelligence), appeared to be serious and well informed; he often came up to discuss matters with us. A tall, rather elegant man, he was very well educated, witty and slightly affected when he wanted to compare his information with ours. In these last few days he had climbed up the stairs to our floor on a daily basis. He appeared a bit worried when he asked us:

"Gentlemen, are you under the impression that something is moving on the other side of the Rhine?"

Actually a few of our penetration agents had just been ordered by their German employers to be vigilant during the next few weeks. They must urgently report any sign of troop mobilization, movement of French army units towards the east, and to check any unusual arrivals of British troops in French ports. In a few days it would be Christmas and the new year 1936. At this point I should pause and sum things up. The phone rang at 11 a.m. and since de Robien had not yet arrived, Darbou answered. I could see by the look on his face that he was quite surprised as he handed me the receiver:

"Robien here, my friend. I'm really very sorry. A silly illness is keeping me in bed for several weeks: I have the mumps! You must excuse me for dropping out on you. I've informed Grosjean and Rivet. Confer with them very quickly to see how they intend to organize the work in our department."

I understood how worried and sorry de Robien was. I attempted to reassure him, at least regarding my good will, since my competence was still an unknown quantity. Darbou asked me about the risks of contagion and also what I was thinking: "We're in a real fix!"

2

Inside the Abwehr

Two months had passed. I was able to handle daily matters as best I could with the help of Darbou and Garnier. I answered letters, followed up on intelligence information, met with visitors, got to know my fellow officers and the staff better, made contact with other offices of the Army general staff, as well as military and civilian magistrates, court officers, policemen and the ministry of foreign affairs. I got used to dictating my mail as I listened to some long-winded person on the phone.

I went to 75 rue de l'Université a few times to visit a dark and dirty little office, spared for a time from the rubble of the war ministry which was in the process of being rebuilt. A very discrete doorkeeper had me meet with young men and women of every age and origin who were "ready to do anything" to serve their Homeland! The Special Services must meet with these "volunteers" who try to get in through a general, a minister, or even the President of the Republic. Mostly I wasted my time during these interviews despite the quite promising smiles displayed by more than a few spirited ladies tantalized by the demons of espionage.

I needed the help of my superiors almost on a daily basis. Grosjean was hard to pin down ever since he was scheduled to leave on April 15, 1936. I didn't want to bother de Robien during his recovery and as he was getting ready to leave. Colonel Rivet therefore became my main support.

His experience and his willingness to help were endless. He was in charge of the department since Colonel Roux had left. I hesitated to prolong our conversations, which were so illuminating to me. His statements were on target:

"Our Service is exclusively a branch of National Defense."

"We look for secrets all the time and everywhere. We protect our own and that's to be your mission."

"Because we look for secrets our structure and our actions must remain secret."

"We serve only the nation; let's not become the pawns of clans or political parties."

Sometimes Rivet would stop and wonder, his statements shifting to current events. His deep knowledge of Germany drew his attention almost exclusively toward the changes taking place there. He asked me to keep him informed about research by the Abwehr and the lists of questions, revealing which issues were on the minds of the Reichswehr and of the Reichsführer.

"Our problem, Paillole, is to find out ahead of time against whom and how Hitler will attempt to make the changes he wants.

"For the moment everything indicates the left bank of the Rhine, whose demilitarization he has castigated as immoral. For several weeks we have observed the preparations made by the Reichswehr in that area: barracks are being refurbished, the Army suppliers are negotiating with the Office of Supplies, logistics are being prepared to supply the troops and so on.

"The future of peace will depend upon the attitude adopted by France and the Allies…"

This was the opinion of the French ambassador to Berlin, André François-Poncet, whose reports to the government confirmed those we were sending daily to the High Command. On March 7, 1936, at 5 a.m., 19 battalions of the Reichswehr entered the Rhineland while 16 other battalions were waiting to see what the French reaction would be before they also followed. The commanding general in charge of the operation opened the secret orders spelling out his mission a few hours before it began. The troops understood what was expected of them as they crossed the bridges on the Rhine.

"We will not accept the fact that Strasbourg will be threatened by German cannon," proclaimed Albert Sarraut. [*]

---

[*] Albert Sarraut was Prime Minister from January to June 1936.

Only the Abwehr was really worried about the true meaning of this statement by the French Prime Minister and German spies were watching very closely. During that spring-like weekend France was relaxing at Barbizon or Deauville and in a few weeks the French people would vote in the Popular Front. England was not about to make any moves and everything ended right there!

As far as we were concerned the event was vastly important and extremely instructive. The conventional phase of political tensions had passed. Germany was now in a permanent state of mobilization, ready to undertake its plans brutally, come what may. The leaders in charge of such operations were to be informed of their mission only at the very last moment. Success in the intelligence war would depend upon knowing the enemy's troop strength, and above all what his intentions were. We knew the main points through *Mein Kampf*, Hitler's thundering speeches and his political positions, all of which were so bold and cynical as to mesmerize our diplomats and paralyze the government.

At this juncture the contribution of counterespionage to the research effort could make a difference if it was able to uncover and stop the work of the Abwehr and find out the ultimate goals of the German High Command by being able to examine its research planning. I was very much aware of the prime importance of this role and I would have preferred to travel to our listening posts in France and abroad to examine with my colleagues how this work was being carried out and try to improve the results. This was to prove impossible! My daily duties were to absorb my time completely and I was not as productive as de Robien. Yet I was able to meet with Gessmann and had read his file before conferring with him. There wasn't much, except for the description of his few contacts with the policemen from 1932 to 1936 regarding the Frogé case for the most part. Once Gessmann testified at the trial, which was held in secret, he remained silent for a long time. He reappeared in April 1935 to identify Lydia Oswald, whom Superintendent Osvald—no relation—was in a hurry to arrest and sentence because of the threat her charming ways represented to our naval officers. She had already been set free, and was known to be traveling from Turkey to Iraq...

At that point, in February 1936, Osvald introduced me to Gessmann and quietly left us alone in a modest little bar right near the Saint-François-Xavier metro station. He was a tall, well-built man, about thirty-five, with good-looking features and elegantly dressed. He spoke to me politely in excellent French and his clear, easy way of answering my questions was a pleasant surprise. I immediately formed the opinion that Gombart, his boss in the Abwehr, must have reacted the same way and it bothered me somewhat. Since I was new to that kind of meeting, I was very nervous and it showed to the point that my contact sensed it immediately. He spent a lot of time talking about Feldkirch, his little hometown, where he lived and which he described in detail, as well as his fear of seeing the Nazis take over in Austria one day. His voice changed when he tried to express his hatred for Hitler's regime.

I then discussed the part he played in the Frogé case with all his mistakes and provocations. Very cleverly he explained his errors as the result of his anxiety to succeed and the fact that he believed in Frogé's guilt. He also mentions his "good relationship" lasting four years with Gombart, whom he described as a good, well-intentioned man who was surrounded by bad people…and I could only agree with all of this. The entrance of the Reichwehr into the Rhineland was only a few days away. Gessmann told me what was worrying the Abwehr, asking me how he should answer questions by his commanding officer regarding France's position if faced with such an event. I hadn't expected the question, so I answered without committing myself:

"France is aware of this threat; it wishes to avoid anything that might be perceived as a provocation. Later on, should the threat become real, French reaction can go, in agreement with its allies, from the toughest military response to diplomatic sanctions…"

I was right on the money! Gessmann's second question appeared more on target. Gombart was seeking information on tank manufacturing at Satory, Issy-les-Moulineaux, and Roanne. He also wanted the tactical data used by French armored units. In asking these questions Gombart, who to my amazement was meeting openly with his informer at his office in Lindau, was referring to a long report written in German. Gessmann had managed to see the signed letter S at the bottom of the last page. He was convinced that the author of the report could only be a journalist residing in Paris. Gombart, who trusted Gessmann, didn't hide the fact that the most important parts of the report came from the transcripts of the meetings of the National Defense Commission at the Chamber of Deputies, which were often held in secret.

I promised to provide Gessmann with the most important parts for him to use at our next meeting set for March 15, 1936, at 5 p.m. Until then he must watch what was happening in France. He was to write, or in case of emergency cable, using the appropriate code words to an agreed-upon address, which was a mailbox for German intelligence located in Vaduz, Liechtenstein. I jotted down the address. Just before parting I offered him money, which he turned down as he disappeared into a metro station. As I walked back to my office, I could only imagine the complicated life of this strange but somewhat charming individual. What was to come out of all this? Sooner or later his dangerous game would have to end, the adventure would stop, perhaps tragically, here or elsewhere ... For the moment I had to be the chessmaster and my Service the only one to benefit from all this.

My report to Rivet confirmed his forecast of a coming action in the Rhineland. I was to contact the 3rd Bureau of the Army High Command to prepare the appropriate answers to the German intelligence questionnaire. These had to be credible enough without damaging national defense. In the absence of an organized plan for distributing false intelligence, the task is almost impossible. My colleagues of the 3rd Bureau, who are very much interested in the Abwehr's questions, agreed with me. We all complained about the absence of a specialized office dedicated to creating plans to artfully deceive the enemy. I shall revisit this issue later on.

We agreed on some information and documents that were likely to interest Gombart and point him toward weapons studies that the High Command already knew it would never manufacture in large enough quantities. I informed Osvald of Gessmann's extended stay in Paris. As usual he would have him followed discreetly. As for myself, I began an investigation in Vaduz through our station in Belfort. We must also find out the identity of "S," the mysterious author of the report Gessmann was able to see. If we could identify him, if the address in Liechtenstein was really being used by the Abwehr... I must say this would lift the funny feeling about Gessmann I was unable to shake. He returned to Lindau on March 16, 1936, and was satisfied with the information I had furnished.

I discussed the entire matter with my boss's new deputy, Lieutenant Colonel Malraison, a clever infantryman blessed with a happy disposition, who had served at headquarters. He strangely camouflaged his bald head by bringing a few strands of hair all the way up to his forehead by combing them from the back.

"The Boss is pleased with your work. He doesn't want to give you an older commanding officer to replace de Robien. I have two candidates in mind, both of them excellent. Lieutenant Lullé-Desjardins, who graduated from Saint-Cyr two or three years behind you and who has the best recommendations. He will be available in two to three weeks. And Lieutenant André Bonnefous, who was in your graduating class. I was very much impressed with him under my command and that of Commander de Gaulle at Trier." I was ecstatic! Bonnefous would be great! But then I thought about it. I was awed to have to take on responsibility for the German section under the present circumstances and with so little experience in my assignment. Malraison reassured me and made a very convincing point.

"The replacement for Grosjean at the head of the *S.C.R.* will give you an excellent superior officer, a top-ranking graduate of the *École de Guerre*, specializing in German-related issues and with experience in intelligence work. With Bonnefous you'll make a smashing team! As for Lullé-Desjardins, he'll fit in perfectly in a special station we intend to set up in Toulouse in a few months with Spain as a target, because of the deteriorating situation that will require the close attention of intelligence and counterintelligence. Bonnefous will be here at the beginning of April."

I was very pleased. With Bonnefous our output would greatly increase. I hadn't seen him since Saint-Cyr but I was sure we would make a tough and successful team. We had been brought up with identical values from similar backgrounds; we were drawn together by that special comradeship that is the trademark of our graduating classes. We would know how to face the daunting task that I was more and more convinced was vital to our country. As I waited for this unexpected help I worked harder than ever, taking no days off!

De Robien, having recovered, came by the office in the middle of January before leaving for a command in Syria. He came to say good-bye and was surprised that he hadn't yet been replaced, but satisfied that I was handling the job. He returned two days later much to our surprise. Through his brother and the Quai d'Orsay, he had obtained an invitation to the embassy of the USSR for the visit of Marshal Tukhachevsky to Paris. The marshal was on his way to London to represent his government at the funeral of King George V on January 28, 1936. He asked to meet with some French "friends," who had been in the same German prisoner-of-war camp in 1915 and 1916 and for Major de Robien, whom he probably knew was part of the Special Services.

"As you might imagine," said de Robien, "Rivet and foreign affairs snapped up the opportunity and demanded that I get this white elephant to speak up. I will find out tomorrow with Perruche and most of all with Josset how to slant the conversation."

I saw de Robien two days later; he was reporting back to the Boss and the S.R. on his meeting with Tukhachevsky.

"He's a simple and direct man; more open than the Russian diplomats my brother had introduced me to. He speaks very little French and poor English; but he does speak German and we were able to chat for quite some time. We reminisced about our months as prisoners of war and about the current situation in Germany. He was aware of my assignment to the *Deuxième Bureau* and wanted to know our opinion regarding the Reich. He fears the political trends and Hitler's policy in seeking to free Germany from its obligations under the Treaty of Versailles. He was clear about wanting to closely check on German military potential and that the prior agreements between the High Commands of the USSR and Germany should be kept in force and effect. He's convinced that the best way to monitor the enemy is to stay in contact with him."

Tukhachevsky was non-committal about the internal situation in Russia but did intimate—de Robien added—that the recent purges initiated by Stalin were causing opposition to the regime, which could be used by White Russians abroad against Soviet interests. Then he asked me what our attitude was regarding the activities and leaders among White Russians in France and in particular General Miller and his deputy Skoblin in Paris. Tukhachevsky was asked to meet with a representative of the general in London and he accepted, guided by the principle that one must keep in contact with the enemy. De Robien was surprised by what he heard, the tone of confident sarcasm with which it was conveyed and by the "bourgeois" demeanor of the general, who appeared to be quite openly hostile to Stalinist methods.

"Something new will be coming out of Russia my friend. I suggest you watch those Russian circles and Skoblin in particular very closely; we have already observed his curious connections to the Germans."

Then de Robien finally took his leave. I was never to see him again but I remember him as a perfect gentleman, possibly too worldly in his approach for a mission that I now know required great attention to detail and an open mind. From Syria he later sent me, along with his best wishes, a magnificent Druse dagger. Later on in 1938 I had the thankless task of telling him that in Sofia, Bulgaria, where he was military attaché, his safe was being regularly visited by Bulgarian intelligence.

What de Robien said intrigued me. Our files indicated that General Miller was the president of R.O.V.S.* following General Kutiepov, who had been kidnapped in France by the Soviet secret services in 1930 and had vanished without a trace. Miller was a cautious, understated individual who commanded respect in some White Russian circles. He had good relations with the German embassy in Paris and since Hitler had come to power it appeared that Skoblin was in charge of maintaining those contacts. Skoblin was quite a strange character. He became a general in 1920 when he was not yet thirty years old, and was now president of the association of the veterans of Kornilov's army and a candidate to take over Miller's position. With his wife, the internationally famous Russian singer Nadia Plevitskaya, he enjoyed a grand lifestyle in Paris. Skoblin was often seen in German circles and his several trips abroad to Belgium and Germany led us to believe that he was probably in contact, if not with the Abwehr, at least with the SD. Plevitskaya, who was older than her husband, and still very beautiful, on the other hand appeared, according to some information difficult to assess, as long being on excellent terms with the Soviets and undoubtedly with the NKVD.

Commander Josset, who was well connected to the R.O.V.S., suspected that the Skoblin couple had a hand in Kutiepov's kidnapping and was in fact working for the NKVD. Police Commissioner Gianvitti, who had replaced the well-known Commissioner Bidet because of the Soviet "Fantomas" espionage case at the political police, decided to place the Skoblins under surveillance and agreed with Commander Josset's conclusions. He was also convinced that their country house at Ozoir-la-Ferrière was bought with funds originating both from Soviet and German intelligence. One year later events were to prove that de Robien's warnings, Josset and Gianvitti's suspicions, and information within our own files were all correct. The facts spoke for themselves.

On June 11, 1937 a terse bulletin from the Soviet news agency TASS announced to the world that marshal Mikhail Nikolaïevitch Tukhachevsky, having confessed to committing the crime of treason, had been executed, along with eight other generals who were his accomplices. Marshal Blücher, on express orders from Stalin, commanded the firing squad. Vyshinsky had used an indictment that would remain mysterious for a long time to come. Some French and German writers have stated that the indictment contained information provided to the Soviets by Heydrich, which had

---

* Association of Former Officers of the Tsar's Armies.

been confirmed by Czech President Edvard Beneš. This information, whether true or false, was intended to prove the existence of deep and secret contacts between the German and Soviet High Commands initiated by Tukhachevsky.

Three months later, on September 22, 1937, a Soviet commando kidnapped General Miller in Paris. A long and difficult investigation, hampered by political interference, succeeded in establishing the circumstances surrounding those events. General Miller had become cautious since the Kutiepov disappearance, and even more so in recent months, since he was suspicious of Skoblin and his shady relationships laced with intrigue. On the morning of September 22, before going to the meeting set up by his deputy, General Miller brought a sealed envelope to the headquarters of the association he headed at 29 rue du Colisée, to be opened in case he did not return promptly. General Kussonski another one of Miller's deputies, received the envelope around noon and was surprised by the way all this was done. Miller did not return that evening.

Kussonski opened the envelope where Miller stated that Skoblin had set up a meeting at a location he described with two German officials whose names he stated. He intimated that this could possibly be a trap. French authorities were unable to recognize any of the names written by Miller in his letter. When Kussonski contacted Skoblin that same night, the latter offered no explanation and disappeared. He was never to be seen again! Miller's family filed a complaint with French authorities. On the evening of September 23, 1937, the Soviet cargo ship *Maria Ulianova* suddenly sailed from Le Havre after loading the contents of a van with Paris license plates. We later found out that the van belonged to the Soviet embassy in Paris. When subjected to questioning, Plevitskaya provided false alibis regarding her whereabouts as well as those of her husband on September 22.

Under pressure from public opinion and the press, the French government was considering the recall of the Soviet ship and Miller's return, since it was by now obvious that he had been kidnapped. Daladier, who had received information from our Services concerning Skoblin's shady reputation, was unsuccessful in getting French Prime Minister Léon Blum to take action. In a politically charged atmosphere, upset by social unrest, the right-wing leagues, the civil war in Spain, threats hanging over peace— all these reasons were good enough to avoid taking action that might undermine a precarious diplomatic status quo that had been difficult to reach. The excuse this time centered on the difficulty in establishing the facts regarding the time the Soviet ship set sail and the time the van arrived at Le Havre. The matter then bogged down and was overtaken by other events.

Just as Kutiepov before him, Miller would soon be forgotten and his case was quickly etched in the "profit and loss" ledger of French sovereignty. Plevitskaya, who played the part of the scapegoat, was found guilty as an accomplice and sentenced to twenty years of hard labor on December 9, 1938 by the Paris criminal court. She died in 1944 at the penitentiary at Rennes while the Germans showed no interest in her case. Had Skoblin been instrumental in the execution of the Soviet generals they would undoubtedly have shown much more interest. My conclusions on this whole matter may appear somewhat more simple than those offered by other French or foreign authors. It may be summed up as follows:

Beginning in 1934 the White Russians were counting on Hitler's Germany to destroy the Soviet regime sometime in the future. This was the origin of the contacts established by Miller and most of all by Skoblin with the Nazis and explains why Miller agreed, even though he suspected something, to the meeting set up by Skoblin with the two alleged German officials. Most likely these were the men sent to kidnap him. As Tukhachevsky told de Robien, he found it useful to maintain relations with the Wehrmacht. He was opposed to Stalin's brutal policies and agreed to or even solicited contacts with White Russians. Skoblin and his wife, who were informers of both the SD and the Soviets, kept them abreast of these contacts, of Miller's plans and his contacts with Nazi officials. The fate of both Tukhachevsky, whom Stalin hated, and of Miller, was therefore decided. Stalin had only to give the signal at the appropriate time to put a stop to this conspiracy, which took place in a few weeks during the summer of 1937.

On the eve of important decisions by Hitler in the midst of political tensions, it was tempting for Heydrich to use the information provided by Skoblin and take credit later on for having played a role in decapitating the Red army. Through channels that remain mysterious, he passed on information to the Soviets, possibly documents confirming Tukhachevsky's "betrayal" and supported by many additional circumstantial details, even of a cloak and dagger nature—such as the Nazi break-in of Canaris' safe in their search for any clues of contacts between German and Soviet generals and the forgery of related documents. This shady initiative by Heydrich was in fact a golden opportunity for the intriguing head of the SD to provide his master Adolf Hitler with additional "proof" of his effectiveness and devotion.

No mention of this matter came up at the Nuremberg trials; however, had Heydrich's involvement been essential it would certainly have been added to the charges brought against the SD showing that starting in 1936-1937 that organization, which was accused of crimes against humanity, was in fact preparing the aggression against the USSR. Neither the defendants nor the prosecutors at the trial of the SD took that angle and the Soviet Union certainly didn't. But where there's smoke there's generally fire; some explanation to this general lack of interest in a case that was rather serious and worrisome must be attempted. It may also be imagined, and I am not alone in this, that secret contacts between Nazi and Stalinist secret services did exist in 1936-1937 and that they would eventually lead to the signing of the Nazi-Soviet Non-Aggression Pact of 1939.

One morning in April 1936, Lieutenant Colonel Grosjean called me into his office. The head of counterespionage generally appeared only for exceptional matters that were of vital importance to the Service...or to his own peace and quiet. I went right in and found Bonnefous sitting there. He hadn't changed a bit and was immaculately dressed, his black hair was perfectly parted, his dark eyes had their usual lively expression and his voice was quiet and serious. We shook hands at length and that handshake was to remain symbolically alive through events, separations, bad times or intrigues that could have divided us. I remembered him as hardworking and intelligent, one of the best graduates of the Saint-Cyr military school, handicapped only by relatively poor health. That was how I caught up with him eight years later, smiling broadly as I introduced him to Rivet, who welcomed him warmly and made him feel completely at ease. Bonnefous very quickly fit into his new mission and a specific case was to get us both involved in the task at hand.

Gessmann was back, and quite pleased about the information he was carrying. He told me about the creation of new *Wehrkreise* and new Abwehr observation posts in Wiesbaden in particular, which was a logical consequence of the remilitarization of the Rhineland and the general rearmament of Germany. The Stuttgart office, which controlled the tiny observation post of Lindau, was now under the command of Major Waag, who happened to be a nephew of Admiral Canaris. New posts were being opened at Constanz, Bergenz, Lörrach, and Sigmaringen. France was being targeted much more, and Italy as well. "It isn't prudent to consider Italy as being completely loyal," said Gombart. It's also very important to work in depth in Austria, where increased Nazi penetration irritated and enraged Gessmann.

The documents concerning the "tank project" excited Gombart, who was quite candid and said that he would find out more after French maneuvers at Mailly and Châlons-sur-Marne. He told Gessmann to continue his research and offered him a lot more money. Gessmann generously handed me an envelope with a real fortune inside, which was to make our accounting office very happy. This time I fully realized how important it was to penetrate the enemy camp. I found it deplorable that besides a small investigating unit under retired Commander Terres in Paris, there was no Special Services office in charge of handling such matters. It had to be set up and in the meantime I was to fill in that gap by beginning to recruit agents myself.

Having studied the Gessmann file Bonnefous agreed with my assessment of the agent. Obviously, in order to gain the trust of the Germans he must have performed some very important tasks for them before Hitler came to power. Gessmann was ideologically opposed to National Socialism and to the Anschluss; he had other interests and was useful to us. Since the Frogé affair he was well aware of the fact that he was known and was being closely watched in France. His immediate problem, apart from the missions he had to carry out, was to make sure that both Gombart and I kept on trusting him. He was clever enough in handling the German, who could have become suspicious after the Frogé business. Gessmann described the strange circumstances by which he became involved in the matter. He told about the tricks he used to avoid arrest by the French. In agreement with Osvald, he brought the Abwehr some first-hand information on the organization of the French police and judicial system while he pursued his fictitious espionage missions. Gombart appeared to be satisfied with the results.

Sensing that I was quite suspicious about the actions of a double agent, Gessmann remained trustworthy and several clues were to convince me for a time of his continued loyalty. Our Belfort station informed us that the address in Vaduz belonged to a tailor with customers all along Lake Constance. The investigator, our loyal and dedicated Jourdeuil, had suspected for some time that the tailor was in fact a German intelligence agent. Some of his "customers" were regularly visiting the offices of the Abwehr in Lindau. Tight surveillance of this mail drop allowed us to intercept messages mailed from Ivry and find out that they were written by a medical doctor. It took us one year to identify that person and make an arrest. We were more fortunate with another letter writer, the spy Berthollet, who was quickly stopped because Gombart had made the mistake of giving him the same mail drop. Some of the Abwehr's top "aces" were to make that same mistake later on, thus revealing some of the most important sources of information for Nazi Germany.

Together with Bonnefous I visited the rue des Suassaies for a meeting with Osvald and his assistants, Linas and Même, to discuss the report signed "S." Gessmann said it was a journalist. There were hundreds of journalists in the files of the Sûreté and the police prefecture, including both French citizens and foreigners whose last name began with the letter "S." Which one could it be? We decided to examine the newsmen who had been allowed to report on the military maneuvers. We obtained about 40 names from the 3rd Bureau of the E.M.A. At the letter "S" we found a Baron von Stackelberg from the Baltic who had to be our man.

We spied on him closely for several months, and opened his mail. When he traveled to Belgium, Switzerland, or Germany our inspector Danger would be waiting for him whenever he returned. Sometimes the inspector would wait patiently in front of a hotel on the Avenue Victor-Hugo while the newsman made love to a young secretary who worked at the Quai d'Orsay, and later followed him once more to a bistro at Les Halles until the wee hours of the morning… Another unproductive night for our investigation. During the September maneuvers we became even more cautious. Like most newsmen Stackelberg was interested in changes in materiel, listened to the summaries of the commanders of the exercises, and took some notes. He returned to Paris without a hint of any wrongdoing. Could we have been making a mistake?

During the winter of 1936-1937 Gessmann became our retriever of sorts. In order to pick up the scent of the prey we had to try to get Gombart to talk. We gave Gessmann some new information on tank supplies and a report regarding the same maneuvers that Stackelberg had attended. He discussed the report with Gombart, who found it amusing because he thought it was so vague. With some pride he extracted from his desk a typed report in German several pages long also signed "S," which was so technical that before transmitting it to Berlin he decided to meet with its author in Bern for further explanations and comments. We increased our surveillance of Stackelberg and at long last our patience was rewarded. Stackelberg boarded a train to Switzerland. One of Osvald's inspectors traveled quickly to Pontarlier to set up a very careful customs search of all the passengers. If successful, we would place Stackelberg under arrest. His production for the Abwehr was too dangerous for us to simply watch him operate. Many long weeks of surveillance had produced enough proof that he was an extremely efficient operator.

Obviously this arrest could compromise Gessmann's position and lead to negative consequences for the little observation post at Lindau, which we also seemed to control rather well. All things considered there was too much at risk in allowing Stackelberg to roam around as a free man and I was not averse to ending Gessmann's career as a double agent. Besides the fact that I am opposed to using that type of informer for an extended period, I had other reasons to reach that conclusion: his game was getting dangerous to him as much as to us. He was not the kind of informer I was looking for to discover what was going on inside the Abwehr. Lindau was a secondary outpost and even though he was clever enough, Gessmann would never handle important information. Finally, I had the impression that if we eliminated source "S" there would no longer be much to nibble on at Lindau.

A baggage check yielded some notes by Stackelberg in German on armored units. The baron insisted this was part of his regular work as a journalist; to us it was enough to take him off the train and back to Paris to the rue des Saussaies. He was pale and disheveled and admitted to his real activity rather quickly because we found a phone number in Constanz, which had already been used by the spy Lydia Oswald, in his address book. Stackelberg had been working for the Abwehr for three years. He was operating as a journalist accredited to the Quai d'Orsay with access to the Senate, the Chamber of Deputies, as well as many official and military functions. Because of their importance, he would hand over his reports to an official at the German embassy whom he met either at the consulate or at diplomatic receptions and who, in turn, was the courier responsible for their transmission to Lindau. The Belfort case, the arrests of Krauss, Lydia Oswald, Berthollet, and now Stackelberg—this proved to be too much for Major Ehinger, the head of Section III F of the Ast in Stuttgart. His investigation uncovered so many mistakes that at the end of 1937 Gombart was given early retirement and the Lindau observation post was shut down.

For quite some time I kept Gombart's farewell letter to Gessmann mailed from Constance on January 13, 1938. I didn't forget what he wrote:

Dear Friend,

I am writing to you from my retirement. For the least three years fate has not been good to me and my hair has turned white.

In this line of work, which I loved above anything else, I learned to judge men not according to the sympathy they may inspire but rather for their qualities. Your qualities were great because you were useful to my mission in spite of all the obstacles. Yet I feel it to be my duty to warn you about a profession that can lead you into taking the most dangerous risks. I still feel enough friendship for you to not harbor any resentment, even though you bear some responsibility for my current position.

Good luck!

Heil Hitler!

Gessmann didn't incur any punishment. I provided him with a new identity and the necessary documents. Through our office in Lisbon in June 1938 we got him a job as an engineer in Portugal under the name of Fonseca. We met him once again in 1941 while he was pursuing his activity as a double agent between the Intelligence Service and the Abwehr.

By early June 1936 I had formed an opinion regarding the usefulness of that kind of agent after considering several cases, such as the Frogé affair. By the end of May 1936 I had also seen the high quality and production of the work done by Doudot as a penetration agent inside the Abwehr. As a reserve officer-interpreter, Doudot had a deep knowledge of Germany, its language, and dialects. He had been part of our services for many years and specialized in counterespionage. We admired the extremely efficient branch he headed in Metz. He knew the German intelligence organization, its methods, objectives, and personnel much better than his opposite number, Major Rudolph, commander of the Cologne branch of the Munster Ast! Doudot was able to infiltrate that branch and earn the trust of its commanding officers. I listened while he described his work to me for over one hour, his eyes shining with pleasure as he told me how he was able to hoodwink his opponents.

"I had witnessed the increasingly aggressive action by German intelligence ever since the Abwehr was created in 1926. In Metz we thought that many spies were slipping through because we didn't know the enemy or his methods. Both Colonel Manges, head of the Special Services branch at Metz, and myself then thought we should attempt to contact our adversaries directly.

"In 1932 I mailed a letter from Luxembourg to the address of Radio-Cologne and inside there was a second envelope addressed to the Intelligence Service where I offered my services for cash. I identified myself as being a non-commissioned officer in the reserves requesting an answer to general delivery at the Luxembourg central post office. One month later I was summoned to a café in Trier. I refused to go into Germany for security reasons. Two weeks later a second letter arrived setting up a meeting at the Koob pastry shop on the Boulevard de la Gare in Luxembourg. I was to be seated at a given time having a cup of tea and clearly reading a Belgian newspaper. That was how I came to meet Kriminal–Sekretär Clövers, who subjected me to a real interrogation, and very carefully checked out my (false) passport like a seasoned veteran. He observed me while I spoke and then left about ninety long minutes later, after setting up an appointment two weeks later at the Rheinischer-Hof Hotel in Sarrebruck. He wasn't alone; Rudolph, an officer from the Cologne Abwehr, had come with him. He had just been promoted to the rank of major and assigned to the Munster Ast.

"I quickly became his trusted informer. Every month he, and after a time his successor, would meet with me in a different location. I was given lists of questions and money… 'Captain (I had just been promoted myself), when you come to Metz you will see the kind of offices we have because of Hitler's money…'"

Doudot laughed and went on:

"The problem is to answer the military questionnaires, and there's no way we could get any guidelines from Paris on this issue. So with the regional military command we cooked up some answers that sometimes got me in trouble with Cologne. The questionnaires related to the Maginot Line, the troops manning the fortresses, and the weapons used. During the recent occupation of the Rhineland, Rudolph was worried and forbade me from finding out the mobilization numbers. Sometimes they asked me to check out information provided by others. In case of emergency I had a phone number in Cologne as well as a code to send messages to a mail drop. I was able to identify several Abwehr officers this way. I have them watched in Sarrebruck or in Luxembourg and I also kept watch over the café in Trier. In less than three years we have uncovered about thirty Belgians and French nationals who were working for those gentlemen."

Thanks to Captain Lafont, an officer in the Metz office, and one of the best technicians in the service, Doudot had been able to infiltrate a reliable agent named Schweitzer inside the Ast in Stuttgart, which was responsible for Lindau. With even more sophisticated intelligence to entice the Abwehr, Schweitzer and Doudot, who displayed truly amazing talent, could have improved both their position and their results inside the two main German sections targeting France.

With Bonnefous now part of the team, I was able to travel more often outside Paris. I went to Lille at the beginning of June 1936. Commander Darbou, the brother of my colleague in Paris, was the very authoritarian and surly head of that listening post working on northern Germany through Belgium and the Netherlands. There was no dedicated counterespionage officer, but all the officers around him were very much aware of the rebirth of the Abwehr. They watched for developments through an excellent penetration agent, Li 159, whom I shall discuss later on.

In Brussels, Darbou introduced me to the head of Belgian security, Mr. Verrhulst, who congratulated me and was very pleased with the excellent results he was able to reach because of the work shared with Doudot and promised me his complete cooperation. But to no avail. The Belgian High Command, just like our own, was not responsive to our attempts at working together and refused any official cooperation with our Special Services. Our Belgian friends were to maintain a strictly neutral policy toward Nazi Germany, whose ambitions and threats were as clear to Verrhulst as they were to us. I returned to Paris, intending to go to Belfort as soon as possible. I was unable to travel to southeastern France at the time. General Roatta, head of Italian espionage, had requested that the French Special Service office in Nice, which was a branch of the Marseille district office, be "put on ice" and the French Ministry of War had accepted to do so rather rashly.

The Italians used sentimental reasons to back up their request for this neutrality on the part of the French. Our service, and Rivet in particular, was extremely irritated because just like the rest of us, he was well aware that Roatta and Canaris were holding meetings and setting the stage for an agreement that would be the prelude to the creation of the Axis alliance. Bonnefous was handling the workload in my absence and in-

formed me that Captain Brun, the oldest member of the SCR and recently appointed to the section next to ours, had requested to speak with
me urgently. He was a rather conceited and not very dedicated officer
who partied a lot.

"Old boy," he said, "Grosjean's 'replacement' came around several
times. I didn't see much of him. He came at odd hours. He's a great
horseman, thin as a rail; you'd think he's no more than thirty! He seems to
know everything. It appears that he was part of the SR downstairs a few
years back. His pseudonym was Saint-George. His name is Major Guy
Schlesser."

"When will he be back?"

"He didn't say, perhaps shortly or eight days from now."

"Did he ask to see me?"

"Of course! When I told him you were in Lille he liked the idea.
Don't change your schedule."

I was surprised, a bit worried, and very curious. That evening, tired
from my trip, from studying the urgent files, and under pressure because
of the growing amount of work that was now becoming part of my
mission, I went home around 9 p.m. I went to bed and was trying to fall
asleep when the phone rang.

"Paillole, hello Paillole. Good evening, Paillole. Could you please come
over?

"Who's calling?"

"It's Saint-George obviously!" (He burst out laughing.) "I'm waiting
for you at the office!"

It was 10 p.m. There were some people strolling along the Boulevard
des Invalides, taking advantage of the warm evening that announced the
coming summer season. Douarin, the guard at the door, and Brochu were
amazed to see me dart passed them and run up the stairs two at a time.
There was a strange melodious music playing throughout the office and
the windows were open wide. Schlesser was waiting for me in riding
breeches and shining boots, his jacket thrown over a chair. We discussed
the Service for hours on end. He already knew most of what I told him.
I listened enthusiastically to what he was saying, knowing it would be the
key to our coming initiatives, which reflected my own thoughts.

"Germany is our target."

"We're not fighting the enemy with the same kind of weapons he's
using."

"We must behave like hunters."

"We must wake up the government, the High Command, and break the lethargy."

"We should adopt the motto of Edmond Rostand in *La Princesse Lointaine*: 'Inertia is a vice, my dear Erasmus, and enthusiasm is the only virtue.'"

It was very late. Schlesser came up to me and, almost standing at attention, he stared at me intensely, looking rather satisfied with his deep blue eyes. Then we shook hands vigorously.

"See you soon, Paillole. Good night!"

I wandered around the empty avenue for a while. I could now sense my mission and myself much better: I knew that something had just changed in my life.

3

Organizing the Resistance

S chlesser's appearance and his determination to get into his new job very quickly compelled me to sum up what we knew about our adversaries. We were already referring to them as the "enemy." Under the spell of such a charismatic and enthusiastic leader who knew how to get to the bottom of things, Bonnefous and I jumped into writing the first paper—to call it a summary would be rather pretentious—describing the German intelligence services. It was far from being as detailed and as complete as we wished; however, it did underline the main points of Nazi Germany's effort in the area and set our own objectives.

Thanks to our penetration agents and Doudot in particular, our knowledge had greatly improved. The interrogation of the spies we had arrested turned out to be quite disappointing: there were few big operatives, and many were shiftless types, degenerates, crooks, homosexuals, or desperate individuals without any money. I couldn't imagine how they could be of any use if not to justify additional appropriations and the need for large numbers of agents. One excellent source was providing our service with increasingly high-quality information, a man we named Asché,* whom Captain Bertrand of the office next door to mine was meeting regularly. Since

---

* Asché was the pseudonym of Hans-Thilo Schmidt.

he had been appointed to the Forschungsamt he was providing us, besides other very important intelligence, with the intercepts and decryptions made by the Stuttgart listening post that was targeting France.

Thanks to his deliveries when he was at the Chistelle,[*] and because of the excellent way in which he was being "handled," our cryptographers were able to read the interceptions of our listening posts like an open book. Schlesser, who had met Asché with Bertrand several times in neutral countries, described that colorful character, who was clever and bold enough to remove the most secret German army mobilization codes from his commander's safe. Göring's Forschungsamt, whose mission and efficiency were no secret to us, was the ubiquitous Nazi eavesdropping service both inside and outside Germany. It listened in on the conversations of all suspected civilians, military, foreigners and German individuals and organizations it deemed necessary. Göring alone decided how to use the messages obtained in this manner.

Again thanks to Asché, our technicians were about to reproduce the Wehrmacht's encoding machine, the "Enigma." Once that task was completed just before the outbreak of the Second World War, Captain Bertrand's section was to achieve unparalleled results using the same research method. French intelligence (S.R. and C.E.) therefore possessed an important weapon in the secret war. Asché was betrayed in 1943 by one of our recruiting agents, Lemoine (codenamed *Rex*), whom he had met several times since 1933. *Rex* had talked either out of fear or under torture and Asché was condemned to death and executed by firing squad in Berlin in July 1943.

The Abwehr's *Group I* had grown into the three traditional research sections (war, navy, air force) with an additional economic espionage and a technical airborne espionage section. This proved how important it was for Germany to build up and improve its air force.

Group II was to become one of the cornerstones of the Abwehr: its mission was political sabotage in foreign countries through the manipulation of the political opposition, as well as dissident factions. We shall see what its effects were to be in France on separatists, pro-German and subversive groups.

Group III handled military security and counterespionage and underwent a spectacular increase. The Abwehr's mission clearly was to protect

---

[*] This was the abbreviation for Chifferstelle, the encryption division of the Reichswehrministerium, or Reich Defense Ministry.

Germany's secrets and develop repressive action. Entire sections were dedicated to protecting the army and the armaments industry. Section *III F* was the most important one, concentrating exclusively on counterespionage. Its mission, similar to ours, was not only to uncover enemy agents but also attempt to penetrate enemy intelligence organizations. Had we provided them with some kind of hint?

Group Z was in charge of managing the central file, mobilization, administration, and finances of the Abwehr.

The offices reporting to Berlin were growing just as fast as the central services. Ast Wiesbaden was active against France through its Trier branch, which was headed by Oscar Reile, * and Saarbrück directed by Dernback, also a counterespionage specialist like Reile. The Hamburg Ast (with branches in Bremen and Flensburg) was increasingly active against France, England and the United States. It dealt mostly with naval matters. For us to check that particular branch it would be necessary to increase our contacts with the British and the Americans, whose intelligence services were totally inactive. About 12 large branch offices of the Abwehr were identified and corresponded to the 12 *Wehrkriese* Hitler had decided upon. Four were permanently targeting France: Stuttgart, Münster, Wiesbaden, and Hamburg. Our study would have been incomplete had it not included the sum total of what we knew about the atmosphere inside the Abwehr and the organizations which carried out and strengthened its actions.

What was more worrisome was the growing influence of the Nazi party inside Germany over the police and administrative offices. The Nazi party was the only legal party since the law decree of July 14, 1933. The SS were fast becoming the most important group within the party, a reservoir of "racially pure" men, who had sworn allegiance to Hitler. "We swear to obey Hitler until death!" Since June 17, 1936 a Führer decree had named Heinrich Himmler the Reichsführer SS, as Chief of the German police within the Ministry of the Interior where Wilhelm Frick was the Minister. This move confirmed the takeover of the Gestapo and the overall German security apparatus by the most extremist elements of the NSDAP.

Himmler had reorganized the police forces into the regular uniformed police and the Security police, the Sicherheitspolizei, or SIPO, which included the criminal police, or KRIPO, and the Gestapo whose men were

---

* Oscar Riele was to head the Abwehr Section III F at the Hotel Lutétia in Paris from June 1940 up to the liberation.

obviously going to become members of the SS if they had not already joined that organization! As for our "friend" Heydrich, besides being already in charge of the security service within the SS (the *Sicherheitsdienst* or SD), he was to head the entire organization. The SD was no longer limiting itself to operating abroad to ferret out anything that could harm or be a nuisance to the regime. The border police, now part of the Gestapo, pursued those investigations it deemed necessary beyond Germany's frontiers.

Suspects of all kinds were often shot; more often they were placed "in protective custody," an elegant euphemism to describe their removal to concentration camps. Our informers had been reporting for two years on the extremely brutal conditions—at Dachau for example—that the inmates were subjected to by the SS *Totenkopfverbände*, or "Death's Head" units. Ninety-five percent of young Germans were grouped under the leadership of Baldur von Schirach in the Hitler Youth organization (*Hitlerjugend*). Steeped in Nazi ideology, they were the recruiting ground for the SS, the SD, and the German army. They adopted the slogans of Nazi propaganda: destruction of the Versailles "Diktat," rearmament, return of the lands with people of German race, seizure even by force of the necessary living space, *Lebensraum*, anti-Semitism.

Alfred Rosenberg, head of the A.P.A. the foreign affairs office of the Nazi party, was in charge of Nazi ideological education worldwide. Josef Goebbels, in charge of "total war" and Minister of Propaganda, disseminated Nazi ideology with extreme mastery and huge budgets. The grants to agencies handling information outside Germany went from 400,000 RM to 4 million RM. Through radio and the press it supported the efforts of the delegations overseas operating mostly under diplomatic cover.* Goebbels, along with his main deputy Hans Fritzche, under the pretense of informing the German press, that included some 2,300 daily newspapers, set up what amounted to a foreign intelligence gathering service which we provided efficient support to the Abwehr. In agreement with Baldur von Schirach, Goebbels forged ahead in targeting his propaganda efforts toward European youth and was committed to rally Europeans to the German side.

Several hundreds of thousands of copies of the Hitler Youth's magazine *Wille und Macht*—Will and Power—were distributed in France in French

---

* The *Eildienst, Tranz-Ozean, Europa-Presse*, and the powerful DNB (*Deutsche Nachrichtenbüro*).

translation and one could even read in an editorial signed by the French ambassador to Berlin this dangerous statement: "German influence fertilizes French thinking"!

Schlesser was furious because he knew how tenuous our relationship was with the ministry of foreign affairs, always inclined to minimize the danger represented by enemy propaganda and espionage inside France and never very cooperative in facilitating the efforts of our intelligence agencies overseas. While we described these frightening signs of change in Germany, Perruche, who was keen and sarcastic, told us about the main military measures taken by Germany contrary to the peace treaties:

> March 10, 1935: Creation of a military air force, the Luftwaffe.
>
> March 16, 1935: Conscription is reinstated by decree; the army will go from 100,000 to 500,000 men; the peacetime army is organized in 12 Wehrkriese, instead of 7.
>
> May 21, 1935: Secret law for the defense of the Reich: training of military personnel and efforts to produce armaments and munitions.
>
> March 7, 1936: Reoccupation of the Rhineland and decision to build the Siegfried Line.
>
> May 27, 1936: Joint decision by Hitler and Göring: "no financial limitations to the war effort."

"What puzzles me," Schlesser would repeat, "is the apathy displayed by everyone in the face of such threats. The information we get on Germany is very specific and during the past few months our intelligence gathering has improved even more. Besides official open diplomatic sources, our honorable correspondents* produce excellent reports on the situation in general, on the political aims of Hitler, the Nazi party and its by-products. It is alarming and our leaders are aware of it."

The S.R. was providing information on changes in Nazi Germany's military power to the Army High Command, which could, in turn, furnish unbiased reports and assessments to the government and the leadership. Captain Stehlin, French air force deputy attaché at the Berlin embassy, was sending us assessments on German rearmament and on the Luftwaffe, confirming and completing intelligence we had received from our field offices. French penetration agents inside the Abwehr were able

---

* H.C.

to uncover the areas the German High Command was focusing on and its drive to gather maximum intelligence on its potential enemies in case of war. In Berlin and in its various branches we were informed of the Abwehr's deep concern during the reoccupation of the Rhineland. We knew that an immediate military reaction by the Allies would have led to the Wehrmacht's retreat back to its former barracks.

"We missed the one opportunity to force Hitler to withdraw and perhaps avoid war," said Schlesser, regretfully, echoing Rivet and Perruche.

Having been on the job for the past nine months I was able to explain my understanding of our mission to our new commanding officer. It was a pleasure to speak with him even though our conversations often lasted late into the night and the "paid vacations" that the Popular Front government had so generously passed in its enthusiasm for social reform on June 7, 1936. The paid vacations had all passed me by!

From our conversations back and forth, Schlesser formed a concept of counterespionage that was unquestionably ambitious in view of the internal situation of France at the time, the structure of its antiquated parliamentary institutions and the meager size of our capabilities. One point did stand out: our mission could no longer be simply repressive. Obviously stopping our enemies was to remain an important part of our task. Gathering intelligence overseas was also an essential function of counterespionage that we had to carry out, triggering police and legal action inside French territory. However, the objectives of national defense had to become much broader.

Since the enemy was preparing for war he needed to discover our secrets and be informed of the nature and size of our reactions at every stage of the fateful march that Hitler had decided upon, and reduce or abort any opposition to his ambitions, no matter how demented they may be. The preventive and essential part of our defensive mission was to protect and keep watch over anything that might be of interest to the Abwehr—which implied providing a clear definition of what a "national defense secret" was. This proved to be a very complex problem for all national institutions attempting to respond to our requests. The solution encountered general skepticism; the easygoing attitude and legendary indiscretion that is so much a part of French national character at every social level also flourished at the various administrative and military echelons. We would be up against messy habits as well as the lack of funds of every administration that always needed more money to buy the cheapest waste paper basket. We needed to end improvisation and business as usual.

A simple rubber stamp marked "Secret" was enough to reassure everyone; no one knew the number of copies made of a very confidential memo and there was no procedure or control as to its dissemination. Documents, like secret objects, were filed (when they are *really* filed…) in offices open to all, within dusty old cabinets made of wood or scrap iron that any key in the world could easily open, as we had experienced in Belfort! To formulate a proper definition of what constitutes a national defense secret and how it must be protected can only be achieved with the consent of those involved. Would we succeed in alerting the French people, and its leaders, of the looming dangers threatening the country and of our duty to protect France?

To inform the nation, beginning with the army, also meant protecting morale and shielding it from some of the enemy's more insidious initiatives, mostly relating to propaganda. Schlesser, whose mission it was to address all these matters, felt it necessary to make an inventory of the weakest areas and make sure they were being properly scrutinized: munitions plants, fortifications, main lines of communication, ports, the locations of army maneuvers.

"The borders," he would cry out, "are as many sieves!" Had those measures been completely and thoroughly enacted the enemy could never succeed. Alas, the world is not perfect, even less so when it becomes necessary to enact regulations that go against the grain of the people who are expected to follow them. There were cracks everywhere within our preventive shield. Those in charge of protecting our secrets were very often the first ones to ignore the basic rules.

During the espionage trials we were involved in to evaluate the nature of the intelligence that had been compromised, I understood how controversial the concept of national defense secrets remained. No precise definition was provided in any law or legal document. In Germany anything the enemy wanted to find out was secret. It was clear, expeditious, and Hitlerian! In France everything led to endless disputes, such as the political and social climate, the personality of the spy or the traitor. Defining what is a secret was not set in stone, but rather subject to change according to the person's position of privilege or responsibility, even within the government. Only a total patsy was virtually assured of being subjected to the so-called "rigors of the law," an expression, which in the year 1936 with Nazism on the rise, had become completely ridiculous.

We were discouraged and frustrated by the chronic weakness in the repression of espionage. A strong and independent system of justice, with a credible arsenal of punishment acting as a deterrent, could be our partner in enforcement; and since national defense was the subject, it should be agreed once and for all that the relevant jurisdiction could only be in military tribunals, that were best qualified and prepared to judge cases in matters of that nature. A specialized police force would be the necessary arm of the law to ensure that repressive measures were properly implemented.

There was a nucleus of extremely competent and highly professional policemen in matters of counterespionage inside the *Sûreté* who understood the importance of our mission. This was the division known as the *Surveillance du Territoire*. Beyond that handful of specialists and a few policemen in the 5th Section of the *Renseignments généraux de la préfecture de police parisienne*, the RGPP,* the ministry of the interior had no personnel dedicated exclusively to the struggle against espionage. This was totally inadequate, considering that these very small units were assigned to long investigations and the time that was required for tailing suspects in just one case, such as the Stackelberg affair. It could become necessary and very effective in some cases to let a spy continue to go about his business, to keep tailing him and unravel the organization he belonged to rather than brutally terminate his activities.

We harbored no illusions as to the results we could conceivably expect from our current defensive efforts. People given to loose talk, the spies, the traitors, were not about to be stopped and France's secrets were slipping away in the process. We attempted to put a stop to this and tried to reduce the hemorrhage. The idea of using disinformation took hold: it was rather attractive to attempt to drown what the enemy really knew within a flood of false information and deceive the opposition while stanching the leaks. In our boss' office, overlooking Paris and its frenetic but so distant life, oblivious to the threatening dangers that loomed, we defined a much broader concept of our mission. A total counterespionage action that could be summed up as follows:

1. Penetrate the enemy and find out his intentions. We referred to this as offensive counterespionage, which was to direct our investigations and planning as well as our defensive action.

2. Set up a protective shield impervious to enemy procedures and capabilities. This role was assigned to defensive counterespio-

---

* Police Superintendent Gianvitti and his deputy M. Martz headed the 5th section.

nage in its preventive and repressive mission. It all implied a definition of what a national defense secret was, the division of responsibilities between the ministries of the interior and national defense, and new legislation regarding espionage.

3. To trick the enemy through a coherent disinformation plan designed and implemented by the offensive counterespionage department.

Schlesser and I agreed to the plan because the threat of war looked like a foregone conclusion. We began taking action in that direction. However, convincing the government, the High Command, the administrative authorities, and our fellow citizens in general of the urgent need to take action looked like an impossible task in the face of the universal indifference to the issues we were so worried about.

"No, Paillole, it's not impossible. We must see people, talk to them and convince them, make alliances everywhere to spread the truth and get them to help." I could see that Schlesser was determined to succeed, like a horseman who intends to jump the fence after the horse has balked a hundred times over. He went on:

"After Paris, we must break out of our shell and make the rounds in the regional branches, the outposts, the barracks, the training grounds, the arsenals, in the fortresses and at the borders...We must show the way to those responsible and make them participate in our efforts... We must pull together with our British, Belgian, Dutch, Czech, and Polish friends. I must set the example and prove how urgent this collective effort must be and give no time to the know-nothings and the skeptics."

He paused to light up his pipe and continued quietly:

"I can't let the S.C.R. go leaderless while I'm away. I just cannot prepare the legislative framework, the administrative and military orders required by our struggle and still direct, supervise, and summarize the tasks performed by our departments. I need a deputy and I thought of you because our work against Germany must be our main task; I was about to say our only task. We will never have the budget to run in every direction! I will give Bonnefous the necessary personnel to cover the German section and the archives..."

When I described our plans a few days later to Police Superintendent Osvald, his comment about Schlesser was, "What stamina and what guts!" I spent days and nights following Schlesser's ideas that I accepted straight away because of their bold realism and I was sometimes overwhelmed by the audacity of his imagination and the unexpected solutions he would propose. Like the time he dragged me to see Rivet, without giving me time to think and introduced me as his "deputy" to the big boss. "It's the best solution," said Rivet who, was probably already in the know and didn't bat an eye.

That was how the year 1936 ended for me. I barely had the time to spend two days in Belfort, where the special service branch was living up to its reputation for efficiency dating back to officers like Andlauer and Devernine during the First World War. Colonel Schutz was in charge and he gave me a warm welcome with the traditional "esprit de corps" that was part of our unit. Since he was about to retire he introduced me to his successor, Major Lombard, whose knowledge of Germany and the Abwehr I found impressive. He was no doubt a very dynamic intelligence hunter, endowed with a spectacular physique and a charming manner, which, I was told, made him quite a ladies man.

Jourdeuil, the counterintelligence chief of the branch, also made an excellent impression. He knew his stuff and was successfully manipulating two or three double agents. I had just enough time to meet some officers: Pourchot, whose blue eyes gave a feeling of great energy, Sérot, a flyer who would later become, despite his own trials and tribulations, a valued and trusted friend and a loyal comrade. Everyone gave the "rookie" that I was a warm welcome, which overwhelmed me somewhat, along with the discovery of a technical knowledge, I was about to say, of a true science for research which I could not even imagine from my office.

I saw Commander Barbaro back in Paris. After some time spent as troop commander, he returned as head of the Marseille branch. His post in Nice had been put on ice in July 1935 following military agreements in Rome between Badoglio and Gamelin to attempt to counter German subversion in Austria! He explained clearly how he had been able to re-open the Nice substation in a few months with the help of Captain Giscard d'Estaing as its commander. In Marseille Captain Guiraud was specialized in German and counterespionage matters. In record time Barbaro and his team were able to update our knowledge of Italy. The Italian army's order of battle was reviewed with such precision that the inside joke was that Mussolini would call up Barbaro to find out the location of any Italian military unit.

This survey of our branches in metropolitan France was very reassuring to me. All they needed were some additional officers to develop the counterespionage section, reproducing as much as possible the productivity of the S.R. itself. At that point Schlesser and I went into the issues of manpower, budgets, and organization of the S.C.R. because before we could "make waves" we had to be able to withstand the consequences. Our organization was unable to fulfill its mission and our needs while our personnel remained so small. I reached the conclusion that one of the secrets of an efficient counterespionage organization had to be complete centralization and a methodical intelligence filing system. The very name of our division—*Section de centralisation des renseignements* (S.C.R.)*—defined its function with precision! Unfortunately everyone was working separately, jealously, and selfishly.

The *Sûreté Nationale* (S.N.) had a central file and I was uncertain whether it included a special file created by the *Surveillance du Territoire*. The *Préfecture de Police* (P.P.) had its own filing system, which also didn't include the small file created by the 5th Section of the *Renseignements Généraux* (R.G.) handling counterespionage in the French capital. Our filing system was very specialized and highly classified to protect our sources and we intended to enlarge it and improve it by adding and merging information. It remained more detailed than the others as far as foreign agents were concerned and incomplete as to the mass of individuals of all kinds and types that constituted a breeding ground for enemy intelligence services to find recruits. In searching for the identity of a suspect we had to consult, beyond our files, those of the S.N., the P.P., the Foreign Legion and the Gendarmerie, or even the customs administration!

While we waited for the impossible central file, new rules were issued to our archivists to ensure that research was conducted as thoroughly as possible. Garnier requested, and we could only concur, a two-fold increase in his staff to reach our objectives and time to set things up. He did obtain some reinforcements and Maurice Piroulas, a top archivist, was added to his staff. New officers were added in a few months to Bonnefous' German section. Mayeur, an air force flyer, was in charge of matters relating to the ministry of the air force while Bayonne, a naval officer, would liaise with the ministry of the navy on the rue Royale, and two officers, Abtey and Challan-Belval, were added to that team. We created an Italian section supervised by Captain Brun to also handle any matters regarding countries other than Germany or Italy.

From now on espionage cases were to be the exclusive domain of military justice. Close cooperation with the military courts was to provide

---

* Department for the Centralization of Intelligence.

us with improved implementation of the law and benefit from the experience gained in previous cases. We had to be included in the drafting of the new legislation to make sure that the sentences the courts handed down were commensurate with the seriousness of the crimes. Major Giboulot, a military justice officer with very high professional standards, joined our staff. Finally an essential innovation was introduced in creating a "preventive defense section" under the excellent Captain Devaux, with the mission of locking up our secrets and defending the sensitive areas. Later on Captain Jacques Lambert, whom I had met in 1932 during a training course at Evreux and whose clear-cut personality had impressed me, became his deputy. Further ahead two more officers were added to this "preventive section," Captains Pasteur and Pommiès.

We were quickly improving our external interceptions and signals intelligence as well as decryption and decoding activities. We didn't have an internal eavesdropping section. The Stackelberg and Lydia Oswald matters proved that certain foreign diplomatic missions were the untouchable extensions of propaganda and espionage. They used their immunity to avoid our investigations and our laws. With the approval of the minister of war, Edouard Daladier, Rivet and Schlesser were able to secure, at the end of 1936, using proof coming from our German section, top secret listening posts inside France to be located at number 2 *bis* Avenue de Tourville. Captain Cazin d'Honincthun and his deputy Lieutenant Lochard, both of them multilingual, ran the listening post very effectively, which would prove to be decisive in many instances. The use of the vast amount of intelligence information provided by this source within the exclusive domain of the S.R. and the C.E. was to be so discreet that neither its beneficiaries nor its victims would ever suspect its existence.

The reinforcement of the S.C.R. was extended to branches where we were able to assign some outstanding officers and non-commissioned officers so they could specialize in counterespionage. Lullé-Desjardins had just been assigned to open an observation unit in Toulouse to handle Spain, which was torn by civil war. His methodical work of penetration inside Spain through Perpignan, Bayonne and through the Pyrénées was to be extremely effective, especially during the occupation of France from 1940 to 1944. Every member of the S.C.R. behaved honorably in the struggle against the Germans from 1940 to 1945 (with a single exception): Lambert would die in combat, Cazin d'Honincthun, Garnier, Challan-Belval, Piroulas were sent to concentration camps; Pommiès created a famous partisan group that fought in southern France before becoming part of the 1st French Army. As for the others, military and civilian men and women, who shall appear later on in this book, were all filled with the kind of realistic energy and dedication to service that Rivet and Schlesser in their different ways knew how to communicate to their subordinates.

During his barnstorming tour of the regional military commands, Schlesser demanded that at a minimum one officer be dedicated to counterespionage in each 2nd Bureau, which would serve as the cornerstone for our organization in case of mobilization. The 2nd Bureau in Paris was under the command of Colonel Mermet, who was lucky enough to have as his deputy an officer of exceptional talent and destined to be a valuable contributor to our service: Captain Brouillard, of the High Command—better known as the espionage novelist Pierre Nord.

The S.R. was also strengthened by a valuable new officer in Captain Henri Navarre, who had just been appointed to the German section. His intelligence and precise and methodical approach made him one of the best section leaders in our service, while Perruche was in charge of the research sections. Rivet's unit began the year 1937 better equipped and with the right energy to undertake its mission, even though it was still far behind the capabilities of the Abwehr. Despite the problems France had to face—strikes, worker takeovers of manufacturing plants, right-wing turmoil, the consequences of the events in Spain, a difficult socio-economic context—the Popular Front government and Edouard Daladier in particular seemed to have understood the nature of the threat coming from abroad. Prime Minister Léon Blum asked to meet with Rivet and set up weekly meetings with General Gamelin, the heads of the Special Services and the 2nd Bureaus of the Army, Navy, and Air Force High Commands.

Unfortunately this excellent decision was not pursued beyond that short phase of the government's initiative. Later, once it was discontinued, government ministers would be in the dark about facts they should have learned about first hand rather than through third parties, and the tendency to use unconfirmed information from often biased sources increased. In the end when it came to intelligence each one formed his own opinion and claimed that he was "in the know." A cabinet minister often listens more willingly to the things he wishes to hear!

The closest assistants of the minister of war, Clapier, who was head of the cabinet, and Génébrier, his chief of staff, were very much aware of the threats to peace and to our national defense. Every day Schlesser or Rivet delivered new information showing growing German espionage and propaganda activity. It became obvious to those officials as much as to us that new defensive measures improving our security were urgently needed. They introduced Schlesser and his deputies to the ministries of the interior, justice and foreign affairs and to the heads of military justice, the *Sûreté Nationale* and the Gendarmerie. Orders were issued to the commanding generals of the military, naval, and air force regions to undertake immediate protective measures of our secrets in the fight against espionage, even before the publication of the regulations setting the responsibilities of the various military and civilian authorities.

Those regulations were some job! We were dedicating our efforts to drafting them non-stop ever since we had agreed to our "battle plan." Schlesser didn't stop making contacts. After having convinced our minister's cabinet he set his sights on the minister of the interior, Marx Dormoy, with whom he had many meetings, along with M. Moiteissier, head of the *Sûreté Nationale*; Castaign, controller general of the *Surveillance du Territore*; and sometimes the inspector general of the *Police Judiciare*, Mondanel. Our first breakthrough came on March 9, 1937. A decree from the minister of the interior set up ten brigades or stations of the *Surveillance du Territore*, reinforcing and reorganizing the command in Paris. These first S.T. stations were established close to our border posts and within the military regions.

The staff of these stations, all of them young policemen trained by the experts of the rue des Saussaies, were enthusiastic and proud to be working for national defense. They were receiving uninterrupted assistance and information they required from our "specialists" for their enforcement efforts while they passed on to us whatever tips they picked up. A defensive curtain was set up allowing us to triple the number of espionage arrests in 1937 (153 instead of 40 in prior years). A close liaison was established between the Special Services of national defense and the *Surveillance du Territore*, between "deep research" and "operations," that would ultimately be extremely fruitful and continued, with few exceptions, during the occupation of France by the Germans. It was to be the cornerstone of security in North Africa and within the operational theaters of the French and Allied armies.

With the wiretaps inside France and the brigades of the *Surveillance du Territore* set up, in a few months we had added two fundamentally important tools in the struggle against foreign spies. As far as I am concerned this was an achievement to the credit of the S.C.R., even though I may be antagonizing some people who claim that it was their doing after the Liberation in 1944. Without waiting for the actual legal decrees to be issued defining both civilian and military responsibilities, the first true resistance to Nazi invasion by counterespionage and S.R. specialists was implemented in the spring of 1937.

Before dedicating almost all our efforts to the struggle against German intelligence, we quickly summarized what we knew about other countries. Obviously this information was rather sketchy. Even friends are not in habit of revealing the secrets of their organization and methods and what we knew was neither necessarily precise nor complete. Commander Bill Dunderdale, a congenial and refined officer, had just replaced Jeffes as the British intelligence representative in Paris. Dunderdale spoke good French and we liked his easy going manner and the efforts he made to foster friendly relations with us. I traveled to London with Bonnefous at Dunderdale's request, where we were given a friendly welcome as comrades in arms and shown around the British capital spending two evenings at a music hall and a concert at the Albert Hall. We spent a few minutes with Colonel Sir Stewart Menzies, an affable and unpretentious man whom I had already met in Rivet's office in Paris. We returned home without having learned much, but then perhaps there wasn't much for us to find out, and also our friends wanted to take our measure in person and see us in action before opening up completely.

Schlesser's arrival tightened our relationship with the British since they had known him for a long time and liked his work at the S.R. Dunderdale, who shared the same kind of openness and enthusiasm as my boss, would visit us often. He readily admitted that British counterintelligence was rather weak and that he wished to get further involved with us. We began sharing some information about the Abwehr, the S.D., the Nazi regime and its methods and propaganda. He was amazed by what we were telling him. Dunderdale had a deputy, a big imposing man with a quiet manner, named Tom Greene who lived in a luxurious apartment on the Avenue Victor Hugo with his wife and two daughters and where we would often meet. In such a comfortable atmosphere our discussions continued far into the night and a true comradeship was established between us. So much so that I became close friends with both Dunderdale and Greene, whom we called Bill and Uncle Tom as well as valued allies.

I slowly came to understand the kind of prestigious organization the British Intelligence Service really was, a true public service dedicated to the defense of a great empire; it appeared almost exclusively directed to its protection. I was therefore surprised to see how the British viewed the changes in Germany and Europe as secondary issues. The I.S. was imperial and stretched across all governmental ministries, but for its research throughout the world it was most closely linked to the foreign office according to the organization chart. The counterespionage service M.I.5 was operating inside Great Britain and its overseas territories; the information gathering service M.I.6 handled research overseas. The United States, whose intelligence service was then practically non-existent, although it would play catch-up quickly later on, relied on intelligence shared by the British.

Rivet, who knew our friends very well and had an excellent relationship with Menzies, was not convinced of the effectiveness of our cooperation. He suggested that we encourage our Allies to be more vigilant in order to avoid repeating the experience of 1914-1918, where the French S.R., because it was better engaged on the continent, had to fill in the gaps for the I.S. Dunderdale helped us a lot in that area, to our benefit in the future. The SIM, the Italian intelligence service, had turned toward the Abwehr since 1936. Gamelin insisted that Rivet attempt to keep our old and moody ally within our camp but Roatta was avoiding meeting with him. On the other hand Roatta's relationship with Canaris was well known to us and the events in Spain helped bring the two men closer together: for the moment Franco, whom they both met several times, would be their common denominator.

Mussolini's rise to power gave the SIM a greater political and police orientation. The head of the Turin office that was assigned to, or rather "against," France was an officer of the *carabinieri*, Major Roberto Navale. SIM's main task was counterespionage and together with the OVRA it was clearly involved in France's internal affairs. The many Italians living in France, the consulates and the above average number of diplomats, were a growing danger because of the increased SIM-Abwehr collusion. The interceptions and decryptions made by Major Bertrand's section, plus the increasingly frequent contacts between Roatta and Canaris since the beginning of the Spanish civil war, were clear indications of the direction their relations were taking.

Ever since the founding of the Cheka in 1918, the secret services were the most solid cornerstone of the Soviet regime. The names used to identify the secret services, be it GPU, OGPU, or NKVD changed little to the fact that they reported directly to the highest government authorities and were responsible for all tasks involving espionage, security, sabotage, and even terrorism. With its immense resources, the Soviet secret service was not bound by traditional or diplomatic behavior of any kind. Following the "Fantomas" affair, and even more after the signing of the French-Soviet defense pact, it appeared that Soviet intelligence had put a damper on its espionage activities in France. However this didn't apply to propaganda or the brutal repression of any opponents of the regime.

For the moment we had no evidence of any Japanese activity, which was to appear later on as a consequence of the agreements signed on November 25, 1936, between Japan and Germany. Wiretaps placed by Cazin d'Honincthun were to reveal the intrigues of Japanese officials at the Paris embassy at the end of 1938 to secure the blueprints of a new French air force fighter engine through a prominent Parisian socialite. We were able to intercept a suitcase full of secret documents only at the last minute. Once the blueprints were safe, the courier was placed under arrest, and after the Japanese ambassador had extended his apologies regarding the matter, the French socialite was set free despite our impassioned appeals. "It's not who you are but who you know..."

The Polish secret service was one of our allies our Russian section thought very highly of. Rivet and Bertrand knew it well since it began helping us with decryptions and intercepts targeting Germany, and they had good things to say about the Polish services that were enthusiastic and very effective inside Poland and overseas. The Czechs by comparison were much more modest and our Prague representative, Major Gouyoux, maintained excellent relations with them. Through the Czechs we were kept informed of the activity of the Munich Ast against Austria. Colonel Count von Marogna-Redwitz, head of the Czech service since 1933, was in contact with Austrian intelligence just as Nazi penetration was increasing. Our Czech friends also kept us informed of the meetings held by the head of Hungarian intelligence, Colonel von Henneye, and Admiral Canaris, a clear indication of how much Hitler intended to court Hungary through Abwehr cooperation. Another issue troubling Czech intelligence was Abwehr penetration of the Romanian intelligence service, which was part of the state secret police. The head of the Romanian secret police, Moruzow, was in effect an "honorable correspondent" of Canaris. The Abwehr's Section II was intent on protecting Germany's access to Romanian oil fields, which were filled with its agents working as engineers, foremen, guards, and other specialists.

We invited our Belgian friends, Verrhulst and his deputy, to visit us in Paris to discuss friendly cooperation. They bowed out as neutrals while giving us assurances that they were as close as they could be to our side and the future would confirm their sincere loyalty to us. The Dutch were just as cautious, even though our branch in The Hague, headed by Commander Trutat, continuing the good work of his predecessor d'Alès, had excellent rapport with Colonels van de Plassche and van Oorschot of Dutch military intelligence. They were very much aware of the threat to their country represented by Hitler's rise to power. Discreetly and without embarrassing his friends, Trutat was able to turn to our advantage the unusually favorable opportunities offered by Holland for intelligence gathering, and recruitment in particular.

Léon Blum's government was toppled by a Senate vote defeating his request for full powers to overcome the financial crisis. Camille Chautemps became prime minister on June 22, 1937, fortunately retaining both Daladier and Marx Dormoy as ministers of war and the interior, and they supported our efforts. The year 1937 ended in turmoil once the CSAR, also known as the "Cagoule," a secret subversive organization, was uncovered and some of its leaders arrested. An intelligence item that mysteriously turned up at the ministry of war implied that some officers of our branch in Nice were involved in the matter and acted as liaison between Eugène Deloncle, head of the CSAR, and Major Navale of the SIM station in Turin.

Schlesser and I went to see Mondanel at the ministry of the interior who was very friendly and candidly summed up what he knew:

"Besides a few individuals, the army is not involved with the Cagoule. We've seized the organization's files and found only one name of a high-ranking officer that I must withhold, but who is not part of your unit. We have agreed with Mr. Daladier personally not to publicize any names of officers without his prior approval. I can tell you that the Cagoulards from Nice, like Joseph Darnand, who often travel to Italy, are in contact with some officers of your branch."

Schlesser traveled to Marseille and Nice. Like Rivet he wanted to be sure that the Service was not compromised and that some officers hadn't been so rash, willfully or otherwise, as to facilitate certain actions by the Cagoule. The investigation discovered that since the Rome agreements of June 1935, which put the Nice branch "on ice," we had suggested to contact the Italian intelligence service in order to keep "better track of Germany"! Captain Beaune, who headed the branch, had taken the opportunity to contact Major Navale of the Turin branch of SIM. Beaune was very much involved with right-wing political groups, sharing the ideas of Darnand, Agnely, Gombert, Paul Esmiol, and other Cagoulards who were active in the Nice chapter of the CSAR. The CSAR's ultimate goal was to seize power by force to fight Communism. Beaune turned these militants into "honorable correspondents," entrusting them with missions in Italy.

Under the pretense of improving the relationship with the Italians, Darnand met with Navale and the head of SIM counterintelligence in Rome, Colonel Santo Emanuele. The Italians then provided the Cagoule with weapons but it was impossible to find out whether they demanded anything in return. It was almost certain that through Darnand, Colonel Emanuele and Major Navale got the CSAR to carry out the murder of the anti-Fascist Rosselli brothers, who were political refugees in France in June 1937. Schlesser was unable to establish Beaune's involvement as an accomplice; however, with Daladier's agreement, he was withdrawn from Nice and sent on a mission overseas. After the defeat in 1940 Beaune returned to France and resumed his relationship with Darnand, who had then become the delegate of the *Légion des combattants* and a zealous supporter of the policy of collaboration with Germany. I tried unsuccessfully to talk Beaune out this in June 1941. In February 1943 Beaune agreed to head the intelligence section of the *Milice*, the odious political police that Darnand had set up as a component of the SOL, the *Service d'ordre legionnaire*, to hunt down partisans and resistance fighters. Beaune was tried and sentenced after the Liberation and did not survive his shameful conduct. It was a painful and pathetic case because Beaune was a brave soldier in the First World War but he broke our rules and dishonored the service.

Schlesser had other reasons for being angry upon returning from Nice because he sensed that there was a lack of trust between military and civilian authorities. Each side suspected interference by the other in its domain. The "Cagoule" incidents were creating a foul atmosphere and Schlesser had also observed during his many visits to local unit headquarters, barracks, and border posts that training in the protection of secrets and counterespionage was being completely ignored.

Late one evening in January 1938, I was tired and stressed by the innumerable rounds I was making in the ministries and the offices of the High Command to convince people to secure assistance and persuade the bureaucracies to be efficient about the security measures we wanted to see implemented. I was relating all this to my commanding officer as he was signing the thick correspondence of the various divisions. Suddenly he stopped, turned to me, and said acrimoniously:

"The indifference, the negligence… It's an outrage! I fear that in the border areas facing Germany local headquarters have neither understood nor done anything. If we have a situation at Metz, Nancy, Strasbourg, and Belfort similar to what happened in Nice it would be very bad! I must go there! I'll see the prefects, the generals; assemble the officers, the 2nd Bureaus. Obviously I'll meet with our men and the policemen of the *Surveillance du Territoire.*"

"When do you plan to leave, Sir?" I asked.

"Tonight…"

"But it's already 9 p.m.!"

Schlesser smiled and went back to his mail, saying:

"I'll be in Metz by 5 a.m. It's the best time to visit a fortress."

"Since you'll be away for a few days, what's going to happen to our meeting with the 3rd Bureau and the disinformation plan?"

"You'll go with Bonnefous," he answered.

"That's not the only thing! Our definition of secrecy is ready to be sent to military justice and to the minister's cabinet office. We'll have to explain it thoroughly."

"I trust you to do that. You should also prepare the changes to the law for the repression of espionage. I'll look at them when I get back."

"You might get snow and icing conditions…"

"I have chains on my tires."

"Our manual on penetration techniques of enemy intelligence organizations is ready. We need your approval before it can be distributed throughout the branches."

"I'll take it with me."

I sensed there was no way that I could get Schlesser to delay his trip to eastern France, so I asked how to get in touch with him.

"Write to 'General Delivery' in Belfort. If necessary, phone our office for me to call you back."

I was to be in contact with him daily and I had to admit that he was right. Nothing could replace personal contact when you must convince people. Transmitting written orders and instructions from afar runs the risk of diluting the best intentions among a mass of useless or longwinded paperwork that was the daily fare of countless civilian and military bureaucracies. It was a fact that everything began piling up just as I was getting some results from penetration agents I had infiltrated into the Abwehr a few months before. I was having almost daily meetings out of the office that required a lot of time. Our workload was relentless. Suddenly Schlesser called me back to his office.

"Should Elizabeth call on the 'special phone' meet with her! I generally have my rendezvous at the bar of the Gare d'Orsay."

"Who is Elizabeth?" I asked.

"Marie Bell, the actress at the Comédie Française. She's due back at any moment from making a movie in Berlin. Listen to what she has to say and tell her I'll meet with her when I get back. I know she was supposed to meet with some Nazi leaders like Heydrich, Himmler and most of all Göring, who loves actors and artists!"

As he was speaking to me he pointed to some instructions directed at the commanding generals of the military regions setting the rules for instruction in counterespionage and training officers at the regimental level.

"You understand, old man," he said, "that before we start circulating this I must go and explain on location what we expect. I'm taking a copy with me. Give the original to Colonel Rivet tomorrow so he can get the minister to sign it. I must get going!"

Three days went by. I met Duperré, a penetration agent whom I was able to get recruited by the Abwehr branch in Münster through an ad in *Le Matin* and *Le Journal* published ten months before. Some very innocuous offers of "discreet loans to military personnel and government functionaries" had attracted our attention. I asked one of my engineer friends, M. Duperré, who specialized in munitions, and who was just as curious as I was, to mail in a reply. One month later he was called to a meeting in Liège, and had "borrowed" 1,000 francs by proving his credentials. He signed an agreement for monthly payments of his loan. Two months later, with the excuse that he was unable to keep up the payments, he asked to meet once again with his "banker," who in turn proved very accommodating and put Duperré in touch with a "friend" who could help out... The matter did in fact get settled in exchange for the delivery of information.

Duperré very cautiously and cleverly succeeded in gaining the trust of Rumpe, the officer in the Cologne annex who was delighted to be working with such a high quality source. Along with the penetration work of Doudot we had our hand in both the Münster Ast and the Cologne annex. So now Duperré no longer had "money problems" but he had created problems for me because I had to feed him information while I coordinated his actions with Doudot and other penetration agents. Fortunately Duperré was the assistant of Colonel Michel, the inspector of the tank corps, who agreed to play along... Before getting the long-awaited disinformation plan he gave me some technical information, which delighted the Abwehr, forcing it to seek out more information about our weapons systems. This was all priceless.

Back in my office I handed over to treasury the funds Duperré had received and wrote my report, which included some observations on the morale of our enemies and their own problems with the SD. I called Rivet to hand in my report.

"Come quickly! I have something to tell you," he said.

The big boss looked very worried.

"Do you know where Schlesser is?"

"He's in eastern France, colonel."

"Well, get in touch with him. He must return the electric blueprints of a facility on the Maginot Line…"

"Which blueprints?" I asked.

Rivet looked relieved.

"That Schlesser character! At 5 a.m. he entered a fortress near Thionville. He saw some blueprints on a table and just grabbed them. Then he offered a cigarette to the sentry on duty, who was looking puzzled seeing a civilian walking around at night. 'My name is Schlesser, I'm an engineer, I'm here to get my briefcase. When you go off duty you can report my visit,' he said. Well, since yesterday there's been a revolution going on here and in the military region! Since the electric blueprint is missing the work in the fortress can't proceed! The 2nd Bureau in Metz had quickly succeeded in identifying the thief but Schlesser had disappeared. The commanding general of the engineer corps was told and in a panic he informed General Gamelin. I can't rest until we've found Schlesser and retrieved those blueprints!

I grabbed the phone and called Belfort. Schlesser returned my call an hour later. I was at my wit's end:

"Major, this is some upheaval! Do you have those electrical wiring blueprints?"

Schlesser gave me one of his hearty laughs.

"I told you… They're not doing their job! Now they know it. Call the head of the 2nd Bureau in Metz and tell him his blueprints are in his steel cabinet, which isn't even locked! He should be thankful he's not getting 30 days in the stockade, under lock and key.

By keeping this up the protection of military secrets would finally become second nature, and it was high time! Once he returned from Belfort Schlesser told me:

"Are you aware, old man, that the construction company, which is working at the location where I pulled my stunt, employs 45 percent foreigners and that most of them are Italians!"

Navarre joined us and was just as outraged as we were because he was also having problems recruiting informers among the men working on the Siegfried Line.

"We were about to make a "connection" with a foreman who was 100 percent German, a pure "Aryan," whose family lives in Germany. He was dismissed from the Siegfried Line only because a very distant relative of his had moved to England over ten years ago!

You could walk around the Maginot Line easily enough. German veterans and their families could use the excuse that they were visiting the burial locations nearby…and so Abwehr agents arrived by bus, without being checked and asked all sorts of questions, took pictures…We made a heroic decision: any foreigner crossing our borders, by train, plane, in a car, or on foot must fill out an entry form that Bonnefous would design. A few weeks later we received a flood of the new forms; each day we went through them and entered the suspicious ones into our files. It was to be a good harvest, yielding excellent results. At the same time we issued instructions to limit, or even prohibit, the use of foreign labor in all industries working for national defense, and any exceptions must have our approval. This was a massive enterprise and the police department helped us unstintingly. However, the problem of checking and keeping watch over foreigners was practically impossible to solve.

On July 1, 1937, we recorded 16,987 German nationals in Paris, a real windfall for Canaris and Goebbels! There were a meager 488 innocuous French citizens in Berlin under heavy surveillance. German embassy and consulate support personnel were entirely made up of German nationals in Paris while in Berlin the staff of our diplomatic and consular offices was not French… "This has got to change!" Schlesser kept on repeating as we faced all these problems at once.

The year 1937 failed to produce any aggressive moves on Hitler's part. We watched a peaceful middle-class gentleman strolling around the Paris International Exhibit—it was Admiral Canaris, whom we had followed from the border to the door of the German embassy where he stayed for a few days. For our amusement and to please him we risked one of our penetration agents. Cazin handled the wiretapping operation. We made an urgent request to meet with the German military attaché. The next day our informer placed another call and the military attaché's answer came after he had checked back with Berlin as to the trustworthiness of the caller:

"You can bring Zigarro."

"Zigarro" happened to be a new casing for the 155 mm shell that our agent refused to take out of France because of the high risk involved! The borders were being watched much too carefully. We would never find out whether "Zigarro" traveled to Berlin inside the diplomatic pouch or in the old beat up briefcase that Canaris carried with him. It was additional proof that German diplomats were actively engaging in espionage but the Quai d'Orsay showed no concern. Some extremely compromising documents came into the possession of our S.R.: a "Kriegspiel" targeting Czechoslovakia and another relating to Austria.

By January 19, 1938 an intelligence windfall confirmed that the Anschluss would take place shortly. Nazi propaganda and the Abwehr's work in France and against our allies were constantly growing. We finally convinced Dunderdale and Menzies that the danger of war was very real. We also lamented the fact that British intelligence had no branch in The Hague for over a year. Would the leaders of MI6 succeed in convincing their government? Once again France was going through a political crisis and had no government: the 103rd government of the Third Republic had been voted out because of social unrest, the problems relating to the Cagoule, the policy of neutrality towards Spain, as well as an economic and monetary crisis.

"So you see, there is something good about the Nazi regime!" The person saying those words was Françoise, a tall, athletic young woman in her thirties. She had deep dark eyes and looked like a strong and passionate type. We were sitting at the Café des Deux Magots while the Boulevard Saint-Germain bubbled over with lively carefree youth. She loved Paris, where she had studied for a doctorate in French and German and was pleased to share some information with me. I was always happy to meet her when she returned from Berlin where she had been teaching French for the past few years. I liked her strong and intelligent personality although she displayed, rather cynically, ideas that were quite close to Nazism. Françoise was the daughter of a retired officer and she loved France and its culture. I had been introduced to her by one of my top recruiters: Jacques Favre de Thierrens, who seemed to know just about everybody. A colonel in the air force reserves, a real hero of the First World War, he was an art collector in Paris, owned a farm in the Gard region and became a painter at an age when others retire. He was attracted to our work, not knowing much about it, and the idea stimulated his imagination.

He came to our office to offer his services during the summer of 1936. He was one of those persons so bold as to be foolhardy and was therefore able to get precisely where their need for action would take them. I was somewhat lost in the chaos of information he spewed out and had the damnedest time sifting through it all. I liked him and wanted to do something with him since I could see where his talents lay and was convinced he would be the ideal "public relations" type. All of Paris visited his artist's studio on the Avenue Matignon, intellectuals, artists, antique dealers, financiers, industrialists, civilians, military men, young and old men and young women… often stunning girls who appeared out of nowhere!

So one day with some difficulty, he persuaded Françoise to come and meet me. She didn't want to betray her employers nor compromise herself, but the way Favre de Thierrens described me as well as his appeal to her sense of duty were very effective in overcoming any hesitations she had. Françoise had chosen sides in the ideological struggle that was shaking the world. Against Communism, which she feared, she imagined a Franco-German understanding and had joined the *Association France-Allemagne* as soon as it was established. Her militant activity had helped secure her employment as a French teacher at a Berlin language institution accredited by the Nazi authorities. Among her students were officers and staff of the Kriegsministerium, the Wehrmacht, and even the Abwehr.

"Canaris is very liberal in reimbursing his men for the French lessons they take with me. After that he sends them for a few weeks at his expense in the various countries where they're to work."

Françoise led a very proper life in Berlin. Sometimes she dated her students. She had a few amorous and short affairs before a more serious one with a Nazi foreign ministry official. She confided all this to me with a kind of brutal candor that was possibly meant to keep me at a distance in our relationship.

"Let them get involved in Austria and in the East. Don't you get involved! They want to bring back their fellow citizens. On February 28, 1938 Hitler declared himself the protector of all Germans wherever they may be. I find that quite acceptable," she said.

Then she discussed the reorganization of the German High Command.

"The War Ministry has been eliminated since February 4, 1938. Blomberg was sacked after a shameful marriage to a prostitute and von Fritsch was fired because he was a pederast! Hitler took overall command of the army and created the OKW, where he placed General Keitel who is close to the Führer in command."

Françoise continued about the Abwehr, confirming some things I knew:

"The Abwehr is also being completely reorganized and Canaris will have more power. He will get an additional section to supervise German military attachés overseas, as well as liaison with the Ministry of Foreign Affairs.

She did not go beyond what her political conviction dictated and thought she was working at bringing about a French rapprochement with Germany by attempting to justify the initiatives that were under way. I never attempted to convince her to do otherwise, which would have been totally useless and contrary to my mission. Up to 1941 I would meet her every two to three months, sometimes in the company of Schlesser, either in Paris or at other locations. She was always passionate and exciting. The events of 1940 led her to cry over what had happened to France and later to Germany; she was either furious or saddened at the widening gap separating the two countries more and more each day. She died in 1950.

On the morning of March 12, 1938, three poorly equipped German divisions entered the Austrian countryside. France, meanwhile, was either taking a hayride or looking for flowers in the forest. We had no government. Rivet, summoned by the deputy commander-in-chief of the army, General Gérodias, had to explain the "unbelievable swiftness" of the German operation. England was also unruffled that weekend and our penetration agents did not notice any undue worry at the Abwehr. Austria was ready and welcomed the German army marching in triumph while Germany did not even bother to reinforce its positions on the Rhine. Göring didn't even interrupt the party he was giving that day and was to explain his cynical behavior at the Nuremberg trials: "The Allies had not moved in March 1936 during the military reoccupation of the Rhineland when Germany did not have the power to block their actions. Logically they would certainly not move two years later when they were faced with a stronger and determined Germany about what was a strictly German matter."

Two days later the second government, presided by Léon Blum, was formed with Marx Dormoy as minister of the interior and Daladier still as minister of national defense and of war. All these comings and goings were to paralyze our efforts and slow down our negotiations. The legal issues surrounding what we required to codify and facilitate our defensive action were still being discussed, such as the definition of national defense secrets, stronger legislation to combat subversion of the country's external security, the organization of the nation's defense in peacetime and at war... And yet Nazi Germany had never been so bold.

One of our reserve officers, Georges Dobrouchkess, who was the fearless type, noticed a car parked at Guyancourt on the road to Versailles, near the military training grounds of Satory. It was 3 p.m. and the driver was quietly filming the demonstration of a tank prototype in front of a group of civilians and military officers. Our friend jumped on the man who happened to be German, grabbed his camera and demanded that he follow him to the nearest police station. The German refused to oblige and a furious fistfight took place under the wary eyes of the civilian and military commission. A gendarme approached slowly and took everyone to the nearby Gendarmerie station. After much discussion Dobrouchkess was allowed to call the 2nd Bureau of the Paris region, which in turn called me. I took Osvald and went directly to the Satory proving ground.

The documents of the individual involved and his ambiguous attitude induced us to take him to the rue des Saussaies. Once developed the film showed many frames of the Somua tank. Some of the workers at the Arsenal were even so obliging as to pose in front of the tank itself. The German's cover was as an employee of the Schenker company, and he admitted that he had been asked to gather information about French armaments by the Ast at Stuttgart. The consequences of our having neutralized Stackelberg were being felt at that branch! Our counterespionage section at Belfort, which had just been turned over to Gendarmerie Captain Hugon, needed to fill that "defection" with a few penetration agents who were operating by the end of 1938. The Satory case helped us convince the Directorate of armaments to at last take tough steps to enforce better security at its facilities. Georges Dobrouchkess who was invaluable as an "honorable correspondent," had a tendency of being impulsive but he did help us film the comings and goings from his office windows on the rue Huysmans, facing none other than the offices of the German consulate.

In August 1937 I was able to latch onto the Abwehr post in Wiesbaden. A Foreign Legion NCO of Yugoslav origin named Friedmann, well regarded by his superiors, had been referred to me by the BSLE. Friedmann wanted to work for the Special Services: he spoke fluent Serb, German,

Italian, and obviously French, and impressed me very favorably. He was smart, had a gift for observation, and was dreaming of an active life of adventure. Since he was also Jewish he wanted to defeat Fascism, the Nazis, and racism. I was glad I gave him a try. He slipped surreptitiously into Germany and declared himself a deserter to the Grenzpolizei (German border police), who then escorted him to Gestapo headquarters at Sarrebrucken.

Following some rather tight questioning and being held under observation for a few weeks, the Gestapo became convinced of Friedmann's "sincerity." We actually contributed in creating this impression by issuing wanted bulletins to all our policemen and gendarmes to be on the lookout for a deserter named Friedmann. We were well aware that Reile, the Trier representative of the Section III F (counterespionage) of the Weisbanden Ast, was getting that bulletin and passed it on to his colleague at Sarrebrücken. A rather distinguished looking visitor who was introduced as "Doctor Becker" then paid Friedmann a visit. After a short conversation he was transferred to Wiesbaden and asked whether he was ready to go back to France on a spying mission with new documents identifying him as Frederking. At first he hesitated, and had to be convinced further, but he then accepted once the "Doctor" made an attractive financial proposal.

The "Doctor" was none other than Major Klein, head of the Wiesbaden Ast, who was just as impressed as I was with Frederking's intelligence. He appeared to trust him rather quickly and trained the new agent in the use of one of the Abwehr's first secret transmitters. Friedmann, alias Frederking, was ecstatic upon returning from Germany. He carried a decent sum of French francs, which he handed over to me, and a letter of introduction from the *Propagandastaffel* for the German tourist office where he began working. His new employers didn't know what his real mission was. A few days after his arrival in Paris Friedmann received a message and picked up a suitcase at the Gare du Nord containing the transmitter. Our technical services quickly went over the device. They had never before seen such a machine and still didn't believe it worked!

Through this channel I was in direct contact with several Abwehr stations and Hamburg was the only one still missing. My luck would improve in the spring. Police Superintendent Gianvitti of the Paris préfecture introduced me to Paul Schlochoff a French citizen of Polish origin who had studied theology but had later decided against the priesthood. I was more impressed by his intelligence and quietly happy disposition than by his tall, lanky appearance. Gianvitti had facilitated his naturalization and was recommending him not just for his good character but also because of his background and knowledge of Germany and its language. Paul Schlochoff had been involved in the toy trade for the past few years. Nothing could appear less conspicuous than that! He represented German manufacturers whom he would visit regularly and every year he would sample their novelties at the Nuremberg toy fair. He was exactly the man I was looking for.

Once Gianvitti and I were able to overcome his self-effacing personality and appeal to his anti-Nazi ideas, he agreed to help me out of gratitude toward France for having welcomed him. He refused the financial rewards I was ready to offer him. I found out through the British Intelligence Service that the Hamburg Ast had been able to recruit several agents through the local Gestapo. An important toy manufacturer was located in Hamburg and Schlochoff was one of its customers. As soon as he arrived Schlochoff visited the police station to make sure his presence was properly recorded. With a naïve attitude that fit in perfectly with his personality and his profession, he explained his travels to Germany and France, the Christmas trees and children's parties he would organize in public and private establishments, at industrial facilities, barracks, ports, etc. He also displayed boundless admiration for the Nazi regime. The police chief had Schlochoff come back several times, encouraging him to talk and accepting a little toy for his son. He asked Paul to be sure to contact him again during his next visit.

A few weeks later, back in Hamburg, he was introduced to a tall navy officer of the Abwehrstelle who immediately asked him to work for him. For Schlochoff that was the start of a successful career as a penetration agent that was to last up to the end of 1943, when for security reasons I ordered him to cease any further activity. He will reappear throughout this book, always loyal and ready to carry out in every circumstance with the same quiet courage the most dangerous missions that an agent of the Special Services can be assigned.

4

Nazi Infiltration

Within two years we had reached one of our 1936 objectives. With scores of penetration agents of different kinds, all properly vetted, I was able to track the Abwehr branches targeting France. Our three branches in Lille, Belfort, and most of all Metz, were also following the same successful recruitment strategy and we were able to collate, complete and cross-check the very risky work our agents were engaging in. While we seemed able to grasp the methods and subjects the enemy was after, I am not as sure that we were equally successful at "drowning" his knowledge of our secrets. We succeeded only partially in stopping the loose talk, the lack of caution, and sloppy habits, as well as keeping the right pace on the insufficient flow of disinformation that we fed the Abwehr with generally positive results. We were still much too weak in offensive counterespionage.

At that point we introduced the Penetration Charter, an awesome new tool along with the guidelines on how it should be used. We had carefully planned the entire process, specifying every step to be followed: recruitment, handling, maintenance, and engagement. At first there was the simple penetration agent coded "W," similar to Duperré or Frederking. Then came the double penetration agent who was given the code "W2," such as Gessmann or a similar SR informer whom we knew had been sent by the enemy to find out the plans and methods of our Special Services. The third part dealt with disinformation but the plans for the preparation of false intelligence had still not been established and never would be. No government entity or military office was willing to shoulder that kind of responsibility and all of them attempted to sidestep the issue.

We therefore had to proceed piecemeal and improvise along the way. We would sort out and coordinate as best we could the kind of information to be submitted to the enemy which was of little interest and mostly useless. It took all the ingenuity of our Ws and many times a certain amount of guts to pursue our attempts to deceive the enemy and whet his appetite with such weak material. The High Command and the government were never able to use the great instrument we provided and that in some circumstances could have forced Hitler to hesitate as to the direction of military operations in 1939 and 1940. I must say that this extremely useful procedure we had perfected was also offered to the British in 1939 and we would improve it together later on as a new weapon called *Force A* in 1942. From 1943 onward, in circumstances that I shall explain later and using our penetration methods, it produced decisive results during operations in Tunisia, Italy, and France.

I could no longer handle all the W agents in Paris along with many honorable correspondents without additional assistance. Many people who were just as worried as we were regarding our situation abroad would visit our offices: Professor Wullus-Rudiger, a specialist of Germany, who taught at the Belgian war college and was a friend of King Leopold; Paul van den Branden, who had entrée to the German embassy in Brussels; the Reverend Abbott Vorage, of Dutch origin, who had been our agent in 1914-1918 and was ready to volunteer his priestly attire and his amazing boldness in fulfilling missions on our behalf. René Mayer, who later became prime minister, offered us the resources of the *Compagnie internationale des wagons-lits*. Hettier de Boislambert visited Schlesser's office before going off to a hunt in Hungary where he was to meet with Göring and other Nazi bigwigs… And in the darkened hallway of the ground floor I also noticed the long shadow of de Gaulle as he was leaving Malraison's office.

How could we oblige so many well-intentioned people with our very meager personnel resources? Perruche at the S.R. was complaining that he was unable to use all the potential agents who were being sent to him. Yet Rivet was still able to recruit a few more officers, like Roger Gasser, who was the trusted collaborator of General Weygand. I was able to pluck an excellent man named Guillaume from the archives section. He was to support me in handling the Ws in Paris and help in using the information they gathered. The ratio of our services to the Abwehr was to remain at one to ten. Just as Françoise had been telling us, the Abwehr had grown into one of the major components of the OKW, known as Amt-Ausland-Abwehr. She confirmed that as the senior officer in the leadership Admiral Canaris had acquired increased authority under General Keitel the slavish and servile executor of the Führer's wishes.

We were like someone running a candy store trying to compete with an industrial colossus. The only weapon we had was the quality of our production. Unfortunately our basic tools were being added much too slowly and the small number of employees too green for the job. Aces like Doudot were quite difficult to find! He had just pulled off a masterstroke. One of his Ws, Schweitzer, who had been working on the Abwehr branch at Stuttgart suddenly died of a heart attack. It came at a bad time while tension abroad was increasing due to Hitler's ambitions about Czechoslovakia. Doudot decided to fill in the gap. Using the typewriter of the deceased, his letterhead and disappearing ink, he announced to the Germans that his "uncle whom he had long been helping in sickness" had died and he enclosed a copy of the local newspaper *Dernières Nouvelles de Strasbourg* bearing the death notice. Among the list of relatives was one Paul Schweitzer, a "nephew." A few days later he received a rather impatient letter asking why the uncle had never before mentioned his illness nor his nephew Paul. They set up a meeting in Switzerland.

"You understand," Doudot told me confidentially, "I just couldn't ignore the matter. Since I didn't want to be recognized and risk losing my contacts with Cologne and Münster, I decided to modify my weight and my face: eyeglasses, a mustache, a little growth under the left cheek and even better a magnificent and highly visible gold tooth which I have a lot of trouble inserting and is the damnedest thing to remove…" He showed me how he managed it. "My first meeting with the German emissary took place in January at Rheinfelden in front of the bridge on the Rhine. The man wasn't an officer but a *Hauptvertaunesmann* (a main confidential representative) and I am certain that he was French."

The traitor questioned the "nephew" for several hours. Doudot knew his "uncle's" business far too well to be tripped up.

"He handed me a large sum of money, orders in the event of a mobilization and some mailboxes to use as addresses in Switzerland."

Just as with Schweitzer, the Stuttgart Abwehr asked the "nephew" to investigate some persons who could be of interest, these were potential spies, suspicious individuals, wheeler-and-dealer types, and others.

"We have no problems with those people," said Bonnefous. "They not only give us the names of our customers but they also pay us for the investigations!"

The employer was so satisfied that some time later he asked the "nephew" to identify possible Abwehr recruits. It was high time to try and unmask this traitor and find out what the Germans actually knew about our air force and any other research. After preparing the operation with the colonel in command of the air base at Essey-lès-Nancy, Doudot told Stuttgart that Master Sergeant Dumoulin was a good potential recruit. Dumoulin was a smart young pilot and very happy to play the game. His profile was that of a gambler who liked women saddled with huge debts and desperately in need of money. Two weeks later Dumoulin got a letter postmarked at Kreuzlingen, in Switzerland, offering him a very lucrative job as the new correspondent of a Swiss magazine with pacifist views that was mainly interested in aviation. He was to mail in his résumé and recent photo.

After some correspondence a meeting was set up at the Gare du Nord railway station in Brussels on Easter Sunday, 1939. Dumoulin got off the 3 p.m. train from Luxembourg, as agreed; he was wearing civilian clothes and holding his cap in his hand when a well-dressed man around forty years old approached him. Speaking perfect French the man introduced himself as Monsieur Martin. They walked into the Ardennaise rotisserie, a restaurant on the Boulevard Adolphe-Max, where there were several Belgian police cars parked discreetly near the railroad station exits. Many very good snapshots of Dumoulin and the German agent were taken. After some small talk Martin asked the flyer to do some aviation research for the magazine about new civilian and military plane models, their technical specifications, the condition of the emergency landing strips in the Lorraine region and their intended use. For safety reasons, Martin recommended using disappearing ink and handed him a bottle along with the appropriate instructions.

"This Monsieur Martin knows the barracks in Nancy better than I do. He even told me the officer's names and their descriptions to make me feel more comfortable!"

Doudot sent us the photos taken in Brussels that proved to be of very high quality. Our counterespionage and aviation officer, Mayeur traveled urgently to Nancy where Sérot, the air force specialist from our Belfort branch, was expecting him. The man named Martin was identified in a few hours. He was actually a reserve officer named Masson, born in 1896 and already in the files of the Belfort counterespionage branch due to his frequent trips to Lake Constance, the favorite location of the Stuttgart Abwehrstelle. "Martin" and Dumoulin were keeping a secret correspondence for some time and the questions asked were becoming progressively more detailed allowing air force headquarters to gauge which issues were of interest to the enemy. Masson's home in Dijon was under surveillance and the letters addressed to his wife were being discreetly opened and checked. Aware of the danger implicit in his espionage activity for the Abwehr, the traitor didn't travel to France for over a year.

At the end of August 1939, during the Polish crisis, we intercepted a card he sent postmarked from Rome and two days later another one mailed from Tunis. The *Surveillance du territoire* was to find Masson in a hotel in Tunis where he had made the mistake of signing the register using the name Martin. He was transferred to Paris where he admitted to committing espionage. His mission was to gather information regarding the French air force's strength in Tunisia and to give that data to the Italian consulate general in Tunis.

"You see, those Italian bastards keep on telling François-Poncet a pack of lies. They have succeeded in convincing the ministry of foreign affairs that they want peace and don't trust Hitler!"

Masson was condemned to death in April 1940, but the Germans were able to set him free just in time in June 1940 and he resumed his work for the Abwehr in the region of Dijon-Belfort. He was placed on our "blacklist" and was arrested during the Liberation when he could no longer avoid the punishment he deserved.

One day in June 1938 I returned from the Place Vendôme at full speed. I had just had a conclusive conversation with H. Corvisy, an important official at the ministry of justice. The essential changes in the law we had requested for so long were about to be issued as a legal decree: the political definition of espionage would be abolished and crimes against the external security of the state were now part of the criminal code. Any act that was directed against France would be considered treason if its perpetrator was a French national, but it would became espionage if the perpetrator was a foreigner. The old classification of the crime of high treason now became a crime of treason against the nation and was punished at all times with the *death penalty*. Daladier countersigned the decree on June 17, 1938 and Schlesser phoned Corvisy, who had been seriously wounded and maimed during the First World War, to express our gratitude and satisfaction.

Another law decree issued a year later, on July 29, 1939, while keeping the essential provisions of the original decree, was to modify the Criminal Code by adopting the concept of a national defense secret in terms identical to those we were using since 1938 for the training of our counterespionage officers, broadening the definition of national defense.

"Information relating to military, diplomatic or industrial matters, which by its very nature must only be known to persons qualified to receive it and must in the interest of national security be kept secret from any other person."

"We have what we need now!" said Schlesser, as he came into Bonnefous' office to give him the news.

"That's great, but now we must put an end to propaganda as well," answered Bonnefous.

In fact, Nazi propaganda was infiltrating France like water seeping through sand. The propaganda was insidious, underhanded and very clever, finding its way into the most divergent political ideologies; it took on certain characteristics aimed at convincing the rabid anti-Communists and attracted those who wished a return to absolute authority, to reassure the fearful and the cowards and encourage the separatists.

"Look at this bulging file," said Bonnefous. "It's all German propaganda! It all comes from Baroness von Einem, whom I am unable to pin down but who moves in newspaper circles and distributes vast amounts of money. We must go after this man called Karl Roos, who is financing the autonomists whether they are Basques, Bretons, and most of all Alsatians. There is also the *Cercle Grand Pavois* located on the Champs-Elysées; they invite every pro-German individual in the Paris café society and spread the good word through the *Comité France-Allemagne* where that maggot of Otto Abetz holds court..."

Schlesser was smiling and happy, our dedication still not what he wanted it to be but he did feel that the service was now jumping out of its lethargy.

"Obviously now we must take measures to protect the nation and the army against all actions intended to break our morale..."

If we failed to thwart Hitler's propaganda our counterespionage effort would yield only disappointing results and encourage all potential traitors. It was Nazi Germany's form of advertising to promote itself as a quality product. We pursued our crusade to seek repressive legislation targeting that mortal danger. Our penetration agents were once again on the alert; the Abwehr was demanding vigilance and information on possible mobilization initiatives. Something new was brewing.

Françoise came to Paris on holiday at the beginning of August and told me that Canaris was visiting Budapest with a delegation of OKW officers. She thought this was to prepare for the operation against the Sudetenland and iron out an agreement with the Hungarians. Once again she repeated, "Let them push on to the east, they will stop eventually!" She was brainwashed by Nazism!

On April 8, 1938 a new highly confidential and reliable source informed the S.R. of an OKW operational plan targeting Czechoslovakia. Gouyoux confirmed this item, coming from Czech intelligence. Rivet felt it necessary to brief Daladier privately about this new situation, as well as the general opinion that France was powerless and wouldn't get involved in a war between Germany and Czechoslovakia. This alarmed the prime minister and he appeared determined to help us react and vigorously counter German propaganda. On August 25, 1938 the S.R. informed the French government that the Nazi operation against the Sudetenland was set for September 25, 1938. We saw the month of August go by with the highest level of anxiety, tension being at a maximum. The S.R. was reporting heightened construction activity along the Siegfried Line and identified all the new works in progress thanks to an air force squadron led by Colonel Ronin that successfully photographed the area, allowing us to complete our knowledge of the fortification works.

Documents filched from the inner sanctum of the OKW showed the German army's order of battle and the planned movements of major units to reach the Czech border. Rivet called us in for a meeting.

"The operation against the Sudetenland is close at hand and it will be launched in spite of the opposition of some German generals. Hitler is determined to pursue his policy of reintegration of all German nationals and territories back into the Nazi Reich." The boss concluded on a somber note: "War is now unavoidable!"

Mobilization orders were being issued. For several months Schlesser and I had prepared the plans to place our counterespionage service on a war footing: our heavier equipment, such as the archives, research and support personnel in each section, was moved outside Paris; personnel was increased, with more officers and non-commissioned reserve officers placed in the military districts of our wartime organization plans. In each main headquarters we set up a plan for the *Bureau de centralization des renseignements*—BCRs—that were manned by handpicked reserve officers and whose mission it was to back up the generals in enforcing their police powers. Our detailed instructions had not yet been issued and were to coincide with the necessary government instructions detailing the functioning of civilian and military authorities, as well as the tools to be used in the fight against espionage. These instructions had been ready for over one year and were bouncing around inconclusively from one ministry to the other, which was exasperating to us all.

On September 26, 1938, Hitler announced to the world his intention of having his troops cross into Czechoslovakia. Then, on September 29, there was the Munich conference and the abandonment of the Czechs. Inside our unit there were highly charged and emotional arguments going back and forth. Many agreed with Rivet that the Allies had lost a last opportunity to compel Germany by force of arms to remain within its borders and abandon its predatory policies. In attempting to save the peace at any price we were losing the war and our prestige. The analysis offered by our Chief was breathtaking:

"German industrial war production is greater than our own. German public opinion is galvanized by easy successes and backs the Führer by 90 percent. It was a good and perhaps the final opportunity to seize the advantage created in the High Command by the sacking of top officers and of General Beck in particular. By turning our backs on the Czechs and on the Sudetenland we surrendered a pivotal stronghold from which to fight and defend ourselves and we will not get it back. All of this," said Rivet as he concluded, "Colonel Gauché and I have repeated over and over to Generals Colson, Gamelin and to Daladier ... Menzies is well aware of it and has duly kept Chamberlain informed ..."

Some of my fellow officers felt that the breathing space offered by Munich could be useful. They were convinced that the morale of the French people was the most important issue: France displayed indifference to what was happening beyond its borders and to the continuous threats by totalitarian regimes, appearing ready to accept Nazi and pacifist propaganda. They saw in the "triumphant" photos of Edouard Daladier's return from the Munich conference proof of all this and hoped that America and the USSR in particular would react because "Russia cannot allow this threat to grow toward the east." All of Europe seemed permeated by a psychosis of powerlessness that overwhelmed masses of people and showed their fear. Governments were hard pressed to shore up their public opinion and cover up the catastrophic consequences of their failures while they accelerated war preparations and tightened their friendships abroad.

The Führer was very much aware of all this weakness and felt confident in his war production capability. He pushed very hard for the recruitment and training of all army units, seeking to play the winning card because of his recent successes and because the game requires him to move swiftly. The second part of the Czech operation was to closely follow the first one. As seen from the intelligence accumulating on our desks, the closing months of 1938 were very dramatic. Preparations for the second act were being made in full view while our Czech friends were filled with anguish. The Prague operation was covered in the west by the heightened activity of German intelligence against France, which had become more aggressive than ever. We counterattacked rather brutally and the success of our penetration agents and our defensive apparatus was enhanced by the lack of caution and the hurry used by many Abwehr "handlers" and "deputy-handlers" who were new to the profession, and mistakes could easily be made by newcomers and inexperienced amateurs. Canaris was paying a heavy price for the huge increase in personnel: the number of Abwehr agents arrested in France went from 35 in 1935 to 153 in 1937 and 274 in 1938.

I was surprised by the poor quality of many of those agents we arrested, stateless individuals, insignificant German types, some hopeless Frenchmen, crooks of all kinds and nationalities, homosexuals—a conglomeration of people without much to offer that had been recruited very quickly made me doubt the effectiveness of the espionage work being undertaken and the seriousness and professionalism of the recruiters themselves. Our Ws were the agents who were holding up well and were very much appreciated by the Abwehr. As for the others always on the run, they would wind up hiding inside official organizations such as embassies and consulates, where they were untouchable.

"It's shameful; our diplomats don't have the balls...," Consul General Loewenbrück told me in confidence. He was a solid Alsatian, as tough as nails at the office of foreigners of the Quai d'Orsay and very close to our service as well. Often he would forget his diplomatic language to sound off against the acquiescence he witnessed in many high officials at the ministry of foreign affairs.

"When it comes to looking into German newsmen, Pierre Commert sees red!" Commert was in charge of the foreign press desk at the Quai d'Orsay.

It would take the arrest in January 1939 of Baron, who was the Paris correspondent of the *Berliner Zeitung,* to force the Quai d'Orsay to accept the facts and allow us to deal with the matter without further delay. Wiretaps had allowed us to find out for some time that the Baron couple was in contact with councilor von Rath at the German embassy, who had already been involved in a few espionage cases. We knew from Françoise (who found this very amusing) that Canaris was getting many reports from Paris concerning our political situation and other Parliamentary activity. Through our W agents we secured a series of phone numbers in Berlin and several German cities that were being used for confidential Abwehr communications.

Cazin intercepted one very short and apparently innocuous call made by Baron to one of those numbers in Berlin at 2 a.m., during the Munich crisis, which was extremely revealing. On January 12, 1939, in agreement with Commissioner Gianvitti of the P.P. we decided to take action. The situation overseas was too serious for us to continue tolerating espionage activities we were unable to check because of the protection offered by embassies and consulates. If the scandal was to involve the ministry of foreign affairs it was just too bad. Baron and his wife were arrested and I was present when they were questioned. In Baron's address book I found two Berlin phone numbers belonging to the Amt-Ausland-Abwehr and I very politely asked Mrs. Baron what she had to say about it. She burst into tears and Baron broke down. At the same time we decided to shut down the espionage network of German news correspondents. Five journalists were arrested and unmasked, including Ihlefeld, who was, along with Baron, one of the most active, with entrée to many French politicians.

The matter caused a lot of commotion; P. Commert questioned his bosses, Daladier demanded explanations and the German ambassador got involved and made one inquiry after the other. But we stood firm. Baron and his wife went to prison along with three other newsmen. Ihlefeld was declared *persona non grata* and we took advantage of the repressive wave to deport from France Otto Abetz, who also was a frenetic Nazi propagandist. There were loud protests everywhere reaching Rivet and Schlesser, who were hard pressed:

"Are you sure your information is correct?"

"Don't start any provocations!"

"Mrs. Abetz is a French national!"

"Watch out for counter measures!"

77

We laughed it off! There was a memo from Daladier's office asking us to submit a report on the matter and to work out the cancellation of the deportation order of Otto Abetz with the ministry of the interior. We wrote an explanation, reaching the conclusion that if Otto Abetz returned to France he would go to jail. We enclosed for the minister and General Gamelin a very revealing report written by Bonnefous on the inroads of German propaganda and the fact that we couldn't stop it, because we had no laws against that form of subversion. The underhanded methods being used to lower France's morale now appeared more dangerous than the initiatives of the Abwehr since they were dividing the French people more and more, dampening the will to resist and increasing political dissension. Our Ws informed us of the tenfold increase in activity within the Abwehr's Section II specializing in *morale sabotage.*

Despite increased repression inside Germany, our informers and honorable correspondents were able to warn us of the incredible increase in the Nazi security apparatus. Under Reinhard Heydrich the RSHA became an all-powerful ministry. It had absorbed the Gestapo, infiltrated the propaganda organizations controlled by Goebbels and Ribbentrop, kept German communities abroad under surveillance, and increased surveillance and espionage under the leadership of an ambitious young SS officer Walter Schellenberg. Pro-Nazi elements in France were multiplying everywhere. The *Comité France Allemagne,* which had been founded by Ribbentrop's protégé Otto Abetz, was organizing lectures, and meetings that would today be referred to as seminars today. Young people, veterans, businessmen, industrial entrepreneurs, writers, journalists, all classes of society and professions were probed, flattered, attracted and subjected to a Nazi seduction campaign while the Paris *Cercle du Grand Pavois* gathered part of French high society. Within all this activity we could see emerging Marcel Déat, Jacques Doriot, Monsignor Mayol de Luppé, Jean Luchaire, Jean-Charles Legrand, and Fernand de Brinon, all of whom would become the vanguard of the 5th Column and, after France's defeat, the High Command of the collaborators with Nazi Germany.

Ribbentrop was delighted by the results of his propaganda and the kind of help he received from some French magazines. He referred to the weekly *Je suis partout* and its founder, Pierre Gaxotte, saying: "He's my bugler!" Bonnefous made all this very clear in his January 1939 report:

...Yesterday German propaganda preceded Ribbentrop's visit to Paris tomorrow with gusts of incense. Later it will, if we are not vigilant, encourage the entire nation to capitulate without putting up a fight...

Our calls to resistance were heeded just in time! The legal decree of February 10, 1939 was to make the struggle against espionage a law according to the methods and concepts we were using and suggesting. It took months of negotiations with the various ministries and the ministry of the interior in particular to finalize the law itself that Schlesser had asked me to draft. In peacetime counterespionage in metropolitan France was the responsibility of the ministry of the interior within the *Surveillance du Territoire*. Counterespionage outside France was the responsibility of the ministry of national defense and part of the 2nd Bureau S.C.R., which in time of war takes over the entire struggle inside and outside France.

The decree set forth the application of defense measures and specified those responsible for:

1. The definition and the protection of National Defense secrets.
2. The instruction of military and civilian personnel for counterespionage.
3. The defense of sensitive areas and facilities that were working for National Defense.
4. The protection of State administrative bodies.

This was a vitally important document that many governmental agencies and administrators were to ignore or set aside. It represented the charter of the Special Services for defense matters and the principles it was based upon remain valid today. The laws of June 17, 1938 and July 29, 1939 were meant to fight against subversion against the state coming from abroad, while the decree of February 10, 1939 was intended to defend France from a mortal danger and stand up to the Axis powers. During the various phases of my counterespionage activity it would remain my gospel. I was to adhere strictly to the letter and spirit of the law whatever the political circumstances or the changing personalities exercising political power, including those our Services depended upon or reported to. The events about to develop were to severely challenge those laws and the men whose mission it was to carry them out. To reach that goal we would often rely solely on our own conscience as soldiers in the service of France.

5

Stopping the Spies

T he treacherous relief that followed Munich did not affect us. Once he had put an end to the lukewarm interventionist hesitations of England and France, Hitler pursued his strategy to annex the remainder of Czechoslovakia to Germany. The SR and our penetration agents, Gouyou, the wiretaps, were all confirming and describing the coming tragedy, which was also being predicted by our diplomats. In January of 1939 our best sources informed us of plans for the complete absorption of Czechoslovakia. The Czech military attaché in Paris, Colonel Kalina, would visit us daily with alarming news. By February it became obvious that the operation was imminent; on March 6, 1939 we advised Gamelin and Daladier that it was to take place on March 15. During the evening of the 14th German troops crossed the border peacefully occupying Prague on the 15th. By March 20, 1939 it was all over and no one made a move!

The dramatic transcript of a secret meeting, which took place on March 16 at the foreign affairs commission of the Senate, had been transmitted in its entirety to the Abwehr, something completely unheard of. Pierre Laval, oddly enough (in truth it must be said that he was no longer a government minister) was the most acrimonious speaker in condemning the lack of reaction by France and its allies. Facing foreign minister

Georges Bonnet, Laval warned of the danger ahead and championed an agreement with Italy:

"What is happening is an abomination… the octopus is spreading its tentacles… The only way to prevent Hitler from taking over Europe is to make a chain from London to Paris with Rome, Belgrade, Warsaw, and Moscow—otherwise Germany will win… In a few months it will be French blood that shall be flowing…"

There was therefore a traitor inside the Senate! Françoise had revealed it to me on April 10, 1939 and added another vital piece of information:

"The Germans have laid their hands on French documents in Prague from the files of the Czech High Command."

I was skeptical. On April 5, 1939 Gouyou after a rough trip through central Europe was able to return to France. With tears in his eyes he described the suffering of the Czech intelligence service that was forced to leave the country after having burned and given orders to burn tons of secret archives that held untold treasures. But Françoise was very insistent, making her point strongly:

"I am convinced they now have the blueprints of the fortifications of the Maginot Line. They discussed them in my presence as they were talking about the Czech operation, which some of those present had been preparing. They said the fortifications are extremely impressive and impregnable. They have no intention of giving it a try!

I asked around the Boulevard Saint-Germain at the ministry of war and was able to verify that in order to help our Czech friends speed up the construction of their fortified lines the French High Command had authorized communicating to the Czech military commanders select technical files of the Maginot Line. We had neither been asked nor were we even advised of such a communication. Schlesser, who happened to be with me, asked Françoise to repeat her story since we couldn't believe our ears. Both Gouyou and Kalina, whom we questioned, couldn't provide any explanations and we had to accept the fact that the Germans now knew the defensive value of our fortifications. This was confirmed by the fact that after May 1939 none of the Abwehr's questionnaires dealt with the Maginot Line. That was when we saw the start of the first intelligence efforts regarding the defensive fortifications in northern France between Sedan and Dunkirk. After his successes and in the midst of the disarray that swept the various governments, Hitler turned his sights on Poland.

By the end of December 1938 Rivet had warned the High Command and the government of this coming jump by Germany. By June 10, 1939 he was able to pinpoint the exact date to the end of August 1939. This time the Führer knew he was risking war because Poland was determined to defend itself and England and France could no longer shirk their obligations. Hitler knew through Canaris that Polish General Kasprzyski was in France negotiating an agreement with Gamelin to coordinate war operations between French and Polish armed forces in the event Poland was invaded. The French government requested that our penetration agents spread this information and it was one the few times the leadership was to remember that these agents even existed. We would go to any length through peaceful means to stop Hitler from carrying out his plans.

"Before moving East the Führer wants to be covered in the West."

The first quarter of 1939 saw a considerable increase in German intelligence activity in France with over 300 arrests in five months! German subversion and propaganda became so intense and more dangerous because of our own weaknesses. While we could check the initiatives of the Abwehr we seemed powerless in stemming the interference and meddling by the enemy in our internal affairs. Resistance to this diabolical activity was always thwarted by indifference, disbelief, narrow partisan political considerations which divided parliament and paralyzed the government, depriving us of the necessary repressive legislation.

"It's serious," said Schlesser. "Canaris, Ribbentrop, Goebbels, and Heydrich are all in cahoots to find and wipe out any minimal resistance to their master's plans and while they're active we're asleep. Paillole, old buddy, I'm afraid we're destined to be a happy few fighting it out against these juvenile delinquents and their dastardly methods for quite a long time. As long we don't get kicked out let's be absolutely implacable!"

We can only be implacable when the law allows it, as was the case for espionage since June 17, 1938. On March 8, 1939 at dawn, Ensign Marc Aubert was executed by firing squad in the ditch of Fort Malbousquet in Toulon. He was the first to be sentenced in accordance to the rigors of the new law. His mother arrived from Lyon the night before in an attempt to beg military authorities for mercy, but to no avail. She cried out her sorrow all night. The Havas news agency published the item in a terse bulletin and I also waited for the announcement at dawn, listening to the radio with a heavy heart. It was the last act of a painful matter when the future of the French navy was decided during the few months of the false peace we were living in. On June 27, 1938, with Schlesser out of the office, Bill Dunderdale phoned me around midnight.

"May I come to see you tomorrow morning with a colleague from London?"

"I'm in my office at 8 a.m. Is it serious?"

"It's serious."

Bill came with Lieutenant Colonel Hinchley-Cook, a jolly red-faced fifty-year-old officer. He cautiously extracted from a locked leather brief-case a thick envelope addressed in French to an Abwehr mailbox in Dublin, Ireland. Hinchley-Cook told me that his service, MI5, was watching the mailbox in question after a request from the FBI. It was discovered be-cause of the matter relating to the ocean liner *Bremen*, belonging to the German Atlantic lines. The officers of the *Bremen* had been involved a few months earlier in a sensational espionage and propaganda case in the United States. I remembered the matter because the Ast of Hamburg had attempted to penetrate the U.S. and the Americans had used the case to alert public opinion and turned it into a commercial success with the famous movie, *Confessions of a Nazi Spy*, which also thrilled hundreds of thousands of French and European theatergoers but failed nevertheless to change their placid outlook.

I looked at the envelope very carefully and saw the postmark from a Paris post office branch.

"Is this the first one you intercepted, Colonel?" Hinchley-Cook was not rushing to answer so I became more insistent. "It's very important to know whether other similar envelopes reached you and what happened to them."

The visitor admitted that "in the wake of the *Bremen* case" another envelope had been opened previously in London, about a month ago. It was placed back in the mail because it merely announced the next mailing. He wouldn't volunteer anything more than that. Hand it to the British! They're gentlemen, they believe in fair play and all that…but would we ever really know what they were thinking? There was no time to lose so I called in Bonnefous. With Hinchley-Cook's agreement we steamed open the envelope and photographed the four pages inside containing informa-tion on the Mediterranean naval squadron and announcing a follow up message. The pages were the kind used by schoolchildren and were hand-written with only a letter A as signature at the bottom of the last page.

We carefully sealed the envelope back up and begged Hinchley-Cook to return home immediately so that the letter would be mailed through the regular circuits. He was a bit surprised by the urgency of our request and disappointed to not be able to sample the virtuosity of some famous Parisian chef, something that would have to wait for another time, since our good friend was driven back to Le Bourget at top speed. He understood that this was an extremely sensitive matter and would forward the next intercepts as soon as they came in. Bonnefous took the photos to the 2nd Bureau at the admiralty's headquarters in the rue Royale. The naval officers were flabbergasted because there could have been only one officer in the Mediterranean fleet able to collect all this information. These were operational decisions taken by the admiralty due to the tension created by German plans for Czechoslovakia. "The Mediterranean fleet can set sail in twenty-four hours." That was the first line of the letter we intercepted. We requested absolute secrecy from everyone.

I dispatched an officer to Lyon for a handwriting test by Professor Locard, who found that the handwriting belonged to a young man about thirty, physically strong, with a weak personality and not very well educated. With our fellow naval officers we searched the listings of the Mediterranean fleet officers, whose last name started with an A and fit our expert's description. This turned out to be a thankless task. Ten days had passed when Hinchley-Cook returned with another letter announcing a very important delivery and requesting instructions and payment. This time we gave our friend the royal treatment but we still had found out nothing. By August tension was at a maximum. A young MI5 officer brought us a postcard addressed to the same Dublin post office box. It had been mailed in Antwerp and was postmarked August 16, 1938. It also ended with a few friendly words. There could be no further doubt that the handwriting matched that of the intercepted letters.

While Bonnefous was unable to locate the right name among naval officers who had requested permission to travel overseas, I ran up to Brussels to see Verrhulst, who agreed in his usual spirit of cooperation, to lend us the hotel registration cards of French citizens staying in Antwerp between August 1 and 16. We knew through our Ws that the German consulate general was the permanent Abwehr station reporting to the Hamburg Ast and its Bremen annex. I suspected that the traitor had transmitted a very large amount of documents through there and that the card postmarked in Dublin was to confirm that his mission was accomplished. In Paris the hours clicked away as we waited for the results of the research by Belgian state security. On August 20 Verrhulst's deputy brought us several hundred cards that Bonnefous and his assistant, Abtey, went through one by one, comparing the handwriting to the sample belonging to the traitor. Suddenly they both darted into my office, looking ashen and excited, holding a card and showed me the incredible sloppiness of the spy. I read:

Name: Aubert
First name: Marc
Profession: Officer...!

Bonnefous rushed to the rue Royale and the offices of the ministry of the navy. He returned very late as I stayed to wait for him. He was rather unhappy: there were several officers on the list with the name of *Aubert* at Brest and Lorient but none of them had the first name *Marc* and none was serving with the Mediterranean fleet nor would fit professor Locard's description. Just to be sure, Osvald also traveled to both cities himself; he also checked the handwriting of the various officers named Aubert, but to no avail. Could the traitor have used a false identity? We still had to check among the officers of the Mediterranean fleet in Toulon for similarities in the handwriting to the letters addressed to Dublin and the hotel card from Antwerp. Osvald handled this very detailed work with his faithful assistant, Inspector Danger. They were traveling with a special mission order issued by the navy's chief of staff, Admiral Darlan.

After several days, on September 22, 1938, Osvald called me. "I've got him! It's an ensign on the destroyer *Vauquelin*, of the Mediterranean fleet. The handwriting, the description and obviously the name, everything matches! There's no mistake possible," said the police inspector.

At the ministry of the navy there was considerable amazement! How could they explain so many negative results from the officer lists? In Paris they had simply decided to *not also* look at the list of the most recent graduates of the naval academy, since their names would appear in the official register only during the coming year. This oversight gave the traitor an additional month of espionage, besides wasting a lot of our time and work. Between August 16 and September 22 Hinchley-Cook sent us an envelope he had intercepted containing new instructions transmitted to the fleet that included its state of alert orders! The value of such information in the hands of the enemy was such that in case of war the Mediterranean fleet would have been seriously threatened. We had to find out what Aubert had passed on and ideally we should continue feeding the

Germans with plausible information that could reduce the damage done by the traitor, with us standing in for him.

We had to arrest Aubert in absolute secrecy—it was the key to the success of this ambitious disinformation plan and for once the highest authorities fully agreed that it was necessary. Bonnefous immediately traveled to Toulon with orders from Darlan. Together with Osvald he reported to the naval authorities at the *préfecture maritime*, since it was that office's responsibility to subpoena and arraign Aubert to face the Maritime Court. Our two men went aboard the warship *Algérie*, anchored at Toulon and informed Admiral Abrial, the commanding officer of the fleet, of their sad mission. It was agreed that Aubert would be arrested that coming Sunday afternoon, the day he was to be on guard duty. It would be easy to avoid the possible curiosity on the part of a few sailors on board the *Vauquelin*. Only the ship's commanding officer was informed and would be present with Bonnefous when Osvald would issue the order to arrest the suspect. He was also to make sure that Aubert's prolonged absence was adequately explained to the rest of the crew.

On Sunday at 3 p.m. Osvald and Bonnefous, both wearing civilian clothes, appeared to be two very interested visitors that the commander was escorting around every part of his ship. Two sailors were swabbing the deck thoroughly. They reached the door of Aubert's cabin in the officer's quarters. The captain was in uniform wearing white gloves and looking very pale. He knocked on the door. A tall strong-looking man appeared in the doorway. They shoved Aubert back into his cabin while Osvald closed the door. The ensign, looking aghast, stared at the three men in silence.

"Aubert, you have brought dishonor to the navy; all you can do now is pay for your crimes!"

It was quite a dramatic moment. Bonnefous grabbed the codebooks open on Aubert's writing table as well as the manuscript pages he was working on. As it was customary in the navy the youngest officer on board would be entrusted with secret documents. With what appeared to be a cynical and at the same time mindless attitude, Aubert took advantage of his day on the watch to finish copying one of the codes he hadn't yet turned over to the Abwehr. As he admitted later, Aubert had traveled to Antwerp to hand over most of the codes used by the fleet! Then he got hold of himself, not feeling any kind of remorse. When confronted with the questionnaires prepared by German intelligence that had been found in his locker, he just shrugged his shoulders! Letters from a woman were also seized. "Those are from my friend, she's not involved," he said. Osvald noted the return address.

Danger and Commissioner Cottoni of the *Surveillance du Territoire* quickly located the girl in Rennes, where she was arrested in her own apartment. Bonnefous returned to Paris. At the rue Royale everyone was aghast. "Had we suddenly been at war the enemy would have read our maneuvers like an open book and we could have faced disaster…" The head of the 2nd Bureau, Captain Samson, who admitted this to us, wanted to make immediate changes to the codes. We refused. That operation must take place quietly and gradually. The "burned" codes must continue to be used until we gave the signal to stop: the enemy was not to discover that its agent had been arrested.

Bonnefous told us what he'd learned in Toulon. Under questioning by Osvald in the offices of the *préfecture maritime*, Aubert didn't take long to make a confession.

"Locard had been right, Aubert was a weak type, driven by sex. In 1937 he met a whore in a brothel in Rennes. She grabbed hold of him twice over through sex and emotions! He thought of himself as a modern day Des Grieux, took her out of the whorehouse and then to Brest where he was naval cadet. He needed money, and lots of it… That's when that son-of-a-bitch got the brilliant idea of visiting the German embassy in the rue de Lille in Paris. Aubert asked for the naval attaché, giving his rank and assignment."

I had never before seen Bonnefous, who was normally a calm and collected person, in such a state of excitement using language normally used in the barracks, as he went on:

"Naturally the Boche understood what was going on and since the embassy is but a way station for the Abwehr, Aubert was ushered in immediately. He offered some very important documents he was carrying but the German politely refused them, telling him to come back in two weeks. He was asked to travel to Antwerp the last Sunday in October 1937 to a hotel they indicated. There he was to be contacted—this defies the imagination—by his real name by someone who would be qualified to speak with him… that's it. The hooker traveled with him so that he wouldn't lose his nerve and he didn't, the bastard. At this first rendezvous he turned over a whole suitcase full of documents. Some were secret, others were confidential but the German said they were all interesting. He handed over 5,000 francs and lots of promises. A lot of hot air! All of it carefully designed to keep Aubert in the shit, forcing him to make more deliveries to Belgium. Another German found out he was going on a cruise aboard the *Jeanne d'Arc* and he handed Aubert the famous address in Dublin."

In a moment of inspiration Bonnefous asked Garnier to look in the file for a backup Rotterdam address they had given to Aubert to be used "in case of war." In three minutes our head archivist came back with the answer: "Mailbox of German intelligence discovered in 1916 and used during the Great War!" So Hamburg-Bremen wasn't better organized than Lindau after all.

"There's no reason for them not to fall for it if I play Aubert's role." This was what Bonnefous proposed, getting more excited by the game. He practiced the traitor's handwriting, rewriting over and over the opening line, "My dear Paul." He rewrote the "A" in the signature but was not to handwrite the entire letter even though it was a perfect imitation. We decided to have Bonnefous replace Aubert. With the assistance of the naval officers we answered the questions Aubert still had left open, explaining to the recipient that the letters would be typed from now on as a precaution. The letters were posted regularly the next day with the help of the PTT and MI6.

His employer was pleased and didn't suspect a thing. He congratulated "Aubert" on his caution and the growing value of his deliveries, paying very generously and even reimbursing him for the typewriter. The banknotes were slipped between the uncut pages of French books shipped from Paris to the address of Aubert's mistress, Marie Maurel, in Rennes. They were intercepted by the PTT and handed over to Bonnefous. The messages sent by the Abwehr and the questionnaires were reconstructed by discovering the printed letters in the text itself with a magnifying glass. We lifted the ones showing that they had been punctured with a pin. It was a long and tedious process but the game was intense and exciting.

For Christmas "Aubert-Bonnefous" explained to the Abwehr that the monthly payments had to be doubled…it was the year-end traditional bonus! Our accounting department was ecstatic, the deliveries were improving, and Hamburg was very pleased. Due to political tension, we were even more cautious with "Aubert-Bonnefous." He understood the danger and proposed to cautiously change the mailbox—one never knows—because in time even the best procedures can be easily discovered. Hamburg was still using the same writing method, ordering the correspondence to be delivered to the counter of a café near the Gare du Nord. The envelope should simply be addressed "deliver to Monsieur Paul."

On January 10, 1939, while Aubert was being judged in secret by the maritime court in Toulon, one final letter was posted to Dublin, announcing that an important package was being delivered on January 31, 1939 to the counter of the café. On February 2, Frahm, a big fellow who worked for the German *wagons-lits* on the Hamburg-Paris line, appeared as usual around 11 a.m. to have a beer. He was "Monsieur Paul," asked for his package and walked away but didn't get too far. Osvald and Danger were waiting for him. Frahm was just a small fish and got 5 years in jail, but the fact that he was caught proved that four months after it had started they still hadn't discovered our caper. The navy had enough time to switch their codes and change their alert plans as well as the mobilization orders. Aubert died bravely, while his mistress was sentenced to three years in prison and disappeared after having served her sentence. She was indifferent to what happened to her lover.

Two weeks after the tragedy another letter mailed in Paris, just like the others, reached the address in Rennes. I opened very cautiously a brand new espionage novel by one of my favorite authors, Robert Dumas. There was no money inside and no messages inserted with pins. Suddenly my paper cutter slipped between two pages and a thin sheet landed on the floor. I picked it up and read a single word written in French: "Compliments." If the sender wished to prove that he knew me well, the choice of the book was a good on, while the congratulatory word was addressed to our counterespionage and I appreciated it. The entire trial had been held in absolute secrecy, not one mistake was made. The attorney defending Aubert was extremely correct in following the rules. I traveled to London to inform our friends and offer our thanks. We discussed the matter at length and the lessons we should draw from it; we also talked about our Ws, about disinformation; and the work we were doing together. Major Cowgill, whom Menzies introduced to me as the Schlesser's counterpart, asked me to return to visit in a very friendly way.

"You are our masters!" he said.

The "masters" still had a long way to go to overcome so many loopholes and weaknesses. The lessons of counterintelligence hadn't yet reached the army or the country as a whole. There was still no military security service; had there been one in Place Aubert would have been identified before doing so much damage and would no doubt have avoided his tragic end. His many approaches to the Rennes police and in Brest to get his mistress' card identifying her as a prostitute withdrawn, his frequent trips to Paris and overseas, and his constant need for money—all these were reasons to draw attention to Aubert, to make sure he was being watched, and had no access to secret documents. I have shown the mistakes committed by the Abwehr, using many "mailboxes" that had been blown, odd and potentially compromising trips taken by an officer, handwritten messages, etc. But were we flawless in our mission to protect the SR?

Perruche shared his losses with us from time to time. A number of our SR agents disappeared. Had they been arrested? Did they run off with the money their handlers had given them or were they just hiding after realizing the dangerous side of their work? We had few answers we could give. The Gestapo was more and more vigilant and our penetration agents were unable to discover the enemy's success in fighting us. Heydrich and Himmler were keeping those facts a jealously guarded secret. It was our mission to vet the persons the SR was planning to recruit, we had to find out things about them, watch them and report regularly on their morality and loyalty to France. This work was only partially fulfilled. The march of events and the pressure of politics were forcing the SR to quickly increase its research personnel. Only too often an agent was being recruited too fast, missing the slow but always thorough crosschecking by counterespionage. We also had few tools to undertake many different tasks and SR security couldn't be our main concern. There was another reason: de Robien led me to understand that some SR officers looked down on counterespionage because of the police aspects of our job. This was a rather simplistic viewpoint that was completely out of touch with reality; nevertheless it was a fact that up to 1936 counterespionage was the poor relation inside the Special Services.

"Good wine turns into vinegar and the older SR officer moves to counterespionage!"

This opinion, voiced by an SR station head in 1935, gives an idea of the kind of atmosphere we operated in before we were able to make our case for the importance of our service after Schlesser took over. For a very long time some SR officers were unable to accept our role as "protectors" and even confide in us. They were to pay dearly for the consequences of that attitude.

On August 15, 1938 an intelligence agent from the Metz station named Heinrich Müller showed up unexpectedly at the usual location of his meetings in the town of Forbach. He was returning from a mission in Hanover. His case officer had told him not come back before August 20. Once he was informed of this return ahead of schedule, which appeared warranted, Doudot decided to interview the man. Müller was uneasy and explained his sudden return by the fact that he was short of cash and couldn't complete his mission. Doudot was becoming more and more suspicious and became convinced that the agent wanted to test how French intelligence worked on a holiday when his usual case officer was absent. Once he had listened to the man with a smile he suddenly said: "Empty your pockets!" The German, very much surprised, did as he was told. He was carrying a notebook with gourmet recipes and Doudot became very interested in one of them: how to make good cakes. You mix 507 grams of flour, 151 grams of butter, 146 grams of granulated sugar, 18 grams of yeast, 30 grams of almonds, 16 grams of milk, 31 grams of raisins, and 2 grams of egg!

The numbers tied in with the regiments stationed in Metz! Müller's attempt to explain the 2 grams of egg didn't even convince him how ludicrous it was to defend himself. Then in flawless German Doudot told him he was going to place a phone call to Wiesbaden, to the number 481-43, to inform Major Heinrich of the Abwehrstelle XII and tell him how incompetent his agent was. Amazed by Doudot's language proficiency and his knowledge of the Abwehr, Müller then admitted he was working as a double agent to answer the Abwehr's questions more efficiently. He would meet his employers in locations well known to Doudot and his men. Had Müller's case officer informed counterespionage that he had been recruited the double game by the spy would have almost certainly been discovered. Once he was informed of the arrest upon returning from vacation, the case officer burst into Doudot's office:

"Who authorized you to arrest my agent?"

"Since you have recruited him he has been stealing money from you, providing you with false information cooked by the Abwehr III F and has been spying on us!"

"So what? Paris is pleased with what we produce."

This was obviously a deplorable kind of attitude topped by a guilty conscience. Sometimes the SR was recruiting without giving counterintelligence time to do its job, which was even more of a problem because identifying double agents infiltrating the SR could have ramifications going beyond the security of the service.

At the end of August 1938 we were informed by the BSLE that a Legionnaire of German national origin, Richard Christmann, had deserted and we were provided with a very detailed description. On November 12, 1938 Monsieur Judas, the French consul in The Hague, was called upon by Christmann, who said he was sorry he had deserted and was asking to return to the Foreign Legion even at the price of the punishment he'd suffer by French military justice. The consul asked him to come back in about ten days and in the meantime he informed Major Trutat, the Special Services representative in Holland, who, in turn, asked the Lille station of the Special Services to meet with Christmann and investigate him as well. Lieutenant Fontès was put on the case. Fontès was a rather tall, smart and perceptive officer, who had graduated from Saint-Cyr two or three classes after me. He had been stationed in Lille recently and had already been to the Netherlands on a few missions.

Through Mr. Judas he met the deserter in a hotel in The Hague and the conversation was to prove Christmann's intelligence and cleverness, along with his knowledge of military matters. Fontès understood the possible ramifications and decided to use him for research in northern Germany and Hamburg in particular. He set up another appointment after handing the German some money and getting a few identity-type photographs. Counterespionage wasn't informed of this recruitment. A few days later Fontès gave Christmann a false Danish passport in the name of Clauss and escorted him to the German border. The agent accomplished his missions well and returned to Holland every month with information about Germany, but always found some pretense to avoid returning to France. In April 1939, Fontès, who was friendly with one of our counterespionage officers recently stationed in Lille, and Bertrand (brother of Major Bertrand in Paris), discussed Christmann, alias Clauss.

Bertrand, being very thorough, passed on the information to us. Our routine file search painted a rather unfavorable picture of the deserter and his antecedents. Could he be an agent provocateur? The SR let us examine his production that appeared normal and well put together, too much even because they often tended to place the emphasis on information that was in the public domain. In order to avoid any indiscretions or mistakes we decided to keep watch over Christmann without informing Fontès. We mixed in his photo with a score of other pictures and show them to two of our W agents working at the Hamburg Ast. The first W was positive he had seen Christmann in a restaurant with Wichmann the station head, as well as with Giskes, his deputy for Section III F. We decided to let Christmann play out his role. By obtaining answers to the questionnaires that we established with the army High Command he was to give us information about the disinformation tools created by Berlin. Christmann thus became one of our first W2s.

I met Christmann some thirty-five years later. He fit precisely his old description by our research of the German intelligence services: medium height, balding, very strong and the silent type. The intervening years had hardly made any changes and his French was excellent. He greeted me politely and deferentially; perhaps he was quite pleased to be having that meeting. He spoke in detail about his missions, pointing out with some pride his own achievements and those of his boss, Giskes, whom he compared to me, surprisingly enough. He still didn't know that I knew he had played a double game.

"I deserted the Foreign Legion because I wanted to serve my country. I was condemned to death by the French."

I interrupted him:

"And by whom?"

"In Algeria, in London…"

"That's not true Christmann."

I told him that since 1939 we had been following him step by step. I took an identity record of his out of my pocket. He was on the "black list" we had disseminated within our services and those of our allies; there was no indication of his "glorious" death sentence. More modest and slightly embarrassed Christmann told me about his work in Holland and his contacts with Fontès.

"The Abwehr wanted to get to know your case officers and your research plans. Once I returned to Germany after I had deserted, the Gestapo sent me to the Hamburg Abwehrstelle. Giskes and Wichmann convinced me that the difficult role I was to play was very important: to return to the French, say how sorry I was and get myself recruited in Holland. My mission was to discover the capabilities of the French SR as well as its objectives in the Netherlands and northern Germany. Fontès, whom I saw frequently and whom I hold in high regard, gave me the kind of job my superiors had hoped for; sometimes another officer, whose name I can't remember, accompanied him.

"Back in Germany I would report to Hamburg all the things I had found out, then I would go on to Berlin where I would meet with a representative of Abwehr Section III D, which specialized in providing material to double agents. I sometimes had to wait for weeks for the answers to the questionnaires that more often than not were totally innocuous. I feared the reaction of the French SR. The events of May 1940 were to interrupt the game. Since I knew Holland very well, Giskes, who had been appointed head of Abwehr III F in that country, took me with him. We worked there very hard from 1941 to 1944."

I interrupted Christmann.

"You were spotted in Paris in 1940 and again in 1944."

"That's correct! I didn't want to miss our entry in Paris in June 1940, but I never did get along with Reile, who was the head of Abwehr III F in France. At the end of July 1944, with Giskes, we wanted to help the Abwehr at the Hotel Lutetia save its files. There was an incredible mess and Reile had panicked. We burned the most important documents and took many others back to Germany. There was much too much left over because of Reile's fear and disorganization."

"Christmann, you must admit that from 1939 to May 1940 you had an excellent position."

"Fontès was paying me very well and the Hamburg Abwehrstelle was also paying me the monthly salary of a regular army officer."

"Believe me when I tell you that your income was largely deserved, compared to the information you produced and the dangers you were incurring since we knew what you were doing all along."

Christmann was now sheepish.

"There was no hint in the questionnaires that Fontès handed me, other than the fear France had of Hitler's policies and the threat of war..."

I then interrupted him:

"There was nothing in the answers provided by the Abwehr other than the desire to convince us of your Führer's desire for peace!"

We had nothing more to discuss. I watched the German walk away, looking cut down to size.

There was a lot of nervousness at 2 *bis* Avenue de Tourville. Robert Coulondre, the new French ambassador to Berlin, came on April 22, 1939 to compare his own pessimistic views with ours. He agreed to allow French consulates in Germany to support our efforts, which required extreme caution to avoid Gestapo surveillance. The French military attaches and their deputies came to share information and their view of the situation, asking for instructions: Didelet, Réa, Stehlin from Berlin; Laurent, Fustier from Brussels; Réau from Belgrade; Herrmann from Stockholm; Trutat from The Hague, along with Stevens, the new British intelligence man in Holland; Leleu and Voirin from Ankara; Parisot and Donati from Rome; Musse and Klobukowski from Warsaw; Bullat from Moscow; Caro from Copenhagen; Vauthier and Bonhomme, who were both working with Pétain, then ambassador to Madrid. All these busy and anxious visitors dropped in at our offices to see us one after the other.

The spring of 1939 witnessed many new SR volunteers and as many chaotic initiatives: the secretariat of national defense wanted to create an economic espionage section; the weapons and technical studies section contacted Colonel Grant of the British High Command. It was setting up sabotage and destruction operations inside Germany! At the ministry of foreign affairs, de Croy and Grimaldi wanted to set up and head a political espionage service overseas; Colonel Le Bris of the 2nd Bureau of the colonial military command wanted to start a research organization; while Colonel Guillaume wanted to start an SR service in Africa. Rivet listened to them all, quieting down the excitement and channeling back to our sections most of those concerned, not without some problems. Since the Aubert case the navy's 2nd Bureau was living in the fear that its secret codes could be in enemy hands. Every week commander Samson, head of the section, would come for fresh news and without telling us directly it seemed that his men had warned him of possible new leaks. Unfortunately the decryptions and wiretaps of Bertrand were to confirm his worse fears. In April 1939 we found out that the Italian secret service had succeeded in obtaining the codes being used by most foreign countries except for Japan and the USSR. It was a real tour de force! Some 16,000 pages had been passed along to the Abwehr, and the Forschungsamt was able to decode allied diplomatic messages as they were being sent.

We warned all our friends and Schlesser stopped everything he was doing to travel to Rome, returning after 10 days.

"I placed decoys at night inside the safes used by our military attachés and they were moved for the naval attaché. So my conclusion is that all the safes are being open or can be open. We made no changes to the way things were done. The new codes are now in a safe place inside the private homes of our diplomats. The ambassador has instructions to slowly dismiss all non-French employees."

We had requested that last measure for years and it took a major upheaval to convince the ministry of foreign affairs! We would later find out that the embassies were never to be completely swept clean, as we had asked. It was necessary to find out exactly what had taken place in Rome and that was no easy task in a difficult investigation. The Italian secret services alerted by the OVRA were very vigilant and we were rather weak in fighting them. In such a delicate matter overseas, whom could we trust? The navy and its codes were once again the target. The admiralty was very proud of the honor of its traditions and wished to wash its dirty linen in private, while foreign affairs felt hurt in its pride. No one could be suspected in Rome without the Quai d'Orsay or the rue Royale reacting violently in ways that paralyze our investigation. It was to take five years but in the end we were able to shed light on the matter. This was possible because in such a case as in many others despite the furious events taking place and the many changes in our good fortune, French counterespionage doggedly pursued its mission. I therefore digress on this specific point.

In March 1942 I met once more with Rosario Barranco, the head of the OVRA in France. The meeting took place in Marseille in the lobby of the Hotel Splendid. The man was refined, subtle, and very fearful. He was already beginning a conversion that would lead him to become one of my best informers. I asked him about Rome.

"Who was it that you had at the Farnese Palace to spy on us?"

"That was a SIM operation."

"What do you mean?"

"How can I explain it to you, my poor major!" This Barranco had always annoyed me with his patronizing expressions full of pity. "In your consulates and embassies you employ a majority of local people. It's easy to place or recruit our agents among them. In Rome the doorman and the chauffeurs of the Farnese Palace are our agents!"

Even though Barranco was boasting I didn't forget that piece of information. On July 10, 1944, after several weeks of questioning, Riccardo Boccabella, who was still the doorman at the Farnese Palace, finally admitted to Inspector Ducros of the security services of the French Expeditionary Corps in Italy that he was the man Lieutenant Bracco of SIM had entrusted with breaking into the allied safes at the beginning of 1939. A happy and easygoing liar, Boccabella had greeted our counterespionage team on June 7, 1944, proclaiming his devotion and his "loyal" past history of service since he had been in the employ of the French embassy since 1928. It was no doubt due to his seniority that our diplomats had been reassured and failed to take our recommendations of 1939 into account.

Well paid by Bracco, the doorman was informing the SIM about Italian personnel our diplomats had recruited; he made the initial contacts, watched things, informed, and stood guard. The young and pretty maid working for our naval attaché was unable to turn down the charm and money offered to her by the handsome "maresciallo," Manca, who was also Bracco's deputy. While the officer was away attending Italian naval maneuvers, the maid handed over to her lover the keys to the office for a few hours. The keys were quickly duplicated and the nighttime visits began immediately with the vigilant help of Boccabella. They were also extended to other offices without my finding out how the keys had been obtained and copied, but a similar procedure appeared to be likely.

The safes had been opened seven times before Schlesser rushed over to Rome in April 1939. Every two to three months Bracco and Manca would photograph the documents they found interesting, placing them back with extreme care. They were so sure of themselves that they never paid attention to the decoys my boss had placed inside the safe. Manca was arrested in July 1944, accused of trespassing and stealing documents. Bracco was never to be found and since the embassy failed to keep any personnel records the maid could also not be identified. Were Boccabella, Manca, Bracco, et al. guilty or not guilty? In good conscience I think they did their duty and I knew who the real culprits were in any case.

6

The Abwehr's Fifth Column

We were increasingly alarmed by the many undiplomatic activities of the German embassy and its consulates in France. Personnel numbers were growing immeasurably. Rudolf Hess' organization of Germans overseas, Goebbels' propaganda services, the German League, the Hitler Youth and obviously the "protégés" of Ribbentrop hadn't been stopped by the deportation of Otto Abetz. All these people were finding a warm welcome within the various German diplomatic offices in France. The Nazi poison was being spread by many slogans: "Germany is no longer claiming Alsace; Germany wants peace; Hitler is the final bulwark against Bolshevism, and favorable to social progress…" This propaganda was intent on anesthetizing public opinion. Pro-Nazi zealots knew no limits: Régis de Vibray, the secretary of the student organization of the *Comité France-Allemagne*, was publicly supporting Germany's position; German and French war veterans who had gathered on Ribbentrop's initiatives swore at Douaumont to keep the peace. At the same time, a few kilometers away, Weber, a German spy was taking pictures of the Maginot Line for the Stuttgart Ast. On the German side of the Rhine a French delegation of victims of the First World War was welcomed with military honors by the same Reichswehr unit that was also working on the fortifications the Siegfried Line. A few newsmen were invited—all expenses paid—to visit Germany and write favorably about it. Writers Henry Bordeaux and Jules Romains mindlessly prostituted their talent in attacking as "warmongers" anyone criticizing the danger that Hitler represented.

From the beginning of 1939, once our report on Nazi propaganda had been distributed, Schlesser and I unsuccessfully attempted to have the ministry of the interior stop and circumvent this flood that was upon us. We were only able, with difficulty, to prevent the distribution of a book by Ferdonnet, a young disciple of Charles Maurras, condoning the abandonment of Czechoslovakia and racism. We always ran into a widespread inertia and misunderstanding at the Quai d'Orsay. Mondanel, just like Castaign and the entire *Surveillance du Territoire*, agreed that the police were powerless.

"The Nazis are bold beyond comprehension," Mondanel, the inspector general of the police judiciare, told us in his high-pitched and sarcastic voice. "I just had the rather incredible visit of a big tough fellow who bullied his way through the front desk claiming that he had a message for me from Himmler. He gave me the Hitler salute, clicked his heels loudly stating his name, 'Bömelburg!' He told me then and there that he intended to set up his office in Paris inside the German embassy: there are military attachés, cultural attachés, commercial attachés, why shouldn't there also be 'police attachés'? I was so dumbfounded that Bömelberg felt it best to add that he'd let me think about it and would wait in Paris for the French government's decision!"

"They're no longer content with spies, propagandists, saboteurs, agitators," added Schlesser angrily. "They need an official Gestapo and SD in France. That's unbelievable!"

Our investigation in Berlin confirmed that Bömelburg was part of the SS, working closely with Heydrich. Mondanel was furious and took the matter to his minister while Rivet informed Daladier. The ministry of foreign affairs was puzzled since it had been queried by both services and consulted in Berlin with Ambassador François-Poncet, who knew nothing about the matter. Everyone was hesitating to make a decision. It took Mondanel's stubborn opposition, backed up by the Special Services, before Bömelberg was informed one month later that he was *persona non grata*, which was a polite invitation to go back to Berlin. The German policeman left in anger and was not about to forget the incident.

In June 1940 he was to take over as head of the Gestapo in the rue des Saussaies, sitting in Mondanel's very office, while Mondanel, a top administrative official was dismissed by the Vichy government, then arrested and deported to a concentration camp by Bömelburg's office. We could only respond to such boldness on the part of the Nazis and to their attempts to destroy France's national morale by using the existing espionage laws that placed very strict limits to what we could do. It was obviously a weak response and as Mondanel would say, "We are just rotting away!" Contrary to their German allies, the Italian special services seemed absent, but we noticed the constant increase in personnel at the embassy and the consulates in the border areas.

The OVRA representative at the Consulate General of Italy in Nice was the very talented police inspector, Rosario Barranco, who gathered information and kept the SIM informed. He had a propaganda role among the large Italian community, showing that it would be natural for the Comté of Nice to be reunited with Italy. With Barranco's help from his post in Turin, Major Roberto Navale was keeping an eye on the activity of our intelligence service. The possibility of a conflict that our ministry of foreign affairs persisted in declaring unlikely and the intense and efficient work done by our stations in Marseille and Nice encouraged Fascist counterespionage to move vigorously and subtly. About thirty of our agents were arrested in the period from the end of 1938 to July 1939; it was a very hard blow. Some of them, like Polacci, were shown photos of themselves having conversations with our SR officers in France while clever double agents caught others whom Navale had infiltrated into our services and who were identified much later. Others had been sent into Italy without the proper training because war was about to break out and we had to work quickly. They took huge risks, like the tourist couple sent to Florence at the end of 1939 to identify new military units and was caught looking too insistently and too closely at a barracks.

In France diplomatic guidelines required caution. We should do nothing that might annoy the Duce, thereby giving him an excuse to join the Führer. Rivet offered an ironic comment to those guidelines as he announced the signature of the "Pact of Steel" by Ciano and Hitler on May 2, 1939. For the moment the Italian intelligence service was making things easy for us; the SIM simply asked the Abwehr for anything it wanted to know about France. Why should they double the risks on the same target? This elementary caution in secret warfare was similar to the way the Italian army behaved on the battlefield. The Abwehr and the SIM worked very closely together in Rome and Berlin but not yet in France, where it was much more dangerous. Canaris and Roatta had an excellent long-term understanding. To be even more efficient the Italian espionage chief was permanently transferred to Berlin, where he was acting as military attaché and also studying and applying the methods that Canaris was introducing at breakneck speed inside the Abwehr.

With our own methods we were in a position to find out as much as, if not more than, Roatta. Our deep research work on the Abwehr was bearing fruit and the German section of French intelligence now had the full plan of the order of battle of German espionage that was being updated daily by our penetration agents. Thanks to this work and the very detailed description provided to us by Aubert, we had identified the officer of the Ast in Hamburg who first trained the French officer to be a traitor: Commander Fritz Unterberg, *aka* Gibhardt, who had been spotted in the last few weeks in Brussels where he had diplomatic cover at the German embassy. This additional Abwehr muscle in our neighbor's capital confirmed what Li 159, our penetration agent at the Stuttgart Ast, had observed since January 1939.

German intelligence was building up its agents hurriedly in Holland and Belgium, attempting to infiltrate pro-Nazi political movements, especially the Belgian Rexist party of Léon Degrelle. From there the Abwehr went after other intelligence and propaganda targets in northern France and England. We now had Unterberg in our sights and followed him to Zurich in June 1940. After a few months spent in Madrid he reappeared as part of the German armistice commission in Casablanca in 1941, from where in 1942 he barely avoided capture by crossing the border into Spanish Morocco. He ended the war as head of the Ast Section I in Lyon.

Analysis revealed all the changes in the enemy intelligence command in Berlin where the Amt-Ausland-Abwehr was now on a wartime footing. Section II in particular—sabotage and subversive activities—drew our attention. Lieutenant Colonel Lahousen, who was more to Hitler's liking, since he was a 42-year-old Viennese and the founder of the Austrian intelligence service in 1936, had replaced Lieutenant Colonel Grosscurth. Canaris appointed Lahousen to his research section after the Anschluss under Colonel Pieckenbrock, who immediately liked the military correctness and gift for organization displayed by his new subordinate. A few months before the Anschluss in Vienna, Lahousen found an excuse to contact the French military attaché. Through a French woman residing in Vienna a discreet contact was established between him and our service. Navarre was in charge of handling this exceptionally important connection, making sure that Lahousen didn't grasp all its ramifications. It was to continue throughout the war up to 1943, when he left Canaris' staff to fight on the Russian front. Even though it reached us at wide intervals, the information provided by this source, regarding the intentions of the OKW in particular, was to be of major importance during that very tense period.

Canaris and Lahousen, contrary to Grosscurth who disliked the idea, decided to increase the scope and size of Abwehr Section II. After the Austrian and Czech experiences, where the manipulation of opposition political parties helped promote Hitler's plans to perfection, the two men molded the Abwehr to fit that kind of new covert action aimed at undermining the opponent's national cohesion. While Goebbels and Ribbentrop were in charge of disseminating Nazi propaganda as it was defined for the most part by Hitler's spokesman Dr. Otto Dietrich, Canaris and Lahousen used opposition political parties in France and in Europe, attempting to penetrate them to channel and increase their influence. The instrument for such action was the *800 Company* founded in 1939 which became a regiment in 1940 and finally the *Brandenburg* division in 1942. It was a training ground for all kinds of saboteurs and the focal point of all the Fifth Columns and units in charge of special undercover missions, such as kidnapping officials and violent attacks behind the lines.

It is interesting to note that, at the end of 1940, Keitel asked Lahousen on Hitler's behalf to assassinate General Weygand because the Axis wanted to stop his initiatives in North Africa. Abwehr Section II was also in charge of murdering General Giraud after his spectacular escape from Koenigstein in 1942. In both cases our services were able to take the necessary security measures, thanks to the information secretly obtained by Navarre while Canaris and Lahosuen refused to take part in such acts of banditry. Even though the Abwehr refused to take on those dishonorable tasks its moral sabotage was continuing vigorously. We learned a lot from the questionnaires that were handed to our agents and the orders issued by Section II of the various Abwehrstellen. The main targets were Alsace, Brittany, the Basque country, Corsica, and North Africa, where the Germans wanted to know the exact strength of separatist and nationalist political movements and identify the militants who could be bought and financed. The objective was to undermine French national unity and weaken our defenses.

It was difficult for us to follow every detail of German actions for several reasons. It was a new way of using covert conflict and our legal, legislative, and security institutions, and our laws couldn't meet that kind of challenge to national sovereignty. Enemy intrusion of that type gave rise to many issues, such as, where did regionalism, separatism, and autonomist movements end? These subtle questions were enough to trouble many people. We sensed that there was a lot of hesitation within the National Security forces. Between the *Renseignements Généraux* and the *Surveillance du Territoire* turf problems began appearing. What were the boundaries of political propaganda? When was national security endangered? Given the laws on the books at that time the only way to end all discussions and polemics was to consider propaganda cases as equivalent to espionage so that they could be dealt with clearly and directly.

We were able to use that kind of approach for some nationalist movements but failed with the PNB (the Breton Nationalist Party)—Breiz-Atao in the Breton language—even though its two leaders, Debeauvais and Mordrel, were known to be in contact with Abwehr Section II. The two men fled to Brussels in September 1939 where they continued their unsuccessful anti-French campaign in Brittany and received financial and other help by covert Abwehr agents from the German embassy. They returned to Rennes with the German army in June 1940, but were openly despised by the Breton population, and the Germans who had been forced to abandon their autonomist policy in favor of collaboration with a united France had become rather indifferent. We were to be more successful in Alsace.

Through our penetration agents we found out that the Ast of Kassel's Section II had set up a branch in Frankfurt-am-Main aimed at Alsace and its separatist movements. Karl Roos, the most vocal Alsatian separatist leader, traveled regularly to Germany and had meetings with officers of the Abwehr branch. Alsace was calm and intensely patriotic in its feelings toward France. We could not allow any kind of agitation take hold in such a sensitive border region. We decided to proceed with Roos' arrest. Under lengthy questioning by the *Surveillance du Territoire* he became clumsy in defending himself and made a fateful mistake. In analyzing a notebook Roos was carrying, our German counterintelligence section noticed that a page had been torn off in a hurry. Our technical services found that the following page had traces of what had been written on the torn page. Lead scattered over the page revealed two phone numbers in Switzerland that Roos had written in his own hand. We knew those numbers that the Frankfurt branch gave to its agents to be used only in case of war. Confronted with the evidence the traitor confessed his collaboration with the enemy and was condemned to death on

October 26, 1939 by the military court in Nancy. He was shot by firing squad on February 7, 1940. The Germans were to display their gratitude after the armistice of June 1940 by changing the name of the Place Kléber, one of Strasbourg's most beautiful squares, naming it after Karl Roos. They also transferred his remains to the castle of Huneburg and tried to make it into a Nazi shrine.

Every week we summarized our workload in Schlesser's office. On a huge map of France little flags with different colors indicated the arrest of enemy agents, as well as the locations of interest to the Abwehr. We noticed that they tended to be more concentrated toward the north. Our efforts were producing satisfactory results with about fifty arrests per month. The stations of the *Surveillance du Territoire* were proving their efficiency. The protection of the country's morale against Hitler's aggression remained the weak spot.

"It's well and good to pick up the small fry and the poormouths of the Abwehr! But what are we *really* doing about society people who openly admire Germany, are spreading its slogans and making it easier to recruit and set up its agents? Nothing is being done at all! Everyone's talking and taking action, using the excuse of freedom of opinion and so remains untouchable. If we don't want to die from all this, our government must give us the tools to defend ourselves…" as Bonnefous repeated time and again.

Nazi slogans came at us in waves, disseminated at random, or I should say stupidly, by French nationals. They went far and deeply harmed us: "Better Hitler than Stalin!" Our efforts to get French public opinion to focus on the enemy's perverse ways and acknowledge the existing threats to peace appeared useless. A few rare posters by Paul Colin, "The enemy is listening," "Keep silent, be suspicious," were ridiculed while people were packing their suitcases for the coming vacation. But there was even more. We received through Rivet, who barely cushioned them, new government and High Command directives to slow down our repressive zeal and reduce our demands for a crackdown on all the help and ease given to the pro-Nazi propagandists. At the end of May 1939, Colonel Duzan, the government's commissioner at the military court in Paris, informed us that his superiors intended to shelve the case against a high-level official accused of delivering secret air force materials overseas. So the Abetz case was back with us once again!

On July 10, 1939, General Decamp came to see Schlesser and me on Daladier's behalf, asking that we cancel the expulsion order of Otto Abetz.

Once again we explained the extent of the damage caused by that agent, who was responsible for spreading propaganda and slogans along with Ribbentrop's money.

"But he's a Francophile and has a French wife!" Decamp kept on repeating, unconvinced by what we were saying. On July 22, 1939, Malraison, Rivet's deputy, was urgently summoned by General Gamelin and returned to my office two hours later. He was ashen and his hair, which was carefully parted under normal circumstances, was unkempt:

"Old boy, we have to cancel the expulsion of Otto Abetz. Gamelin's threatening to have you all reassigned—Schlesser, Bonnefous and you."

"A real opportunity for all of us, colonel! But as for Abetz you can forget about us making any changes whatsoever."

I handed over to the beleaguered Malraison a lengthy new report about Abetz and his dangerous activities. Abetz was a young fine arts teacher from Karlsruhe steeped in French culture. In 1931, along with Jean Luchaire, a reporter working at *Notre Temps*, Abetz became the founder of the first Franco-German university association. Baldur von Schirach, the head of the Hitler Youth, saw possibilities in Abetz and made him a convert to Nazism, then introduced him to Ribbentrop. Abetz broadened his activities and made connections with French writers and journalists as well as war veterans. For eager Frenchmen who agreed to closer ties to Germany he organized meetings and visits to meet with Hitler himself and saw it as an honor. He was the editor of the *Cahiers franco-allemands*, which were printed in Karlsruhe and distributed in France.

Nazi propaganda had found the cultural vehicle to support its penetration. It was to manipulate the good faith of Frenchmen, such as Henry de Montherlant, who understood his mistake and publicly denounced the dangers of Nazism. With the *Comité France-Allemagne*, Otto Abetz became the leader of a huge attempt at seduction. Among the well-known personalities were Georges Scapini, Fernand de Brinon, Professor Fourneau, Jules Romains, Pierre Benoit, Louis Bertrand, Henri Lichtenberger, the Duc de Broglie, the Marquis de Chambrun, Count Melchior de Polignac, Jean Goy, Henri Pichot, Jacques Benoist-Méchin, Bertrand de Jouvenel, Sacha Guitry, Régis de Vibray, Pierre Drieu La Rochelle, Darquier de Pellepoix, and Monsignor Mayol de Luppé, who was awarded the Legion of Honor with much fanfare on May 14, 1939.

Because of his ability to corrupt and mystify the elite, Abetz looked like the engine of a psychological aggression supported by innumerable private and public organizations. Hanesse, the German air force attaché, and Faber, the diplomat at the embassy, tried to approach and seduce our more conservative politicians. A few Nazi organizations were under Otto Abetz's direct control: the Brown House at 3 rue Roquépine in Paris, with its branch offices in other cities; the French section of the National-Socialist Party located in the annex of the German consulate in the rue Huysmans; the Labot Front group, with over 900 members just in the Paris region and sixty newsmen among them—all of them zealous propagandists for Hitler. The German University Bureau organized cultural exchanges; the German Chamber of Commerce had 500 members scattered all over France and helped place Abwehr and Gestapo agents inside German or French businesses. The German Tourist Office on the Avenue de l'Opéra and the German Catholic and Evangelical churches in Paris were also part of the vast network orchestrated by Otto Abetz. The citizens of the Reich were under the obligation to take active part in the propaganda effort and in case they refused the punishment could be fierce: loss of German nationality and seizure of any property located in the Reich.

I read to Malraison the closing sentences of the document: "Through its ubiquity, whether it be overt or covert within our country, Nazi Germany is spreading disarming slogans while it builds an image that consolidates and commands respect for its superiority. Who could fail to notice that even within its defensive shield, France seduced and blinded feels it must turn to the German company, Siemens, to build the electrical wiring on the Maginot Line?" To which Bonnefous added:

"Colonel, I think the Abetz case is open and shut and that you will provide us with instructions to neutralize that entire menagerie!"

On July 29, 1939, less than one week after sending in that new accusation, the government closed one more gap, preventing our repressive action. A new legal decree (Parliament was totally incapable of passing laws regarding issues affecting current policy) completed the criminal code, finally allowing the punishment of acts harmful to national cohesion. Separatism and intelligence on behalf of foreign countries could now be punished in peacetime as well as war.

On August 2 we studied the implementation of that decree, which had been obtained at the last minute after much insistence, thanks to the support provided by Corvisy.

"We must cut off efforts at propaganda," wrote Schlesser. "There's no time to waste. We must quickly solve a few egregious problems, starting with Baroness von Einem, who will serve as an example."

The day before, intelligence coming from Asché and from source Z, which kept us directly informed about the OKW, both confirmed that the military operation against Poland would take place during the final days of August 1939. While returning to our offices (which the archivists were already emptying of the most important files to be shipped to our wartime HQ located in Gretz) we harbored no illusions as to the effectiveness of what we were about to undertake. It was now very late and the harm had been done. In the courtyard of 2 *bis*, after many requests, military engineers were completing a concrete air raid shelter. Two workers were loading some wooden planks on a truck. I had been walking past the men for three months. We knew each other and said hello.

"We're off! So you've got your bunker, it's a very good construction but it'll be useless!"

"Why do you say that?"

"Because Hitler doesn't give a hoot about us! And we don't care at all about Danzig!"

Bonnefous was angry:

"Naturally the baroness has flown the coop! The desk clerk at the Hotel Meurice said he hasn't seen her. She succeeded in eluding Gianvitti and the policemen who were tailing her and now that the decree of July 29 would have allowed us to grab her, she gets away! It's disgusting!"

Fortunately, because of the constant surveillance she was subjected to since December 1937, we succeeded in identifying most of her contacts. Gianvitti's deputy, Inspector Martz who was keeping her under his watch, told us:

"That baroness has sex appeal. She's about fifty years old but you'd think she's no more than thirty. She sees many people, Frenchmen, Germans, diplomats, members of parliament, journalists. She invites them all to cocktail parties and dinners and her suite at the Meurice is the most luxurious of all. She pays all her bills on time and her husband, an Austrian socialite from Vienna, is nowhere to be seen. She comes from a very prominent German family from Cassel and her father, Baron von Scheurenschloss, just died."

With the help of the doorman at the Hotel Meurice we put bugs in her suite, but she was very cautious and never had conversations that we could listen in on. The few people she had upstairs spoke in very low voices covered by a radio that was permanently connected to a music station.

Tension was now extreme and war was plainly inevitable. The baroness would not return to Paris anytime soon and we made a list of the

French citizens who appeared to be involved in her propaganda efforts. Two newsmen, Aubin from *Le Temps* and Porier from *Le Figaro*, had traveled to Berlin where they had been in contact with Winkel, who was on Goebbels' staff in charge of newspaper propaganda in France. In agreement with the police prefecture we decided to arrest them and what they told us went far beyond our worst fears. Aubin, whose real name was Perroux, had been working at *Le Temps* since 1911 where he was head of the news department. He looked respectable enough and at 66 he was an officer of the Legion of Honor. Aubin admitted that he had been introduced by the baroness, whom he had met in 1937 at a party at the German embassy, to the office of Dr. Goebbels. Winkel gave Aubin a three-million-franc subsidy to orchestrate a pro-German press campaign. Even though *Le Temps* also published articles decidedly critical of Hitler's policies, in particular after the Anschluss, Aubin received an additional million francs in 1938 as a bonus for his effectiveness and did not provide many details about that money, which must have been shared with other propaganda agents.

Poirier, formerly an administrator of *Le Temps,* had become the administrative director of *Le Figaro*. He also readily admitted to his dishonorable conduct and that he had agreed to spread the basic tenets of Nazi propaganda. The Nazi Reich had granted him an annual subsidy of 3.5 million francs. In 1938 he was paid 3.6 million francs, 100,000 more as a bonus for his efforts. Crushed by his shame Poirier was to die of a massive heart attack in jail right after his confession. The Nazi propaganda machine had paid eight million francs in 1938 (roughly three million dollars) to two French newsmen to confuse and prepare public opinion to accept Hitler's coming acts of piracy.

"Eight million! What do you think of that?" said Bonnefous. "Plus the millions spent by the baroness at the Meurice and elsewhere, the millions Abetz was distributing for Ribbentrop, and the millions coming from Canaris that we fortunately control for the most part... plus everything we *don't* know about! It's enormous!"

The Aubin-Poirier case led us to another thread that would allow the unmasking of the traitor inside the Senate that Françoise had told us about. By keeping a tight watch over the German embassy at the rue de Lille on April 26, 1938, we saw a Frenchman later identified as Bouillaut leaving the building to meet two other individuals in a nearby café. The three were followed and quickly identified. One was Amourelle, a stenographer at the Senate and formerly part of the Prime Minister's secretarial staff. He was in his 40s and connected to extreme left-wing groups. A few days later Bouillaut traveled to Amsterdam by plane. We warned Trutat, our station chief in The Hague, who had the man followed. Bouillaut visited the German consulate and the next day he was in Brussels, from where he phoned Amourelle. We recorded the conversation. The two agreed to meet in Brussels with a German named Bauer who was a well-known agent of Dr. Goebbels and was also in contact with Aubin and Poirier.

The arrests and confessions of Bauer and the two German agents prompted us to question Amourelle and his two friends. A search yielded Trotskyite propaganda and the blueprint of a revolutionary newspaper, *La Carmagnole*. Amourelle admitted that he was expecting funds from Germany to finance that paper and its anti-militarist propaganda. He was confident that Bouillaut and Bauer could get the money from Winkel in Berlin to cover his subversive activities. Only Germany could finance what he called his pacifist campaign and which he described quite cynically: refuse to answer the call to mobilization; general strike; and sabotage in defense related factories.

We were sure we had found the traitor who had passed along to Berlin the transcript of the secret meeting of the foreign affairs committee of the Senate on March 16, 1938. Amourelle understood the extreme danger he was in and strongly denied any contact with Nazi officials other than for propaganda purposes. The research we undertook in the wiretaps of the German embassy showed that on March 20, 1938 councilor Rahn received a message at 8:45 p.m. informing him that Michel Sextius had completed his task. Amourelle's address was 17 rue Sextius-Michel. Rahn was the propaganda specialist at the German embassy. Even though wiretap secrecy would not allow us to use that information, Amourelle was forced to admit his contacts with Rahn and having passed on political information. The 3rd Military Court in Paris condemned him to death on May 29, 1940. He was executed by firing squad in Bordeaux on June 22, 1940.

On the same day, May 29, 1940, Aubin was sentenced to 10 years of forced labor and the reimbursement of all the money received from Germany, plus a 20,000-franc fine and the loss of civil rights for 20 years. As for Baroness von Einem, she was condemned to death *in absentia*. French counterespionage found her and she was arrested in Salzburg on December 9, 1946. On March 19, 1947, her lawyer Gorsse argued in front of the Paris military court that the crimes were not punishable at the time they took place because the decree became law on July 29, 1939. The baroness was acquitted!

Less than two years after Germany's surrender, we were ready to forget Nazism's most cunning and deadly methods that blinded the French nation and helped spread the gangrene eating away at its patriotic spirit, preparing it for treason and defeat.

7

Forecasting a War

Paris was deserted. My concierge was sitting on the doorstep enjoying the cool evening before turning in. It was 9 p.m. and I walked to
my office where I would be on duty until the next morning.

"Always at work, captain?" the concierge asked. "You're wasting away
your best years! When will you take a vacation?"

I walked away waving good-bye. That Saturday, August 19, 1939, was
hot and humid and I felt oppressed. The day before Rivet informed the
High Command and the government that the attack on Poland was set to
take place between August 26 and 29. We spent the 17th and 18th preparing our mobilization, calling up our reserves, and packing up the archives
that were to leave for our advanced HQ at Gretz on Monday. The guard
around the 2 *bis* building had been strengthened. On the ground floor,
near the trunks, I saluted Captain Louis, Major Bertrand's deputy. Cables
were flowing in and a professional was required to decode them quickly
and pass them along so that the officers in the sections could work on
them immediately. Lochard, Cazin d'Honincthun's deputy, was working
on the wiretaps. He was a big fellow with a dark look beneath his tinted
glasses, and who could speak every language in Europe when he con-
sented to do so!

Our correspondents from Berlin and Moscow were informing us of unusual contacts between the two capitals. During the night a telegram announced the departure to Russia of an official close to Ribbentrop. We informed the Quai, which appeared to have already been alerted by Coulondre and Naggiar, the French ambassador to Moscow. With the help of Polish intelligence, we were following political developments by the hour and the concentration on the eastern border of fifty-six German divisions, including five armored units. At 8 a.m. on Sunday, August 20, Friedmann informed me he was returning to Paris and wanted to see me urgently. I met him later at the Bois de Boulogne. He was very alarmed in coming back from Berlin where he took a ten-day specialization course in radio near Brandenberg.

"The Abwehr II has set up a training camp for special units. I heard them speaking English, Dutch, Polish, Russian, and even my own language, Serbian!"

Being the curious type, he noticed a group of men dressed in Polish uniforms among the many civilians. The reason for his hurry and excitement was the instructions he had been issued: to look out day and night for signs of mobilization. He was given a large sum of money for the informers he was to recruit in various barracks in eastern France and an additional radio transmitter with daily contacts.

"What should I transmit?" he asked.

"Say that France is totally quiet."

"That won't look so good," answered Friedmann. "I'll give myself away if I send that message after what I saw and heard in Berlin and Brandenburg."

"I'm serious and it's the truth! I'll let you know if there's any reason to change."

He was still complaining as I drove him back to Paris. I told him that my deputy, Gilbert Guillaume, would see him the next day and keep in contact. On August 21 at 11.30 p.m. a momentous announcement was issued by the Havas news agency regarding the imminent signing of an agreement between Germany and the USSR. Twenty-four hours later TASS announced that Ribbentrop was traveling to Moscow. Cazin and Lochard were recording the wiretaps of amazed officials at the Soviet embassy in the rue de Grenelle and the surprised comments of the unidentified Frenchmen they were. On August 24 at dawn, both agencies, DNB and TASS, broadcast the news of the signing of the German-Soviet Non-Aggression Pact during the night and that very evening we received information that a secret protocol that was part of the pact provided for the division of Poland between the Nazis and the Soviets. As Rivet commented:

"This is a monkey wrench for the Communists. It is an underhanded diplomatic deal that will not make Poland's life any easier, not to speak of our own. Our generals in Moscow must be feeling ridiculous."

He was speaking to Menzies, who nodded and looked very worried. He had just arrived from London with Cowgill. The head of the Intelligence Service clearly stated his government's concern and was attempting to find out France's position through Rivet. The British government had issued very firm instructions to its ambassador in Berlin. Sir Neville Henderson met with Hitler on August 22 to inform him of England's resolve to be at Poland's side in case of war. Like Rivet, Menzies didn't believe that kind of threat alone would be sufficient to prevent war. The two intelligence chiefs decided to tighten and improve our liaison that had to become permanent and secure.

Schlesser was traveling on a mission to prepare and speed up the mobilization of our counterintelligence services within the military districts. Cowgill and I, in Schlesser's absence, were summing up what we knew and what we could do. The high probability of war in the short term prompted Paris and London from the end of June to intensify their resources and contacts. Cowgill was very accurate and methodical, even though a bit slow and his very blue eyes had an ironic look under his heavy eyebrows. His French was just as awful as my English but fortunately Dunderdale was working with us, functioning as the interpreter. Bonnefous presented our analysis of German intelligence and our study of moral sabotage in France by the Nazi services and the Abwehr II. Our British visitors were very much surprised. I spoke about our penetration agents—W and W2—and the results they were producing. I also insisted that the Intelligence Service use the same method intensively, especially in Holland which had become the favorite hub for the Hamburg Ast's actions into the English-speaking countries. Cowgill agreed and requested that I return to London as soon as possible to give his officers some additional technical information, which I promised to do. I much appreciated the candor of the head of British counterintelligence; the friendship and trust that had grown between us was destined to continue into the future. We were to work loyally until victory was achieved, putting all our cards on the table. With Menzies' approval, Cowgill was to demonstrate his understanding throughout our ordeal. He gave us his help by being steadfast, efficient, and always tactful—qualities that will never be praised highly enough.

The French and British alliance had been reestablished in 1938, *ipso facto*, making all the excellent relationships that had existed for a very long time with British intelligence officials. There was no doubt that the friendly contacts existing between the two services contributed greatly to rekindle the alliance. Unfortunately no serious defense or war plan had been issued after the agreements that would also include Poland. Just before war broke out there was no one heading the military side of the coalition, where the French army was to play the main role. Maurice Gamelin, the chief of the general staff, appeared convinced that our defensive military doctrine, so loudly proclaimed, and the strength of our fortification system were both correct. Gamelin did even better than the government's and Parliament's expectations in stating his belief that the French army, shielded by the Maginot Line, could wait for both the war industry's increased output and help coming from our allies. He renewed those assurances on August 23, 1939.

The intergovernmental meeting presided by Daladier confirmed France's obligations toward Poland. Air Minister Guy La Chambre was optimistic about our air force, "whose readiness should no longer prevent the government's decisions." During the meeting held that day none of the participants mentioned a possible German attack through Holland and Belgium. Yet at every meeting of the Superior War Council, the permanent Committee of National Defense, and the Cabinet, the consequences of German rearmament and the possibility of an attack through Belgium were brought up.

"He has good ideas…has trouble making decisions…and never puts his foot down!" complained Rivet, who once again relayed Gamelin's procrastinating and evasive answers regarding French mobilization. "Were we to remain part of the Ministry of National Defense and War or attached to the High Command that had moved to Vincennes? We'll be in an extremely awkward position," continued Rivet, "because General Georges, the commander of the North-West theater of operations, also wants us to be under *his* command!"

Georges possessed a brilliant and sharp mind and was a truly outstanding chief of staff. During a recent trip to Alsace, along the banks of the Rhine, Churchill was able to measure his worth and maintained friendly relations with him. There was a rumor that his serious injury during the murder of King Alexander of Serbia in Marseille had drained him of his energy and willpower. Colson, chief of staff of the ground forces, was a pale carbon copy of Gamelin. He was the one on paper in charge of regulating, checking and using our work in addition to the 2nd Bureau, whose head was the excellent Colonel Gauché. Admiral Darlan had made a reputation for himself as a bold and capable sailor. The officers under his command respected him and were proud of the renewal of the French navy, thanks to Darlan's efforts. General Guillemin was in command of the air force that had excellent personnel but, despite what Guy La Chambre was saying, with equipment in short supply, both in quality and, most of all, in quantity.

In spite of the open border from Longwy to the North Sea the Abwehr's research in that area, the intensive work by German intelligence in Luxembourg, Holland, and Belgium, and all the historical precedents, our defensive posture taken on the Maginot Line would not change. The High Command considered various maneuvers beginning in September 1939 should the Wehrmacht violate our neighbors' neutrality. However, we could only attempt to outline our response. Why go any further when no one wanted to believe that the German army would attempt to pass through the Ardennes and when it was impossible to plan a coherent security system with the potential victims, the Dutch and the Belgians, who were steadfastly neutral? The order to build some lighter fortifications to cover the northern border was issued. Major Darbou, our "lion" in charge at Lille, said ironically:

"The Belgians, like the Luxemburgers, want to ward off thunder and lightning. They give proof of neutrality by building fortified works in every direction, even facing *us*. The least we can do is build the same facing them. In the meantime Hitler is doing whatever he pleases and when the time comes he'll force everyone to agree."

Time was running out. The Abwehr questionnaires were getting more and more frequent from every direction. They all confirmed that German intelligence was on high alert and wanted to be informed instantly about French reactions in the face of events that were about to unfold in the east. Research was concentrating more and more on northern France. Personnel had doubled in a few weeks at the German embassy in Brussels and the German legation in Luxembourg.

"Since war is around the corner we must wipe out the last of the Abwehr's potential," said Schlesser. "All operations being planned or already underway must be wrapped up immediately."

We attacked the German intelligence service with no holds barred, as the enemy later acknowledged. Since we expected the worst case we carried on as best we could. There was a heavy silence hovering over the unit. From time to time Rivet would hurry through the hallway carrying a heavy briefcase. He would take one of the staff cars that always had their engines running and drive off to the rue Saint-Dominique or the Boulevard Saint-Germain to deliver our latest information and comments, unsure of the effectiveness of our warnings or getting the attention of those responsible. In our overheated and poorly ventilated offices everyone looked serious and tense. Not one of us dared make any predictions regarding the outcome of the coming war. Facing a Germany that was in overdrive and completely geared toward military effort, where we had been witnessing the firm and ominous resolve to make war for so long, the allied reaction appeared hesitant, slow, and pointless.

The weekend of August 26-27 went by without the start of Hitler's planned operations. There were some final attempts at negotiations initiated by the British. Mussolini himself was hesitating to join the Führer in war. On August 30 the Poles informed us that they were mobilizing. Border incidents were increasing and for the first time special commando units of the Abwehr identified by our Ws and by Friedmann began appearing. In Silesia, at Beuthen and Troppau, German agents—both Abwehr and SD—wearing Polish uniforms, secretly crossed the frontier into Poland, causing panic and gathering information. Some of them were gunned down on their way back into Germany, since the Wehrmacht hadn't been informed when it intercepted them.

At 8 p.m. on August 31 came the final and most disgusting plot. An Abwehr commando led by five or six SD officers under the command of SS officer Helmut Naujocks attacked the German radio transmitter at Gleiwitz. All the attackers were wearing Polish uniforms and after a brief firefight they occupied the radio station. A German broadcast a message in Polish, threatening and insulting to Germany. As he left a few minutes later, Naujocks deposited a bloody corpse at the entrance of the radio station. Heinrich Müller, head of the Gestapo in Berlin, had provided the dead man. This was the incident Goebbels was expecting in order to denounce the "Polish provocation" to the world and justify a punitive action on a grand scale: war!

The next day the Wehrmacht hurled its fury on Poland; two weeks later Soviet troops would follow suit. On Saturday, September 2, Prime Minister and Minister of National Defense and War Edouard Daladier had Parliament vote the funds necessary for mobilization. At 5 p.m. the next day, a few hours after England, France declared war on Germany.

"We declare war so as not to have to fight," said my colleague Brun ambiguously. Could he also have been under the spell of Nazi propaganda?

Poland was crushed in less than one month and Warsaw became a martyred city. On September 12 at Ilnau, Hitler called a conference aboard his special train with Keitel, Canaris, and Lahousen. Ribbentrop was also present. The head of the Abwehr reassured Hitler regarding the situation on the French border facing the Wehrmacht. Hitler then issued orders of unbelievable brutality, which Keitel accepted without flinching. In less than eight days the Polish campaign must end and reach the demarcation line agreed to with the Soviets on the Vistula, the San, and the Bug rivers. All resistance must be annihilated. The Jews were to be put to death.

Hitler ordered the Abwehr to identify and support political movements within the USSR that were hostile to the regime and then to manipulate Ukrainian nationalist organizations. Hitler was thinking in the long term and believed in his tactic of causing political deterioration. Once this news reached us at the end of October 1939 we were still light years from surmising that the Nazi dictator was in fact getting ready for Operation *Barbarossa* (the code name for the invasion of the USSR). On September 9 six French divisions entered German territory between Bitchie and Sarreguemines without opposition, even though our W agents had told us on September 6 that the operation was known to the enemy. Gamelin had decided to go ahead with the plan anyway. It was intended to be a limited offensive that both the High Command and the government saw only as having political value. Our soldiers stopped once they reached the Siegfried Line. It was a diversionary thrust without any vigor, which didn't surprise anyone. The Poles, in their martyrdom were well aware that there was no way it could relieve them. While Canaris ironically derided the timid and useless French move at Ilnau the same day, the Polish government through its ambassador in Paris protested against the lack of support from its allies. He would receive no reply.

A second similar operation, set up in haste to the west of Sarrebruck, failed to take place because the complete collapse of Poland upset allied plans. French divisions in front of the Siegfried Line were ordered back to their home bases in front of the Maginot Line. Only a few vanguard units stayed in German territory but the Wehrmacht drove them back into France on October 16, 1939. It became clear that the Germans would not cross the frontier. My friend Besson, who took part in those short engagements, told me:

"Our men were great. I was amazed at how the Wehrmacht was able to maneuver. How brave, tough, and youthful their men were and the way they pushed us back into France. It's going to be hard, very hard!"

On the opposite bank of the Rhine, in Alsace, huge posters were being set up and our spotters could read, "Germany will not attack France." From the Stuttgart radio station Ferdonnet was preaching about Germany's good intentions and telling his fellow citizens to go home. There were also many rumors spread around of negotiations being underway.

"As you can see," said Brun, "they don't want to slug it out. I hope we won't be silly enough to start knocking around the area."

"I could really kill that guy!" Schlesser later told me angrily.

8

The Fifth Bureau

Since August 28, 1939, our units with the most personnel had been relocated to CP Victor at Castle Pereire, a huge old mansion on the road to La Ferté-sosu-Jouarre. The castle was a rather pretentious affair located some forty kilometers northeast of Paris, hidden deep inside a dark and damp park but an excellent location to store our archives and the large personnel, which had now been doubled with recruits. They would eat, sleep, and work on the same premises and get very bored since contact with the outside world was extremely rare. It was the studious and silent atmosphere of a monastery where Colonel Malraison was the chief, looking after the place, making sure the food was good, telling ribald stories, and keeping things peaceful.

The smaller staff of the SR and the SCR remained at 2 *bis* Avenue de Tourville with Rivet, as part of the command and the dynamic air force section. The head of the air force section was Colonel Ronin, an easygoing and efficient commander, with his deputy, Major Pépin, one of my younger comrades from Saint-Cyr, an enthusiastic and brave man to the point of being foolhardy and sacrificing his life in one of the final dogfights in June 1940. The lighter staff of the SCR that Schlesser and I were in charge of was made up of reserve officers with the right profile and personality to allow permanent liaison with the civilian ministries. Guy Perrier de Féral and Yves Cazeaux had been important officials at the ministry of the interior and were responsible for all the many delicate issues there.

The state of siege had been decreed following mobilization, giving military authorities the responsibility for police protection while the military handed to civilian authorities the duties it no longer wanted to discharge, meaning most of those outside the military areas. We now had full responsibility inside and outside the country for all problems regarding espionage. We also had to spearhead repressive action that was facilitated by the excellent relations we had with the *Surveillance du Territoire* and Military Justice. However, enforcing harsh preventive measures was to be the source of ever increasing conflict as the specter of deadly warfare dimmed and many began harboring the crazy illusion that the war would end without a battle. The measures we wanted to enforce appeared to them as just more of an inconvenience and inappropriate.

There were clashes with the ministry of the interior when we wanted to muzzle the supporters of Nazism and fight defeatist propaganda and when we closed the borders with neutral countries, or when we demanded a whole series of measures restricting the freedom of German nationals or of countries friendly with the Reich, or when we wanted to reinforce the security checks of personnel working for national defense. There were conflicts with the ministry of foreign affairs when we denounced activities by foreign nationals that were favorable to Germany, carried out, thus incurring restrictions. There were disagreements lasting several months before we could expel Italian consulates from military areas where they were operating as observation posts for the Abwehr.

There were conflicts with the economic ministries who disliked the strict protection targeting sabotage and espionage; and with the ministry of PTT (postal service, telegraph, and telephones) that held us responsible for the increased difficulties and extensive use of postal controls and wiretaps, causing technical problems and a flood of complaints. The security of a mobilized nation was being enforced amid indifference, skepticism, and even hostility. The legislation defining its general conditions and applications, such as the decree of February 10, 1939, were much too recent to be understood by those in charge of enforcing them and no detailed set of instructions had as yet been issued, just as no special mobilization exercise had been put into place. Fortunately many very capable civil servants, such as Loewenbruck at foreign affairs, Lange at the PTT, Mondanel at Interior and Corvisy at justice, helped us and understood we had to recommend or enforce defensive measures.

"If we could only speak in the name of any kind of authority," Schlesser would complain. "We've been at war for one month. In theory our unit, the 2nd Bureau SR-SCR, is no longer operating and the 5th Bureau that was supposed to take over as soon as mobilization occurs hasn't been formed yet! This is an inconceivable situation given the crushing responsibilities we have to face."

Rivet was also livid, and our service was completely disoriented, caught between the commander in chief and the minister of National defense. Finally, on September 25, Gamelin ended the arguments and resolved the issue by ordering the creation of two 5th Bureaus, one reporting to Daladier and the other reporting to himself.

"That's all we need to create even more confusion and make me resign!" was our boss' comment.

The threat worked and Daladier moved faster than the commander in chief by having the president of the republic sign a decree on October 3 making the 5th Bureau report to him through General Colson, who headed the minister's military staff. In order to avoid being surprised by instructions they wouldn't like, the High Command had Gamelin sign a note dated October 15, 1939, describing how the 5th Bureau was expected to operate with the commander in chief and the two commanders of the theaters of operations: General Georges in the main North East theater and General Noguès in North Africa. These conflicts and rivalries caused delays and forced us to have two headquarters far apart from one another and thus complicating our work and lowering morale. On top of that technical controls—postal, telegraph, and telephone—which had been set up during mobilization all over France were part of our responsibility and for which we were completely unprepared. All this at a time when the government, without admitting as much, wanted to allow many offices to continue to work as in peacetime, causing a number of incidents on a daily basis.

On September 22, 1939, Daladier himself was interrupted during a telephone conversation that a censor, listening in, found was too indiscreet! The incident whipped up a storm around our unit creating more interest than all our reports on Nazi propaganda.

"It's absurd!" complained Schlesser, in whom I detected weariness of it all.

We were able to convince Rivet to negotiate the autonomy of those cumbersome auxiliary services. He succeeded in mid-October by having General Jouart take command in close contact with us. We had to dispatch an officer as liaison and Schlesser used the opportunity to get rid of Brun. CP Victor was not affected that much by all these events. Bonnefous was given reserve officers to fill the unit, including two men from Lorraine who had been well trained in Metz: Captains Johanès and Lutwig. Because of his technical knowledge and leadership ability, Johanès became deputy to the head of our German counterespionage section.

The stations on the flanks in Lille and Belfort facing Belgium and Switzerland had been reinforced. The Metz station had been withdrawn to Paris with the exception of Doudot, who kept up his special missions in eastern France. Colonel Crest de Villeneuve became the head of that station in Paris with my classmate Simoneau as his deputy. A solid unit under Gilbert Guillaume and Abtey took over most of the penetration agents I had recruited. The pressure of events finally brought about the kind of organization we had long wanted in Paris, but since a lot time had been lost and we had added too many functions, we also were responsible for the weakness of our new mobilized unit.

I have mentioned the broader problem we encountered in getting the definition of "national defense secret" accepted and our obligation to defend ourselves against espionage and moral sabotage. I have mentioned the weakness of our service and must also point out the problems the army was facing with respect to enemy subversion. A few months prior to the beginning of the war we succeeded in getting a few officers specialized in counterespionage stationed within the 2nd Bureaus of the military districts. We had no time to do more. In September 1939 most large units were still using the same security procedures they used during the First World War. We were never able to set up a single alert exercise to demonstrate to the commanders the inadequacy and weakness of that old type of organization in the new context. "We're always one war behind the times!" complained Schlesser.

Schlesser took it upon himself to travel everywhere, attempting to improve the territorial organization of our counterespionage. The mobilization of the BCR representing us within the commands of the military districts took place adequately because of Schlesser's presence but, nevertheless, he was unhappy about the static way our units were set up.

"It's an army of bureaucrats, my dear Paillole! You'd better take a tour with Lambert to make sure their coats don't smell like mothballs!"

We were wrong to laugh because the BCR missions were to be carried out very well by those serious, quiet men who proved to be totally devoted to their duty. Thanks to their preparation and knowledge of laws and regulations and their personal charisma they were able at times to get more out of local military and civilian administrators than all the piecemeal instructions coming from Paris could. They defended themselves from enemy threats thanks to the brief summaries we provided listing German intelligence initiatives. They hunted down suspects using our information cards on specific persons to be watched and got both the police and the justice system very effectively involved. Their role was to be essential in the military areas, where the larger units didn't have the tools to fight the special kind of war the Nazis were waging on us and yet those units were the prime objectives of the Abwehr. In order to make up for that loophole, Schlesser was able to mobilize into the BCRs in the north and northeast some exceptionally talented officers who were very quickly able to fulfill the task they had been assigned; for example, the district attorney in Lille, Cassagnau, and Colonel Gérar-Dubot of the reserves in Amiens who overcame some unexpected wartime situations and whom we will meet again later on in this book.

While we had a good territorial security system thanks to the quality of those additional personnel, it was also necessary to give the armies themselves as soon as possible the modern tools of warfare for military security and military police units in particular. When I told Bonnefous about my worries regarding the inadequacies of our system, he noted:

"Don't worry, at the pace things are going we have time to think about what we should do when our victorious armies will chase the enemy outside our borders!"

He was quite satisfied with the results of what he referred to as his "plant" since there was more than enough material coming in from the BCR stations, from wiretaps and decryptions that he compiled around the clock into finished products, and he was correct in his statement. Major Bertrand's service was also providing high quality data that was often decisive. Not far from CP Victor, Bertrand had requisitioned the Château Vignolles, renamed CP Bruno. French personnel had been reinforced and since February 1939 Bertrand had added some Spanish-speaking specialists from a group of Spanish republicans who had acquired German and Italian codebooks. In addition, starting in November 1939, they got additional help from about 15 Polish cryptographers with experience on German and Russian traffic. A British intelligence officer was permanently assigned as liaison with us and a teletype kept us constantly linked to London.

We were intercepting foreign radio broadcasts day and night and CP Bruno was able to complete and centralize the production of listening posts scattered all over France. The listening unit of the army in North Africa was part of counterespionage by seeking out covert radio stations. Thanks to our penetration agents Bertrand had been able to identify the radio traffic by enemy spies for about one year. Besides a few transmitters we controlled, only one Abwehr transmitter was uncovered in France prior to the defeat in June 1940. We discovered it in March 1940 near Amiens while the position-finding service that had been set up for the first time by the *Sûreté Nationale* during the mobilization was just beginning.

In July 1939, just before the war began, after several years of working together with our Polish and British allies in particular, Bertrand's service succeeded in rebuilding the "Enigma" encrypting machine used by the Wehrmacht for its coded radio traffic. From then on hundreds of coded messages were being intercepted and decrypted day and night, providing the High Command the most precise information about the enemy's order of battle, the activity of the air force, their orders and operational reports, etc. By "covering" secret radio traffic we could check the effectiveness of our penetration agents who were using radio transmitters provided by the Abwehr. We also discovered that we had succeeded in preventing the arrival in France of agents with transmitters, only one was uncovered and arrested, as I have already stated. He was a French citizen named Sprotte who was able between September and November 1939 to send twenty-four messages regarding troop movements in northern France and railway traffic. We discovered him starting with the ninth message. It took us fifteen more messages to locate him and have him arrested by the *Surveillance du Territoire*. Sprotte was executed by firing squad six months later. The operation allowed us to seize six transmitters built into suitcases with codebooks and blueprints. They were used by my counterespionage services and in July 1940 wound up being the sum total of our transmission equipment. I must admit how weak our technical services were, since before 1940 they were unable to provide us with any kind of portable and inconspicuous type of radio.

At dawn the military aircraft flying me to Marignane airport near Marseille was still deep in the thick October fog. Inside the rudimentary and ice-cold cockpit I was thinking about my mission in North Africa. Two days before Schlesser had told me how worried he was:

"No one can tell what might happen. We have to be in a position to function no matter what takes place on the battlefield, even if Paris must be evacuated and North Africa is cut off from France. Two immediate precautions must be taken: first we must make sure we can quickly move our tools, namely the files and the archives. I'll order the engineers to manufacture three to four hundred boxes that are easy to handle. We'll have a trial run with CP Victor. The second priority is to prepare a fallback base that's distant enough and able to function even if the files and archives can't be moved or are destroyed. Go to North Africa, to Algiers, without making a fuss about our plans. Just think about the possibility of this happening and prepare for it in any case."

From Marignane a navy seaplane flew into Algiers harbor around noon under a broiling sun. Colonel Delor was waiting for me on the pier. He was very well dressed in civilian clothes and wore a magnificent bow tie. As we left the port a street merchant offered me some oranges and a dark-eyed child trotted behind me with his shoeshine box. Delor drove me up to Telemly, where he lived high above the white city.

"What brings you here my friend?" he asked.

I knew the head of our Algiers station very well and had paid him several visits since 1936. He was an excellent host who knew how to smile, talk and extend promises, making every meeting very pleasant but also mostly disappointing. His station's work was rather superficial and his initiatives for counterespionage were lacking in imagination. The distance, the sunshine and his easygoing disposition encouraged a kind of euphoria, treating serious matters a bit cavalierly. Would he understand now how important the mission I was about to entrust him with in Algiers actually was?

"Colonel, since mobilization there is a BCR in Algiers. Colonel Schlesser wants us to take a look at his effectiveness and he wants me to help you beef up the counterespionage personnel working for you."

Counterespionage was practically nonexistent and I had some trouble convincing Delor to immediately take on two or three officers. Much to my surprise I discovered that he had a rather large filing system and some important archives. The head of the BCR at headquarters of the military district was Colonel Badin of the reserves, a former regular army officer who hadn't done much for a few years after becoming one of the more successful local attorneys. He knew his stuff and had excellent relations with the *Surveillance du Territoire* in Algiers. I also met Police Commissioner André Achiary, the local commander. He had a great personality;

he was young, open, brilliant, and very much aware and pleased to be of assistance to national defense and to the army. He was a dynamic auxiliary we could count on. Delor found an alibi to explain away the weakness of our counterespionage section: he relied on Achiary for all his security concerns.

I jumped on a plane to Tunis. Colonel Niel was in charge and had a completely different approach. Clever, high strung and sarcastic, he looked at me with a sly and suspicious attitude as if he were seeking to discover deep down some secret ulterior motives and the real reasons for my visit. The station chiefs in Africa were like Chinese mandarins: very much aware of their prerogatives and authority they were jealously protective of their peace and quiet. They don't like the *missi dominici* at all. Delor who was more of a man of the world but didn't show it; Niel, who could be brutal and sarcastic, made no attempt to hide it. He demonstrated interest in our problems and was on top of the situation in Tunisia. I didn't take any of his attitudes seriously and got a complete and very intelligent report from him on the security situation in Tunisia, which was good. He obviously wished to ignore Delor and his work remained isolated and would be sent directly to Paris. He discussed Italian activity rather passionately and the measures he took with the local BCR and the *Surveillance du Territoire* to fight it. After I thanked him for helping us arrest Masson, I was at last able to break the ice and he became friendly. Niel took me to meet the resident general, Eric Labonne, a relaxed and courteous man, very much the Quai d'Orsay type. He ambled around the sitting rooms very casually as he carried a basket containing four small kittens that were playing with a cork!

"He doesn't give a shit about anything," Niel whispered in my ear. "The important thing is that he lets his staff work with me."

On my way out I shook hands with one of the staff, M. Jamet, who said our station chief was very effective.

Back in Algiers Delor was still happy and welcoming but I concluded it was necessary to beef up his station with experienced counterespionage personnel and use his files and archives as the fall-back base of our documents should we have to retreat. By sending copies of our files, we would beef up his system along the most vitally important documents from France. The coordination of all counterespionage work being done in North Africa was insufficient and now became urgently necessary. In order to overcome these problems and avoid any personal conflicts the initiative had to come from the newly created chief of the North African theater of operations, General Noguès, commander in chief and resident general in Morocco. I traveled to Rabat. One of the general's staff, Colonel Bertrand (no relation to our Bertrand) welcomed me. He was responsible for the 2nd Bureau and the BCR of French forces in Morocco. He was interested in security issues and was knowledgeable about specific problems within the country and North Africa. He accompanied me to my meeting with General Noguès.

Could it be that the general was particularly interested and intrigued by the Special Services? Or did we hit it off on a personal basis because of our common origins from the Pyrenees region? Or did the general appreciate my respect for his fine intelligence and quick grasp of the situation? Be that as it may his friendly attitude towards me at each one of our meetings led him to speak confidentially. Even though the general had only limited confidence in the Sultan, he kept tight control over the situation in Morocco. The Sultan's sympathy for the Istiqlal nationalist party was worrisome. He listened carefully when I told him that the Abwehr II was very much interested in Moslem national movements and of the relationship between Balafrej, one of the leaders of the Istiqlal, and with the Grand Mufti of Jerusalem, who in turn was in constant contact with Berlin and the Abwehr. We discussed North Africa's position in the war and he thought his title as commander-in-chief to be more theoretical than effective for the moment. Noguès was above all a diplomat and his flexibility was well known to everyone. He handled Algeria and Tunisia tactfully and cautiously while mobilization took place without a hitch in North Africa. He was satisfied with Tunisia's defenses if confronted with a possible attack by Italy. The fortified line of Mareth on the Libyan border was solid.

During a friendly lunch with Mrs. Noguès and the general we discussed the situation in France and he was not very optimistic. The lack of action by the Allies during Polish affair had been a big mistake.

"The absence of a second front is regrettable. Our industry will never catch up with Germany. I can support an allied effort from here; I only need to keep a minimum of troops to counter the Italians and any German attack if necessary."

I told him that out of caution we needed to set up a much larger counterespionage base in Algiers and asked him for his support.

"It's the wise thing to do. You can tell Rivet and Schlesser that I'm issuing orders so that you get everything you need. I'll awaken Delor and make sure your services are well coordinated throughout North Africa."

Captain Luizet was waiting for me in the lobby of my hotel in Rabat. He was our representative in Tangier since June 1939. I had briefed him at length in Paris before he left as to the counterespionage work he was going to undertake. Tangier was a cosmopolitan town open to every type of trafficking and a haven for all kinds of spies. British, Russians, Germans, Italians, and Spaniards, obviously, were all present but didn't want to be unmasked as such. They were all keeping watch on Gibraltar, the straits, the Mediterranean, and on their neighbors! The Abwehr used it as a hub for action in North Africa while Canaris was negotiating with Franco for more sophisticated bases at Ceuta and Melilla in Spanish Morocco. Luizet was a curious type and had already thought through all these problems.

"There are all kinds in Tangier," he told me. "All intelligence services are filled with crooks. They drink up the sunshine, report on things everyone is well aware of and gamble their money away in private casinos, that some them even own. The only thing I'm really worried about are the regular visits of Moroccan nationalists to the German consulate. I spot them and pass their names along to Boniface and Bertrand. But I'm bored and I envy you for being in France. I have the impression of being out of the fray in this decadent and safe world. I'm thinking of asking to be relieved and I'm thinking of Captain La Paillone."

I disagreed and told him we knew about Abwehr directives to work on North Africa. Luizet must penetrate that dangerous German action that he agreed was very ominous. I returned to Paris via Oran. With my boss I wrote orders to all our BCRs and stations in France to begin sending copies of files and counterintelligence information to Algiers as of November 1, 1939. Schlesser was to travel around to verify that this very important directive was properly carried out. There were quite a few reactions to it: some people feared for the security of the information while others didn't want the extra work. We ignored them all and no one could imagine how vitally important that decision would be a few months later.

9

The Lost Battle

We were now about to face the enormous tragedy. Rivet called us to a meeting on October 13, 1939 and said in a steady voice:

"The decisive clash with us that Hitler has called inevitable is about to begin. Its exact date depends upon him and him alone since the Allies have decided to not take the initiative. We have an impressive amount of information and teachings regarding the Polish campaign. The High Command knows what to expect as to the technique and power of the German army. The massive use of tanks and air force was no surprise to us even though it was for the Poles and for our military leadership. The German military intelligence list of questions leaves no doubt in our mind that the Führer intends to go around north of the Maginot Line. We have to figure when and how. Hitler has also just confirmed to his generals his decision to attack"—Rivet was referring to the October 9, 1939 conference where Hitler decided to study Plan Yellow, the attack through Belgium—"as soon as his offensive forces are ready. The troops that had been engaged in Poland moved back west, replacing some lesser divisions, which until then were facing. The German High Command was reluctant to start anything until the Wehrmacht's strength had doubled, meaning at least 100 regular divisions and 10 armored divisions. This wouldn't take place immediately and we have a few months' reprieve."

Rivet and Schlesser pointed out the nature and dangers of this pause.

"This will put us to sleep and demoralize us, as the new Nazi propaganda initiative proves," Rivet said. "To play for time, using it to paralyze our forces is the Führer's current objective. He'll even use the help of the Soviets and do anything to favor subversion and pacifist campaigns in France and among our neighbors. The idea that the war can end without a fight is being spread around very effectively! It's the Trojan horse intended to set up a successful final attack. Don't harbor any doubts whether or not this attack will be launched and it will happen only when Hitler decides."

Just before the declaration of war the measures taken against enemy propaganda and the arrests of Aubin, Poirier, Amourelle, Roos, and others had stopped antinational activity and dampened any pro-German zeal. The Nazi-Soviet pact and the brutal treatment of Poland confused political circles, including the Communists, and put a stop to antimilitarism. Only a few faithful apostles actually continued to believe that the agreement between the Germans and the Soviets actually served peace, the fate of Poland, and the Allied cause.

As Françoise told me, after leaving Berlin on September 1 it was an unnatural agreement that would only last long enough to settle the Polish matter and establish peace in the west.

"You mean without a fight?"

"Yes, without a fight if the Allies accept the fait accompli and the olive branch Hitler intends to offer."

"Otherwise?"

"Otherwise it'll be all out war. A terrible war because, believe me, they're determined and strong, very strong. They'll never give up on the victory they've achieved in the East."

I was annoyed at the assurance displayed by Françoise. She understood and apologized for her abrupt candor. We agreed to have her try to return to Berlin one month later by traveling through Switzerland where her friend had arranged to have her contact the German embassy in Bern. Events in the east had impressed the French people and mobilization went much more smoothly than we had expected three months earlier. Jacquot, who was still in charge of morale within the Minister's cabinet, informed us of the government's satisfaction. Paradoxically he was able to justify the positive effects of the Nazi-Soviet pact:

"This pact among gangsters to do harm has disgusted everyone. The impact on public opinion has the advantage of forcing people to face up to reality and the dictator's bad faith. I can feel a jolt toward national unity and civic duty. If America steps in and we immediately go to a vigorous offensive we can force Hitler to retreat and perhaps the Russians will jump on his back."

But the only real new offensive was initiated by the German intelligence services. The Ast branches working on France had all been increased tenfold and the Abwehr stations working in the west were beginning to set up special commando units similar to those that had been used against Poland. In the neutral neighboring countries, German consular and diplomatic offices were filled with new "officials." The German embassy in Brussels had grown to frightening proportions and three Abwehr sections were present while most of our W agents were being "handled" by untouchable "diplomats" inside Belgium. A sort of secretary and hostess named Gertrud Beckmann was setting up meetings, reimbursing expenses, typing reports and discreetly keeping close track of the work done by that special group of people. In Lille a penetration agent who had been working for us since 1937, named Hengen (Li 159), was able to establish friendly relations with her through a number of little gifts and flattering comments, which apparently were well deserved.

In Luxembourg, the Nazi von Radowitz headed the German legation and was working on the local German minority. But the effort was unsuccessful, because local authorities, while maintaining their neutrality, were working discreetly with us helping our research and surveillance work. On November 17, 1939, M. Blum, Luxembourg minister of justice, asked Rivet for our services to take part in the surveillance of the German border and set up an alert system. Our boss traveled to Longwy where we had a small outpost with a branch inside Luxembourg. With these instructions, Captain Archen the head of the Luxembourg branch and Commander Vernier who was in charge of communications, met with Pierre Dupong, head of the Luxembourg government. They agreed to set up along the Luxembourg-German frontier about 10 radio transmitters provided by the French army. This took place in a few weeks with the help of technicians from the Luxembourg PTT. Local policemen were handling these advanced signal posts. Police Commissioner Schlitz of the Luxembourg *Sûreté* was watching over these installations as he engaged in the fight against Nazi propaganda and espionage with Doudot.

During the historic night of May 9-10, 1940, starting at 7:30 p.m. minute by minute, the network was announcing the preparation of the attack that began at 4:35 a.m. on May 10.

"It's a shame we couldn't do the same in Belgium and Holland," said Rivet when he came back from Longwy.

Abwehr II was now going flat out: besides the posters calling for peace on the Rhine and the reassuring broadcasts by the traitor Ferdonnet, were new posters and loud speakers preaching camaraderie and peace to our forward positioned troops. On December 16 Rivet attended the conference held by Gamelin and the leading officers of the staff of the High Command at the fort of Vincennes. In moving words Rivet denounced German efforts to destroy the French army's morale as well as that of the population and voiced his opposition to the distribution—in vain it turned out, since the deal had already been made—of 10,000 radios to the soldiers who could use their time in other ways than to be fed Hitler's propaganda so easily. Leaflets and newspapers printed by the enemy were flooding local authorities, elected officials, journalists, teachers, and students. Special lots printed by the West-Information press agency in Stuttgart were being destined to Britanny. The leaflets were being mailed from Holland, Belgium, Italy, Spain, Sweden, and Norway and we were seizing batches of them every day. On September 15 there was a shipment from Antwerp; on October 10 our station in Chambéry intercepted 42,000 of them; on November 1, 2, and 29 we seized leaflets just about everywhere carrying Ribbenrop's pacifist speech made in Danzig.

After the leaflets there were the recordings sent to hotels, cafés, restaurants. The Belgians were pretending not to notice; the Swiss became alarmed and refused to be the go-between while the mailings coming from Spain bore the stamp of the official censor of the Franco regime! Marshal Pétain, France's ambassador to Madrid, summoned Rivet to see him in Paris where he had returned and was informed of this collusion by the Spaniards. Not expecting much success, he promised to lodge a protest with Franco. Following his meeting with Pétain, Rivet told us:

"Spain is openly hostile to us; its leadership is completely favorable to Germany and Italy."

After the mail there were the planes, the little balloons spreading flyers with peace messages praising the Nazi-Soviet pact over the frontlines and in the town in north and northeastern France. One and one half million flyers in French and Arabic were targeting our North African troops, especially the Moroccan units. We were able to seize three-quarters of them. We also observed the contacts between the heads of Soviet and Nazi propaganda units in Geneva and in Brussels. Faber, who worked both for Goebbels and Lahousen, was in the same position in the German embassy in Brussels as he had been in Paris. His former colleagues in France, Friedrich Sieburg and Krug von Nidda, were spearheading with him this German-Soviet collusion that was quite surprising. They targeted the same entities, used the same distribution centers and propaganda agents.

"To think that we had asked for the arrest of that team back in April 1939!"

To those bitter words Schlesser criticized the failure of our foreign affairs in terms that I am unable to put in print. Another traitor named Saint-Germain was working for Lahousen at radio Stuttgart. The inevitable leaks by other Frenchmen were used very cleverly: "Radio Stuttgart knows…" … "Radio Stuttgart announces the news" … and the French people who were listening would end up believing those broadcasts. I could hear the outraged comments by some very serious people in Paris who had "found out" by listening to radio Stuttgart that the 3rd Battalion of the 21st Infantry Regiment at Saint-Dié had just gone to the front line. When we investigated, the news item had appeared two days earlier in a newspaper located in the Vosges region. Pacifists, defeatists, fascists, antimilitarists were active because the way we were waging war was deeply confusing to a public opinion already shocked by the brutal defeat of Poland and the lack of action on the part of the French army. The peaceful and almost friendly attitude of the German army confirmed to our troops the insidious idea that they had been mobilized for nothing.

On January 20, 1940 Rivet delivered to Gamelin, Colson, and Daladier a new report regarding the propaganda offensive to undermine French morale. He recalled the speech he had given on December 16, 1939 at the High Command Headquarters; his conclusion was actually a warning:

"Germany finds a willing vehicle in Soviet propaganda, which is an accomplice in this renewed offensive. At a time when at the front and on the home front among the military and civilians, morale is weakening because of the weariness of a harsh winter season, our obligation to rebut each lie is even more important. All those who have been emboldened enough to resume their destruction of morale must be stopped and brought to justice. There is enough time to repair the malaise that creates favorable conditions for enemy propaganda. That's the price we must pay to prove that it's impossible to defeat us without fighting!"

On January 25, 1940, Daladier's chief of staff, Clapier, requested the basic data that we used to draft the report. One month later Daladier appointed a "conseiller d'état,"* Mr. Delfaux, to coordinate the country's morale services. Schlesser had a meeting with Delfaux and returned irritated and angry.

"One more sorcerer's apprentice!" he railed. "Had he been named a year ago he could probably have done some decent work but he knows nothing! Nothing about our services, nothing about the ministry of the interior, nothing about the enemy. He sticks his nose everywhere and wants to inject his weird views on technical controls, propaganda, border surveillance, the protection of manufacturing plants, and everything else! He's messing up everything! He reminds me of a traffic cop who's lost in a wild traffic jam and whose only solution to everything is to blow as hard as he can into the whistle they gave him!"

This coordinator who created complications, confusing some things and messing up others showed the uselessness of his action on morale. The government was aware of the problems caused by Delfaux' innovations and readily accepted his resignation on April 24. Two months had been enough to show that you cannot improvise in our specialty. We would hear nothing more about protecting the nation's morale and our report until May 5, 1940. Georges Mandel who had just been appointed minister of the interior in Paul Reynaud's cabinet, asked to read our reports on Nazi propaganda on that day. The copies we gave him were to disappear with him in the maelstrom that was about to strike a few days later.

Lahousen, the commander of Abwehr II, which continued its antimorale campaign, was now concentrating his energies on an offensive aimed at Luxembourg, Belgium, and Holland. The destruction of communications among those countries and France had been set up since January 1940. Leaflets to be showered over the three countries were printed and ready. Nazi "diplomats" in Brussels were openly courting extremist and pro-German political movements, which had already been identified, while ambassador von Bülow-Schwante was unsuccessfully attempting to curb their aggressive behavior. The results of this propaganda were very clear within the V.N.V.—the National Flemish Association—that used German funds to create defeatist cells in some military units. Anton Müssert, the Dutch National-Socialist leader, requested and received even

---

* "State Councilor": the equivalent of a Supreme Court justice in the U.S.

more financial support while his daily newspaper, *Volk en Staat*, repeated Dr. Goebbels' propaganda line.

The subversive effort was spreading while Hitler imparted his aggressive orders to those in charge of mobilization, to the arsenals, and to industry. Germany had, on the one hand, to make sure that the Allies' rearmament efforts didn't succeed in catching up and, on the other, to lower their dedication to war even more as the fateful hour drew closer. Disinformation efforts ran parallel to the usual propaganda. The Nazi strategy of anesthetizing its opponents became so effective as to reach perfection while we were unable to identify the person pulling the strings: was it Goebbels, Ribbentrop, Keitel, or Himmler? German intelligence services made sure the strategy was successful through Wehrmacht propaganda, the RSHA through the SD, the foreign office through its "reinforced" diplomatic and consular representatives, and Canaris through Abwehr II, which played a key part in the scheme of things. The Abwehr II was coordinating the propaganda efforts of various Nazi agencies and the clever mixing of truth with falsehood was becoming a real daily headache for Rivet and the rest of us. It wasn't easy to sift through the torrential flow of information reaching our unit since the end of the Polish campaign, to separate lies from truth and convince our commanders that we were assessing the situation correctly.

There were rumors of plots against Hitler; about generals opposed to the Nazi regime; of initiatives by military or civilian officials to start peace talks; of offensives and alerts at the borders; new and secret weapons; sabotage, and so on. Every day there was a new conundrum for us to solve, and every day Rivet would calmly proceed to defuse the bombs, set the facts straight, and reassure everyone. We didn't deny the existence of what was called German "resistance" to Hitler's adventurism. We even detected in those on the opposite side many reservations about Nazism. However, Oster, Lahousen, and Canaris, to name some of them, were quite incapable of being disloyal to the Führer or to betray their country. That's what we told Perruche when he asked for our opinion on the many rumors that were going around.

"That's what I believe as well," said the head of intelligence about the traditional generals. "Their opposition and pacifism is a lot of nonsense! They're just tickling public opinion with those tales. They're all too proud of their victories, too well disciplined to oppose any of Hitler's plans except to say that it might rain on the western front."

Perruche was alluding to an item he had just received. The Wehrmacht High Command always wanted to save time by being on top of its attack preparations and added to the pretext that it was not sufficiently well prepared (which the Führer steadfastly rejected) by asking to wait for better weather. The rumors of false peace initiatives, false plots and so forth were being spread around constantly everywhere, from Sweden to Switzerland, some landed on Menzies' desk, others reached Rivet. Much to Churchill's anger a false rumor coming from Holland reached the intelligence service on November 9, 1939. In Paris in May, Trutat had introduced us to Major Stevens, his British colleague from The Hague, who was new to the Netherlands and became keen on using penetration agents. In spite of Trutat's entreaties, Stevens used a double agent known to us whom we didn't trust. The man convinced the British intelligence officer that a group of German generals was plotting to eliminate Hitler and would attempt to negotiate an honorable peace. He offered to introduce Stevens to a representative of those generals. The matter fascinated British intelligence and Lord Halifax himself understood its importance. Stevens was authorized to cautiously meet the German representative.

On October 21, 1939, accompanied by his deputies Betz and Coppens, Stevens met the man in the little Dutch town of Venlo, very close to the German border. He was a pleasant young man, tall and blond: Walter Schellenberg, the fiery SS officer and protégé of Reinhard Heydrich. They discussed a trip to London of one of the generals in the plot and the hope that reaching a conclusion to the conflict in this manner would be attractive to the British government. Britain would agree to welcome a qualified negotiator but the only precondition was that he must be vouched for by an important German political figure—like Göring, for example?

Two of our W agents reported the Abwehr's irritation at the initiatives taken by the SD that overlapped its own prerogatives inside Holland. Indications clearly pointed to the Stevens case and once again we informed our friends of our fears in the matter. To no avail. On November 9, 1939 following a strange attempt on Hitler's life in Munich, the matter reached its tragic conclusion. Schellenberg and the British intelligence officers had an appointment in a bistro in Venlo to settle the details of the trip to England. A Gleiwitz-type commando grabbed Stevens and Betz and dragged them both into German territory. Then shots were fired and Coppens was killed. Schellenberg returned triumphantly with his two prisoners whom Goebbels immediately portrayed as hostages captured after a fierce battle in retaliation for British intelligence's involvement in the Munich attack on Hitler. It read like the plot of a novel. But what was real was the fact that negotiations with British intelligence had reached a point requiring the Germans reach some kind of conclusion, even a brutal one, because they were unable to satisfy British demands. Furthermore, the Abwehr and the SD now identified Coppens as really being Klop, a Dutch intelligence officer acting as the permanent liaison between the Dutch and British intelligence services. It was an excellent opportunity to prove that Holland was collaborating with the British and therefore justify, when the time came, any military action against it.

The Dutch were embarrassed about protesting the violation of their territory while the British were furious and swearing "they wouldn't fall for that again." Hitler's deputy Rudolf Hess was to experience the British attitude when he parachuted into England on May 10, 1941, just before the attack on Russia, and perhaps with Hitler's agreement to make another peace attempt. Churchill, however, refused to listen and had Hess locked up.

A few days later a new peace attempt cropped up. On November 14, 1939, Henry Mann, an American citizen, recommended by the U.S. military attaché, paid us a visit. He came to our offices at 2 *bis* Avenue de Tourville at 11 a.m. and no one knew anything about him, but we had no reason not to doubt his *bona fides*. Mr. Mann had traveled from Berlin via Switzerland and had been in contact with German generals who claimed they feared Hitler's policies. One of these, "F" (whose name I am unable to reveal since I could not reach him), asked Mann to check out the attitude of allied military leaders and see if they were interested in seeking ways towards peace. Rivet was skeptical and informed General Georges. On November 16, Gamelin, whom he met at Vincennes, told him that after a conversation with the minister he decided to take no action on the matter. The excuse we gave Mann was that the contacts were not at a sufficiently high political and military level to warrant any follow up.

Mann returned to 2 *bis* on December 13 after a short visit to Germany to report on his failure both in Paris and London, where they were still in shock following the Venlo incident. He also relayed the threatening comments made by his disappointed contacts and some idea of Hitler's vast projects of establishing hegemony over Europe.

"Nothing new," said Rivet, as he filed the matter away. He was immersed in reading the Paris dailies that were announcing an imminent a German attack on Belgium.

"Why have any censorship at all?" complained our commanding officer. "This new trial balloon was pierced a few days ago. I wonder how it is that the papers could be informed about it!"

The ministry and the High Command were asking questions within the hour. We had to check the information and be sure of its origin.

"We're wasting our time," sighed Schlesser.

Actually for the past three months we were fighting rumors, biased news, and the disinformation campaign the Abwehr had unleashed. These false alerts were forcing us into endless checking and exasperating reports to the High Command and the government who were both affected negatively by the news and by their own devices. Many top officials persisted in relying on their private informers who were thought well if not better placed than the professionals we were meant to be. These parallel services were having a counterproductive effect since they could not be checked and were for the most part out of control. They were the nightmare of every regime, favored by all politicians and military leaders and it's impossible to measure the kind of damage they were doing. The Abwehr was spearheading those maneuvers, and our Ws were being asked to spread rumors of attacks, which the Wehrmacht coordinated with a few troop movements on the ground.

"It's the best way to find out the reactions of the Allies and the neutrals"—Rudolf was telling Doudot confidentially—"because the more they're on the alert the less vigilant they'll be the day we really attack!"

The first alert came on September 26, 1939. German troop concentrations were flagged to the High Command, no one knows by whom, in the area of Aix-la-Chapelle.* Gamelin was worried and we reassured him and once again presented to him and to Generals Georges and Bineau the enemy's military deployment according to our ongoing observation: there was little risk of our having to face a serious offensive before the end of winter. Rivet was summoned to Vincennes eight days later because of insistent rumors of an attack on the Maginot Line. Reinforcements had indeed been sent in and military intelligence had seen bridges under construction on the Rhine and the Saar. Our crosschecking and information from our Ws led us to conclude that this was a disinformation initiative. On October 22 Swiss authorities secretly let us know that they feared their border will be breached during the night of October 23-24, but our outpost at Belfort was able to reassure everyone.

---

* Aachen.

At the beginning of November, King Leopold visited The Hague. Both the Dutch and Belgian governments were worried about German troop concentrations north of Aix-la-Chapelle. Our Ws were unequivocal: that specific threat was being magnified to reinforce the current peace offensive and they also reported back that the Abwehr was expecting a Soviet military action against Finland. On December 2 the Belgian military attaché in Berlin announced an imminent German attack on the western front. He got the information from Colonel Oster, a close collaborator of Admiral Canaris. Rivet once again was able to dismiss the news, but the reprieve was short lived. On January 12 Gamelin summoned our boss to a meeting of the generals of the army. The King of the Belgians had sent a note to the French commander in chief about a coming German offensive on the western front. The note was part of a document that the Belgians had seized and thought genuine, but we were not told how or why. The next day and the following night High Command Headquarters was badgered incessantly and the Belgian military attaché came urgently to Vincennes to confirm the innumerable initiatives taken in Brussels to inform the French military attaché. They still had no details regarding the origin of the information or the precise sector that was threatened. Our Belgian friends also told us of the arrival of four divisions, including two armored to their positions for an offensive. According to an investigation by our observers in Belgium and Holland there was nothing going on at all. Our W agents confirmed that the German embassy was quiet, as were the various Abwehrstellen. Despite these reassurances the Belgians decided to evacuate Eupen and Malmédy as well as Verviers, calling to arms their reservists while the garrisons of Gand and Brussels moved closer to the border with Germany.

Things calmed down during the night of January 15, 1940 and Belgian authorities never told us the origin of the documents that caused the alert. We had every reason to suspect that it was part of the files that were found in the cockpit of the German plane that was forced to land at Mechlen-sur-Meuse in Belgium on January 10, 1940, when it lost its way in the fog over the Meuse River. King Leopold and his chief of staff had issued strict orders that the incident was to be kept secret to avoid any damage to Belgium's relations with Germany.

On March 12 our intelligence services detected movements and reinforcements on the rear of the German front lines. Curiously enough some comments by Lahousen, which we were obviously supposed to hear, reached us through the usual channels on April 10 at 9 a.m. They were announcing an offensive to start on the following day. Christmann, our W2, had passed on a similar item to our observation post in Lille at the beginning of March, but we were not to be taken in by this disinformation. It was to be the last one. On April 12 Schloschoff gave me some very important intelligence; the Ast in Hamburg had given him an urgent mission that had to be completed before April 20. On the axis Sedan-Charleville-Saint-Quentin-Amiens he was to identify any obstacles, measure the width of the river crossings, the condition of the embankments, estimate the carrying strength of the bridges, the troops, and make a list of the gasoline dumps.

For the Abwehr the German offensive was now going to take place during the first days of May. The operation was intended to be devastating enough to bring the Wehrmacht on the banks of the Seine River in less than one month.

"They're extremely confident and sure of themselves!" said Schlochoff. "This time it's for real."

I hurried over to see the boss. The quality of the informer and the exceptional quality of the information were enough to make an impression on Rivet while the SR was constantly reporting the arrival of reinforcements between Trier and Aix-la-Chapelle, facing the Ardennes. He took me to Esbly, the new headquarters of the High Command since the beginning of February. General Petitbon, who happened to be my old geography instructor at Saint-Cyr and Gamelin's chief of staff, saw us. He listened carefully to the information my boss and I provided.

"I shall inform the commander in chief. He's meeting with the British, who are as concerned as we are about what's going on in Norway."

The Germans had occupied Denmark and invaded Norway on April 8.

"Go straight and inform General Georges," added Petitbon. "I'll call him so that he'll see you immediately."

At La Ferté-sous-Jouarre Colonel Navereau, head of operations for the Headquarters of the northeastern front, met with us. He was a 45-year-old graduate of the École Polytechnique, a calm, serious and very courteous man. His huge desk was covered with maps that had multiple markings on them. He was silent and kept on looking at the maps while Rivet made his presentation. Then he puffed on his pipe a few times.

"I find it strange," he said. "I see the importance of what you're saying, but it contradicts other information we have that leads us to believe that the main German thrust will take place more to the north, through Holland and northern Belgium."

General Georges came in. He was friendly, unassuming, with a keen eye behind his thick glasses. He spent a long time with Navereau, examining the possibility of an offensive through the Ardennes toward Sedan. Then he thanked us and left without sharing his thoughts. I was to see Georges and Navereau again in Algiers in 1943 and we discussed that meeting of April 13 that they both remembered very well.

"We had to choose between several possible dates and directions of an attack; the one you brought to us was the good one. We didn't think so at the time and that's a shame! We never gave enough importance to the information provided by the Special Services. Perhaps by sending Giraud's army into Belgium we had followed political considerations much too quickly under pressure from the Belgians and the Dutch."

On April 20 German intelligence operatives left their posts in Belgium and in Brussels in particular. Information provided by the SR, the wiretaps, the decryption services, our Ws—everything confirmed the threat hanging over Luxembourg, Belgium, and Holland, while there was bad news regarding the fate of the French and British expeditionary corps in Norway. Daladier and Gamelin went to London on April 28 to examine with the British, who suffered heavy losses in ships and planes, the decisions they should make in that sector. Italy was also a big worry for the High Command. François-Poncet was sending messages that sometimes sounded reassuring, and at other times worrisome, but always rather ambiguous. We were ordered to be particularly vigilant about Italy.

We took advantage of that state of mind to clamp down on many Italian agents of the SIM and indirectly on the Abwehr. In Lille the head of our counterespionage section, Colonel Robert-Dumas, and his deputy Lieutenant Rigaud had a field day! With the wholehearted support of the local *Surveillance du Territoire*, directed by Superintendents Dubois and Blémant, they had easily pinpointed suspicious connections made by the Italian consulates. The wiretaps and mail checks worked wonders and between April 15 and 30, eighteen Italians were forced to admit that they had espionage missions between the North Sea and the Ardennes. The Italian ambassador rushed to the Quai d'Orsay to register his protest against these unfriendly actions. Our reply to the ministry of foreign affairs by giving them the list of our agents under arrest in Italy and proof of the unfriendly actions the Italians had undertaken against us. We also recommended to French military courts to ignore any diplomatic entreaties.

Daladier (since March 21 he had been replaced by Paul Reynaud as prime minister and was now minister of foreign affairs) was now back from England. He summoned Rivet and myself to his office on April 29. Looking very confident, with his deep Midi accent, he told us he was getting disturbing information from Switzerland about the relationships of some French politicians with German and Italian officials. Daladier was very enigmatic, and we thought he was referring to François Piétri and Pierre Laval. He recommended that we tighten our watch of the borders and check the reasons for traveling in and out of neutral countries. He was very worried about Italy's doubtful position. It was a short meeting and the minister was pressed so hard by his staff that from time to time they came looking into his office, motioning for us to leave.

Big news on May 1, 1940: Mr. Viénot, a member of parliament and former government secretary, had just been appointed head of propaganda at the Ministry of Information. He paid us a visit, asked for our files on Goebbels' organization and the Abwehr, and shared some of his plans. He seemed sincerely dedicated to cooperating with us, but could he reverse the trend? The British were now convinced that a German offensive was in the offing. On May 2 there was a meeting of the heads of 2nd and 5th Bureaus of French and British military intelligence at the British embassy. We compared our information to that of our allies and communications were strengthened even more. The security of British troops operating in France would be the responsibility of our BCRs, which would also have additional British intelligence officers on staff.

Bertrand's section, thanks to the Enigma machine, was able to predict preparations for air attacks on our airfields on a daily basis. On May 6 the forward post of German intelligence out of Stuttgart in Luxembourg retreated. Every piece of information on May 7 and 8 confirmed that the Wehrmacht was ready for an offensive. Hitler's order was expected at any moment. Doudot wanted to be in the front seat and traveled to the city of Luxembourg on May 9. On May 10 Vernier's Luxembourg network reported back that the bridges on the Sûre and Moselle Rivers were being occupied at 3:35 a.m. and that the Wehrmacht would be passing through one hour later. At 3:50 a.m. the post at The Hague signaled that the Dutch border had been breached in the areas of Arnhem and Roermond. Colonel Oster had once again secretly passed on the news the night before to the Dutch military attaché in Berlin but this time he was correct. The Dutch High Command informed Trutat immediately that night.

Abwehr commandos from sections II and III were the first to enter at multiple points into Luxembourg, Belgium, and Holland, taking over strategic crossings where they attempted to seize secret archives and those they suspected of being agents of the Allied intelligence services. Many airfields in France were bombed while paratroopers were dropped into Holland and Belgium. In some areas dummies were parachuted in to scare the local population into a panic, while other Abwehr II commandos undertook sabotage missions deep behind our lines and were guarding points essential to the Wehrmacht's passing through, such as bridges, tunnels and so on. That morning Giraud's troops entered into Belgium and their motorized units reached Antwerp and Tilburg. Until the night before no specific talks were possible with the Belgian High Command.

Within four days Holland was defeated and there was talk of a betrayal by the 5th Column!

Suddenly by May 14 the German offensive increased in violence in the Ardennes on the Meuse River. The cities of Mézières and Charleville fell to the enemy. We were informed that lapses had occurred among some French divisions at Sedan. Gamelin called Rivet, sounding worried because of rumors of another German offensive at the Swiss border, and the attitude of Italy appeared to be a problem.

"I was able to reassure him on that score, at least for now," the boss told me. "The lightning advance by the Wehrmacht into the French Ardennes and the bad behavior of the army when facing armored units and the air force are a worry to him."

During the night of May 15-16 German motorized units were sighted towards Laon and Saint-Quentin, following the itinerary Schlochoff had indicated and that we had provided to the High Command on April 13. I was in Lille for the past forty-eight hours, where with my fellow officers of the *Surveillance du Territoire* I took part in the detailed "search" of the diplomatic train that had been formed in Brussels to repatriate the German ambassador and his staff. The train was passing through France on the way to the Swiss border via Reims, Chaumont, Besançon, and Pontarlier. In spite of the immunity protecting the convoy, Schlesser and I decided to ignore the inevitable protests of the ministry of foreign affairs and to subject the passengers to rigorous controls. Some of them were old acquaintances of ours even though the big guns had left Brussels as early as April 20. Obviously each one of them had a perfectly valid diplomatic passport, while the ambassador indignantly reminded us that what we were doing was completely illegal.

"We shall retaliate in kind," he said arrogantly to Robert-Dumas and Rigaud, when they politely informed him about our decision to search the train. And then he added, "The Belgian diplomatic train out of Berlin is waiting inside Germany at the Swiss border. It shall be allowed to move only if we all, and I mean *all*, are treated with respect and safely escorted into Switzerland."

In spite of the threats uttered by our "customers" they were forced to get off the train and transfer to the offices of the *Surveillance du Territoire*. There were two individuals of exceptional interest to us: Gertrud Beckmann and Otto were both at the top of our list of German intelligence agents. Gertrud was a beautiful German woman about 30 years old, blonde, with stunning blue eyes, who spoke French but refused to volunteer any information. She stonewalled our questions for two nights and three days and gave us names of Abwehr agents who had left Brussels on April 20, thereby avoiding having to reveal anything that might compromise her service. She made no mention of our penetration agent Hengen (Li 159), which was proof enough to us that she wasn't telling us everything she knew.

"She's very, very good," Blémant told me. He was in his shirtsleeves, and gallantly offered her a sandwich and a glass of beer.

Otto was much more excited. He was an imposing man about 40, elegantly dressed wearing bright yellow leather shoes. He was carrying a diplomatic passport in the name of Hermann Brandl, which was precisely the way he was identified in our files. Using the pseudonym of Otto he was the Brussels factotum of Colonel Rudolf, whom we were to encounter once again in July 1940 as head of the Abwehr in France. It was a good catch. We had no reason to pamper this individual whom we had been watching since 1936 nor take into account the recently issued diplomatic passport he was brandishing. He was trying to impress us by saying that he was related to Hermann Göring.

"That makes things much worse for you," said Robert-Dumas, who then proceeded to recite the list of our grievances against him.

Otto had been in Brussels since 1925 and had been recruited by the Münster Ast in 1933. He was engaged in all kinds of espionage. Under commercial cover financed by the Abwehr he had been specializing for a few years in recruiting agents and more recently in training radio operators. Little by little he broke down and Blémant who took over after Robert-Dumas, wrote down his confession and gloated over his cowardly behavior. Otto revealed among other things, the existence of a spy in the area around Mons to whom he delivered a radio transmitter and receiver. Our inspectors raced into Belgium and retrieved the "pianist" along with his beautiful wife, a young woman from the island of Java. The man was a harmless looking 70 year old who displayed his card as a ham radio operator to explain why he owned such a contraption. Unfortunately for him a search allowed us to discover the codes used to transmit messages and Otto's confession was overwhelming. Both appeared to be very well informed about covert German radio transmission techniques.

We informed PC Bruno and Bertrand joined us to question Otto, who gave him useful technical information. We wanted to hold on to him because he had an encyclopedic knowledge but despite the clear proof of the way diplomatic immunity had been abused in this case, the German ambassador refused to allow the diplomatic train to leave without the spy. Best of all the Quai d'Orsay agreed with the ambassador! The King of the Belgians himself issued a protest and the Swiss ambassador took several steps since his government was responsible for the exchange of trains and was growing impatient. Additional threats of retaliatory measures were more than enough to convince our ministry of foreign affairs to give in. Orders came from Gamelin, then recommendations from Rivet, and just silence from Schlesser. I finally decide to have Otto accompanied back to his train compartment. Blémant was beside himself with anger.

"Captain, let me accompany Otto on the train!" The young superintendent explained his plan to me.

He would set up an awful mishap during the trip at the risk of his own life but he wouldn't miss his target! I had a very hard time talking him out of that project while Otto, sitting quietly in a corner, was watching our comings and goings, green with fear as he realized that his life was in the balance. In the end Rigaud decided to accompany the spy himself. Later on, ten and twenty times over I was to bitterly regret not having followed Blémant's proposal. Hermann Brandl, still using his pseudonym, was to move triumphantly to the rue Adolphe-Yon in Paris at the end of 1940. With the blessing of Canaris and Rudolf he was to take part in a massive looting of the French economy for over two years and the infamous "Bureaux Otto" he created were to plunder on a grand scale whatever could be found on the black market, trafficking in gold, diamonds, leather, and precious metals. The colossal profits he garnered were to be used to finance the other Abwehr activities in France.

In 1943 at the request of the Vichy government and on orders from Göring, Otto had to stop his economic theft. His buying offices where that other trafficker Joinovici often appeared were shut down. The grand total of his activities was in the range of 50 billion francs of this gigantic enterprise and Otto only retained a meager five percent commission for his services! Rich and idle Hermann Brandl was now more than ever before deeply involved in a career as an Abwehr auxiliary agent. He was associated with a young Belgian, Georges Delfanne, whom he had indicated as one his correspondents. Delfanne was immediately arrested by Belgian security but he was freed on May 16 by an Abwehr commando unit. Brandl then engaged in tracking down resistance networks with a zeal and cruelty similar to those inhuman members of the Bonny-Lafont gang.

Delfanne would become famous under the sinister name of Masuy; he moved into an apartment on the ground floor of 101 Avenue Henri-Martin in Paris. On January 5, 1944, in Paris, he succeeded in having Colonel Bertrand arrested. (Bertrand had become the head of our covert intelligence network, which was codenamed "Kléber.") Our comrade would owe Otto his life! The gangster recognized him as one of the officers who was present in Lille when he was being questioned on the diplomatic train and knew the fate Blémant had in store for him. He felt grateful that his life had been spared and decided to set Bertrand free. Under arrest in Germany, Otto hanged himself in his cell on August 6, 1946. As for Delfanne-Masuy, he was executed by firing squad in Paris along with two accomplices, who unfortunately were French, on October 2, 1947.

On May 14, 1940, after another initiative by the King of the Belgians, the diplomatic train resumed its itinerary to Switzerland. It was high time because after three days and two nights conditions on board were becoming very unsanitary. I spent May 15 in Lille analyzing the information we had obtained, making sure with Robert-Dumas, Rigaud, and Blémant that the intelligence was properly disseminated. I really liked Blémant, then a 32 year-old policeman. Direct, enthusiastic and with a determination in his eyes that convinced me he could also be pitiless. He was a man of action who was disgusted by procedures and half measures. He despised his own boss, Superintendent Dubois, about whom he didn't mince any words:

"He's a bum! Once he's had a few drinks, which means twelve hours out of twenty-four, he squirms and sobs about everything. He backs off and gives up as soon as you talk back to him! This train story drove him crazy because he's so fearful of being blamed for anything."

That was not a problem for Blémant! At 7 a.m. on May 16 he came to my room, freshened up and smelling of cologne. I had been awake for a long time; the German air force was flying above us and the sirens were blaring all over town. I couldn't hear any anti-aircraft fire.

"Captain, we must leave. The news is very bad. The Germans are moving from east to west toward the sea; they might cut off the road to Paris. Travel as close to the coastline as possible. Do you want someone to travel with you? It seems the Germans are using paratroopers in civilian clothes ahead of the troops."

"Where have these been sighted?"

"Just about everywhere toward Saint-Quentin, between Péronne and Amiens…"

"Let's get going!"

We left in three cars and spent the morning and part of the afternoon scouting the region, pistols in hand. We were questioning the Gendarmes, local officials, farmers… Nothing! And yet everyone told us that they saw German planes dropping paratroopers far away. At about 3 p.m. we uncovered the key to the mystery: a few kilometers west of Péronne at Herbécourt two German pilots bailed out of their plane, which had been hit. They were arrested by the local Gendarmerie who handed them over to the army where they were being questioned. Blémant and his detectives left me since they were more or less reassured about my fate. Long lines of refugees filled the roads to the west and going south; they looked harassed and thought they saw Germans everywhere. Taking country roads I got to Montdidier and reached Paris through Clermont and Creil at about 8 p.m.

Schlesser was sad and nervous. I reported on my mission and the alarming rumors going around. News from the front was depressing and the insinuations about the damage done by the phantom 5th column were trying his patience.

"I'm going to leave for a few days. I have to travel on the spot to understand what's going on. I was very firm with Rivet this time and asked that he name a successor. I proposed Major Guy d'Alès, who had been stationed at The Hague before Trutat. He's available and ready to come and knows this place very well. I'm sure you'll get along very well with him."

I was astounded by this sudden decision. Rivet confirmed that Schlesser was about to leave.

"Be sure not to spread the news; we want to avoid any problems within the service. Your commander is convinced that he'll be much more effective in an armored unit. He feels good about the SCR since you're here and d'Alès has agreed to come on board. I can't hold him back because at the rate things are going he might very well quickly be dealing with a disorganized army and not find a command worthy of his talent."

The boss was depressed for the first time and I felt he was truly discouraged.

"You must burn the archives you don't need and prepare the service to fall back. I'm thinking of Montrichard on the Loire River. I've sent Bergeat to look things over and prepare the barracks."

This time I was horrified. While I was involved in my espionage cases in Lille I had not followed the big picture very closely. It was of catastrophic proportions. Our Ws, who were returning through Switzerland or Italy as best they could, were telling us that inside the Abwehr everyone was euphoric. "We'll be in Paris by Bastille Day!" was the comment Duperré heard from his employer. The mission he was given said it all: find out the locations picked for evacuation by the French government and the military commands. Identify emergency airfield south of the Loire River! Schlochoff was ordered to Marseille to observe ship movements in the harbor. On May 19 at 7:30 a.m. the Havas News Agency announced that General Weygand had been appointed as commander in chief of the army. Gasser, who was Weygand's chief of staff, told us later that the meeting with Gamelin upon taking over had been dramatic. Gamelin was crestfallen, spoke of his strategic mistakes, and admitted defeat. The situation was getting worse by the hour. General Giraud and his entire staff had been taken prisoner. Saint-Quentin was under German occupation and our stations in Lille and the BCR had retreated to Caen. Schlesser was back and exhausted. He traveled the length of the broken front and witnessed an incredible mess and was now waiting to be given a command and for d'Alès to arrive. He summed up his impressions in the presence of Rivet.

"Weygand's appointment gives us some hope, but everywhere I was hearing talk of treason, of paratroopers, 5th columnists, the failure of the SR and the command. The men and their officers are convinced that they've been the victims of secret manipulations and these rumors are rampant among civilians and the military alike. They accuse us and if we aren't careful these tall tales will become the alibi for those who *are* guilty and we'll be singled out as responsible for the disaster."

I was shocked by his violent conclusion. I got Gérar-Dubot on the phone; he was still in Amiens, unaffected by it all. When I spoke of treason, paratroopers, and the 5th column, he just said these were hallucinations, an incapacity to act, and a royal mess. I contacted all the BCRs and their answers were the same everywhere. No sabotage could be found anywhere and I was fearful of ridicule in reporting the complete calm of the Special services on the home front. I decided to sleep in my office and at 10 p.m. a statement from the minister's office (Paul Reynaud, since March 21, 1940) informed us about a paratrooper drop by the enemy in the area between Pacy-sur-Eure and Evreux. It appears that the news was coming from the local préfecture.

I traveled alone by car towards Evreux with my headlights off. Just past Bonnières a powerful car passed me on the RN13 highway and I barely avoided it by veering right, almost crashing into the ditch. I was able to follow the car for a few kilometers at top speed. Suddenly it looked like the car was heading off the road. With an incredible noise it crashed into a roadside hut that was completely destroyed. I stopped and got out of my car. A large truck coming from the opposite direction also stopped and the driver came up to me. A man covered in plaster emerged from the ruins of the hut that thankfully was empty; in the night I was unable to recognize him. As we got closer to him he began screaming:

"There they are! The Krauts are here!"

He pointed to the truck and ran away across the fields.

"He's nuts," said the truck driver as he went back to his rig.

At 3 a.m. I reached Evreux and went straight to the barracks of the 2nd cavalry regiment. The officer on duty whom I had awakened looked like he'd been through a nightmare. He knew nothing so I went next door to the barracks of the Republican Guard. The commanding officer, who just got out of bed, looked at me completely surprised. He quickly got dressed and went with me to the gendarmerie, then to the police station, and finally the préfecture. By now it was 5 a.m. and I was beginning to look like a person spreading panic. The chief of staff of the prefect whom it was difficult to find confirmed that the gendarmerie at Pacy-sur-Eure had in fact reported the evening before that enemy planes had been flying low and that a commando had touched down in the Eure Valley, near Cocherel, not far from Pacy. The gendarmes there had been on patrol all night but saw nothing. We found them exhausted and more frightened by my presence than by the supposed enemies in the neighborhood.

We all went back out with them to search for the phantom commando. I spoke to the farmers who witnessed the paratroopers bailing out; their stories were not very clear and sometimes contradicted each other. I came to the conclusion that three unknown planes flew in very low around 4 p.m. and the paratrooper drops appeared to have taken place near Evreux. I suddenly realized that there was an air base nearby. I rushed over there and the counterespionage officer who was very much surprised to see me said that there had been parachute exercises the day before between 4 and 6 p.m. and that it hadn't been the first time. What attracted no attention two weeks before was now suspicious following the panic spreading because of the Wehrmacht's lightning victories.

When I returned to Paris on May 23, Schlesser appeared somewhat reassured. The BCRs were indicating a situation that could be called normal if wartime events hadn't caused amazement and fear everywhere. He had returned from Gretz where he saw the retreat of heavy support units to Montrichard on the Loire River. A train under heavy guard was used to evacuate the archives and the files that were packed in strong boxes. The King of the Belgians had surrendered on May 27. A large contingent of our troops was encircled inside the Dunkirk pocket and was attempting to embark in order to get to England under the escort of the British navy and the RAF. German bombing of the port city was relentless and the evacuation took on a dramatic turn and ended on the morning of June 4.

On the same day Ybarnergaray, the minister of state for security, summoned Rivet and me to a meeting. He was very forceful and promised to support our efforts against antinational subversion as well as against what he called the 5th column. I told him that we had looked all over France for the clandestine army that was orchestrated by Hitler's secret services and hadn't found it. We had searched in vain for spies and saboteurs that were embedded in our society since before the war to suddenly appear and destroy France. Ybarnegaray nodded and went on stubbornly:

"But then the 5th column?"

"The 5th column, sir, is everywhere and nowhere. It can be the defeatists, the antimilitarists, pro-Nazis, the Fascists, the autonomists, the separatists, and elsewhere it could be the German minorities, Abwehr commandos ahead of the Wehrmacht, and often it's the weakness of the regime, the blindness or inability of those in power. The diabolical Ger-

above
Colonel Louis Rivet, head of French
military intelligence, 1936-1944.

right
Admiral Wilhelm Canaris, head of the
Ausland Abwehr, 1935-1944.

above
Sir Stewart Menzies, head of the British
Secret Intelligence Service (MI6), 1936-1953.

right
SS Gruppenführer Reinhard Heydrich,
head of the *RSHA* and the *SD*, 1939-1942.

William J. Donovan, appointed head of the
Office of Strategic Services (OSS) by President
Roosevelt, 1942-1945.

SS General Walter Schellenberg of the *RSHA* foreign espionage section; became head of all German espionage in 1944.

above
Lydia Stahl, who seduced her way into French naval secrets in the 1930s.

below
Military quartermaster and German spy Frogé with his lawyers in 1935.

above
Lydia Stahl and her attorneys.

below
For Lydia Stahl's accomplices and their lawyers, Maurice Garçon, César Campinchi, de Moro Gaffieri, Klotz, and others, a spy trial in Paris in 1935 was also a photo opportunity.

above
M. Ross, head of the Alsatian
Autonomist Party.

right
Navy ensign Marc Aubert, executed by firing
squad in Toulon in 1939 for espionage.

above

Paris, 2 *bis* Avenue de Tourville, HQ of military intelligence. The *Deuxième Bureau* was located directly under the dome of the Invalides; the concrete wartime shelter was in front of the entrance.

left

Colonel Guy Schlesser, head of the German section of the SR 1933-1935, and of the *Deuxième Bureau* counterespionage, 1937-1940.

above

Major André Bonnefous, head of the German section of counterespionage, 1937-1940; deputy to Major Paillole, 1941-1944.

left

Commander Bill Dunderdale, British Intelligence Service representative in Paris, 1936-1940.

left

Captain Doudot—France's top spy catcher —was head of counterintelligence in Metz until 1940 and a *TR* officer in North Africa, 1940-1944.

below

Claude Dansey, deputy to Sir Stewart Menzies at MI6.

Leadership in crisis: Edouard Daladier (*with cigarette*) and Camille Chautemps just before the French government left for Bordeaux in June 1940 during the fall of France.

Admiral Jean-François Darlan, commander of the French fleet and later prime minister of the Vichy government. Assassinated in Algiers on December 24, 1942.

right
General Maxime Weygand
replaced General Gamelin on
May 19, 1940.

below
General Charles de Gaulle in
London on Bastille Day, 1940.

Pierre Laval, Vichy prime minister and main promoter of collaboration with Nazi Germany, making a speech in August 1942.

Hitler and Pétain shake hands at Montoire on October 24, 1940, the symbolic meeting that launched the policy of *collaboration*.

Nazi ambassador to Vichy Otto Abetz.

Collaborator Jacques Doriot, wearing a German uniform, was the founder of the PPF and a major promoter of the French LVF volunteers fighting in the German army in Russia.

man propaganda was always there to exploit what helps the greater Reich and weakens its opponents. It's the deadly virus everyone tries to isolate to explain and justify the disaster at hand or to oneself. The anesthetized France, morally defeated, was beaten militarily on the ground it had decided to fight on. She woke up under the blows, wounded and disoriented, powerless and miserable. France was trying to understand and searched for an explanation among that grab bag containing the clever tricks of the other side and the alibis of those who had been defeated, and she found the 5th column!"

10

The Downfall and Our Revolt

O n June 3, starting at 3 p.m., the Luftwaffe was bombing the airfields and industrial centers around Paris. Citroën and Renault were the main targets, suffering 906 casualties and 254 killed. Inside the concrete bunker of the 2 *bis* we silently waited for the end of the air raid. Since May 26 we knew about operation "Paula" through the Enigma machine and our services warned Vuillemin, who could only fight back with some very weak antiaircraft guns. The bulk of our air force fighter planes was involved in the battle raging once again on the Somme River. Back in our offices we were commenting bitterly about our weakness.

Schlesser summoned me to his office and introduced me to d'Alès, who had just arrived. The new SCR head, a man of average height, looked very distinguished, even though he was slightly round shouldered in his full dress uniform. He was easy to talk to, good-natured, talked with me quite simply, and his dark eyes kept on looking at me.

"I'm not very well acquainted with your specialty," he said. "Guy told me about your reputation for being very competent. I'll be right behind you to help pilot the ship. Be sure not to make any changes in what you're accustomed to doing."

I thanked d'Alès and listened to Guy Schlesser.

"Paillole will describe to you what we've done to provide a defensive shield at last. To do this we had to fight a two-front battle, one against espionage and the other against propaganda, or rather the sabotaging of the country's morale. I think we succeeded in winning the first battle and I'm sure we lost the second. The political nature of the struggle placed it beyond our jurisdiction. As soon as one treads on the sacred right to freedom of thought and expression even governments become paralyzed. The Nazis know that very well. They hit the bull's eye by favoring and manipulating all kinds of opposing groups. In the future our powerlessness will be denounced as the inability to act or even as collusion! No such problems exist in Germany, Italy, the USSR, but it did exist in Holland and Belgium and you can see with what results."

D'Alès interrupted to ask a question:

"What role do the Abwehr and the Gestapo play in all this?"

"Paillole will fill you in. I must leave now. What I want say to you is that our service has neither the size nor the importance it requires. We do great work in our two specialties, the SR and Counterintelligence; the rest is rather thin. After months of meetings with the British and with our naval officers we were unable to organize the blocking of the Danube to disrupt the German oil supply. On the other hand the boss under orders from Gamelin wasted hours in talks with a madman about using fungus in German potato fields."

He stopped talking, seemed to hesitate for a second, then warmly shook hands with both of us.

"I shall come back; we shall see each other again and we'll do many things together!" Then, having said all this very quickly to hide his sadness and trying to spare us our own, he walked away. That room where Schlesser's presence was felt whether he was there or not, suddenly appeared very empty and d'Alès, seeing that I was somewhat emotional, brought me back to reality.

"Tell me about the Abwehr and the RSHA."

I unfolded my organization chart of German espionage. It was a military and political machine ten times larger than ours. After Keitel, Canaris was the most important officer of the OKW, as well as a diplomat who has the Führer's ear.

"The RSHA has grown recently and is the great strength of the Nazis. It looks into everything and everyone, competing with the Abwehr in political espionage and counterespionage."

I then showed d'Alès the RSHA organization chart and we spoke for a long time about our work, its problems and the current situation. He was easy to talk to and we were both on the same wavelength, becoming friendly after that initial positive meeting.

The German offensive kept up its threatening pace. Information about the Italian position remained contradictory and the Quay still harbored some illusions. There were ongoing negotiations regarding the exchange of our spies who were prisoners. The two governments had approved the idea and the Special services were given the task of finding the right formula to make it happen. The boss gave me that mission and told me to get in touch with my Italian contacts to assess what they were they had in store for us. I telephoned Nice to set up a meeting with the Italian officer in charge of the negotiations, Major Roberto Navale from Turin. In the afternoon the station let me know that Navale could meet me the following day at 11 a.m. at the border between Menton and Ventimiglia. I took the blue train that evening and reached Nice at 6 a.m. on June 6. The superintendent of the *Surveillance du territoire*, Simon Cottoni, who was responsible for my personal security, was expecting me. He stopped his car just before the border crossing, posting a few other policemen and I walked ahead alone in the "no man's land." A civilian with a rather heavy step walked in my direction from the Italian side: it was Navale. In a friendly way and a bit ceremoniously he asked me to walk past the gate and have a talk with him comfortably in a building nearby where the Carabinieri were garrisoned. I agreed. Cottoni was observing the scene. I could see him pacing up and down in front of the French barrier. He looked worried and not at all reassured by this sudden decision. What if the Italians were attempting a caper like Venlo?

"Captain," said the major in excellent French, "I thank you for taking the trouble. Would you agree to sign the exchange document I've prepared? I see that Mr. Cottoni has brought our men with him."

I was stunned. "Which men?"

The expression on his face changed completely and his smile disappeared. He mistook the policemen Cottoni (whom he appeared to know fairly well) had brought with him for the Italian prisoners he was expecting.

"Captain, you mean you don't have my four men with you? Your four Frenchmen are here and I can deliver them to you if—"

"Major," I interrupted him, "there's a misunderstanding. I'm here to agree to the conditions for an exchange but not to proceed with it."

The Italian was disappointed and told me so, but he suddenly had a flash.

"But perhaps you could make a phone call to have them freed and transferred here. We could make the exchange tomorrow."

"It's not that easy. I need at least several days, if not weeks."

"Well, then it's not going to work," said Navale plaintively.

Without a doubt he had organized a triumphant return for his four liberated spies.

"Why won't it work?"

I could see that the Italian was having trouble answering me, so I insisted.

"In eight days I may be able to return with your men."

"It'll be late, captain, much too late."

"You mean because we'll be at war?"

He nodded yes with a theatrical bow of his head and shook my hand at length as he declared his love for France.

"Politics, captain, politics!"

I asked the question once more, forcefully.

"How much time will you give me?"

"Four days."

He realized that he talked too much and added,

"Well, possibly a bit more. Everything can still change for the better."

"Please let me go and make a phone call to find out if I can get something done in such a short time."

I ran back into France. Cottoni was relieved. I ran into the customs office and called Rivet on his private line. I was lucky to find him there.

"It'll happen on Landry's day!" I said.

Silence. Rivet was looking at his holiday calendar: Saint-Landry was June 10.

"Are you sure?"

"Absolutely sure!"

I could hear the boss's painful reaction over the phone, his anguish at this stroke of bad luck and his disgust at the cowardly behavior of the Italians. I returned to take my leave of Navale and told him that I was unable to get a firm date. He was very insistent.

"But captain," he said, "if you don't come back too late, the 12th or the 13th of June, for instance, I could possibly get something done. I'll return here between the two lines with a white flag and a bugle. We'll sound the 'cease-fire' and you'll meet with me."

He understood from my expression the kind of contempt I felt for him. With sweeping gestures he assured me that nothing major was to happen in the area near Menton before June 19 or 20.

"By then, captain, the war could well be over."

I took my leave rather abruptly but still avoided a permanent break because I wanted to have every opportunity, no matter how slim, to proceed someday to a prisoner exchange. Future events were to prove me right.

Back in Rivet's office in Paris I met Colonel Barbaro, who had just returned from Esbly where everyone was greatly alarmed. He barely missed the bombing of the High Command Headquarters. The information provided by the head of the Marseille section confirmed what I knew and put an end to any doubts regarding the Italian attitude that had very unrealistically been kept up. Bad news kept coming in and increasing. The Germans were now at Rouen and everyone was falling back on Paris. At 4 p.m. on June 10 the central services were evacuated in trucks from the building at 2 *bis*. I remained behind alone with Rivet and another officer, Reserve Captain Henri Verrilhe. I walked through one office after the other from the cellar to the attic, there was nothing left anywhere. I kicked around the heaps of ashes in the courtyard where we had burned the papers. Back in Schlesser's old office which d'Alès occupied for just a few hours I messed up the combination of the safe which was now useless and in a childish move I put a cartoon by Hansi inside it, reading "Long Live France!"

Verrilhe joined me; I liked his common sense and good judgment. We listened to the radio without commenting as the sound of artillery could be heard in the distance. It was dark everywhere. None of our actions could prevent this disaster. Five years of work and youthful sacrifice to reach this result? Anger and sadness were overtaking me when suddenly Rivet reappeared like a shining light. He had been at the minister's cabinet as it was being evacuated and saw Weygand, who was talking about an armistice! A supreme war council was to take place the following day at Briare with Churchill and Eden attending.

"It also seems," said Rivet confidentially, "that General de Gaulle, the secretary of war, is examining the possibility of redoubt in Brittany where the French army could hold out. Weygand asked me to think about how the Special Services would operate in such a scenario. What a time for anything like that!"

The boss was feeling overwhelmed and asked us all to get some rest before we moved out of Paris. For the last time I dialed from Schlesser's direct phone line and through some miracle it was working; an operator came on the line. I was able to call our stations and the BCRs and was fortunate to find our stations of Lille and Amiens that had been able to fall back. I was able to give our new orders to everyone. The station at Toulouse and the BCR in that city, where I asked our fellow officer from the SCR Devaux to go and represent us, would be receiving all our messages and mail for the moment. We were to remain in contact with Toulouse, which would always be able to inform the stations and the BCRs of our movements and transmit our instructions. These final instructions during that anguished night made me feel sick. I could sense the anxiety in the voices of my fellow officers; many were asking me what they should think about the situation. I told each one that come what may, our mission would go on.

I went home, washed up, and packed a suitcase. I didn't sleep and left Paris driving my Citroën with Verrilhe. We were wearing combat uniforms and helmets. There was a thick cloud of smoke covering the empty city. At the Porte d'Orléans cars full of refugees converged from every direction and a haphazard and miserable convoy got under way on the RN20 heading slowly south. We were able to pass them using our uniforms to the maximum effect.

"We don't look so good," said Verrilhe, "running in our uniforms faster toward the rear than these poor people!"

I also felt uneasy and anxious. We reached Montrichard through some smaller and empty roads. Garnier had set up his files and unpacked the archives in a requisitioned building. The phone operators tried to reopen the lines and a young sergeant set up a field telephone in the office I was sharing with d'Alès. I had already noticed how exceptionally smart and well prepared that NCO was at 2 *bis*, his name was Marcel Taillandier and later in 1943 he was to set up and lead the Morhange resistance group. Bonnefous and his German section began catching up on the mail and whatever I had brought back from Paris. The atmosphere was heavy, the front was breaking up and as soon as we arrived we had to start thinking of evacuating Montrichard. We began looking for trucks to ship the archives and the personnel since we could no longer use the railway system. And which destination should we pick? We finally settled on the camp of Courtine near Ussel in the Creuse region.

"We must inform High Command Headquarters," said d'Alès.

"Never mind," answered Rivet. "They took off without giving a forwarding address."

During the night of June 15-16* a violent booming raid sent us all down to the cellar. Medical corpsmen found forty people killed, most of them refugees. We loaded the archives as fast as we could on the new trucks we had succeeded in prying loose from the car pool the day before, then we took off. Around noon we learned from the radio that Pétain had been named Prime Minister and had asked to negotiate with Hitler. It was a brutal shock. Someone who loses a loved one after witnessing his long agony feels the hurt and at the same time the macabre relief death provides with the end of all suffering. The flow of refugees rolled on with us to the south. Suddenly a rain of bombs dislocated the ragtag convoy. Three low-flying planes turned back towards the east. They were Italians.

"Bastards!" roared Verrilhe.

By nightfall we were on the road, silent and hurting, making our way slowly to the south. Occasionally we would fall asleep. On June 18 d'Alès summoned us to a meeting at 8 p.m. at La Courtine.

"I tracked the High Command at Ussel. They don't know what they'll do nor where they'll go next. There is no further news about the army that is now in a rout. I shall ask you to make one more effort. We'll leave tomorrow at 7 a.m. and go to Bazas on the Garonne River, south of Bordeaux. I sent Lambert ahead to prepare your barracks."

Rivet reached us at Bazas at 8 p.m. on June 21. Looking depressed, he described the awful atmosphere at Bordeaux where the president of France and the government had been evacuated.

"It's impossible to find out what's going on. It was every man for himself. Don't wait here for more than forty-eight hours. Armistice conditions will be extremely harsh and I fear you may be in the area the Wehrmacht intends to occupy. If there's no way to find a ship at Bordeaux to go to Africa we'll try Port-Vendres, Marseille, or Toulon. If not we'll have no other solution than to continue our fight clandestinely."

The armistice with the Germans was signed the next day, June 22, 1940. It was to become effective after the signing of the armistice with the Italians that was still being negotiated. There was a clause confirming the dissolution of our services and a deathly silence permeated our barracks. From the office next door we suddenly heard a voice:

"Honor, common sense, the interest of the Homeland compelled all free Frenchmen to keep on fighting wherever they are and however they can."

---

* Paris had fallen to the Germans on June 14.

It was de Gaulle speaking from London who hardened our resolve as we had decided the day before at Bazas: *to continue fighting wherever we are, however we can.*

"Meet me tomorrow at the seminary called Bon-Encontre, just outside Gane near Moissac," said Rivet. "Send the archives to Brax, near Toulouse where Malraison is located. He'll save everything and you should destroy whatever you don't need."

A piece of bad news reached us: the Germans had seized the files of the High Command (and not those of the 2nd Bureau as it has often mistakenly been written). The train they were loaded on was blocked at La Charité-sur-Loire because of the destroyed railroads and bridges. A small Wehrmacht unit that was looting supplies in railroad stations noticed the convoy by accident. It was a godsend for Ribbentrop and Goebbels. The political and diplomatic importance of those files was far greater than any military value they may have had. We reached the seminary at 1 p.m. on June 23. The father superior who directed the school was standing in the center of the courtyard with his hands behind his back as he looked at our odd convoy. The trucks and automobiles spewed out men and women, military and civilians of every age and unit. Some of them were carrying their weapons and the others were staying close to their luggage at all times.

"This looks like the 5th column," said Lambert, who was always very surprised by the special appearance and discipline of our unit.

I respectfully approached the priest who looked at me warily.

"Father, this is the second half of the 5th Bureau Colonel Rivet told you about."

He interrupted me rather abruptly:

"Sir, I really don't know what this is about. I ask you to leave this seminary immediately. Its ultimate destination has nothing whatsoever to do with yours.

He spoke without expecting an answer and turned around. My units scattered about. We found our colleagues from 2 *bis* and from CP Victor and Bruno. Our distressed situation tightened friendships and acquaintances. I would never be able to gather up my unit if we had to leave once again. I found Rivet in the lunchroom and told him about the wary welcome I got. He answered:

"The father superior had been informed that I was requisitioning his establishment. Don't you worry about him. There are empty dormitories you should take over."

I quickly complied; the free space was adequate and the father supe-rior had disappeared. I reported back to Rivet and had a bite to eat: bread sausage, but I didn't have time to taste the cheese, which was a really excellent Cantal. The good Marandet, who handled the logistics, ran up to us in a panic because the father superior wanted to see us in the court-yard. The priest was leading a delegation of First World War veterans with a colonel of the medical corps as its leader, a rather heavyset fellow with a handlebar moustache. He summoned us to leave the premises, which were desecrating by our presence. It was unheard of! We spent over an hour arguing the matter. Rivet lost his legendary calm and con-cluded the meeting with the good old French word: "merde"! The armi-stice with Italy was signed on June 25, 1940. Pétain made a speech and the whole disaster was now a fact. We all gathered around the monument to the war dead at Bon-Encontre where the old veterans also took part and remained there in silence for a long time. Rivet spoke to us in his low voice and set each one's duty straight: we must continue to fight against the invaders. We all swore to do so.

PART TWO

THE RECOVERY

July 1940–November 1942

11

The TR—Clandestine Counterespionage

W e had to work quickly. In the lunchroom of the seminary of Bon-Encontre, we were still feeling the pain of the ceremony at the monument to the war dead and it showed on our faces, where you could read humiliation and rejection. Rivet spoke to us.

"Our fate doesn't simply end right here. France has been awakened by the brutal tragedy and can see that there is a part of retribution in its demise. It's time to recover. Too many clever calculations, the fixation on a sketch,* or some kind of oversight have given the temporary victor a portion of territory along with French Africa and an embryonic army. Who will be ready to believe that this armistice army will accept its own shameful fate with any more docility than the Reichswehr in did 1918?"

We listened in silence to his words because they expressed what we were feeling. He went on:

"You can be sure that this army will provide our undercover intelligence and counterespionage services with the kind of support and cover that the Reichswehr had given once before to the Nachrichtendienst. Those

---

* There was a map being passed around in Germany in 1939 showing the limits of Hitler's ambitions in Europe. It also indicated the "Demarcation Line" inside France!

like ourselves who can fight on must not wait; our action must continue and remain secret and invisible. No other attitude is acceptable. Suspending hostilities for us is worse than an unforgivable mistake; it would be tantamount to infamy. I expect each department head to come up with recommendations for me by tomorrow."

For the last several days d'Alès, Bonnefous and myself had been thinking through various scenarios we could consider because of the armistice and our determination to continue with our mission. There was no doubt that the pro-Nazi factions were now, thanks to the German victory, about to gain enormous influence on the government and the administration of the country. There was no doubt that both the Abwehr and the RSHA were going to take maximum advantage of the situation. I was also aware of the comment made by the SS Bömelburg upon arriving in Paris on June 22, 1940:

"This country must be bound and gagged. We need 30,000 agents here as soon as possible."

I knew about the Abwehr setting up its offices at the Hotel Lutétia in Paris under the command of Colonel Rudolf and the mission given to Reile, the head of Section III-F, to continue the struggle against us and against anything that might be useful to the British in their pursuit of the war. I also knew that the clever Otto Abetz was about to be appointed as Hitler's ambassador to ensure the overall stranglehold of Germany on France with unlimited resources to do so. Too many of our fellow citizens were likely to fall victim to so many negative and detrimental influences. The atmosphere of the end of June 1940 was a web of darkness. Individual fates, just like the fate of the nation, were floating in the long night dotted by many contradictory or attractive slogans and words. Within this moral disarray we were able to guess that the wish of the vast majority was to seek ways and means of resisting the oppressor and shake off the occupation and its constraints. To serve the enemy was still and would remain a BETRAYAL. We were determined to show the nation through our clandestine actions whatever the consequences were to be for us, whether the French state was powerless or failed to live up to its duties towards the country.

This view of our mission in addition to the fact that our services were to be dissolved and that every action hostile to the invading army was to cease meant that counterespionage now needed two separate organizations that would continue to complement each other: one remaining secret, on the offensive, always targeting with a view of opposing the

Axis secret services; in liaison with the Allies; and ensuring the protection of the intelligence services; the other organization was to be overt, defensive in nature, and part of the new army under the pretense of defending it against anti-national subversion. It was to provide cover for the clandestine Special Services, helping them operate (providing funding, automobiles, etc.) and openly working on the information brought in by the secret organization. If the state of siege law was to remain in force, this institution could channel and even control the incidents of attacks on the external security of the state that were handed by the police to the military courts.

D'Alès stepped in at that point in our discussions:

"Paillole, I think you must take over the clandestine operation and be responsible for our files and archives. Neither must fall into enemy hands, come what may. You know the enemy very well; you've had experience with research, recruitment, and agent handling. There's another reason prompting me to place you in this position: you're almost certainly known to the Abwehr. Should you be listed in any official document you could very well compromise it altogether. I'll be the head of the 'above ground' organization, and since I'm new to counterespionage I'll need the help of Bonnefous and Lambert."

"Let me think this through for a few hours, major, and I shall give you my answer tomorrow before noon."

We parted. I was tempted, since I had originated the idea in the first place. I still thought that an older officer in the intelligence service who knew Germany well and had experience in the nuts and bolts of covert action would be better qualified to take on that responsibility. I was thinking about Lafont, who had been in the service since 1920. I talked to Rivet about it but he disagreed.

"That would be a mistake, Paillole, old boy. I'm not saying that someday you might need somebody like Lafont at your side; but today the clandestine work you must carry out is not just about discovering and handling agents. There's the gathering and analysis of intelligence inside an occupied France, with all its implications in the way of administrative know-how and personal contacts at the service head level, which you have had experience with in the past. There's North Africa, where you have the best connections and the liberation of the country that you're well placed to prepare for since the Allies know you and are well disposed toward you. Believe me when I tell you that you can succeed in this task."

I was not able to calm down during the night. Being independent, taking the initiative and even adventure didn't displease me but would I be strong enough to take on such a vast enterprise? If I was to accept, I was determined to change the pre-war structure, where the SR (intelligence service) and the CE (counterintelligence) were mixed in the stations and required a very bulky staff that was bound to draw too much attention. How would such a split be viewed even though in my mind the protective mission of counterintelligence was to remain unchanged? I was awakened by a ray of sunlight at 6 a.m. and I suddenly remembered that Schlesser had indicated to me as he was transferring his command that M. Préaud of the land engineering section in the ministry of agriculture could be an HC candidate. (HC stood for honorable correspondent, a person working benevolently for counterespionage.) I found out at Agen that his office had been evacuated in that general area.

"He's the brother of one of my old classmates," said my former boss. "A good man. If you ever should need an introduction at the ministry of agriculture, be sure to use my name."

How did he ever get such an idea that I found to be a stroke of genius in retrospect? Perhaps in discussing the 5th column of fungus that some weirdo in the army High Command wanted to throw on Hitler's potato fields. It was not the right time to visit people but in agriculture just as in the army people get up early in the morning! I decided to go and by 8 a.m. I was having a meeting with Préaud. He was very pleased to meet me once I told him who I was and who recommended, me as well as what I had in mind. My plan was simply to place a secret service inside the rural engineer corps, something that could be rather turbulent to say the least.

"What I would like to do is to use your cover and approval but I wouldn't want this to be any source of problems for you as director."

"For God's sake, captain," Préaud answered, as the high government official he was, "in the present circumstances it's not the problems we should worry about but the struggle to get rid of the enemy. I'd be guilty if I didn't help you. We just have to find a solution that's coherent and effective. Tell me what you have in mind."

"Could you provide space within your offices for my officers and myself in Marseille, Lyon, Limoges, Clermont-Ferrand, and Toulouse? It's very urgent!"

Préaud thought for a while, then said:

"Let me discuss this with my deputy, whom I trust implicitly. Come back around 10 a.m. One more point: how many people are you talking about?"

I was afraid to give him exact numbers and my thoughts were not yet very specific, but he was quite helpful:

"Don't be afraid to tell me the truth; we'll always find a solution."

"Five to six people in each city with a big cast iron cabinet of files that'll quickly become lethal. As for Marseille, that's another story. I plan to go there myself with about fifteen people, thirty tons of archives, and a very large filing system."

He listened quietly and walked me to the door, where we shook hands. "See you later."

At the café next door I thought the problem through once again. I hadn't thrown around the names of cities and the number of my staff haphazardly. I saw Marseille as the headquarters of this clandestine organization. I knew the city very well. It was easy to reach and get lost in. I had childhood friends there, like the Recordier brothers, and my friend Superintendent Osvald was chief of police. The ministry of the interior had transferred the personnel of the *Surveillance du Territoire* of Lille to Marseille and the excellent Blémant was also on location. Finally, it would be possible at any time, if necessary, to transfer our men and the archives to travel to North Africa, where I planned to keep a permanent liaison. Captain Guiraud, the counterintelligence specialist for Italy, was hoping to continue his mission in the Marseille-Nice region that he also knew very well.

The Belfort station was now in Lyon. My Saint-Cyr comrade Captain Hugon had succeeded in bringing in his counterintelligence staff to keep watch over his traditional targets of Switzerland, southern Germany, and northeast occupied France. The counterespionage section of the Lille station, headed now by Emile Rigaud, was already in Limoges, working on Belgium, northern and western France and Paris. Captain d'Hoffelize, head of counterintelligence in the Toulouse station, was determined to pursue his work in Spain, extending it to the ZO (Zone Occupée) and southeastern France. It was absolutely essential to have a counterintelligence station in the Vichy area, where the government was planning to move. Colonel Mangès, former head of the Metz station, and Captain Johanès, at a Clermont-Ferrand, were ready to take on the Occupied Zone, eastern France, Luxembourg, and northern Germany. As I was waiting to have permanent locations for the services I could securely store the archives in the cellars of the Roquefort cheese works.

At 10 a.m. sharp I met with Mr. Préaud, who was smiling and introduced me to his deputy. He made an offer that I immediately accepted.

"It would be difficult and dangerous to slap the label of rural engineers on you. Our personnel would inevitably be curious and I fear gossip and rumors. But there's no objection within our services to have a private company whose mission in its branch offices is to undertake rural works under our supervision: draining the countryside, maintenance work on rural sewage system, cleaning up the woods and forests, waterways, and so forth."

"This is relatively simple work and we'll supply you with manuals that will make your people look legitimate," said Préaud's deputy. "I'll meet each one of our local managers in the cities you've chosen, to recommend that they help you. Here are some letters confirming the existence of your "Société des Travaux Ruraux," accrediting it with our services."

I was ecstatic and satisfied by my success and must have stammered as I thanked Préaud and his deputy. Now that I was determined to complete the task the toughest part was ahead, but it was a good start and a very encouraging one. I told d'Alès about my discussions.

"So you agree to take this responsibility?"

"Yes major, give me two or three days to talk this through with my fellow officers and look into the details. By July 1 at the latest, the *Société des Travaux Ruraux* will be operational."

The officers of the counterintelligence stations all came to Bon-Encontre. They were anxious to know their fate. All of them had recontacted their agents and it didn't look like we had suffered that much damage. On the other hand the Abwehr commandos had freed many spies from prison because the penitentiary system had not been able to transfer them to safe places fast enough. German repression was very harsh and the mobile military courts of the Wehrmacht were handing down tough judgments in a few hours. Friedmann, who had managed to find me at Bon-Encontre, told me that there had been seventeen death sentences in Paris on June 24, including our comrades Le Fèvre, Maiseran, and Guille. On June 22 I had been able to reach the BCRs that had been evacuated or were located in the Free Zone and I had ordered the burning of their archives. I can still hear Gérar-Dubot's wrenching comment: "Eight months of work up in smoke! What a waste, nobody wants to be demobilized. We'll go on!"

I was unable to tell such men that the 5th Bureau of the Army High Command and the BCRs were now dissolved. The reservists were to be sent back home, we would call upon them later on. Rivet approved of my organization plan and its camouflage within the rural works. We had to deal with salaries and other such issues, and the comrades, who were as much a part of this adventure as I was, had to be assured they would have enough to live on. I was going to answer all these questions on July 1, 1940, the day I summoned Captains Guiraud, Hugon, Johanès, d'Hoffelize, and Rigaud to tell them what I expected of them. We had enough money. Rivet confirmed this when I told him that his Paris apartment had been searched at 3 p.m. on June 24 by two Abwehr officers.

"Our secret funds are untouched, but they're not endless. As soon as the command is reorganized I'll secure your funding."

The regular army officers would be able to request a complete discharge from the army or a furlough because of the armistice, giving them partial pay; we were to make up for the difference, giving out of our funds. The reservists would get a salary at least equivalent to their rank but obviously we couldn't ensure that this would be attractive or that the future would be secure. My comrades were undaunted by these material issues, and they all wanted to continue their mission. I left d'Alès and Rivet to deal with the army's future and traveled to the castle of Brax near Toulouse.

Part of the service was there with our archives, which had been reduced from thirty-five to thirty tons. The excellent Garnier, looking as black as a chimney sweep with soot, told me that there was nothing more difficult and boring than to burn compressed files covered with dust, especially when these are useless like the interminable negotiations between France and its neighbors to modify the borders. I asked him to get the boxes ready to be shipped to Roquefort. An old lady who thought I looked very tired offered me a bacon sandwich. Her name was Mémé, and she was the custodian of the castle. Later on she was to take very effective care of our clandestine comrades. Radio technicians were sorting out electrical wiring and equipment I couldn't identify in the courtyard. Major Arnaud was good naturedly overseeing this work, that was more akin to being an antique dealer in a flea market. I was disappointed when he told me he couldn't give me a single portable radio transmitter and receiver, but he did provide a very large one that I earmarked for Marseille. The NCO who was cleaning it up and had a pleasant fair looking face was Simonin. I told him what I was doing and asked whether he'd like to join me. His eyes shined with enthusiasm:

"With great pleasure, captain!" As an aside he told me, "I hid a small transmitter prototype and I'll give it to you."

"Well, Simonin, confidentially I have sex radios in my baggage that are a gift from the Abwehr."

On June 30, five trucks reached the cellars of Roquefort under escort, where Garnier and his archivists became cheese workers to stand guard around the archives. On July 1, 1940 at 4 p.m. in the lunchroom of the seminary at Bon-Encontre, I informed my comrades of memorandum number 1 creating the TR—*Travaux Ruraux* (it became the name of clandestine counterespionage until the liberation of France)—and naming them directors of the CE stations undercover, with the title of "rural works engineers." These were: Rigaud (alias Richepin) in Limoges TR 112; Johanès (alias Jansen) in Clermont-Ferrand TR 113; Hugon (alias Hurel) in Lyon TR 114; Guiraud (alias Georges-Henri) in Marseille TR 115; d'Hoffelize (alias Daubray) in Toulouse TR 117.

Headquarters was to be in Marseille, which I christened Cambronne! Guiraud, along with another officer from my central service, Roger Corvée, went looking for office space while I became the director of the *Société des travaux ruraux* (Rural Works Company) under the name of Philippe Perrier, born on November 8, 1904 at Blida (Algeria). I became older, which made me appear more serious. My orders were very simple:

1. Continue the fight against Axis espionage services.
2. Penetrate pro-Nazi and pro-Fascist organizations.
3. Liaison with British intelligence and support to pro-Allied initiatives.
4. Inside the so-called Free Zone (Zone Libre or ZL) surveillance and penetration of enemy armistice commissions.
5. Clandestine action to remain compartmentalized and centralize intelligence at Cambronne for analysis.

The TR organization in North Africa would be set up once I had more information about our potential from the overseas army beyond the 100,000 men authorized in France itself. "Professor" Doudot was already working on a mission to start up the main TR station in Algiers that would centralize information—TR 119. He was at risk in France and had succeeded in leaving Marseille on June 20, 1940. At my request he'd taken twenty trunks of CE archives coming from the regional head of the BCR, representing the most important intelligence we had gathered since the beginning of the war. Along with the archives in Algiers they were to be the cornerstone of the general archives I planned to assemble in North Africa to face any new situation. Three "specialists" were going to become available, Bertrand and Fontès from Lille and Breteil in Toulouse, and I was going to ask them to take on TR stations in North Africa. The most urgent task was to penetrate the Abwehr stations that were being set up in France itself.

Reinforcing our capabilities in Spain was also a priority since we had seen increased activity by German intelligence. Spain and Portugal were to become the most important locations for us to communicate with Africa and London. The former Toulouse station under the command of a brilliant intelligence officer, Lullé-Desjardins, who wound up in a concentration camp in 1943, had managed to set up networks to cross the Pyrenees with correspondents in Madrid, San Sebastian, and most of all Barcelona, where our honorable correspondent, Hector Ramonatxo, was completely at home. That evening the boss assembled us all for a very moving farewell dinner with the reserve officers of the demobilized central services. We were to reestablish contact with them later on, mostly in the ZO (Occupied Zone). They would become the backbone of the clandestine services. I sent my staff to Marseille to set up the Headquarters of *Travaux Ruraux*. My deputy was Challan-Belval, a young reserve officer who was excellent in our specialty, and had been helping Bonnefous and myself since 1938. Since he was also an agricultural engineer he could help answer any kind of questions about our "expertise." With his deputy, Major Giboulot, Challan-Belval's job at the CE was to sift through intelligence, separating the items to be kept secret with the TR, to be used later on, from the official information that was to be turned over to the police and the courts.

Renée Morel Schlesser's experienced secretary came to work for me and Simonin became my radio expert. Once Garnier and his team arrived at Cambronne the TR headquarters included about fifteen people and to ensure maximum security everyone was to live on the premises. I transferred Guillaume from my Paris office and Klein, who was Doudot's former assistant, to TR section 115 in Marseille. Both of them were well versed in working on Germany. The TR was starting off with twenty penetration agents inside the Abwehr. About sixty former agents or honorable correspondents in Paris, in the ZO (Occupied Zone), and overseas made up the staff of our offensive and clandestine CE, now known as the TR at inception. The corps of rural engineers was very effective, especially in Marseille where it rented a large house, big enough for all personnel and the archives of TR headquarters to be kept under one roof. It was known as the Villa Eole (later destroyed by the Germans in 1943), and was located out of town, near the mouth of the Huveaune River on the beachfront, with huge rooms, several garages and an enclosed courtyard. A guard's house allowed us to check everyone entering and exiting the premises. Mr. Lévy, the owner, wanted to show me around, telling me how pleased he felt to be able to rent his house to a company working with the ministry of agriculture. He looked at the water works plans in the Camargue that Challan-Belval had had time to hang on the wall above a drawing table.

"After so many disasters, sir, France will come back only through a return to the soil."

Lévy introduced me to his daughter and offered her services as a stenographer in my company. He really wanted to trust me.

Curious to see the new headquarters the TR heads traveled to Marseille to deliver their first intelligence items. Everyone confirmed the detailed preparation by German intelligence for the Wehrmacht's attack on France. Special Abwehr troops had been on the ground everywhere alongside the German army when they were not actually preceding it. Everywhere the commandos of Sections II and III (sabotage and counterespionage) had taken on their objectives. In Paris the searches and arrests were growing markedly. The central archives of the *Sûreté Nationale* in the rue des Saussaies had been seized and in the other cities and towns in the provinces the teams organized by Reile (Abwehr III F) grabbed enormous quantities of documents. Osvald had taken over the "Bishop's residence," as the Marseille police forces was referred to. He assured me that the secret files of the *Surveillance du Territoire* had been evacuated and burned.

Abwehr III could count on some very tough teams within the Wehrmacht to fight against espionage in the occupied countries: the Geheime Feldpolizei or GFP, was the secret military police which, for the moment, kept the Gestapo out of any counterespionage cases in France.

"The Germans are teaching us what we should have been able to do," said Schlesser.

He had tracked me down in Marseille. Where wouldn't he have succeeded in doing so? My former commanding officer was on his way to Pau, awaiting a command in the armistice army and told me about the fighting and how he was able to escape from the Occupied Zone. He listened to my description of both our retreat and the Abwehr's offensive methods.

"We should have been doing that! We just declared war without a clue or really wanting to fight. To help Poland we stayed put!" And he added seriously, "There's no other solution but to gather what remains of our army and throw it into battle once the British and the Americans will be able to make war in France. That's Weygand's idea. It could possibly also be Marshal Pétain's and we have to help them make it happen."

Since July 10, 1940 the national assembly had made Marshal Pétain the head of state and of the government while Weygand was minister of national defense. Gasser was Weygand's deputy, confidant, and our go-between. Time was passing and for an entire month we were living like nomads without being able to work. With our archives still at Roquefort, without official cover or contacts with our allies, without effective communications among us, it was impossible to use the intelligence that promised to be very rich. I decided to get things moving faster and traveled to Clermont-Ferrand and Vichy to meet with Rivet and d'Alès. I took a detour through Toulouse to hug my mother who had been without any news from me since I had left Paris. In her small apartment on the Place Saint-Georges she was giving shelter to Lullé-Desjardins, whose real duties she knew nothing about. She also didn't know much about what I was doing other than I worked at the ministry of war. She was very upset by the defeat and worried about my future. I was able to reassure her by saying that I was no doubt going to remain a civil servant working in Marseille. That pleased her but the way she said good-bye from the top of the staircase led me to believe that she hadn't been completely convinced by my explanations.

"Promise me that you'll be cautious!"

12

The Armistice Army and the BMAs

Y ou had to be cautious in the defeated Vichy. I came to the end of July 1940 with my false identity, a threadbare civilian suit, and my very firm and realistic plans. A show-off government of sorts set up by Laval under the enemy's watchful eye attempted to conform to the "New Order." Obviously, Laval, the cunning presumptive heir of Marshal Pétain, was to have the greatest political influence. But the proud Admiral Darlan, frustrated by all this, wouldn't stop intriguing. On July 3, 1940, the British fleet opened fire on French warships at Mers-el-Kébir, Algeria, sinking or damaging several vessels and killing 1,400 sailors. Between the pro-German Laval and the anti-British Darlan a struggle for power was in the offing. The prize was whatever was left of France and success depended on the cooperation of the occupying power. All of Marshal Pétain's prestige couldn't change that deplorable reality.

Some institutions disappeared and others made their debut, some new faces appeared and old political hacks weighed the risks and potential benefits of the new regime. A colorful crowd gathered under the awnings of the requisitioned buildings, while the now rare and crowded hotels emptied their guests into the streets. The cafes were filled with scheming and useless individuals, satisfied civilians, officers with too many decorations, lost refugees and worried-looking persons who had come to Vichy for the water treatment, along with salesmen, brokers, political arbiters, and bizarre prophets. I took my leave of this decadent and obnoxious world. In the town of Chamalières, hidden inside an understated garden where Rivet and d'Alès had moved with an embryonic staff, I found the Hotel Saint-Mart. Bonnefous and Lambert, locked in a small room, showed me without much enthusiasm the tenth organization chart of an official defensive service similar to the "Abwehr 1925" model.

"The Krauts will never let us copy what they did," sighed Lambert.

"The army must protect itself somehow," answered d'Alès. "I've spoken with Gasser, who told me that Weygand has approved this type of organization. We'll find out soon enough, since the boss has an appointment with him at noon."

At 5 p.m. Rivet returned.

"I handed Weygand our project," he said. "He agreed to a covert SR and a CE unit using a centralized bureau of anti-national subversion as cover. Its mission would be to maintain army morale. He's thinking about a special status for clandestine personnel and there'll be some pulling and tugging. First, coming from the Germans to create this Bureau of anti-national subversion. Weygand says that he'll succeed in getting approval from the armistice commission in Wiesbaden through General Huntziger, who's negotiating the creation of a new army. There'll be opposition, for sure, from Admiral Darlan, and above all from Minister of the Interior Adrien Marquet, and Pierre Laval, who don't even want to hear about any kind of actions against Germany. Finally, we'll need the approval of Marshal Pétain. Weygand is convinced this final obstacle will be the easiest to overcome."

I expressed some doubts, but Rivet reassured me.

"Weygand's position is very clear: the war isn't over. The armistice is only an interruption of the fighting. His exact words were, 'Come what may, the line of conduct your services must follow is that of the army itself, meaning that Germany must be considered the enemy and England as an ally.'

"And," the boss added, lowering his voice and sounding worried, "with such views being confirmed by other facts (for example the instructions given to the various regions to hide a maximum of weapons) I fear that the general will not be minister of national defense for very long. One way or the other we must set up a project of some kind as long as he's there."

I was impatient to contact my former colleagues inside the service. Perruche and his SR were hiding in Vichy. He told me:

"My dear director, the best place to hide a fortune is in the thieves' cloakroom!"

The air force SR of Ronin found a building in the village of Cusset, near Vichy while Cazin d'Honincthun had a quiet room just above the Vichy post office where in a few days the postal employees had set up five wiretaps that could listen in around the clock for our benefit on enemy representatives (armistice commissions, diplomats, Gestapo, etc.) and their conversations with the outside world. A few months later that surveillance was extended to all long-distance phone lines between France and Germany. The technical know-how and patriotic feelings of the postal employees allowed us to tap into the Paris-Metz and Paris-Strasbourg phone line cables and listen in on enemy communications with Germany. This was to be known as source K, transmitted daily to the British by radio.

Through Weygand's help Bertrand was able to purchase a large estate near Uzès in the Gard region, known as "Cadix," where he was able to rebuild and set up his decryption service. He retrieved his foreign technicians (seven Spaniards and fifteen Poles) who had been evacuated to Algeria as a precaution. While the Enigma decrypting machine was more operational, Bertrand's services were fully operational once again by September 1940. "Cadix" was able to accurately collate and complete the information provided by the TRs about the German intelligence services, such as the Abwehr, RSHA, armistice commissions, police forces, gendarmerie, etc., but also to facilitate the control of the penetration agents' work by intercepting their messages to the Abwehr. It was to be our most productive and most secure liaison with British intelligence.

During the first quarter of 1942 we intercepted and decrypted 150 cables concerning the Russians. Some of the cables revealed the issues of interest to the Abwehr and its penetration of Soviet intelligence units operating inside France. These decoded cables were given to the diplomatic representatives of the USSR in Vichy but Bertrand was unable to establish a direct radio link with Moscow. Most of the intercepts of "Cadix" were the work of the radio-electric control group that had been officially created in July 1940 by a Captain Romon of the engineer corps as an excuse to check the subversive groups. That group was to tap into almost all the communications of the Wehrmacht and the Gestapo, under the very nose of the enemy's control commissions and to our benefit.

Captain Romon was arrested in December 1943 and executed by firing squad in Heilbronn, Germany, on August 20, 1944.

At 52 Avenue d'Italie in Clermont-Ferrand, Mangès and Johanès were able to set up TR section 113. Colonel Mangès wanted to let his younger fellow officer become the head of the section. Both men were impatient about our inability to repress the many acts of treason they were able to uncover thanks to the many networks of informers and the wiretaps set up by Cazin.

"The superintendent of the *Surveillance du Territoire*, who is living upstairs, is a nice guy," Johanès told me, "but he can't do anything officially. He showed me a memo dated July 12 from the big boss of the *Sûreté Nationale*, Mr. Didkowski, stating that 'the armistice interrupts any action against German espionage'!"

"That's outrageous!" said Mangès indignantly.

"But there's a lot to be done urgently," added Johanès. "The German armistice commissions at Clermont, Vichy, and Royat are getting offers of services and denunciations on a daily basis."

Johanès also told me about a very serious case.

"Cazin told me about an Italian who's calling the German commission at Clermont quite often. I was able to identify him one day when he had an appointment with the Krauts. He's a laborer who works on a farm near Issoire. I found out through Kerhervé, the captain of the gendarmerie in that town, a terrific fellow, that in an unused barn on the farm there are two 47mm anti-tank guns, two 25mm anti-aircraft cannon, and several hundred shells. The French army originally hid all these weapons with the help of the farmer and Captain Kerhervé. So now the Italian has just made a phone call for an appointment at 6 p.m. tomorrow with a Wehrmacht handler to take him on the premises. What can we do?"

The *Surveillance du Territoire* is just waiting and not a single policeman will act openly against the orders issued by Didkowski. The fate of that poor farmer who had five children was in the balance and the weapons were going to be seized. No one could legally judge and imprison a spy who was an Axis citizen and also a traitor to the country that was giving him work.

"What can we do?" Mangès looked at me with his steely blue eyes while Johanès remained unflappably calm as he was in the most tragic circumstances. I looked at them both and nodded as I shrugged my shoulders.

"Understood," said the head of TR 113.

A few months later a peasant at Parentignat near Issoire found a skull that some crows had brought to the foot of a tree. An investigation started and through a strange set of circumstances it was to take place at the same time as a second investigation because the Wiesbaden armistice commission had issued a search request to the *Sûreté Nationale*.

"I don't understand why the policemen came to see me," d'Alès told me as he discussed the matter during a trip to Marseille. "They were asking if I knew anything about an Italian farm hand that was working around Issoire. Does that ring any bells with you?"

"I really wouldn't know, major. It's true that Italy is pursuing a glorious but difficult war against the Greeks. All able bodied Italians must have gone straight to the recruitment offices and that must have been what happened to your man."

"I guess that must be it," said d'Alès.

It was now August and I had time to take a trip to Algiers to explain our projects to the military authorities and prepare with Colonel Delor, head of intelligence and counterintelligence in Algiers, and Doudot the setting up of a covert counterintelligence station known as TR 119. The Italian commissions were everywhere. Colonel Verneau (who was later to become the chief of staff of the army at Vichy and head of the Amy Resistance organization (ORA) and died in a concentration camp in Germany) was at the time head of the French armistice delegation in Algiers. He told me that instead of 200 Italians, which had been agreed to, there was actually twice that number. About one hundred teachers came from Italy to set up schools in Tunisia. All these people were involved with the local population spreading Axis propaganda, looking for weapons stores and spying generally!

"It's both the OVRA and the SIM in full force," as Doudot and his partner Achiary, the superintendent of the Algiers *Surveillance du Territoire*, were telling me, "but you can be sure, captain, that we will make their lives very miserable, especially if you can convince the military courts to give us a hand."

The "Victors," as my two fellows referred to the Italians, were operating in Constantine, Algiers, and Oran and nothing they did escaped our surveillance. They had informers in the hotels where the Italians were staying. Several penetration agents were infiltrated at the Aletti Hotel, the headquarters in Algiers of the head of the Italian delegation. I was able to meet with General Noguès who traveled in from Rabat to permanently shut down the High Command of the North African theater of operations. He was very bitter and openly stated his disappointment at the way the battle of France had ended.

"Every day, Paillole, between June 17 and June 24 I phoned or cabled to the government and General Weygand to let them know that we should keep on fighting from here with the air force that had retreated here and the navy that was still completely operational. I could've held out for a long time. I insisted and begged without any results. I even told Weygand to come over here and lead the armed forces of the French empire. They would not or could not hear me."

With a dejected expression Noguès extracted from his briefcase a document that he asked me to read. It was a copy of cable he had sent to Weygand on June 25, 1940. I can remember the closing sentence: "I shall remain at my command post to fulfill a mission of sacrifice that fills me with shame and in order to avoid cutting France into two opposite camps. I am requesting to be relieved of my command."

"As you can see, Paillole," Noguès added sadly, "nothing will ever be the same as before in this country. We've offered the sight of a defeated France. We'll have a lot of trouble to keep our authority over the indigenous populations that are so sensitive to prestige and strength. Since June Axis propaganda has been spreading and has a very easy time doing so. Try to explain to Weygand and Marshal Pétain at Vichy that if we want to hold on to North Africa we must fight against these enemy incursions, reinforce the army and appoint well-known and prestigious generals as its leaders."

After my meeting with Noguès and seeing that the other military leaders that I met in Algiers shared his views, I told Doudot, Achiary, and Colonel Badin of the reserves who was a lawyer in Algiers and former head of the BCR not to wait for official instructions from Vichy to keep the war against the Axis going. They all agreed with me, and the government's representative at the military court also agreed, to pursue all espionage cases that we would refer to him. That decision was to be enacted less than one month later.

The presence of a German Luftwaffe officer who was a guest in a hotel in Sétif was reported back to TR 119. He claimed to be part of the armistice commission enabling him to visit the airfield at Aïn Arnat but there was no such German commission in what was an Italian area at the time. It looked suspicious and Doudot traveled to Sétif and had the officer summoned to police headquarters under the pretense of checking status. A tall, dark man with piercing eyes and an arrogant manner, he reported in a Luftwaffe uniform but didn't wear it well enough. Dudot lashed into him in flawless German:

"Who gave you the idea to come here and impersonate me?"

"Heil Hitler. To whom am I speaking?"

"Shut up, they could be listening to us. Give me your documents for safekeeping and be sure to answer the policemen's questions using your true identity. I'll handle everything else."

The man extracted some notes he had taken about Aïn Arnat, Constantine and the location around Sétif. He requested that they be sent to Major Kunze-Krause, the Abwehr representative at the armistice commission in Aix-en-Provence. A few weeks later the military court in Algiers condemned the spy to death. We considered that first verdict as France's justice and will to fight for its honor. It was an act of defiance in the face of the invader that had a positive effect on our official and covert counterintelligence officers. The extremely severe sentence served as an example for other similar trials. Unfortunately a very careful censorship that could almost be construed as working for the enemy never allowed the publication of those judgments or their execution. Most Frenchmen inside and outside France, and many friends of France would never find out about them and still do not know that the lost battle didn't stop our struggle. I returned from Algiers very much impressed by what Noguès had told me; and when I told Rivet, and then asked him about the status of our official services, he remarked:

"Still no news. I feel a kind of passive resistance to our projects just about everywhere; we're thought of as interlopers of sorts."

"I've told the regular army officers of the former BCRs to remain at their posts," said d'Alès. "I sent Lambert and Bonnefous to secretly tell them, just as you've done in Algiers, what General Weygand is thinking. That way they can start working on how to solve their problems."

I could wait no more and we had to get back to work. I had the archives transferred from Roquefort to Marseille. The trucks of the cheese factory delivered our boxes into the courtyard of the Villa Eole.

"You can just imagine the kind of Marseille humor to be had with those 'tons' of cheese!" said Garnier. "Twenty-four hours later the archivists were working and Cambronne was operational."

Guiraud came to see me about his station, TR 115. He was a very hard working, self-effacing little man who knew his job inside out and was all the more successful because he didn't stand out in a crowd. He had established a liaison in Nice and Marseille with a British intelligence officer, Captain Garrow. I told him to keep up that connection and even though he was no longer part of the SR he still had excellent relations with the station in providing intelligence. Major Jonglez de Ligne took over the former BCR and navy Lieutenant Viret was in charge of camouflaging the equipment at the regional level. There were no problems with police chief Superintendent Osvald, Dubois, and most of all Blémant at the *Surveillance du Territoire* gave TR 115 all the assistance I could expect. During the first days of August I again left for Chamalières where the Hotel Saint-Mart had changed completely since the administrative and technical services were now working with Rivet. Everyone was in civilian clothes and there was a sign on the door saying "National Bureau for the Return to the Land." Agriculture was an inspiration to the service!

"Yes, but you don't even have any gasoline!" said Gérar-Dubot who was visiting from Limoges. He was chafing at the red tape and the slowness of the bureaucracy as well as the uncertainties of his own fate. I tried to reassure him and told him he had to stay in Limoges at least until the armistice army's defense services could be set up. I promised that he would be free by August.

"But we'll not let you go completely. We're counting on your help in Paris. Your many press relations can open up a lot of doors to us."

"We'll see," answered Gérar-Dubot. "At the moment we're standing still while the Krauts are working hard."

There was some news, however. Weygand had approved a secret charter for the officers of the Special Services. It was sent to Marshal Pétain, who signed it on August 31, 1940. About fifty specialists, including my TR regular army officers and myself, were taken off the army lists and given assurances that we could continue our mission without any prejudice to our military career.

"It's a guarantee for now and it also indicates that the Marshal agrees that we should pursue our work," said Rivet, as he locked the document in his personal safe.

The project of a single clandestine service had to be scrapped. Darlan was adamantly opposed to it because he wanted to have his own independent intelligence service that he could set up to suit his plans. The undersecretary of the air force wanted his intelligence service to be on its own and Ronin, who was in command, was highly qualified for the task. His work targeting Axis air forces was once again operational and the army's intelligence service under Perruche was working in isolation. The idea of a service against anti-national subversion (*Menées Antinationales—*

MA) was agreed to and was to cover the three intelligence units—army, air force, and navy. The *Travaux Ruraux* were not mentioned out of caution and it was agreed that the army would handle counterespionage for all three branches of the service. The law decrees making these projects official were signed on September 8, 1940. Rivet remained in active service through a decision by General Colson, undersecretary of war, and his mission was to coordinate the MA service, army intelligence of Perruche, and the clandestine counterintelligence of the TRs. D'Alès was to become head of the MA, now part of the cabinet of the ministry of national defense and a BMA (*Bureau des menées Antinationales*) was set up for each military area. A short document described the mission of that service: "The protection of national defense secrets and protection of the army from any subversive activity." That mission didn't allow any action by the MA outside the armed forces.

On September 10, 1940, d'Alès gave Weygand a list of officers having a special status as well as that of the regional offices of the MA. All of them were known for their intense patriotism as well as for their competence in counterespionage matters. In order to create a model office of the MA in a delicate border region (facing Switzerland and the demarcation line), d'Alès appointed Bonnefous as head of the station at Bourg-en-Bresse. With the final approval by the minister of national defense on September 11, 1940, our defensive organization was finally ready to start working. Gathered at the Hotel Saint-Mart on the evening of September 12, the BMA heads listened to Rivet, d'Alès, and myself describe what was expected of them beyond their mission as it was specified by the decree.

— Protect the army against espionage and antimilitary propaganda (the BMAs were never to encounter any serious instances of communist or antimilitary propaganda).

— Provide cover for the covert organizations of the army (SR–CE–CDM, standing for camouflage of supplies) search and delivery of resources–men (HCs among our reserve officers) and supplies to help them in their action.

— Analysis of the counterespionage intelligence gathered by the TRs using the *Surveillance du Territoire* and the military courts if required.

— Protection of patriotic and pro-allied organizations, screening of police procedures of military justice for the internal and external security of the state.

Each BMA would have three to four officers and as many NCOs at the location of the military division. The corps commanders were to appoint an MA officer in each regiment or isolated unit. We were very clear about the need to work cautiously in order to avoid compromising secret work and the obligation to remain strictly within the military field. The BMAs must not in any case encroach upon the police, who remained the only responsible service for all investigations and arrests. They had no tools to proceed with their own investigations and actions outside the army. This was clearly essential to avoid any friction with civilian authorities causing them to change their minds about the fragile existence of our organization. We insisted heavily on this point once Gasser had informed us that General Weygand would soon leave the government. This meant that we'd become much more vulnerable despite the solid connections we had created.

On August 10, following a discussion between Rivet and the new minister of the interior, Marcel Peyrouton, and a rather energetic demand by Weygand, Didkowski was appointed prefect of the department of Isère and replaced by Chavin. The new director of the *Sûreté* had to cancel the instructions issued by his predecessor forbidding the struggle against Axis espionage. I made an effort to meet with Castaing, who was still in charge of the *Surveillance du Territoire*. He hesitated to enter the fray.

"What do you expect the Germans to look for in France? They can go anywhere they please; we have nothing to hide anymore," he said.

I had reacted vigorously.

"How can you say that? The war continues. The Gestapo's hunting down good Frenchmen! The Abwehr's recruiting spies and is still working against us and the British. Treason will spread everywhere if we don't react."

"And what will we do with the Axis spies?"

"You'll hand them over as usual to the military courts that will decide their fate. I can guarantee that."

He smiled and appeared convinced by my words of self-assurance. A few days before, Gasser had me meet Chasserat, the head of military justice and the gendarmerie who had immediately agreed with Weygand's rule that the armistice was only a temporary interruption of hostilities, that the British were our allies, and the Germans our enemies. Together we reached the logical conclusions: national defense remained a reality with all its secrets, and the BMAs were supposed to protect them. Because of the state of siege the military authorities were to remain responsible for the fight against and repression of all espionage.

"I'll instruct the military courts to handle these matters quickly and secretly," Chasserat promised me.

Before leaving his office I made a request.

"Am I allowed to ask for the help of the gendarmerie?"

"Yes, no question about that."

In my presence he phoned General Fossié, the deputy director of the gendarmerie, so that he would see me immediately. The general had previously shown interest in counterespionage activity and he now readily accepted the idea of the participation of the gendarmerie in our work against the Axis and authorized delegating personnel within our TR stations as well as using his internal mail system to route our own communications.

"I'm ready to trust you, Paillole. You'll handle these issues man-to-man with those officers of mine you deem necessary to your missions. The gendarmerie as a state institution must not be caught red-handed in hostilities against the Axis. It would give the enemy an excuse to cancel the armistice agreements and impose new and harsher ones. If any of my officers has any doubts, encourage him to come and have a confidential talk with me!"

I was beginning to set up our organization for its repressive mission by assessing the kind of sentencing that would be applied for espionage and treason. The ministry of justice handled those issues and I had discussed the matter with our friend Henry Corvisy, who was at Vichy. I was happy to see him with his proud demeanor, made even more impressive by his many First World War wounds. I told him about the covert and official decisions we had made and his face opened up.

"Good! Soon I'll be in charge of criminal affairs and pardons, so you can count on me! Neither the Marshal nor my minister will ever tolerate treason. Regarding those sentenced, your victims who are dearest to the enemy will be shipped to North Africa, way out of his reach."

In the waiting room outside Corvisy's office I saw Cassagnau, former prosecutor at the supreme court of appeals and also head of our BCR in Lille. He had just been appointed head prosecutor to the court in Riom and had come to meet the minister, Raphaël Alibert.

"I need a day of your time," he told me. "The chief judge of the court, Mr. Caous, wants to meet you."

"Why is that?" I asked.

Cassagnau pushed me quietly into the hall.

"Laval has decided to have us put those responsible for France's defeat on trial. What he really expects us to do is put his political adversaries on trial. I find this washing of dirty linen under the watchful eyes of the enemy disgusting. I accepted this job to ensure the defense of the truth and nothing else. I intend to demonstrate that your services had no part in our defeat whatsoever. This is a matter of prime importance; please help us make sure it's indisputable."

I was to see prosecutor Cassagnau many times after that. I handed him proof of our efforts to stop the sabotage of French morale, the theft of France's secrets, and our attacks on the political and military objectives of Nazi Germany. One day in April 1941 he had me meet with Judge Caous in a quiet little inn of Paillaret, just a few kilometers outside of Riom. For several hours the two men had me describe the nature of our struggle. I condemned the monstrous goals of Nazism, its methods that were at once anesthetizing and cruel, the crazy and obstinate will displayed by Hitler, and his cynical preparation of aggression as well as the uselessness of our warnings.

"Your honor, before you try those responsible for our defeat, shouldn't the court put on trial those who were responsible for the war?

"That seems logical to me," said Caous.

I went on:

"Who *is* responsible for the war? The dictators, Fascism, Hitlerism; but also their accomplices here and elsewhere; those who willfully or not just let them go on. They're coming out in the open today; you'll identify them without much trouble and I'll help you do so."

Both were honest and brave men to have the truth stand out. But the enemy and the instigators of the trial had no intention of seeing themselves in the role of being accused and they took advantage of a request for additional information to interrupt the proceedings at the start of 1942. The trial was never reconvened, or at least not until Nuremberg.

While d'Alès was completing the MA organization I was still looking for help, which took me to the army general staff. There was an atmosphere of revolt against the Germans that the commanding officer, General Picquendar, supported and that was vigorously stimulated by Colonel Baril, head of the 2nd Bureau. The German section had been secretly reconstituted at Lyon where it was continuing its work of analysis on German war capabilities through information it received from Perruche's SR. The British were the main beneficiaries of this intelligence through the American embassy at Vichy. I met Major Mollard, who was later sent to a concentration camp in Germany. He was in charge of camouflaging weapons and supplies (the CDM). He was a clever officer, full of enthusiasm as he gave me the details of the work he had been doing with Weygand's approval since July 1940. He asked me to keep a watchful eye on his men and their work.

"If you agree, I'd like to move my most important civilian office to your quarters in Marseille* that was used as cover for armaments and repairs of hidden military hardware.

This took place and secret phone lines to Cambronne connected the Marseille agency of the CDM. D'Alès gathered some very good officers at the central MA office at the Hotel Saint-Mart: Lieutenant-Colonel Bonoteaux, Captains Heliot and Delmas (who all died in a concentration camp); with Lambert (killed in action at Belfort in November 1944) and Mayeur for the air force and Bayonne for the navy the team had a clear and realistic vision of its mission. The MA offices within the military districts were just as good: Mercier** and Roger** in Clermont-Ferrand; Bonneval in Châteauroux (he was to become General de Gaulle's aide-de-camp); Bonnefous and Denaenne *** in Bourg-en-Bresse; Vellaud*** in Lyon; Jonglez de Ligne** in Marseille; Devaux and Proton*** in Toulouse; and Blattes*** in Montpellier. Everywhere the BMAs would hold fast in their mission to stop the enemy. By the end of September 1940, the MA organization was operational, the TRs were organized, and counterespionage was moving ahead.

My thoughts in the overcrowded train I took back to Marseille became clearer. I could see a glimmer of hope after three long months of chaos and uncertainty. This defensive organization, built with difficulty and as fragile as it may appear, was a new beginning in the struggle in our mission and our duty as Frenchmen. The impulse was there and it was irreversible. By adapting to a de facto situation we were not seeking to serve a de facto political system. We wanted to use the legal system to its extreme limits and later we would take action according to the circumstances of the war. During the ordeal that had plunged France into defeat and chaos we felt free to act according to our conscience in the country's best interest. One phase in the life of the Special Services of National Defense was over; a new one was beginning, still imprecise as to its limits, but very clear as to its objectives.

---

* The *Société Dubourg* and Cie, headquartered at Avenue Ferdinand-Flotte in Marseille, a dealer in agricultural machinery and gas generators

** Deported to Germany.

*** Died in a concentration camp.

13

Counterespionage Faces the Enemy

I t was barely autumn and we immediately faced our first challenges. Weygand was forced out of the government. The direction he was giving to the armistice army, the rebuilding of the Special Services under the mask of the BMAs and his narrow interpretation of national duty made him a target to the enemy and its cohorts now in power. He was given a government mission in French Africa. Some people were to see this exile as a fall from grace, others as a provocation and the enemy as a threat but Weygand turned it into something positive because of his tenacity. For the moment his departure left a difficult void in Vichy as far as we were concerned. General Huntziger replaced Colson on September 14, 1940, and the ministry of national defense had not yet been reestablished.

Rivet visited Cambronne and shared his impressions following his initial talk with the new minister of war.

"He's not comfortable with the MA service. As far as he's concerned France is defeated. She must loyally execute the clauses of the armistice that he signed at Rethondes and this means no initiatives against the Axis and no help to the British."

"The opposite of what Weygand was telling us?"

"Not quite," answered Rivet. "I can sense that his patriotic conscience is bothering him and I'm confident that I can get him to accept our existence. But it will be a tight game and we must avoid putting Huntziger in front of any 'tough cases'."

Good old Rivet! I suddenly understood why he came to Cambronne. It was because he feared the potential fallout from our repressive actions. Following the death sentence given to the spy in Algiers, a new case was making the rounds in Vichy. Some wiretaps set up by TR 115 on the German armistice commission, housed since the beginning of August at the Hotel du Roy René at Aix-en-Provence, confirmed the existence of an Abwehr station headed by Kunze-Krause. My men had no trouble slipping two agents into that Nazi cell. One of those agents "denounced" the existence of an arms cache in an abandoned quarry near the Esatque. The Germans duly seized the cache that had been set up by Giraud, which contained some older light machine guns and several boxes of ammunition. The snitch was congratulated and introduced to a young officer in civilian clothes who was Kunze-Krause's deputy. They asked him to observe ship movements in the ports and the loading of ships. The other W from TR 115 offered his services in writing saying he had pro-German feelings. He described himself as a former naval officer who found what had happened at Mers-el-Kébir revolting; to the Abwehr this was a prime recruit. His job was to check on what remained of the French Mediterranean fleet at anchor in Toulon. During their contacts with the armistice commission in Aix-en-Provence they both noticed that their young employer often commented on information he had been receiving from another one of his informers. Stricter surveillance of the Abwehr officer revealed that without using any kind of tradecraft he was meeting with a little man often accompanied by a beautiful young girl in the bar of the Hotel Terminus in Marseille.

The *Surveillance du Territoire* identified the man as Silberstein, a German-Jewish refugee who had been living in France since 1935. In 1939 in Paris he made contact with a German embassy official named Faber. He often traveled to Toulon with his girlfriend, roaming around the harbors, or near the barracks near Marseille and Forts Saint-Nicolas and Saint-Jean.

"Well, what should we do?" asked Blémant. "This is a very good opportunity to test our defensive system and show the Vichy authorities the double-dealing that goes on with the armistice and show the Germans that we are on top of their games."

To pull off a first espionage case against the occupying power inside France just three months after the armistice was a unique opportunity for me.

"Arrest him when you think he's about to meet with the Kraut and let me know right away."

Two days later the *Surveillance du Territoire* called me in because Silberstein and his mistress had just been arrested. They had the detail of the merchandise loaded the day before on the ship *Ville d'Oran*, that was leaving for Algiers, as well as the inventory of the troops garrisoned at the Endoume barracks in Marseille. Silberstein's diary carried the phone numbers of the armistice commission at Aix-en-Provence.

"He's a tough guy," Inspector Piani, Blémant's assistant, told me. "I've been asking him for the past two hours why he had such information on him but he won't respond and is ignoring me completely."

"I'll not handle him anymore; I'd end up beating him!" added Blémant.

I analyzed the Silberstein file at Cambronne and found enough detail to show him that we knew all about him. I walked into Piani's office with Blémant. The girl was sitting down and smiling, her huge blue eyes lit up her face. She was smoking, with her legs crossed, defiant.

"How can she sleep with that lecher?" asked Blémant, pointing at the little bald man standing by the window and ignoring all our comings and goings.

"Silberstein, you're an Abwehr V-Mann and we've been following your activities since 1939."

I described what we knew about his life, including his meetings with Abwehr representatives at Aix-en-Provence. I'll never forget what happened next. The German came up close to me and looked me over.

"I have nothing to say to you!" he hissed. "You're nothing but a defeated officer of a nation of fugitives." Then he spat in my face.

The policemen jumped the man and I had some trouble in preventing him from being lynched then and there. On my way back to the Villa Eole in the car I sat petrified in the back seat, shaken by the humiliation, while my driver Pfister, who was worried by my silence, tried to make me discuss that awful scene! What kind of abyss have we sunk into to deserve that kind of treatment! That Jew, who was being hunted everywhere, spat out his betrayed hopes and threw up his contempt. What kind of sacrifices will we need to endure to regain our dignity? I hadn't measured the magnitude of the disaster until then; the wound burned inside me and filled me with a vengeful anger that I could feel was potentially devastating. Jonglez de Ligne, the head of the BMA, drafted a report to back up the order to indict Silberstein and his mistress. The military judge Ronsin (who was later deported to a concentration camp in Germany) had the couple locked up at Baumettes prison and expedited the matter because Blémant's summary was damning for the two spies. Two days later Huntziger, who had been informed by the armistice commission, summoned d'Alès to find out what he knew about Silberstein's fate.

"He's under arrest for committing espionage, general."

"Call Rivet. This is incredible!"

Rivet got the same treatment as d'Alès and was asked to investigate in Marseille. Once I had informed him of the facts he congratulated and encouraged me and returned to Vichy to report back to Huntziger. He called me the next day.

"This time, old man, they understood. Tell the court to continue its work; the minister is letting it run its course."

I told Blémant the whole story and he drew his own conclusions from the case.

"We're a bunch of softies, captain. This time it didn't end up so badly. Silberstein is in the 'slammer' but we're on a tightrope. The day will come when *we'll* be going to the 'slammer' if we keep it up."

I attempted to explain to the policeman that we must force the state to uphold the crimes of treason and espionage if we want to help the country reject the pressure applied by the Germans.

"Okay, okay," grumbled Blémant. "But there are other ways to oppose the enemy and make the French people aware!"

I agreed with what he was saying. Had the Silberstein incident taken place anywhere other than in the police department's offices it would have, no doubt, reached a very different conclusion. Sooner or later we would have to restrain enemy agents ourselves without going through proper legal channels.

"Dear Robert, I harbor no illusions about the strength of our official security agencies. It'll take very little to switch them around: pressure from the enemy, changes in the men who are in power. But you have to agree that we must take things to the limit. Furthermore, we can discover whatever is solid within the state organizations that we work with."

I sensed that Blémant was just about ready to leave the police force to unburden his conscience and go into violent clandestine action, so I made my plea more pressing:

"I need you in Marseille. Stay at the *Surveillance du Territoire* as long as you can work in a way you like. Using the cover of your job, I must prepare a covert organization for repression. We'll set it in motion when we can no longer act through other means."

"Ask me whatever you want, captain. I'll handle your group. You'll be satisfied!"

"You must need money…?"

"That would be too much! I wouldn't drain your meager resources, so don't even think about it. I can find money if I have to. I told Guiraud how I would have dealt with Silberstein had I been alone. He turned green… So you must understand that I can't let that good man have any more nightmares. I only want to deal with you alone."

I don't know whether the decision taken by Blémant and me in October 1940 had any influence on his lifestyle, or if it finally drew him into the "mob." There are some dark corners one never reveals even to a friend. It was clear that there was a strong friendship between that man and myself that was without a doubt rooted in our common concept of patriotism. During almost daily contact up until the liberation of France we never discussed anything other than our fight against the German invaders. The passionate Corsican fire in his blood and an iron-willed personality stood out from the steely look in his eyes. I was surprised by his generosity and his brutal candor was attractive. He was tactful enough to never mix his other activities that had nothing to do with our struggle. He wound up being murdered in the Provence region on May 5, 1965, like an "honorable gangster." Nothing ever troubled our friendship or the trust I knew I could place in him.

Just two weeks after that conversation Blémant introduced me to his father, a rather colorful character with a carefully tinted black goatee and a mock adventurer's attitude.

"Dad was a lawyer in Valenciennes, but as long as the Krauts are there he won't go back. He's going to live with my sister in a house I've just bought near the beach, not too far from where you are in a small inlet of Pointe Rouge." He then added in confidence, "I also bought a little boat and keep it at the foot of the stairs that go down to the beach. That's how we can get rid of cumbersome packages."

He couldn't have been more cautious, but where had he found the money to do all that? The three of us were just finishing lunch in the back room of the brasserie called *L'Ami Fritz* at the top of the Canebière. Two men came up to our table, a very big fellow and a shorter, rounder type, a pair of funny-looking characters. They sat down at our table without asking for permission.

"This is the Boss," said Blémant, pointing at me and then introducing the two. "Big Louie and Little Pierre. You can count on them just as you can on me. I have 'liberated' them."

Blémant senior walked away. It was a discreet kind of family and Robert went on:

"Captain"—I was wondering why he even mentioned my rank—"both of them have been wiseguys and want to be whitewashed. They've decided to place themselves at your disposal. I hadn't told you before because I wasn't sure they'd come today."

The two looked friendly enough and Big Louie seemed intelligent. His massive frame dwarfed Pierre, who looked crushed in his chair. Both were about 35 and pretty well dressed.

"Captain," said Louis Raggio,* "I've done all the bad things in the book. My own mother doesn't want to see me any more. She's old. I want to prove to her that I deserve forgiveness. I'll do anything you order against the Krauts. I want to bring her back a military medal or some other proof that I did my duty properly as a soldier in this dirty war before she dies."

Pierre also told me he wanted to do something "clean" in order to rehabilitate himself. I was a bit disconcerted. Blémant had gone too fast in his search but I couldn't discourage the two fellows.

"I congratulate you on your patriotic feelings. I'll most certainly need you. But the things Robert will ask you to do on my behalf won't get you a medal—not now at least! It's going to be hard and probably dangerous."

"We know that," cut in Big Louie. "All we're asking is to be able to do work for the army because we know the army's clean." (I was now beginning to figure out why Blémant mentioned my rank.) "Robert and I thought you'd probably need to have a base in Vichy for yourself and your men. I can buy a small hotel with a bar and a restaurant right in front of the railroad station. My wife can help me before she has the baby. At the same time we can make a living because there are a lot of people in Vichy. I have to give an answer within a week, that's why we took the liberty of coming today."

---

* Louis Raggio died near Paris in 1974. One of the last times I saw him was for his daughter's holy communion, where I "presided" at the moving family ceremony with Fourcaud. Big Louie was very proud to show us what a repentant mobster could accomplish with will power and courage.

Raggio's proposal was attractive enough. I approved it and we agreed to a next rendezvous. Blémant drove me back to the Villa Eole feeling some satisfaction after the meeting.

"I know the hotel Big Louie wants to buy; you can be safe there and use it as much as you need."

I could see that Big Louie was sincere. Serious events took me to Vichy at the end of October. I was welcomed in his hotel as a true member of the family. Since September the TR reports that were routed to us regularly by the gendarmerie mentioned increased Abwehr activity in Spain. Pieckenbrock—head of Abwehr I in charge of intelligence gathering—and Canaris traveled to Madrid and Algeciras in August.

"The SR," said d'Alès, "has recorded German troop movements toward the Pyrenees border. Franco has increased his forces in Spanish Morocco, where there are 100,000 men."

Through decryptions Bertrand was able to tell us that the Abwehr II's Brandenburg regiment was on alert and in training at the Valdahon camp in the Jura region of France where Lahousen was traveling on inspection. Those were the ideal shock troops for an attack on the fortress of Gibraltar. TR 117 station in Toulouse reported increased enemy intelligence activity at Hendaye and San Sebastian. One of our Ws, Françoise Fidalgo, had been able to penetrate the German consulate general used by the Abwehr in that Spanish city. She also became friendly with Kurt Grande, the SD representative in Biarritz and found out from him about Nazi plans for Gibraltar. The air force attacks, the blitz that Göring had started on August 13, 1940, had stopped and the Seelöwe plan—the landing in Great Britain—was shelved on September 17. All indications were that the Führer was now concentrating on seizing Gibraltar. Spain, however, hesitated in getting involved and set as a condition to its possible entry into the war the recognition by the Axis of its "rights" in French Morocco and part of the province of Oran in Algeria.

It seemed very likely that the war was about to spread. On October 23, 1940 Hitler met with the Caudillo, Francisco Franco, in Hendaye. The following day it was the famous handshake at Montoire: Pétain agreed to the policy of collaboration with Germany. Perhaps France will be required to let German troops pass through the Free Zone! The British would certainly not fail to react. The United States would no doubt blockade Spain, whose economy was in dire straits. All these scenarios could have dramatic consequences for us. The first thought was a total occupation of France, perhaps with renewed hostilities and a break with North Africa where Weygand would certainly fight any Axis military initiative.

We had to plan for our falling back to Algiers and ship out our files and archives. To load everything in Marseille and travel by regular cargo was extremely dangerous. All ports and ships were under constant surveillance. I couldn't run that kind of risk. I went to Toulon. A few weeks before, when I was setting up our W in Toulon to check up on the German commission in Aix-en-Provence, I met the head of the 2nd Bureau of the naval region, Captain Nomura. He didn't like the British but that was nothing compared to his hatred of the Germans. He was in complete agreement with our penetration game and gave us some pointers to help us into the Abwehr. I told him about my concerns.

"Can you approve loading thirty tons of archives on one of your ships going to North Africa?"

"It can be done only with the consent of the admiral in command of the Mediterranean fleet. Such a large shipment can't be loaded in secret and I fear the admiral will want the approval of the High Command."

I knew full well and admired the fight rules our sailors were following and didn't dare press on any further. I decided to go to Vichy to negotiate the transfer.

"In the meantime, commander, can you help me ensure the security of our crates and the personnel guarding them?"

Nomura thought for a while.

"Yes, certainly. I think you can even use the navy prison within the arsenal as independent and discreet offices."

"But if the evacuation were not authorized by your High Command and if there was a real threat to our archives…"

The sailor stopped me:

"I will take responsibility to either guarantee that they're shipped to North Africa or, should that be impossible, that they be completely destroyed with your approval."

Upon my return to Cambronne I gave orders to pack up the thirty tons of archives in their crates once again. One of my officers went to report to Commander Nomura the next day to prepare for our convoy's arrival. On October 28 I met with Rivet and d'Alès at Big Louie's in Vichy. We examined the situation at length.

"Colonel, I can't accept responsibility for the safety of the archives if they remain in France. If the navy High Command approves, we're ready to load them aboard ship in Toulon."

Rivet immediately went to see the head of the 2nd Bureau of the navy, Captain Samson, and explained our situation. Rivet returned two hours later, distraught. Samson asked Darlan for his approval but the admiral categorically refused, without any possibility of his changing his mind.

"Bastard," muttered d'Alès.

I phoned in the bad news to Nomura and he understood my allusions and my determination to hide my "packages" somewhere. He was very calm and collected as he reassured me he was not very surprised to hear what I was telling him:

"Send in your 'merchandise!'"

I trusted him and deep down I thought I'd be able to find a solution in Toulon to ship the archives to North Africa. The move was a blow to our work and Challan-Belval told me his problems:

"I had just cleaned up the Abwehr filing system and was about to tackle the RSHA!"

Renée Morel also complained:

"My special file will be interrupted!"

She proudly showed me the boxes where she was indexing carefully what she referred to as her "bastards." Those were individuals identified by our TR stations who had relationships with the enemy and who sooner or later would have to answer for their actions. We agreed with Garnier that a daily liaison would be maintained with a Cambronne archivist and that urgent and important matters could lead to research inside the crates. I left and informed Rivet and d'Alès about the transfer of the archives and to settle several matters I considered vital:

— the transmission to the British of operational information generated by my TR stations;

— liaison with our covert SR colleagues in the army (Perruche) and the air force (Ronin);

— coordination between TR stations and in particular TR 112 (Limoges) and 113 (Clermont-Ferrand). Both were working in the Occupied Zone north of the Loire and Paris, where I was ensuring that they didn't interpenetrate each other.

Rivet, worried about his unit's survival (he also had the weakness of shying away from being tough on his subordinates), repeated twice to me that he was forbidding any direct contact with London.

"We must play it close to the vest," he said. "Huntziger just summoned me about the threats and accusations leveled by the Germans. They claim that we're letting the British use clandestine radio transmitters. So I'll handle contacts in Vichy with Dupuis, the Canadian minister, and Bob Schow, the U.S. military attaché. We'll pass things on to our friends through them; and we'll use the diplomatic pouch for liaison with British intelligence in Lisbon and Bern. I'll also ask London for a radio transmitter for myself. You'll give me your messages. Paillole, you understand that any slipup could wreck everything. We must avoid taking risks because of too many contacts with our friends."

I understood but I was not convinced. Without disregarding any of Rivet's recommendations I pushed for faster contacts between TR stations and our allies. In Marseille the problem was resolved through Captain Garrow of British intelligence, and Toulouse was in contact with the British consulate and the Intelligence Service in Barcelona. In Lyon, TR 114 had established with Major Lombard of the neighboring SR station a way to get our military intelligence out through Switzerland. In Clermont-Ferrand TR 113 was in contact with our honorable correspondent, van den Branden, a Belgian, who had been close to many U.S. diplomats in Brussels before the war. He had succeeded in reestablishing those connections in Vichy. In Limoges TR 112 and its Paris branch TR 112 *bis*, were both connected to British intelligence agents and the first Gaullist agents, to whom they passed on (directly or through others) operational information.

At the end of 1940 clandestine radio transmission techniques were still rudimentary. The few transmitters being used were bulky and difficult to hide. It took a lot of nerve to haul those cumbersome machines around and operate them, as the very first agents of the Free French were about to do. I ordered Captain Abtey to travel to Lisbon.

"Make contact with Bill [Dunderdale] through the British embassy and find out from him how we can improve our communications."

That meeting took place at the Grand Hotel in Marseille in September. I gave Abtey identification documents in the name of Jacques Hébert. It was an excellent cover, as an actor, part of Josephine Baker's show. Josephine had volunteered her services to us in 1939 and she diligently accepted the kind of risks she had to take with youthful enthusiasm and agreed to a tour of the theaters in Portugal. Just before he left I gave Hébert intelligence we had gathered on the German army in western France, the air fields, the ports, the landing barges and other preparations for a coming attack on Gibraltar. I also gave him some items we had received from our Ws about the Abwehr's intentions to infiltrate into England: Russel, the head of the Irish Republican Army, and two Frenchmen from Brittany, were to be dropped off by submarine on the southwest coast of Ireland. A group of Abwehr II agents was to land in Wales, on the coast west of Swansea in November 1940. The mission was to take over the Welsh nationalist movement and Scottish separatist groups.

I also drew our friend's attention to the fact that spies were being sent to Great Britain via Yugoslavia and that the Abwehr III was planning to infiltrate provocateurs into the intelligence networks operating in France. Abtey-Hébert transcribed part of this information in disappearing ink on the song partitions used by Joséphine and memorized the rest. He reached Lisbon at the beginning of November and made contact with British intelligence. Six months later at the request of the British and with my approval he moved to Casablanca, where he became an employee of the Compagnie Chérifienne d'Armements—a Moroccan weapons company. He was to continue his liaison mission while he kept watch over the activities of German intelligence and helped prepare the landings of November 8, 1942 with the U.S. vice-consuls Canfield and Bartlett.

At the beginning of March 1941 Major Bertrand, sent by Rivet, traveled on a mission to Portugal to meet Bill. At that time both Ronin and Perruche already had radio transmitters provided by the British. Bertrand would get a radio transmitter and receiver as well as the quartz and codes required for a direct line between our central service and British intelligence. The radio was shipped to Vichy in the diplomatic pouch and set up at "Cadix" because of the urgent nature of the information originating from the Enigma machine decryptions. Connected to Rivet by radio he was to send to the British an average of eight to ten messages per day equaling three hours of transmission between March 1941 and November 1942. Besides these outside communications there were also those within France itself. On October 15, 1940 Simonin came down from his perch in the attic of the Villa Eole.

"Could you come with me, sir?"

I was puzzled as I climbed up into the attic. There was the huge radio transmitter and receiver I had seen in Brax. Simonin smiled, put on the earphones and began sending a series of messages. Suddenly I could hear the choppy response on the earphone coming from a mysterious correspondent.

"Who is that?" I asked

"That's Algiers, sir. In a week I'll also have Toulouse and Clermont and a little later Lyon and Limoges. After that I'll try London."

All six of the Abwehr's suitcase transmitters were now being used. I congratulated him and ordered:

"Be sure not to use those radio connections except in emergencies or to check that our network is working; I don't want to risk our being located."

These cautionary measures were necessary because of the enemy's listening posts, and also by the French police forces themselves (anything could happen) that had radio-locating equipment in a few rare cases. The connection with Algiers was the most vitally important one. Through Guiraud I met an Air France pilot, Mr. Viret, who worked on the Marseille-Algiers route. He agreed to carry our mail twice a week in both directions and thanks to him copies of the information gathered by the TRs and the slips established by Cambronne were centralized in Algiers.

Our knowledge of the Abwehr's organization in France was growing. The Hotel Lutétia in Paris was the general headquarters and Colonel Rudolf, an old acquaintance from the Münster Ast, had about 200 people, plus some hotel employees. They were having a roaring time and the champagne was flowing non-stop in a joyful atmosphere! Major Waag of the Stuttgart Ast was directing intelligence of Section I in Spain and Portugal. The threat to Gibraltar coming from Section II headed by Colonels von Brandenstein and Eschwege was also confirmed. Major Reile head of Section III F had a strong counterespionage team with Leyerer, Wiegand, Radeke, Scheide and others. Captain Bulang was now at the rue des Saussaies where he oversaw a unit of some fifteen experts who were harvesting the archives and the complete files of the *Sûreté Nationale*. The research was centering for the most part upon on anti-Nazi and Communist groups. Other teams were doing the same thing under SS supervision, in the archives of the police préfecture and the ministry of foreign affairs at the Quai d'Orsay, where Göring set up princely accommodations for himself when he would visit Paris.

To all this documentation should be added the papers of the French High Command that were seized at La Charité-sur-Loire, and one can gather an idea of the extent of the knowledge the Germans had acquired about the secrets of French policy and our domestic affairs. A few technicians specialized in radio locating techniques were also available to Reile in his search for clandestine radio transmissions. A new element was the

opening by the Abwehr in Paris of a few apparently commercial enter-
prises that were actually used as recruiting centers for all kinds of individuals. The worse kind of French, Arabic, and foreign gangster types were
used to infiltrate intelligence and resistance organizations. I identified some
of the names from our reports: the Belgian André Folmer (alias Jean Richir),
who had been one of Riele's men since 1938, was living like a king on the
fashionable Avenue Hoche with his deputy, Jacobs, who was also Belgian.
Hermann Brandl, alias Otto, had been brought in by Rudolf to open the
infamous purchasing bureaus. Using that as a cover the Abwehr was financing its services and recruiting its agents and provocateurs with the
help of the Belgian Masuy and the Swiss citizen, Max Stöcklin. Among
these was a Frenchman, Frédéric Martin, also known as Rudi de Mérode,
who had been condemned on October 10, 1936 to 10 years in prison by the
Strasbourg military court and then freed by the Abwehr in June 1940. Max
Stöcklin was a strange character and we knew that he was in contact with
the Abwehr since 1938; we arrested him in 1939; in June 1940 the advancing Wehrmacht freed him; he was the cleverest recruiter used by German
intelligence. He introduced several gangsters he had met while in prison
to Radeke and one of them was the infamous Henri Lafont.

One day in April 1942 d'Hoffelize, the head of TR 117, suggested
that I meet with Max Stöcklin.

"He attempted to approach Taillandier* in Toulouse and is trying to
set up purchasing offices in my area.

"What do you expect to get out of such a lout?"

"He knows about you and wants to give you some information. I promised that he wouldn't be harmed should you agree to meet with him."

D'Hoffelize was so insistent about the matter that I couldn't disappoint him. Surrounded by Blémant's watchful thugs who had mixed with
the crowd, I met Stöcklin at the end of April 1942 in a nondescript café on
the Canebière. The Swiss was tall, elegant, almost distinguished looking; he
seemed almost too sweet and nervous to me. I got right down to cases.

"You're working for the Germans. You're lucky you're not in jail.
Why do want to speak with me?"

"Mr. Perrier, I know what I'm risking in meeting with you, but I trust
Mr. Daubray ** and his word as well as yours. I want to break away from the

---

* He was a sergeant who had been forced to retire and used to be a radio
specialist at 2 *bis* Avenue de Tourville.

** Pseudonym used by d'Hoffelize.

Germans. They're taking advantage of me because they got me out of jail in July 1940. I can give you information about the Bony-Lafont gang. For the past year they've been operating out of 93 rue Lauriston and are working for the Gestapo. As long as they were, like myself, working for the Hotel Lutétia, they were behaving more or less correctly. Now we're outraged by their thievery. I know they intend to move into the unoccupied zone, to Toulouse and Marseille. They have you in their sights, so watch out!"

I thanked Stöcklin. His offer of service only increased my revulsion for such a character, who was the epitome of the double agent negotiating his future. As he left the only promise I made to him was that I would let him cross back into the Occupied Zone without being arrested. I gave orders to Daubray to break all contacts with him.

"You really are much too proper," Blémant told me once again.

A bug under the table recorded the conversation, while a photographer was discreetly taking a picture of the Swiss agent for our records. Since he was near the top of our "blacklist" he was finally terminated in 1944.

On October 25, 1942 one of my "safe houses" at 10 Place Saint-Georges in Toulouse was searched and ransacked. On November 12, 1942 two more safe houses in Marseille, in the rue du Coteau and the Hotel Petit Louvre, were also "searched" and ransacked. Blémant was ready to swear on his gangster's honor that the Marseille mobsters were not involved. Perhaps Stöcklin was sincere and I let a very valuable recruitment slip by. We identified five more Abwehr stations in the Occupied Zone: November 1941 the Ast at Saint-Germain-en-Laye was able in to neutralize and subsequently turn against the British the intelligence network run by the Polish commander "Armand" (his real name was Czerniawski) that reported via Lisbon, as well as to our SR through Mathilde Carré. Simoneau called her "La Chatte" (The Cat). She had been introduced by a fellow officer from the 2nd Bureau, Major Achard-James, whom she had met in North Africa before the war. Mathilde Carré was trained and handled by Simoneau in intelligence gathering and she helped our SR with the work that was being done by her network on behalf of and financed by British intelligence. After she was arrested she worked for the Abwehr and tried to get Simoneau to come to Paris by proposing a meeting with an interzone card but our counterespionage was able to break into that attempt because of the unusual swiftness with which the card was issued.

The Angers Ast was operating with deadly accuracy in western France and Brittany; one of its first victims was navy Lieutenant d'Estienne d'Orves, who was executed by firing squad on August 29, 1941. At the Ast in Dijon I thought I had identified under the name of Gertrud Burckhart the former secretary of the Brussels Abwehr, Gertrud Beckmann, whom I had questioned in Lille. Colonel Ehinger was in charge of the Dijon station that was responsible for the region around Lyon, and would concentrate on fighting *Combat*, the resistance movement created by Henri Frenay. In 1943 Ehinger succeeded, with the assistance of local policemen, in dismantling our SR station in Lyon where fourteen officers among our best specialists were arrested; some were sent to concentration camps and some executed by firing squad.

Major Rumpe from Cologne was the head of the Bordeaux Ast. Our penetration agents and mostly Li 159 met with him often in Paris where he demonstrated his keen interest in women and gourmet food. The Bordeaux station just like Brest also had additional specialists from Hamburg working on Great Britain and the United States. Canaris took advantage of the fact that Spain had occupied the city of Tangier to set up an Abwehrstelle for North Africa. An Abwehrstelle was identified at Brussels with its Sections I and II working on Great Britain and Section III on Belgium and northern France. That section was to be responsible for the dismantling of the Red Orchestra* in December 1941 as well as of British intelligence and the French resistance network known as *La Voix du Nord*. Faced with the enemy's commitment and the activity of pro-Nazi French groups, the TR stations were developing their own intelligence capabilities in the Occupied Zone and in Paris. This additional work required that we increase our personnel and we had to count on younger officers who were very idealistic and completely non-partisan. The communist Médéric and the "cagoulard" Saint-Jacques (Maurice Duclos) were both ready to commit themselves completely against the German occupier when the time came.

The new generation of specialists that I later called "Young TR" was given the very dangerous mission of using new liaison procedures we ordinary would not have used in our service and the losses were to be very heavy. The lack of experience in covert operations was an additional handicap for those men and the careful presence of the veteran officers would often not be enough to avoid the losses. Courage, the attrac-

---

* The "Rote Kapelle": code name given by the German counterintelligence organs to the group that delivered valuable military secrets to the Soviet Union.

tion of dangerous activity, the love of action and enthusiasm were all qualities that were required and necessary for the youths who were volunteering to enter the fray with us. But these very qualities were often in contradiction with necessary caution and it is the commanding officer's duty never to forget that fact. "Remember to be suspicious!" Was I strong enough to resist the generous impetus of these fellow officers who were only slightly younger than myself? Two officers who were very different but just as passionately committed worked to support Rigaud (TR 112) and Johanès (TR 113) in the Occupied Zone and in Paris. At the end of July 1940 I asked Rigaud:

"Do you have someone in mind for Paris?"

"Perhaps," answered Rigaud. "I'll be sure in a few days if the comrade I'm thinking about confirms his intention to join us. He's been extremely helpful since I've been stationed in Limoges. He managed to get us seven crossings of the demarcation line, the last one through a baker from Pranzac who delivers his bread into the other zone. We hid our papers inside the loaves."

A week later I met with Lieutenant Maurice Martineau, a Saint-Cyr graduate, one of my "young men." Robert-Dumas and Rigaud had worked with him in Lille where he had fought very bravely. The way he avoided being taken as a prisoner of war demonstrated his aplomb and more importantly a keen sense of observation and the ability to take action. The young man was of medium height with a sweet adolescent face and his large inquisitive eyes gave him an even more naïve and youthful appearance.

"Mr. Richepin* told you what we expect. Do you understand the dangers and difficulties of your mission?"

"Thoroughly, Mr. Director. I've known Mr. Richepin since the beginning of 1939 and I know your line of work. I find it wonderful and with my bosses I could go anywhere on any mission!"

I told him about the Abwehr, the RSHA, propaganda, the pro-Nazi Frenchmen and I quickly figured that he grasped what was in store for him. After some additional training with Johanès at Clermont-Ferrand, Mr. Pelletier (Martineau) opened TR 112 *bis* at 6 rue Jadin in Paris. That was on September 15, 1940. Ten days later on September 26, Eugène Martin, a traveling salesman, arrived at the Gare de Lyon and checked into the Hotel de la Haute-Loire on the rue Guisarde, where he took a

---

* Rigaud's alias.

room on the rear courtyard. That became the headquarters of TR 113 *bis*, a branch of the Clermont-Ferrand station directed by Michel Garder, alias Eugène Martin, whom I was to meet on November 30.

"As we agreed," Johanès told me, "I arranged for you to meet the guardsman who's managing the Paris branch."

He was shivering in his office on the Avenue d'Italie in Clermont-Ferrand. Colonel Mangès had a bad cold and more a blanket over his back as he chewed on a cigarette butt and cursed both the Germans and the traitors. Trimouillas, his secretary, who looked blue in the face from the intense cold, was banging the typewriter keys harder than usual to keep warm. Trimouillas was a police inspector from the *Surveillance du Territoire* whose commanders had passed him on to us because they were unable to quiet down his anti-German passion. It was dark, and we could scarcely see each other through the cigarette smoke. Suddenly the door swung open and a character looking like a laborer stood at attention.

"Michel Garder," said Johanès, "the guard I was telling you about: TR 113 *bis*."

Heavy coat and jackboots; he was a young man, no more than twenty-five years old; his eyes were full of enthusiasm and I liked his vigor and easy going manner. I congratulated him for joining us and he laughed a little as he told me he was only doing his duty.

"How did you cross the demarcation line?"

"In the Dijon-Clermont-Ferrand express train, under a third class seat."

I recoiled.

"It's a good method," said Johanès. "The Krauts check out the sleeping cars and the first-class cabins looking for doctored *Ausweise** but in third class they aren't so thorough!"

"Mr. Jansen** asked you to check and penetrate pro-German groups. How's that coming?"

Garder told me what he had found out and summed up all the items he had sent us for the past two months:

"I took as a deputy a fellow officer from the 11th guards regiment. He was able to join the MSR*** The movement is disseminating propaganda in favor of collaboration while other friends are inside the 2nd Bu-

---

* Travel authorizations.
** I.e., Johanès.
*** *Movement Social Révolutionnaire.*

reau of the PPF* of former communist Doriot, and the RNP** that Marcel Déat has created to support the press campaign in favor of national-socialism and he's not that soft on Marshal Pétain or the government that he considers too timid. I also think that *Parti Franciste* is about to be launched by Marcel Bucart to rally all those in favor of integral Nazism. I'll find out more when I return to Paris."

He explained all this with great precision and knowledge. I could see that the young man knew and mastered his subject very well.

"The guardsman is not telling you the secret of his boots," said Johanès.

Garder explained that he was hiding the documents he carried in his shoes.

"I also brought some military intelligence items for Mr. Séjourné *** that are of interest to the British."

"My dear Garder, I really don't like to get missions mixed up. Don't ever compromise your own security because you get involved in the matters of another section!"

Johanès cut in, rather nervous about this.

"This is an exception to allow 113 *bis* to receive some funding from our friends of the SR. Don't forget that Garder, before joining our unit, was working for Navarre and Simoneau."

What could I say? We were far from being flush with money and we had to pay dearly for our informers in Paris. TR 112 was doing the exact same thing. Martineau added a full time air force reserve officer, Marcel Thomas (he was to die in a concentration camp), who had been trained in counterespionage in the Paris BCR under Colonel Mermet. His tradecraft was excellent and he had many acquaintances. Within the broad range they covered, Martineau and Thomas were looking mostly for Abwehr, RSHA and auxiliary stations! It was a lot to cover; too much even considering the sometimes messy energy displayed by that team. Thanks to Gérar-Dubot TR 112 had an efficient network in Belgium headed by Jeff Dehenin, a Belgian police superintendent.**** Once he returned to Brussels he became the king's attorney (prosecutor) at the end of July 1940.

---

* *Parti Populaire Français.*

** *Rassemblement National Populaire.*

*** I.e., Simoneau.

**** He was executed by decapitation in Dortmund, Germany, on October 8, 1943.

Practically the entire Belgian gendarmerie was helping with his counter-espionage work. Unfortunately he took on too many assignments that were not directly related to his mission. Very much involved in the resistance movement, Dehenin was in contact with British intelligence and Belgian minister Paul Henri Spaak. On top of that he asked TR 112 to set up escape networks for Belgian officers to the Belgian Congo as well as for British pilots to Spain and Portugal. How could we stop this massive flow and reduce the risks involved? It proved to be impossible. During those initial months of the occupation there were few fighting resistance units and those that were apparently organized were used for the widest number and most noble tasks.

Captain Ansot, the former deputy of Gérar-Dubot at the Amiens BCR, maintained the liaison between our Belgian network and TR 112 on a weekly basis. Its counterespionage activity covered the French department of the Nord and the Pas-de-Calais. Back in Lille he returned to his job as head of personnel at the daily newspaper *L'Echo du Nord.* In the town of Saumur, Deputy Prefect Milliat, who was one of our reserve officers, was an excellent contact and served as a relay for Limoges, while Martineau and Rigaud had found in the Desmarais Oil Company in Saumur an excellent HC named Madelin. Along with Police Superintendent Eprichard and despite the fact that he had seven children, Madelin was happy to get involved and take action. Thanks to him we made contact with the photographer Decker, who was expecting the arrival of an emissary from London, his own nephew Gilbert Renaud, also known as "Rémy," the famous "secret agent" of the Free French.

"What should I do when Gilbert Renaud comes over?" Martineau asked me.

"You'll help him without identifying yourself or modifying your mission."

A few weeks later Rémy was meeting with Decker in Saumur. Rémy was to succeed with dogged determination in creating a remarkable intelligence network later called the "Confrérie Notre-Dame." Martineau came to see me.

"This guy Rémy looks like an amateur. In any case he's very likable and extremely bold. De Gaulle's 2nd Bureau has given him the mission to set up an intelligence network in the French regions where we're already working. He's got lot of money and a radio transmitter. He asked Decker to help provide a cover for his radio technician, Bernard Anquetil, who's a mechanic from Angers. Decker asked Madelin and I authorized our friend to hire him in the oil company. I don't think Rémy has anything to send back to London yet. Would it be alright with you if I were to hand him copies of the operational intelligence we centralize in Paris?"

"Of course! But on condition, once again, that neither the TR nor yourself appear in any way."

If everything worked smoothly we would soon have an additional connection to London, which was a first link in working with the Gaullists, an excellent omen. Madelin traveled with Rémy to Paris and in a café of the Place Saint-Michel, using the name of Vautrin, he introduced him to Martineau's deputy, Marcel Thomas. Rigaud, who had just returned from Paris, reported on the newly established connection.

"Martineau witnessed the entire meeting between Rémy and Vautrin from a table nearby. Everything went very well and Vautrin said he was representing a group of former officers, which is the truth. He gave Rémy a sampling of our material and explained what else we could provide. Rémy was so pleased that he offered him a monthly fee of 100,000 francs."

"I hope Vautrin refused the money," I said.

"No, Mr. Director, because it looks like Rémy is rolling in cash and he offered that 'manna' with such insistence and so cleverly that it was impossible to refuse."

I couldn't help smiling and Rigaud went on:

"Vautrin promised to provide one dispatch per week. Meetings with Rémy or his representatives will take place in the Dupont cafés. We'll switch locations in the same order as they're listed in the phone book."

The connection was very valuable for Rémy and extremely useful to us. In May 1941 Dehenin informed us that one of our old acquaintances, Jamars, an Ast Brussels agent, was given the mission to infiltrate his network and other groups working for British intelligence in Belgium and northern France. He was attempting to uncover the system used for escapees and their routes to England. We tried to tell Dehenin to make him feel comfortable and that the head "office" was located in Marseille.

"To get him to come into the Free Zone he must be convinced that we're the real thing," said Dehenin. "We must be able to prove, for instance, that our Marseille man is an important person and is in contact with London, but you must act quickly because that bastard is doing a lot of damage in Belgium."

Rigaud was able to suggest to Jamars to request confirmation of a meeting with the "the head of the Marseille base" through a BBC message that he would write himself. It was Anquetil's radio that was to transmit to London the text of the message, "Albert is waiting near the canal." Jamars listened to the BBC and heard the message. He rushed to take the train. He was out of luck! A routine check by the Lyon *Surveillance du Territoire* (Triffe) allowed them to stop some travelers whose documents required additional "examination of their status." We had a photograph of Jamars since 1938 and the policemen had no trouble identifying him. He had been also traced in Brussels by the TR and drawn into the Free Zone through a BBC message transmitted by a Gaullist agent. Denounced by the BMA to the *Surveillance du Territoire*, he was arrested and tried by a military court in Lyon that sentenced him to death. The repressive mechanism was working!

The intelligence deliveries we provided to Gilbert Renaud increased even more because the suppliers often had very quick confirmation of the effectiveness of their work. This was especially true for the *Madelin* and *Maintenir** groups that TR 112 *bis* was using.

"We almost ran into a big problem," Martineau told me. "One of our 'honorable lady correspondents' was organizing erotic rendezvous in her Paris apartment in the rue Pierre-Demours. Occasionally she also provided drugs to her friends. One of her faithful customers is a young German navy officer—we can't reveal his name. Thomas was able to meet him at our friend's house and was able to 'recruit' him, offering cocaine and money. His production is of the highest quality. This time he just gave us for twenty-four hours the defensive plans of the city of Dieppe. We handed them to Rémy, who was unable to pass them back to us in time. The officer solved the problem by setting fire to his office! We came very close!"

"How does Rémy get those kinds of documents on to London?"

"He makes microfilm and gives it to the couriers."

"I hope he's pleased?"

"More than ever—he just doubled our monthly fee!"

Bernard Anquetil was working much too hard. In July 1941 I found out that sadly enough he was arrested by a Funk-Abwehr, the radio-detecting unit. He proved how brave he was and revealed nothing that could have harmed the Rémy networks and the TRs. He was condemned to death on October 15, 1941 by the military court of *Gross Paris* and was executed by firing squad on October 24, 1941 with four other patriots: Bonnard, Grossin, Keller, and Henry. Martineau's energy made me very

---

* Student group headquartered at the Place Saint-Michel in Paris.

uneasy. He was adding some "ancillary work" to his basic counterintelligence and intelligence gathering: for instance, burglarizing Georges Mandel's apartment that was now occupied by the RNP. He also had Guingouin, a new courier (he was from Châteauneuf-la-Forêt, and later became an FTP colonel and mayor of Limoges) crossing the demarcation line to give Rigaud the stolen documents. By extending his actions and taking on too many tasks he was risking losing control of his contacts. I feared for his security and that of his station; this was also Rigaud's impression, since he traveled to the Occupied Zone to help 112 *bis* whenever possible. During one of his trips outside Limoges, Rigaud was replaced by Martineau, who met our W agent Li 159 (Hengen). The Paris Ast had given Li 159 the mission of setting up an Abwehr network in North Africa and recruiting radio operators. That chance encounter, contrary to every rule of compartmentalization, was to have very negative consequences.

On Friday, December 13, 1940, at 11 p.m., our friend Mondanel—as head of the *police judiciaire* in 1940 he set up a special section for the surveillance of Germans traveling to Vichy and kept us informed—accompanied Pierre Laval to Châteldon, where he was placed under house arrest. Pierre-Etienne Flandin became minister of foreign affairs. D'Alès led me to understand that there could be reactions coming from the Germans.

"Be vigilant," said the head of the BMAs.

Sure enough the next day the demarcation line was shut down to everyone including the highest-ranking civil servants and government ministers. Two days later Otto Abetz paid a visit to Marshal Pétain, and then had Laval set free and took him to Paris. Admiral Darlan was now the top political figure. Was there any reason for us to rejoice? His initial decisions left us wondering: Fernand de Brinon, the mastermind of collaboration policy, was appointed delegate general of the government in the Occupied Zone. The *Groupes de Protection* (GP) of the ministry of the interior (a kind of Vichy praetorian guard) played a key role in the December 13 purge, and were dissolved. The man who had set them up was Colonel Groussard, former commandant of the Saint-Cyr military academy. He was a friend of Ronin and d'Alès and inspector general of the *Sûreté Nationale*, now forced to resign.

To allay the suspicion and irritation of the German occupiers, Darlan seemed to take a flexible attitude that appeared openly slavish. The wiretaps were disheartening and also revealed the preparation of a meeting between Darlan and Hitler.

"No one understands which way he's going," d'Alès told me as I met him to find out about the situation at Christmas 1940. "We don't trust Darlan. I met Groussard, who's ready to work with the British and de Gaulle. He claims Huntziger agrees and is planning to go to London. The admiral must be kept in the dark. He has some of the old GPs on his secret staff. He wants me to transfer the officers who are now available into the BMAs and highly recommends Lieutenant Warin, a young energetic officer you can trust, like Martineau. Do you think we could send him to Marseille and then transfer him into the BMA under Jonglez de Ligne?"

(In 1944, at the liberation of France, Warin changed his name to Roger Wybot and became the head of the *Surveillance du Territoire* at the ministry of the interior.)

"I think it would be useful, major. BMA 15 has a lot of work and needs men."

"He's on good terms with Fourcaud, one of de Gaulle's representatives, whom I've met several times.* He wants to work with us. It would be a good thing if we had a relay near you in Marseille."

"This fellow Fourcaud, very bold and a real go-getter," said d'Alès, "should try to hold back a bit more. I get the impression that he's met just about everyone and certainly anyone who counts in Vichy where he announced his ranks and attributions to all who would listen. If he's not more cautious, one of these days he'll get us into trouble and land himself in a jam."

Ronin, the head of air force intelligence whom I met in Vichy, confirmed the work he was doing with the British. He was passing his intelligence to Bob Schow or to the British air attaché in Lisbon through the diplomatic pouch. Suzy Borel (who later became Mrs. Georges Bidault) was a family friend and worked at the ministry of foreign affairs where she helped getting this work done and often did it herself. Ronin was generous enough to offer me the use of his connection. He also stated, but I was more skeptical about that, that his stations used the BMAs and TRs for their protection. Perruche of army intelligence said much the same thing. What was really happening was that the scattering and isolation of each branch of the service, the lack of access to the archives, and the difficulties in having safe communications didn't prompt our fellow comrades to follow our security regulations. Few potential agents were

---

* Captain Fourcaud was to become deputy director of the SDECE in 1946.

being passed on to Cambronne to be investigated prior to recruitment and this also applied to the TR stations. This regrettably lax attitude was due to covert working conditions created by the German occupation and would also have very serious consequences.

"How about spending New Year's at my brother's house in Fez?" said d'Alès, who had just been promoted to lieutenant colonel.

"Colonel, with great pleasure."

Conditions in France were confused and serious enough and the importance of Africa was so critical that we thought it necessary to use that pretense to meet with General Weygand. The general had been in Algiers for two months. Through a wiretapped confidential conversation of Lahousen we found out that Abwehr Section II had been given the mission to assassinate Weygand, who was Hitler's bête noire. We discreetly informed Gasser, the general's chief of staff and our friend, and with Navarre, who was head of the 2nd Bureau, arranged for his protection. The general was very amiable with us; he was dressed in uniform, and had a simple and direct approach.

"You're correct in creating your back-up here and to think ahead about using this as a fall-back area. I'll tell Gasser and Navarre to give you every form of assistance. It's urgent that one of your representatives should be on my staff. We must organize the directorate and coordination of the Secret Services in Africa under the guise of the BMAs."

The general's statement went beyond our wishes and I discussed Darlan's opposition to the transfer of the archives that were still in Toulon.

"Don't try and do it anyway; the admiral would find out sooner or later and your services and yourself would feel the consequences. That shouldn't stop us from finding some discreet and safe locations …life goes on! That will be one of the missions of the man you will appoint on my staff down here."

We had to locate a technician who could only be someone with knowledge of our services and familiar with Africa. Lieutenant Colonel Chrétien was appointed, and reached Algiers in March 1941 after training at the central MA office and at Cambronne. Before leaving Weygand we discussed the situation in France, Africa, the Italian, German, and Spanish initiatives, and the threats hanging over Morocco.

"Go and pay Noguès a visit. I agree with him that we should oppose any enemy intrusion by force. I feel that the mass of the Muslim population is now reacting the right way. However, Axis propaganda remain, very active and the Destour had stopped its agitation in Tunisia. From his prison cells in Marseille, and Lyon Habib Burguiba had been preaching moderation. In Algeria there were no major problems and the nationalist leaders including Ferhat Abbas and Messali Hadj, were quiet."

The general hadn't mentioned that the loyal attitude of the indigenous population in Africa was essentially due to his personal prestige and the will that he expresses with firm and benevolent determination to keep the area out of the enemy's reach. He confirmed his commitment to us:

"The meddling by the Italian armistice commissions into our sovereignty is intolerable. I asked Navarre to watch them. Be sure to give your services clear orders to stop those encroachments. I also recommended that the military courts hand down quick and unrelenting justice against propaganda, espionage, and treason that benefit the Axis."

We had proof that those instructions were being applied to the letter. A sergeant of the Algerian infantry's 1st Regiment, Ouadani Abdelkader, had just been executed by firing squad in Algiers. At the request of a German intelligence recruiter he had faked an escape of North African POWs from a camp in the Landes region in France in September 1940. Traveling through Toulouse and Marseille he wound up at his unit's headquarters in Blida, south of Algiers. He was having what looked like an amorous correspondence with a lady named Boutheau, which had been set up in Toulouse by the Bordeaux Ast. Néron, our W agent, discovered her (he was a penetration agent in contact with Rumpe, Sibelius' deputy, who was head of the Bordeaux Ast). Néron had been friendly with Rumpe since 1937 and that mailbox was under the control of TR 117. The disappearing ink used by Ouadani didn't hold up to the chemical tests. The traitor was very intelligent and had a gift for observation; he was passing along everything he knew about the army in Africa, including the mobilization instructions Weygand had given to the North African units. He described the training of the regiment and the location of weapons depots. Even though the letters were unsigned, the BMA of Algiers under Lieutenant Colonel Labadie had succeeded in identifying the author in a few days.

Since August 1940 we had been using rather elementary rules in dealing with all the soldiers who had escaped from German POW camps. All of them were being questioned. Those whose escape appeared to be suspicious were kept under surveillance. That was the case with Ouadani because the story of his escape was inconsistent. Rather than crossing the demarcation line at the closest point around Dax, he had gone to the crossing 150 kilometers north at Langon. The justification of that long and dangerous trek through the Occupied Zone had not been convincing. What had really happened was that Rumpe had kept Ouadani in training in Bordeaux for two weeks, sending him back into the wild without anticipating carefully enough how plausible a return through Langon would appear. Such a rudimentary way of recruiting, training, and fielding agents could only end in failure. It was the method used by Abwehr stations in France and all of them had been ordered by Canaris to set themselves up in North Africa as fast as possible.

Most of their spies meant to go to Africa simply threw themselves into our defensive shield. It was disaster from October 1940 on and it would grow with six spies arrested in October, eight in November, seven in December 1940, twelve in January 1941, fourteen in February—to reach the record numbers of thirty-one in April 1941, fifty-two in April 1942, and four hundred thirty-two in the last quarter of 1942, of which there would be sixty-nine death sentences that were carried out by our firing squads. The Abwehr understood the strategic importance of the Mediterranean and of French Africa too late. Its efforts to penetrate the area were unsuccessful, proving once again that in intelligence gathering improvisation doesn't work.

We traveled to Morocco as Weygand suggested and on January 1, 1941, we were visiting d'Alès' brother in Fez, where he was in charge of Arab affairs in the area. He told us about the impact of German propaganda on the Istiqlal party. One of the Istiqlal leaders, Ahmed Balafrej, often visited Spanish Morocco. In Meknès I paid a visit to Colonel Bazin, who was the government commissioner at the military court. Since he had been a judge in criminal court in Paris he knew what to expect from Nazi espionage and had five German espionage cases on the calendar and three Spanish cases. There was no need to recommend that he be firm: out of the seven trials there would be four death sentences.

Noguès received us with his usual courtesy and had noticed, as we did, German intelligence efforts in Morocco. He was expecting that two officers, Auer and Klaube, who had just arrived in Casablanca, to oversee the switch that would soon replace the Italian delegations. The Resident General attributed that decision to the intrigues and lack of caution of those he called the "Gaullists."

"The actions [of the "Gaullists"] and their loose talk has the German led to think that there would be an Anglo-Gaullist action in French West Africa and Morocco. The Germans don't trust the Italians to foresee it and act against it," said Noguès.

What the general didn't tell us, but that the BMA in Rabat revealed, was that the police force had orders to act against Allied and pro-Gaullist groups with as much energy as against the Axis. The work of Section TR 120 that I set up in Casablanca with Breitel in charge was not easy. While d'Alès was in a restaurant with his brother in Casablanca, I was having lunch with Noguès. At the end of the meal when we were alone I told him about the threats hanging on Weygand's life.

"That can't be possible!" he said, very upset. "Do you think they would dare?"

I took advantage of his reaction to tell him about our plans to reinforce locally and asked for his support. As always I found him to be very understanding but skeptical about the possibilities of the army authorized by the armistice. He longed for times past and regretted what he called "the lost opportunity of June 1940" and accepted the current situation with a kind of fatalism. He appeared skeptical as well about the way the war would end, France's future, and that of the Maghreb. I could not predict how he would react.

14

Resisting the Germans

The TR stations were beginning to notice a clear revulsion to what was called "Vichy." The role that Weygand had given to the armistice army lacked credibility. No one doubted that the military leaders were in good faith but people didn't trust the government in power and were worried about the handshake between Hitler and Pétain at Montoire. Beyond our W agents and the usual honorable correspondents (HCs) the cooperation of individuals was due more to the fact that we pursued an independent and rather brutal repressive policy than because we were part of the army. The assurance that intelligence provided about the enemy would reach the British and not Laval or Darlan contributed to a large part to the effectiveness of our recruitment. I explained this to Rivet and we paid a visit to army headquarters where he introduced me to Lieutenant Colonel Baril, the new head of the 2nd Bureau. He was having a conversation with Major Vautrin of the infantry. I was about to take my leave.

"You're welcome to stay. Have a seat."

It was a warm and spontaneous welcome and the two officers were both tall, in excellent condition, and seemed to be very intelligent.

"I help your organization on the coast, Paillole, and I like working with Guiraud and Chotard.*

---

* The head of the Nice annex of TR 115.

Vautrin's compliment made me feel comfortable. Then Baril said:

"The British are holding out very well. The Italians are getting whacked in Greece and their navy just ran away when it had to face the Home Fleet! The Americans are sending us a new ambassador, Admiral Leahy, a personal friend President Roosevelt's. It must mean that the president wants to get a clear picture before he gets involved, and we can help him do that."

"Which is why we came here to see you," said Rivet. "On the SR and counterintelligence levels there's no problem. We'll give the Allies everything we have. There's the part the army can play. Paillole tells me that the mission of the army is still confused, or at least misunderstood in the Occupied Zone."

"We must make that very clear and prevent the Krauts from doing as they please. Let's go and meet with du Vigier."

We followed Baril to the office of the head of the 3rd Bureau, a tall, lean lieutenant colonel who was very calm and collected.

"Everything needs to be done and I know it won't be easy," noted du Vigier. "We have to figure out which scenarios to consider. Where and how do the Allies plan to reenter the continent and with what kind of forces? What do they expect from us? We have a small army and we should be able to increase it by calling up the reserves. That's what Carmille is setting up in Lyon.* We have to be able to arm our men and Mollard is camouflaging weapons and supplies. We also must be informed and protected and that's your job," the colonel smiled at us. "This army must also be able to operate in the Occupied Zone and that is not yet the case."

I interrupted him:

"The action into the Occupied Zone should be coordinated with patriotic initiatives that are cropping up everywhere. That's how the action and existence of the armistice army will gain credibility and yield results."

"It's true," noted Baril. "I suggested my men help one of the officers who's about to leave the army to join the underground resistance.** Here, d'Alès, Ronin, and myself are in contact with others who are taking similar initiatives, like Groussard, Loustanau-Lacau, Faye. I advised them to be cautious and use the BMAs as protection and I understood that's what they're doing."

---

* Using the National Statistics Service as cover, Controller General Carmille (who later died in a concentration camp) was preparing for the secret mobilization of 300,000 army reserves.

** Baril was talking about Henri Frenay.

I confirmed what he said and added:

"There's a permanent contact between the BMA and Loustanau-Lacau in Marseille with the approval of Colonel Granier, the regional chief of staff."

"This is all very good," said du Vigier, "but the game is dangerous. Give me a few days to organize my work and the position of the High Command. Come back to see me in one month."

The TRs were now operational and functioning secretly—at least that's what I thought until an incident caused me to think otherwise. Roger-Corvée, one of my Cambronne associates, told me what he'd seen at the Officer's Club in Marseille where he would occasionally go for lunch.

"I met a lieutenant from the colonial army who's been furloughed because of the armistice. He seems to be doing the same thing we are."

"What do you mean, 'the same thing'?"

"He told me he was working with a secret organization that was fighting the Germans and asked me if I wanted to help."

"Who is this lieutenant?"

"I didn't take down his name; I think he's opening a travel agency specializing in Africa."

"What did you answer him?"

"I didn't. I let him do the talking, listened, and that's it."

I was about to go to the club myself to meet this individual when a few days later Jonglez de Ligne, head of the BMA, came to see me.

"My dear director, be careful. I have the impression there's a lot of talking going on in your shop."

"What do mean? Can you spell it out?"

"One of my friends, Lieutenant Chevance, who has been furloughed by the armistice, met a mysterious captain in civilian clothes at the Officer's Club. He was intrigued and got him to talk, then offered to give him a job in a travel agency he's setting up. The officer answered that he wasn't free and had an assignment in a secret counterespionage service. Since no one from the BMA besides me goes to the Club I thought it could possibly be one of your men."

I immediately thought of Roger-Corvée and summoned him to my office.

"You haven't told me everything about your conversations at the Officer's Club, have you?"

I must have asked the question somewhat roughly because Roger-Corvée stammered, became red as a beet, looked at Jonglez desperately, and then said theatrically:

"Sir, I failed in my mission and my honor, I know what I must do!"

"Just a minute. What you must do is bring that travel agent to me, under any kind of pretense, tomorrow between 1:30 and 2 p.m. at the Cintra bar on the Quai des Belges."

That was how I met Maurice Chevance at the beginning of 1941 and I immediately felt I could trust him. He had an open and pleasant face. No affectations and was completely self-assured. I confirmed what we were doing.

"We're hunting down Axis spies. Do you wish to help us?"

"I really would but I must ask my commanding officer for permission. It would be best if you met him."

"Who is he? Where?"

"He'll be here at the end of the month. I'll let you know through Roger-Corvée."

"You know who I am and what I'm doing, so tell me who your commander is."

"That's impossible, Mr. Perrier. I'm not authorized to reveal his identity."

I didn't push any further and as we left Chevance I told Roger-Corvée to note the lesson an "amateur" had just given the two "professionals" we were supposed to be.

"Please," said Roger-Corvée, "this is a very tough lesson. I won't set foot outside Cambronne without your authorization."

On January 2, 1941, in mid-afternoon, I was at the Cintra waiting for Chevance and his commanding officer. I was amazed! I saw him with Henri Frenay, one of my former Saint-Cyr mates. Our happy surprise turned to laughter and we talked at length. I didn't have to tell Frenay what we were doing; he knew it through Chevance and Dr. Recordier, who was putting him up and who was the brother of my childhood friend Maurice Recordier. He was also informed through Rivet, with whom he was in constant contact at Vichy, where he was also one of Baril's associates.[*] Frenay explained his view of the resistance organization, the libera-

---

[*] Maurice Recordier was not simply the discreet doctor of the TRs, but also a most reliable and trusted HC. I would sometimes live at his house, where I would meet his brother, Henri Frenay's personal friend.

217

tion of France and the country's rebirth. We agreed to work hand in hand and help each other out. Chevance and Challan-Belval were to keep our communications going. Frenay then shared his ideas with me and we had a spirited conversation during which we disagreed in a friendly way.

"I shall not stay in the army. Despite the patriotic feelings of most of the regular army men, it obeys leaders and a government that takes its orders from the enemy. Not only will it remain paralyzed in trying to decide whether to resist or not, but it's also approving the policy of collaboration."

"As weak as it may appear, there's hope of rejoining the struggle against the Germans. That hope is what's keeping the armistice army going. Should officers such as yourself leave, it'll have no reason to exist and could run the risk of becoming an auxiliary of the Wehrmacht."

"I think so, my dear Paillole. I would not want to be in the position someday of having to choose between the military duty to obey, meaning discipline, and the duty that my conscience dictates. Even with people like Rivet, d'Alès, Baril, du Vigier, and so many others, the army will sooner or later become subjected to the will of the Germans. The rebirth of France demands another kind of action on a very different level. We must call every social class to resistance; we must fight with everything we've got, and not only against the Germans but also against the regime that's willing to accept their dictates. We must be willing to fight even though it might mean bloodshed. Perhaps we will need martyrs, but that's the price we must pay to stand up again."

"No question about that! But if we have to convince our fellow citizens and the rest of the world that the enemy is still our enemy, the fighting spirit must be kept alive and rekindled inside the government's administrative offices, the army, and the police. If the best elements of that resistance go away, as you plan to do, the consequences will be very serious."

"There'll always be some of them left and from the outside we must help them every way we can."

Chevance listened to us carefully and approved both approaches.

"In your own ways you're both striving toward a utopian ideal."

Perhaps he wanted to bring us back down to earth and started taking a more familiar tone when he asked me:

"What do you plan to do?"

"Use the government structure to fight the enemy. That's what my service is all about. We must make sure the Vichy police will arrest German spies and that Vichy courts will hand down sentences, and that the armistice army will provide the firing squads to execute them. When that will no longer be possible, we'll know that we must act in a different manner. I understand Henri worrying about the future of the armistice army, but I repeat, there is the hope, even though it might be vague, that the army can get back into the fight and liberate the country. Our duty as regular army officers is to make that happen."

Frenay was thoughtful and looked at me intensely. He was very sentimental about the army and for those, like me, who had kept the faith. He had made his decision and he respected mine.

"The most important thing is that our efforts add up to each other. For the moment your efforts are the most important ones and it's our duty to help you succeed."

"One last question. Have you contacted de Gaulle?"

"No."

"What's your position as far as he's concerned?"

"Wait and see, but I know we'll certainly need him one day."

I could only admire Frenay's determination and his moral rigor. The organization chart of his plans (scores and scores of military sections, regions, departments, and zones) seemed very ambitious to me and underlined the rigid thinking of the *Ecole de guerre*. His fear of being some day out of synch with the duty to obey orders didn't bother me. For the moment the armistice army had no other mission than to prepare for the struggle to liberate France. I felt comfortable with the mission and if we were given a difficult mission under pressure from the enemy I would have no trouble in taking action as a rebel. I informed Rivet of the meeting.

"He's leading the charge in a plumed helmet and white gloves," was the boss' comment.

"We've got to help him, colonel, if only with technical advice about intelligence gathering."

"Of course, I think he contacted Simoneau. He's got a contact in the 2nd Bureau in Lyon in the German section and his representative in the Occupied Zone, Captain Robert Guédon, who has already seen Husser [*] and Mercier[**] I'll also meet with him."

In March 1941 Rivet made Frenay an offer to add our efforts to his. Because of what I considered to be unreasonable caution he refused the

---

[*] Head of the covert SR section in Châteauroux.

[**] Head of the German section of the covert SR in Vichy.

proposal while praising the clandestine SR. The changes inside the government and the administration were symptomatic of a malaise that I thought was created by the enemy as well as the intrigues of Admiral Darlan. He met with Hitler on December 25, 1940. Paul Baudoin and the minister of justice, Raphaël Alibert, both resigned in January and Pierre-Etienne Flandin was to also resign on February 9, 1941. On February 25 a government reorganization that was approved by Otto Abetz made Darlan head of four ministries, including foreign affairs and the interior while Pierre Pucheu became secretary of state for industrial production. Laval let it be known after meeting with Marshal Pétain that he had refused to be a state minister.

Commander Rollin, a navy officer, was Darlan's man inside the police department, in control of the *Surveillance du Territoire*. Another navy officer, Rodelec du Porzic, was police commissioner in Marseille and Osvald told me that he was as anti-German as he was anti-British. Our archives, still in Toulon, could not be easily accessed and Nomura was hesitant to hold on to them.

"If someone finds out, we could be running some considerable risks." I insisted.

"You're sure we can't ship them secretly to North Africa?"

"It's risky. I can't make that decision," answered the chief of the navy's 2nd Bureau. "What I heard from the ship commanders and from Admiral de Laborde was rather negative."

Too bad! I decided to bring everything back to the Villa Eole, an operation that took place on February 13, 1941. I thanked my archivists.

"I'm growing tired of turning you into freight forwarders running so many risks with these archives. The situation is unclear; sooner or later we'll have to evacuate Cambronne. I'll ask you to let me know which files you agree to destroy, for example those predating 1914: since it's getting cold we'll have something to heat up the fireplace. Then take from the general file anything that's potentially current. Renée Morel will condense everything into special archive crates."

The selection was a lot of hard work requiring scrupulous attention and a high level of specialization. Garnier, Piroulas, and their team were to get it done in less than one year. Starting on February 15, 1941 the janitor, Douarin, kept an endless fire going behind my back in my office! The archives were reduced from 30 to 20 tons while I kept looking for discreet locations to hide them in case of emergency. I finally decided upon a large isolated farm at Lédenon in the Gard region, about 30 kilometers north of Nîmes and owned by Favre de Thierrens. Garnier and one of his archivists, the gendarme Saint-Jean, were to take refuge there at the end of October 1942 with the 20 tons of paper. The special archives were about 300 kilos packed in boxes that were rather easy to handle. They could always be moved to the country house belonging to Recordier's parents at Eyguières, about 30 kilometers northwest of Marseille. The Germans captured the Lédenon location in July 1943 in circumstances I shall explain later. Garnier and Saint-Jean were sent to concentration camps while the boxes at Eyguières were found intact during the liberation of France.

It was high time to prepare the next prisoner exchange with the Italians. Guiraud had informed me on August 28, 1940 that Major Roberto Navale, who was still head of the Italian counterespionage in Turin, wished to resume the negotiations that had been interrupted by the war. Police Superintendent Simon Cottoni had transmitted the request through the Italian armistice commission in Nice. I had hesitated for some time before taking on the negotiations myself. My secret activity seemed incompatible with the resumption of an official contact using my new identity. After giving it some thought it was simple enough to show the Italians written orders under my name, allowing me to negotiate the matter as the representative of the army High Command. I was also disgusted at the thought of having to face Navale as a defeated army officer after the stab in the back the Italians had inflicted on us.

"You can possibly save some of our men; you must forget your misgivings," d'Alès had told me. "Just imagine the anguish of our fellow citizens who have been jailed once more in who knows what conditions after expecting their deliverance for a few days at Ventimiglia in June 1940."

Finally, I informed Navale of the French government's agreement. The appointment was for the first few days of October just outside Menton. Navale was there once again in civilian clothes. Without any handshakes and every bit as embarrassed as I was, he asked me ceremoniously to ride in his car to take me to the casino. With a heavy heart I saw the deserted streets and the silence that permeated the humiliated little town.

"I understand your sadness, captain. Politics is quite a despicable thing."

"It's my understanding, sir, that you wish to take up the exchanges where we left off in June."

"Precisely, but I shall no longer be the one you'll negotiate with since I'm leaving my post. I wanted to welcome you myself and introduce you to my successors after telling you my personal regret about leaving you under such circumstances and offering my deepest sympathy."

Respectful of my silence for a moment, his face showing an emotion that could have been either real or feigned, Navale went up to a servant and whispered a few words. Two men in civilian clothes then appeared. One of them was tall, thin, and elegantly dressed, he was the infamous Rosario Barranco, the OVRA's representative in Nice since 1938. The second man, whose name I was unable to catch, had a shaved head, wore a monocle, and was very broad shouldered in his tight-fitting suit; he looked like a Prussian officer from 1870. He could have been a German with the mission of examining me close-up and checking on the meeting. Navale suggested a date to meet again and see to the exchange of prisoners once and for all. I proposed January 1941 since I knew that the administrative red tape would be long in France. We met again as agreed and Barranco, who came alone, was relaxed and sure of himself; he said that on his side everything was ready to proceed with the exchange. We agreed to a date in March 1941.

It was a wonderful day for my fellow French citizens—Garapon, Salmon, and Rosa—and for me as well on the Union bridge at Menton-Carnolès. Everything went smoothly but my compatriots looked very thin. There were too many other Frenchmen rotting inside Italian jails. The pressing steps taken by the families to the head of state or the ministry of foreign affairs were given to me by Rivet. Some of them were quite alarming. I met Barranco again in an attempt to have other exchanges. The Italian response was disappointing, demanding that we hand over not just those Italians who had been condemned for espionage before June 1940 but also political refugees, including Pietro Nenni, the Italian Socialist leader who had taken refuge in France. I refused to go down that path and the negotiations dragged on endlessly. Finally, after many discussions and much good will on the part of Barranco, I was able to obtain a second exchange and then a third on January 28, 1942, leading to the freeing of Sabran, Fould, and Polacci, who had been sentenced on December 18, 1939, to sixteen years in prison by the Special Court for the Defense of the Sate in Rome. A fourth exchange took place in March 1942, freeing Gaggero, Gasiglia, and Valori. It was to be the last because our supply of Italian detainees sentenced for espionage had ended.

Barranco was becoming increasingly friendly and trustful. He talked a lot and made no secret of his anti-German feelings that I kept feeding as venomously as possible with tidbits about the Abwehr's mistrust of Italy. Little by little I began thinking that with patience and perseverance I could perhaps alter the nature of our relationship. Barranco knew many secrets and was very good at his work as a political informer and OVRA observer. We knew all about his activities thanks to that fly on the wall Lisa, a smart chambermaid whom the very clever Gallizia, our associate at the Nice SR, had succeeded in infiltrating into the Hotel Continental where Barranco was working. She was picking up the trash for us and gave us carbon copies, scratch pads, and torn papers that the OVRA boss in France had forgotten to incinerate.

Even though Marseille was not part of the Italian occupation zone I would invite him from time to time to come and have a *bouillabaisse* and he began coming to visit more frequently under the guise of having a good time. To avoid his wasting time looking for mediocre intelligence, I would provide him with balanced reports on the situation and public sentiment in France. Baril gave me some reports with statistics proving that Germany was on the way to being defeated and was basically rotting from within. Written in Baril's style it was impressive enough and made Barranco feel wobbly. He conscientiously translated the batch and sent it on to Rome, which we could verify, thanks to Lisa.

The production was so impressive that the SIM was unhappy about it. Since I was surprised by this fact Barranco explained that SIM was now headed by General Carboni and Colonel Tripiccione, who had both taken over after Roatta left. The SIM also included besides the intelligence service itself, a sabotage service that reported to the secretary of state for war and a counterespionage service that was more or less independent and led by Colonel Emanuele. Italian counterespionage had been involved in France through the Cagoule, taking advantage with great skill in the opportunities this provided to penetrate the French intelligence service itself. That was how so many of our agents in Italy had been arrested in 1939. The counterintelligence service that Navale belonged to was a rival of the OVRA, much like the RSHA was the rival of the Abwehr. The OVRA as a political organization tended to want to take over the security work and tried to replace the counterespionage service of the SIM. I understood Barranco's ambitions: having succeeded in eliminating Navale he wanted to take over all political and counterespionage work in France. I decided to help him do that.

Barranco was rewarded for his excellent work with money and promotions and in his own way he thanked me for it. In April 1942 he warned me about an ex-informer at TR 115 named Angrisani, whom he said was an agent of the Germans and the Italians. We were to find out that this information was in fact correct when the Italians occupied Nice in November 1942. Angrisani was responsible for the arrest of French patriots in the area and was executed in Nice in April 1943 on orders coming from the BCRA in London. Our comrades had decided to extend our repressive actions at the right moment. Barranco was probably impressed by how much weight I had lost and provided me with many sacks of macaroni and kilos of Parmesan cheese that were a feast for us at Cambronne. And then what had to happen did in fact take place. One evening in September 1942, in an isolated corner of the lounge of the Hotel Astoria in Marseille, I told him to stop being the ally of a defeated Germany and become the friend of France, which was already involved in the fight to free itself and that he should take part in. He listened attentively and silently since he was far too clever not to understand the meaning of my words. Months of approaches and human contacts had set up the great moment that an officer of the Special Services goes through with a high degree of anxiety. It's the pay off. What would the man's reaction be to the proposal? I looked at Barranco intensely; he didn't move, and in the most natural way in the world he simply shook my hand. The next day I introduced him to Guiraud, who was to handle the liaison between us from now on, turning him into an exceptionally productive HC.

Rivet and d'Alès summoned me to the Hotel Saint-Mart at the end of March 1941. As agreed we were to meet with Colonel du Vigier to try and define once and for all the covert action of the armistice army and the build up of its forces in the Occupied Zone. We went over the various possibilities before that meeting, important to our future and to that of the army. Rivet described the SR under Perruche. Major Navarre, who was the head of the German section, had left for Algiers to be on Weygand's staff. Major Mercier was replacing him. Major Le Trotter headed the southern section centered on Italy, and Lochard—who was to become the military attaché in Moscow—was in charge of the Russian section. Darlan demanded that we create an Anglo-Saxon section and we had to comply. Rivet appointed Captain Luizet (he was to become Paris police chief after the liberation), who took advantage of that position to make some discreet contacts in London. The five SR stations in France were located in the same cities as the TRs and while the work of both divisions was highly compartmentalized, the relationship was good and this also applied to the air force SR headed by Ronin.

Communications with British intelligence used several radio transmitters (including the one used by Bertrand that had been activated a few days before) and French and American diplomatic pouches out of Lisbon and Bern where Allen Dulles was working as a very active U.S. "diplomat." We had a very efficient assistant military attaché in Major Pourchot in Bern as well. The Wehrmacht, Luftwaffe, and Kriegsmarine orders of battle were tracked and updated daily and forwarded to the 2nd Bureau (Baril) and to the Allies. My summary of activity for the first seven months of TR activity from July 1940 to February 1941 was:

— 78 persons had been exposed and "handed over" to the BMAs and arrested by the *Surveillance du Territoire*;
— 6 persons were working for Italian intelligence;
— 4 persons were working for Spanish intelligence;
— 68 persons were Abwehr agents looking for arms depots, seeking to identify British or Gaullist networks, keep watch on the armistice army, and "identify the 2nd Bureau officers"; and finally to penetrate North Africa to observe military activity and take over Muslim nationalist movements.

Among the sixty-eight Abwehr spies handed over to the military courts, there were four military men on armistice furlough, including one captain, five Muslims, and nine German nationals whose disappearance worried the German embassy.

"Don't worry," said d'Alès without flinching. "When I'm asked I either don't answer or say that I have no knowledge."

None of us, neither Rivet nor I, ever mentioned the half dozen or so "packages" that we had given to Blémant and that had been permanently "lost." The German and Italian armistice commissions were trying to trace them while Abetz bombarded Vichy with protests. All three of us had noticed the rather messy activities of British intelligence and the Gaullist SR and we tried to help them both.

"Last month," said d'Alès, "Maurice Duclos* returned from London. He broke his leg when he parachuted over the Dordogne. We had to fish him out of there! It was no joke because the entire area knew about it and Rollin wanted to "cash-in" on the deal. In the end, with Rigaud and Martineau we succeeded in getting him out of jail on March 13. I think he linked up with Martineau in Paris. Is that correct Paillole?"

"That's correct," I answered. "They agreed to exchange information through Duclos' cousin, Marc Vaisseaux. Along with Rémy he's our contact to the Gaullist SR."

---

* Also known as Saint-Jacques.

"There's also Fourcaud," said d'Alès, "who's wandering between Perpignan and Marseille where he meets with Warin.* I don't understand why he hasn't come to see me yet. I suspect he's going to create problems for us."

"There's also Colette Lucas, our former secretary at 2 *bis* with her friend Samson, who worked with Trutat at The Hague," said Rivet. "I was able to pry them out of Rollin's clutches. I had to swear they'd stop working for the Gaullists to get them out on bail in Marseille. They're both working with Weil-Curiel, a lawyer from Paris."

"He was just locked up with a few others by the Germans, but he'll get out, colonel," I said.

"Why is that?"

"Because he'll use his good relations with Otto Abetz."

"How do you know all this?"

"I just met Françoise once again," I replied.

I found the amazement of Rivet and d'Alès funny because I had traveled to Paris between March 17 and 20 without telling them.

"You would have forbidden my taking the trip!"

The boss smiled:

"You'll tell me the whole story after we meet du Vigier. For now, I conclude from our conversation that we must coordinate all these very well-intentioned initiatives; otherwise it'll surely get very nasty, including under our own roof."

In du Vigier's office we also met Baril, who gave a very clear summary of the situation.

"Hitler has given up on his plan to attack Gibraltar. Franco was holding back and is very frightened of a potential British blockade, since Spain is 100 percent dependent on the United States for all its supplies. We've reached a turning point in the war and the Führer is beginning to have some nightmares! No invasion of England, failure of the blitz, no assault on Gibraltar or invasion of Spanish Morocco and the Italians are getting their asses kicked by the Greeks. The British and the Free French are giving Germany a hard time in Africa. The Axis surrendered in Somalia and Tobruk and Leclerc is at Kufra. Several large German units have been withdrawn from France to help the Italian heroes. The Afrika Korps is operating in Libya under Rommel's

---

* Lieutenant Roger Warin, alias Wybot, who had just been appointed to the BMA in Marseille.

command and will not be able to extricate itself. American industrial production is working at full capacity for Britain and the U.S. Congress has voted the Lend-Lease Law on March 11. I'm ready to bet that the Americans will enter the war before the end of the year."

Baril was great at winding people up. D'Alès, who had just been on a trip to Algeria with me to hand over command to Lieutenant Colonel Chrétien (who later went to Algiers in March 1943 to become head of counterespionage for North Africa), mentioned the fact that the Germans had arrived in Morocco and in the Italian armistice commissions in Algeria.

"It looks like the Wehrmacht is as distrustful of Weygand as it is of the Italians and is worried about military action in French North Africa."

Du Vigier was listening intently.

"I couldn't find out exactly what the British strategic plans and tactics are. Any scenario involving the French army's involvement should the Allies land in North Africa or France itself or elsewhere can only be conjecture as things stand today. To be able to work productively we need to talk to our allies. What do you think?" he asked Baril.

"In whose name and for what would we be talking about?"

"In the name of the army High Command, naturally!"

"Would that be enough?"

"I will have Picquendar and Huntziger's agreement no doubt and through them we may also get the Marshal's blessing."

"You're forgetting Darlan! He can stop everything."

"He's an opportunist and he'll always be in time to jump on the bandwagon."

D'Alès discussed the issue of the problems raised by the many solicitations the officers were being subjected to by people and groups of the resistance.

"What we're doing should be enough to end all this agitation," said du Vigier.

"I find it difficult to hold back Loustanau-Lacau and Groussard," said d'Alès. "Those go-getters who didn't wait for us to take action. Groussard told me that he had Huntziger's approval to go to England with the support of Fourcaud and Loustanau. He wants to set up an intelligence and resistance network with the British and the Gaullists."

"Good God!" cried Rivet. "What intelligence? With whom and with what?"

For once Baril reassured the boss calmly.

"It's not such a bad thing if Huntziger takes that kind of initiative. If Groussard goes to London he'll speak for the minister and his trip will have a political slant above all else. He knows us too well to know not to step on any toes."

Du Vigier returned to the main point of the meeting.

"The first step is to send one of our men to Washington and London to bring back information and inform our friends. How about André Poniatowski? I can be in touch with him tomorrow and I'm almost certain his answer will be positive."

Everyone knew André Poniatowski. He was a reserve officer and an industrial entrepreneur specializing in armored tanks and tracked vehicles. He spoke fluent English and was related to some important American families (Princess Poniatowska was Averell Harriman's sister-in-law). His son had just escaped from France to join a fighting unit in England. He was to be killed in action in Holland at the end of the war.

"Excellent choice!" said Rivet, echoing everyone's opinion. With his friend d'Aulan, Poniatowski supported anti-German resistance in the Aisne region and he was totally dedicated to the cause.

Baril added:

"Poniatowski must not go empty handed; I'll give him a report summing up what we know about the enemy."

"I'll set up his mission with Rivet and Baril. He could begin in the United States as Bob Schow suggested."

"The preparation and execution of this mission will take weeks and months. We can't wait for the results to start reorganizing covert army actions of a 'departure,' using the Wehrmacht as a scenario. I'll study the possibilities and they'll be finalized once Poniatowski returns. Paillole, do you have plans for what could be done in the short term in the Occupied Zone?"

Of course I had thought about the problem and Frenay confirmed that in order for any recruitment attempt to work it had to be made with British support.

"That's why Poniatowski will negotiate with the British," said du Vigier.

"Abwehr III and now the RSHA are stuffing the patriotic organizations with *agents provocateurs*. Ideally we should be able to ensure the security of the groups that have to be set up. This means that my services must be informed about any planned contacts and that we can verify that they're genuine. In many cases this will be impossible."

Such clandestine action would run the risk of being discovered by the Germans. They must not be given the opportunity to trace anyone back to the army High Command. The head of such an organization must be located outside Vichy, giving the impression of being an individual initiative by former officers, for instance Frenay.

"What do you suggest?"

"An officer with covert experience should be the head. He should have access to counterintelligence archives and be located far from Vichy. Why not in my organization in Marseille? At least initially during the gearing-up period."

"Who do you think fits that description?"

I answered without hesitating.

"Lambert!"

D'Alès reacted when he understood he was going to lose one his best men at the central service of the MA, but with great sportsmanship he approved.

"Paillole's right, it's a good choice. I'll tell Lambert to make his way to Cambronne and have Bonnefous replace him on my staff."

That was how the self-defense groups were started (*Groupes d'Auto Défense*—GAD) and by the end of 1942 they were the core of the ORA (*Organisation de résistance de l'armée*).

"So Paillole, tell us about your rendezvous with Françoise."

The long working session with du Vigier hadn't made Rivet forget my trip to Paris and in d'Alès' office. I gave a full report.

I hadn't seen Françoise since October 1939. Unexpectedly her Berlin diplomat had not asked her to return to Germany but rather that she stay in Switzerland. She was back in Paris following the armistice and informed me through a letter mailed in the Occupied Zone to one of my mailboxes at 16 rue Gambetta in Toulouse. In a second letter at the beginning of March she said she wanted to have a meeting at the usual place—the Cafe des Deux Magots on the Boulevard Saint-Germain through a simple message left with the cashier twenty-four hours before the meeting. I asked Johanès, who was the only person informed of my trip, to organize a passage of the demarcation line at the Veurdre between Lurcy-Lévis in the Free Zone and Saint-Pierre-le-Moutier in the Occupied Zone. During the night of March 17-18 I crossed the Allier River before the bridge at Veurdre. By 7 a.m., after traveling in a milk truck, I reached the railroad station at Nevers. The crossing was perfectly organized. It was mostly thanks to Master Sergeant Lenoir, who was in command of a squad of republican guardes mobiles checking the line at Lurcy-Lévis.

Early that afternoon I left the message for Françoise at the Deux Magots and I met her on March 17 at 7 p.m. She hadn't changed: still holding on to her pro-German ideas, yet sincerely French and saddened by our fate. She guessed how painful it was for me when we saw a young Luftwaffe lieutenant and a beautiful, if a bit too made up, young Frenchwoman sit at the table next to ours. She clumsily attempted to play down that encounter.

"I can assure you that the Germans are sincere when they want to get closer to France!"

I cut her off and asked what she was doing. Since January 1, 1941 she was working as a secretary and interpreter at the German consulate on the rue Huysmans. She worked for Dr. Posselt. Her friend (I later learned they were married) was a councilor at the German embassy working for Otto Abetz. She was always so discreet that she didn't tell me his name or anything about their affair. Was he informed about her meeting with me or not? She didn't tell me, but what she asked indicated that it could possibly lead to "someone well placed."

"There are in Germany 290 French agents who have been found guilty of espionage," I continued. "In France there are 198 Germans who were sentenced for espionage before 1940 and held in the Free Zone. Why not negotiate an exchange?"

D'Alès interrupted me:

"True, we got a list of 198 names to be let out, but we were never asked about an exchange."

"It's blackmail," said Rivet. "Our agents were arrested before 1940 in Germany. We don't even know how many of them have really disappeared: were they executed, or imprisoned? Their fate is totally secret despite our research. What did you answer Françoise?"

"More or less what you've just said, colonel. Very disappointed and irked by my comments about the hypocritical nature of the request she promised me a list of those Frenchmen arrested before 1940—which in any case will never be produced. To smooth over the bad feelings at the beginning of our meeting Françoise told me about her life in Paris, the people she was meeting, the receptions given by Otto Abetz and by Westrich, the embassy councilor. Little by little the meeting became more relaxed and I found out many things."

First and foremost she discussed the organization and establishment of the RSHA in France. Françoise was convinced that the Nazi intelligence service would replace both the Wehrmacht and the Abwehr before the end of 1941 because of the way it was infiltrating and taking over everywhere. Heydrich was still in charge in Berlin and his direct representative in France was Dr. Thomas, with an office at 57 Boulevard Lannes in Paris. Dr. Knochen was in charge of the six RSHA sections working in France and had his offices at 72 Avenue Foch. The two most dangerous sections were IV and VI. Section IV was the Gestapo headed by Bömelburg, with an office at the *Sûreté Nationale* in the rue des Saussaies, was involved in hunting down the communists; he was in possession of the files of the *Renseignements Généraux*, the *Sûreté Nationale*, as well as the *Police Judiciare* and also defensive counterespionage with Kieffer and Döring. The Abwehr III F (Riele) was taking on more and more of an offensive counterespionage stance, much like the TRs, using all kinds of penetration agents while Abwehr I gathered only military intelligence. Section VI gathered political intelligence; and Nosek at 11 Boulevard Flandrin was in charge and well introduced in all Parisian circles. He was charming, very well educated, and spoke flawless French.

There were RSHA branches being set up in the Occupied Zone as well as the Free Zone, and Françoise mentioned Rouen, Dijon, Bordeaux, and Biarritz, where the SS Kurt Grande was handling the liaison with Spain that confirmed the intelligence provided to us by our W agent Fidalgo since August 1940. The Nazis had three observers at Vichy: Geissler, working for Section IV at 125 Boulevard des Etats-Unis, and Detering as representative of Section VI. Dr. Reiche was reporting directly to Heydrich in Berlin about everything happening in the Free Zone. Françoise was happy to describe the heavy and intricate Nazi organization and she kept on giving me more details.

"Kieffer and Döring pride themselves in having complete control over all attempts at setting up espionage networks. I was able to find out through them about the arrest of a group of patriots, which included Mr. Weil-Curiel, who is thought to be a very old friend of Mr. and Mrs. Otto Abetz, and Section IV is getting ready to set him free."

I asked Françoise the location of her meetings with the two "gentlemen."

"At the office in the consulate, with my boyfriend in the bars and sometimes at the Marquise de Polignac, who has been organizing cocktail parties for the Germans in Paris at the restaurant *Alexis*, owned by the Corsican Pierlovisi in rue Notre-Dame-de-Lorette in Montmartre. The food is good and they don't require ration tickets. There are lots of people you can meet there: artists"—she gave me about ten names— "newsmen, politicians (I even noticed Georges Bonnet there), and naturally the entire SD group: Knochen, Bömelburg, and Nosek, with their friends Doriot, Carbuccia, Carbonne, Spirito, Léandri, Luchaire, and many others. At Nosek's request at the end of October 1940, I set up a trip to New York for Mr. James Freddy MacAvoy of Standard Oil. He traveled through Spain and Portugal. I wonder why the SD encouraged that gentleman to return to the United States when he was perfectly happy in his villa at Cap d'Antibes, where he would meet with Florence Gould, who often crossed between the two zones.* She was getting her *Ausweis* from Klingeberg, the director of the *Deutsche Nachrichten Büro* in France, who in turn obtained them from me."

Françoise went on endlessly about those Frenchmen who favored collaboration with Germany and was very understanding regarding those she considered sincere. Noticing my puzzled look she hesitated and said she also despised the newspapers and those Frenchmen who were shamelessly working for German propaganda, like *Radio-Patrie* with Jean-Hérold Paquis, Pierre-Antoine Cousteau, Algaron, the dailies *Paris-Soir* with Gerber, *Le Petit Parisien* with Claude Jeantet, and above all *Le Matin*, where Richard de Grandmaison was taking 5,000 francs a month to spread the Nazi poison. On occasion she would visit the offices of the Propagandastaffel on the Champs-Elysées. She found out that the Germans had stopped any support for the Breton autonomists while the propaganda effort had been doubled in Alsace, within the Muslim groups and especially in French Morocco. Just before leaving she underlined what she thought was most important.

"You have to trust Germany because she is our best barrier against Communism. You'll see. You must explain to the Marshal that he must make his peace with Hitler and bring back Pierre Laval, who is the only sincere politician and a true statesman. Darlan's doing what he can but has no political stature. The embassy even thinks he gives in too easily, making the Germans suspect that he is just an ambitious man with little character…"

"That's very true," said Rivet. "That being said, Paillole, you shouldn't run the risk of being nabbed in the Occupied Zone. Did you ever think of

---

* Gould was to have problems after the liberation of France because of her relationship with Klingeberg and another German friend named Vogel.

all the things the Germans could find out from you should you get caught and weren't strong enough to resist?"

I was urgently called back to Marseille where I found Challan-Belval and Guiraud deep in conversation with Blémant.

"We have to make a decision about Bardon, sir."

"We've been holding him since March 24," said Blémant, "and can't get anything out of him. Are you sure you can trust your sources?"

For the past three months the travels of this individual from Paris to the Free Zone were being pointed out to us by the observation posts on the demarcation line. Bardon was an aeronautical engineer and an air force reserve officer who was also a friend of Dieudonné Costes, the hero of the 1930 crossing of the Atlantic from Paris to New York. The pro-Nazi opinions displayed by Costes led us to watch him carefully; later, in September 1942, he was to travel to the United States on a mission for the Abwehr. Our Paris stations informed us about his close ties to Pierre Constantini, the head of the pro-German group "La Ligue Française" and who also acted as an Abwehr recruiter. Bardon, who had many friends and acquaintances in the Free Zone, was socially involved with influential people in the aircraft and other industries. He had been seen at the officer's clubs. In December 1940 our W agent Duperré gave us the description of a man he had seen several times in Paris at the Institute for Scientific Research. The man would meet with the head of the air force department of Section I of the Paris Ast, Dr. Heinrich Braun. The description fit Bardon perfectly. At the end of February 1941 the TR section in Marseille had found out that our client was at Istres and Marignane.

"He's extraordinarily bold," said Guiraud. "He's been asking passengers returning from Algiers all kinds of questions! What's even more serious is that he's been trying to recruit in the Hautes-Alpes area a young volunteer of 'Jeunesse et Montagne.'* We told the young man who reported the incident to keep up the connection, but it couldn't last. Bardon found out very quickly that this branch of the youth camps was actually a cover for future air force officers."

I asked Guiraud to give the matter to the BMA to get the *Surevillance du territoire* involved and check out Bardon very closely. We agreed that the arrest would have to take place once he had decided to return to Paris and so it happened in the railroad station at Avignon on March 24.

---

* A cover organization to begin the training of some 10,000 youths to fly gliders and other aircraft.

"He showed us a valid set of papers from the Institute for Scientific Research in Paris," said Blémant, "authorizing him to set up correspondents in the Free Zone for that organization. We searched him completely and he was carrying nothing at all."

So then I asked:

"What about his luggage?"

"We went through it; one bag with some laundry and the traveling kit with toiletries. He's got a package with some old shoes. Do you want to see that? They're in my car."

Blémant went out to get them and all four of us looked again and found nothing.

"We always look at the contents," Guiraud said, "and never what's used to carry them."

This time we took the suitcase apart. It was a shame because it was covered in rather smart-looking black leather. Nothing.

"Go ahead," I told Guiraud, "and don't forget the package that contained the shoes."

I jokingly handed him the hyposulfite detector. He smiled, took the brush, and spread it diagonally on the rough paper laying flat on my desk. Suddenly we can read letters, lines… Guiraud went faster and we read a report with notes along with a rough drawing of the region of Gap-Briançon in a corner of the paper.

"What a bastard!" growled Blémant.

The traitor had revealed the locations of the camps of "Jeunesse et Montagne." He was also giving details about the school in the town of Uriage where Dunoyer de Segonzac was setting up the future officers of the patriotic youth. Finally, he provided intelligence on the maneuvers of the 51st infantry regiment at Larzac and the garrisons at Nîmes and Avignon. Bardon was forced to admit that he was working for the Abwehr. Constantini had recruited him during their meetings with Dieudonné Costes. Rissler, a member of the Institute for Scientific Research, was giving him the Abwehr questionnaires in Paris and provided cover through his organization. He had seen Dr. Heinrich Braun only once and would not see him anymore. I don't know what ever happened to Rissler, who disappeared after Bardon was arrested. The case proved that we had to protect all the new state entities sharing the same ideals as the armistice army that were capable of providing some kind of assistance. General de la Porte du Theil allowed us to take action inside the youth movements *Chantiers de Jeunesse* and *Jeunesse et Montagne*. Police Superintendent Ravaud was the head of the 2nd Bureau of the *Chantiers* and remained in constant contact with the TR (Johanès) and the BMAs.

"My dear old man, it was great of you to put forth my name."

Jacques Lambert had just arrived at Cambronne.

"The MA red tape and the problems with Rollin, with Darlan's cabinet staff, the stupid comments we hear all day about the BMAs—they were all getting to be unbearable to me. I'm really pleased to jump right into things. This GAD business is quite a task. How about going to Auch to ask Schlesser for his advice?"

I agreed. Schlesser was in command of the 2nd Dragoon regiment and welcomed us with great enthusiasm. It was the pleasure of seeing old comrades once again but mostly, I thought, because he relished being at last involved with the clandestine service against the enemy the way he wanted it to be. He thought it justified his choice in betting on Weygand's army after all. Our sometimes passionate and violent conversation, reminiscent of old times, went on in the hotel where we were having dinner.

"Can you help me recruit some people?" asked Lambert.

"If asked for volunteers, you'd get the entire regiment. What is it you need?"

"First of all, a discreet secretary to work in Mr. Perrier's office at Cambronne. After that I'll be looking for a few officers to help with recruitments in the Occupied Zone."

"As secretary, I have the man you need: Master Sergeant Heinrich, a great guy. I'll send him over in a few days. As for the officers I have to think about it."

It was 1 a.m. and by now we were the only ones left in the lounge when suddenly the door opened. An NCO and two German soldiers walked up to us and asked for… rooms for the night! Lambert was laughing and Schlesser gulped down his *armagnac*. I went to wake up the manager who complained but wound up giving the unexpected guests their rooms in a clattering of jackboots through the hallways. The little incident had us all wound up so we went outside to relax. The German truck was parked at the door and it was empty. Lambert lifted the hood, felt his way around the engine block, and then I heard a cracking sound as he must have pulled the electrical wires. I took out my jackknife and bored holes in the tires.

"You bunch of juvenile delinquents," said Schlesser chuckling. "Get out of here! You're making my life more difficult; I bet the Krauts will come over to the 2nd Dragoon regiment to get their truck fixed!"

At Cambronne Lambert and Heinrich, who had just arrived, were going through my special files looking for names of potential recruits for the GADs that hadn't been taken by the TRs.

"This is a starting point. Later we'll recruit on our own and Heinrich will check out the files."

"Fine."

With the help of Schlesser and du Vigier, Lambert was able to recruit volunteer officers who were responsible for a sector of the Occupied Zone: Lejeune, du Passage, Dionne, Hallard, La Chapelle, Derringer, and later Dullin, Beaufort, etc. To recruit faster for the GADs du Vigier asked Major Lecoq of the 3rd Bureau to organize escapes from POW camps in Germany. The BMAs and TRs took part in that work by providing the required documents (ID cards, documentation for civilian workers, German marks, etc.). The Clermont-Ferrand BMA, with a group specialized in such operations, put together 700 packages to help prisoners escape and bring in 130 escapees in six months between May and October 1942. Major Derringer of the GAD with others would be instrumental in the escape of General Henri Giraud from Königstien fortress by preparing his route and hiding places in Alsace. Paris was Lambert's main objective and he sent over there two very intelligent and brave officers, Hallard and Dionne. I made the mistake of allowing them to contact the head of our Paris station 112 *bis*. Martineau was getting impatient to not be able to introduce some very eager patriotic people to a specialized organization. He wrote to me: "We're losing face."

Lambert was cautious not to send his two men into "a void." I gave in and in a few months I was to find out bitterly the disastrous consequences of our mistake. On May 20, 1941, Groussard was secretly trying to reach London with the rather noisy help of Fourcaud. The "Alliance" network that was directly connected to British intelligence was to expedite, among other great feats, the secret departure from France of General Giraud in a submarine on November 7, 1942.

André Poniatowski reached Washington without a hitch with a French passport issued by Marshal Pétain's cabinet. Both of them had the personal approval of Huntziger and perhaps the blessing of Pétain himself.

Presumably Darlan knew nothing of all this; and yet Rollin, the admiral's henchman, bragged that he was tracking Groussard's travels when his rendezvous with a British plane failed several times near Gaulhet. Groussard finally succeeded in mid-June and got to England through Spain and Portugal. The two men's missions were completely uncoordinated.

"The mess goes on," complained d'Alès. "How can we expect to be taken seriously and not be battered by bad luck?"

I felt positive about Poniatowski's mission. He represented an official organization that was really functioning in all areas of intelligence gathering and counterespionage. As an armored division officer he could share with the Americans whom he would initially meet the lessons drawn from the Polish and French campaigns by the French High Command. He was also personally a very distinguished man with an engaging personality and many American officials remembered the important part played by André's father, Prince Poniatowski, in helping build up the U.S. Army Air Corps during the First World War. There could be no doubt as to his loyalty and political independence.

At the War Department he met with chief of staff General George C. Marshall, Undersecretary of State John J. McCloy, and James Dunn of the State Department. He visited the Fort Knox training camp for armored units preparing for duty, gave technical lectures, and was able to convincingly refute some of the lies that other Frenchmen were spreading about their defeated country's behavior. He also got permission to send a permanent delegation of the French High Command to the United States. The War Department requested that either Huntziger or Picquendar countersign the agreement, something neither of them would ever agree to do. Before leaving the United States, the British military attaché asked Poniatowski to travel on directly to London. On June 22, 1941, Operation *Barbarossa*, the German attack on the USSR, was suddenly announced and Poniatowski decided to return to Vichy to report on the first part of his mission and receive new instructions from the High Command. He found Baril ecstatic.

"Now they've really screwed themselves! They didn't want to fight on two fronts, so now they've got three and soon four. I can assure you, Poniatowski, they're finished and we must play our hand very quickly!"

They drafted a report on the excellent work done and Poniatowski began preparing his mission to London in an upbeat mood. However, things didn't look so good since July 15, 1941. Groussard was back from London where he had met Churchill and Maurice Dejean, a former French SR officer at the embassy in Berlin, and who was now de Gaulle's diplomatic advisor.[*] He also met Passy, head of de Gaulle's 2nd Bureau in London and later chief of the BCRA along with several other officials.

---

[*] Dejean would later become ambassador to the USSR.

Rollin, acting on orders from Darlan, arrested Groussard. The police searched his rooms, grabbed some documents and also arrested other so-called "accomplices" while Groussard was under house arrest at Vals-les-Bains in a place called La Châtaigneraie, along with some other well-known political figures.

Neither Huntziger, whom he represented, nor Marshal Pétain, who had "maybe" approved of the mission made any comment. It was a humiliation for the minister of war and a major setback for Groussard's organization as well as major problem for the Free French networks. In his repressive zeal Rollin also arrested Loustanau-Lacau on June 18 and Fourcaud on August 28, 1941. The arrest of Loustanau-Lacau marked the end of an ill-fated attempt to incite the French army in Africa to rise up against Vichy—something our BMAs were involved in, especially the Marseille station. Loustanau was still the wild conspirator of "La Spirale" and his hotheaded disposition led him to try to get the army to revolt in 1938 against the subversive actions of the Communist party. Now his energies were focused against the German occupiers.

Loustanau was no doubt overconfident about the support he thought he had from Marshal Pétain because he'd served under the Marshal in Paris. Since 1940 he had started his own one-man crusade that was well thought of in army circles such as Baril, Rivet, Ronin, and d'Alès. He was very persuasive and had a handful of devotees like Marie-Madeleine Méric, who later married Fourcade. He recruited some agents and sent them off to gather intelligence about the enemy, which he quickly turned over to the British, helping them start up the "Alliance" network.

In January 1941 Major Faye, deputy head of the air force in North Africa in Algiers, joined Loustanau and Beaufre from Weygand's cabinet, followed by others, mostly flyers. These tough men wanted to see action once again.

The fact that Weygand was in Algiers, plus the enthusiasm displayed by Faye and Beaufre, led Loustanau to believe in April 1941 that the French army in Africa could break away from Vichy with British support. He had confided in our friend Colonel Granier, chief of staff of the XVth Military District in Marseille, who was just as impetuous as he was. We were also "involved." The head of the BMA Jonglez issued orders under the name Lambin, a wine merchant, allowing Loustanau to travel to North Africa to set up the operation. The TR service created the necessary false travel documents. At the end of May 1941, Loustanau, Faye, Beaufre, and a few representatives of the three services (army, air force, navy) met in Algiers to prepare a plan of action that had been submitted to British and American representatives. They hoped that Weygand would join once the plan had been set in motion. Alas! One of the officers revealed the entire plot to the police and the *Renseignements Généraux* and everyone in Algiers was quickly informed, including Admiral Abrial, the Governor General appointed by Darlan. Weygand was unable to quash the matter. Loustanau, Faye, and Beaufre were arrested and on October 15, 1941 found guilty and sentenced to two months in prison, and then released. Loustanau was captured once again on July 18, 1942 and sentenced to two years in prison without Marshal Pétain lifting a finger for him. After that Marie-Madeleine Méric took over the "Alliance" network. The Algiers BMA with the help of the brave superintendent of the *Surveillance du Territoire* Achiary was able to have Loustanau escape and avoid revealing the orders issued by the Marseille BMA.

A few weeks after those events the second arrest of Loustanau could uncover our part in the Algiers plot. D'Alès, who was both furious and worried, commented about the arrests.

"Darlan and Rollin are bastards—that's something we know! But the other characters are not so swift and they'll wind up getting us involved!"

It was a clear warning. Would Huntziger and Piequendar leave us in the lurch as well? Du Vigier requested a meeting with both of them at the beginning of August and we anxiously awaited his return.

"Quite a miracle," he told us out of breath. "They both agreed to have Poniatowski go to London. Huntziger even wants him to meet the Marshal before he leaves. "He'll arrange to schedule the meeting."

We were stunned. What was going on? Was it some impulsive reaction of our minister against Darlan? Or a decision by the Marshal's cabinet? We were never to find out

"It's like flying into the fog at night," was Baril's comment.

On August 2, 1941 at 5 p.m. Poniatowski met Marshal Pétain at the Hotel du Parc and that same evening he gave us his verbal report on the meeting.

After a few words of welcome and a handshake, the Marshal discussed the agenda of our meeting

"'So, you've traveled to America. What are they saying about us?'

"The *us* in this context referred to *him*. He had read my report and noticed the part that referred to the attacks against him in the American press. He sounded annoyed and mournful at the same time.

"'But they do know who I am over there; some of them were under my command in 1918; they know me…'

"It became harder for him to express his thoughts. He turned the pages of the report at random.

"'Do you really think the United States will enter the war?'

"I answered that Americans were not in the habit, as businessmen, to commit huge capital investments to build armament plants and manufacture weapons only to help one country even if that country was England.

"'That's strange,' he said. 'The reports coming from Henri Haye* lead us to believe that America is deeply affected by serious economic and social problems. According to what he says, the majority of the country is opposed to U.S. participation in the war. The funds you mention are much higher than what the ambassador tells me. Your numbers of combat aircraft are ten times higher than his. If what you say is true, Henri Haye's attitude is absurd!'

"Then he suddenly switched to a different topic.

"'Why are the Americans so convinced that there are Germans in Dakar?'

"'They get that impression from rumors by Frenchmen in exile and the attitude of some French citizens,' I told him.

"Pétain then returned to the idea that was haunting him.

"'You feel the Americans will enter this war? If that happens, they can't possibly concentrate their troops in Great Britain, which is too small and vulnerable. They must land in North Africa. They have no other choice. If we could know in good time, we could take advantage of that event.'

"I seized upon that opening," said Poniatowski, "to say that it was my main reason for meeting with him.

"'I'll tell General Laure to study that issue with Picquendar.' He then went on to discuss the situation in Syria. He wanted to be sure the Americans understood that he was under an obligation to oppose by force any military action by the British and the Gaullists.

"I gave the Marshal an inconclusive answer. He wasn't listening to me anymore. His mind had wandered away. Was he tired? Was it a clever device to avoid delicate questions? I don't know. Darlan's arrival interrupted the meeting.

"'I'm sorry. I must chair a cabinet meeting. Come back to see me. Get in touch with General Laure.'

---

* Vichy's ambassador to Washington.

"He got up and slowly walked to the door, then turned around and traced his steps back, took my report and slipped it into one of the drawers, which he locked, and said, 'It's safer that way!'"

Poniatowski never saw Pétain again. His trip to England and a second trip to the United States were approved by Huntziger and scheduled for mid-November 1941. On November 12 the minister of war was to die in an airplane crash on his way back from North Africa. The plane crashed in the Gard region and the causes were never clearly established. Was that tragic ending the prelude to the end of the armistice army?

Poniatowski arrived in London at the end of November. He was given a friendly welcome by our allies and met the head of British intelligence, Sir Stewart Menzies, and his deputy, Sir Claude Dansey, and through them the representatives of the War Office. A working plan was drafted within three weeks to be submitted to the French High Command:

1. To allow the study of future joint operations involving the French army three French staff officers were to be sent to the War Office in London. They were to provide all useful information for the reinforcement of the armistice army; the potential of the GAD; their needs in equipment and supplies and the maintenance requirement plan, etc.

2. Permanent connections to be established through U.S. diplomatic pouches transiting through Bern. A first radio transmitter and receiver will be given to Poniatowski for direct contact with London. It was brought from Lisbon to Vichy in the French diplomatic pouch and, starting in December 1941, Major Brantès, the French military attaché to Portugal, was in charge of it.

3. Communications between the SR and counterintelligence increased with the receipt of new codes and radio transmitters.

There was only one disappointment in that mission: for security reasons that were probably exaggerated the British asked that André Poniatowski refrain from meeting anyone besides the persons brought to him by British intelligence—contrary to our instructions and his repeated requests, our envoy was unable to meet with General de Gaulle and his intelligence staff, which was to have very negative repercussions for the future of our relationship with the FFL.

Poniatowski's second mission was to be interrupted, just like the first, by a major event. The day before his departure for Washington the Japanese bombed Pearl Harbor, attacking the U.S. fleet. He was recalled to Vichy on December 10, 1941. On December 11 Germany and Italy declared war on the United States.

The representative of the French High Command had just returned from London when Jean Moulin, de Gaulle's envoy, arrived on a mission to France. He parachuted into the Provence region on January 1, 1942. His mission was to "unite within the Free Zone all those elements that are resisting the enemy and his collaborators." Before meeting with anyone he went to my friend Recordier's and I was told of his arrival. He was to meet many people, but not with us. Why?

Perhaps he was following some awful partisan instructions, but Jean Moulin lost an opportunity to remove the wall of misunderstanding that already separated us from the Gaullists in London. He simply ignored us. And yet at the very moment when the envoy of the Free French went about his mission and tried to reach Henri Frenay, we were able to rid *Combat* (the name of Frenay's resistance group) of one of its unreliable members who could have jeopardized everything. It was just one operation among many others that allowed us to remove and punish traitors who were undermining those patriotic Frenchmen working in secret.

The incident is worth recounting. At Lyon the clandestine counterintelligence station TR 114 kept watch over the local SR station and the resistance groups that it was able to warn of any potential dangers threatening them. Hugon, a talented technician, was in charge of the station. He was austere and demanding as well as abrupt in his ways but his professionalism was unquestionable. Jourdeuil was his deputy and also a very good man. They ran a network of agents (HCs) in the Occupied Zone and counterespionage covering eastern France, Alsace, and Switzerland. The W agents in Belfort were still operating and had found most of their employers at the Ast in Dijon. Dulac (alias Danton), one of our oldest and best technicians, ran a TR 114 substation in Mâcon. Every month it provided us with the *Fahndungsnachweis* (a list of suspects distributed to the German police that allowed us to warn several hundreds patriotic Frenchmen), thanks to a brave woman from Alsace, Madeleine Folzenlogel. She was arrested and deported on May 28, 1942 to a concentration camp in Germany. Jean Dupont, her liaison agent with TR 114, was executed on July 30, 1943.

In November 1941 TR 114 found out that one of the couriers in a resistance group was working for the Ast in Dijon. Our penetration agent

"Y," whom Hugon had placed in 1938 in the Ast Stuttgart, was still working with the same officer handling him since August 1940. It was Hauptmann Hans Binder, alias Alphonse Mercier. The meetings were taking place alternatively in Switzerland or in Dijon, but also in Paris where Mercier used an apartment at the Porte Champerret. Starting in September 1941 the German began coming to Paris more frequently. He had a new apartment near Saint-Augustin. All the travel and frequent stays and the change of residence intrigued "Y." He was able to find out that Mercier decided to move for security reasons, saying the 2nd Bureau had spotted him. He took many precautions to check on a resistance group where Section III F Dijon had successfully planted a V Mann very recently. Every week the man carried the group's mail in the van he used to make deliveries between Lyon and Paris and back.

Generally Mercier would catch up with him inside Paris, always at different locations. He would check out those papers that were of interest and photograph the messages and documents and the van would leave once again. That information was enough for us to alert the Lyon BMA. A rigorous surveillance of the demarcation line was ordered and effected with the help of the gendarmerie. We identified the owner of the van within one month, one Henri Devillers, an employee at the Messageries Hachette. I was amazed and disappointed to find out that Devillers was a courier for *Combat*. There was no way we could let him keep up his criminal games. In agreement with Hugon, who like me didn't think the arrest of Devillers would unravel our W, the TR asked the BMA to urgently ask the *Surveillance du Territoire* to step in. During the first days of January 1942 Devillers was arrested. Superintendent Triffe, head of the *Surveillance du Territoire* in Lyon, was a master at the art of questioning. The man broke down rather quickly and admitted to committing treason. I asked Triffe to inform Henri Frenay immediately and he did, through Henri's very good lady friend, Bertie Albrecht.

"A bad break," commented Cherance, whom I advised in Marseille.

We were both thinking of the risks hanging over the heads of Jean Moulin and Frenay.

The file on the matter was overwhelming and the damage to the *Combat* group was serious. The head of the Lyon BMA, Descours requested that the general in command of the 14th military district sign an order to open an inquest for endangering state external security. The reason deserves to be mentioned.

"A paid agent of an enemy espionage organization, Henri Devillers, gathered and obtained secret information relating to national defense."

The case went to trial very quickly and the traitor was condemned to death by the Lyon military court. I informed d'Alès so that Corvisy would present the request for a pardon to Marshal Pétain. Devillers was executed by firing squad on April 16, 1942 at Fort Monluc in Lyon. Justice took three months from start to finish. Three days later German embassy councilor Rudolph Rahn took an urgent initiative with Pierre Laval, who had returned to power a few days before. We found out what had been said, thanks to Cazin's wiretaps and bugs.

"We were informed of the arrest in Lyon of a good Frenchman [sic] who was of special interest to Ambassador Abetz. He should be freed immediately because he's in danger."

"What's his name?"

"Henri Devillers, Mister President."

"I'll take care of it."

Rivet, whom Laval immediately summoned, could only confirm that the execution had taken place.

"So that's another dirty trick of your BMA. We'll have to do away with them," said Laval, who was seething with rage as he showed Rivet the door.

"Y" saw Mercier once again but made no mention of the Devillers affair. Later on the Abwehr officer would tell his agent confidentially that he had to leave a Paris that "had become meaningless and much too dangerous." [sic]

In the very sincere book by Henri Frenay *La nuit finira* I found out that one of the members of the *Combat* network, Jean-Paul Lien, a railroad worker originally from Alsace and who had moved to then Free Zone, had told Bertie Albrecht just before Devillers' arrest about his contacts within the Abwehr. The circumstances by which Lien had found out about the betrayal, at least the way he described them, were so suspicious that the greenest member of counterespionage would have recognized and demanded a "situation review" that would have unmasked Lien's true personality, since he was already working for the enemy. Lien also managed to penetrate the "Alliance" network. We would have discovered that he was already in our files under a different set of circumstances that should also be explained just to prove the essential role played by the centralization of information in the struggle against espionage and treason.

Starting with the first months of 1941, we began gathering a lot of information regarding the gangster-type methods enemy intelligence was using to penetrate patriotic groups in order to destroy them. Abwehr Section III used some very unscrupulous intermediaries to do their recruitment, either because the Germans didn't want to have to manage and supervise a huge army of informers or because they were just too shady to be involved with and were very well paid and given orders that would bear no discussion: Otto Brandle and Masuy, André Folmer and Jean Jacobs, Henri Lafont and Max Stöcklin and many others. These individuals became even bolder because the Germans in the Occupied Zone covered their depredations. They began venturing into the Free Zone and North Africa. One of Lafont's men was supposed to establish a spy network in Algeria, but he was arrested in March 1941 and executed by firing squad in Algiers a few weeks later.

In Marseille we were given the opportunity to experience how efficient and bold these gangsters working for the Abwehr really were, following the kidnapping in Toulouse by one of Lafont's teams of a Belgian the Germans were looking for. One of our W agents, code named "Angevin," had allowed TR 115 to lure one of the best German intelligence agents into the Free Zone, well known to us but whom we couldn't catch, a Belgian named Jean van de Casteele. He became interested after we fed him some false intelligence about the reestablishment of the 2nd Bureau and the possible recruitment of agents in Marseille.

Blémant came to the Villa Eole several times to keep me posted on the very meager results of the questioning. He finally suggested that we simulate suicide and put an end to that spy's career.

"He's one tough guy, major! He's brave enough to jump out of a window to avoid talking. Believe me, Mr. Perrier, that bastard won't tell us anything we don't already know. If we hand him over to the military courts I know he'll manage to complain to the Krauts. He's a top man!"

I disagreed and turned the matter over to the BMA. The order to prepare the case allowed military judge Ronsin to lock van de Casteele up in Baumettes prison. Ten days later a master sergeant of the gendarmerie and a gendarme took the prisoner to see the judge to start the questioning. Since then we never saw van de Casteele or the (fake) gendarmes again. Blémant was furious and started to let off steam in front of me.

"That's really great! He'll tell the Krauts everything we do. It'll cause a huge scandal and Rollin will blast every one of us!"

"It won't be so simple, Robert. But you're right. It's high time we changed our methods. I'm determined to find better ways to take action more vigorously in the Occupied Zone and at least force the Abwehr gangsters into being more discreet."

Blémant was beaming.

"So we finally get to the point," he said. "Mobster vs. mobster it is. I'll take care of it."

Blémant paid me a visit toward the middle of June. He was mysterious and to the point:

"I found what we need."

"What do you mean?"

"Two tough guys ready to carry out your orders."

"Who are they?"

"Emile Buisson and Abel Danos."

I reacted when I heard the names of those two known bandits who had been living on the margins of society for years

"What can we get out of them? These are low-life mobsters. I'll not be their alibi," I said.

"We've tested these guys out. They were involved in the stick-up of the rue de la Victoire on February 24, when four thieves attacked an armored car in broad daylight, making off with 3.8 million francs, one bank employee killed, and the other seriously wounded. We can't hire choirboys or rich kids from the 16th arrondissement in Paris if we need to be efficient. Le Grand Louis will be with them, and that's a guarantee. Meet with them so you can make up your own mind."

The following day as I was finishing dinner with Blémant in the back room of "L'Ami Fritz" at 11 p.m., Louis Raggio arrived with Buisson and Danos. The first one was about 40 years old, of average height, rather thin, with a swarthy skin color; his eyes were shiny and constantly moving. The other one was a massive type with a heavy head and a savage look on his face; he could not have been more than 28-30 years old. I had a negative impression. Their eyes looked away and I fired some questions at them.

"Robert tells me that you're ready to help us in the Occupied Zone. At what price?"

Louis Raggio answered.

"Tell us what it is we have to do. Then you be the judge as to what they deserve."

Danos appeared to be in another world and Buisson's high-pitched voice confirmed what Grand Louis had said. I had thought about two possibilities before our meeting: if the guys appeared to deserve our trust I would send them to the rue Lauriston where Lafont and his gang had just moved in. Otherwise I would simply test them in a minor case where Raggio would run smaller risks.

Since January 1940 an Ast-Dijon officer named Mercier, the man we were looking for, had moved to the 4th floor of a building at the Porte Champerret in Paris.

Our penetration agent "Y" was keeping us regularly informed of the individual's activities. He was recruiting agents, had a secretary, led a high flying social life, was involved in the black market, and met so many people that if "something" were to happen to him it would be difficult to guess its origin.

"Bring me Mercier's files and the documents that are in the living room."

"Is that all?" asked Raggio, staring at me.

"That's it. I want neither noise nor messy situations. If you succeed I'll consider you for other operations. Careful, because even though Mercier is absent the apartment is still occupied. I shall expect to see you again in one month at the most."

The month went by and I became very impatient. Little Pierre, who was running the Hotel Vichy while Grand Louis was away, had also heard nothing. In the middle of July he called and said: "we're on for tomorrow night." I knew it was where the commando would return and I quickly went to Veudre where Raggio and I had planned our rendezvous. At 2 a.m. sounds outside indicated Grand Louis' arrival. He was alone and carried a large suitcase. We walked silently to my car at Lurcy-Lévis and drove to Vichy.

"It wasn't easy, major. Buisson got nabbed on the train going up where he was arrested by German police. Danos was no longer as confident. I had to shake him up and get everything done on my own. Luckily the fifth floor apartment just above Mercier was free for rental and with the excuse of refurbishing it I sent two painters, Danos and Rocca-Serra. It took us a long time to figure out what was going on downstairs. In the end we succeeded in completing the mission only the night before last. There was a guard in civilian clothes that we tied up without hurting him and I packed everything that could be of interest to you in this suitcase. Danos preferred to stay behind in Paris with Rocca-Serra. I don't think you should count on those two anymore."

I dropped Raggio off at his house. He was exhausted but pleased to make me an excellent cup of coffee, while Pfister, my driver, was ready to take me back to Marseille.

I was in a hurry to examine the contents of the suitcase and start using them. On the back seat of my "Citroën traction avant" I had installed a small table, allowing me to work in the car. We drove off at sunrise, oblivious to the beauty of the landscape. I immediately went to work on the documents.

There was just about everything, invoices, bills, receipts, love letters, filing cards, numbers. I searched frantically for any incriminating documents and for secrets regarding the work of the Abwehr. I was disappointed. Mercier was not the easy-going sloppy person I had imagined.

I kept on looking and by now we were into the Rhône valley under a hot sun. Pfister was silent. When we reached Cambronne around 1 p.m. Giboulot and Challan-Belval were fooling around the courtyard with our guard dog, Nénette. Challan-Belval took the suitcase that I handed to him with a disappointed look on my face. He came back smiling two hours later.

"There's some good stuff in there, Mr. Director!"

He handed me some documents and a few letters in German. One of those letters, which had no letterhead and came from Bordeaux, was in Lien's name. He was also being recommended to the addressee (Mercier no doubt). We immediately indexed Lien's name along with many others we discovered in the suitcase and would remain inoperative inside our files much too long because we had not been told at the end of 1941 what Bertie Albrecht knew.

The Paris police arrested Abel Danos on July 19, 1942. Fearing that he'd have to pay for his crimes, he wrote to Bömelburg offering his services and to denounce us, Blémant, Raggio, Police Superintendent Chenevrier and me, as being the leaders of a vast anti-German organization. Chenevrier barely escaped arrest by the Gestapo and we became friends. One of the reasons he was deported in 1943 was because of the many ways he had helped me. Rollin fired Blémant. In August 1943 in Marseille he got a surprise visit from Nosek that had been arranged by the bosses of the Marseille underworld, namely Carbonne and Spirito. He did not fall for the SD's trap to lure him into the Occupied Zone. Raggio joined the maquis. Devoted and reliable he continued his intelligent and valiant rehabilitation. As for me, I changed my identity and my home address once again. By the end of 1942 Danos joined Henri Lafont at 93 rue Lauriston. He became the French Gestapo's bloodiest executioner and was to die on the guillotine after the war. He even tried to bring up the services he rendered to the cause of France. Buisson went to the gallows on February 28, 1956.

"Well Blémant, what do you say about those mobsters of yours?" I asked.

"They were a bunch of weaklings, major."

15

Initial Clashes

L et's look back for a moment and catch our bearings.

Over one year had passed since the Germans had occupied France and we could clearly see that the public had become disenchanted with Marshal Pétain. Hatred for the enemy occupying the country was increasing. German espionage and propaganda efforts were on the rise under Nazi supervision.

While our defensive net in the Free Zone and in North Africa proved to be efficient—and this was vitally important for the future—what we could accomplish in the Occupied Zone without police support (the *Surveillance du Territoire* was not allowed to take action in the Occupied Zone) and paralyzed by the German presence, remained unsatisfactory. As I have stated previously, you cannot improvise in the field of intelligence and even less in counterespionage. We resorted to attracting into the Free Zone the individuals we considered most dangerous. They were handed over to the military courts or sometimes to the more summary justice of the TR and Blémant. Those we couldn't reach were put into our files; they would pay later on, something that didn't look too promising at the time.

Looking back and reading the published accounts and history of that period have convinced me of the disastrous consequences created by insufficient communications between our services and the initial members of what became the resistance.

I deplore the frequent absence of a unified initiative for protection and security. Initiatives such as those of Loustanau-Lacan and Fourcand in contacting d'Alès in 1940 or of Frenay when meeting with me in January 1941, could have led to a common initiative and should have been encouraged rather than derided and sarcastically dismissed by London. In 1941 there were very few well-structured groups of patriots. They had little experience but a lot of enthusiasm and their example spread very quickly. The dangers they faced were proportionate to their aggressive recruiting and other efforts. The most important ones were in the greatest danger.

The scum on the Abwehr and RSHA payrolls were infiltrating these resistance movements. We were able to stop scores of every kind of traitor that we brought to justice in the Free Zone.

These were (alphabetically): Adt, Allard, Balloli, Police Superintendent Bachelet, Bellune, Henri Blanche, Bier, Borkeloh, etc., including Raoul Lafauvie, Jacques Max, Pinon, or Ramsteter had infiltrated the British intelligence service to be able to reach England. Most of the time they were provocateurs endangering our networks and the most active friendly networks:

> — Jacobs, Richir's deputy, was introduced by Reile into the Gaullist networks of Saint-Jacques (Maurice Duclos) and Rémy. We arrested Jacob in 1942;
> — Devillers, a traitor on the payroll of the Ast in Dijon to destroy *Combat*. We executed him by firing squad in 1942;
> — Morel (handled by Scheide, Reile's deputy), who destroyed our Paris station 112 *bis* and could only be brought to justice after the liberation of France;
> — Delobel, the destroyer of the British networks and "La Voix du Nord," was handled by the Paris and Brussels Ast. We arrested him in 1942.

The "Alliance" network that the BMA covered as best they could in the Free Zone was unable to withstand the repeated attacks of the Dijon Ast with the help of the traitor Lien. The "Interallié" network of Armand and La Chatte would fall victim to Hugo Bleicher of the Ast of Saint-Germain-en-Laye. We were be powerless to protect it despite the recommendations of Simoneau and the arrest of Van de Casteele in Marseille. The summary of German intelligence that was produced by my service in 1944 concluded that Bleicher probably used the pseudonym of Van de Casteele to travel to Marseille on a mission and escaped under amazing circumstances.

I explained all this to Rivet. We had reasons to be satisfied but also to fear the increasing instances of treason and the weakness of our services. I also pointed out the growing hesitation displayed by the police regarding repression and the suspicious attitude of the police force towards the army in general, especially the BMAs:

"Colonel, are we really being backed up by our minister?"

"I can't explain it," said Rivet. "Huntziger is mixing apples and oranges. Whenever I meet him he's distant and cold, yet I know he really approves of what we're doing. We found out during Weygand and Gasser's visit to Vichy in June and July 1941 that Huntziger was moving bravely towards a stronger position against the attacks by Darlan on our services and the BMAs 'that were preventing his policies, from being enacted.'"

Until his death on November 12, 1941, Huntziger was to be our strongest supporter. Darlan had signed a French-German protocol of agreement under pressure from Hitler when they met on May 11, 1941.

In exchange for some humiliating peace promises Darlan allowed the enemy to use the bases at Bizerte to supply the Afrika Korps and Dakar for its submarines. Weygand, with Huntziger's assistance, succeeded in part in stopping these moves at the last moment, but not some dangerous concessions, such as the purchase of trucks and food supplies for the German army in Libya, the transfer of heavy artillery pieces, and the opening of German consulates in Casablanca and Algiers, destined to be espionage and propaganda centers. What Françoise had predicted took place: Darlan in discussion with the Führer was forced to agree and risk what he referred to as "the last chance for a rapprochement with Germany." Darlan confirmed in his actions what he told the cabinet on May 14, 1941: "If we favor British policies France will be crushed... I have chosen and will not deviate from that choice through offers of a ship full of grain or oil." During a cabinet meeting on July 15 Darlan made a statement that was violently critical of the BMA and concluded with a request that they be urgently purged of certain elements along with the army officer corps.

Huntziger protested and Weygand reacted so vigorously that his words were being repeated outside the cabinet and around Vichy: "I refuse to be involved in what you call a purge. There are enough degenerate individuals inside the government to handle that kind of police work similar to the decadent period of the Roman Empire and heap daily insults on America and England."

"I'm really afraid," said Rivet, "that Weygand, whom Hitler was ready to have assassinated, will not be able to resist the admiral for any length of time, as he is subjected to German pressure. In any case, it's open war between us and we are henceforth considered the 'bête noire' of the regime!"

This was very true. On July 16 Darlan authorized Rollin to search Colonel Ronin's office. Our friend had miraculously succeeded in evacuating his radio transmitter but he was placed under arrest in spite of the vigorous protests of General Bergeret, minister of the air force. Huntziger was indignant, and ordered the BMA to oppose the searches with force if necessary. By using a lot of new men Darlan went about setting up a new police force and intelligence services devoted to him. To lead the new intelligence service (named *Centres d'Information Gouvernementaux*—CIG) Darlan appointed, quite surprisingly, General Roux, who had just been freed from a POW camp in Germany. He was the former head of the 2nd Bureau (SR-SCR) who had welcomed me into the service at 2 *bis* Avenue de Tourville in 1935. Roux was much too friendly with Rivet and told him about Darlan's aggressive attitude. Soon Roux left that position but for a few weeks he tried to slow down the reforms that were being enacted by the government, using all his expertise at exercising bureaucratic obstruction, which he had mastered perfectly over the years.

"It's the engine without 'Roux,'" said d'Alès ironically.

Admiral Dupré, Darlan's chief of staff, replaced Roux and was determined to take action. His first decision was to tell everyone how indignant he felt that the BMA had not yet been purged. His second decision was to travel to Marseille to investigate "that covert counterespionage that has been creating so many problems" [*sic*]. The third decision was to dissolve the visible parts of the anti-German military iceberg, starting with the BMA's. We shall revisit this further ahead.

On July 18, 1941 Pierre Pucheu was appointed secretary of state at the ministry of the interior. A graduate of the Ecole Normale Supérieure, he had a brilliant mind and huge ambitions. He had worked in private industry since 1926 and had innumerable contacts in big business as well as an uncommon craving for power. He was to prove this very quickly in his new position, where he made many decisions affecting the police forces, including the gendarmerie, so they would be concentrated under his control. He created special brigades to hunt down resistance fighters more efficiently, bringing the urban police forces under the central control of the government, setting up special anti-Jewish and anti-Masonic police, and special police for economic crimes. He created the special section of the court of appeals and the state courts to pass judgment without the right of appeal through an expeditious procedure and under German control of all cases referred to as "terrorists."

The men chosen to head the *Sûreté Nationale* were appointed on the basis of their devotion rather than their administrative or police competence. They were invariably infatuated with themselves and lusting for power. At the grass roots the police were torn between the directives they was being given and their deeply patriotic feelings, and seemed unable to understand what was happening. Many officials remained favorable to us and were ready to continue the fight against the enemy within, but we had to admit that we were completely "short circuited." The government was against us, including the ministry of the interior and the police force. Any defensive action we took brought protests and dressing-downs. On the other hand, when our men were caught by the enemy inside the Occupied Zone they were used to denounce our opposition to the policy of collaboration and requesting sanctions against us.

Rollin told d'Alès that he wanted to meet with me. Why not? He tried to welcome me as amiably as possible with a rather forced smile.

"I wouldn't want you to run into problems, major. I must ask the *Surveillance du Territoire* to act more objectively and stop tolerating any networks that are in contact with London. How can Admiral Darlan respond to German demands if he's constantly reminded by the occupation authorities of hostile acts whose existence in the Free Zone is practically official?"

"Mr. Director, you know that the Germans are displaying quite a lot of hostility. The *Surveillance du Territoire* can't react to espionage and treason in favor of the enemy as to the help our patriots give to the Allies. I really don't think it's within its jurisdiction at all."

Rollin was nervous and again tried to smile.

"I'm sure you have no doubts about my anti-Nazi feelings. Right now we must save what we can and avoid terrible reprisals. Groussard and Loustanau, just like Frenay and Ronin of your group, are very clever. Their actions won't amount to much, but they place us in an impossible situation with the Germans, who are aware of everything. No matter how one feels about these men, we're compelled to step in. It's the very policy of the government that's being challenged, and it's for the government to decide its own policy without any interference from the military."

That was a clear allusion to the BMA. The tone was becoming adversarial and I answered somewhat obnoxiously.

"As far as I'm concerned we're still at war and the counterespionage function is part of our duties."

"Not for very long, major."

The meeting was over.

The following month a decree restored all police power to the ministry of the interior, making official a de facto situation that had been created by Darlan's coming to power. It looked as though the police were not bothering André Poniatowski—perhaps it didn't know the real motive for his trip to the United States and the one we were preparing to England. Were the police turning a blind eye? Or were they waiting to gather more evidence of the "army conspiracy" before making a move?

We were asking ourselves these questions when several incidents made our position much worse. On August 8, 1941 Captain Gilbert Turck parachuted from a British plane near Mont Luçon and was wounded upon landing; at the same time Jacques de Guélis parachuted as part of the SOE, specializing in sabotage. Two peasants warned the *Surveillance du Territoire* through the gendarmerie and Rollin got involved! Turck says he was working with one of our men, Major Brochu in charge of covert sabotage. Brochu was also located in Marseille and had an office near Cambronne for security reasons.

Turck was an officer of the corps of engineers, mobilized into the Special Services in 1939. Rivet and Brochu had sent him to England on July 3, 1940, along with Major Humphrier and three other British SOE officers transferred to our service at the beginning of the war. After intensive training the British sent him back to France to consolidate our communications and prepare various sabotage operations in the Occupied Zone.

Warned by Brochu, Rivet was negotiating with the police. However, Rollin was very bitter, asking Rivet to take responsibility and write a report. On August 11, 1941 Rivet wrote that Turck could only return to France by pretending to accept a mission for the British. He closed the report by asking for Turck's release. Rollin pretended to believe Rivet's story and freed our officer. Turck went to work and the police did not relax their surveillance. On June 11, 1942 Vichy handed Turck's file to the Germans, along with a few others. Turck was then arrested in Paris on July 7, 1942 and deported to Dora, then to Bergen concentration camp in 1943.

The traditional atmosphere of trust that had existed between the *Surveillance du Territoire* and the *Services Spéciaux* was seriously shaken.

I told Blémant the story and he nodded, knowing that he would soon leave the police force.

"Once I go, be wary of Léonard and Piani. They're good guys but are quite spineless and will execute Vichy's orders even against you!"

For the moment Leonard was absent. He was in charge of the Marseille police brigade. On the evening of August 28 Blémant came to Cambronne, out of breath.

"Major, just as I told you, they arrested a man at the Gare Saint-Charles. They had been following him for several days. The worst of it is that at the same time they also arrested Lieutenant Roger Warin of the BMA. I've told Jonglez.[*]

A few minutes later the head of the BMA arrived just as upset as Blémant.

"I was able to talk to d'Alès by phone. He told me to tell you that tomorrow he's sending over his deputy, Lieutenant Colonel Bonoteaux. I saw Warin and I scolded him! He's a wonderful young man but he behaves like a child. The other man under arrest is Fourcaud. He's been wandering around the area for some time. Warin has known him for about one year, when he worked for Groussard. They hold meetings without taking any precautions."

A very bad break!

With previous cases still making waves we now had a problem because Warin, Fourcaud, and Groussard could also implicate d'Alès, perhaps even Poniatowski, the High Command, and Huntziger. Rollin had to be chuckling.

"He certainly has no intention of playing the case down," said Bonoteaux, d'Alès's deputy. "He just sent in Superintendent Linas, his best detective, to lead the investigation. D'Alès asks that you use your influence on Linas to try and keep that idiot Warin and the BMA out of it. We really should find out if the *Surveillance du Territoire* has found out about Poniatowski's mission while they were undergoing questioning and searches following Groussard's arrest. That was the origin of the case ending with the arrest of Fourcaud. We're counting on you to do damage control."

---

[*] Head of the BMA in Marseille.

That afternoon I went to police headquarters and saw Blémant coming out of an office where I could hear some heavy discussions going on.

"They're disgusting," he said. "Thank God you're here! I'm leaving. It makes me sick!"

I let Linas know I would like to speak to him. I knew that intelligent and brilliant policeman since 1935, and we handled many counterespionage cases together. His clear and precise investigations were used as models at the time and with Osvald there was no better team to unravel an espionage case, even the most complicated ones. He often asked for my help in his police investigations. I had not seen him since June 1940, but I knew and regretted the way he applied all the orders he received to the letter. I could very well imagine that with his policeman's experience he was playing cat and mouse with the often naïve skullduggery of the British and Gaullist networks he was after. He immediately understood the reason for my visit.

"Major, I'm very pleased to see you."

Was he remembering our old friendship or did he realize how much harm he could inflict on us and on me in particular? Or was my visit a reminder that the military was still master of its own house (for the moment at least). As soon as I asked, "What's going on?" he immediately answered:

"Unpleasant business with one of your officers."

"What has he done?"

"I don't know. He'll tell you himself. As for Fourcaud, he's not defending himself too well. He lives in a fantasy world. He doesn't want to tell us why he went to see Admiral de Laborde in Toulon. He also says he's on a mission for de Gaulle to meet top people! But he won't say whom! You understand that he's not making my work any easier!"

"Why is he under arrest?"

"It's because of the Groussard Case."

I stopped asking questions. There was no "accidental" meeting at the Gare Saint-Charles even though Fourcaud was not hiding his true identity. He was being very openly "covert"!

I entered the room where he was being questioned. He was standing, very pale with his arms crossed over his chest. He looked rather confused and I understood that he'd probably not been well treated since the day before. His dignified attitude was in contrast with that of some of the policemen. I liked Fourcaud and felt sorry for him so I asked Linas for permission to speak to him.

"Sir, you claim to be on an important mission from General de Gaulle to an important French official. Can you tell me who that is? I will inform that person."

I was afraid that he might name Huntziger in front of Linas. But that was not the case. Fourcaud was reassured by the fact that the room was now quiet and the police detectives who were questioning him relentlessly were gone. He answered courteously.

"I'm not authorized to tell you."

I could see that to defend himself he was using the many contacts at the highest levels he had in Vichy. He intimated that neither Linas nor myself were competent to receive such information, which was a state secret.

I didn't insist. The case could not be handled any further in Marseille. After all, I could put the BMA out of the loop and be assured that Fourcaud was treated well and didn't say anything that could compromise us. I asked him:

"Do you wish to go to Vichy? No doubt you'll find there the person you're looking for."

"Yes, is that what you want?" asked Linas. Fourcaud nodded. It was over and I shook hands with him. Before going into the other office where Lieutenant Warin was being questioned the policeman stopped.

"What should we do with that officer?" he asked me.

"He belongs to the army. Just write in your report that you handed him over to the military authorities that were requesting him. We'll see if anyone dares question *that*."

That solution was a way out, acceptable to Linas. Warin sheepishly gave me some contradictory explanations. He was too smart not to understand that he placed us in an extremely delicate situation.

But I liked his reactions and his love of action. His training for clandestine operations and counterespionage could be useful, even though it was still rudimentary. We would consider him again after the storm had passed. I asked Jonglez to take his officer back and to put him to "pasture" for a few weeks and informed Bonoteaux, who was traveling back to reassure d'Alès and Rivet. Toward the middle of September Osvald returned from a mission to Vichy. He told me about the depressing atmosphere in that fake capital.

"My dear director, I have to tell you that I saw Linas and Fourcaud at a café acting like two buddies. Can you picture that?"

"Quite frankly no, but it's just as well."

In December I saw Warin again. He could no longer remain at the BMA nor in Marseille; some kind of punishment was required. I offered him an important job in the Paris TR and he asked to think about it. A few weeks later I learned he had left for London; I was to see him again in Algiers in August 1943. He told me about all the problems he had with the Gaullists because of his stay at the BMA and his glowing praise for our counterespionage organization. All this didn't prevent him from gaining de Gaulle's trust and, once France was liberated, being appointed head of the *Surveillance du Territoire*.

"You've awakened our calling!" as Luizet was to tell me once he'd been promoted to prefect of police in Paris in August 1944.

The year 1941 was ending. In a year and a half we multiplied our manpower by ten: 500 new agents or HCs, who were unpaid, worked at 7 TR stations in France and North Africa that were now operational. Our main thrust at penetration was directed at enemy efforts to gather information and take action in the Mediterranean and in Africa.

Besides the positive operations by two TR stations in Algiers and Rabat, the stations in France were also successful. Two operations were notably fruitful. One was due to the vigilance of the BMAs; the other because of the experience of our W from Lille, Li 159, and his case officer Rigaud, head of station TR 112 in Limoges. On April 12, 1941 Captain Soutiras of the Toulouse BMA was questioning POWs who had been sent home for health reasons. It was a routine task that we took seriously because in every convoy we would run into some men faking illness and carrying out Abwehr missions. They were to report back to the armistice commissions that paid them for their services. Most of the time the POWs who had agreed to play the role of informers to be returned home would inform the M.A. officer in charge. The spy was often discovered during questioning; for example, the POW in excellent health who visibly did not warrant repatriation. This time Soutiras noticed a very strong-looking legionnaire. After some lengthy questioning he found out about his German origin, so without a doubt he'd been slipped into the lot with a special mission.

His name was Drach and after some time he acknowledged the fact. He had been captured in May 1940 with Giraud's army. The camp commandant had pointed him out to Lieutenant Wieland of the Stuttgart Ast. Since he was considered a traitor in Germany he could only remedy his desperate case by working for the Abwehr. For six months he'd been trained as a spy, learning Morse code, cryptography, using secret ink, radio transmitters, and receivers. He was given the identity of another legionnaire from a neutral country who had died. He was part of a group of six other French POWs who had been trained in the same manner to be sent to the ports of North Africa and Spanish Morocco to check on maritime traffic and the straits of Gibraltar. Besides a very good salary they were also promised a 20,000-franc bonus for every British or American ship they identified along with its load. Wieland added that if they betrayed Germany they would be executed sooner or later anywhere they might try to hide. Drach was faced with a terrible dilemma, between the threat from Wieland and the offer by Soutiras.

"I'll make sure you don't get court martialed, which would mean the death penalty if you return to your legionnaire's faith and serve France."

Drach also had a wife and 12-year-old girl in Sidi-Bel-Abbès. Soutiras used that pawn as well.

"Very well, captain, I'll tell you everything."

He extracted from his knapsack Flaubert's *Madame Bovary* and indicated the pages he was to use to encipher his messages. He also showed his rubber stamps filled with special ink and revealing liquid.

"Once I reach Algiers I have to check the help wanted section in *L'Echo d'Alger*. As soon as I see the ad, "Looking for chauffeur/delivery man between 50 and 55 years of age," I must go to the Aletti Hotel and pick up a suitcase left with the concierge in my name. The suitcase will contain a radio transmitter-receiver. After that I was to move to Spanish Morocco."

"Who are your six companions?"

Drach hesitated at first, then gave us their names. At that point, Soutiras informed d'Hoffelize, the TR 117 head in Toulouse. Drach now felt reassured and quickly switched sides. He was intelligent and clever enough to grasp the importance of his mission and all the advantages it could provide him and his family.

D'Hoffelize confirmed the positive impression of Soutiras. After checking our files I agreed to using Drach as a W on a trial basis. The only caveat was to get the Abwehr to agree to posting its agent temporarily in a French port, like Oran. I wanted his initial activities to be carefully monitored. If everything went well we would proceed to set him up in Spanish Morocco. D'Hoffelize handled Drach's initiation himself. The other six V Männer were identified: two were in North Africa, two others in Marseille, and the last two in Tarbes. One after the other they were arrested, sentenced, and shot. Their radio equipment became part of Simonin's stock.

The Paris Ast was trying to set up observers in the southeastern part of the Free Zone and North Africa. Rumpe, who had been transferred to Bordeaux, had informed the Paris section Ih (specialized in intelligence on ground troops) of the high value of its agent Hengen (Li 159). Since 1937 Hengen's production had been very interesting. His reports since July 1940 indicated that he was as devoted and insightful as ever. In August Rumpe had given him a precision Leica camera. He would return from his missions in the Free Zone with interesting information and microphotos of original documents regarding the military organization of the Limoges sub-district. Rigaud of TR 112 was providing the documents with the approval of the division's command. Since the same documents were being provided officially to the armistice control commission in Wiesbaden, the Abwehr was simply getting its information ahead of time and faster than the commission. Rumpe's successor saw Hengen as not simply a top V Mann but a potential recruiter as well.

In April 1941 Hengen asked him to identify an informer in southeastern France to gather intelligence on Toulon and the port traffic. Fulfilling Ast Paris' request was like child's play. They were so satisfied that by July 1941 they asked that Hengen recruit agents for North Africa. The objective was to keep close watch on General Weygand's army, its morale, its training, and the weapons it used. The informers would have to be excellent radio technicians because they would all have transmitters. An NCO from the Marseille garrison, Richez, who had been part of the 43rd Infantry Regiment in Lille where Rigaud had met him, filled the Abwehr description perfectly. He was described as being slated for transfer to Algeria. Richez accepted enthusiastically and was given a radio. Under our supervision he handled the first radio transmission for the Abwehr Marseille and Paris in August 1941 before he left for North Africa.

A second technician recruited in Algiers in September 1941 would also receive a radio transmitter and was part of our effort to disinform German intelligence up to August 15, 1944.

We were able to hit the enemy very hard: 4,500 persons suspected of being in contact with Axis intelligence had been placed on file. As of December 31, 1941, some 316 spies had been arrested and handed over to military courts, 16 had been executed by firing squad, about 10 had "disappeared," and 50 had been sent to Algeria to escape German controls. Lieutenant Colonel von Sibelius head of the Bordeaux Ast was transferred. His fiascos in the Free Zone and Algeria were unacceptable, he was in disfavor, and his private life was dissolute.

On April 22, 1941 Mrs. Marcelle Touzin, his mistress, was arrested in Toulouse along with her mother, Mrs. Boutheau. They were managing a very hospitable hotel located 3 rue du Moulin-Bayard. It was a drop-off point and mailbox for agents of the Ast Bordeaux. TR station 117 in Toulouse was in charge of checking the place. A few months after Sibelius, Rumpe was destined to a similar fate. In spite of their many years of experience both of them had behaved like amateurs in the Toulouse matter. The "seven-year itch" enhanced by the excitement of victory and the full-bodied Bordeaux wines didn't spare them.

In August 1940, in Paris, Marcelle Touzin, a very pretty 30-year-old woman who was getting a divorce, had met Sibelius' secretary, whose lover managed the restaurant *Le Bec Fin*. The Germans, in need of bilingual personnel, hired the young woman, who originally came from Alsace. She went to Bordeaux where she charmed the Ast head, who used her as his secretary and assistant. He had not succeeded in taking her away from her Parisian boyfriend, whom she saw every weekend. The secretary invited Marcelle Touzin to visit Bordeaux, where she met a graying fifty-year-old man of medium height and slightly overweight: it was Sibelius. He introduced himself as a journalist and spoke very well. He had money and was somewhat melancholy because his secretary was attached to her boyfriend. Marcelle became his mistress but Sibelius was not to be caught playing the jilted lover role twice. He invited Marcelle to come and stay in Bordeaux.

"That's impossible," said the beautiful woman. "I can't leave my mother alone in Paris."

"No problem," he said. "Bring her here with you."

Mrs. Boutheau, the mother, was a very wily middle-aged woman and came to stay with her daughter. There's a good chance of being bored living in a provincial town after being used to the capital. Sibelius was well aware of this and introduced the mother to another fifty-something bon vivant type. The rich food from the Aquitaine region had turned the man into a happy type and his red face was framed between two oversized ears, which were those of a professional, since they belonged to Major Rumpe, deputy director of the Bordeaux Ast. The foursome didn't go unnoticed in the black market restaurants. Neron, our W and "friend" of Rampe, had noticed him and had pointed him out to us in October 1940. While the Abwehr was having a good time and enjoying good food we were on a jockey-type diet and the heads of my TR stations didn't feel like laughing at all.

"I have the two couples in my sights," said d'Hoffelize.

He'd asked Gilbert Getten, one of his best HCs, to keep watch over them. You can be in love and still think about your business. But you can't go on for weeks of partying collecting your payroll, pilfer secret funds, and fail to produce anything.

The two buddies were thinking how they could use their new girl-friends, who in turn were no doubt planning their future because it's not an everyday occurrence to find such nice men with so much money—the master race!

"What if you found a cushy job in a big city in the Free Zone and I paid your expenses? What would you say?" Sibelius whispered to the two women. Mrs. Boutheau, who had previously lived in princely luxury, thanks to her charms as well as her daughter's, at the Hotel Bristol in Paris, felt an irresistible attraction for the hotel business.

"Why not?" asked Sibelius, who was also thinking about an observation post in the Free Zone, a discreet relay for agents and a mailbox.

Marcelle was not that shy either and soon she'd be bringing back intelligence from the surrounding area. The two women took off for Toulouse with 200,000 francs.

"Should anyone ask where you got that money you'll say you won the lottery," said Rumpe. He made out an *Ausweis* for travel to the Pavillon de Flore in Paris to get their loot. Sibelius' valet, a North African named Max Ali, took the luggage to the railroad station where French counterin-telligence officer Getten (in Bordeaux) was observing the scene.

In Toulouse a realtor quickly produced a wonderful deal: the "Biarritz Hotel." Without raising any objections Mrs. Boutheau paid the 300,000 francs in two installments, plus another 100,000 francs to refurbish the place. The inauguration at Christmas 1940 took place by candlelight with champagne flowing. The customers began arriving. The letters were also coming in, like those from Ouadani, a sergeant under arrest in Blida whom Rumpe had recruited. His arrest was kept secret in order to avoid com-promising that precious source of information for the TR.

Marcelle Touzin traveled around. She liked the little game that brought in easy money. We followed her to Montauban, Avignon, and Marseille. In Toulon a secretary at the arsenal kept her informed on ship move-ments to Dakar. At Châteauroux and Francazal some flyers gave her de-tails on the camouflage of air force materiel. This expert young girl was becoming dangerous. We couldn't control everything at the hotel. We also noticed several visits by a man named Lien again! We couldn't find his address and were never to see him again until after the war when he was executed.

On April 15, 1941 we gave the Toulouse BMA the necessary information for the *Surveillance du Territoire* to go after the two treacherous women. A few days later they were arrested with six accomplices and a number of Sibelius' agents were identified and filed in the Occupied Zone.

Our successes were not always so pleasant. From May 14-27, 1941, we had the satisfaction of tearing down the espionage network of Major Helmut-Hasse-Heyn, who was under orders from the Paris Ast to set up a post on the Mediterranean coast. We arrested twenty-six agents, twelve of them Germans, and seized eight radio transmitters—a windfall! Hasse-Heyn was himself arrested and sent to Oran where he had been sentenced to death. A lightning intervention by Otto Abetz, who threatened to shoot nineteen hostages as reprisals, forced us to back down. On April 8, 1942 the major was handed back to German authorities.

In June 1942 there was another disappointment. Subjected to the same kind of threat we were powerless to prevent the return of Jacobs (alias Meunier), the deputy of Folmer (alias Richir). We succeeded in luring him into the Free Zone in December 1941 and obtained a death sentence from the military court at Montpellier. The two buddies succeeded in infiltrating the Gaullist network of Saint-Jacques (Duclos) and the Belgian network of General Genotte. Their boss, Reile of Abwehr III F, could pride himself, thanks to them, in having arrested between October 9-30, 1941 some 962 persons!

The enemy was not sparing us at all. In October 1941 part of our Belgian network was destroyed, its leader Dehenin and eight of his men were arrested. They fell victim to a provocateur, the same one no doubt who sold the Genotte network. These arrests caused that of Ansot in Lille and harmed our efforts in Belgium. A tragedy took place on November 15, 1941 when Martineau, the head of our TR 112 *bis* station, was arrested in Paris at the Café le Triomphe on the Champs-Elysées. Two GAD officers, Dionne and Hallard, who were with him but still unknown to the Germans, were also arrested and then deported to concentration camps. Rigaud had returned from Paris a few days before. He had met Martineau and brought back many reports.

The activity of 112 *bis* was enormous and very scattered, a lot of counterespionage intelligence but also operational information for Rémy, Duclos, the air force SR at Limoges, etc. Rigaud and Martineau were both unaware that one of Riele's agents had penetrated their network. Sergeant Morel of the air force had been recruited by 112 *bis* to research information on the air force and provide help for Ronin's service. He was a traitor already in contact with the Paris Ast and had been meeting with Riele's very efficient colleague, Scheide, since the beginning of October 1941 in a room of the Grand Hotel. Rigaud barely avoided arrest

Martineau resisted the rather decent questioning by the GFP and the Abwehr for a very long time. Since he was being held in complete secrecy his closest collaborators knew nothing about his arrest until the beginning of December. Because of his confession the consequences were immediately very bad. Later, once Martineau was condemned to death on August 29, 1942, he agreed to work for the enemy to save his own life; scores of arrests were attributed to him. But he made the inexcusable mistake of not trying to alert us about the awful situation he was in.

In August 1943 the SD arrested him for the second time. The Germans themselves were skeptical about the loyalty of double agent Martineau and since they could not make up their minds they decided to deport him to Dora concentration camp. The statements of those who were to suffer because of him, the discovery of German archives, the often contradictory questioning of Abwehr and SD offices, added up to many troubling facts on Martineau's attitude in 1942 and 1943 that on June 15, 1950 he went on trial at the Paris military court. One newspaper reporter said it was "the Hardy case of the 2nd Bureau but tried in secret." Just like Hardy he was acquitted without the whole truth being divulged. A magnificent soldier, resistance fighter, and Machiavellian double agent, or simply a miserable victim of the secret war?

The court had issued its judgment

The month of November 1941 that saw so many mutilations of my service was to be fateful to the armistice army. The SR also went through a series of mishaps. D'Autrevaux (alias Amblard) and Froment of the SR station in Paris appeared to have fallen victims to a double agent. Their network had been under attack. Desserée, one of Ronin's excellent informers, was arrested in Paris and was executed by firing squad in 1942. On November 17, 1941, Mathilde Carré (The Cat), who was liaison for Simoneau (deputy to Colonel du Crest de Villeneuve head of the clandestine SR station in Vichy) with the Allied network of Roman Czerniawski (Armand), was arrested in Paris with her boss. Hugo Bleicher of the Saint-Germain Ast was responsible for the case and sixty-six other people were arrested after the capture of Armand's files in his apartment in Montmartre.

On November 12, 1941, Huntziger died in a plane crash and Darlan temporarily became minister of war.

On November 20, 1941, Weygand was suddenly ordered back from North Africa. The Germans had demanded it. Admiral Darlan also wanted it and Marshal Pétain agreed. Weygand refused any kind of reward and lived for a time in Grasse, then in Cannes before being arrested with his entire family by the SD on November 22, 1942, on the road to Gueret and thence to be incarcerated in Germany. General Juin, whom Pétain had requested be liberated from a POW camp, was appointed head of the French army in North Africa. Juin didn't enjoy the power, the prestige or the strong personality of his predecessor. He was, however, a realistic and intelligent military leader, very well liked by the troops under his command. On December 20, 1941, Juin met with Göring in Berlin to examine the possibility of supplying Rommel's Africa Korps through Tunisia and how to defend the French protectorate in Tunisia in case of an Allied invasion attempt.

"Your General Juin is clever and resourceful as a negotiator. At the German embassy they say he made no promises and that he would be as problematic as Weygand for Germany."

Françoise was telling me this when I met her in Toulouse, where she was visiting with her father for New Year's 1942.

"Be cautious. Berlin has sent precise instructions to Paris to step up the fight against terrorism. The Führer's convinced that the Wehrmacht isn't tough enough. On December 7, 1941, he decided that the Wehrmacht would no longer be solely in charge of repression. That's very serious. Any case that is not concluded in France or Belgium within eight days— and by concluded I mean by firing squad—will be handled by the RSHA. Those under arrest will be secretly sent to Germany with no information given as to their fate. They must disappear in 'Night and Fog.'* Hitler's answer to terrorism is terror itself."

Françoise was worried and suffered because of her ambiguous position and what she referred to as the "misunderstandings between the French and the Germans."

"As you can see, everything's grown worse since the Soviets are at war. There have never been such levels of violence on both sides."

I know where she was leading the conversation. She wanted to attribute all the ills to the communists and echoed Goebbels' propaganda. I asked her what would be the likely reaction of the Wehrmacht.

---

* *Nacht und Nebel.*

"There won't be any other than the strict compliance with the Führer's orders. I know of no German officer capable of having any other attitude. Whether they are Nazis or anti-Nazis, they remain disciplined and very proud of the military successes of the Reich."

Françoise was very accurate in her assessment. On February 2, 1942, Admiral Canaris signed—under the OKW letterhead—the order to the Wehrmacht for the application of the sinister "Night and Fog" decree. It stated that "the only persons who will appear before military courts in occupied territories are civilians whose sentences will be issued within eight days and carry the death penalty. The others will be handed over to the RSHA and transferred secretly to Germany." The head of the Abwehr concluded that terrible order with a revealing statement:

"It's the only way the Führer can hope to intimidate those in the occupied territories." Much has been written about Admiral Canaris' attitude towards Nazism. If he sincerely feared the consequences of Hitler's policies he never took any steps to counter them effectively. One thing is certain: he served the Führer loyally up to the moment he was no longer trusted by him.

At the end of 1941 and the beginning of 1942 the Nazi party took another decisive step toward absolute power while the Wehrmacht progressively abandoned its traditional prerogatives. Through the increasing intrusion of the RSHA in the occupied countries, the repression took a turn for the worse and adopted the cruelty that had been the trademark of Nazism for so many years. We must regretfully conclude that Canaris will remain associated to that crime against humanity.

16

North Africa and the Secret War

"They're through, I tell you!"

At bridge, Baril picked up the last set of cards of the grand slam he just made against Rivet and me. We were in the small apartment of the head of the 2nd Bureau as we attempted to figure out the situation during the first few days of February 1942.

"They're finished," repeated our host, and he painted a picture according to the information provided by Perruche:

"Between June 1941 to January 1942, in six months, one million dead or missing, plus the wounded, the sick, and the frostbitten feet! That's three million of the elite! You understand what I mean: the best they have! Plus materiel lost or abandoned and that 12th Bavarian Cavalry that let 7,000 horses die in the Ukraine! Well," he chuckled, "if on April 19, 1941, two months before the Germans attacked his countrymen, the Soviet military attaché had believed Perruche and me the whole thing would be in the bag!"

I don't know what the famous Red Orchestra—which the Abwehr was in the process of liquidating in Brussels—could have passed on to Moscow before *Barbarossa*. Clearly, our SR hadn't stopped warning the Soviet embassy in Vichy since January 1941. The move to the East of twenty divisions, four of them armored; the German High Command document spelling out the Red Army's order of battle, obtained by one of our agents; the occupation of Bulgaria on March 1, 1941, and in April the German attacks on Yugoslavia and Greece revealed by reliable sources as steps in Hitler's vast "Drang nach Osten"* program. Finally, the massive quantity of interceptions and decryptions revealing in May 1941 that the offensive was about to begin.

"We must conclude that Nazi propaganda was as effective on the Russians as it was on us in putting them to sleep until the very last moment and forcing them to withstand such defeats before they were able to react. Read this," said Baril, showing me the conclusions of his report to Picquendar and for the government. Bob Schow also got a copy.

At the start of 1941 we could still believe that the war could end in Germany's favor. In 1942, of the three outcomes that could end the war, an Axis victory, a compromise peace, an Anglo-American victory, the first can be resolutely considered impossible. If Germany cannot break Soviet resistance during the summer of 1942 and reach the oil reserves of the Caucasus there is no question that the Axis will have irretrievably lost the war...

"Paillole, do you realize what conclusions the various parties will draw from these facts?" asked Rivet.

I kept silent as I waited for the comments.

"Well, these are the conclusions: we'll all be fired! Du Vigier is trying to go to Algeria where General Juin is asking for him.** Baril and I expected the axe to fall; others would follow d'Alès, Bonoteaux, Perruche...

"There was no way we could follow through on the British requests transmitted by Poniatowski. The poor man was battered by questions from London and tried unsuccessfully to corner Picquendar in the hallway! Everyone was turning the other way! Rather than a stiffening of positions or the reversal that could be inferred in reading Baril's reports they were studying the offers of a separate peace the Führer is making to get rid of us by giving up Alsace and Lorraine one more time. Hitler had gone completely crazy. In spite of his Russian fiascos he asked his general

---

* "Push to the East."

** Du Vigier was transferred in February 1942 to Mascara, where he set up one of the first armored units in North Africa.

staff to prepare for an attack on Turkey. His generals are showing signs of disarray! The Allies are not yet ready to take advantage of the situation as in the first major reversals suffered by the Wehrmacht. It's too bad because some people get used to losses just as they get used to pain. They overcome them! Without being able to exploit them quickly the Allies are running the risk of a longer war.

"It was a risk for us as well," Baril concluded. "There was no further hope for the army in France. The best possibility would be an Allied invasion before the end of the year to open a second front. I don't think that's possible in France. But I do see it happening in North Africa. What Pétain said to Poniatowski seems logical. I kept on telling Bob Schow and Admiral Leahy. Since they want me out, I'll get myself a command in Algeria ready for action."*

It was the end of the armistice army project. Once the army had been decapitated and had no contact with top Allied military commanders, no general plan, it would be up to the individual regional commanders to take whatever positive initiatives they could. It could only seek to save its honor, but how could it do that?

"We must at all costs keep and develop the GADs," said du Vigier, just before leaving for Algeria. Verneau, the new army deputy commander, agreed and General Frère was ready to command that secret army.

It was now impossible not to turn towards Africa. I was determined to increase our presence and our men as I seriously considered moving our main services to Algiers.

"Go back there," said d'Alès, "but move quickly. I can tell that the days of the BMAs are numbered. You'll have to find something else to replace them and me."

"Something else?" I asked, tensing up and looking at d'Alès.

"Yes, old man. It's useless to avoid facing reality. The admiral has decided to get rid of us for months. Look on top of that armoire."

I could see a shoebox.

"There are about 150 letters or notes inside that box coming from the minister's cabinet, from Rollin, from the minister of foreign affairs, and from the Armistice delegation," he said. "Those are 150 instances where we're reprimanded; where I'm requested to find x, y, or z and have them freed from detention; where they protest the arrest of Axis spies; where we're threatened if we tolerate pro-Allied propaganda in the army;

---

* Baril was transferred two months later to lead a regiment in Algeria.

where I'm asked to punish the BMA head in Toulouse—the excellent Devaux—because he was late in transmitting to a military justice proceeding against a Gaullist network. So I grabbed those 150 letters, put them in a box and sat on them. I know they want my head and I know they'll get it. Make haste in North Africa because when you come back you'll have to replace me."

"Replace you? You must be joking. And what about the TR?"

"Put someone in charge and keep an eye on it."

"Oh yes, Paillole, I know you can get an officer of your choice for TR. Rivet promised one."

"But colonel, are you being serious? If the BMAs are dissolved it's not in order to replace them by the same thing with a different name."

"First of all, this is not an immediate thing. You must also understand that most of the defensive organization represented by the M.A. service will have to survive no matter what. You're the most qualified man to find solutions. Rivet agrees with that assessment."

"What? Both of you discussed this without speaking to me?"

"We had to, he's just as threatened as I am. Obviously we'll hold out as much as we can and the MA Service will operate until the last possible moment. When you return from Algiers you'll give me your conclusions and how you see the future. You'll also give me a name to head the TRs. I hope to still be here and you can change your command in Marseille."

I felt desperate. Ever since November 1941 I was tracking with the dreadful agony of the armistice army. Some said it was like a bad dream. The armistice army was full of good will and readiness for sacrifice. One had to consider the unusual concentration of bad elements within and without that sapped its energy and its potential for success. It was indeed the scapegoat of a defeatist regime. The MA organization was under attack and mortally wounded. The sudden realization that I would have to face a crushing fate alone at a time of such complete uncertainty was too heavy for me. D'Alès saw my weakness and grabbed me by the shoulders.

"Come on, old man, there's no other solution."

In the seaplane that once again was taking me to Algiers I had some time to think. A beautiful young woman was the only other passenger. I heard her name called in Marseille: Mrs. Faye. I introduced myself as Mr. Perrier and we traveled in silence. She was absorbed in a book and I had my notes and thoughts. I had often taken that trip since July 1940 but this time I understood its importance and the extreme seriousness of the situation.

The scenario of an Allied initiative in North Africa was the most realistic. During the long flight—the seaplane took four hours to cross the Mediterranean—I attempted to define my problem.

First the enemy: in December 1940 the German High Command, fearing the potential revolt of the French colonial empire once Weygand had been appointed to Algiers, drafted a plan for such a contingency. It was called Operation *Attila* and it included the occupation of the Free Zone.

In January 1941 some of our W agents and Friedmann in particular learned from Section III of Ast Paris that German intelligence was in regular contact with important Arab political figures. The Grand Mufti of Jerusalem, Amin al Husseini, as well as the Prime Minister of Iraq, Rachid el Gailani, had long been refugees in Germany and used an organization for propaganda and intelligence (OMI) that was financed by the Nazi Reich. It covered an area from Casablanca to Tunis, and from Cairo to Damascus. The Sultan of Morocco was personally informing the Grand Mufti of events in his country. The German consulates in Tangier and Tetuan, where the Abwehr used a very active pseudodiplomat named Krüger, were additional links for German intelligence. When Hitler was informed of these results at the end of January 1941 he expressed his satisfaction to Canaris.

On November 22, 1940, the Axis had very cleverly published a manifesto in favor of the independence of the Arab peoples. The Grand Mufti was the champion of that struggle and a heavy propaganda campaign orchestrated by Abwehr II and the SD was aimed at the Arabs. Hundreds of thousands of leaflets were distributed in North Africa within the Muslim regiments and we had noticed mounting desertions. The Arab broadcasters of Berlin radio, Yonnes El Bakri and Takiedine El Hillali, were preaching revolt and had been involved in the troubles that hampered the British in Iraq in 1941, endangering communications between India and Egypt.

The Abwehr adapted its organization to this kind of activity. The Amt-Ausland-Abwehr set up within Section Ih West SR group specializing in North Africa and the Middle East. Major Franz Seubert (pseudonym Angelo) was in charge, using the Grand Mufti's network with offices at Abwehr headquarters in Berlin. Muslim émigrés in Italy, Germany, and the occupied countries, as well as the POWs from North Africa, were being actively recruited.

Nazi infiltration of North Africa was growing. In early 1941 German "liaison officers" were sent to Algeria and Tunisia in the Italian armistice commissions. The German armistice commission replaced the Italians in Morocco. Under the command of Major Hoffman some expert Abwehr officers arrived in Casablanca: Major Christmann, Navy Lieutenant Perault-Frappart. Navy Captain Gibhardt, the man who had recruited Aubert from the Hamburg Ast, replaced the latter in June 1941. With the opening of consulates in Algiers and Casablanca, by the end of 1941, the German organization was complete. There were diplomats such as Avers, who engaged in aggressive intrigues and propaganda in the French and Moroccan populations. The Abwehr also had informers and radio stations located beyond our control in Spanish Morocco. The German consul general in Tangier, Wiedmann, was in charge of propaganda, sabotage, and intelligence in French Morocco. His questionnaires were very similar to those used by the Abwehr.

We were faced with a massive effort that could surely hamper or even compromise Allied action in Africa. Since my services were unable to operate effectively in Spain and Spanish Morocco we had to place a sufficient number of W agents to fight falsehood with truth. Morocco was therefore at the center of the Abwehr's worries; it faced TR 120, the clandestine counterintelligence station (with Breitel, Doudot, Abtery, and Guillaume, who had left Marseille), as well as the BMAs with many young officers who later were to be of great value to my service. They were a positive influence on the *Surveillance du Territoire*. Unfortunately Superintendent Dubois, whom I had met in Lille and whom Blémant didn't like, was not like Achiary (in Algiers). Dubois could be easily influenced and was indecisive, his attitude toward German initiatives was weak and he showed no any leniency toward patriotic Frenchmen.

The Italian armistice commissions (*Commissione Italiana d'Armistizio*— CIA) in Algeria were kept under strict surveillance, their radio and telephone communication were tapped and their officers were sometimes "protected" in strange ways. Admiral Boselli, head of the CIA in Algiers, and his deputy experienced it one summer evening in 1941. They were suddenly attacked by strangers swinging blackjacks on the beachfront and were only saved by the slow arrival of two policemen on patrol. Weygand asked Navarre to investigate with the ST, but it only led to more "protective" measures and recommended that the Italians not leave their offices. It was in effect a form of house arrest.

Espionage was still being severely opposed. The Algiers BMA noticed large sums of money being spent by a French service secretary at the Algiers armistice commission. The wiretaps uncovered the man's relationship with German commander Schmidt, the "liaison officer" to the CIA. Achiary arrested him moments before going to a rendezvous. Two secret documents signed by Weygand for the instructions of reservists and their mobilization were found on him. An accomplice with a radio transmitter and receiver provided by Schmidt was also arrested. One month later both traitors were executed.

Counterintelligence was in good hands in Tunisia as well, where Captain Fontès, formerly of the SR in Lille, took over the clandestine counterintelligence station TR 121 as of June 1941. Despite reinforcements from France, we had too few specialists in North Africa. As soon as I reached Algiers Chrétien pointed this out to me. I sent him new officers, like Allemand, whom I found efficient at the Clermont Ferrand BMA. He was to handle the archives that were safely hidden in the family factory of Jacques Chevallier in Algiers. Chevallier was drafted into my service in 1943 and later became mayor of Algiers and secretary of state for war in the cabinet of Pierre Mendès-France in 1954. In 1944 he was representing my service in Washington.

That evening I had dinner at Achiary's house and resumed the conversation we had in Marseille in September 1941. At the time he had told me in confidence about the initiative he'd taken with some friends to get back into the war in North Africa. I had also told him about the army's plans after the armistice and we agreed to remain in contact for that resistance action. This time I could only tell him about our disappointments in France. The main reason for my trip was to prepare our services in North Africa for a possible allied landing and to set up the central counterintelligence services in Algiers.

"This is what we're hoping for. We're in contact with Robert Murphy and his vice consuls. Jacques Lemaigre-Dubreuil is handling the negotiations with the Americans. Henri d'Astier de la Vigerie is in charge of the British and the Gaullists. You must know him since he was in the reserves in your unit. We're in contact with the army through Colonel Jousse, the Chantiers de Jeunesse with van Haeck, the academics through Capitant, the foreign service with Saint Hardouin, and our movement is growing."

"What about Chrétien?"

"We don't wish to bother him; we know the delicate situation he's in. It would be wrong for us to draw him in prematurely. Naturally when it becomes necessary we'll bring him in."

"What do the Americans think of your initiatives?"

"They're helping us and are very encouraging. They are giving us money and radio equipment. We give them the information they need. We're friends: Boyd is a veteran of the first World War and a widower of a French woman, Rounds was a pilot in the Lafayette Escadrille, King and Knox were officers in the French Foreign Legion, and Knight is a former student at the Sorbonne. They're not professional diplomats, except for Murphy. Their main mission is to create good will and quite frankly they've succeeded."

"Can you think of someone to lead operations if we get back into the war here?"

Achiary's answer proved he was aware of the trends in North Africa.

"The incidents at Mers-el-Kébir, Dakar, and Syria are still resented by the army. This means excluding any Gaullist for the moment. What we need is a great soldier who can win over the army, the Europeans here, and the local population."

"Weygand?"

"He'd be the ideal and the Americans sounded him out in his retirement at Grasse. Murphy indicated we shouldn't count on him: he's too old at 75 and will take no initiative without the Marshal's approval."

"Juin?"

"He was freed by the Germans and recently met with Göring, which doesn't look good to many of us."

"Noguès?"

"He has too many political enemies and like Weygand won't move without the Marshal's approval."

"So who?"

We all looked at each other, puzzled. The solution could come from the outside perhaps. Someone said Giraud. I had already heard the name of that great soldier inside the 3rd Bureau of High Command. Colonel du Vigier ordered Commander Lecoq to organize prisoner breakouts in Germany. General Mast, who had been freed from Koenigstein, provided the blueprints of the fortress and useful information about the surrounding area

The next day I reported to General Juin at the Villa des Oliviers near Algiers. Captain Dorange, whom I had met in Morocco before the war, introduced me. The new commander in chief was direct and informal. He quickly understood the purpose of my mission.

"Nothing of what was going on before me will change. You can count on my support."

He spoke simply and sincerely. Juin rose and walked me to the door then stopped and with his good hand grabbed my arm.

"I trust all my officers but tell Chrétien to see me personally anytime there's a delicate issue to settle and be sure to tell him to keep me informed about any Allied plans."

I spent a few hours in Tunis where Fontès informed me about possibilities in Italy and Libya. He was experiencing severe problems with the Residence. Admiral Estéva was not too anxious to punish Axis propaganda and espionage. His reputation was that of a simple man caught up in the policy of collaboration.

"He's the eunuch type," said Niel, the head of the Tunis SR, always sarcastic and irreverent, and asked to sit in on my final conversation with the head of TR 121 so that he could avoid "my territory being tampered with." He continued: "The military is just as castrated as he is. There's a nonentity running things here: Colonel Christian du Jonchay of the air force, Estevas's chief of staff. He's even more of a collaborator than Laval himself! He doesn't stop playing dirty tricks on us. A few days ago one of our groups was attempting to sabotage an Italian oil tanker in the harbor of La Goulette. Our frogmen got caught. You'd think they'd try to hush the matter up. On the contrary, we found out that du Jonchay apologized to the Italian armistice commission head and promised to have the guilty men punished."

"And the MA office didn't step in, colonel?"

"He's shaking! The result is that the network* that was informing us regarding the Afrika Korps and also the British intervention forces in Malta has been decapitated! Had de Lattre stayed here things would have been very different!"**

Very quickly Fontès confirmed the negative reaction at the Residence.

"Despite Weygand, the German army is being supplied through Tunisia. Crates are arriving in Bizerte without being checked. They're being shipped to Libya in French trucks that were requisitioned."

"That's collaboration," thundered Niel. "It's disgusting!"

I flew to Casablanca in an overloaded dual engine Goeland aircraft. We went over the Roman ruins of Volubilis and the mosques of Fez. In the distance the djebel Ayachi was covered with snow and stood out for a

---

* The Mounier group used the services of Muslims like Naïri Saïd.

** After a stay of five months in Tunisia, General de Lattre de Tassigny had been recalled to France and assigned to Montpellier in January 1942.

moment in the horizon. Every time I went to Morocco I had a feeling of grandeur and balance. The beauty and variety of the Maghreb all appeared concentrated in this land. I appreciated the charm of the ancient cities protected by Lyautey from the disorder and depredations of colonization.

Breitel the head of TR 120 was in close personal contact with Colonel Eddy, representing American intelligence, who was posted in Tangier.

"He's quite a happy character! He has huge funds and we work hand in hand. We both "manipulate" our penetration agents into the Tangier and Tetuan Abwehr where Colonel Recke has just arrived. He gives me the stories the Allies want to feed the Krauts and I tell him what I know about the Germans."

I congratulated Breitel even though that disinformation effort should have been directed and coordinated at a higher level. There more than anywhere else I could feel our weakness and the absence of contacts with the British. As in Algeria and Tunisia wiretaps and intercepts were working perfectly well around the clock. A microphone hidden in a chandelier in an office on the second floor of 226 Boulevard de la Gare in Casablanca allowed Captain Parisot to listen in on the conversations of the German consul general in his office. A similar feat let us listen in on the meeting at the Jamaï Palace in Fez between the German and Italian armistice commissions in Casablanca, Fedala, Meknès, and Marrakech. TR 120 was spying on Abwehr personnel in Casablanca in the matter of secret arms caches. This was how we uncovered the spy Boris Loevchine, a lieutenant of Russian origin in the 1st Foreign Cavalry Regiment. The German consul general was told about his arrest in Rabat on April 15, 1942. He was freed under the threat of reprisals. Back in service with the Abwehr after a few weeks' training in Paris his mission was to organize agents infiltrating via Perpignan and Barcelona into England and North Africa.

Another spy, named John Dollar, who came from the Baltic but was originally Swedish, managed to get hired as a tennis instructor by the French Residence in Rabat at the beginning of 1941. The information he obtained from his students, most of them officers and functionaries, was relayed to the Abwehr in Tetuan ordinarily through the German consulate general in Casablanca. Our technicians were eavesdropping on conversations between Dollar, the consul, or his aides. He was arrested and confessed because of our knowledge of certain details of his activity: the sums of money the Abwehr had given him. He was incarcerated in Rabat and freed ten days later because of German pressure. To top things off, the steamer *Maréchal Lyautey* took him back to France where he recovered from his adventures before going to Madrid to work for German intelligence once more. We owed this irritating outcome to the director of Moroccan *Sûreté*, who told the German consul in Casablanca:

"The police had to arrest Mr. Dollar. If Germany wants him extradited we won't oppose the move."

I was never able to discover whether the French official did this on his own initiative or not.

Before I left North Africa I met Chrétien in Algiers. The morale of the armistice army was our main concern in the face of a potential Allied landing. The overwhelming majority of the army was anti-German. But it was also true that the army was still under the shock of Mers-el-Kébir, Dakar, and Syria. In the mess halls, the officer's clubs, and at headquarters I could hear the Gaullists and the British being blamed.

"It won't be much fun," said Chrétien, "if the Allies land before we've had a chance to placate those resentments and if somehow the Marshal can't give the green light to resume the fight against the Germans."

The truth was that most people still trusted the French head of state, Marshal Pétain. The Mediterranean sun somehow smoothed over some of the more painful aspects of the policy of collaboration even though they were so obvious as in Tunisia where supplies going to Rommel's army did not go unnoticed. In France the hand-to-hand battle with enemy intelligence and its French auxiliaries was such that not a single French family was spared the harshness of that clash and its consequences. Hatred of the German occupiers overshadowed any other consideration.

Before boarding the plane I found it necessary to tell Chrétien, whose direction and steadfastness I liked, about pessimistic rumors concerning the end of the BMAs. He wasn't surprised. Perhaps Rivet and d'Alès had also informed him of their plans, because as he shook my hand he said:

"If the bosses must leave, I hope you'll grab the joystick!"

17

The End of the BMAs

I couldn't stop thinking about the upheaval in the service that Rivet and d'Alès were predicting, the possible increase of my duties and my replacement as the head of the TRs. I had tried to imagine what could happen if for any reason I was to disappear. No doubt some of my old colleagues who knew the ropes, like Bonnefous, Guiraud, or Hugon, could fill in quickly. I had discussed the possibility with Guiraud, whose good judgment, technical know-how and high moral standards I liked. He wasn't game and felt his background didn't fit the job. He was also afraid to deal with problems on a national level. Hugon felt the same way. Furthermore, I felt that to take such specialized officers away from their tasks in the current circumstances was a mistake. The very focused TR work was producing good results, but I knew how fragile it was and the importance of human relationships in personal contact work. Bonnefous was handling the MA issues rather easily and was not involved in TR work. Also, I knew I would need him in an expanded mission predicated on the liberation of France and the official reestablishment of our services. He would be assigned to other missions, not just as my deputy.

I looked within the neighboring SR for a specialist with a knack for counterespionage—someone like a younger Mangès, whose transfer wouldn't jeopardize effective operational research. There was also the problem that my replacement shouldn't have a rank that could create delicate seniority or superiority issues. Inside our service, in fact, specialty and expertise come before rank. Mangès and Johanès proved it at TR 113 in Clermont-Ferrand. But still we had to avoid embarrassing situations that could get out of hand when authority had to be used directly, which would have to be the case between the future TR head and myself. All these caveats seriously limited the scope of our search. I told d'Alès as much when I reported on my mission to North Africa.

"I think we have your man! Captain Lafont, alias Verneuil, who just returned from Central Europe with Lieutenant Colonel de Villeneuve. I don't think there are any openings at a high level right now inside the SR."

I had met Lafont several times in Paris and Metz. We were friendly and beneath his somewhat ordinary appearance, his common sense, and humor he revealed a keen intellect and good judgment. He had been in the service for some twenty years, not because he'd found a niche but because specialists of his type were exceptional. It goes to the credit of their commanding officers to discover them and hold on to them. Working with Doudot in Metz many times, he had shown interest in counterespionage. He knew Germany and its intelligence services as well as I did.

"You couldn't make a better choice," said Rivet. "Lafont is a remarkable SR officer and an excellent comrade in arms. I hope you can get him."

"Since his return from Budapest I don't think he has a specific assignment."

"That's what you think. But that's not what his commanding officer Lieutenant Colonel de Villeneuve thinks. I'll talk to him and hope he'll understand the importance of the mission we're offering his man."

Back at Cambronne a few days later, while I was assessing the multiple bad breaks we were going through from all sides some, good news finally came over the phone.

"You'll get Verneuil in two to three weeks, just give him time to swing around. It wasn't that simple," said d'Alès, "and I suggest you write a very nice letter to de Villeneuve if you don't want him to become your permanent enemy."

Ever since my return from North Africa bad news kept pouring in from Paris and the Occupied Zone. The arrests of Dionne and Hallard, and most of all that of Martineau, had disastrous consequences. After Pierre Besson, a captain in the Paris fire department; after Dimitri de Zubalof, Fabienne Courtaud, Odette Andrieu, Mrs. Darboy, at the end of March 1942 there were the arrests of Germaine Winisdorfer, Gérar-Dubot's sister-in-law and then Gérar-Dubot himself. The disappearance of that HC deprived us of an important agent. Besides his innumerable contacts as an important news writer, his knowledge of all intelligence functions gave him very important status in the service. Had we expected too much from him? Had we also tapped him too many times because of his accommodating personality? Dehenin, Ansot, Rigaud, Martineau, and I had all understood his strong personality and used and abused his experience.

I could see the void his absence created in Paris and thought my dream of making him head of our Paris station once France had been liberated could very well fade away. Deported to Cologne in Germany, Gérar-Dubot, after being roughly treated as a prisoner, did in fact return and finally took over the job I had always thought should be his.

I also expected other consequences from the sad Martineau case. I always assumed that the enemy can immediately know anything one man knows as soon as he's been arrested. It's a rule too often neglected and of late Rivet reminded me about it in rather strong language. After a general warning to the TR and SR I took a number of steps. We closed TR 112 in Limoges. All of its personnel and archives were transferred to Clermont-Ferrand. Rigaud, the head of TR 112, was by now "burned" in France and he left for Tunis after passing his duties over to TR 113 and Johanès. Anything even remotely connected to 112 *bis* was viewed with extreme suspicion and we had to act as though the enemy had succeeded in penetrating deep into that station. Finally, I decided to take advantage of Verneuil's arrival to move command post Cambronne, since Martineau had visited the Villa Eole.

Our troubles began to increase in Belgium and northern France after the arrests of Dehenin and Ansot. A single case would have multiple and extremely serious ramifications, affecting not only the forbidden zone in the Nord, but Paris and the entire Occupied Zone as well, due, unfortunately, to overlapping covert activities! No one, us included, could properly channel and maintain the necessary discipline of such strong spontaneous patriotic fervor.

Since December 1940 two Englishmen living in the Nord using French pseudonyms had organized intelligence and escape networks that for the most part wound up in Marseille with Captain Garrow...and TR 115! They were quite successful because of their accent and reputation (being from "the Intelligence Service"), which delighted their recruits and those of Major Möhring, head of Section III of the Brussels Ast. It was child's play for him to infiltrate all kinds of double agents within those organizations.

The more active of the two British agents and perhaps the leader of the team was Richard Godfrey, a tall blond 40-year-old man. Using the name Joseph Deram he lived with his mistress in Lille and for some contacts he would use the pseudonym Harold Cole.

In December 1941, Möhring felt the fruit was ripe enough to be picked. Godfrey was arrested and with the help of Scheide—Reile's deputy at Section III F of the Paris Ast—who came from Paris expressly where the British networks had many contacts, they quickly turned the British agent, using his codes and radio transmitters. From then on he continued his work as Delobel under the control of Ast Brussels and the Gestapo. There were multiple arrests as well as interceptions of parachuted goods and people instigated by the Abwehr. In March 1942 the Ws of TR 113 and 113 *bis* figured out Delobel's criminal role. One of them sighted him in a nondescript Citroën that we knew from its license plates belonged to the SD of the Avenue Foch.

Garder and Johanès were working to get the traitor to travel into the Free Zone. With the excuse of setting up an escape network to Switzerland one of our agents got him to come to Lyon where the *Surveillance du Territoire* arrested him on June 1942. Unfortunately Delobel had succeeded in placing Möhring's agents within resistance networks he controlled. One of them infiltrated the resistance network, *La Voix du Nord*.

He was someone we actually knew already but failed to recognize immediately, thereby allowing him to do enormous damage. René Besson was a former detective on the police force in Longwy. He was already one of Riele's agents before the war whom we had uncovered in August 1938 because of his frequent trips to Germany. A search of his office revealed that secret documents, such as memos from the ministry of the interior, arrest warrants for espionage and other sensitive papers, all had a central crease in them. To stuff them in his pocket Besson reduced them in size, a telling detail that forced him to confess. He was lucky to have gone to trial before the death penalty had been instituted. Riele freed him from Clairvaux prison in June 1940 and he went back to work for the Abwehr, where he reported to Delobel. He would be tried again in 1952 when he was discovered holding a job in an explosives plant under the name Debraye after a routine check into the poor quality deliveries to the ministry of national defense, his favorite target.

Besson was executed by firing squad in March 1955. The Delobel-Besson team was responsible for five hundred arrests and deportations and fifty persons killed.

More bad news hit us again. For about one year every two to three months TR was shipping to England via Spain a number of sapphires, stopwatches, and other Swiss made precision devices. Our allies needed those highly valuable and expensive items for the navy and air force. In March 1942 Lieutenant Liebert of the Dijon Ast found out about those shipments and seized about twenty crates at the French border with Switzerland. That route was permanently compromised and the damage was very serious. Our revenge was to slip to the Swiss police the identity of the three Germans who had originated the denunciations of that traffic to the Dijon Ast. They were arrested at the German-Swiss border by Swiss authorities and incarcerated in Bern until the end of the war.

We retaliated by arresting Guy de Voisin, the husband of Corinne Lucharie (the daughter of the collaborationist editor Jean Luchaine of the Paris daily *Nouveaux Temps*). De Voisin was trafficking in gold coins with the Germans and the police were able to seize four million francs worth. This distracted us from counterespionage but not for long. All these events were used by Darlan to accuse the BMAs. At meetings at the Hotel Majestic in Vichy, Pucheu kept on complaining about the negative effect of the 2nd Bureau and its members, who will all be "hunted down without pity." And yet not so long ago Pucheu had met with Henri Frenay in an attempt to entice him with the help of Rollin and his wife.

"These are the contradictions of a rudderless government," was Rivet's comment.

Rivet also had to explain why on the road between Marseille and La Ciotat there was the badly burnt body of a known collaborator. Then on March 23, 1942, General Picquendar summoned the boss.

"It's quite simple," Rivet recounted later. "This time it's over. The BMAs are being shut down. D'Alès and I were fired and Darlan didn't dare tell me face to face. It appears that despite his repeated orders we didn't 'purge' ourselves. There are new incidents coming in every day in the Free Zone and the Occupied Zone. I have to go back to Picquendar to discuss the closing down of the service."

On March 25 Rivet went back to see the chief of staff, rather disgusted by the situation.

Then a sudden change. Rivet was asked to stay in Vichy! D'Alès was to take over his new command in Limoges on August 1, 1942. The BMAs were to continue functioning until a new less visible structure was found. However, Perruche and Baril were asked to leave as soon as possible.

"Baril's memos have infuriated the government," said Picquendar. "Gathering information about Germany is a hostile act that cannot be tolerated. It's bound to spark untold reprisals."

"The new event is that Laval will soon return to power. It's the end of all the dreams of the 'crown prince,' who is smart enough to let other people do the dirty work of liquidating us officially and meanwhile leave just as many problems for his rival to solve!"

So we had a reprieve until Laval's return as head of the government on April 18, 1942. The new secretary of state for war was General Bridoux, who had been my equestrian instructor at Saint-Cyr. What I remembered most about him was his brutality, his gold studded horsewhip, and his bowlegs. Along with becoming vice president of the Council of Ministers, and minister of foreign affairs, Laval also took over the ministry of the interior. René Bousquet became the general secretary for the police.

Admiral Darlan, now reduced to commander of the armed forces, was very bitter about losing power and prestige. Two of his assistants took advantage of the situation, "silently and without waving the flag," as Rivet said.

Admiral Battet was the head of Darlan's military cabinet and General Revers was chief of staff. Quietly at first, and later on more decisively, they both acted to prevent any more of their boss' mistakes as well as the complete disappearance of our services which they used to give the admiral a clearer picture of the war situation. Strange as it may sound the military services that had suffered because of the admiral were now used by him against Laval. He talked about his purge and how he was going to pursue it according to a plan obviously conforming to Franco-German policies.

During the whole month of May 1942 Darlan, along with Battet and Revers, had to withstand the assaults of Laval, now prodded by Otto Abetz and Geissler who had just discovered the wiretaps that TR 113 had placed inside his office. I quickly read through the transcripts that Cazin d'Honincthun gave me:

— Geissler was furious with Bousquet when he discovered he was being recorded. He demanded punishment of those guilty.

— Rudolph Rahn, German ambassador working with Abetz, to Rochat, head of the foreign affairs cabinet: "...here's a list of 2nd Bureau officers who are involved in current espionage cases..."

— Abetz to Laval: "...hostile acts against us must stop. Your services are acting as if the Führer had made the mistake of restoring its sovereignty to France..."

On June 3 Laval summoned Rivet. D'Alès and I were waiting for him when he returned, pale and exhausted:

"There was no real clash, simply a discussion at cross-purposes. The Germans are saying that, although officially terminated, our secret services have kept their structure and operations. They have the proof. They want it to stop. Laval got angry and he suddenly asked me, 'In truth, colonel, what are you doing? What's going on?' I told him candidly that we had to protect our secrets and needed to find out other secrets. The Germans are flooding us with spies.

"'What do they want to find out, since we're not hiding anything from them?' Laval asked me.

"'They want to know whether you're being straight with them, Mr. President,' I replied.

"Laval gave me a dirty look and then said:

"'Ever since I took over there have been nothing but bad breaks. But with you entire walls come crashing down.... I don't want this to happen anymore. I told the admiral there are too many hotheads... There are many Frenchmen like you who dream of saving the country and are undermining my policies.'

"A phone call from de Brinon interrupted Laval, who was getting annoyed. He stood up and said:

"'If you want to tell me something, call Rochat.'

"The meeting was over and had been much too matter of fact," Rivet said.

"As I left the office," he continued, "I went to see that fat Buffet, the head of RG,* for some solace. I asked him directly about the distribution of a "Wanted" poster concerning Turck in the Occupied Zone and among the Germans as well. I thought he was about to have me arrested when I hinted that someday he'd have to answer for that."

Buffet was executed at the liberation of France.

Our boss defended the special services tooth and nail against the adventure where France was being led. One last time he would face up to Laval when a document from Berlin informed us that Hitler demanded

---

* *Renseignements Généraux.*

285

150,000 French workers instead of 30,000 as we had been previously told. Rivet told us about that meeting that took place on July 10, 1942.

"The president was sitting down with his hat on. He didn't look at me and let me stand. I felt him tense and ready to bite.

"'What do you want?' he asked.

"'I wish to show you the evidence of Germany's bad faith. It's about 150,000 French workers…'

"'Just a minute!' interrupted Laval in a vulgar tone of voice. 'I still have the murder of Devillers bothering me. Abetz doesn't stop complaining about it. I'm fed up! We must stop your activity, which has no reason to exist. Rahn has proposed collaboration between the intelligence services of France and Germany as is practiced by the police forces. To reap the harvest of my negotiations I have decided to make some real concessions to the Germans.'

"It was unbearable. Slowly I reached the door to escape that nightmare and left without saluting."

I handed over my duties to Verneuil in May 1942 and together we visited the TR stations. Everyone welcomed him very politely and warmly. He knew how to make the men feel comfortable and hold their interest with his knowledge and reputation. He was starting with excellent chances to succeed. During the tough times ahead he was able to steer his unit very cautiously, no doubt better than I would have. We left the Promenade de la Plage and moved Cambronne to an inconspicuous house in the western outskirts of Marseille. I added new men to the central service of the TR: Bernard, from Saint-Cyr, cold and reserved; Morhange a graduate of Polytechnique, full of fire. Lambert, and Heinrich had left. Lambert, who could feel the coming changes, asked for a command in North Africa. My classmate Lejeune replaced him at the head of the GAD. The arrest of Dionne and Hallard threw cold water on the High Command that gave Lejeune very cautious instructions. With the help of Revers Commander de Beaufort at the High Command was able to make up for the weakness of the instructions so that the GAD would keep up their efforts.

D'Alès called me: "I'm expecting you at Saint-Mart no later than July 1." Before traveling to Limoges the head of the BMA went to all his stations to explain his departure and told the men they would be continuing their mission with me in different ways. Even though the TR service couldn't be in better hands than with Verneuil and that I had set it up, I still felt unhappy to leave that unit where I had lived intensely for the past two years. To break direct contact with my men with whom I had ties of personal friendship, overcoming danger together and sharing secrets...

"Don't regret this too much, major," said Verneuil, who understood what I was thinking. "The hunters will become the prey if the war goes on."

We analyzed at some length what we could expect from now on. The involvement of state agencies in our missions would be getting closer to zero. We had to replace our relationships with individuals instead. Two years of work allowed us to take stock of those connections. Our repressive action would change in character and since it was now entirely our responsibility it would have two possible outcomes:

> — One, immediate and violent. A self-defense action to the life threatening aggression by enemy intelligence and its auxiliaries. It meant a generalization of the Blémant method. We called that D-Response;
> — The other, stretching in time and following legal procedure as we waited for France to return to the normal course of justice after its liberation. That meant accounting for the crimes committed. We called it F-Response.

Compiling lists of suspects became very important. My conversation with Verneuil was interrupted by the arrival of d'Hoffelize, the TR head in Toulouse.

"I have a lot to tell you, sir. First of all, Fernand, my W agent in Dakar, has just been summoned to Angers. They're asking him to smuggle two Abwehr teams into Africa."

Fernand was one of our penetration agents from before the war and since October 1940 he was to inform the Ast station in Angers of what was going on in AOF (French West Africa). The British and Gaullist attempt to land in the French colony in September 1940 encouraged the enemy to broaden its intelligence capabilities in the region. Fernand was also supposed to watch the neighboring British colonies. Using a commercial cover (he was the local representative of a well-known brand of oil products) he corresponded with the Abwehr through two mailboxes in Paris and traveled to France every three months to meet his German employers. His position was strong. He was very well paid which was very useful to TR 117 and through him we found out that following the Dakar fiasco the OKW and the Abwehr had orders from Hitler to prepare for the occupation of French North Africa in case there was a second attempt at a landing.

With the approval of the army High Command we provided him with information on French military forces in West Africa in terms that were intended to interest and reassure the enemy.

"This time," said d'Hoffelize, "Fernand has a big job in setting up two teams of spies: one of them is to scatter between Sidi-Bel-Abbès, Tlemcen, and Oujda*; the other will proceed to Saint-Louis, in Senegal, and Dakar. My W agent will put them up in Marseille in various hotels and inform the CAA** in Aix-en-Provence. Each team will get two radio transmitters which will be delivered to their hotels."

"It sounds like fiction," said Verneuil.

"Fernand must first activate the team destined for Algeria. It seems that the identification papers of the agents are genuine. They're using commercial and industrial cover. The team going to AOF will go in later and Fernand is to travel with them, since only one team member is acquainted with Dakar. He must guide them and set them up."

"They're crazy!" said Verneuil, rubbing his hands. "They sound like amateurs."

"For your induction into the TR this is a very special gift!"

"There's a problem," said d'Hoffelize. "My W won't be able to leave right away. His wife just passed away near Toulouse. She leaves him with three young children and two old parents he must care for. I reassured him."

"It's obviously too bad, but it can't be helped! This will force us to take the more radical solution of a sweep in Marseille. I hope that Léonard*** will go along."

I was about to walk Verneuil and d'Hoffelize to the door.

"Let's go to the BMA and get Jonglez involved in this."

"Not so fast, Mr. Perrier. I have more important news. I'm in contact with Taillandier again."

I remembered the sergeant of the engineer corps who had specialized in communications with us. I had seen him last in July 1940 at Brax where he was about to be furloughed because of the armistice. D'Hoffelize had informed us a few months before that Tallandier had been tapped by Max Stöcklin to set up a purchasing bureau for Otto in Toulouse.

---

* In Algeria.
** German armistice commission.
*** A member of the *Surveillance du Territoire*.

"What are you going to do?"

"You spoke about D-Responses?" Verneuil asked.

"Yes, so?"

"He's the man we need in my area," said d'Hoffelize. "He wants to work with us on condition that he not be tied to a desk and can slug it out with the Krauts and their friends. Do you agree?"

Verneuil was listening. His eyes were now strangely fixed and heavy. I asked him, his answer was cautious.

"In principle I agree. I don't know Taillandier."

"I'll go to see him."

He turned to me, bit his lips, and said:

"Your job is quite out of the ordinary. The decisions we agreed to with the head of the BMA made it possible in June 1942 to grab fifteen spies the Abwehr had intended to place in Africa, plus four suitcase transmitters with quartz and codebooks that we also seized."

We learned a lot from questioning the spies, and they greatly enriched our files: six agents were members of the PPF (*Parti Populaire Français*) and had undergone training in two radio centers in Paris, 11 rue Desbordes-Valmore and at 77 rue de l'Assomption. Then they went to Garches for more training, where the Forschungsamt had its eavesdropping center with some sixty people. All radio messages that had been intercepted in France (both in Occupied and Free Zones) were decrypted and used by Ast Paris Section III F under Oscar Reile. Two Muslims who were to go to Algeria were former POWs released in 1941 from the Andernos camp near Arcachon. Four other agents who had been recruited by Colonel Weber of the Angers Ast went through sabotage training for three weeks at the castle of Rocquencourt in the western suburbs of Paris. All of them had covers to justify their being sent to Africa: some were "employed" by the Societé Intercommerciale at 7 Place Vendôme in Paris; others by the Societé de Transport Routier at 65 Champs-Elysées in Paris. Their mission was to set up a transportation network in French West Africa (AOF). They had funds to purchase trucks. There were also two Germans from the Schenker Company who were to open an agency in Tlemcen or Oujda.

The matter must have caused an uproar at the Hotel Lutétia, with Otto Abetz and the armistice commission in Wiesbaden! Ten days after those arrests, Major Ronsin, the military judge preparing the case, told Jonglez that the German armistice commission had requested the names of the German nationals who were being held at the Baumettes prison in Marseille.

"What should I do?" asked the head of the BMA.

"Answer that there are none!"

Two days later, following that negative answer, a commission of members of the CAA came to the military court to visit the prison.

"Ronsin is panicking!" said Jonglez over the phone. "What should we do?"

"Tell the Krauts to come back tomorrow. We'll help them complete their mission. Today is impossible, since there's no one to take them around.

We then met with Jonglez to set up the next day's script. There were nine German nationals accused of espionage at the Baumettes and seventeen big wheels.

"Excellent. That makes twenty-six, the full load of a truck with four gendarmes."

The next day was open house at the prison. The warden welcomed the control commission with a smile and the buildings were searched high and low. Common criminals took the place of spies while a closed truck with police cars front and back was driving around Marseille.

"The prisoners were very happy with their tour and asked if they would do it again," Jonglez told me.

"A good start for Verneuil into the nitty gritty!" said d'Alès when I told him about it at the Hôtel Saint-Mart on July 1.

As he had requested I came to take final orders. I stayed in a very modest hotel at Ceyrat near Clermont-Ferrand. Bonnefous and his brave wife had been staying there for a few weeks before I arrived. I didn't know what would replace the BMAs but in my mind the structure and organization of a new counterespionage (CE) unit were taking shape. Bonnefous was to become my first deputy. His main role would be to prepare for a return to a territorial and operational counterespionage service with a view toward military operations and the liberation of French territory. The service we would create would only surface at first in a very small part ("like an iceberg" said Bonnefous). Verneuil, second deputy, head of the TR, would be in charge of the offensive CE inside France that would remain completely covert. Chrétien would head the overall services of the CE (both offensive and defensive) in North Africa and he would continue to welcome the central service retreating to North Africa should there be an Allied offensive.

For the moment d'Alès and Bonnefous were handling daily matters at Chamalières as they supervised an MA service about to disappear. The problem was to proceed with its liquidation without disrupting our work and I wanted a new organization to be in place within two months.

"It won't be easy," said d'Alès. "Rivet is shunted aside and despite the fact that Revers is covering us we're still very wet!"

"There are many complaints and recriminations," added Bonnefous. "Look at this stuff!"

He handed me a list of twenty-seven spies who were German nationals or claimed to be Germans. Sadly, among them I saw some real Frenchmen, from Alsace and Lorraine whom the Germans considered to be of German nationality. They had all been condemned to death by our military courts. The Nazi Reich wanted them back and was threatening awful reprisals. Ten hostages to be shot for every German spy we executed!

In the group was Bömelburg's secretary, Radomir Smrka, a former Czech pilot, who had just been arrested in Marseille for espionage, as well as the diamond broker Marcel Villain, who had denounced those groups working for British intelligence. They had not yet been tried.

"You can be sure that we're not about to hand over those characters and a few others. Villain will be tried in two days. The German request will dispose of him even faster."

On July 3, 1942 the Lyon military court sentenced Villain to death.

"Careful about reprisals."

"No way," answered d'Alès. "We have the means to reciprocate and the Krauts know it. Villain is a French national. They won't get him."

Among the prisoners were the British citizen Richard Godfrey (Delobel); Georges Schweyer, NCO at the 24th Battalion; Joseph Moser, an officer; Fréderic Strohm, a policeman in Algiers; Jean Wagner; Coster; Stockman; Stolz—all condemned to death for treason.

"You haven't seen the best one!" said Bonnefous, waving a memo from General Bridoux, minister of war. "A request to extradite someone named Doudot, alias Toussaint, from Lorraine, and therefore a German national. He's being accused of espionage and of breaching the security of the German Reich!"

D'Alès took the memo that he called "toilet paper" and placed it in the famous shoebox:

"The bastard who sent that deserves to be shot!"

Johanès, the head of TR 113, heard I was around and quickly came to see me at the Hôtel Saint-Mart. He had just found out that Section III F of Ast Paris knew about the TR organization and the part played by the BMA. Reile had issued orders to step up the repression.

"Good timing," I replied, to reassure Johanès. "We do away with the BMA, the TR changes its location, and Mr. Perrier is no longer in charge of *Travaux Rumaux*. (The Abwehr had not yet discovered my true identity.)

"Yes major, but it does prove that those of our comrades who were arrested talked."

"We'd always factored in that possibility. You should take precautions. Martineau spent some time in your shop. Leave the Avenue d'Italie, go elsewhere, change your identity, and have everyone else do the same. Where is the Dynamiter? I'd like to see him." Captain Thiry was nicknamed Dynamiter and came from the sabotage section under Brochu. Since 1941 he had found a strange sideline in undertaking the execution of traitors and small sabotage inside the Occupied Zone, working alone. He had shown me his plans when he offered his services.

"You see, Mr. Perrier, when you have no accomplices you can't do much, but at least you're sure you won't be betrayed."

I hired him and sent him to TR 113 where Johanès had him undertake a few punitive actions and some sabotage of enemy materiel such as a truck belonging to the Funk-Abwehr that he had exploded as it was parked near Moulins.

"He's a bohemian of sabotage," answered Johanès. "You never know where he is or when he'll return."

"I'd like him to leave his mark in Paris on the Société Intercommerciale, on the Place Vendôme, or the Société des Transports Routiers on the Champs-Elysées. We can't allow those so-called French companies to continue to work with impunity for German intelligence. You can also mention the castle of Rocquencourt, where the Abwehr conducts a sabotage school."

My wishes were to be fulfilled. Thiry the Dynamiter destroyed two trucks belonging to the Société des Transports Routiers and was able to sabotage the phone lines of the castle of Rocquencourt. He would pay for his daredevil attacks with his life.

I had to return suddenly to Marseille to face an "inspection" by Admiral Dupré, who had replaced General Roux as head of the of the CIG (*Centre d'Information Gouvernemental*) because Darlan, against the wishes of Revers and Ballet, wanted to keep it active despite its messy anti-British and anti-MA activity. Had Dupré been told of the existence of the *Direction des travaux ruraux* in Marseille by the Germans or by Rollin? What was he looking for?

"I have no idea," said Rivet, as he asked me to return to Cambronne to contain the damage.

"I don't see it as having dire consequences, colonel. Verneuil has left Villa Eole. I'll show an empty building to the admiral should he insist."

Dupré was a kind of soft giant. He summoned me through the Marseille BMA to meet at the prefecture in the office of the police commissioner, Rodelec du Porzic. The initial contact was icy.

"You work for the Rivet organization? What's your job?" Dupré asked.

"We investigate and produce reports on foreign intelligence services."

"Where do you get the information?"

"From the BMAs."

"But the BMAs are scheduled to be shut down as of August 1."

"That's why we're also closing our service in Marseille," I said.

The admiral shuffled his shoulders as if something was bothering him: "Where were your offices?"

"At Villa Eole, 23, Promenade de la Plage. Would you like to visit the premises?"

Dupré agreed and came to our former "Cambronne," where the driver Pfister and his family were still living. I had warned them about this strange visit. Everything was clean but empty.

The admiral quickly walked through the rooms with his hands behind his back. Then he suddenly asked me:

What are you planning to do?"

"I don't know. I'll follow Colonel Rivet," I replied.

"He is a nobody now!"

"Then I'll report to his successor."

Dupré looked at me sideways, shrugged his shoulders, and walked out without shaking hands.

I returned to Chamalières and informed Rivet.

"Colonel, I'm told you're no longer anything."

"Perhaps it's true, old boy. I'm waiting for Colonel Pététin, who's coming from Nice to take over from me, but I don't even know who appointed him. Baril's going to Algeria. Perruche has been transferred to Lyon. Delor, the man with the bow tie, is replacing him without my being given the reason. D'Alès' deputy, Binoteau, is also gone. So you see it's a big purge!"

"What about Picquendar?"

"He's a lightweight! He also left the army High Command. Even though he faded away for a few months and informed Laval about our objectives and the part Poniatowski was playing—in spite of all that he was also fired!"

The "hush hush" information brazenly offered by the former chief of staff had some immediate consequences. On July 10, 1942, Poniatowski was summoned by the "President," namely Pierre Laval, who subjected him to the usual anti-British tirade and his faith in Germany's victory. Poniatowski was stunned.

"So you wish to return to America, sir? My son-in-law is American but the United States refuses to give him an entry visa."

The monologue ended with something that sounded more like a warning: "Go at your own risk." Three days later I found out that the name André Poniatowski was broadcast to the police for surveillance and subject to arrest in case he attempted to leave. It would be in vain that Poniatowski's radio linked to British intelligence tried to obtain more information. The French armistice army remained silent while the Vichy government created the "Tricolor Legion" to fight in German uniforms against the USSR. The memorandum from the ministry announcing the anti-Bolshevik unit came with the one announcing the end of the BMAs as of August 1, 1942. Both were being discussed around the army and at headquarters. An excerpt from the secret diary of General Bridoux reveals the true nature of relations at the highest levels.

> June 1942. I saw Rahn. We agree to the exchange of intelligence. The mindset of the army's High Command worries him. We discussed the size of Allied espionage networks in the Free Zone. We decided to take repressive action together.

In mid-June the heads of the BMAs were assembled at the Hotel Saint-Mart. Rivet and d'Alès took their leave and explained the position of our services and of the army; confirming the mission I had received and their confidence in me. The orders remained unchanged: we shall continue! But how? Revers, whom I met at the Hotel Thermal in Vichy, told me:

"Don't ditch anything! Find a way to gain time. The admiral wants to take over your services for his own reasons. Bring me a plan at the beginning of August."

Could it be that the storm Darlan had hurled at us six months earlier had died down? It now seemed to be directed against his rival and successor Laval. What strange twists can human nature indulge in when ambition and pride overtake statesmanship and transform at any time yesterday's truth into tomorrow's error? I understood the sadness and puzzlement of the BMA heads and tried to reassure them:

"You shall continue to provide your watchful service inside the army. Your counterintelligence mission is confirmed. Military courts shall continue to punish treason; I have the assurance on this point of the director of military security, Chasserat himself. Keep a minimum of personnel only and stay in contact with your men who have been transferred back into the ranks, men you feel can be used for future clandestine action. Before the end of August I promise to give you precise directives."

D'Alès left the following day and brought us together one last time. I could see real sadness under his forced smile, but his words swept any of my fears away:

"You're a natural in this business, Paillole, and you'll do it better than I!"

He walked slowly away. I felt suddenly alone and needed the silence to understand the extent of my responsibility: to carry on our struggle, to create a new CE service ready to play its role in the military action we saw coming and in a liberated France. Above me there was a gray area and a government that cleared its decisions with the enemy. With me I had a team of determined friends and against us a cruel and furious enemy. The situation was confused; the French people were suffering, the resistance was divided and being hunted down. What were we to think of de Gaulle and his negative remarks about the BMAs?

"Well, old man, shall we get to work?" asked Bonnefous, drawing a line on the past.

18

The SSM—Military Security Service

"The 5th Bureau was officially dissolved but the officers remained at their posts, dedicating all their energy to continuing to fight...

"Espionage activity continued, using the same personnel with the same anti-German bias. The real BMA activity was known to the agencies of the Reich; therefore that organization was dissolved and replaced on August 24, 1942 with another organization called *Service de Sécurité Militaire* (SSM). This new entity was theoretically only enabled to fight disorganization inside the French army. In practical terms it was functioning as a real counterespionage service that was only partly overt."

I did not disagree with this report by RSHA Group V1 SS Standartenführer Hermann Bickler, dated July 18, 1943. He was a former lawyer from Strasbourg, and we had arrested him in 1939 before the war. He was part of the lot of prisoners freed by the lightning advance of Abwehr III commandos. Assigned to Paris as a colonel just after I reached Chamalières, Bickler received his mission to oversee us from Himmler himself.

The slow death of the BMAs, the increasing activity of French and Allied intelligence services and resistance groups, the increasing threat of military action in the west compelled Hitler and Himmler to step up Nazi pressure in France. SS Brigadenführer Karl Oberg was appointed to take over this effort in Paris. The RSHA took the lead over the Abwehr in gathering intelligence as well as the repression of its enemies. The Reile results appeared unsatisfactory. The failure of Section I (intelligence) and II (sabotage and propaganda) in North Africa was obvious. RSHA group VI was to double the Abwehr before replacing it completely.

At the end of July 1942, I met Françoise once again in Lyon. She requested that meeting at the bar of the Hotel Terminus at the Gare Perrache. She was far too smart to still believe in a possible German victory. Her new line was a compromise peace to "avoid Soviet predominance."

"Laval has the right idea, let that be known around your circles."

She was loyal as always and recommended that I be more cautious than usual.

"Oberg summoned Colonel Rudolph, the head of the Abwehr in France," she continued. "Along with Rahn they studied how to fight against sabotage, attacks, and espionage effectively. It seems that most intelligence networks are based and have their headquarters in the Free Zone. They've decided to force the Vichy authorities to make all of that stop or else they'll intervene directly. So be careful."

We continued to make small talk and I felt she had something more to tell me. She took my hand and had me sit down again.

"There's something else. I can't keep to myself one more terrible thing, but I ask that you keep it secret. Hitler has ordered the murder of General Giraud!"

"Are you sure of this?"

"Absolutely, but don't ask how I know it."

"I respect your request. Let me just say that a French woman like you shouldn't remain an accomplice to such assassins."

She turned pale, stood up as if she'd been insulted, stumbled, and left me. I was never to see her again.

I rushed over to see Hugon the head of TR 114 in Lyon.

"Do you know a trustworthy officer with guts and who can be transferred to Giraud's entourage?"

Hugon wasn't surprised by my question. Since his colorful escape the general was living near Lyon at Sainte-Foy-Lès-Lyon. He made no bones about his anti-German feelings and his intention to lead the resistance in the Army. TR 114 and the Lyon BMA had informed us many times before about the police surveillance of Giraud and his family. I knew his clandestine 2nd Bureau commander, Major de Linarès, who had been one of my instructors at Saint-Cyr. I had met him at the beginning of July in Vichy.

"I'm thinking of Captain Vellaud," said Hugon. "He's at the Lyon BMA, but actually works for me. Loves his job and has to be held back. What do you see him doing with Giraud?"

"Keeping the liaison with us. You know as well as I that the general likes to push very hard. Laval has him in his sights and we must keep him out of any traps. Send Vellaud to Vichy as soon as you can."

At the beginning of August I met a strapping infantry officer in a well-cut uniform, energetic and keen; just the man I was looking for. After swearing him to secrecy I told him about the threat hanging over General Giraud and asked him if he would take on the task of ensuring the general's security in liaison with us. He accepted the assignment.

I wrote a short personal note to de Linarès, agreeing to Vellaud.

"Give this to de Linarès and inform him confidentially about your mission."

A few days later de Linarès called on me at Vichy. I confirmed Hitler's criminal projects and asked that he trust Vellaud.

"I know him, he's the perfect choice," answered de Linarès.

"Keep me informed of the general's intentions and what he plans to do and keep anything Vellaud tells you to yourself."

"I promise."

On August 6, 1942 Darlan summoned Rivet. He called me urgently to his office to tell me about the meeting. He looked happy and more keyed up than usual.

"That meeting had been set up by Revers…unbelievable!"

I was curious. What had happened?

"Darlan was very relaxed when I met him. He said: 'I've just had an altercation with President Laval regarding the secret services. I took the matter to the Marshal, who sided with me. I said that if I could take over whatever remains of those services that had by now been purged [*sic*], I'd make sure that the government would no longer have any complaints about them.' At that point," Rivet continued, "he handed us an organization chart where the three SRs * were placed under a single commander reporting to Darlan and the CE as Revers hinted was in on the change. 'What do you think of this?' asked Darlan. 'It looks good,' I answered. 'So go ahead and set it up with Revers!' he said. It was like a bolt from the blue. I got up and

---

* Army, navy, and air force.

told him, 'You forget that I've just been sacked,' 'Forget about that,' he said. 'I need you. I'll see you tomorrow.' The admiral left and in the office next door Revers pressed me to accept the challenge by saying, 'The future of our secret services depends on it. Accept!' What do you think, Paillole?"

"You must accept, colonel, and act quickly to save whatever we can still save."

Rivet, back in the saddle, was now heading the three SRs and counte-respionage.

With Revers and Ballet I worked at preparing the legal decree of August 24, 1942 that placed the new SSM under my command. The visible components of the SSM were minimal: only one or two officers to every military division. The mission no longer mentioned anti-national subversion but protection of the army from espionage and sabotage. In an unprecedented manner in the history of military defensive services I made sure that for the first time the three armed services were unified for security matters:

— Bonnefous will be responsible for the army;

— Colonel Serot, a great soldier and a real specialist in intelligence matters, will be in charge of the air force;

— Captain Jonglez de Ligne (brother of the former Marseille BMA chief) would create military security in the navy.

On August 28, 1942, I had the satisfaction of assembling the group leaders of the SSM and TRs. I told my audience of a coming Allied initiative and had reason to believe that it would take place in Africa. I had come to that conclusion from my contacts with American representatives at Vichy and Bern. It was also confirmed through the confidential discussions with Colonel Eddy that we received from Breitel, head of TR 120 in Rabat, and other attempts with General Giraud to have him lead a military coup in North Africa to coincide with the Allied landings. I also received information from Achiary, who kept me informed of the contacts made by the "Group of Five,"* with Robert Murphy, United States

---

* Jacques Lemaigre-Dubreuil, director of the Huiles Lesieur; Rigaud, his representative in Algiers; Henri d'Astier de la Vigerie (reserve officer of the Special Services); Colonel Van Hecke, former HC of the Special Services in Belgium and head of the "Chantiers de Jeunesse" in Algeria; de Saint-Hardouin, a French diplomat stationed in Algiers.

consul general in Algiers. I knew that such an operation by the Allies would lead to the occupation of the Free Zone by the Wehrmacht. My instructions were to prepare for those events as follows:

— The TR were already completely covert and would continue their mission inside France and radio links to Algiers must be permanent;

— The African stations would tighten relations with the Allies and must work autonomously in case of a break between Africa and France. I had Chrétien meet with Revers to confirm the need for direct contact with Murphy;

— The SM stations must be ready to go completely covert until the liberation of France and acquire good knowledge of their territory with increased personnel;

— My part would be to negotiate with the Allied High Command the collaboration of French security, and counterespionage services with Allied intelligence.

The results of that extremely important meeting were:

— French sovereignty could only be reestablished if we could provide security at the theaters of operation and inside the liberated territories;

— For now our mission was to oppose enemy intelligence, preventing them from entering French Africa and convincing them that Axis intervention in French North Africa was not beneficial.

Our penetration agents were to be responsible for convincing the Germans. We agreed with Verneuil to convey the message to the enemy that the French army would defend itself against any aggressor. That idea was reinforced by the transfer to North Africa of elite officers, the training of the army in Africa, and unfortunately by the blind repression undertaken in Morocco against the Gaullists and Allied intelligence in spite of us. Our disinformation offensive underlined the importance of the efforts made by the British and the Free French in Libya and Tripolitania. The resistance of General Koenig's Free French forces at Bir-Hakeim in June 1942 proved the high fighting spirit and quality of those French troops. The threats of an offensive into Sicily and southern Italy increased—Barranco agreed with that conclusion and would prompt calls for help by the Italian command. With the British pressuring Cyrenaica, and Montgomery's victory at El Alamein on October 23, 1942 opening up Libya to the Allied forces, the Italian distress calls became more and more strident.

With their renewed spirit our services took most of our defensive shield back into action, including the *Surveillance du Territoire*. In a few weeks, from August to October 1942 about 100 enemy agents were arrested, nine were executed, including a German of Hindi origin, Eric Dutt, who was condemned to death on October 6, 1942 by the Montpellier military court. Dutt was a spy for the RSHA Group VI and was attempting to reach North Africa. We also arrested Bostroem, Léon Drai, Marc Dreesen—all foreigners infiltrated into the Free Zone to identify Allied and Gaullist intelligence, check war ships docked at Toulon, check the garrisons at Pau, Auch, and Toulouse, and check our aircraft manufacturing.

"I have two important pieces of information for you, major.* One bad, the other good," said Johanès, who had urgently asked to speak with me.

"Let's have the bad one first."

"The Paris military court has sentenced Maurice Martineau, Dimitri de Zoubalof, Fabienne Courtaud, and Jeanne Jeunet to death on August 29."

I remained silent. I was crushed.

"We must try anything to save them! Maybe an escape?"

"I'll tell the German authorities that if they're executed we shall also respond with reprisals. I shall meet with Rivet so that he can reach Darlan, Laval and, if necessary, Marshal Pétain himself."

The contacts were made in September and led nowhere. We then learned to our amazement that Martineau had been pardoned and set free.

On November 12, 1942, the day following the complete occupation of the Free Zone by the Wehrmacht, the hapless Dimitri de Zoubalof was executed in Paris.

"Come on, Johanès, make me feel better. What's the good news?"

"We caught Gerhard Schmidt!"

This Schmidt was German and a friend of Otto Abetz. Since the spring of 1941 he was the manager of the Transocean Agency at Vichy. Françoise had told me at a meeting in Paris in 1941 that he had exit visas to travel to Dakar. Johanès was checking his mail, which seemed unimportant and limited to his commercial activity. Chemical tests were inconclusive and revealed nothing suspicious. His correspondent from the AOF

---

* I had regretfully abandoned my pseudonym in taking my new assignment.

sent very long typed letters every month and it was the length of these otherwise meaningless texts that Johanès and TR 113 found intriguing. He looked at an uninteresting letter even longer than usual. After the standard checks he ran his hand over the paper, which bulged slightly because of the dampness of the steam used to open the envelope in that instance, and against my instructions. He was surprised by some smaller bubbles his fingers could feel as he touched punctuation marks. Usually the stroke of the typewriter keys tended to depress the paper rather than create a tiny bulge. He used a magnifying glass and thought that the top of those punctuation marks looked less smooth than the others and stood out compared to the whiteness of the reverse side of the sheet. Using a microscope they found the stenographic letters of a report. Compiled and listed were military intelligence reports on AOF, the French air force in Thiès, and the British colonies of Gambia, Gold Coast, and Nigeria.

The spy, of Dutch origin in Dakar, revealed to the newly appointed military security officer the secrets of his work method. He would type his Abwehr reports on thick sheets of paper. A photo reduction machine would reduce the page to the size of a dot. A tiny stamp of the same size would remove one or more periods typed in the regular letter. In the empty spaces the spy would insert the microreduction of his report. It was very meticulous work, requiring extreme care and thick commercial sheets of paper (weighing eighty grams) and all the special equipment that Schmidt had brought with him on one of his trips. Having been tipped off by the bungling investigators, the Dutchman had enough time to hide his equipment before being arrested.

Those unfortunate mistakes prompted me to send d'Hoffelize, who was an experienced CE officer, in October 1942.

Time was flying and I sensed that events were about to overtake us. Chrétien and Achiary in Algiers, Breitel in Morocco, Schow in Vichy, Giraud in Lyon, Ronin, and Bertrand were all informing us about Allied intentions. The British-Canadian landing at Dieppe on August 19, 1942, limited in scope but extraordinarily bold was a kind of limited dress rehearsal full of useful information. A few days later Poniatowski met Revers for a final attempt with the British. The admiral's switching sides in our favor did not go unnoticed—we had obviously informed them as it happened. When our friends noticed the bold moves made by General Giraud and his assurance in being able to summon the army's support they wanted to find out the real story. Their question was clear: "Will the armistice army be strong enough to support Allied efforts to take over France's Mediterranean ports?"

The Giraud plan had no doubt been passed on to the Allies by Murphy and Tuck (the U.S. chargé d'affaires in Vichy since President Roosevelt recalled Admiral Leahy to Washington). The answer to the British and Americans was drafted by Revers and Verneau (the future leader of army resistance who died in a concentration camp) who had succeeded Picquendar as head of the army High Command. The answer was scrupulously honest:

"The army, like France itself, is going through difficult times. The High Command has just been overhauled. No serious plan can be studied. Nor can any formal commitment be taken. If the Allies go to Africa they shall be received with enthusiasm and will be offered help, provided a legal French authority can issue orders to the armistice army."

That was the final message. Did Darlan see and approve it? As a witness to those events and close to both Revers and Verneau I say he did not.

At that very moment Pierre Laval was telling an indignant France that he wished for a German victory.

As Rivet commented:

"Laval has chosen his side but the admiral is playing both sides. He keeps the emergency exit hatch open in every situation."

19

Treason and Double Cross

To facilitate communications with German authorities Darlan sent his trusted staff member Admiral Dupré to Paris. That was his answer to the calls from Karl Oberg and Ambassador Otto Abetz. The purpose was to seek true cooperation with Abwehr officers in the area of intelligence gathering and counterespionage.

I found out about the trip and the meetings. I don't know whether Canaris himself was present, but I do know that he appreciated and supported the move. Dupré called me as soon as he returned to Vichy and I didn't think anything positive would come out of such a strange meeting.

"Major, it would be useful if from now you could on provide me with the information you have regarding British and pro-British activities."

Dupré noticed my surprise and added, no doubt to reassure me:

"The admiral asked me to draft summaries on the matter."

"I'm not the person to ask. You should go to your own 2nd Bureau admiral."

Dupré was slouched in his armchair and began shifting his shoulders in a now familiar fashion.

"What's important to Admiral Darlan are espionage activities."

"I don't know of any. I fail to see what the Allies would want to spy on us for."

Dupré looked more and more agitated and was clearly embarrassed.

"That's not what I mean. I was referring to our activities against Germany."

There it was. I got up and felt my face contract, going pale.

"You must allow me, admiral, to inform Colonel Rivet of your request and also to inform the commander in chief himself," I said.

Dupré also rose to his feet:

"As you wish. Remember, that in the current context the commander in chief is the master and that he calls the shots."

"Double cross," yelled Rivet, who was outraged as I told him about this conversation. I had already told him about Dupré's contacts with the Abwehr. Like me he had no doubts that the present request was the result of commitments made to the Germans. I decided to not respond.

"You're right! I'll see him and Darlan tomorrow. I'll be open with them and we'll see how far their treason goes."

The next day Rivet told Dupré unhesitatingly "what we know" and asked him whether the answers to the questions were for the Abwehr. The admiral looked puzzled and confirmed that the Germans asked him for information about the British and Americans. The boss stopped listening and ran to Darlan. He returned one hour later to relate the conversation.

"I found out that Admiral Dupré is gathering intelligence on the Allies to hand over to the Abwehr!"

"They're embarrassed right now," answered Darlan, who tried to keep calm. "I want to keep them 'amused.' I'll give them some useless straws. However, Dupré is wrong to make any demands of your services."

We found out that with Darlan's approval Dupré was passing on to the Hotel Lutétia (Abwehr headquarters in Paris) intelligence coming from the navy's 2nd Bureau taken from wiretaps. I had no idea of their value. The only consolation in these shameful compromises was that the Germans were admitting their own weakness in asking Darlan for intelligence on the Allies. Starting at the end of August 1942 several troubling details were brought to my attention including something even more serious!

On August 28, 1942 two German cars followed by a French car with policemen from the air and radio ministries surveyed the Landes region near Aire-sur-l'Adour and then up to Pau. At the beginning of September a French officer with an order from the war minister's staff requisitioned the castle of Charbonnières near Lyon. I was able to identify Captain Desloges. Two days later the castle at Bionne near Montpellier was also requisitioned following the same method. Then the Desloges mission went on to requisition buildings in Limoges, Pau, and Marseille.

Two hundred blank national identity cards were signed by an official on the staff of René Bousquet* and were handed over to Geissler, the head of the Gestapo at Vichy, during the first week of September. Finally, a message from Françoise informed me that in August two French generals met with Rahn and Reile in Paris and appeared to have signed an agreement. Then on September 15, 1942, the curtains parted completely when I found out through Blattes, the military security officer in Montpellier, that twenty-three automobile license plates were reserved by the Hérault prefecture and given to Desloges.

With the government's agreement the Germans were preparing the intrusion of the Abwehr and the Gestapo into the Free Zone. Since Desloges was using an order from the minister's cabinet I asked to meet with General Delmotte, who was in charge. He was a young, very courteous and distinguished general. I told him what I knew…and that he must have already known full well!

"General, to allow the Abwehr and the Gestapo to operate in the Free Zone is against the clauses of the armistice. It's also a crime against state security and those who are involved will have to answer for it."

Delmotte listened to me very carefully and the rapid movement of his deep blue eyes indicated how nervous he really was as he saw the magnitude of the bad situation that seemed to surprise him. He got up and took out a map of France where he pointed out some large red dots:

"These are the transmitters working for the British," he said in a hushed voice.

I could see Lyon, Marseille, Vichy, Nîmes—four towns where we also had our stations; about ten in all were scattered throughout the Free Zone. The general said in a halting voice:

"I've met your counterpart, Colonel Reile. That's correct, but don't go thinking that I met with him alone. President Laval didn't want Admiral Darlan to start negotiating with the Germans without our being in-

---

* Secretary general of the police at the ministry of the interior. [NDT]: René Bousquet was implicated in various anti-Jewish actions taken by the French police in assisting the Nazi arrests of Jews. He went on trial in Paris but was murdered on June 8, 1993.

formed. I only accompanied Admiral Dupré on the mission he was undertaking for the commander in chief."

Delmotte stopped and looked at me intensely as if he wanted to convince me of his sincerity.

"We could only accept Reile's demands. The Funk-Abwehr had pinpointed those transmitters from the Occupied Zone. The messages have been decrypted and everyone proves to the Germans that they're being spied on and that something is brewing. It's vital for them to stop this radio traffic. One can easily understand that! They've requested permission to intervene in the Free Zone since we don't have the means to do so. They hinted that if we refuse to collaborate Hitler will order the invasion of the Free Zone."

The threat that General Bridoux's chief of staff was relaying to me was no idle menace. It had been palpable since the end of August; two Wehrmacht divisions had arrived in Dijon with Marseille as their objective.

"Rest assured, Paillole, we had no choice. Perhaps we shouldn't have tampered with the situation. That wasn't my minister's choice, but rather the admiral's!"

The general then lowered his voice again and said:

"If your stations are threatened tell them to keep quiet. I gave you a fair warning!" He looked relieved.

I left the Hotel Thermal, where the ministry of war had its offices, deeply distressed. How could such fine soldiers be so blind or intoxicated to become a party to such a criminal game just a few weeks or days before what could be decisive operations? I warned the SRs of Delor and Ronin and obviously "Cadix" who would inform London. I asked the SM and TR officers to inform as many people as possible about the looming threat the networks were facing. I ordered a halt or limit to a minimum all TR radio broadcasts. With Hugon we organized the surveillance of Charbonnières, which was the enemy's main station that included Hauptmann Frey, the goniometric specialist and Hauptmann Schmitz of the Abwehr, and an RSHA representative named by Bömelburg with Bousquet's approval. On September 17 we were informed that Kieffer a CE specialist was also present. Captain Desloges was the liaison between German intelligence and the French authorities.

We found out very quickly how many units were being sent into the Free Zone where each commando included:

— A 10-man SD team from the rue des Saussaies in Paris—the headquarters of Section IV Gestapo of the RSHA under Bömelburg. The team leader also headed the commando with the RSHA in charge.

— A team of the Funk-Abwehr also coming from Paris: fifteen men with twelve cars, three vans with tracking equipment camouflaged into commercial vehicles, nine touring cars, most of them black Citroën 11cv. All these vehicles had French license plates from the Free Zone. The team also had portable tracking devices for close range localization of clandestine transmitters.

— An Abwehr team sent by Hotel Lutétia Headquarters with two representatives of Section I (intelligence gathering) and two from Section III F—Reile. Scheide was part of the Marseille team. He arrested and questioned Martineau and clearly used the opportunity to review his information and investigate us. But he was to have a hard time because we had moved.

— A team of French policemen from the *Surveillance du Territoire* to make arrests and go through procedures under SD supervision. There were a total of 200 Germans using French identity papers.

When I told all this to Rivet, he cried out:

"He's a criminal!"

Suddenly we had a real emergency: Ronin's station had been identified! He had to move at a moment's notice because despite all our warnings he had continued to broadcast. I returned to Delmotte to protest the invasion and the first results of German investigations: three stations captured in Feyzin, Rochetaillée, and Châtelguyon. He admitted that he was powerless and very worried.

"I'm not responsible. Ask Darlan!"

Revers and Battet were outraged. They were able to get me to meet with Darlan on October 14, 1942. Rivet came with me. The admiral was in civilian clothes, stout and red faced. He was trying to be cordial and a regular guy. He told Rivet:

"So, colonel, did you save your service?"

"Not for long, admiral! Paillole will explain the terrible threat we're facing and an intolerable encroachment on our sovereignty that's already very much under fire."

I told the admiral how enemy teams had become active in the Free Zone, my meetings with Delmotte, and our fears. He didn't appear surprised by my report. Revers had briefed him in advance and his reply was both clever and cynical:

"I didn't want to leave the door open to this government that's handing the Germans everything they want. It was planning to collaborate with them for intelligence and counterespionage. I found out about their negotiations, managed to short circuit them, and limit the damage."

We looked at each other, completely stunned! What gall! After a long silence Rivet asked Darlan if he had read a memo he, Rivet, had sent to him through Revers.

"That memo, admiral, shows how criminal this enemy intrusion into the Free Zone really is. We are running the risk of cutting the Allies off from any kind of information inside France when they seem poised to undertake decisive operations."

"Ah! So that was your memo? You wrote that American ships were setting sail. Strange thing. Do you believe in 300 ships in the Atlantic? I don't! The Allies can't do a thing now in Europe. They don't have enough tonnage for a large operation."

Again I observed Rivet's tense face, drawn by anger. Darlan's observation showed his own ignorance. It was reassuring about the value of the information Dupré was passing on to the Abwehr. Perhaps that mistaken opinion about Allied capabilities was actually a very sophisticated form of disinformation. The admiral went on.

"I'm ready to help the Americans if they're reasonable," he said. "I told Leahy as he was on his way back to Washington: 'I'll never do anything against you. Bring 3,000 tanks and 3,000 planes to Marseille or somewhere else and I'm your man.'"

That wasn't about to happen anytime soon.

Rivet nodded in assent.

"Colonel, believe me, the German army is strong and has not yet been really defeated. It's in France's interest that the war go on that both sides use their resources, the British first and foremost, our worst enemies."

This was said in a hateful tone of voice. I attempted to place a word.

"But admiral, we shall also be bled white!"

"No, no, and no; not if we know how to steer ourselves! The best course is to avoid shortening this war or take sides openly too soon."

Rivet and I got up, and before leaving I tried to secure Darlan's promise to stop exchanging information with the Abwehr and the intrusion of German tracking devices into the Free Zone. His reply was disappointing:

"Tell Delmotte on my behalf to give those instructions to Desloges. We must limit the scope of those German teams. I'll talk to Bridoux about it!"

Outside a cold rain made us shiver as night fell and Vichy looked dismal.

"We can expect nothing from these people," muttered Rivet. "They're all liars!"

That meeting had deeply affected us. I left Rivet to run to the army High Command to see Verneau and Olleris, the deputy High Commander. I told them what I knew and Verneau tried calmly to reassure me:

"We'll probably not be of much use if the Allies landed. Yet I've decided that the army will uphold its honor. We're preparing something; come back to see us at the beginning of November, we'll need you then."

Back at Louis Raggio's hotel where I went to warm up I met Superintendent Chenevier, one of our best detectives and a reliable friend!

"I was looking for you, major. Buffet got orders to keep an eye on you and have you arrested if you try to leave France."

"Well, well. What's new?"

"They say you're Blémant's boss and are behind the Bernolle affair."

"What do you mean?" I asked.

"Bernolle was kidnapped by Blémant's men and delivered all tied up to the Marseille police," Chenevier said. "Leonard, the head of the *Surveillance du Territoire* in Marseille, filed a report here and asked for instructions. Bousquet's answer was to set Bernolle free and arrest Blémant and his men. Since you're a big fish they're using the big guns."

"Where's Robert,"* I asked Grand Louis.

"In hiding, don't worry."

"Good! Thanks, Mr. Chenevrier. Here's my picture. Please make me an identity card in the name of Billaud; this is what you write on the card. If I think I'm in danger, I'll go underground with a new identity."

"Yes, major. You'll have your documents tomorrow. If there's anything new I'll tell you."

Chenevrier was true to his word and got me that precious card. Many of these brave actions would land him in a concentration camp. I went to see Grand Louis in his kitchen and asked again:

"Where's Robert? I want to see him!"

"Wait here, major."

---

* Meaning Blémant.

He shut down the restaurant and closed the shutters of the kitchen where he had me sit down, and disappeared. A few minutes later he was back with Blémant, who was ecstatic to see me. He was as gaudily elegant as ever and wearing so much cologne that it managed to overcome the smell of Mrs. Raggio's french fries. There was no way he could fade into a crowd!

"Bousquet and Buffet can try all they want; they'll never catch me."

"What happened?"

"Do you remember before you left Marseille you had asked me to nail the Bony-Lafont team?"

I remembered, of course. For months Blémant was idle and anxious to extend his punishment to the entire Marseille region. I had put him on the trail of the rue Lauriston team—the headquarters of the French Gestapo of Bonny and Lafont in Paris—whose brutality was becoming intolerable. Danos had also recently joined them.

To penetrate the Paris "underworld" Blémant had used Renucci, one of his Marseille "associates," a great friend of Palmieri, a boss with contacts in Group IV–Gestapo and VI RSHA Intelligence. Renucci had also contacted Nosek, the most active officer in Group VI, who in turn took him to the center of the French Gestapo. At the same time at the end of May 1942, Bonny had recruited one of his former colleagues, retired superintendent Jean Bernolle. Bernolle became the gang's No. 1 informer, spotting the best targets for the Gestapo as well: denouncing resistance fighters, Jews, kidnappings, blackmail, robberies, and more. Business was good and in a few months Bernolle had stashed away some three million francs.

Blémant was disgusted by the policeman's treason and encouraged by Palmieri and Renucci, who opposed Bonny-Lafont as rival gangsters. Blémant decided to lure Bernolle into the Free Zone and kidnap him. We thought up a scenario that would entice the enemy to introduce him directly into the French-German mafia. Then he'd make sure to nail Bernolle. Renucci told Nosek that Blémant had been asked by the 2nd Bureau [*sic*] to make contact with Group VI of the RSHA. The German was very interested and summoned our friend to Paris. Robert, fearing arrest, refused to go, but Nosek wanted to make contact at any cost. A meeting was set up in Marseille at an apartment belonging to the gangster Spirito.

On one side with a gun in his pocket was Blémant and the two Renucci brothers, and facing them Nosek, Carbonne, and Spirito. The German proposed to Robert working together "only against the British." In exchange he'd agree not to bother him should harm come to any German agents or should any of them disappear." They were offering a whitewash of all his poor conduct.

Blémant asked to think it over.

Nosek was back in Marseille in September and had lunch with Blémant, who promised a yes or no answer the following month. However, he preferred the contact be a less conspicuous one than a German like Nosek, someone like Bernolle for example. Among former cops it would be easier to get things done. When Bernolle came to Marseille at the beginning of October Blémant wanted to take him on the traditional boat ride. He told Verneuil, who talked him out of it. If the police questioned Bernolle they would have surely found out some interesting things; they had to deliver the traitor to the *Surveillance du Territoire*

But that didn't account for Leonard's hesitations, the orders to "close their eyes" given to the *Surveillance du Territoire*, as well as Laval's determination since the Devillers case to avoid any further incidents with enemy agents.

"You see, major, your successor is just like you—he makes people make mistakes. I was on the police blacklist so I couldn't be present at Bernolle's questioning. I delivered the package and nothing else. The payoff is they wanted to put us in jail. Next time I'll handle the Noseks and Bernolle's my way."

When I told Bonnefous the story his comment was:

"It's over! There's nothing more to hope for here—look!"

He showed me a memo from Corvisy informing us that the 118 German spies sent to North Africa were handed back to the Germans. Laval transmitted the German memo threatening reprisals, with some added requirements of his own.

"We can do nothing more," said Bonnefous, "other than prepare our revolt as we wait here or elsewhere for the return of the rule of law."

20

The Eve of Battle

Bonnefous and I worked non-stop to prepare the guidelines for Military Security (SM) and its counterespionage mission inside the army and in the liberated parts of the country.

"Hopefully this won't take too long," said Verneuil, "we can't stay undercover forever!"

For the past few weeks Allied action in North Africa was becoming more focused. I knew for a fact that it was to take place before the end of the year 1942, probably during November. Colonel Eddy, who was William Donovan's* representative for North Africa, intimated as much to Breitel and asked him to step up our help. The head of TR 120 came confidentially to obtain my approval.

Following that information and other indications, from Schow and Sabalot the U.S. naval attaché in Vichy, I assembled my station commanders on September 23 and 24, 1942. We analyzed what the consequences of an Allied landing in North Africa and the occupation of the Free Zone in France would be. Chrétien was present and he was to play a key

---

* William Donovan was the head of OSS (Office of Strategic Services), the precursor of the CIA.

role from then on up to the moment when our services would be merged. While I was impressed by the flexibility and efficiency of what he had accomplished in Morocco and Algeria, I had to conclude that the same was not true in Tunisia. The distance, the very different characteristics of each country of the Maghreb, the individualism that unfortunately takes on an exaggerated importance—all this weakened Chrétien's hold on his two flanks (TR and Military Security) in Rabat and Tunis.

Since General Juin's command was limited to North Africa and Chrétien was on his staff, he had no input in French West Africa. That was an intolerable situation. I decided immediately to dispatch d'Hoffelize, the head of TR 117, one of my best specialists, to Dakar. He was to improve counterespionage results and concentrate on Algiers where Chrétien would be heading the station and managing the African services while we were waiting to reorganize the central office.

In the liberated territories the state of siege was to be enforced. French authorities were to take over the police military security, counterespionage, the struggle against sabotage and other secret enemy activity. Our Allies would therefore respect our sovereignty only if we took over those missions seriously. Our activity took on a truly national dimension and I wanted all my comrades to feel that way. It must become their main objective just as it was mine; until France's ultimate deliverance it guided every one of our actions.

To make sure Chrétien had good backup in Algiers I transferred two tough officers originally from Lorraine who had been in the dissolved BMAs (Captain Dullin, whose cover was "burned" in France). Colonel Sérot, my deputy for air force security, was to join them later. During the first few days of October I made a final attempt with the navy to ship our archives to North Africa. What Darlan could not tolerate as prime minister, Darlan as commander in chief of the French army could very well accept, in order to oppose the civilian government of Laval.

"Why not?" said Rivet, when he asked the admiral. But he returned discouraged.

"Unbelievable. He refuses again! There's no reason to run away!" said Darlan. He said he couldn't understand why we would hand over to the British what we had denied the Germans."

"Well, I understand what's going on," said Verneuil, who was present. "I'm off to Marseille. I'll put the archives in crates and ship most of them to Lédenon."

He was back by October 17, 1942, and confirmed that about twenty tons of historical archives were transferred to the country estate of our friend and HC Jacques Favre de Thierrens. Garnier and his assistant Saint-Jean set up shop quietly, one posing as a gardener and the other as caretaker of the estate.

At the army High Command Verneau and Olleris were undecided and unsure of the thinking of some military leaders. Since Poniatowski informed London about the uncertain allegiance of the armistice army they were out of touch with the Allies.

"Giraud would like us to protect an Allied landing on the coast of Provence," explained Olleris, "but nothing proves it will take place. In any case we're counting on you for our security and contacts overseas."

Verneuil brought all the TR heads to see me on October 19. The uncertain future of the armistice army was on everyone's mind in spite of our efforts to minimize their anxiety.

"How do you expect us to be useful in all this confusion?" said one of them. (I was insisting that all internal and overseas radio contacts be maintained no matter what happened.)

"Of course," answered Verneuil, "but with all those Kraut tracking teams it's extremely dangerous!"

All station heads agreed with him and hesitated to run the risk of endangering their main work of intelligence gathering for transmissions that didn't seem as important as the urgent operational messages. I knew that our radio technology was far from able to elude the dangers threatening us with modern detection devices. We must improve our methods and our capabilities and create new well-trained specialists in this fight to the death.

It was impossible for me to resolve that problem immediately in France without Allied support. Meantime improving communications with North Africa through Spain became an extremely urgent requirement. We had to set up a TR station in Barcelona. On Sunday October 25, 1942 at 7 p.m. I arrived in Toulouse with Verneuil to settle the problem, get d'Hoffelize to French West Africa, and reorganize TR 117 following those two decisions.

I found my mother trembling and in tears. Her apartment had been ransacked while she was gone. It had been thoroughly searched but nothing was missing. I told my poor mother to rest at Portet-sur-Garonne, a few kilometers from Toulouse, where we had kind-hearted relatives who upheld the simple traditions of honor and hospitality of a family that had been decimated by many wars. Often during the German occupation my comrades and I were to count on them and they always came through.

D'Hoffelize readily took the African assignment knowing that his deputies Berthaud and Reynard—who were both to die in a Nazi concentration camp—were highly qualified to manage TR 117. The *Gendarmerie*, under Captain Abadie's command in Toulouse, would help them without fail, acting as if he were under my command. For the Barcelona TR station I was planning to appoint d'Hoffelize once he completed his mission in Africa, so in the interim I asked August Larquier to take the position. He was an HC of TR 117 who was very well thought of and agreed to take on the assignment, asking for three weeks to organize his personal affairs.

Three weeks sounded like a long time. I got a message from Vellaud on October 27 informing me about the meeting at Cherchell and that the operation in North Africa was now at hand with General Giraud's participation.[*] I quickly returned to Chamalières to meet with Larquier before he left. While in Toulouse I met two HCs of TR 117 who were to become friends: Edmond Michelet de Brive, who worked for Frenay, and Gilbert Getten, a brave officer in the reserves who was strongly motivated by ambition and pride. I was to set him up in Paris in July 1943 to build our station, which had been reduced following the arrest of Martineau and his friends.

Verneuil also contacted Taillandier to plan a very targeted repression in the southwestern region of France that I shall describe later on. At the Hotel Saint-Mart I found out through de Linarès about General Giraud's upcoming trip to Algiers. The possibility of an Allied landing in France had been shelved. The general asked me to authorize Vellaud to take part in the trip and I agreed! He was to "report" to Chrétien and work in liaison with him.

On November 6, 1942, at 3 p.m. Rivet summoned his department heads at Vichy: Delor, SR and Army; Ronin, SR and air force; Samson, 2nd Bureau navy; and me. Also present for part of the meeting were Pététin Rivet's deputy on a temporary basis and Villeneuve SR station head in Vichy.

---

[*] On October 22, 1942, General Mark Clark, Eisenhower's deputy, had a meeting in the town of Cherchell in Algeria with General Mast, commander of the division of Algiers and General Giraud's representative. Together they went over the conditions of an Allied landing in North Africa.

I had triggered the conference when I requested orders from the boss in the event of a German occupation of the Free Zone. Such a possibility appeared to be imminent according to our penetration agents—it was the confirmation of the warnings issued by the SR.

"How will you react to such an event?" Rivet asked each one of us.

"My service is 'burned,'" answered Ronin. "I think the safe thing to do would be to move everything to Algeria or England where we could pursue our work."

"The army SR is ready to function since it's completely underground," said Delor with quite convincing self-assurance. Samson didn't believe in a complete occupation and in any case he would follow Admiral Darlan's orders. Without offering too much detail I explained the moves we were making in France and Africa with the *Sécurité Militaire* and TR. Nobody mentioned the Allied landing in North Africa. Was it because of ignorance, caution, or suspicion? The meeting broke up with a kind of "each man for himself" as the only directive.

I was overcome by a wave of uncertainty and saw that Rivet had the same unpleasant feeling. The attacks he had been subjected to, his progressive retreats, the men and decisions forced upon him, the uncertainty he experienced regarding his own future, as well as that of the Special Services and of the army itself, had shaken his self-assurance and authority. He was now completely dependent upon our initiatives.

Starting November 1, 1942, the TR station in Morocco was working with the OSS and the staff of General Béthouart—the commander of the Casablanca military region—in preparing Operation *Torch*, the code name for the landings in French North Africa. The operation included disinformation directed against the enemy by our W agents to focus attention away from Morocco and toward Tripolitania and Malta. The Germans and their auxiliaries came under increased surveillance set up by commandos to secure as many enemy files and stop any opposition to the Allied operations.

Chrétien informed me of rather disorganized pro-Allied groups in Algiers that became so obvious that Vichy sent an investigator, Police Superintendent Bègue. His report was about to expose the entire "plot" had the *Service de Sécurité Militaire* (SSM) not intercepted and altered its conclusions making them sound ridiculous.

There was also a lot of activity around Giraud at his residence outside Marseille. Once again the SSM had to step in to smooth over the edges and reassure Darlan. The admiral had been warned by Laval himself, who was worried and intrigued by Lemaigre-Dubreuil's* travels back and forth from France to North Africa. It was another opportunity for me to meet with Admiral Darlan to complain about actions of Abwehr and Gestapo teams inside the Free Zone. With a tired wave of his hand he admitted he was powerless.

"I've just returned from Algiers. I warned the Americans against a premature operation in Africa. Whatever some people may say or think, they don't have the means to undertake such action."

I didn't answer and took leave of Darlan, whom I wouldn't see again.

On November 4, 1942 at 5 p.m. I was in the office of Olléris when Verneau came in:

"What should we do?"

"Without any knowledge of what the Allies intend to do we have decided to call up the reserves and have the troops leave their garrisons as soon as the threat of occupation of the Free Zone is confirmed."

"They'll take up defensive positions in the mountain regions and harass the enemy. The 15th division in Marseille and the 14th in Montpellier will fall back to the coast to establish two bridgeheads on the Var, and the other in Roussillon. They could eventually help in case the Allies landed."

I couldn't hold back my amazement:

"But, general, a landing is out of the question."

"Perhaps. But if we resist enough, and we'll certainly try all we can, the Allies will come to our rescue if only to evacuate our forces by ship. Giraud promised me he would ask them."

"You should go to the region of Alès in the Gard as soon as there's an alert on the demarcation line," said Verneau. "We'll join you there."

Major Clogenson, head of the 3rd Bureau, was to confirm the decisions of the two generals when he sent out their orders. On the evening of the 5th Rivet called me. London notified us by radio that Operation *Torch* was about to begin. British intelligence suggested that we immediately evacuate the very valuable decryption personnel and the Enigma machine to North Africa or England. This took place almost entirely during the first weeks of 1943.

I prepared to evacuate the Hotel Saint-Mart. The stations were warned and I set myself up in Vichy to receive SR intelligence as quickly as possible and above all the interceptions of radio and telephone conversations

---

* Jacques Lemaigre-Dubreuil was the liaison between Giraud, Murphy, and the "Committee of Five."

on German lines. As of November 6 all indications were that as far as the OKW was concerned the convoys that had just left Gibraltar were about to reinforce Malta and British troops in Tripolitania. We intercepted an Abwehr message sent in plain language—due to confusion or sloppiness, who knows?—on November 7 at 6 a.m. that was still pointing to Malta and Tripolitania with a hint about Tunisia…

Barranco tried to reach me. He was in a panic and I had Guiraud tell him that the French "2nd Bureau" agreed with the Abwehr's assessment! That afternoon Revers confirmed to me that the Germans were uncertain and that in the morning they had asked Dupré about French opinions on the issue.

"Malta, Tunisia, or Tripolitania—right admiral?"

"That's what we think," said Dupré, who, like his boss Darlan, had fallen for a colossal disinformation campaign that we carried out on our own with the agreement of the Allies.

I asked Revers to inform Picquendar about the hidden weapons to be distributed to resistance groups as soon as the armistice army left its garrisons.

"OK but which groups?"

"May I ask that you inform Frenay to meet with you and settle that issue?"

"Fine."

A few days later I informed Chevance in Marseille.

"Oh great! Henri* will be very pleased!" Both Chevance and Frenay were going to try to solve one of the most difficult problems the resistance faced through that connection. The representative of *Combat* met with Revers who duly recommended him to Picquendar as promised. Ever since the "Poniatowski case" and the fact that he had been kicked out of the army's High Command he was unable to take a position and resorted to hiding behind Mollard who then could only ask General Frère, his commander, for approval. Giraud had named Frère to head the ORA (*Organization de Résistance de l'Armée*) and more time was wasted. While the military leaders who were still in control of a few army units wasted their time debating hierarchy and seniority issues that had long been overtaken by events, the Abwehr and the Wehrmacht would grab one-third of the weapons stored in the Free Zone. Another third was to be destroyed, and the remaining third would go to the resistance and the ORA.

---

* Henri Frenay.

On November 7 at 10 p.m. Verneuil told me that the Abwehr and the *Surveillance du Territoire* had arrested Marie-Madeleine Méric, Faye, and some of their friends in Marseille. That team from the "Alliance" network had set up by radio the escape on a submarine of General Giraud and his son, with Beaufre and Vizet, his staff officer. The radio hadn't stopped transmitting despite our calls to caution. Faye was to reveal to the French policemen[*] the start of Operation *Torch*. He begged to be taken immediately to Vichy to inform Marshal Pétain and have the armistice army fight the Wehrmacht when it entered the Free Zone. With General Brécart, the grand chancellor of the Legion of Honor, he was able to secure an immediate meeting with Marshal Pétain. He pleaded in favor of Faye and suggested that Pétain leave for Algiers...to no avail! Faye was arrested. The army was disoriented and damaged; it did not move against the enemy. Against its wishes and its destiny the army would fight its friends. An entire generation of soldiers full of hope and dreams was wasting away; but only for a short time because the best were to prevail in the end.

---

[*] Meaning Léonard Piani and Superintendent Théus (Blémant's successor). The entire ST team in Marseille later helped Marie-Madeleine and her friends escape.

PART THREE

DELIVERANCE

November 8, 1942 – November 20, 1944

21

The Turning Point
November 8, 1942

At dawn I was exhausted but happy. I spent the night of November 7-8, 1942 trying to get news and contacting my stations. Laval, who had been told by René Bousquet, the secretary general of the police, refused to believe in the Allied action in North Africa. I couldn't resist waking up Delmotte to tell him about the landings.

"Impossible!" he cried. "Can you repeat, Paillole?"

"The Americans are landing in Morocco and Algeria," I said.

"That's impossible! They dared! What a mistake! Believe me, this time they'll lose the war!"

At the same time in Algiers, Darlan, who had been visiting his son on his deathbed, was told and in a fit of anger lashed out at Robert Murphy:

"Bastards! We'll fight!"

In London de Gaulle was informed by his chief of staff, Billotte, and was also outraged:

"Bastards! I hope the Vichy people will throw them back into the sea."

Some news filtered in by the afternoon. There was fighting in Morocco, and in Algeria. It was awful; all our efforts were useless if the end result was fighting our allies, something Marshal Pétain appeared to approve.

I went looking for Rivet.

"He flew away!"

Pététin told me sarcastically that he went to Istres and North Africa with Ronin, Beaufort, and a few other air force intelligence officers. Revers confirmed the news and didn't know what was going on in the Mediterranean, other than that Admiral Darlan was in charge of French interests.

"Weygand has just arrived, I hope he's able to convince the Marshal to go to North Africa while he still can. It's the only way to stop the fighting."

"And what about the army inside France, general?"

"The only solution is to fight if the enemy enters the Free Zone."

The head of the Vichy intelligence station, Lieutenant Colonel du Crest de Villeneuve, was expecting the invasion at any moment. He thought it was for November 10 and was amazed at the boss' sudden departure.

"Once the Krauts come into the Free Zone I'll go and join him. In such circumstances the intelligence service must be present in Algiers."

"That's not what Delor and Pététin seem to want."

De Villeneuve's only answer was to shrug his shoulders in disgust. On November 9 we finished moving out of the Hotel Saint-Mart and the personnel began its journey. I was to hook-up with them the next day at the *Sécurité Militaire* in Montpellier where Olleris was supposed to contact me. I left Captain Delmas alone at Chamalières to maintain our liaison with Vichy. I recommended to Corvisy to do everything he could to evacuate all enemy agents under arrest to Algiers and free the patriots who were incarcerated.

"I hope the ministry of interior will open wide the doors to the camps where patriots are being held!" was his answer. By November 20, 1942, seeing that Corvisy had not succeeded, Bonnefous, without informing General Bridoux, was able to send to all government officials in the military courts of the former Free Zone a memo requesting the destruction of criminal files regarding British or Gaullist cases and the immediate liberation of persons involved. That brave initiative angered the minister's cabinet and forced Bonnefous to go underground. During the night of November 9-10 we arrived in Montpellier and the 10th went by without any Wehrmacht intrusion. Bonnefous went to Istres all day and to Marignane airport to try to quickly make a round trip to Algeria in an attempt to meet Rivet, who had flown out that morning. I was able to reconnect with my stations. There was no news from Verneau and the High Command other than what Delmas was telling me by phone: they had left Vichy for a command post further south. Could they be traveling toward Alès? At 5 a.m. on November 11, 1942, another phone call from Delmas:

"This is it, major. The Krauts are in Vichy!"

"What about Verneau, Olleris, and the High Command?"

"Everyone's here!"

"In Vichy," said Delmas.

I called Pététin, who confirmed the news jokingly.

"The rooster returned and all the chickens followed him back to the coop," he said. "You can only do the same as everybody else!"

This time I was floored. Everything had collapsed! General Bridoux returned from Paris and simply cancelled the orders given by the High Command and everyone accepted! It was unbelievable! I found the mediocrity of such an ending revolting. It made the entire project look unrealistic and far too ambitious. Suddenly a sentry called me.

"There's a phone call for you, major."

"Paillole, Paillole? Hello?"

It was Schlesser! Once again he had been able to track me down. That friendly voice was comforting even though what he asked was inconceivable and saddening.

"You tell me what to do, old man! The Krauts are coming! Are we going to let them grab us like a bunch of cornered rats?"

What could I answer?

"You received no directives from the High Command?" I asked.

"None! No one thought about us. And you?"

Had I told him what was on my mind, I would only have added to his worries.

"Colonel," I said, "we're carrying on here and elsewhere as always. I'm going back 'up there' to try and see and understand. I shall advise later on. The Krauts are landing large forces in Tunisia. There's fighting in North Africa. We have to go there, my place is over there!"

"Under Darlan's command?"

"There's Giraud!"

Verneuil came into the room and listened while Schlesser kept on talking over the phone.

"Can you authorize me to ask your TR station in Toulouse to help me disguise my regiment to reach North Africa through Spain?"

"Of course. You mean the whole regiment?"

"Naturally, old man. Why not? Why not?"

"He's got guts!" said Verneuil. "He told me he lost contact with Algiers despite Simonin's efforts and the awful risks he was taking."

On November 9 I had fortunately been able to pass on a personal letter to Chrétien through Captain Luttwig, who flew to Algiers with our most confidential files on enemy intelligence (memos, lists of suspected agents, etc.). I repeated my orders for cooperation with the Allies and asked that he temporarily take command of counterintelligence and military security until I was able to reach Algiers. Blattes, head of military security in Montpellier, came to see us. He said that General de Lattre had left with some of his units.

"He's hoping to create a bridgehead in Roussillon. In any case he will not surrender to the Germans without fighting."

So there were still some military leaders with a sense of dignity and honor. De Lattre's initiative would fail because of contradictory orders from Vichy. The general was arrested and sentenced on January 9, 1943 by the state court in Lyon to ten years in prison for "having abandoned his command and attempted treason." Darnand took part in the proceedings.

I asked Blattes to temporarily hide our men in a hospital in town. I now became Bernard Billaud, accountant. A German motorized unit appeared suddenly between Saint-Flour and Issoire and passed me. The men were young and silent; some of them were sleeping in the cars. I felt cheated by the sight of my prey doing what it pleased; I was like a frustrated hunter. At 7 p.m. Vichy was dark. I quickly went to the Hotel des Bains where I met Olleris; his eyes were tired and he sounded exhausted.

"My friend, we've been betrayed. Bridoux issued orders that superseded ours and almost everyone followed him. All we could do was acquiesce. It was pitiful!"

I had a question for him.

"General, what do you and General Verneau intend to do?"

"Demobilize the army as best we can," he answered. "Save as much equipment as possible. Remain in touch with those available to join the GAD and prepare for guerrilla action. We'll follow the directives that General Frère will receive from General Giraud."

"You're not thinking of going to London or Algiers?"

"We can't leave our comrades," he replied. "And you, Paillole, what do you intend to do?"

"My place is in North Africa. Once things are settled here I plan to go to London to see where we stand with the British and the Gaullists. I'll seek an agreement with them regarding security in the liberated territories and inside the army and regarding our struggle inside occupied France"

Olleris smiled and whispered:

"I envy you!"

He asked me to wait and then came back with Verneau. The general was quiet, his eyes betrayed a lack of sleep and he congratulated me for my resolve.

"Don't forget to see Revers and agree with him about the liaison with Giraud," he said. "I give you *carte blanche* to do the best you can for your unit and for France. I wish you good luck."

They both walked out with me. Olleris, who must have been emotionally battered, gave me a bear hug but his eyes were filled with tears. A few minutes later I was in Revers' office. He was in control of himself and tried to deal with a very confusing situation. There was little news coming from Algiers. He was meeting with Bridoux, who was filling in for the commander in chief. Revers was to find out what the Germans intended to do with the armistice army.

"Come back to see me tomorrow morning. I'll know more."

I found Villeneuve, who was determined more than ever to go to Algiers and Pététin, who was into crazy projects to create a new SR.

"We'll work in liaison with the Abwehr and we'll 'double-cross' the Germans."

I quickly left to avoid hearing anything else. Through a side door at the Hotel Thermal, which was the headquarters of the secretary of state for war, I slipped into a room that the sergeant of the gendarmerie guarding the hotel held ready for me at all times. In spite of my being completely exhausted my mind was wandering.

The crucial event that was shaking the world; the miserable end of the army in France and its resurrection in Africa; the new scope of my mission—all this was running through my mind and occupied my thoughts.

How could Verneau and Olleris, both of whom I admired and whose high-minded diligence and patriotism I respected, think of rescuing at the last minute a project they had decided to shelve only a few weeks before? Was it incompetence, cowardice, and treason on the part of some leaders who did not deserve the confidence placed in them? No doubt. But there was also complete ignorance of the rigorous pragmatism of the Allied command and the thorough precision of its tactical methods. Operation *Torch* had been planned since July 1942. In August, due to the pressing insistence on the part of Giraud, the planners had thought of adding a move into France itself with the participation of the armistice army. British intelligence had asked through Poniatowski about the thinking at the French High Command. The disappointing but honest answer put an end to that idea. From that point on the decision was made to limit the operation to North Africa. Nothing would possibly change that decision and the Allied command was doing everything to ensure the success of the operation. First of all there was the secret preparation and the element of surprise.

The secret had been kept from the enemy. I had some cause to be proud of my service's success in denying the Abwehr access to North Africa and to sources of information.

The secret was kept from the French army High Command and French military leaders, since the armistice army's participation had been cancelled and was now under the nervous scrutiny of the Germans.

The secret was kept from Giraud, who was told of the landings only six days before but without any operational details.

The secret was kept from de Gaulle, whose troops couldn't participate and whose entourage could be indiscreet.

Most of all the secret was kept from Darlan, whose thinking was well known to the Allies and whose close staff was in contact with the Abwehr.

The secrecy that was required and strictly enforced was irritating to some people who chose to consider themselves as suspect for whatever reason. The secrecy surrounding the operations was a textbook case in point but it couldn't ensure surprise by itself. The huge armada's movements couldn't go unnoticed and the enemy had to be deceived as to its destination. The work of our penetration agents at that critical point of Operation *Torch* became particularly useful.

Secrecy and surprise are not the only ingredients for the success of an operation. There is also the knowledge of the enemy that allowed the filtering and the direction of our efforts. Planted inside the OKW with deep sources of information within the Reich and its satellites, able to seize and decrypt its messages, French intelligence (SR), against all odds, had maintained until then a regular production of detailed information. The Wehrmacht's order of battle, along with the navy's and the Luftwaffe's, had been carefully updated, as well as the Axis's industrial production. The British, the Americans, and the Russians benefited regularly from our service but there was also something more! Intelligence, the secrecy of the Allied plans, the tricks of disinformation, the powerful military forces engaged would probably not have reached their optimal results without a number of factors that were specific to the enemy.

The first and most important factor in my view was the absolute priority given by Hitler to the Eastern Front and his determination to reach the Caucasus at any cost by the spring of 1943. The second factor was Italy's failure in the Mediterranean theater of operations with which the Axis had entrusted her. Germany considered it secondary and the Wehrmacht only became engaged in the area to shore up the shortcomings of its partner. On October 10, 1942, an intelligence item I had gathered took on special significance. Rosario Barranco had insisted on meeting with me that day. He was back from Rome where he had reported to the Duce and his government on the results of his three-month mission to Spain. His conclusions were summed up in four points:

— Spain was lost to the Axis.
— Spain was the next target of the Anglo-Americans.
— The Axis could no longer win the war militarily.
— There was no hope for a compromise peace.

The Italian government and the High Command (Badoglio?) had reached some conclusions and gave Barranco the following instructions: 1. Tighten relations with French intelligence to establish contact with the British-Americans (which was what he was attempting to do); 2. Dispatch to England one of its most highly placed HCs of unimpeachable stature to find out the reactions of political and government leaders[*]— and Winston Churchill in particular—in case of a coming Italian switch of sides that could go as far as a declaration of war on Germany. History will record that as of October 1942 Italy was dropping the Axis, and fortifying the Brenner Pass.

A final element explaining the German attitude in October and November 1942 was the failure of its intelligence operations. Some writers have gone so far as to attribute it to treason by the Abwehr and especially by Canaris. That's absurd. Despite his enigmatic attitude, which came from his personality as much as his position, and despite his fears regarding Hitler's bold policies since 1939, Canaris was never guilty of betrayal.

---

[*] Neither Barranco nor the British ever revealed the identity of this very important anti-Fascist, who could have been one of those left-wing Italian politicians whose extradition had been requested by Italy to the Vichy government.

He served along with the Abwehr scrupulously and with sometimes exaggerated zeal because of Germany's success and its need to remind everyone even at the price of the most brutal methods. The Abwehr knew about and forecasted Operation *Torch*. I can base this statement on two facts: first, since July 1942, our wiretaps revealed that Germans in Morocco were worried; and that they repeatedly asked for German troops to be sent into the French protectorate; and second, in September and October 1942, the Sultan Sidi Mohamed Ben Youssef (later King Mohammed V, "Compagnon of the Liberation") had warned the Grand Mufti of Jerusalem, himself an Abwehr agent, about a coming American offensive in Morocco. Was this simply loose talk by diplomats? Possibly. I was always under the impression that American diplomats went too far in the way they attempted to win over through confidential information some Moroccan circles. Breitel had warned Eddy of that tendency.

This information gathered and transmitted by the Abwehr was compared to other sources and also the disinformation we had concocted. Despite its value they were missing the inescapable points, the absolute proof guaranteeing them absolute credibility of any information. Canaris didn't possess direct information by a "plotter" operating to welcome the Allies into Morocco or the cooperation of an agent placed highly enough to have access to confidential discussions between Mast, Lemaigre-Dubreuil, or the papers of Robert Murphy. He didn't have Loevchine in Rabat, Ouadani in Algeria, and the hundreds of spies that we caught in our dragnet.

Without the capability of providing information that was absolutely certain, the Abwehr could only give the OKW and the Führer a choice between several scenarios. Like every politician in the world who is confronted with a similar problem, Hitler picked the scenario that best fit his views—what I mean is the one less likely to disturb his plans. Supplying Malta and Cyrenaica were plausible objectives and had the advantage of not upsetting his strategy in the East. Even Darlan didn't escape the rule that when it comes to intelligence the pride of ambitious political leaders tends to transform their hopes into reality. Blinded by his hatred of England the admiral readily accepted—along with his 2nd Bureau—the easy explanation of supplying Malta because it confirmed his mistaken conviction that the Allies didn't have the strength to open another front. On the morning of November 7 that was how he saw the situation in the Mediterranean and his staff and Admiral Dupré so informed the Abwehr.

The German reaction was too weak, came too late, and was insufficient. This was the turning point in the war. It was also the turning point of the Abwehr and its leader. As Germany sank progressively into its fate and realized that defeat was inevitable she looked for those guilty of treason. Hitler's hour was not yet at hand but Canaris' was.

The defeated France of 1940 cried treason and accused a nebulous fifth column. The Nazis used the army as their alibi; the RSHA would have the Abwehr. While North Africa was falling into Allied hands, Germany's best resources were being bled to death from a huge wound 2,500 km wide on the Eastern Front. It was too much! The responsibility of the head of the Abwehr was to be violently proclaimed in proportion to the enormity of the defeats. Who could defend an intelligence service incapable of penetrating the secrets of Operation *Torch* or those of the Red Army and the industrial capability of the USSR? Not even Keitel, although he knew how Canaris had warned about Italy's weakness and had been against the deadly extension of the war to the East. Isolated and attacked from all sides he saw his star and his service sink under the Nazi attacks. In February 1944 the party stood up against the army and Hitler fired Canaris. The RSHA took over the Abwehr. A few months later, on Sunday, July 23, 1944 Walter Schellenberg the young SS officer in charge of the Reich Intelligence Service, arrested Canaris at his house at Schlachtensee. At dawn on April 9, 1945 Canaris was hanged at the Flossenburg camp. His SS executioners divided his clothing while his naked body burned into ashes.

22

Spain

November 8, 1942, was the turning point of the war for the Axis and the Abwehr; it was also the tidal wave that changed our lives. Until then our service as the heir of the 2nd Bureau (SR-SCR) in peacetime and of the 5th Bureau at war had been able to operate with its traditional research methods. The "lines" connected in Paris had been very quickly reconnected in Vichy. The only big change was the addition of networks inside the Occupied Zone. Our problem was to transfer outside France for the benefit of the operations command our intelligence gathering and analysis capabilities. This was essential to our pursuit of the war. Rivet needed to rebuild his control over the SR, which for the moment was rudderless. Villeneuve wanted to bring him that element when he came to join Rivet. As for counterintelligence, before I left France to negotiate with the Allies the location and responsibilities of my service I had to set up with my fellow officers of the SM and TR the new covert way of working. I needed the scope of their requirements and to maintain their permanent contact with me.

At Chamalières I found Bonnefous and Verneuil during the evening of November 12. They were unhappy and greeted me in a somber mood. Bonnefous, who felt less tight with me, expressed his irritation and the worries of our fellow comrades at the distressing condition of the army that we were much too optimistic in thinking that it was capable of defending its honor.

"So what do we do?"

Verneuil silently asked me the same question as he nervously clasped his hands. My answer was unequivocal:

"We continue!"

I recounted my day to them.

I spoke at length with Revers. The fate of the army in its garrisons was being discussed. We were negotiating about an armed camp near Toulon to resist with the fleet out of reach of the Wehrmacht.

"One more asinine idea," said Bonnefous.

"That was our opinion as well," I said. "I shall summon Jonglez, the head of Military Security at Marseille, to warn him about that rattrap. We have confirmation that the fighting against the Allies has ended in North Africa, but in Tunisia the situation is very serious. The Krauts are landing large forces and Estéva's letting them in. Revers understands that the demobilization of the army is due in a matter of days. He's asking us to tighten our contacts with the resistance groups and to help him and General Frère meet with the main resistance leaders. He requests that the GADs, with additional elements coming from the demobilized army, coordinate their clandestine action with those groups. I told him about my intention to travel to London and from there to Algiers and he agreed. He wants me to tell Giraud about other steps taken by the ORA*; it was the first time I heard that expression coming from Revers—the GADs were the origin of the ORA. Revers wants me to visit him again before I leave."

My friends all looked much more relaxed now: this time things were clear. Our mission remained unchanged but was no longer prey to the desperate situation in France or the confusion in North Africa. In France our mission was inside a resistance organization; in liberated Africa and in the army it was to recapture its national purpose. We divided our tasks: Bonnefous would prepare the secret military security service before the liberation, which meant keeping a permanent link to the resistance. With the help of our HC Michel Flandin, a professor at the Lycée of Clermont, he was to meet Raymond Aubrac of the group called *Libération*, a resistance organization created by Emmanuel d'Astier de la Vigerie in 1941,

---

* *Organisation de Résistance de l'Armée* (Army Resistance Organization).

just as Guiraud and Jonglez in Marseille were in contact with Chevance of the *Combat* group.

Verneuil was to move the TR headquarters from Marseille to Issoire. I could always contact him through our friends, Captain Kerhervé (who was to die in a concentration camp), the gendarmerie commander, and through Dr. Roubille. The activity of the TR stations was focused on the new Abwehr and RSHA initiatives inside the Free Zone and no doubt the TR organization would have to adapt to this larger enemy network. My job was to keep the whole section functioning and coordinate it with North Africa for best efficiency. I was planning to leave at the end of November.

I went to Raggio's hotel in Vichy to sleep. At 10 p.m. Chenevier was there and told me that Buffet, the head of the criminal division, was working with Bömelburg to purge the Free Zone. He had a copy of a list of suspects to be arrested and I was prominently listed under both my real name and the pseudonym of Perrier, along with Rigaud, Johanès, Hermann, and a few others. This didn't affect me at all and I thanked Chenevier.

I spent November 13 and 14 examining each individual situation of the TR and SM station heads and I introduced Jonglez, the head of military security in Marseille, to Revers. The armed camp at Toulon was a real rattrap to be avoided. Jonglez, beyond his regular duties, tried to forecast any invasion attempts by the Wehrmacht and kept the general informed. He told me that two of my safe houses in Marseille, rue du Coteau, and the Hotel Beaureau, had been vandalized.

"The problem, according to Blémant," said Jonglez, "and he's adamant, is that no one from Marseille participated in the break-in. He thinks a team from the rue Lauriston* was guilty, taking orders from Bömelburg or Nosek."

"I'm going to see Blémant; you can tell him."

"In Marseille?"

"Of course, in Marseille I shall also meet Chevance and Guiraud."

"Beware major, after missing you once and twice the third time could be your turn!"

"We shall see!"

I agreed to let Villeneuve leave with me. André Poniatowski was to join us. I decided to travel through Spain, study the TR station's progress

---

* In Paris, headquarters of the French Gestapo.

in Barcelona and then travel to London via Gibraltar. We were to meet after November 26 in Perpignan.

On November 16 I took leave of Revers and reassured him of the connections we were making between ORA and the resistance organizations. In early December Bonnefous, Verneuil, and Mercier met Aubrac several times, traveling to Lyon with him to meet Emmanuel d'Astier de la Vigerie on December 23, 1942. D'Astier understood the importance of my comrades' initiative and proposed that Revers go to London. In early January 1943 Bonnefous and Mercier organized a meeting in Vichy between Aubrac and Revers and at Royat with General Frère. Aubrac organized the general's plane trip but other reasons didn't allow the general to travel and Revers was irritated and disappointed. When on January 14, 1943 I radioed to Revers that Giraud agreed for him to come to North Africa via London, he rejected that invitation, telling Captain Mercier, whom I had sent over, that he wished to continue his work on ORA inside France. He refused again on February 5, 1943, when through Michel Thoraval, another emissary of mine, I repeated the order given by General Giraud (which had not been easy to obtain). Looking back I'm convinced that Revers lost an opportunity to create a truly united and confident resistance in France. Perhaps General Revers with his realistic and accommodating approach could even have lessened if not avoided the growing conflict between Giraud and de Gaulle.

My unit was to maintain and expand its links to the resistance that appeared much better structured by the end of 1942. Beyond *Combat* and *Alliance*, with which we had direct connections, besides *Liberation* where we had made contact, we felt it necessary to meet General Delestraint to study the security requirements of the AS (*Armée Secrète*), the secret army that he headed. Verneuil's deputy, Captain Mercier, had several talks with Delestraint at Bourg-en-Bresse. At the end of April 1943 he was introduced to Olleris and on May 10, 1943 Mercier again organized a three-hour conference between himself, Delestraint, and Olleris. An efficient collaboration was agreed to between the secret army, the ORA, and our counterespionage services (SM and TR). But just one month later the move toward unity was suddenly halted because the two main leaders of the secret military organizations, Delestraint, head of the AS, and Frère, head of the ORA, were both arrested by the Gestapo on June 9 and 13. Those who opposed merging the military and civilian resistance groups were able to slow down the process and were not part of my unit.

I left Chamalières for Toulouse on the morning of November 17. I had asked Terres and Ramonatxo to prepare our trip to Spain. With André Poniatowski, who was in contact with the British, we agreed to accept the offer British intelligence extended to Ramonatxo to handle our travel from Barcelona onward. I saw Larquier, who was now ready to take over the station. He had perfected his counterespionage techniques with Berthand, who was replacing d'Hoffelize. We gave him a list of our HCs in Barcelona. I told him we would meet at the British consulate after December 1, 1942. He was to ask for Mr. Billaud. I hugged my mother and had some trouble convincing her that I was still some anonymous bureaucrat in Marseille.

I was in Marseille on November 21 and Blémant confirmed that Reile's deputy Scheide and Nosek were both in town. Blémant was having a hard time avoiding them because the Bernolle affair put him in the spotlight and he was in danger. I advised him to leave France and go to Algiers where I would need him. Because of Hitler's order to the Abwehr to kill Giraud we had to tighten the security around him and Blémant was eminently qualified for such a task, which would free Vellaud, whom I needed for other missions.

"Yes, major, but who'll take care of my team here? Who'll keep the liaison with Verneuil and Guiraud for your D operations?"

"You'll have to find someone, Louis Raggio for example."

"I'll see. In any case I have a lot to do so don't plan on seeing me for three or four months."

The underworld was a very secretive place and I didn't press the issue.

I was unable to meet with Chevance, so I handed Guiraud a letter of introduction for him to General Revers. I was pressing them to agree to hand over the hidden weapons to the resistance fighters. Finally, the head of TR 115 would inform Barranco that I was gone once I reached Algiers. I left Marseille on November 26. When I reached Montpellier I suggested to Koenig, the excellent superintendent of the *Surveillance du Territoire*, to join me in Algiers with some of his policemen. He agreed. In Perpignan I met Villeneuve, André Poniatowski, and one of his friends, the journalist José le Boucher, who was also on Buffet's list. He was coming with us. Verneuil was also present and reassured me on the work being done by the TRs and gave me some news. Reile was in Vichy to attempt to get the French police involved in his counterespionage operations in the Free Zone! The Abwehr was busy setting up Ast stations in Lyon, Marseille, Toulouse, and Limoges. Then Verneuil stopped, appeared hesitant, and then said:

"I'm worried. I think Martineau is betraying us. He's running around free. A few days ago he was seen in Limoges and also Clermont-Ferrand. He was trying to meet his old comrades but Johanès threw him out."

"That's very serious! Order Johanès to break all contact and take the most stringent security measures."

"Major, you should beware as well. They're looking for you. The Germans are now in charge of patrols along the Spanish border and have reinforced their stations in Spain. The RSHA is extending everywhere and is becoming ubiquitous. There's a man called Barbie in Lyon; Dunker, also known as Delage, in Marseille; Redzek in Toulouse, Barcelona, and Madrid."

The TR head, who was a bit older than I, kept on insisting that I be cautious.

"Be cautious! You must succeed. We only have enough money for one more month. You know how weak our radio capability is. We must be linked through you to an unquestionable military authority. We can only hold out if we're sure that our work is useful."

We walked through the darkening streets of Perpignan. Under an awning a young woman was kissing an SS of the *Das Reich* division.

"That's disgusting!" said Verneuil

I found the scene humiliating and clenched my fists. Verneuil and I were quite affected by the necessary separation. Across the Pyrenees lay the unknown, an adventure. What was I to find in Spain, in London or in North Africa? I tried to reassure Verneuil:

"You shall hear from me before the end of January."

"Please avoid taking too many risks. You're the only one who can rebuild our service."

On November 27 we found out about the tragic end of the armistice army. The Wehrmacht's attempt to grab the fleet in Toulon failed and the fleet scuttled itself. Admiral de Laborde refused to obey Darlan and sail to Algiers. The barracks obeyed orders from Bridoux and Delmotte, our soldiers remained inactive, and were overtaken without a fight. Weapons were confiscated; some equipment was hidden, some flags were burned, others hidden. The soldiers were free to go. The "demobilization" that Verneau and Olleris were hoping to carry out "correctly" to save for the resistance whatever could still be saved was nothing more than an outrageous shutting down of Hitler's orders.

"We're none too proud," said Villeneuve, as he listened to the radio communiqués. During the night of November 28-29, 1942, we crossed the border, ducking past two patrols of German Feldgendarmerie. Our guide was a Spanish railroad worker who had been recruited by Ramonatxo, and took us from the Tour de Carol to the railway station at Puigcerda. We hid inside the tender of a locomotive and reached Ripoll in broad daylight. It was cold, and a canteen full of rum kept us warm. Huddled in a coal shed inside the station we had to wait until noon to board the local train to Barcelona. Our guide gave each one of us a railway ticket and we broke up to board the railroad cars among a large crowd of noisy travelers. I slipped into a corner and pretended to sleep to avoid answering the woman next to me. She was holding a basket on her lap and I could see the red crest of a rooster.

Two civil guards boarded the train at one point and walked through the aisle. Even though I kept my eyes closed I was expecting the worst to happen. But it didn't. We reached Barcelona and followed our guide at a distance. Through narrow winding streets we reached a building where we were welcomed by a rather heavy set hostess whose true profession couldn't be mistaken. All we had was some ice-cold anisette, but no food or drink since we left the Tour de Carol. That night a Spanish man picked us up in a car to drive us to the British consulate. The city lights were blinding and the nightlife on the Ramblas was surprising since we hadn't seen anything like it in a long time.

British consul Farquarth gave us a warm welcome and a young French speaking attaché explained that we were now under the jurisdiction of British authorities. We had to be extremely cautious and avoid arousing the Spanish police. Before moving on to Madrid we stayed comfortably in the house of the consul's chauffeur. I felt much better after a night's rest and very early in the morning I slipped outside with a map of Barcelona in hand to seek out the HCs that TR 117 and Larquier had listed for me. I didn't succeed and returned exhausted. Poniatowski and Villeneuve were worried by my long absence. I started off again the following day and this time I was more successful. I was able to meet some HCs who were to be very useful to Larquier. When I returned I found my friends very worried. An unannounced visit by Farquarth's deputy confirmed that the chauffeur was reporting on us. My absences couldn't be tolerated and I was to go to the consulate immediately.

"We asked you to respect our hospitality," the young man told me in an angry and surly tone, "and you just walk off without telling us, breaking every rule of caution. If this goes on the consul general told me to tell you that we can no longer help you and that you'll be on your own."

"Fine," I replied. "Kindly ask the consul to give me an appointment to see him."

Alone with Farquarth I explained my absence and my determination—no matter what should happen to me—to act freely. I thanked him for his hospitality and asked that he inform General Menzies and Commander Dunderdale in London about my conduct.

Twenty-four hours later the consul general asked me to forgive his deputy and told me to act as I saw fit. He provided me with a car and a charming secretary, and on December 5 Auguste Larquier came to see me in her office, the day before we were to leave for Madrid. Larquier found the consul and his secretary very helpful in setting up our TR 125 station and sending our mail to London or Algiers. In August 1943 I had Hector Ramonatxo back him up and concentrate his escape networks in Catalonia in Barcelona. Jean-Louis Vigier, who later became a senator from Paris, managed one of them. All the escape networks needed the cooperation of the gendarmerie, especially in Saillagouse with Botet, its commander. Reverend Leblond was our informer in the Spanish enclave of Lliva. Through Ramonatxo our service could count on some cooperation from the Spanish police and intelligence service. All this meant that our solid support structure helped our HCs in Barcelona: Fort, Buscail, Pellerin, Bouyat, Canal, and many others.

In Madrid I had accommodations in the comfortable apartment of the first secretary to the British embassy, a young and pleasant gentleman. He was very considerate, no doubt in an effort to prevent me from getting into trouble.

"We must be careful not to compromise the embassy or our escape networks," he told me confidentially. "Should you wish to meet with certain people, I shall be pleased to welcome them here."

It was a charming way to make me swallow the fact that I was under control as to my activities. I made no mystery that I wished to meet Colonel Malaise, the French air force attaché in Madrid. I had heard that he was very active in the resistance and that Ronin of the air force intelligence was using him. He could also be of help in getting Larquier started. Malaise turned out to be an enthusiast, and French escapees were fortunate to deal with him. He was able to draw a maximum of help from the British and American embassies and he ignored the Gaullists. The information he could give about North Africa was vague, but he was reassuring and very helpful.

"Be assured I shall travel to Barcelona soon and will meet with August* and give him all the help he may need, especially to send your mail to Algiers. Do you know Monsignor Boyer-Mas, who is, in principle, connected to the French embassy?"

"No," I replied. "In Perpignan I was told that he was close to our services."

"You should meet him. He's a real prince of a man!"

"I'd be delighted, but here I am under house arrest on my honor. Could you ask him to please come and pay me a visit?"

Monsignor Boyer-Mas was the perfect man of the cloth. The ease and authoritative way he spoke, a bit affected at times, stood in stark contrast with the humility of his appearance. He looked quite thin and distinguished in his black robe when he offered me his services.

"I expect Vichy in the next few days to authorize the opening of a representation of the French Red Cross in the Calle San Bernardo," he said. "You shall be at home there. I'll also be able to help our fellow citizens who have been stranded in Spain to reach North Africa."

"Monsignor, you should expect a flood of young Frenchmen. Colonel Schlesser spoke to me about his regiment."

"My gosh!"

"You should be on the lookout particularly for personnel belonging to the Special Services. A cover provided by your agency would be extremely useful to us in Barcelona. On the other hand, we could also help you identify among the escapees those who are enemy agents."

"Excellent, excellent," said the priest. "All this shall be done."

"I'll tell Larquier to pay you a visit as soon as possible. But how will the Spanish authorities react to such initiatives?"

"You shouldn't worry. I have friends at the ministry of foreign affairs and the interior, plus my robe will work wonders."

Boyer-Mas stunned me with his self-assurance but he was able to deliver what he promised. Thanks to him—and to us in part—some 20,000 young Frenchmen transited through Spain to join the French army from 1943 to June 1944, four times more than from July 1940 to December 1942.

---

* Larquier.

Dressed as Canadians on the run we reached Gibraltar on the evening of December 15, 1942. Major Codrington of British Intelligence was waiting for us and set us up in the fortress. There was a lot of activity on the airfield: every few minutes the landing strip would suddenly emerge from the darkness with thousands of beams from projectors on the rock lighting up for a landing or a take off.

From time to time we heard the muffled explosions of underwater mines that shook the port area. The town was quiet and the shops were filled with Spanish-made goods. The next day Villeneuve and Le Boucher took a plane to Algiers.

"What should I tell Rivet about your plans?" asked the colonel.

"I'm off to London. I shall come to Algiers as soon as possible."

The governor had invited Poniatowski and me to lunch. I spent the afternoon walking the streets and watching British soldiers play soccer. Poniatowski went to bed early. After playing bridge with some British officers I was crossing the deserted hallway to my room when a young man suddenly appeared and smiled. When two Frenchmen run into each other overseas it's rare for them not to start up a conversation...

"Good evening," I said.

"Good evening."

"Are you French?" I asked.

"Yes. And you?"

"Me too," I answered.

"Are you going to Algiers?"

"No. I'm going to London. And you?"

"To Algiers for now."

"Are you coming from France?" I asked.

"No, from London."

There was a moment of silence; the young man wanted to know who I was and I told him.

"Oh! You're Major Paillole! I'm really happy to meet you and I salute you. They're expecting you in London; we were afraid for you. We knew that the Krauts and Vichy were both looking for you. Passy offered the British to help you."

"You know Passy? Who are you anyway?" I asked.

"Fred Scamaroni. Up to now I handled my region, Corsica."

"Are you going back there?"

"Yes, but not immediately," he answered. "First, I'm to accompany General François d'Astier de la Vigerie to Algiers."

"What's he going to do there?"

"Quiet, major...that's a secret."

We parted company laughing. Scamaroni was very likeable and the contact was a good omen for my London trip and what I was trying to accomplish. Perhaps the secret mission of General d'Astier, whom I didn't know, had to do with bringing together the Frenchmen in London and Algiers. I was ready to cheer on such a move by de Gaulle.

above
René Bousquet, general
secretary of the French
police under Vichy.

right
Lieutenant Colonel Rémi
Robelin, deputy chief of the
Vichy guards, was tortured
to death by the Gestapo in
July 1944.

Major Paul Johanès, head of the covert counterintelligence station *TR* in Clermont-Ferrand, was sent to a concentration camp in 1943.

left

The Gestapo murdered Major Marcel Taillandier, leader of the *Morhange* counterintelligence action group in southwestern France in 1944. This photograph was in the Gestapo's wanted file.

right

Captain André Fontès was one of Taillandier's first deputies in the *Morhange* group. This photograph was also part of the Gestapo's wanted file.

left

Colonel Gérar-Dubot, one of the longest serving agents of French intelligence, headed the Amiens office of the BCR in 1939-1940; HC of the Paris *TR* 1941-1942; head of the Paris BCM, 1943-1944; then chief of the Allied counterintelligence office (BICE) in Germany in 1944.

Louis Baril, head of the *Deuxième Bureau* at the High
Command, 1940-1942.

left
Major Chrétien, head of
counterintelligence in
North Africa, 1941-1943.

right
Robert Blémant, police superintendent at the *Surveillance du
Territoire* in Lille, 1938-1940, and
Marseille, 1940-1943; headed a
counterintelligence action group
in southeastern France; then
headed Giraud's security in
Algiers, 1943-1944.

left
Major Gilbert Getten, the *TR*
man in Bordeaux in 1940-1942;
also headed the *Gédéon* group
in Paris in 1943-1944.

Colonel Oscar Reile of the Abwehr, head
of counterintelligence in Trier, 1937-1940;
and in France at the Hotel Lutétia in Paris
1940-1944.

top

Navy Captain Fritz Gibhart (Unterberg), who recruited French ensign Aubert in 1937 for the Hamburg *Ast.* Stationed at the German consulate in Casablanca, 1941-1942; then in Berlin, Lyon, and Lake Constanz.

right

Lieutenant Maurice Martineau, head of the covert counterintelligence station *TR 112-bis* in Paris, 1940-1942.

below

Major Henri Navarre was head of the German section of the *Service de Renseignement* 1937-1940, and later head of the Deuxième Bureau with General Weygand in Algiers, 1941-1942; head of military security in France, 1943-1944.

above

"Cambronne" 1940-1942, HQ of the Travaux Ruraux *(TR)* located at 23 Promenade de la Plage in Marseille. The Germans destroyed the building in 1943.

below

Paul Paillole's false identity card, signed by Police Superintendent Charles Chenevrier on September 19, 1942. Chenevrier was arrested and deported to a concentration camp in Germany in 1943.

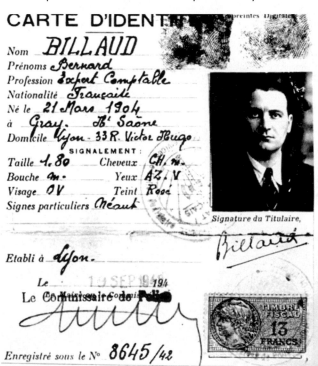

right

Commander L'Herminier, the daring skipper of the submarine *Casabianca* until 1943.

below

The *Casabianca* had a crew of 6 officers and 79 men.

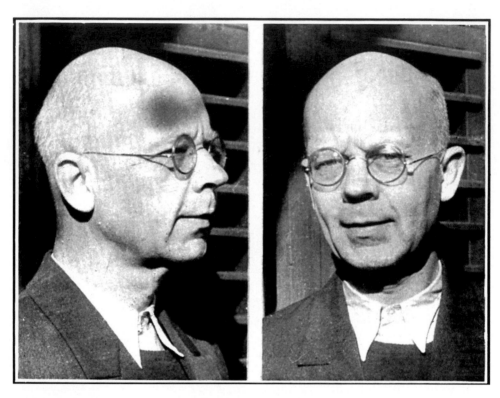

SS General Karl Oberg was *Höherer SS und Polizeiführer* in France, the "personal representative of H. Himmler, responsible for the French police and setting up French SS units."

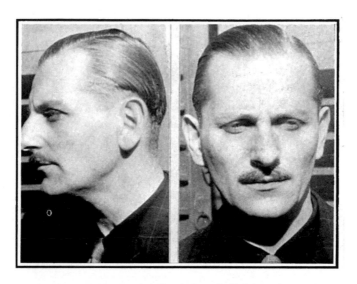

SS Sturmbannführer Roland Nosek, born in Zwickau, August 11, 1907, "specialized in political intelligence in France and had countless secret informers at every level of society."

SS Sturmbannführer Herbert Hagen was head of section VI of the *RSHA* in Paris, also known as *Einsatz Kommando Paris*.

Retirement ceremony of General Rivet at El-Biar HQ in Algiers on May 6, 1944. From the left: Colonel André Serot, Colonel du Crest de Villeneuve (head of army intelligence), General Louis Rivet, and Paul Paillole.

Jean Moulin, one of the leaders of the French resistance, captured and killed by the Gestapo in Lyon in 1943.

Henri Frenay, former army captain and leader of the *Combat* resistance network.

above

Algiers, December 1942. General Eisenhower speaking to Admiral Darlan, who would soon be murdered; General Giraud (*with cane*) and General Noguès (*on Giraud's left*).

below

At the Casablanca conference in January 1943, Roosevelt and Churchill were able to reconcile Giraud (*far left*) and de Gaulle (*second from right)* for a short time.

23

London

As of December 17, 1942 I was still in Gibraltar. I was getting impatient and complained to Codrington.

"I'm wasting my time!"

"Don't worry, you leave tomorrow. You have a pleasant surprise!"

What did he mean? I went back to my room. The door next to mine was open, a man whose back was turned to me was unpacking. I saw it was Ronin! A very good surprise indeed; he was very happy to see me!

"This isn't bad at all! Beaufort told me two days ago that you were in Lisbon!

"His information is sometimes thin. Give me some news from North Africa, colonel."

"Things are very confused with Darlan, Giraud, and the Gaullists. You'll see for yourself. Rivet will tell you the whole story."

"Not right away. I'm off to England tomorrow."

"What?"

Ronin suddenly looked somber; he was disappointed and angry.

"You mean you're not going to Algiers?" he asked.

"No, I'm going to London."

"But Paillole, old boy, your commanders are in Algiers and they expect you there."

"Colonel, I have too much respect for you and Rivet so I intend to be clear. Since November 8, and possibly even before, I've had no other commanders than my conscience and the service. I took on *alone*, without orders from anyone, the responsibility for a national mission that I have every intention of completing. That responsibility takes me to London, first to ensure the survival of the service, and then to create the conditions of its work in the future. I shall return to Algiers when things clear up and then I'll fit into the operational units of the French and Allied forces."

Ronin listened without interrupting me. Then he laughed and gave me a bear hug.

"You're right; I'd behave the same way if I were you. Just promise not to do anything that could appear to the British or the Gaullists as proof of a disagreement between us."

"What does that mean for me?" I asked.

"To coordinate what we're doing. I'll tell you what I intend to do, you tell me what you want to do. I'm going to London as Rivet's deputy to officially reorganize the SR and our liaisons with British intelligence."

"You'll meet with de Gaulle?"

"No. Darlan and Giraud don't want me to."

"I intend to see him. Nobody can stop me."

"Please, Paillole, wait until you've spent some time breathing the air in Algiers. I can assure you that both the British and the Americans wouldn't take very kindly to a clash between ourselves. If you meet with de Gaulle now, you'll place Rivet and me in an impossible position."

He had become very insistent; I could see that he was both unhappy and irritated. So the wave of November 8 hadn't swept away disagreements among Frenchmen. It was a shame. It was also true that Darlan's presence as the head of French North Africa was something hard to accept.

"You'll see old boy," continued Ronin, who was just as puzzled as I was. "You'll see! We had to use the unexpected presence of the admiral to free the army in Africa from the criminal orders it was getting from Vichy. He's promised to step aside. We have to play the game now!"

"The game! Again and again! It's killing us. My men in France can't stand being eternally victimized by these murky situations and political intrigues. They must ally themselves with the men who are resisting. I'll meet with Passy."

Ronin agreed to that.

"OK, we'll see Passy. In return for that concession promise me you won't attempt to meet with de Gaulle now. Promise me also that you'll join Rivet as soon as possible."

I promised.

Perhaps my friendship and admiration for the older officer, Ronin, made me make a mistake. There were more and more obstacles on the way to French unity.

On December 19, 1942 at 1:45 a.m. a bomber flew Ronin and me to England, while Poniatowski arrived in London two days later. At about 11 a.m. we landed at Hendon where the gigantic Uncle Tom (Mr. Green), Bill Dunderdale's deputy, met us with a big smile. Without any formal entry we left the airport and his car drove us to London. A few moments later we were in Bill's office where there were many bear hugs and congratulations. Ronin went on to his hotel and I went to the Hyde Park Hotel. I had dinner at Green's home with his family and Bill was also present. There were innumerable questions about France and North Africa. Finally, an understanding Uncle Tom took me to my hotel where I crashed in bed, totally exhausted.

When I woke up the next morning I had a pleasant surprise: new underwear courtesy of my old friends. For some time now the meager reserves I carried around were coming to an end and my nightly washings had destroyed socks and handkerchiefs.

Before going to the office of British intelligence I went with Uncle Tom to a ready-to-wear shop. I found a very nice suit that I gladly traded for the worn out wardrobe I had been wearing for a whole month. Well dressed and rested, I felt ten times better and pleased to join my British friends. We were to set up with Felix Cowgill our joint counterintelligence work in North Africa and outside. General Menzies was extremely solicitous when I paid my respects that morning and assured me the full cooperation of his service. That evening I had dinner with Claude Dansey[*] and with Menzies himself. Sir Claude was a rather strange character, the power behind the throne at the Intelligence Service; without a doubt he was close to the government within the service. Menzies appeared deferential toward him and he spoke with an air of authority. The conversation quickly came to our attitude toward the Gaullists. They

---

[*] Dansey was Menzies' deputy for SR matters, with the title of "Deputy Chief of the Secret Service." The other deputy for security matters was Colonel Valentine Vivian, also "Deputy Chief of the Secret Service."

were both relieved when I spoke of pooling our resources and that I wished to meet with Passy. "You're right. He's very good," said Sir Claude.

Menzies seemed more reserved. He had just read reports from Algiers that were pessimistic about the state of mind regarding the Gaullists. He didn't want to appear to be taking sides in the growing political conflict that we couldn't even imagine in France. He only wished for unity, and hoped that "Passy's SR would merge into the Rivet organization." Clearly the head of British intelligence felt deep friendship and admiration for the French service and its head. Dansey asked:

"What do you think of the situation in North Africa and Darlan?"

I didn't know how to answer and got around the question saying that not having enough information I was unable to form an opinion. The discussion took a technical turn and I explained my views about the way the service should be organized. Two points appeared extremely important where we had to work in unison: the centralization of counterintelligence data and disinformation targeting the enemy. A completely independent direct radio line, between Algiers and London, would link my services to Cowgill. It would be called *Cub-Minor* and would be working day and night from January 1943 to August 1944. A special service was set up within the Allied High Command to prepare disinformation actions to confuse the enemy. Together with British intelligence we implemented those plans through our penetration agents called *Force A*.

From February 1943 to 1945 *Force A* was to play a permanent and often decisive part in major military operations in Tunisia, Italy, and France. Following our exchange of views, I was convinced that there would be cooperation on an equal footing between French and British counterintelligence services. I also sensed that Menzies wanted us to handle all security matters inside French territory within Allied operations areas as soon as possible.

"The Americans will need you. Their counterintelligence service is still inexperienced," said the head of the Intelligence Service.

"It'll be a crucial point to avoid having AMGOT,"* said Dansey

"For the moment your representatives in Algeria and Morocco are working very well," added Menzies "And then there's Rivet!"

---

* AMGOT stood for Allied Military Government in Occupied Territories, the military government for the administration of occupied territories, replacing all local government administration.

These projects and plans were to make a counterintelligence station operating in London an exceptionally important requirement that would grow as operations in Europe got underway. I was convinced that such a station was to play a key part in reaching an agreement with the Gaullists to merge our services. I promised the head of British intelligence I'd give the job to Bonnefous, whom he knew and liked. Bonnefous had also served, prior to coming to the 2nd Bureau SR-SCR, under de Gaulle's command. The general had often praised Bonnefous in the past.

I took my leave and was delighted with the result of those initial meetings. I was deeply touched by the courtesy and thoughtfulness of the chiefs of British intelligence; they never had a derogatory word toward my country. "France is in difficulty but she's picking herself up and we shall help her." Not a single word that might wound my pride as an officer and a Frenchman, nor anything to prevent an agreement between the Gaullists and ourselves. I immediately recaptured with them and their subordinates who came spontaneously to congratulate us for our work and my escape, the old spirit of comradeship.

On the evening of December 23 a thunderbolt struck while we in London: Darlan had been assassinated. "It's serious," said Dunderdale "The Americans may react negatively to this. On the other hand, for you Frenchmen an obstacle to a rapprochement between London and Algiers has been removed."

From the moment I arrived I kept asking Bill to introduce me to Frenchmen who could be sent into France very quickly because Verneuil was expecting news, money, and radio equipment from me. "I need a young Frenchman, someone dedicated and smart with some training in covert action and completely trustworthy."

"A rare bird!" chuckled Bill.

"We're scouting everywhere for your diamond in the rough, wherever French people congregate," said Uncle Tom.

By December 24 he called me to announce triumphantly:

"I think I found your man: a young fellow who worked in France for a covert group under SOE. He came to England in June 1942 to join the FFL and has just completed training as a paratrooper and radio specialist. He's available now and is raring for action; he also loves the idea of working for the 2nd Bureau."

Right after Christmas day I met this young, fair-haired adolescent, who seemed very shy. He looked so young that I cut the initial interview shortly after it began and went to see Dunderdale.

"You can't be serious! I can't hand over a mission as difficult as this one to a mere child, no matter how worldly he may be!"

"You're mistaken. Michel Thoraval is very much an adult and he's been through a lot."

I returned to my candidate determined to find out for myself and spent the entire afternoon asking him questions. I described the mission in the darkest terms possible, outlining the risks and dangers involved. But all that was useless. He had an answer for everything. By the end of our chat he was even more willing and determined than at the start of our meeting. His shyness had evaporated and I was looking at the young man I had been searching for.

"It's true," I told Uncle Tom, "he's a real jewel!"

He still had to be trained in the techniques of pick-up—the creating of emergency landing strips for clandestine landing and take off inside France—to prepare him for the mission I was about to entrust him with.

On January 19, 1943, at 2:30 a.m. Michel parachuted near Issoire. He hid his gear and waited in hiding for daybreak to meet with Captain Kerhervé and be accepted as my envoy. Then with the officer and Dr. Roubille, who used his car for professional reasons, they drove to meet Verneuil and his top deputies: Mayem, Johanès, Hermann. He handed them my correspondence, radio gear, and 500,000 francs loaned by British intelligence that we would repay one month later.

In a matter of hours, with an ecstatic Simonin, he established contact with London and Algiers. He met Olleris, Revers, and Frère, who all gave him their correspondence for Giraud. On February 18, 1943 having successfully completed his first pick-up operation, he brought back to London messages that were reassuring me as to the dedication and efficiency of the TR.

I met Passy on December 27. Ronin came with me. I thanked him for his interest in my fate and he congratulated me on my escape. I was impressed by what he said and his assurance when he said it. He had a deep, pleasant voice and his blue eyes looked young but some premature hair loss also made him appear older. I expressed my wish for unity.

"We have no counterespionage service," answered Passy "and no real experience as far as SR and intelligence gathering is concerned. In the merging of our services you're eminently qualified to provide the technicians."

Ronin didn't say much. He was listening. After an hour of friendly conversation I had the feeling we could get along. Especially where counterespionage was concerned there were no problems and I was a godsend for the BCRA. At the time the BCRA had an internal security service of the FFL, headed for a time by Warin, alias Wybot, who had given it the grandiose name of "Counterespionage."

"General de Gaulle knows that you're in London. Would you like to meet him?"

"Not right away," injected Ronin. "We shall report back on these meetings. Colonel Rivet will draw the conclusions as the political situation between Algiers and London evolves."

"As you wish," answered Passy dryly.

I was somewhat embarrassed by Ronin's refusal and informed Passy of my plan to set up a liaison station in London headed by Bonnefous.

"The British trust him and his effectiveness. General de Gaulle knows him well. I would hope that he could very quickly merge our services with your help. He's best qualified to make sense of the huge volume of information coming to you and the British from France that pertains to our security and counterespionage. He'll also handle liaisons of that part of my services that'll be set up in England."

Passy, whose priority it was to work on France itself, discreetly suggested that I establish my headquarters in London. I didn't see things that way. Algiers had been prepared for a long time to play that role and had both the personnel and the necessary archives. I added a point that I thought Passy found convincing:

"Some French territories have been liberated, where a French authority has been established. General de Gaulle will visit them, the sooner the better. The French army is fighting with the Allies. The head of military security and counterespionage should be located in French territory near the commander in chief."

There was another motive for my position. The BCRA was dependent upon British intelligence and had to use all its contacts and radio transmissions for its actions in France, so that our friends knew every message. This was not the kind of solution I found compatible with the nature of my mission and my idea of French sovereignty.

I did use the British for the Thoraval operation though. I was happy about that and was ready to start over every time it would become necessary. The Allies never refused to help me but it was urgently necessary to attempt, through specifically French organizations, to ensure the independence of my service. Menzies, Dunderdale, and Cowgill understood this legitimate wish. The only ones who could not possibly understand, having no knowledge of counterespionage work, couldn't share my concept of dignity and modesty whereby Frenchmen should wash their dirty linen amongst themselves.

24

Algiers

On January 2, 1943, at 3:30 p.m. I landed at Maison-Blanche airport in Algiers. I had flown out of England on the night of the first and still have dreadful memories of that seaplane trip to Gibraltar. Alone inside the huge plane I had been in freezing conditions for about ten hours, jostled by stormy weather conditions and the sudden turns of the plane that was after enemy submarines. An awful bout with airsickness that also affected the crew had destroyed me. In my haste to get on the ground I forgot my suitcase on the plane that took off immediately with my beautiful *Made in England* suit and my new underwear!

I was now back in Africa, choked up with emotion and worried at the same time. A stopover at the American base in Oran revealed the gigantic equipment and supplies capabilities of our Allies as well as their strange culinary tastes. Like everyone else I was given, in the same plate, a helping of chickpeas, some artificial jam, and a serving of corned beef. A slice of bread like a piece of cotton was my fare with all the other GIs, all of them very relaxed, wearing jockey style caps with the brim pushed up in their own irreverent way. My first impression was one of power, informality, and benevolence. An American officer found me a driver who took me from Maison-Blanche airport to 17 rue Charras in Algiers where Ronin told me I would find Rivet. It was a nondescript little building; the offices were narrow and sparsely furnished. I found Villeneuve in charge of army intelligence (SR) and I met Captain Trautmann, who had arrived the day before to head the navy SR:

"We're not many but we have men of quality. You were the one missing!" said the Boss, as he gave me a warm welcome.

It felt as if we'd never parted and I told him at length what I had been up to since November 8. He approved my actions and was very encouraging.

"You'll find a situation that hasn't been cleared up after Darlan's death. Our comrades, who were more or less involved with the Allied landings, have been shunted aside: Baril, Monsabert, Mast. In Morocco Béthouart was placed under arrest with your man Guillaume and a few others. We had a hard time getting them out of jail. The heads of the *Sûreté* in Algeria and Achiary have been incarcerated in Laghouat since December 30."

I was stunned and stopped him.

"But colonel, the *Surveillance du Territoire* has no chief. What does Chrétien say?"

"You'll see; he was powerless. All these officials are involved in Darlan's assassination. General Giraud was appointed by the Imperial committee—composed of the governors and residents general in North Africa and West Africa, plus General Giraud himself and Bergeret—to succeed the admiral as high commissioner and commander in chief of the ground forces. Actually General Bergeret is in command of interior affairs that are even more complex and troubled since the Count of Paris arrived in Algiers. He was at the center of many intrigues. Bergeret asked me to tell you to go and see him as soon as you arrived. Go tomorrow with Ronin."

"What about my service?"

"In spite of this confused internal situation it's solid and efficient. Relations with the Allies are good. Most sabotage attempts by the Krauts or the Italians have been nipped in the bud. We had about twenty of them on the railroad tracks, all of them inconsequential, mostly in the area and the bridges around Constantine. A few agent infiltrations by the Abwehr or the SIM on the ground or by parachute were quickly located. The Muslim population is quiet."

"What about France?"

"I've been in radio contact with our SR comrades for the past few days, but we don't have much news. We were able to send a mission to Corsica on December 10 that included Griffi, de Saulle, and an American from OSS named Brown. Our submarine, the *Casabianca*, which had avoided the scuttling at Toulon, took them over; the skipper, Commander Lherminier, is an ace and the crew is fantastic."

Word of my presence got around; Allemand and Vellaud came by, the former handed me a requisition ticket for a room at the house of a lawyer in Algiers, M. Genty. He was to take me to El-Biar where Chrétien was expecting me at military security headquarters. Vellaud told me that his job as Giraud's bodyguard had become superfluous. Viret, the orderly, was always at the general's side and was jealous of his position. Vellaud was impatient:

"I'd like to go back to my TR job in France."

"We'll talk about that once you've trained about ten more officers like yourself over here."

'Really? I can begin right away?"

"Of course," I answered. "I need tough guys ready to go to France and set up links to North Africa and London. Find yourself a space and look for volunteers. Follow up with Allemand and local military authorities, especially Major Grossin.* The operation must begin quickly; starting next week we'll set up counterespionage training sessions, radio transmissions, parachute training, and pick-up."

Vellaud was beaming when he left us and we drove to the Villa Jaïs at El-Biar.

Chrétien was set up in a large Moorish style room with a fire burning in the fireplace while he quickly explained in detail the conditions he faced in his mission without ever interrupting his security and counterespionage work.

Of the twenty-odd penetration agents in North Africa about half had radio transmitters and continued to maintain contact with the Abwehr, allowing us to check its objectives. It seemed all the more urgent that *Force A* be created because enemy questionnaires were becoming very specific. The answers had to fit into Allied battle plans. We also had to "reassure" Abwehr II about its sabotage efforts by giving some information about a few destruction initiatives its agents (our Ws) had undertaken. Chrétien had succeed in enforcing the state of siege law and the requirements in the decree of February 10, 1939 regarding counterespionage organization in time of war; military security could now count on the

---

* Pierre Grossin was later promoted to the rank of general; he headed the military cabinet of the president of France, Vincent Auriol; and was finally appointed Director General of the SDECE.

police forces and the gendarmerie. The *Sécurité du Territoire* and the technical controls were under our command in Algeria but what we were still missing, as in 1939-1940, was a purely military security organization. I knew we would have to create such an organization and draft the regulations limiting its jurisdiction and the status of the police forces that would be placed under our control.

The French Special Services had retreated from Tunisia, leaving behind a number of agents who had gone to Le Kef. We were informed that a group called "Phalange Africaine" had been created, and that Christian du Jonchay, Admiral Estéva's chief of staff, was one of its promoters. The elements for the Phalange were recruited in France and Tunisia among members of the SOL (*Service d'Ordre Légionnaire*) led by Joseph Darnand and Jacques Doriot's PPF. They took part in a few battles alongside Axis forces but were routed in April 1943 in the Medjerda Valley and subsequently disbanded.

In Morocco General Noguès contended that the country's special statute allowed him to avoid remaining under the authorities in Algiers, especially for security reasons. Finally, a stricter policing of the border with Spanish Morocco and the coastline, as well as entry and exit points from North Africa and West Africa, were urgently required. There was a huge amount of work to do but we'd have full Allied support. After a few days to catch his bearings, Chrétien was able to get his service recognized by everyone. He had full power over security and counterespionage in Algeria. The Allied High Command, OSS representative Colonel Eddy, and British Intelligence Service representative, Major Trevor-Wilson, trusted Chrétien completely.

The results confirmed Rivet's satisfaction. German General Nehring, commander of Axis forces in Tunisia, was unable to stop the retreat of General Barre's units of the French army toward the west to join the Allies. Canaris was ordered to strengthen his assets in North Africa and paralyze Allied efforts. Abwehr I was no doubt satisfied because of the work of our penetration agents and was active close to the front lines in the area around Constantine and the border between Algeria and Tunisia. Abwehr II attempted to block our lines of communication in the east and destroy fuel and other supply dumps. Spies and saboteurs were recruited on the run mainly in Tunisia and many Arabs were drafted without any technical training. Practically every one of them would defect to the Gendarmerie once they reached Algerian territory. Some of them were turned, mostly those who were best prepared and those who were most sincere, and we were able to use these newly found Ws to check on the sabotage the enemy was planning.

The bulk of infiltrations by enemy agents was taking place along the sketchy front lines of southern Tunisia and the region near Constantine. Some commandos were flown in on gliders, others used submarines, and on rare occasions they would parachute over the lines. These enemy attempts didn't amount to much and the results were insignificant. The only significant operations in the initial phase were on January 16 and 19, 1943. At Bouira a railroad bridge was damaged, but not enough to interrupt train traffic. A ditch was destroyed at M'Zita by five men who parachuted in (an Arab, a German, and three Frenchmen who were members of the PPF).

All this was far from the triumphant results announced by Abwehr II. An OKW message we intercepted on December 21, 1942 offered a glimpse into the kind of objectivity and sincerity of the men on Canaris' staff: "Our actions against enemy communications are unqualified success—124 [*sic*] Arabs were condemned to death in Algeria where they were found guilty of sabotaging the railroad tracks. Muslim hostages are being arrested by the hundreds."

"This gross misrepresentation of the truth reminds me of an incident," said Sérot as he handed me that intercept. "In Belfort in 1937 an agent of German origin had walked in to offer his services to sabotage German industrial plants. From time to time I was getting messages announcing fires, an explosion, or some destruction. A few days later I read accounts of these incidents in the German newspapers that he'd send me. The mishaps were said to be accidental or the result of negligence or other mistakes. The fact that sabotage was never once considered made me suspicious. Then I discovered the whole scheme. Because one of his friends who worked at the DNB German news agency, our agent took note of any accident that could pass for the result of a criminal act and he would then give me the news before the DNB would broadcast it to the press. The two fellows were doing the same thing with several other intelligence organizations, thereby pocketing some nice amounts of cash."

Fraud has always prospered within intelligence organizations. What was real in any case were the results our services could show following November 8, 1942: 904 suspects had been arrested (propagandists, spies, and saboteurs). Among them we discovered some leaders of collaborationist groups, Abwehr, and RSHA, SIM, and Spanish intelligence agents; there were 266 persons suspected of working for Spain under arrest. It resulted in an implacable repression: 189 death sentences, of which 57 Arabs (far from the Abwehr numbers), 62 Frenchmen, 22 Spaniards, 19 Italians, 8 Germans, and 21 others. But along with these positive results there was one disappointment: radio contact with the TR in France was still cut.

"In spite of our calls we still can't raise Simonin," said Allemand.

It was a serious situation and one that made me think of our technological weakness. I regretted not having been able to fix that problem prior to 1941. So we had few pieces of news from France, which didn't appear to bother anyone because the attention was focused on what was happening in Algeria. Only one message, dated December 26, 1942, from Auguste Larquier in Barcelona through Malaise in Madrid, reached Algiers. It contained news of TR 117, of the situation in the Pyrenees region and mapped out what the station knew about Abwehr and RSHA organizations south of the Garonne River to Montpellier. Auguste had successfully completed setting himself up and was now able to observe enemy activity in Catalonia and keep up communications with France—especially with Getten, who was about to set up his post in Paris.

With an introduction by de Linarès I reported to General Giraud on January 4, 1943 at the Palais d'Été. He cut a tall, imposing figure at the far end of the large room where he had set up his office. He greeted me in an unexpectedly familiar way, sat near me, and crossed his long legs as he came right to the point.

"The Americans had no clue as to what our theaters of operations were like. Since Tébourda (where in the wake of a Panzer attack the Germans took some 700 American prisoners) they've understood what the enemy is all about. But they must not let up the pressure. I'm off to Constantine and the front shortly. Rivet told me about you and your service. I congratulate you and confirm your appointments. Come and see me often and keep me abreast of what's going on in France. You've just returned from England? What are they saying over there?"

"That the French must be united and that you have to get together with de Gaulle," I answered.

"Not so fast, my young friend. It's not as simple as that. I was able to turn the French army against the Krauts and it's now bearing the weight of German pressure, but it remains fundamentally anti-Gaullist. The Axis is dispatching more and more reinforcements and the military situation is far from settled. I can't run the risk of weakening our position. Some militant Gaullists are agitating in a clumsy way. They're confusing the public and harming our war effort by worrying the Allies. Meet with Bergeret he'll tell you more."

In de Beaufort's office I saw Major de France, who had been part of Pétain's staff until a few hours before November 8, 1942, when he escaped with General Bergeret and de Beaufort. They introduced me to Bergeret who was with Ronin. Suddenly the general said to him:

"You'll temporarily replace Rigaud at Interior and Paillole will take over general security, replacing Henri d'Astier de la Vigerie."

Rigaud was an assistant to Lemaigre-Dubreuil and a former member of the "Comité des Cinq"; he was also the secretary of the interior, a sort of ministerial job. Ronin started laughing:

"You can't be serious! I haven't a clue! You should appoint Paillole!"

Bergeret didn't appear to like his former classmate's objection. I could see the general was serious and worried: his face was drawn and his blue eyes looked tired. He reviewed the internal situation that he found very worrisome:

"There are intrigues everywhere," he said. "We have reason to believe that after murdering Darlan they wouldn't stop at murdering Giraud. The Americans are afraid that may happen as well and they're asking us to take forceful steps to ensure law and order behind the lines. If we don't succeed quickly enough we'll wind up under AMGOT."

"Arresting the heads of Algerian security forces have given a bad impression of both a lack of order and insecurity," I commented. "How could it be that such highly qualified officials as Achiary and Bringard are in prison?"

"I'm not sure they were accomplices to the murder of Darlan. But what I do know is that they're part of the political unrest that destabilizes our authority. As for Rigaud and Henri d'Astier de la Vigerie, among others, I think they were both involved in all these matters; they're both as slippery as eels. You see, I can't trust any of the people here."

Bergeret looked at me.

"So Paillole, will you take the job?"

"I didn't come all the way to North Africa to become a policeman or engage in politics," I protested. "My mission's a very sensitive one, requiring all my efforts. What would my comrades in France think if I abandoned my post?"

Bergeret looked puzzled and turned to Ronin, who agreed with me.

"Paillole's right. We can't sacrifice a vital mission for something we're not trained for. Why not give the job to Chrétien? He's better informed than we are about what's happening in Algiers; he knows many more people than we do."

"That's just the point," Bergeret interrupted. "He knows too many people. I thought about it and it won't work. Furthermore, Juin and Giraud don't trust him. We need someone from outside Algeria not involved in local intrigue."

There was a long silence that Bergeret finally broke:

"Paillole, will you take on at least the investigation into the murder? We must get out of this situation."

More than any other reason I felt bad because of Achiary's arrest. It was a mystery to me. I could imagine how it must have confused the *Securité du Territoire* when we needed it to be very efficient. Allemand warned me the day before against the negative effect on the Algiers police force that was paralyzed by all this. The *Sécurité du Territoire* suspected military security of having cut off its head and was not cooperating whenever we approached it.

Was our defensive shield, so long in the making, going to grind to a halt? Perhaps I could do something to stop what was going wrong.

"General," I answered, "I accept the appointment. But in a few days I'm expecting the arrival of my British counterpart, Colonel Cowgill. I've asked him to come over to set up our work together, so I must complete this mission in a few days and have time to prepare for Cowgill's visit."

"You're free to act as you see fit. Everything you require will be available to you."

In the military plane, a Goéland that took me to Laghouat, I studied the file that Rigaud had given me. It was as thin as the few explanations the mysterious secretary of the interior gave me in a whisper. I came to three conclusions: both the investigation and the prosecution of the murder of Admiral Darlan had been badly botched; the appearance of the Count of Paris in Algiers was strange; the measures taken against the heads of the police and a few others had nothing to do with the Darlan murder.

In the camp in Laghouat where they had been locked up, Muscatelli, Bringard, and most of all Achiary all greeted me as their savior. With the spontaneity and sincerity that always existed between us, Achiary confided what he knew and what he thought happened. I was convinced that others had masterminded the plot. They had not only put an end to what the Americans called "a temporary expedient" and wanted to cut the umbilical cord to Vichy, but hadn't yet decided whether to replace the admiral with the Count of Paris. They unscrupulously set up and then turned their backs on an adolescent, who sacrificed himself. (Bonnier de la Chapelle, who murdered Darlan, was part of the "Chantiers de Jeunesse." He was executed by firing squad on December 26, 1942.) They acted without scruples and like cowards. Muscatelli and Bringard noted that to have their monarchist plot succeed they had to neutralize the defenders of Republican order that they represented.

It made sense as an explanation, yet I was certain that Bergeret, who had signed the arrest warrant for the policemen, was not at all an accomplice in such a twisted plot. It would require for the plotters to take advantage of his good faith and the confusion created by Darlan's death.

On my flight back to Algiers I decided to request three immediate decisions to stop any *ad hoc* decisions, end political agitation, reassure the police, and restore it to its mission of national defense: free the prisoners in Laghouat, ask the Count of Paris to leave, and begin a real investigation into the case.

Bergeret saw me at his home when I returned that evening. He was impressed by my conclusions and approved them. The order to free Muscatelli, Bringard, Achiary, and the others was issued. Ronin was ordered to accompany the Count of Paris to the border with Spanish Morocco with every appropriate courtesy. A new investigation into the murder of Admiral Darlan was also ordered, to unravel the circumstances and responsibilities in the case.

"How do you see the investigation succeeding?" asked Bergeret.

"It can only be undertaken by military judges who will have the same independence as you required of me."

Two officers from military justice in Morocco, well known for their integrity and experience, were appointed two days later to begin their investigation: Colonel Laroubine, as prosecutor, and Major Voiturier as judge.

"I thank you, Paillole. Return to your regular duties. I only request that you help the officers of the court in getting on with the job. It's not an easy one." As I was leaving Bergeret a sentry announced Mr. Harold Macmillan. "Stay here," ordered the general. "You'll see for yourself how difficult things are for us. At Eisenhower's headquarters Macmillan is Churchill's eyes and ears."

The British official was an imposing man, about forty-five, with a dour look on his face. He appeared surprised to see me there and Bergeret reassured him.

"Major Paillole is the head of our counterespionage and security service. He just returned from France and London."

Without further ado and with a gruff manner that was very undiplomatic, Macmillan went right to the point.

"The general* is still worried about your internal situation," he said.
"He thinks you're not in control. We still don't know anything about the
plot that eliminated the admiral."

"That's exactly why I ordered Major Paillole to find out the truth,"
answered Bergeret. "He just handed me his initial conclusions and we've
made a number of decisions that will be effective in the next few days."

"General, it's very urgent. We shall be forced to take extremely serious measures if you're unable to keep law and order internally, impose
respect for the law, and return to democratic ways of government."

Bergeret was startled.

"What do you mean?"

"We cannot accept the fact that North Africa is still under the Vichy
regime. You're still holding political prisoners and your attitude toward
the Jews and the Muslims is incompatible with a democracy."

Macmillan was correct no doubt, but it was a French problem. I
couldn't stand all this hectoring and discreetly took my leave.

A few days later Judge Voiturier issued indictments against Henri
d'Astier de la Vigerie, the Abbott Pierre-Marie Cordier, and Police Superintendent Garidacci. The judge told me:

"The first one gave the order and provided the funds for the execution: 2,000 dollars was found on Bonnier de la Chapelle, taken from some
40,000 dollars that Henri d'Astier de la Vigerie had in his possession.
Major, can you tell me where those dollars came from?"

"Give me the numbers on the bills and I'll try. What do you have
against Cordier and Garidacci?"

"Cordier provided the weapon. As a priest he gave confession to
Bonnier de la Chapelle before the murder to ease his conscience. As for
Garidacci, he took Bonnier's complete confession but withheld it at the
trial since it implicated d'Astier and Cordier as being responsible for the
murder. The chief of police was the one who hatched the plot; a priest
was an accomplice in an execution; a policeman was obstructing justice.
And that's not all," added Voiturier. "There is also a man named Alfred
Pose, a director at the BNCI bank and the Commissioner of Economy
and Finance, who had the Prince as his guest. I also remind you, major,
that we'd like to know where those dollars came from."

---

* Eisenhower.

Then Cowgill arrived in Algiers on January 8, 1943, as promised. I gave him the numbers on the dollars without expecting too much due to the well-known secrecy of the British Intelligence Service. By January 20, 1943, to my complete surprise he told me that the dollars had been given in December 1942 to the financial services of General de Gaulle. An authorization to take the money to North Africa was issued to General François d'Astier de la Vigerie, Henri's brother. His presence, along with Scamaroni in the fortress of Gibraltar, was now clear. It was obvious that the Intelligence Service wished to be absolved of any responsibility in the matter now that there were rumors in Algiers about its part in the Darlan assassination.

By September 1943 the case was closed. Henri d'Astier went on to fight in Italy in the French army and was decorated with the "Croix de Guerre." Cordier was given the medal of the "Resistance" and Garidacci was fired from the police force.

Voiturier came to see me at El-Biar at the headquarters of military security:

"I'm now out of work, major," he said. "Can you help me?"

Fortunately his hobby was to tinker with little radio transmitters that could be used by our clandestine services. He stayed in our service for some time; I owed it to him.

As for Laroubine, he was more to the point:

"You got me into a bizarre mess. Now 'they' would like to throw me out!"

25

Military Security
and Counterespionage in North Africa

I was finally able to concentrate on my mission. I wanted to isolate myself from the obsessive and depressing atmosphere of Algiers. Rumors were rampant despite the decisions that understandably consolidated Giraud's authority and reassured the Allies. Intrigues were being hatched and then faded away; the cafés and bars were filled with many idle people coming out of the woodwork, having hushed conversations. The cocktail hour at the Hotel Aletti was full of individuals predicting what was about to happen, choking the atmosphere with news be it true, false, good or bad. Events in North Africa were on everyone's mind and many an imagination was running wild. The Gaullist movement was slowly making headway with expert handling, giving rise to different kinds of reactions: "He'll come." ... "He won't come." ... "The Americans don't want him" ... "The British don't want him anymore."

In the confusion the voice of France remained silent, whereas in London it could be heard loud and clear. I could see it happening in my own service. Allemand, Sérot, Luttwig, Vellaud, d'Hoffelize—all my comrades from France could feel it and were asking me to react. I also wanted to but it wasn't that simple. There was real administrative anarchy in the improvised capital. No state administration had prepared or planned to fall back on Algiers. Impromptu officials hovered around the newcomers who were running governmental services. At first they were residents of North Africa, then little by little they included more escapees from France. Some centralized government agencies were packed up and used as a dumping ground for all kinds of draft dodgers and ambitious types. Improvisation was the most positive trait of this embryonic state administration that lacked traditions or archives.

There were constant clashes between military and civilian authorities, both having overlapping responsibilities, neither of them with any experience of the laws on the state of siege. Despite Chrétien's efforts and existing rules, the Gendarmerie would be a bone of contention for a long time, just like the police force, the internment camps, deportations, and repatriations.

Despite the endless resources of our legal arsenal, which remained unused or simply ignored, the officials incessantly hammered away, issuing decrees, orders, and instructions of all kinds. In such conditions we were to ensure security and engage in counterespionage! Therefore we could rely only on ourselves because we possessed trained and experienced personnel but in very small numbers and could count on a few men and organizations, such as the *Sécurité du Territoire* and the Gendarmerie, on archives that were thankfully up to date and on the favorable disposition of our Allies.

In this chaotic environment the *Sécurité Militaire* appeared as a kind of bastion of legality that everyone ignored and of national traditions that seemed old fashioned. Some negative commentators chose to see it as a kind of surviving entity of the Vichy regime, as if the French Republic's laws on security and counterespionage were not valid and independent of any particular political regime. In truth some treacherous Frenchmen in Vichy, for a variety of reasons, joined with the Abwehr in labeling our activities Gaullist and attacked them as such. A humorist summed things up best:

> "Gaullists in Vichy."
> "Vichyites in London."
> "Giraudists in Algiers."
> "The only people who call us Frenchmen are the Allies and the Boche!"

It wasn't until April 24, 1944, that General de Gaulle, as President of the French Committee of National Liberation and Commander in Chief of the Army, signed interministerial instruction no. 8000/DSM, which I had drafted together with Jacques Soustelle* to restate and impose upon everyone the fundamental security regulations and the struggle against espionage that we tried to maintain and enforce since 1939. Oddly the defensive apparatus de Gaulle made official in April 1944 had its origin in the decree creating the *Sécurité Militaire* that had been signed in August 1942 by Revers under Darlan's orders. It was the end result of the doctrine of unity of action that our service had to follow to ensure national defense, no matter which political regime was running the country. It was also noteworthy that instruction no. 8000 made reference to the legal decree of February 10, 1939, which was the basis of France's fight against espionage and signed by Daladier, and the application instructions to the armed forces codified on May 11, 1943, in Algiers by Giraud.

I thought things through in my office in the rue Charras. First of all, the connection to France had to be reestablished and strengthened by radio and by courier. I expected much and was not to be disappointed in the Thoraval mission. The Barcelona station was growing and the mail coming from France through Spain was arriving weekly. We still needed a direct connection between Algiers and France. Air connections from North Africa were very difficult due to distance and the lack of experience of American flyers. I therefore looked to the sea. The *Casabianca* was just returning from its expedition to Corsica. I went to see Lherminier.

"Commander, if I secure the navy's and the Allies' approval, do you think you could land or bring back a group of my comrades off the French coast?"

The "Pasha" didn't hesitate for a second.

"That would be fantastic!" His very thin energetic face was full of enthusiasm. "But your guys over there have to tell us whether or not the location we wind up choosing is being watched by the Krauts! That kind of task is much more serious than Corsica, where there are only Macaronis—none too brave."

To be able to deliver what Lherminier wanted we had to reestablish relations with TR 115, which seemed possible. For the last twenty-four

---

* Soustelle was Director General of the Special Services, overseeing the *Sécurité Militaire*.

hours our calls were being answered in Marseille. Guiraud's station sent a very short message and then fell silent again, no doubt out of caution because German direction finders were very active.

I discussed my plan with Rivet and on January 7, 1943 he got General Giraud's approval. However, to get the navy to approve it took all of our friend Trautmann's diplomatic skill. Only in February did a first group land at Cap Camarat. The service inside France had to be reinforced as much as the communications, and I remembered Verneuil's warning:

"Make haste! The longer we wait, the better our chances to go to the gallows."

Clearly we couldn't hope for France to be liberated in the course of 1943. The Americans were making war forcefully and step by step; for now, the Mediterranean front was a handful for them. To reinforce the TR meant creating a network parallel to the old one, a "TR jr." I still had to replace Bonnefous as head of the clandestine *Sécurité Militaire* and begin its network into the old Occupied Zone. Vellaud, who reported to me, was in charge of creating and setting up the "TR jr." network in France. By the end of January 1943 we had recruited about twenty officers in North Africa, and as many NCOs and civilians, all of them volunteers, chosen because of their patriotic sense of duty, their courage and aptitude for our type of work. Two training centers were opened: one inside Algiers for technical training of counterespionage personnel and military security; the second in Guyotville within the Allied training schools for parachute jumping and pick-up operations.

The first teams were ready by March 1943 to be taken to France, either by submarine in the Mediterranean, or through either Spain or London to parachute in or pick up. For the time being we coordinated our efforts with the Allies. Getting *Force A* up and running was pressing and that was the main reason for Cowgill's visit to Algiers on January 8, 1943. I met his deputy, Major Trevor-Wilson, a little man about forty, intelligent with a sense of humor, and a kind of exaggerated politeness. He was a "bon vivant" and liked France, especially French women. Until he left Algiers at the beginning of 1944 he would be a loyal friend to my unit. The same could be said of Lieutenant Colonel Stephens of the U.S. Army, who was handling the liaison with my services. He was a reserve officer, trained at the Staff College—the counterespionage branch of CIC—since 1940, a well-informed and keen observer who truly believed in French sovereignty.

With these specialists, plus Colonel William Eddy (the OSS head in North Africa), we discussed our objectives and what each one could do. The

Americans were very well equipped and extremely helpful. Their security and counterintelligence personnel were well staffed and active. They were short on experience regarding our problems and had to adapt to our kind of secret war. American "SCI units," or "Sections of Counterintelligence," were scattered among the large U.S. Army units as specialized groups. Deep intelligence gathering was done by the OSS, headed by Colonel William Donovan. In fact, at the time the OSS was just starting in Europe and Africa, but it took a powerful and fundamental leap forward.

For the moment the British appeared to be the leaders of this Anglo-Saxon double team. They had excellent personnel resources and a world-renowned reputation, great traditions, and without a doubt unparalleled experience of what was now occupied Europe. The British secret services were the masters in action operations, liaison, and communications as well as using every possible means to gather operational intelligence.

For our part, with fewer resources, we had a mastery of counterespionage that had been confirmed since 1940. We knew the enemy's organization; the activities of enemy intelligence services and their auxiliaries in Europe and North Africa were included our reports, our files, and archives. We had a proven defensive organization in theaters of operations that we knew well and that had been tested. Our offensive capability was surprising to our Allies. Our penetration of the enemy didn't simply have a defensive capability to increase our knowledge of him and paralyze his work; it also revealed what the he knew, what he feared, and at times what his intentions were. Through disinformation it allowed Allied commanders to orient the enemy's decisions to a certain extent.

The large number and quality of our penetration agents facilitated the immediate creation of *Force A*. British General Dudley Clark was in command at General Eisenhower's headquarters. Together, Americans, British, and French officers and men drafted plans for false information and set up various disinformation methods—fictitious military operations, strategic information leaks, false scenarios and so on—which were to support the information disseminated by our W agents. The Ws were recruited among those agents best suited to gain the enemy's trust; their tasks in wartime operations will be part of a separate chapter.

It was time I traveled to Morocco; Cowgill and Trevor-Wilson came with me. It was necessary to coordinate our forces and make some of our external services work hand in hand in Morocco as they did in Algeria. On January 12, 1943, we stopped in Oran, where a longer resistance to the Allied landings left some bad memories. We wanted to be sure that a renewed spirit of trust between the French and the Allies now existed and that security conditions were good. Oran was a sensitive focal point because of the concentration of large American units, the huge volume of traffic at La Senia airport, and the vast naval base at Mers-el-Kébir.

The local TR station used a few penetration agents into the Abwehr in Spanish Morocco. My Saint-Cyr classmate Forest was heading military security as best he could. That evening we had dinner in the general's mess. Everyone was asking questions. They wanted to know what was going on in France, in England, in Algiers and I told them about the dangerous and necessary work being done by our services in France, the difficult connections that we needed to improve.

At the end of the table a young ensign from the airborne was looking at me intently. He was Yves Le Hénaff, one of the general's aides de camp, and he looked like a very eager, passionate man. Later that night I discussed once more the life of my men, how I escaped through Spain, the adventures of the *Casabianca* and its mission to Corsica. The next day Forest drove us to the airport. He took me aside.

"Le Hénaff came to see me this morning," he said. "He knew I was going to see you. What you said last night affected him very much. He'd like you to use him in France. I can assure you that he's completely trust-worthy. When can you see him?"

"Will his general let him go?"

"Certainly."

"Tell him to come and see me in Algiers as soon as I return from Morocco, after January 20, 1943."

On January 21, Le Hénaff was in my office. He was very intelligent and eager to fight the enemy immediately. His attitude helped me over-come my hesitations because of his youth and lack of experience. We then got into a real nuts and bolts dialog, this young man and I, without any artificial niceties, wherein two men simply compare problems and establish links. It is only through such a person-to-person connection that we discover the mystery of how the Special Services really work.

"Someone will recognize you and identify you," I said.

"I'll change my looks!"

After four months of training in England and plastic surgery to alter his face, Le Hénaff parachuted with his radio in the Finistère region of Brittany on the night of June 14-15, 1943. For eight months he was to be the tireless leader of our TR jr. network and organizer of our connections to England by sea. On the morning of February 8, 1944, a raging storm would finally have the better of his incredible courage.

His sailboat, *Le Jouet des Flots*, with its main sail torn away, and damaged by the rocks at the Pointe du Raz, was to hit the beach at Plogoff. Not all of his thirty-seven passengers, among them RAF pilots, members of the resistance and officers like the future General Jouhaud, were able to save their lives. Bollaert, a delegate of the committee of Liberation in France, Pierre Brossolette, an envoy of the BCRA in London, and Challan-Belval (my former deputy at the Marseille TR, whom I had called to Algiers) were arrested with Le Hénaff.

To avoid breaking during interrogation, Pierre Brossolette jumped out of a window at the Gestapo building on Avenue Foch. The heroic efforts of Germaine Richard failed to free "Fanfan" from the prison at Rennes. He was to die of asphyxiation in the boxcar taking him to Germany in 1944. Only in 1972 was I able to hand the Legion of Honor, awarded posthumously, to his brother. If it is true that it's not part of our tradition to seek praise and beg for rewards, it is also true that it's not in the tradition of official institutions to recognize the sacrifices of the best among those who served their country.

We arrived in Rabat on January 13, 1943, to be welcomed by Breitel and Doudot, the heads of TR 120. They were still angry because Unterberg (alias Gibhardt), head of German intelligence within the Casablanca armistice commission, succeeded in slipping away.

"He was able to run for it with the help of some French policemen."

We had to agree that the French army and navy's resistance to the American landings created a very unclear situation inside Morocco for a few days. Military security in Rabat was under the command of Captain Maurice Dumont, a young, smart and reliable man who understood his responsibilities and was able to carry them out. He was also aware of the importance of centralizing technical work in Algiers.

On January 15, 1943, while the British were having a meeting with their colleagues and the Americans, I met with Noguès. The Resident general was bitter and disappointed at being kept out of the events of November 8.

"Your services should have warned me!"

Just like General Juin, he accused Chrétien of not keeping him abreast of the news at the right time.

"But general, he was bound by secrecy and actually everyone else knew nothing about the details of the operation."

Nogués didn't believe me and went on:

"The end result of all this is an irreparable lack of trust between the Americans and myself, as well as a number of unacceptable interventions by them in political and economic areas."

Before leaving I confirmed my fears to the general regarding the Sultan's attitude. He was still keeping the Grand Mufti informed and the Abwehr appreciated the information. The Resident, with a slow movement of his arms, seemed to be telling me there was not much he could do.

Our journey back to Algiers from Fez would have been routine but on the morning of January 18, 1943, our plane, a military Goéland, missed the take off. In the brutal crash my rear seat went forward and I hit head first on the door leading to the cockpit. My face was covered with blood and my nose was crushed and out of joint, so I needed the services of the surgeon at the military hospital to reconstruct my face as much as possible. Fortunately my two British guests were unscathed; the pilot had been severely injured and was taken to Casablanca.

I returned to Algiers in time with my battered nose to put a stop to the many rumors that were beginning to go around: it was an attack, it was sabotage, Paillole was in a coma. Allemand, who was constantly with me, was happy to report Michel Thoraval's success in parachuting into France near Issoire. Contact with Verneuil was reestablished and I was overjoyed in reading the first messages sent from London from our special "Cub-Minor" radio. In my absence Vellaud continued to find enough volunteers to start up the TR jr., especially in those areas where the old TR consisted of HCs or a few agents like the Nord region where there was a gaping void following the arrests of Dehenin and Ansot in 1942, and Brittany where I wanted to set up regular links to England. That would be one of Le Hénaff's missions. The regions of Vendée and the lower Loire had been hard hit by the arrests following Martineau's. Trautmann brought me a young sailor, Lieutenant Lavallée. He had shown his worth in several war operations and I was impressed by his calm determination and felt I could trust him. He went to England for training and was parachuted into France with his radio operator in 1943.

In the Nord region and in Belgium we were lucky to have a young man from Sainghin near Lille, Lieutenant L'Heureux, a Saint-Cyr graduate whose two stars on the recent Croix de Guerre spoke for his bravery. He wanted to be back in action and felt homesick at the same time. After three months of training he was parachuted in May 1943 in the Somme with his deputy Bellet and his operator Le Douguet.

Our TR network was quickly rebuilt around this group named "Joy," which could count on the help from local networks like *La Voix du Nord*. His long messages came in regularly from London. L'Heureux, Bellet, and Le Douguet were arrested on March 12, 1944 during a pick-up operation in Maurepas in the Somme region. They never returned. Men like Dr. Betrancourt, Verdun, and Louis Christiaens, who was later a deputy and cabinet minister, took over.

One morning in September 1944, in Paris, an old and shy man look-ing forlorn came to my office.

"I'm the father of Lieutenant L'Heureux. We have no more news. Do you think he's still alive?"

I didn't know what to say. I could only tell him how proud I was to have had his son under my command and thank him for giving France such a fine soldier. The old man stood up.

"Major, if he's not coming back his mother and I will at least have the satisfaction of knowing that he did his duty well."

Lieutenant L'Heureux died of dysentery at the Ellrich prison camp on December 17, 1944.

At the same time these TR jr. missions parachuted or were picked up, we used the moonless nights to begin our submarine operations on the Mediterranean coasts. During one of those nights, on February 5, 1943, the *Casabianca* chose to land at Cap Camarat, near Saint Tropez, the first TR jr. team created in Algiers. As group leader I was lucky to have an old hand and a counterespionage specialist in Guillaume, who had finally been freed after his arrest in Morocco with General Béthouart in November 1942. The two of them, with the help of TR 120 and a few patriotic Frenchmen, had tried to avoid the clash between the French and the Americans by neutralizing General Lascroux, supreme military commander in Morocco. Their attempt had failed and Noguès had ordered them to prison in Meknès.

The team's radio specialist was Lieutenant Caillot, who later became head of my communications section in Algiers. Brown, an American, was also part of the group. He looked and spoke like the kind of secret agent one sees in films, but he was also exceptionally brave and strong, as well as an excellent radio technician. I carefully prepared what was, be-sides the American radio equipment, an essentially French mission. On January 22, 1943 I had lunch with Lherminier and his deputy, Lieutenant Bellet, aboard the *Casabianca*: an excellent menu of sardines, corned beef, and peas from a can. We discussed at length the best spots to land and Lherminier liked the "Wolf's Lair" between Cannes and Nice.

"We have to be sure the Krauts aren't watching too closely, ever since Giraud left from there on November 5, 1942."

"Tonight I'll ask our TR station in Marseille to check the area and be ready to receive our men when they land," I said.

"I'll need an answer before I leave, at the latest by February 1. The night of the 4th to the 5th is a full moon; at the most I can still do it on the night of 5th to 6th."

"Suppose I have no answer by February 1?" I asked.

"You can route a cable via Gibraltar."

"Why via Gibraltar?"

"All the sailings are checked and tracked by the Allied admiralty," said Lherminier. "If we want to avoid being shot at by the British our route has to be known and tracked. All messages to ships at sea for Allied vessels are centralized in Gibraltar."

"If I have nothing?"

"Well then, either we come back or we risk the operation. What do you think?"

What kind of question was that? I preferred to avoid answering.

I was watching Lherminier, who was having trouble standing up at the table where a map of the Mediterranean coast and sea depth was detailed. He was suffering intensely but refused to show it. I asked him:

"If I'm told that the "Wolf's Lair" is under guard by the Krauts, what do we do?"

"We either come back or risk the operation somewhere else. What do you think?" he asked.

Another embarrassing question.

"But commander, you must have a suggestion?"

"I found a spot that's not as good as the "Wolf's Lair" for us, but the coast is much more difficult to patrol. There is little risk of finding any Krauts there. It's a wild spot of the Maures, Cap Camarat."

Lherminier showed me the village of Ramatuelle, above the cape, and a point in the water on his map named "Escudelier Rock."

"We could try there. But it'll be no picnic for your men! They'll need to climb up at night with their gear through the rocks and the shrubs. Then they might lose their bearings in the confusion of the underbrush. It's OK by me but it'll be tough for your team."

"My men," as the Pasha called them, were extremely tough. I knew how determined they were to succeed. Caillot and Guillaume knew, as I did, the reason behind their mission. It would be an insult to them to hesitate. I therefore agreed.

That evening we failed to contact TR 115 on the radio. We started over on the night of the 23rd. Finally, at 1:50 a.m., on the 24th, Marseille station got the message. He agreed to inspect the "Wolf's Lair." We waited for his answer every night. I was becoming increasingly nervous due to insomnia, a result of nightly German bombing raids over Algiers and Lherminier could sense it. He gave me another twenty-four hours.

"Whatever happens, we'll sail on February 2 at 10 p.m. I can't wait more than that. I also have to take two other guys to Corsica."

The fateful day arrived and I was rather ashamed because Marseille hadn't broadcast a thing and the team that was about to leave was certainly less confident than myself. The identity papers we had forged were far from perfect and there were no ration cards available. They were all carrying very large packs. I had to hope that Guiraud would be there to help them. I accompanied them on board where Master Sergeant Bozzi and radio operator Chopitel, who were to become part of the SR team headed by Griffi (who had landed in Corsica in December), were waiting. Lherminier was there to greet us, as calm and relaxed as the skipper of a pleasure boat. Almost without a sound the *Casabianca* slipped away from the dock and vanished into the night.

We were waiting anxiously for a message from Marseille but by February 3 nothing had come through. The 4th was about to end when at 11 p.m. Marseille station signaled that the "Wolf's Lair" was heavily patrolled and occupied by the enemy, concluding: "Landing impossible." We barely had time to transmit that message to the Admiralty, since February 5 was the last day that could still allow the submarine to make a landing.

At 2 a.m. on February 5, 1943 off Cap d'Antibes the *Casabianca* got my message retransmitted by Gibraltar: "Billaud informs reconnaissance unfavorable." At 11:30 p.m. the submarine stopped some 300 meters off the coast where the dingy dropped off Guillaume, Caillot, and Brown in a tiny inlet off the Escudelier Rock at the foot of a sheer cliff full of thorny bushes that made up Cap Camarat. They had to climb up, hide their gear and first reach Saint-Raphaël, then on to Marseille. Then they returned later for the gear, the mail, and money for the old TR, and set up the new radio transmitters. It all got done smoothly, with the exception of Guillaume's dislocated ankle. A new radio connection to Algiers was established on February 10 at 11:45 p.m. It was the first clandestine radio hook up that was one hundred percent French between French North Africa and France.

André Poniatowski returned from Morocco on January 26, 1943. He took part in the Anfa conference between Roosevelt, Churchill, de Gaulle, and Giraud, and acted as advisor and interpreter for Giraud.

"The boss did well," he told me. "He listed his military requirements and got what he asked for. We'll get enough to create an armored division and whatever we need in Tunisia. De Gaulle arrived late, which made everybody nervous. He proposed a kind political dualism: he'd be Clemenceau and Giraud would be Foch!"

That kind of compromise didn't impress me favorably. In any case Poniatowski did bring back a vital piece of news: the British and the Americans agreed to recognize French sovereignty in French Africa. This meant that Algiers would be officially recognized instead of Vichy. It also meant that we won out as far as security and counterespionage were concerned. Could our work have played some part in that recognition?

Since January 30, 1943 Giraud officially confirmed the special services organization under Rivet's command. The headquarters of the intelligence services and military security (DSR-SM) located in the rue Charras was placed under the direct command of the commander in chief. The organization chart was similar to what we had in August 1942 in Vichy. De Villeneuve replaced Delor as head of the army SR. Trautmann was head of navy SR, Ronin of air force SR. I headed the security services and counterespionage. We had recreated most of our services. I successfully created links and communications networks that would be enhanced and intensified in March and April 1943. The SR and the ORA could use them until they had their own systems.

"Now that we're making a new appearance and that our existence was acknowledged at Anfa, Dansey and Menzies are asking me to come to London," said Rivet when I went to see him with the news of the *Casabianca*'s successful mission.

He returned from England on February 20, 1943 following a ten-day trip.

"I met Passy. He agrees in principle to place the intelligence arm of the BCRA under our group. He must get final approval from de Gaulle. He suggested that I go and see him but I declined."

We were just going around in circles. I felt that the heads of British intelligence had requested the trip to London to put an end to that dual allegiance. I told him as much.

"But there's no dual allegiance of the SR, my dear Paillole," he said. "At the most our services complement each other only inside France. You better than anyone should know that the SR's mission is to gather intelligence in depth. All along in 1940, 1941, and 1942 we doggedly pursued our operations outside France, inside the OKW, within Hitler's closest entourage, as well as other German leaders. You've gone after the Abwehr, the RSHA, and the SIM just about everywhere. It's not only inside France, where, I admit, the BCRA has a very large capability in the same target area, that's the priority of our SR. Logically the merger should take place under our roof, to benefit the only organization that's capable of providing information as completely as possible to French and Allied commanders. But this implies something else, that is, a political merger. My feeling in London was that this was not going to happen tomorrow. De Gaulle and his leadership don't appear ready to stop their polemics against North Africa. They point to it as being full of internal disagreements and close to fascism. Massigli and Dejean, whom I met with several times, both deplored that kind of thinking."

Rivet made me understand that there wasn't much more to be done than let time mend all those fences

Schlesser had successfully escaped through Spain, while he "waited for his regiment to follow"; he traveled with me to Constantine and Le Kef in Tunisia, where I found Fontès and Rigaud of TR 121. We were indignant to find out about the arrest of General Giraud's daughter by the Germans in Tunis; she was married to Colonel Grangé and the mother of five children. Mrs. Grangé died in a concentration camp on October 23, 1943.

Military security that we set up in the larger military units using reservists was able to carry out its mission. Some Axis intelligence infiltration attempts were neutralized along with their radio transmitters. Three agents were turned against their former employers and would be used in our disinformation work against the Abwehr. A tragic cable came in from Beirut on March 8 where Baril had perished in a plane crash. It was an irreparable loss and Mast was seriously injured. Both men were still being penalized because of their pro-Allied positions in November 1942 and were en route to Syria on a fact-finding mission

Since February 5, 1943, General Giraud was civilian and military commander in chief. On March 14 he formally stated his policy for war and peace. He announced his plan to return to a democratic form of government and cancel the decisions taken by the Vichy government. However, Bergeret, who had been part of the Vichy Government and had not taken part in drafting Giraud's speech, didn't agree with several points. Bergeret and Rigaud then resigned.

Giraud didn't wish to let the Gaullists have a monopoly of the "Action" part of intelligence and appointed Colonel Lardin of his staff to create an "Action Service." He was thinking of giving the ORA a mission in France and creating new networks. Rivet, Villeneuve, and I met with Lardin on March 18. He was full of enthusiasm and good will but had no experience of action inside France and no operational capability. He wished to use us and the *Alliance* network, a suggestion that came from Faye to Giraud and Ronin at the end of February.

We could immediately see the dangers inherent in being associated with the project. By going in that direction we would be straying away from our mission and increasing the dangers to our comrades. We warned Lardin, and then Giraud's cabinet chief, de Linarès. To multiply such initiatives could lead to more rivalry—and that was, unfortunately, the right word to use—between the Gaullists and ourselves. In France they would cause confusion, conflicts, disorder, and anarchy when the ORA was attempting to create ties to resistance organizations.

Our cautious counsel was not to be heeded. A Special Services directorate was set up with Ronin to be the "umbrella" of the "Action" unit as well as DSR-SM. It had its headquarters in a small building annex of the Palais d'Eté where Giraud was residing.

Some real patriots like Malaise or Dungler, were encouraging the staff members and Giraud himself into adventurous missions in France. Soon these plans were shelved as boy scout heroic dreams. It was high time to merge the Special Services as a prelude to a larger and more complete merger. Bonnefous, who came on my staff on February 23, 1943, was able to confirm how necessary it was and reminded me of what we had started in France.

"We did everything to get closer to the resistance groups and have the ORA meet with them. In December, with Aubrac and Forestier,[*] we met with Emmanuel d'Astier de la Vigerie in Lyon. At his request I introduced Aubrac to Revers in Vichy and to Frère in Royat. At that meeting General Frère voiced his full support for General de Gaulle. After that I met General Delestraint in Bourg. He was favorable to our activities and wanted to meet with Frère or his deputies. Alice[**] managed to bring him Olleris."

---

[*] Head of the secret army's combat section.

[**] Bonnefous' wife.

"You see things are progressing."

"If the mess here continues, everything we've done won't have amounted to anything. In the meantime the Krauts are hunting us down."

In fact, Geissler, the Gestapo's man in Vichy, was looking for Bonnefous and his wife, who had to take refuge in the Northern zone. Bonnefous had made it out in the first successful pick-up operation by Michel Thoraval with the help of our radio operator Simonin and Antoine Herrman, now one of Johanès' deputies. The single-engine Lysander landed at 1 a.m. at the field of Boën-Feurs in the Loire region. A large amount of TR mail left very little space in fuselage for Thoraval and Bonnefous.

In that mail were reports on Abwehr and RSHA infiltration of the former Free Zone. We also found details on the activities of the collaborators and the creation on January 31, 1943 of the "Milice Française" by Joseph Darnand, with its mission to stop all "the forces of darkness" [*sic*]: maquis, saboteurs, intelligence networks, resistance, and communist networks. We could readily understand Verneuil and our other comrades' worries as they heard about the strange competition between the French in London and Algiers. All of them wanted information about a situation they couldn't accept. They all wished—the word wasn't strong enough—unity among the Free French and common directives to pursue the struggle.

Bonnefous was just the right man to facilitate the necessary merging of the ourselves and Gaullists. He showed me the handwritten letters he kept from Colonel de Gaulle that demonstrated how amiable they were. Following that correspondence, my friend felt encouraged to pursue a counterespionage career against Germany since 1936.

"I'll do everything to make it a success," Bonnefous told me as I drove him to Maison-Blanche airport on March 24, 1943.

He was off to the position I had assigned to him in London where Cowgill and Menzies were impatiently expecting him. He had shaved off his mustache, which used to make him look like the actor Fernand Gravey. I told him he was wrong but he answered:

"It looks better. I don't want to go to England to be in the movies."

On arrival he met Passy and requested a meeting with General de Gaulle. He was received on Easter Monday 1943 at Carlton's Gardens. It was a disaster! Still affected by it, Bonnefous told me the details sometime later.

"There was no doubt in my mind that de Gaulle had been misled by some biased reports. He was icy and remained seated. He didn't hint once at our friendly relations lasting thirteen years.

"'So Bonnefous, what are you doing in London?' he asked.

"'I'm representing the French counterespionage and military security services.'

"'Ah! So you're an agent of Vichy?'

"'How can you say such a thing? I report to Colonel Rivet and Major Paillole. I'm here to reinforce the liaison with British intelligence and your BCRA.'

"'So then, you're a British agent? Very well! You may go, Bonnefous.'

"I was aghast. At such words and such childish accusations the look on my face betrayed my indignation.

"De Gaulle got up and walked me to the door of his office and said:

"'One day, Bonnefous, France will settle accounts with those who served her well.'

"'But general, all we ask is to collaborate!'

"'Collaboration is not the point.'

"With those words I was out the door and flabbergasted!'"

I was just as surprised as Bonnefous. The unfair reaction to a step that we had taken at our own initiative indicated to us the depth of misunderstanding we had reached in spite of ourselves. Will pride and sectarian attitudes overshadow reason and national interest?

I felt I had to tell Giraud of our failure and he drew his own conclusions:

"I told you. It'll be quite difficult to reach an agreement. We're not on the same wavelength. Here, we say 'our only goal: victory!' and over there they say 'our only goal: power!'"

The extremely disheartening internal situation among the French didn't dampen our determination to carry on with our mission. I did my best to keep all those disappointments to myself and limit the damage to my comrades' morale. I kept on hinting to everyone that unity was coming slowly.

In the meantime Bonnefous kept his contacts at the BCRA in London. His agreement with the British allowed us to create what amounted to a sub-directorate of military security in England, allowing for far greater counterespionage intelligence sharing, connections to France, and preparing for future military operations for the landings to come. The new organization of my services was now taking shape. Our research covered all enemy territory, including the occupied countries. Verneuil's old TR and the Barcelona TR were communicating with us on a regular basis. Vellaud's TR jr. was being set up and its initial missions were taking place and growing with each passing month. The TR stations in Africa were extending their research beyond Africa and kept on maneuvering their penetration agents. They played a key role in the creation of *Force A*.

The original military security network was growing clandestinely to cover all of France. Its mission was not to gather intelligence, but acquire information for when it was to surface. I asked Colonel Henri Navarre to take over that post and also keep up the liaison with the ORA and the security of the clandestine organization. It was my luck that he took the position. The Directorate of Military Security in French Africa under Lieutenant Colonel Chrétien supervised the territorial branches with additional reservists and military police.

Achiary and his deputy Loffredo, who were cleared of any political fallout after the Darlan assassination, helped us greatly with the *Sécurité du Territoire*. In March 1943 Chretien told me he wanted to command a fighting unit, an understandable request for a military professional. Obviously, since I had a lower rank, my presence in Algiers created a sometimes-delicate situation. Once Chrétien left, I reorganized the unit and moved out some individuals who were too much into the Algiers "scuttlebutt." Every office was centralized at El-Biar, where I enlarged the facility. The Directorate of Military Security in French Africa then changed to Directorate of Military Security (DSM). I was attempting to set up priorities for our work in France and our actual involvement in military operations.

The DSM organization chart in April 1943 took that priority into account:

— A section under Captain Scheider was preparing the landings in France in liaison with Navarre: preparation of instructions, reading files, training military security personnel assigned to operate in France.

— A section under Captain Emile Bertrand and de Lannurien, working with Verneuil and Vellaud, was in charge of TR intelligence gathering and disinformation for *Force A*.

— A section under Captain Caillot in charge of communications and clandestine radio transmissions.

— A section under Captain Jouannais to analyze counterespionage intelligence for repression, reports, lists of suspects, files and archives.

— A section under Major Combes and Captain Berthin was to protect secrecy and the most vulnerable areas, and analyze the effects of enemy propaganda.

— A section for instruction (it was to train 150 officers at military security centers) and to produce monthly reports for the High Command and the government.

— A section under Superintendent Achiary handled police-related issues and was in charge of recruiting and training personnel for the *Sécurité du Territoire* and military police whose charter I prepared. We created a police academy in Guyotville. One hundred policemen were given the special training required for our missions.

Other sections handled various functions: mail, administration, supplies, etc.

Colonel André Sérot, a man of great experience whom everyone liked and respected, became my deputy. Allemand was my chief of staff and Jacques Chevallier handled relations with the Allies, which were to remain excellent. William Donovan himself came with Captain Eddy to Algiers from September 10-15, 1943, to tighten our relations with American intelligence and offer all the practical support we needed. Besides the easygoing Captain Miller, Donovan assigned, as liaison, Captain Holcomb, a young officer with hard combat experience in the Pacific, where he'd been seriously wounded.

The Directorate of Military Security was operating as of May 1, 1943. It remained impervious to the city's rumor factories and indifferent to all the intrigues as it focused on monitoring France and its coming liberation.

26

Sabotage and
Propaganda in North Africa

The enemy was fully aware of the importance of the fighting in North Africa and the Abwehr had greatly stepped up its efforts. The most spectacular attempt took place on January 21, 1943. Four groups of eight men—three Germans, two Frenchmen, and three Arabs—were flown aboard two Ju 52 aircraft to the landing strip of Zeribed el-Hamed in southern Tunisia. They were under arrest twenty-four hours later; two groups were to engage in sabotage, another in intelligence, and the final one in propaganda.

The Germans were all former Foreign Legionnaires and had become POWs in 1940. By agreeing to work for the Abwehr they were being given a chance to wipe the slate clean of their sins against the German fatherland. The Frenchmen were card-carrying members of the PPF, having been recruited by Paris party leaders Fossati and Robert at the PPF convention in November 1942. Sent to Berlin-Rangsdorf, they were given sabotage and intelligence gathering training. The Arabs were Tunisians who had been for the most part forced to join and were in charge of acting as guides for the groups. Sabotage equipment included explosive packages varying from 500 grams to 2 kilos, each with a magnet to apply them to railroad tracks. The thirty-two Abwehr agents were condemned to death or given life sentences at forced labor; seventeen were summarily executed. Requests for pardon were inoperative in matters regarding state security. There would 268 saboteurs, including 204 Arabs, arrested up to the liberation of Tunisia in May 1943, of these thirty-five were executed by firing squad. Their most successful sabotage actions at Duvivier, Sbeitla, and Tabarka against railroad tracks and gasoline dumps were inconsequential.

Thirteen intelligence agents of Abwehr I, one of them with a radio, were discovered in January and February 1943. They infiltrated into North Africa, either through the Tunisian "no man's land" or from Spanish Morocco. Only one of them parachuted in, Yvon Jeanne, the man carrying the radio. Jeanne was sentenced to death on February 4, 1943 and executed February 6. Maurice Perrod, who had volunteered to join the air force in Casablanca on January 8, was sentenced to death on February 6 and executed the following day. We had Perrod in our files since 1941. TR 112 *bis* had checked on him because of his relations with the Gestapo in the rue des Saussaies in Paris and his travel to Germany. The military security officer at Casablanca air base had been very keen in having the archives checked and through clever questioning got the traitor to confess. He was supposed to hand over his intelligence findings to the Spanish consulate!

In North Africa our penetration agents were the main sources of the Abwehr, which kept sending over questionnaires and money in a few parachute drops that were the joy of our stations in Africa. Enemy propaganda remained one of our biggest headaches. It was clever, insidious, and hard to pin down. I was facing it again under those new skies with the help of many bad Frenchmen and a favorable atmosphere due to indifference, skepticism, and lethargy. Night and day radio broadcasts from Berlin, Paris, Melilla, Bari, and Tunis were spreading their poison. The Algerians and Moroccans were listening out of habit and responded to the well-known topics regarding their political and social aspirations.

Anti-Semitism and the desire for reforms and independence were being used cleverly:

— "The first measures taken in North Africa canceled the laws protecting you from the Jews…"
— "A handful of imperialists will turn you into slaves…"

As well as the perfidious warning that resonates oddly some sixty years later:

— "If the Anglo-Americans win, the Arabs in the Middle East will have to live with the creation of a Zionist state…"

Anti-Communism was awakened:

— "They are freeing the Communists, while your leaders are imprisoned…"

From Paris Doctor Bentani, president of the Muslim members of the PPF, was calling on his fellow Muslims to revolt. From Bari the Grand Mufti of Jerusalem called for the Axis victory that "will give Muslims their independence and a better life."

When we met in Madrid on April 3, 1943 Barranco was not talking about victory. On March 15 I received a long letter from Guiraud through Barcelona. Barranco wanted to meet with me. He was going to be in the Spanish capital between April 1 and 6. I could reach him with a conventional message addressed to the Italian consulate in Madrid. I got the green light from Rivet and Giraud on March 26. Saint Hardouin gave me diplomatic cover to travel to Spain to negotiate the repatriation of French nationals who were being held in internment camps. Only Sérot at DSM knew the real reasons for my absence. I gave my colleagues the excuse that I was going with Rivet on an inspection tour in Tunisia of some fighting units. To cover my tracks my boss came to El-Biar himself to drive me to the airport. He traveled toward the East alone.

I reached Tangier where our station chief, Major La Paillone, a classmate of mine, secured my passage to Cadix in Spain. I informed Barranco of my arrival and following an endless all-night trip I met him at Atocha station around 9 a.m. With a discreet movement of his head he signaled me to follow him. I could sense he was nervous and fearful of being followed. His car was parked in a semi-deserted street. At that hour Madrid was still asleep. I got in next to him and after a few greetings he drove out of town to the banks of the Manzanares Rivet. A torrential rainfall kept us in the car while we talked.

"I had to see you. Italy's position is untenable. Tunisia is lost. If we succeed in eliminating the Duce and fascism, do you feel we can obtain a separate peace?"

"Have you been ordered to ask me such a question and by whom?" I asked.

"My superiors called me to Rome. They asked me to meet with you. I think they in turn are following orders from top political and military leaders, such as Marshal Badoglio."

I remained silent; Barranco looked at me.

"My superiors wish to prove that they're sincere," he went on. "They've authorized me to reveal information that they're asking you to keep secret. They've seen a photocopy of a long letter sent at the end of January 1943 to Krüger, the Abwehr station chief in Tangier. The Sultan of Morocco wrote it in person. He was reporting on the situation of Allied troops in Morocco and gave a detailed account of what took place at the Anfa conference. He's also requesting the immediate support of the Axis to help Morocco achieve independence."

The revelation confirmed what we suspected and was extremely valuable!

"How did your superiors manage to see such a document?" I asked.

"Because of its diplomatic importance and because it concerns the Mediterranean, Ribbentrop gave Ciano a copy and he showed it to my superiors."

Could it be possible that Ciano himself knew of my contacts with Barranco and how that piece of intelligence could be used for my benefit?

Barranco was becoming impatient and repeated the question.

"Do you believe in the possibility of a separate peace?"

"You must understand that I'm not qualified to give you an answer," I replied.

"Promise me that you'll consult your superiors. You can let me know their reaction through Mr. Guiraud or meet me here."

I promised and Barranco relaxed. He did have one more pressing question for me.

"Major, after Tunisia it's going to be our turn, correct?"

The *Force A* plan that had already been approved sought to convince the enemy that the next Allied objective could be Sardinia and southern Greece. With some sleight of hand I offered my opinion.

"Yes, I do believe it'll soon be your turn. Perhaps Sardinia, because it's just opposite Rome."

I also added the idea that the Allies might revive the 1918 plan and invade Europe and Germany through Greece and the Balkans. Giraud had explained such a plan to us ten times over, especially to the TR jr.

officers before they went on to their assignments in France. I recited the lesson I had memorized and concluded:

"That would probably best avoid the difficulty of landing operations in Western Europe where the Axis is very well organized."

Barranco agreed and was full of bitterness against Germany as bearing responsibility for all the troubles of France and Italy.

"Our country is as much under occupation as yours. I'm being watched by the RSHA in Nice, while the Abwehr sent a country squire to shadow me: Captain Hans Buchholtz, who reports to the Lyon Ast. He happens to be a crook wearing a monocle."

Barranco gave detailed information about Abwehr and RSHA networks in southwestern France.

"Tell your friends to beware of the Marseille Gestapo," he said. "I met Hellwing, the chief, and his deputy, Ernst Dunker, *alias* Delage. They know about Jonglez and Guiraud, whom I warned. Dunker, whom you had arrested in Tunis at the end of 1940, is very angry at your service and says he was roughed up!"

Soon Barranco's warning would prove to be true! He drove me back to near the railroad station and shook both my hands before departing.

"There are Germans everywhere around here," he warned me. "Don't be too conspicuous!"

I was not about to. I took the first train back to Cadix and by April 6 I was again with Rivet in Giraud's office. While traveling through Morocco, without revealing my source, I again confidentially warned Noguès about the Sultan.

The political problem Barranco represented went beyond the competence of our commander in chief. He assured me he would discuss the matter with Eisenhower. Two weeks later he told me:

"The Allied governments would inform the Italians directly."

I asked Guiraud to tell Barranco that he didn't need to travel "because an answer was forthcoming from higher up."

On May 25 U.S. newspapers carried a statement from Churchill: "The Italian people would act wisely by getting rid of the Duce and Fascism."

On July 25 Mussolini was removed and placed under arrest without getting any help from Ciano, his son-in-law. On July 28 the Fascist party was abolished and Badoglio took over the government. On September 3 an armistice was signed between Italy and the Allies, near Siracusa in Sicily.

Since my return from Madrid we increasingly alerted authorities about the seriousness of enemy activity among Muslims, and Moroccans in particular. On May 10, 1943 the conclusion of our monthly report contained this warning:

"The wave of nationalism is growing, fanned by enemy propaganda. The unity of nationalist Moroccan movements is taking place with the encouragement of the Sultan and German help. It is high time that the central government reasserts its authority. The initial step should be to set its course regarding Muslim policy."

But was there a real central government? Giraud was waiting for de Gaulle, who arrived in Algiers on May 30, 1943. We just kept on waiting. Our warnings, and we were not the only ones to voice them, were to remain unheeded the only meager result being the interception of enemy broadcasts.

On June 5, 1943 in Rabat, Gabriel Puaux, who had not been prepared for such a mission, replaced Noguès, who no longer had enough authority and did not enjoy the trust of the CFLN. The nationalist parties were now regrouped under the Istiqlal. The Sultan was their leader and a well-structured organization was secretly set up with weapons coming in from the Spanish zone. Funds came in from wealthy Muslims and the Abwehr provided the rest through Tangier, Melilla, and Ifni. The Sultan's call had been heard! A penetration agent was able to find out in September 1943 the extent of the enemy's objective: to begin a general insurrection after the French and Allied troops had left for other operational areas. Fez, the religious center, was to be at the center of the troubles. The head of military security in Fez, Captain Devosges, knew both Islam and his area too well and understood the kind of threat we faced. There were fanatics in the Mosques who were preaching a religious war. At the beginning of January 1944 Devosges ordered the arrest of some of the most vocal leaders, a decision that came after the arrest of arms smugglers, spies, and propagandists, leading to the execution of ten Moroccans in November 1943 and as many in December.

That was the spark that caused the explosion. On January 11, 1944, the Istiqlal delivered to the Moroccan government, the French authorities, and foreigners the manifesto of the Moroccan movement for independence. At the same time demonstrations started all over Morocco: Marrakech, Casablanca, Salé, Port-Lyautey, Meknès, and Fez, along with acts of violence against all Europeans. On January 29, 1944, nationalist leaders Balafrej and Mohamed Lyazidi were arrested. We had known their relations with Germany for over a year and military security had requested that the French Resident put a stop to their activities. A revolt began in Rabat and Salé. The crowd stormed the méchouar,* asking for the Sultan's support and a European on a bicycle who happened to be crossing the square was brutally murdered. Bloody confrontations kept on increasing. Captain Dumont, head of military security, explained the situation to General Leclerc and described the tragic weakness of the civilian authorities. A few hours later, tanks of the 2nd French armored division that was garrisoned outside Rabat came to reinforce the police, who already had two men killed and wounded many.

Violence engulfed all of Morocco. In the sacred religious city of Moulay-Idris the rebels identified one of our penetration agents and brutally had his throat slit. The army unit in Fez had to retreat from the Arab quarter because it was too weak and was being attacked on all sides. General de Suffren had to use artillery fire to put down the rebellion but it would take over a month to restore a semblance of peace and quiet to the country. Hundreds of people died in a premeditated revolt that had been prepared with enemy assistance. Had it started three or four months later, in May or June 1944, after the army and the 2nd armored division of Leclerc had left North Africa, the consequences could have been much worse. We had not witnessed such fanaticism since the early years of French presence in Morocco.

Military security's investigation revealed the existence of a structured revolutionary organization with an intelligence section, a police force, military courts to punish the opposition, communications, medical units, and assistance to the families of those who became the victims of the revolt.

René Massigli was promoted commissioner of foreign affairs within the French Committee of National Liberation on June 3, 1943. Giraud and De Gaulle had set up the CFLN. At the end of January 1944 Massigli went to Rabat in an attempt to resolve the political problem. I also went there to analyze the scope of the damage, find its origins, and try some solutions. I met with the Resident General Puaux, who was stunned and overtaken by the magnitude and violence of the revolt. His comment, true to form, was:

"I knew nothing!"

Back in Algiers I asked to be received by General de Gaulle. Gaston Palewski, his chief of staff, saw me instead. I explained how the Germans

---

* The méchouar was and still is the main palace of the king of Morocco in Rabat.

were responsible but also the very heavy responsibility of the French administration. I understood from something Palewski said that nothing would happen:

"France is our main target. Here for the time being we cannot do more or better; we just don't have the resources."

Events were flying by; one pushing away the other and the Moroccan fires that were the warning of worse to come were quickly forgotten. In my report of May 10, 1944 I concluded that since operational areas were now far removed, North Africa had drifted back to its Mediterranean calm. Using a new vocabulary the pre-war partisan political games were back in play.

As I wrote, "If it had not been for the front pages of the newspapers about the Russians advancing and some news regarding the Italian campaign, the press in April could well have us believe in a very traditional Easter fortnight. While the easy chairs in the oasis welcomed some top leaders taking tourist trips, a myriad of meetings issued fantastic plans for some time in the future. Those who had just escaped from France were frightened and surprised."

27

Disinformation and Military Operations

anaris was puzzled, suspicious, and filled with anxiety. There was no denying that some of his networks were penetrated and misled. But which ones? And who were the traitors? He knew that his mistake had been to push too many stations in France to try at the same time for a late and forced recruitment effort. How could he disentangle truth from falsehood in such a complex situation?

He wanted to return to a more methodical type of research, specialize a single station on the North African operational area, and insist on the genuine quality of the intelligence gathered. He picked Paris for that job. Rudolf and Reile both combined professionalism and caution. They were going to use the potential of the PPF as much as possible. Doriot's party had its back to the wall and could only look forward to an Axis victory. A masterful counterespionage operation was to confirm the efficient functioning of Reile's service and prove to the head of the Abwehr that some of his agents were actually double-crossing him.

Early in 1943 the unraveling of the Martineau case encouraged Reile's wily deputy, Scheide, to order the arrest of Li 159-Hengen. He happened to be one of our best penetration agents, as well as one of the earliest and most highly regarded Abwehr informers. Rumpe, who was his case officer since 1938, kept on defending him until June 1943 when the archives of TR 113 were discovered in Clermont-Ferrand. Rumpe had to admit that perhaps he had "been fooled." Hengen always denied everything, and didn't reveal a single clue that could have harmed us. He was deported and died in Mauthausen concentration camp.

That arrest started a chain reaction, because Hengen had been a top recruiter for the Ast of Paris and Bordeaux. He had been so efficient—and that was our good fortune—that the Germans were unable, or never dared, to find out how deep the problem went. The head of the Abwehr was to candidly admit that he had been betrayed. Belgian historian Léon Papeleux discovered in examining OKW archives that "Canaris informed the OKW that enemy intelligence services were engaged on a very large scale in feeding false information to the Germans."

I had to draw my own conclusions after Hengen's arrest. How far would the revelations of Martineau and his unfortunate comrades take the Germans? Three W agents recruited by Li 159 in southeastern France couldn't be warned in time and were caught by surprise by the enemy. Our W network in North Africa had been partially dismantled. All penetration agents that Hengen had recruited, except for one who had penetrated the Bordeaux Ast without his involvement, had been burned. We still kept them active if only to see what the enemy intended to do. They were useless for *Force A*, whose W contingent was cut by one third.

There was another reason Canaris was compelled to increase his resources in North Africa.

When the Axis alliance was cemented Italy's SIM requested the Mediterranean basin as its territory. It functioned efficiently in Tunisia, poorly in Algeria, and was not operating at all in Morocco. The strategic importance of Morocco and its proximity to Gibraltar encouraged the Abwehr at the end of 1940 to focus closely on the area with the support of the Spanish intelligence service. We saw one of the best German intelligence experts, navy Captain Fritz Unterberg-Gibhardt, the recruiter of French navy traitor Marc Aubert, arrive in Casablanca in 1941. With the assistance of Major Christmann he set up intelligence and propaganda networks covering the entire kingdom.

The quantity and quality of Abwehr intelligence gathered in North Africa therefore decreased from west to east. The elimination of Hengen's recruits made the situation even worse. The few spies that had been sent to North Africa after November 8, 1942, by parachuting in or by infiltration, had either been arrested or surrendered on their own. Those carrying a radio were of such poor quality that even if we stretched our requirements they were useless to us as penetration or double agents. Therefore German intelligence, in order to satisfy the OKW on the Tunisian front and to report more generally on the eastern Mediterranean where Italy's increasingly wobbly attitude was worrying Hitler, had to rely on our W agents.

All this was discussed with our British and American Allies of *Force A* in Algiers on April 7, 1943. The disinformation directives we received from the Allied command had us focus on Tunisia as an immediate objective; and Italy as a second one later. The first order of business was to support General Alexander, the commander of Allied forces in Tunisia, in breaking enemy resistance. Rommel and von Arnim were hanging on to the Djebel Zaghouan* and the Tebursouk mountains. They were doggedly defending northeastern Tunisia, meaning the approaches of Cape Bon, Bizerte, and Tunis itself.

Force A had to convince the enemy of an Allied and Free French attack towards Tunis coming from southern Tunisia, hugging the coastline with navy support. We had to get the enemy to send some of its troops from the north and especially to the center of the front where two Panzer divisions were blocking any British army advance in the direction of the real attack on Medjez-el-Bab-Tunis. Three W agents with radios were to carry out the disinformation. One of them had been in the service since 1941 and lived in Le Kef and was to have an identity card as a war correspondent for the newspaper *L'Echo d'Alger*. He was observing troop movements and recording the very frequent indiscretions of Allied command posts.

Another W had been in Algiers since the start of 1942. He worked at Maison-Blanche airport where he was in air traffic control. The third man was one of those who had been parachuted in during January 1943, Chouali ben Larbi, a gem among the informers the Abwehr, had quickly enlisted in Tunisia! He had been a sergeant in the Algerian Tirailleurs and a magnificent French soldier and had become a prisoner of the Germans in November 1942 near Béja. He was alert, intelligent, and a keen observer, something his German interrogator quickly understood. He was offered training in intelligence work.

"Why not? We'll see what happens," he said.

When he reached a POW triage camp in southern Tunisia, Chouali was selected by an Abwehr officer for technical intelligence and radio training at the center of Berlin-Rangsdorf.

---

* Arab: mountainous region.

In January 1943 he learned mostly how to use the radio transmitter-receiver and observe what was going on. He encoded and decoded scores of messages. During the night of February 14-15, 1943, he parachuted near Médéa in Algeria. He had a radio and about 50 gold "Louis" coins. He buried his radio and codebooks and went to the gendarmerie where he was greeted with skepticism in spite of the gold coins that he showed to prove he was being truthful. The chief of the brigade informed the mayor of Médéa, who happened to be none other than Colonel Grosjean, former head of the SCR at the 2nd Bureau in 1935, now living there in retirement since 1938!

Chouali was sent to us, questioned and tested to make sure he was being sincere. Doudot, whom I had brought back to Algiers to supervise our W agents, was checking the agent's work. The listening post under Major Black was intercepting messages around the clock. The British were intercepting those we failed to catch, since they had the Enigma machine and Major Bertrand's decryption specialists. Our check of all transmissions was therefore very exacting. In a few days Chouali contacted the Abwehr. His mission was to check the port area and, because of his origin, to report on the morale and movements of North African troops.

The intelligence we let him transmit was very well received in Berlin. Starting April 8, immediately following our *Force A* conference, we asked Chouali to report the arrival in Algiers and Bône of British reinforcements and supplies. Later he broadcast that the reinforcements were headed for southern Tunisia. On the night of May 2-3, 1943, he sent a message we had prepared indicating Sousse as the final destination of those reinforcements.

The other two Ws were providing corroborating intelligence. At Maison-Blanche airport they spotted planes heading toward southern Tunisia. At Le Kef there were "rumors" of an allied attack in southern Tunisia between the coast and the djebel Zaghwan. At the same time *Force A* was directing columns of closed but empty British trucks, enough to move an entire division as the Axis air force was watching. During the night of May 4-5 von Arnim withdrew one of the two Panzer divisions that were guarding the Medjez-el-Bab-Tunis line and quickly sent it south. On May 5 the Allies attacked in the center and the north with 800 tanks and 500 planes. Tunis and Bizerte were liberated May 7 and von Arnim surrendered with 250,000 men and a mass of supplies on May 12.

Beyond operations in Tunisia *Force A* also had a distant objective: to draw attention away from Sicily, the next Allied target. The disinformation plan was meant to convince the enemy that what was being studied was the invasion of Sardinia and Greece. The plan was sketched out at the end of March and I had even been able to drop a few hints when I met with Barranco in Madrid. The final approach was decided at the April 7 *Force A* meeting.

On the night of April 28, 1943, on the Atlantic coast of Andalusia, not far from the town of Huelva, a British submarine dropped off the dead body of what looked like a British officer. The ocean tide beached the body in a small inlet where some fishermen found it on April 30. It looked like a flyer who had been shot down, possibly somewhere in the Mediterranean.

Investigators found out from documents on the body that his name was Martin. Other official documents coming from London were addressed to General Harold Alexander, commander in chief of Allied forces in Tunisia. One document hinted that after the Tunisian campaign the supreme Allied command was considering landings in the Peloponnesus in Greece, and Sardinia. *Force A* was well aware of the close ties between German and Spanish intelligence; they were constantly exchanging information. Everything led us to believe that the Spanish High Command would inform the Abwehr.

We reached the first objective of our disinformation plan and on May 12, 1943 Dieckhoff, the German ambassador to Madrid, was told by the Spanish foreign minister about the discovery at Huelva. The Spanish military command vouched for the authenticity and credibility of the documents found on the body. It was now our turn to use penetration agents, and we prepared two new men for this operation unrelated to the previous one. The first W had lived in Algiers since 1941. His production had been regular and the Bordeaux Ast, where we introduced him after Sibelius left, thought he was completely trustworthy. The second W was a new man we recruited from Tunis the day after the city's liberation.

On that day Gilbert, head of the best espionage network ever established by the Abwehr in North Africa, came to us spontaneously, telling military security what his mission was and offering his services. I was informed and after studying and thinking the matter through for twenty-four hours I decided to go along with it. I gave the responsibility to the excellent team of TR 121, run by Fontès, Rigaud, and Captain Parisot, the son of General Parisot, former air force attaché to Rome.

This was not the usual way we recruited our penetration agents. I ordinarily didn't trust "walk-in" individuals who revealed the missions the enemy had entrusted them with. Gilbert was to be the exception to that rule. He'd been deputy police commissioner in a large town; I had met him in France at the end of 1941 and remembered him as a likeable fellow, a bit excited perhaps but clashing with his superiors on ideological grounds so much that he was forced to resign in 1942.

He worked with a kind of zest we found comical, and he tried to live an adventurous existence as much as he could rather than fulfill a routine set of tasks. He was also a career military man, a Saint-Cyr graduate with an impressive record for bravery during both world wars, many citations, and the Legion of Honor. His rabid anti-communism and taste for action had led him to join the LVF right after being fired from his job. In January 1943 he became a follower of Doriot and was friendly with Beugras, who was in charge of intelligence for the PPF. Using a purchasing office as cover he set up a clandestine organization based at 5, Avenue Marceau in Paris for the purpose of establishing relations with North Africa, organizing PPF members and their sympathizers to engage in propaganda, sabotage, and intelligence gathering. A first mission, named "Atlas," was to go to Tunisia where it would fan out and work under Allied occupation. The Germans agreed to provide the funds if the operation was under Reile's command and focused exclusively on military intelligence. They required a real leader to take charge and Gilbert accepted the challenge.

He was intelligent, ambitious, and devious. He knew the Axis was doomed. In this opportunity for adventure he claimed to have found a way to serve his country. My feeling was that above all he felt he could play a title role as he wiped his slate clean. But that didn't really matter. The network he brought us was exactly what we needed to fulfill our objectives and to turn it on our enemies. I decided to play a game that looked as if it would be very competitive.

Gilbert reached Tunis by plane with a team of four men on April 25, 1943. Major Wilhelm Christmann of the Abwehr, a specialist of North Africa, with a pointed nose and thin lips, was part of the team and got Gilbert started. Christian du Jonchay, on the staff of Resident General Admiral Estéva, was very helpful in paving the way. False documents were easily provided. Gilbert rented a modest apartment where he could claim he had arrived before November 8, 1942, using his wish to flee the German occupation in France as his alibi.

Just before the liberation of Tunisia Gilbert did everything possible to get the Germans and the PPF to trust him. He executed their orders on time and saw to it that contacts had been established as requested with several Arab caïds* and with Henri Queyrat-Doriot's delegate in North Africa, who had just returned from training in Berlin, and with other PPF and SOL sympathizers. As agreed with Reile, Gilbert joined the French army in Tunis as a major. Each of his four teammates was to encounter a different fate. Leduc had been recruited by Gilbert himself in France and was his second in command. He was dedicated, discreet, and trustworthy and was to be mobilized to serve headquarters.

Albert was the radio operator, however; he had been recruited by the PPF and Gilbert couldn't vouch for him. There was no way to get rid of Albert, who couldn't be trusted; the Abwehr had recorded his radio touch. He had to continue transmitting and be kept in the dark about his leader's true allegiance. Same thing for Falcon, the radio mechanic. Duteil was the fourth man and a tough guy. He was a former second lieutenant in the LVF and had been in combat in Russia. He had been recruited by Beugras and worked as his secretary for several months as the eyes and ears of the PPF; he was incorruptible, suspicious, and he had to be eliminated neatly and quickly. We set up a trap for him.

Gilbert introduced Duteil to one of his officer friends, who was anti-American and anti-British. The two men became friendly. One evening after a good dinner the officer took Duteil to his office at division headquarters. They were going through some papers when sentries appeared. Both were forcibly dragged to the *Surveillance du Territoire* and questioned separately, in total secrecy and rather roughly. Once Duteil was shown all the information we had on him, he quickly confessed. Some one hundred suspects were identified—PPF and SOL militants, collaborators, Abwehr, and SIM informers, including a police superintendent. After a hard night the traitor even accused Gilbert and his men! A map in his pocket led us to an enormous cache of sabotage equipment. Without telling Gilbert, he had buried it near Hamman-Lif in a patch of olive trees belonging to a PPF militant. Once he had told us everything we had to avoid any kind of indiscretion or escape, so Duteil was immediately sent off to England and not heard from again.

On June 10, 1943 at 8 a.m., the same day as Duteil's arrest, and for the first time after many attempts, Albert succeeded in making the connection with his German correspondent. Gilbert was pretending to expect the worst. He demanded draconian precautions from his team for-

---

* Caïd: local Muslim official.

bidding them to go to Tunis or to see anyone. They received coded messages in locations that were always different and the places used for broadcasts also changed often to avoid detection.

Albert was working as an electrician for one of our HCs in Tunis, who didn't ask any questions but kept us informed of all his movements. Falcon had a job at the communications depot as a repairman. Even though it was down to three broadcasts per week, radio work was exhausting, requiring long nights and cumbersome changes in location. Albert, who was holding a regular job during the day, was beginning to look very tired. His boss hired an assistant, a radio specialist from our service that the Abwehr didn't object to. He would check and monitor all of Albert's radio broadcasts. Should any kind of break occur, we were guaranteed to remain in contact with the enemy.

Our penetration vehicle was now in place. In order to justify the origin of the information Gilbert was transmitting he claimed to have found several of his old-time fellow officers and also friends in high places in Tunisian circles. Both Abwehr and PPF felt comfortable with his reports. Then the disinformation campaign got underway in earnest. Gilbert signaled the preparations at the port of Bizerte. There where rumors in Algiers about a coming operation in Sardinia that our man fed directly to the Abwehr. In the inner lake at Bizerte wooden landing barges were being lined up in huge numbers by *Force A*. Several times enemy air reconnaissance flew over Bizerte to take pictures despite the somewhat haphazard anti-aircraft shooting. A few nights later massive bombing raids targeted the fictitious concentration while the real landing force was being prepared at Sousse some 150 kilometers to the south.

On June 17, 1943 the operation Gilbert had announced as a diversion began. The Allies landed on the tiny island of Pantelleria, located in the middle of the Sicilian straits. One of my officers, Marc Renaud of the TR, was killed during that brief but violent action. His mission like that of the "Shock TRs" later on that went in with attacking Allied forces, was to secure enemy archives and personnel belonging to intelligence units. Starting June 20 the Greek resistance movements, tipped off by British intelligence, completed the disinformation campaign with sabotage actions to lines of communication and supply dumps.

On July 10, 1943 the Allies landed with little opposition on the southeastern coast of Sicily. Palermo was taken on July 17. Once again we needed to measure the effectiveness of our disinformation efforts in influencing Hitler, the OKW, and the Abwehr. We pursued those efforts until the end of the war. The relative ease of the initial landing in Europe confirmed the enemy's weak resistance that could be partly due to surprise. Belgian historian Léon Papeleux notes that Goebbels reports in his diary on May 25, 1943 a revealing conversation he had with Admiral Canaris, confirming that the head of the Abwehr was convinced the attack would take place in Sardinia and in Greece.* It has also been established that that scenario also convinced Hitler as well.

I needed to know for sure so I asked Colonel Reile if the Abwehr had figured out that the "Atlas" groups had been turned and, if that was the case, the date it found out. Reile answered me on January 3, 1974:

"I understood they had been turned about four to five months after the radio operator had started broadcasting." Four to five months after meant October or November 1943.

At about 4 a.m. on November 23, 1943 a Heinkel that had left Montpellier dropped an Abwehr agent by parachute near Enfidaville, not far from Tunis. He was to contact Gilbert. The pilot had failed to land on the strip prepared by the "Atlas" team with the help of TR 121. Reile's emissary, Caron, was close to Beugras and had the trust of the PPF. Lost in the countryside he wandered in the night after burying his radio equipment. Since he didn't know Gilbert's address he appeared early in the morning at division headquarters where a rather indifferent sentry who had no security training gave out the major's home address without much ado. Caron reached Gilbert one hour later, hungry, exhausted, and rather battered from the parachute jump. The leader of the "Atlas" group took care of him and gave him a place to sleep. Gilbert, meanwhile, went through his clothing and in a seam found a code and a signal number which he copied.

Once he woke up Caron congratulated the team for its excellent results but said that from now on he would encode the messages himself and give them to the radio operator. Albert was no longer operating the radio. Once the Caron expedition was announced as imminent we found it necessary to get rid of Albert, because he could become an obstacle to us in checking Caron's work. Gilbert had previously met Caron in Paris in PPF circles and didn't trust him; he planned to watch Caron very closely without arousing suspicion.

On November 1, 1943 we requested a general census of all military reservists and Albert was subject to the draft. Gilbert's attempts to get him

---

* See Louis Lochner, ed., *The Goebbels Diaries* (New York: Doubleday, 1948), p. 394.

off were useless and poor Albert had to go where his assigned regiment was garrisoned in French West Africa! One of our technicians replaced him a few days later and everything continued smoothly. Caron was extremely well intentioned toward the entire "Atlas" team and its leader. He asked many questions and was often away. In the evening he encoded his own messages and gave them to the radio operator to be sent to the Abwehr. We had the copies and there was no doubt that he was spying on Gilbert. For the moment his crosschecking confirmed what "Atlas" was reporting. Actually the crosschecks mainly took place in high-class brothels during wild orgies with several willing young women. Caron handed Gilbert some 200,000 francs but there was no reason to believe that he had retained a sizeable amount to fund his personal requirements. In spite of Colonel Reile the Abwehr was confident and reassured. After five months of radio messages from "Atlas" the Germans were completely bogged down. Our services now had radios and money and thanks to the penetration agents they could grab those being parachuted in, intercept the ones landing from submarines, and either take their places or make them disappear.

Once Sicily had been completely occupied, on August 16, 1943, Calabria, located at the extreme tip of the Italian boot, became the next Allied objective. Italian troops facing Sicily included two German divisions defending the Straits of Messina that were between three to twelve kilometers wide. *Force A*'s mission was to draw a maximum of those troops further north toward the heel of the boot. Gilbert was still a major and had an important position at headquarters in Tunisia. On August 5 he informed the Abwehr that he had successfully placed his deputy into Sicily:

"Message 55/20—Have identified unique opportunity to place 24 into Sicily and get information."

Leduc was part of the commission for the repatriation of the Italians and could travel throughout the island. He was in daily contact with the Allied command but unable find out about all British and American preparations, all the while informing his boss through the regular mail. He would write down the information he got from *Force A* on the back of regular memos in disappearing ink. Gilbert then would transmit to the Abwehr. Caron was observing the perfect clockwork of the team. Starting August 15 Leduc sent a message that Montgomery's staff was looking at the area near Crotone and the Gulf of Taranto. That information was then confirmed by Allied aerial reconnaissance around Crotone. Gilbert's deputy repeated the warning on August 20, giving details about

British forces being assembled near Siracusa for that operation. Caron himself had been able to get it from a British officer who was a bit tipsy and part of a unit that operated in the Gulf of Taranto between the tip and the heel of the Italian boot.

The two German divisions moved toward the north from August 25-30, leaving Calabria for Crotone. Montgomery and his VIIIth Army then landed in Calabria on September 3 with no opposition. The demoralized Italian troops put up no resistance. Three German Panzer divisions stationed between Naples and Salerno were rushed south. They had been fed the idea by *Force A* that this was a diversion before the main Allied attack in the Gulf of Taranto. On September 9, General Mark Clark landed the American Vth Army in the area of Salerno, thereby threatening from the rear the German troops that had gone further south. The Germans were suddenly forced into a fast retreat to avoid encirclement.

Allied forces had now established themselves on the continent of Europe and Naples would be occupied on October 1, 1943. Subtly and intensely the disinformation game was growing steadily and helping the Allied command. General Dudley Clark, head of *Force A*, was rewarded with a spectacular promotion, for which I congratulated him in the name of my entire service. He answered me in a letter dated December 15, 1943, which I wish to reproduce because it proves how important the role played by French counterespionage was in military operations for the liberation of the continent.

Dear Major:

It is with great pleasure that I received your letter No. 1367 dated December 11, 1943, and I wish to express my deepest thanks for your kind congratulations on the occasion of my promotion. I am also very grateful for your mention of the spirit of cooperation existing between our two services. I am very much aware of the fact that this happy outcome is due to the great enthusiasm and great professional expertise that you and many French officers have demonstrated in the pursuit of our united effort for a common cause. It would have been impossible for us to fulfill our task without the DSM's generous and disinterested help.

Nothing could have been more agreeable to me since taking command of *Force A* than to see French and British officers working together toward a common goal: to ensure the defeat of our common enemy. And I think of the day when we can together finish the task on French soil.

Let me add how much I hope that you most particularly and the DSM officers who are working closely with you successfully conclude the work we are all concentrating on.

I remain convinced that it is because of them and you that we were able to achieve the results that were the basis of my promotion to a new rank.

Very sincerely yours,
Dudley Clark

The Anzio landing had been secretly prepared and was successful on January 22, 1944 because we were able to convince the Wehrmacht that the Allies would attack in central Italy.

Operation *Overlord*, the invasion of Normandy, took place on June 6, 1944. *Force A* had mixed truth and falsehood in compelling the German XVth Army to remain inactive until July 1944 in the north since it feared a new landing in the Pas-de-Calais. It was finally during the landing in southern France on August 15, 1944 that we used a wave of concocted information. Starting in June of that year the Abwehr was expecting an Allied offensive in the Mediterranean—*Force A* had been announcing since May preparations in North Africa and Corsica. Schellenberg, the new chief of German intelligence, encouraged Reile to build up his capability in North Africa and Gilbert was requesting reinforcements.

The final effort came on July 27, 1944. On that day a four-engine Junkers plane took off from Athens at 8 p.m. with a crew of five and three agents from German intelligence and the PPF. At 2 a.m. on July 28, the plane turned around the Pont du Fahs, west of Tunis, as it looked unsuccessfully for the landing strip prepared by the "Atlas" group that had been warned several days in advance. An agent bailed out but had trouble landing: he twisted his ankle and broke two ribs. Gilbert had heard the plane's engines and kept his signal lights on even longer. He was exasperated by this new failure and informed Paris, complaining about the incompetent flyers and the useless risks he was forced to be exposed to. He was expecting an answer when at 9 a.m. there was a knock at the door. A man wincing with pain and limping badly introduced himself.

"I'm Le Moco. I'd like to talk to Mr. Mathis. I've just arrived from Paris."

Gilbert was suspicious.

"I don't understand. Who are you? Why are you coming here?" he asked.

"I come from Beugras. I waited this morning at the post office in front of box number 41. Someone opened up at 8:30 a.m. As agreed I asked to talk to Mr. Mathis and they brought me here."

Post office box number 41 belonged to the "Atlas" group and was known to the Abwehr and the PPF. Mathis was the correct password. Gilbert was now reassured.

"How is it your pilot didn't see the lights of the landing strip?" he asked.

"Unfortunately he didn't! I landed in a village some seventeen kilometers south of Pont du Fahs. A truck full of vegetables on its way to Tunis stopped. Fortunately the driver saw my parachute; he stopped and rushed out to help me up. I was groggy and we talked. He was an Italian, an older man. I flattered his fascist feelings and his hatred of the Allies. He helped me buy my equipment and drove me to Tunis. I thanked him with some money and promised him more to make sure he kept quiet."

Gilbert was alarmed and suddenly very worried. That Italian could talk and endanger everything.

"Do you know his name and address?" he asked.

"Yes, of course, since I must give him some more money. Here it is."

"Wait for me here. Please rest up and make yourself at home. I'll be back."

The head of "Atlas" went out and alerted TR 121. One hour later, unable to grasp what was going on, the Italian was locked up alone in a cell at the *Surveillance du Territoire*. He would have to wait in a camp in southern Tunisia for the war to end. Gilbert then went back to talk with Le Moco.

"We flew over southern Italy, then turned toward Algiers," Le Moco said. "Over Boufarik, some thirty kilometers southeast of the capital, two other agents bailed out, an Arab and a *pied noir*."

"Was someone expecting them?" Gilbert asked.

"No! If they get arrested, which is probable, their orders are to admit everything and play the game of being turned. They are to signal that they're under enemy control by inserting 'QBU' in a message. I was to do the same if I got caught and was forced to broadcast."

What Le Moco had planned for did in fact happen. The noise of the four-engine plane was heard in Algiers. A search of the area was on when the two spies were arrested in Boufarik! Sitting on top of their radio suitcases in front of the police station, they were waiting for the door to open to tell their story. It was the end of July and the landings on the southern coast of France were at hand. We were too far into the disinformation operation to start using fellows we didn't know. Yet it would have been fun to make them into W2s and find out the enemy's reactions to broadcasts that were flagged as being made under control. We were playing too tightly to run such a risk and locked both men up until the end of the war.

Gilbert and Le Moco went to the spot near Pont du Fahs to dig up the buried equipment. It was a mother lode! 97,500 dollars, 500,000 francs, two suitcase radios, codes, one-time pads, and the hourly schedules of the radios to be set up in Algiers and Oran with the two men who had landed in Boufarik plus Le Moco and Caron.

This was an excellent opportunity to get rid of Caron. We were constantly fretting that between two orgies he might uncover our game and blow the whole thing apart. He knew about Le Moco's arrival and the instructions from Paris. From now on he was meant to be working out of Algiers. He was delighted; with his pockets full of cash he'd be able to afford all the girls he wanted without incurring any of Gilbert's criticism. But his dream was to be short-lived! It ended when he got off the plane from Tunis at Algiers' Maison-Blanche airport. A few weeks later in a ditch at Fort l'Empereur he paid the price of treason.

"You, my dear friend," said Gilbert to Le Moco, "are meant to go to Oran."

"I beg your pardon, sir. I feel that my mission is accomplished."

"What do you mean?"

"I'd like to go back to my family in Morocco. I took this mission to get back home. I don't think I have what it takes to do what you do."

Gilbert was intrigued and started questioning him at length. He was a former cavalry NCO who was really impressed by the leader of "Atlas." He was sincere, rather mediocre, but trustworthy. A quick check in Morocco proved he was telling the truth and that his family was also loyal. After a discussion with TR 121 Gilbert told him the truth about his role. Le Moco was relieved and agreed to help and played the game with enthusiasm. He told us everything he knew about the PPF organization and Reile's activity. He proved his sincerity by revealing what he thought were two missions of the Abwehr into North Africa we didn't know about, to Algeria in August 1943 and the other to Morocco in December 1943. In Algeria it was an Arab, a former POW parachuted in with a radio near

Sétif. He was arrested when he applied for a ration card because all such requests were under our control and the spy couldn't stand up to questioning by Achiary. The second case concerned a German who spoke perfect Arabic and had been dropped near Guercif. We were warned of his arrival by a TR jr. station in France. We picked him up with his suitcase radio and four million francs in gold coins.

The "Atlas" team with the added participation of Le Moco, became an integral part of our network of penetration agents in charge of protecting the Operation *Anvil-Dragoon** on the coast of southeastern France. The staff work taking place at the Ecole Normale at Bouzaréa near Algiers was under French security protection and American counterespionage. The Allies had assembled an incredibly rich collection of documents. Thanks to French intelligence, to the air force and the navy all the most minute details of the coast between Port-Vendres and Menton were reproduced inch by inch, from the water tower to the smallest location for small arms use. The enemy's order of battle was being kept up daily with fantastic precision.

"It's an incredible achievement," General de Lattre would tell me as he was finishing preparations for the 1st French Army at his headquarters in Holden near Algiers.

Force A's mission was to mislead the enemy about the destination of the huge armada that was about to head north from North Africa, from southern Italy at Taranto to Brindisi, Sardinia, and Corsica. We had to convince the OKW that the real objective was to land in the Gulf of Genoa behind Kesselring's army, still very strong in the Apennines and north of Florence. The idea that we would attack those same forces from the Adriatic was also being circulated. Starting in June Gilbert began spreading news that was to have a devastating effect:

"Allied operation in the Adriatic and Gulf of Venice is being studied... the objective is Austria through the Brenner Pass..."

The Abwehr reacted instantly: "Information is of immense importance—continue research and broadcasts. We are requesting that the Luftwaffe avoid bombing Tunis and Bizerte to avoid problems for you." And in point of fact Tunis and Bizerte were no longer bombed! The 1st French Army's landing on the island of Elba on June 17-18, 1944, could

---

* At first named *Anvil*, the landing in southern France will be named *Dragoon* beginning August 1, 1944 at the request of *Force A* to mislead any intelligence gathering on the part of German espionage.

have been interpreted by the enemy as a first step toward Genoa as our W agents in Algiers and Oran were secretly broadcasting.

Leduc, Gilbert's deputy, was supposed to be mobilized and sent to Italy with French troops that were to take part in the Genoa operation. "Atlas" had confirmed that threat. A whole chain of ships checked by *Force A* between North Africa and southern Italy kept AFHQ's (Allied Forces Headquarters) objective uncertain. Starting August 10, 1944, the enormous naval concentration took shape northwest of Cape Corse. During the night of August 13-14, 1944 General Alexander Patch, the commander in chief, gave orders to head for Genoa. Our listening posts revealed that Kesselring's Army Group C was placed on alert. The Wehrmacht was taking up combat positions on the Italian Riviera. By the night of August 14 the fleet was only three hours from the port of Genoa and shrouded by fog and darkness. Suddenly, at 10 p.m., the ships veered 120 degrees to the west and at dawn of August 15 it was facing the French coast. The landings were beginning.

For the past hour the attack TR group led by Captain Boffy, that had parachuted in with the first elements of the British-American airborne division, was hard at work near Draguignan, close to the command post of General Neuling, German army commander for the area between Menton and Marseille. With the help of our underground comrades it was about to attack the local command posts of the Gestapo and the Abwehr. The enemy was battered by surprises, disappointments, and defeats, yet in February 1944 Hitler made a desperate move: a revolution of the intelligence services that many Nazi hotheads were requesting since the end of 1942 was decided upon. The party had finally overtaken traditional military services: the Amt IV of the RSHA took over the Abwehr. The Kriegs marine was attempting in its humiliation to understand the reasons for so many failures. It provided an explanation on March 23, 1945, when it sent its report to Schellenberg (head of Amt IV of the RSHA) and the Führer:

"The percentage of inaccurate reports (69%) and the confirmed reports (8%) forces us to admit that an increasing number of our informers are double agents who are providing us with information coming from the enemy."

The planned disinformation continued into the battle of France. De Lattre used it to smooth the 1st French Army's entry into Belfort and Alsace. On October 20, 1944 he wrote an order, "Instruction number 3 bis personal and secret," aimed at a wide operation on Alsace through the

Vosges, the Schlucht, and Bussang, ignoring the passage of Belfort. At dawn on October 31, a TR penetration agent went up to advanced German positions in the forest of Champagney in the Haute-Saome and later told us what happened:

"I was taken to the regimental commander. I made them understand my true mission and requested passage to Belfort where I was to hand my Abwehr boss an extremely important document. A few hours later, when I could barely move, I was able to complete my mission and be congratulated by my superiors."

The copy of the "directives" written by de Lattre had been sewn inside the lining of his jacket. He explained that he had obtained the valuable document at Guillon-les-Bains at the headquarters of General Béthouart with the help of a young soldier who was the staff secretary at the headquarters of the 1st Army Corps. German General Black, the commander of Army Group G, examined the document confirming the reports of German air reconnaissance that had reported convoys heading towards the southwestern flanks of the Vosges Mountains… Fictitious command posts were set up at Remiremont. The 5th Armored Division ostentatiously showed that it was preparing for an attack towards Plombières. Finally, from Switzerland another W agent handed to the Abwehr on November 7 a copy of "Orientation Directive Number 4" by General de Lattre, explaining the reasons to pursue the thrust of the 1st French Army through the Vosges. How could they not believe them?

Between November 8 and 10 General Black reinforced his defenses in the Vosges and neglected Belfort. When at 11:20 a.m. on November 14, the attack burst out of a snowstorm toward Héricourt and Belfort, the German command was convinced it had to be a diversion. By the 16th the Germans understood the size of the French effort—too late! Alsace was now wide open. German General von Oppen, in command of that key area, was to say:

"The French command benefited from complete surprise. Among the many signs that convinced us that the attack wouldn't take place through the Belfort passage there were the detailed directives of General de Lattre that had been found on one of the prisoners…"

With German resistance ending, *Force A* and the military disinformation effort were also going to cease. The Abwehr stopped the fight:

"We end our broadcasts stop many thanks stop we will meet again in better times end."

That was to be the last radiogram received by two of our W agents on February 18, 1945. Most of the others had no further reaction from the enemy for several days. (Actually it all ended on March 1, 1945 at noon.) Gilbert, our last penetration agent still operating, got a final eerie message:

"Number 32—Inform our friends of the vow sworn in front of the dead body of Jacques Doriot: let us swear allegiance to Doriot who died for the popular socialist revolution. Let us swear to dedicate all our strength to our struggle for the supreme sacrifice—End."

On February 22, 1945 in Mangen on the road to Constance, Doriot, who was the only Frenchman traveling in a car filled with Germans, had died in violent circumstances that remain mysterious. Had the car been hit by machine gun fire from a plane? Had Doriot been shot in the back of the head?

That ending is similar to the Abwehr's own downfall. Powerless to stop the growing actions of patriotic Frenchmen in France, unable to penetrate Africa despite the help of French volunteer desperados, unable to find out our secrets and of separating truth from falsehood, the Abwehr had been defeated and destroyed in February 1944.

By inheriting the Abwehr's ruins and murdering its leader, the RSHA made the odious agony of the Third Reich even bloodier.

28

Counterespionage
and Military Security (SSM) in France

U nder the leadership of Karl Oberg and Dr. Knochen the RSHA had
spread its presence throughout France. Group IV–Gestapo headed
by Bömelburg was in charge of the repression of espionage (Kieffer); of
Communism (Schlüter); of the Resistance (Wentzel); and hunting down
the Jews (Roetke). RSHA Group VI under Bickler was a political intelligence organization with sections specialized in Anglo-American and Eastern European countries. Most of its activity was concentrated on France
with the SS Sturmbannführer Nosek. Technical divisions made up the
rest of this powerful organization: agent training, radio communications,
false documents, files, etc. There were advisers to the PPF, which had
become the most important recruitment area for German espionage. From
the beginning of 1943 every single Abwehr initiative was under the scrutiny of the Nazis. RSHA stations had been set up in the main French
provincial towns and the Gestapo had replaced the GFP (Geheimfeld-
Polizei—a kind of military security created before 1939 by the OKW at
the request of Admiral Canaris).

Reile's services—Section III F, divided by region into "Kommandos"
with numbers starting at 300—had to request the RSHA's help to resolve

the police aspects of the espionage cases initiated by the Abwehr. January 1943 was the turning point, signaling a much more brutal struggle against French patriots. Active French participation through Darnand's Milice, the French Gestapo of Bonny-Lafont, Doriot's PPF, and many others turned the enemy's repression into something even more hateful. In that revolting list I must not forget to include the *Service de répression des menées antinationales** headed by Detmar. It was the reincarnation of the Vichy anti-communist Police Service, with offices at 69 rue de Monceau in Paris since 1943 from where it spread its terrible jurisdiction. Initially called the MA, it was possible to confuse some uninitiated or malicious persons with the military BMAs dissolved by Vichy in 1942 following German requests.

We had to face that daunting and potentially very deadly assemblage had the various groups not also been rivals and had the military and politicians collaborated loyally with each other by pooling their files and done better research. There were many indications of the anarchy that existed.

By gathering intelligence from questioning our comrades under arrest the Abwehr on May 28, 1942 was able to make a complete and nearly accurate analysis of our secret organizations MA-TR and SR. I was correctly listed as head of clandestine counterespionage (CE) known as the TR. The list was completed in March 1943 and in July established a very accurate organization chart of my services in France and in Africa. At around the same time (July-August 1943) the head of the RSHA in Paris had his stations in France prepare a ten-page report on the activities of the French Special Services since the armistice. I don't know how Lafont managed to get the copy that he sent to me in Algiers in September 1943. The writer didn't know how much the Abwehr already knew. Among many inaccuracies a few pieces of information *were* correct:

"This secret service targeting the German intelligence service was known to and supported by the French government. From the start Marshal Pétain, head of state, was informed of its existence, as was established in a letter addressed to him by General Weygand dated December 7, 1940."

I am described as having functions I never had, such as being "Head of French Intelligence." There was a notation proving the Abwehr hadn't yet found out: "The dissident SR headed by Rivet and Paillole is now (in 1943) called: 'Center for African Contacts.'" It's also a fact that Nosek, who worked on the report, had no illusions about efficiency of his own

---

* Service for the Repression of Anti-National Activities.

intelligence work. Today he readily admits that "most agents recruited by the RSHA in North Africa took advantage of it as a way for them to travel back home." The document ended with what was a warning for us: "We must look for those men who are natural born intelligence operatives and neutralize them."

Obviously both the Abwehr and the Gestapo knew about the two main operatives in our counterespionage organization in France: Navarre and Lafont (Verneuil) but since the files were not properly regarding them, this was no doubt the reason they saved their lives.

Lafont had been in the enemy files since 1921. Notation number 130 of April 29, 1921 of the State of Hesse first recorded his espionage activities and police reports from Berlin periodically noted his intelligence work. Despite this the 1939-1945 Abwehr and Gestapo files didn't mention his past activities and placed him under various other identities and functions. One card that I have seen dated 1944 by the Gestapo says that he was the head of *Alliance*—which was really directed by Marie-Madeleine Méric.

Clearly that kind of research couldn't be effective regarding a man as expert and cunning as the head of TR in France. Navarre, whom the enemy often mistook for the "Navarre" network set up by Loustanau-Lacau, relates how he was able to take advantage of the lack of coordination of German defensive services:

"A few weeks before the capital was liberated two Gestapo agents went to the ministry of war in Paris and requested the address of Lieutenant Colonel Navarre. They claimed that Navarre was one of the leaders of the Resistance and was living in Paris under the assumed name of Blanchet. Two days later two Germans—no doubt from the Abwehr—came to 138 Boulevard Berthier, where I was living as Blanchet and asked the concierge for Colonel Navarre. The concierge answered that he had no tenant by that name. They demanded to see the register of all the tenants without any reaction to the name Blanchet."

Nevertheless, despite those mistakes, the German repressive organization with some occasional help from Buffet and his Vichy police, at least those elements still willing to follow his orders, was to wound us badly. But they would not succeed in destroying us! Navarre, Lafont, and their staff were able to avoid many traps but there were also other reasons they survived. The attacks on our services, far from draining their resources, actually stimulated their efforts instead. While the Abwehr had to look into the garbage cans to find a motley crew of adventurers, traitors, crooks, and gangsters, we were using the French elite and the top elements of the army. When we lost one man, two would come forward to take his place. Our mission went ahead and our organization was spreading. Rocked by hatred, fear, and desperation, the enemy tried unsuccessfully to instill terror. It was an implacable fight between two opponents, one of whom had lost his old set of principles that we had retained: "Nachrichtendienst ist Herrendienst."

The storm broke out during the first months of 1943. TR 117 station in Toulouse was decimated, and the head of our Perpignan substation, Terres, was arrested, as were later on Reynaud and Proton. The head of Military Security (SM) in Montpellier, Blattes was caught in December 1942. Every one of them was replaced.

Following the arrest of Li 159 (Hengen), who was still not talking, the net was closing in on Johanès (TR 113) and the remaining parts of TR 112. Martineau, now under Abwehr control, came roaming around Limoges and Clermont-Ferrand. On June 5, 1943, Johanès was arrested along with his son, part of his family, and that of Mercier's. Our best radio technician, Simonin, was being followed by Scheide and tried shooting it out, but he also ended up a prisoner. Files that had not been well hidden were seized and used to incriminate Hengen. Scheide claimed he had found "the names of eighty-seven double agents." But we actually never had more than half that number! These losses were still very serious. A few weeks later, following up, no doubt on information coming from one of our tortured comrades, Geissler, who was in charge of the repression, showed up at Lédendon and grabbed our archives. Garnier and Saint-Jean were deported with the archives to Czechoslovakia where, oddly enough, they were never used. They wound up in July 1945 with the Russians, who refused to return them. Perhaps the enemy already knew that any current information had been deleted from those archives. The Germans looked unsuccessfully for the special TR files that we had buried at Recordier's farm in Provence.

That series of setbacks as well as basic caution prompted me to order putting on ice our old penetration agents working inside France, like Schlochoff, Duperré, Angevin, and several others. Friedmann was too confident and didn't want to end his mission inside the Paris Abwehr. He was arrested and beheaded with an axe. Our SR comrades also went through difficult moments. In February and May 1943 Lombard, the station chief in Lyon, was arrested along with most of his comrades. These were officers of the underground German section of the 2nd Bureau disguised as employees of the Technica Company. Their files were discovered except for an important one hidden with the Abbot Vorage in the Massif Central Mountains. Klaus Barbie—the head of SS Section IV–Gestapo of the RSHA in Lyon—was looking unsuccessfully for that file. He arrested Henri Mortier, the Abbot's young driver, and deported him. Mortier knew where that treasure was hidden and had the courage to keep silent.

Hugon and TR 114 were spared during those raids but they were also forced to reduce their activity. The results of the first six months of German occupation of the Free Zone impacted us very heavily and Reile could claim a real victory! It appeared that half our clandestine CE was knocked out. But that was to underestimate Verneuil and my comrades. The TR leader took the necessary step to scrap the old organization and replace it with a new one. Names of flowers (dahlia, peony, gladioli) replaced the numbers of the old TRs. New men as committed as the old drew the lessons from what went wrong! "Big" Mercier in the north and "Little" Mercier in the south, and Guiraud in the southeast were going to be on the lookout all over France. Some travelers like Mayeur swept up mail and messages and Verneuil from the Auvergne region directed and centralized the work. He provided the results to the DSM through the TR jr. channel, which had grown exponentially under Vellaud, possibly even too fast by cutting corners on security.

Following Michel Thoraval, Guillaume and Caillot, who in January and February 1943 brought new orders and supplies (radios, codes, money) several TR jr. stations opened each month. By July 1943 the old TR and TR jr. stations covered all of France and complemented each other without ever merging.

Navarre also covered France, crossing the demarcation lines over fifty times, and opening in each former military district a clandestine SM station. While that work was relatively simple in the former Free Zone where our old SM had started the network, it became extremely difficult in northern France. New men had to be recruited and trained. Since Paris was vitally important we were fortunate to have Gérar-Dubot, the former news editor and administrator of the newspaper, *Le Journal*. He succeeded in setting up a clandestine BSM (*Bureau de Sécurité Militaire*) in the empty offices at 100 rue de Richelieu, using part of the former employees of that large daily newspaper. Even before the Germans evacuated Paris, the BSM joined the insurrection and fulfilled its mission.

The problems of working inside France and the need for Lafont, the head of the TR, to take added precautions while strictly limiting his objectives led me to lighten the mission of counterintelligence. When I left France I sensed that Vichy was poised, once all of France had been occupied by the Germans, to "take advantage" of the new situation and collaborate more closely with the enemy. That's what I feared would happen under the Bridoux-Delmotte team.

An April 1943 message from Lafont, coming from our monthly submarine link between Algiers and Cap Camarat, provided me with a secret document from the secretary for war in Vichy. It was a project to coordinate intelligence gathering in North Africa, together with German special intelligence. Were they going to subvert the military and turn a few dimwits into traitors? We had to stop that dishonorable attempt. It was impossible to give that added mission to TR 113 without endangering the station because of Hengen's (Li 159) arrest and Martineau's double game. I told Johanès, who unfortunately didn't heed my advice, to stay away from Clermont-Ferrand and Vichy and lay low for some time. TR jr. set itself up, but its knowledge of counterintelligence was rudimentary. It was in no position to spread itself so thinly when its activity involved external radio broadcasts and links. The only solution was that I take on the matter myself and have an officer recruited in North Africa to penetrate the criminal organization.

Among the growing number of volunteers, there was an air force officer who appeared eminently qualified for the mission. Captain Rodrigue Pimont was deputy to the head of technical control (mail, telephone, and telegraph) in North Africa and therefore in constant contact with my services that he knew quite well. Even though he had a very important job it didn't fulfill his need for action. He had a master's degree in literature, was a pilot, and a flight instructor; he had worked for me in Rabat from October 1940 to July 1942, and liked our activity. He was thirty-five, very courteous, and highly intelligent. A rather big man, his elaborate form of speech led people to believe he was a civilian rather than a soldier. I couldn't ask for anyone better to attempt to penetrate the monstrous Vichy plans. He was very calm and deferential as he sat in front of me.

"I'm going to offer you a thankless and dangerous task," I said.

"That's what I expect!"

"Our goal is to worm into an organization that's recruiting among our former army comrades a whole set of spies and saboteurs meant to operate for the Abwehr in North Africa."

I explained to Pimont what I knew and what I expected. Face to face we spoke in the kind of man-to-man dialog where each man takes stock of the other and makes his own decisions.

"You'll have to leave Algeria as a deserter and risk incrimination."

"That's how the game is played."

"You must cross the border between French and Spanish Morocco at your own risk, with neither money nor luggage!"

"Fine."

"Once in Spain you'll have to ask for help from the Vichy authorities and give the impression that you're ideologically opposed to Algiers and the Allies. You'll have to be vocal about your hatred for your superiors, and of me."

"No problem," he answered.

We both laughed and relaxed like partners in crime. Everything looked simple and turned out to be so, because this W agent was a very clever operator.

After two months' training Pimont left Algiers on July 1, 1943 with another officer just as gutsy as himself. I told him just before he left, "You can reach us anytime through a TR jr. station. Don't try to find out where it's located or the frequency used. Never have any pieces of paper on you that might give you away. Should you face a problem, wait two to three days before contacting TR jr. Just play for time and say anything you want about Algiers and myself."

Pimont reached France on July 17. The French consul in Melilla (Spanish Morocco) gave him a travel document and funds to get to Madrid. The French embassy sent him to the German embassy where he was given a warm welcome by Dollar, the RSHA man in Spain. He was given travel documents and an entry visa for France. Following my instructions, Pimont reported to the Hotel Thermal in Vichy—where the secretary of state for war had his offices—and to Colonel Brun. Our old friend from 2 *bis* was now inspector general of technical controls. He was welcomed, congratulated and introduced to Pierre Laval himself on July 20, 1943. He spoke about North Africa, anti-communism, and proposed a propaganda project. He did it so well that Laval was taken in and introduced Pimont to Creyssel, head of propaganda. Later he was to promote Pimont to be a deputy-prefect in Rouen!

With that kind of backing all the doors opened wide. Our W found out that one of his former classmates, a Foreign Legion officer, was setting up research on North Africa with the Germans. Was that the beginning of the treacherous espionage operation? His friend in Paris was happy to see Pimont and told him about a mission he was preparing with the Abwehr. Three French officers and a radio operator were to go to Morocco soon, following a three-week training period in Berlin.

"Since you've just returned from North Africa, you should help us."

"What do you want me to do?" Pimont asked.

"Show us where to land the 'Hannibal'* team and how to fade into North African circles to find military intelligence. The best thing is that I introduce you to our instructors."

Pimont agreed.

Captain Gehrke and Lieutenant Mühlmann were from the Münster Ast and we knew about them since 1938. They had never set foot in North Africa and were far from feeling secure about the preparation of the "Hannibal" commando. The miraculous appearance of Pimont was a godsend. So they hired him, listened to what he had to say, and paid him handsomely. They trusted him. From then on Dick's messages (Dick was Pimont's pseudonym) reached us regularly and on time from TR jr. station (Larva), operational since July in Marseille. The connection was made by Christian Durrmeyer, a brave and enthusiastic young man.

We found out that the three officers, former members of the *Légion Tricolore* and later of the LVF, had been recruited by the Abwehr by official French services that were advertising for those units. These traitors were officers working for Vichy to recruit volunteers for German intelligence. They were: Agostini, one of the leaders of the LVF; Girod, a salesman in North Africa for the *Légion Tricolore*; and Christian du Jonchay, who had returned from Tunis.

On October 14, 1943, at 8:50 p.m., Larva transmitted this message from Dick:

"Hannibal mission to parachute on October 16 between 2 and 3 a.m. 10 kilometers southwest of Oujda."

I didn't want to let those miserable traitors have time to decide what they should do. Perhaps they would surrender to the police on their own? Or try to fulfill their criminal mission? I was not about to run that risk out of respect to my uniform. I asked Achiary, head of the *Surveillance du Territoire*, to be at the location and nab the commandos as they touched ground. On October 16 at 2:15 a.m. the team bailed out of a Condor plane. At 4 a.m., either subdued or defiant, they were handcuffed and being

---

* The name of the operation.

questioned by our policemen before being turned over to a military court. Notwithstanding what they told us, we had every reason to believe that they intended to fulfill their mission in Morocco: gathering political and military intelligence, disseminating propaganda aimed at the Arab population, sabotaging the railroad tracks. A huge amount of supplies had been sent in by three small parachutes: a fifteen-kilo radio transmitter for short-wave signals over long distance, a generator powered by a pedal creating continuous electric power weighing twenty kilos, a number of accessories (twenty-five- and thirty-five-meter antennas, soldering equipment, etc.) all weighing eight kilos.

The manual for the radio operator indicated that he was expected to work night and day with a correspondent located some 2,500 kilometers away. The frequencies were designed to make it impossible to hear the broadcasts in North Africa, except at a very short distance—less than five kilometers.

"Not audible perhaps but with that kind of hardware they were certainly visible! How could they expect to carry it around without being seen? And then look at the documents they're using," Achiary said.

The false identity cards were poorly executed. The three men were supposedly living in Oran but working in Morocco and border crossings with Algeria had to be justified and authorized. The travel permits were signed "Allied Authorities" while in fact only the *Sécurité Militaire* was handing out those authorizations.

"That's encouraging," chuckled Sérot. "They're even worse than we are at creating false documents and they know nothing of what's going on here."

In one of the spy's pockets we found some addresses of mail boxes in Melilla and Tangier, disappearing ink formulas and a list of radio supplies, ammunition, weapons and explosives that were to be parachuted in upon request. Why not use it? The radio operator on the team made a good impression; he was an NCO who had joined the group under pressure by one of the officers. A few days later under our control he was able to contact his German counterpart. He sent some messages and in January 1944 requested additional supplies and equipment. We intercepted and shot down the enemy plane during the night of February 2-3. One month later we started all over again and shot down a second enemy plane. Meantime, Pimont informed us of two other traitors being sent in to North Africa. Caillat was arrested in November 1943 and Barbat in February 1944 as they were touching down.

In addition to this extremely valuable counterintelligence, Pimont was also transmitting military intelligence he gathered from the Abwehr officers such as those he sent us on December 7, 1943 through TR jr. Marseille:

Number 47 - Decisions at Rommel conference in Paris.
1. In event of landings Rommel to take tactical command-stop-Rundstedt territorial command.
2. Allied landings expected mouth of Loire or Mediterranean Gulf of Genoa-stop-channel coast considered improbable by Germans due to large fortifications. Signed Dick.

Too good to be true! That message which I handed to *Force A* made us all very happy. The second part was an excellent omen for the success of our disinformation campaign. I also had a growing feeling that the Marseille TR jr. and Dick himself were both in danger. Guiraud, head of the old TR for the Mediterranean region, told me he had recommended to Avallard, head of the Larva station, to be wary of a Belgian named Max de Wilde. Guiraud had introduced him to me in April 1942 when he offered us his services. There was a strange look in his eyes, a sweet little smile on his face, and his clammy handshake was rather repulsive. Furthermore, he had a whole confusing laundry list of explanations, unrealistic promises, former relationships—all made him smell like a double agent. We had thrown him out, and now he was back inside the Larva team. I had nothing tangible against him, but his insistence on being part of our organization simply added to my negative impression.

In January 1944 I asked Pimont and Captain Avallard, head of Larva, to return to North Africa. In February again I asked Avallard and Pimont to return because their mission was completed. Both men were oblivious to danger and very passionate about their work. They felt stimulated by their success. I was simply being ignored and had nothing to back up my recommendations. If only I could go and get them, convince them. But unfortunately in Algiers at the time we were in the midst of a major crisis. The de Gaulle-Giraud dispute had reached its apex. The merger of all the Special Services (the traditional units and the BCRA) was an all-important issue being debated and each general wanted to effect the fusion for his own benefit. My service and myself as an individual were being discussed. I therefore could not leave, fearing that the place would be either turned upside down or set on fire! So, many years later, I still wonder why we were so cursed as to tear ourselves apart so violently.

Pimont was arrested on April 2, 1944. What I had suspected did in fact take place and Max de Wilde was a traitor (after the liberation of France de Wilde was sentenced to death). He was working for Dunker, *alias* Delage, deputy director of Section IV–Gestapo of the RSHA in Marseille. One day in January 1944 he had taken the Larva codes, photocopied them, and returned them. The Germans found out as they decoded the TR jr. messages that there was a French agent inside the Gehrke Abwehr team. They therefore were able to identify Pimont. The Paris RSHA ended its report to the military court on May 24, 1944 with this conclusion: "Pimont has been the cause of great harm to the Reich. His betrayal resulted in the arrest of all our agents in North Africa." On June 27, 1944 he was condemned to death and the sentence was sent to the Führer. (All capital sentences of regular army officers were always subjected to Hitler's personal decision.) He was to be saved because during the German retreat the military court was to lose both the file and Pimont himself as it waited for the Führer to decide. He was transferred from one prison to the next until he wound up in Amberg where American troops would free him on April 24, 1945.

Avallard was not to be so lucky. Once he finally made up his mind to return to Algiers he was arrested in Paris on April 26, 1944, during his parting visit. He died in a concentration camp.

In August 1948 we asked Roskothen, the former German military court president who sentenced Pimont to death, what he thought of the French officer:

"I felt I was dealing with a 'true' French officer of the old school. I asked him how he could have betrayed the members of the 'Hannibal' mission, who were his fellow officers. I felt I had to translate his proud answer for the other members of the court: 'Die sache des Vaterlands geht vor!'*

"He tricked the German intelligence services by risking his life. As president of a military war court I had to sentence him to death. Man to man I could only admire him."

In spite of our losses—Michel Garder, head of the Paris TR, was arrested in September 1943, a consequence of the arrests of Martineau and Johanès—counterespionage production of the TRs in France was increasing. At the heart of the Vichy and Paris administrations, with new W agents inside German and collaborationist organizations, our services

---

* "The cause of the Homeland comes ahead of any other feeling!"

were providing Algiers with a mass of intelligence being added to our "criminal accounting" and enriching our reports to the government, the High Command and the Allies.

The links to France were of prime importance. I wanted them to be secure, frequent, and increasingly under all-French control. Ever since Lherminier had opened the submarine link, the "tube" to Cap Camarat worked every month on moonless nights. The Larva TR jr. station provided the teams to receive the sub—helped and protected by the police network of Michel Hacq (formerly of the *Surveillance du Territoire*)—and the "maquis" fighters in the Maures mountains, who were helping and protecting the loading and unloading operations of our men and their equipment.

Air operations (pick-up and parachuting in) were no longer slapped together haphazardly. Michel Thoraval had trained specialists in signaling the landing strips. A paratrooper, Captain Boffy, and his deputy Ribollet, now helped him. Every month on moonlit nights we relied on the incredible experience and dexterity of British flyers. On the coast of Brittany Yves Le Hénaff was handling naval connections to England while another naval officer, Lieutenant Lavallée, was attempting to do the same in the Vendée region. The Pyrenees and Spain were still the preferred passage for our couriers and any Frenchman who wanted to join the French army's fight.

Our escape routes were much more developed thanks to the courage and selflessness of customs officers and gendarmes—particularly those at Saillagousse—making the heavy transit between Algiers and France was slow and regular with good results. We had to make sure it was protected on both sides of the Pyrénées. On the Spanish side we reinforced the Barcelona TR station with radio operators and personnel. D'Hoffelize was now in charge; as former head of the Toulouse TR he was best qualified to tighten our counterespionage activities in southern France and Catalonia. The involvement of Monseigneur Boyer-Mas with the Spanish government in Madrid and that of Foret and Ramonatxo in Barcelona were of prime importance and allowed us to work in peace and quiet. Spanish police were increasingly inclined to close their eyes on our activities that were often quite obvious.

On the French side things were very different. The enemy was aware of the heavy traffic through the Pyrenees and that the region around Toulouse was a gateway for escape and a resistance center. There were maquis being formed all around the area and the Ariège in particular. An army of German policemen under the command of SS officer Retzek was hunting down the freedom fighters with the help of the intelligence unit of the PPF and other collaborationist groups, such as the Milice or the RNP. We were hit very severely. Roger, whom Lafont had appointed to replace Delmas and Proton, had been arrested in June 1943. But thankfully Gilbert Getten and his network were still operating. They were connected to Barcelona through Toulouse gendarmerie Captain Abadie. Taillandier, hunted by the enemy, felt isolated, ever since the total occupation of France when he got involved with the *Combat* network. In 1942 D'Hoffelize introduced him to Captain Pélissier, who was part of *Combat* and the department head of the secret army. He took part in camouflaging weapons and searching for intelligence for our services and for Frenay.

Thanks to the U.S. Army Air Corps we were able at the end of May 1943 to parachute near Carcassonne de Gasquet, a TR officer, whose mission it was to rebuild and reinforce our services in the area. He was to connect them to Barcelona and link Taillandier to TR jr. De Gasquet's arrival changed things radically for Taillandier. He understood the importance of his mission in protecting the paths through the Pyrenees, summed up as follows: "Paralyze the enemy and destroy the traitors." The use of D measures was to be systematic but in accordance with our rules: all decisions were made by Lafont or by d'Hoffelize in Barcelona, except in urgent or self-defense cases. A report was always sent back to Algiers.

In June 1943 Pélissier reinforced Taillandier, now known as Morhange, with André Fontès and the very effective resistance fighters of the *Combat* group. That was the first active part of the Morhange group that was hiding at the Chateau Brax. The good work done in the Midi region of France quickly reduced Gestapo activity and any collaborationist enthusiasm! Just like Getten, who was able to infiltrate the Milice, Morhange's men got into the PPF, the RNP, and even the Gestapo. Achille Viadieu was responsible for that feat in August 1943. We were now able to pinpoint and hit individuals using reliable intelligence. Through Barcelona I was being sent the transcripts of the judgments and the D measures ordered by the TR. On October 9 there was a "trial" of several members of the intelligence unit of the PPF, and Morhange had succeeded in stealing its files. Police Inspector Arsaguet of the *Surveillance du Territoire* undertook the investigation; a judge from Toulouse headed the court. The main culprit was a captain who had been responsible for the arrest of some thirty freedom fighters and in May 1943 he allowed the destruction of part of the camouflage unit led by Taillandier. He was executed by firing squad with his accomplices at dawn on October 10, 1943. The questioning of these traitors and the examination of the files provided the Algiers DSM with a wealth of counterintelligence material.

But in July 1943 Vichy appointed as head of the Toulouse regional police a man whose brutally repressive policies against resistance fighters in Lyon led us to put him on the list of dangerous individuals deserving D measures. The tragic events that took place in Lyon leading to the arrest of fourteen intelligence officers, including Jean Moulin and many other patriots, were enough to prove either his direct participation in the repression or at the very least the assistance he gave to the enemy. In the Technica case the treasonable behavior of one of his subordinates had been lethal to us.

I warned my Toulouse comrades against that police official and alerted the Morhange group to be very careful, and I wanted to show him how much we approved his clean up action and our active participation. Blémant had escaped from France and was now in Algiers, he was in the army and part of General Giraud's personal security detail. He was already well acquainted with the North African underworld and offered several times to provide the services of repentant gangsters. He introduced me to one of them in July 1943, whose determination and candor I liked. His ancestors were from Alsace and refugees in Algeria following France's defeat in 1871. Alphonse Alsfasser was a strong young man, a loner with intense patriotic feelings, like Blémant. The *Surveillance du Territoire* confirmed my favorable impression. In August I called him in.

"I need a real tough man to go to Toulouse and take part in repressive action against traitors and show how determined we are to defend ourselves using the same methods as the enemy!"

"I'm at your orders when and where you need me," he answered.

I told Alsfasser how to contact Taillandier through Inspector Arsaguet. I showed him the file on the Toulouse police chief and the messages we had received from France and London demanding that he be stopped. I accompanied him to the "tube" in September 1943. In a jaunty way he told me how happy he was to serve his country and got into the submarine. At the end of 1943 Alsfasser found Arsaguet at home in Perpignan. A few days later Arsaguet introduced Alsfasser to André Fontés, Taillandier's deputy in Toulouse. From then on the Morhange group began preparing down to the last detail for its punitive mission.

The comings and goings of the police chief were carefully recorded: he would leave his office in the Place Saint-Etienne at about 8 p.m. to go home, a house at the crossroads of two streets far from the center of town. He traveled down deserted avenues, the Allées Verdier and the Place du Grand-Rond. Taillandier and Alsfasser decided to take action on the evening of October 16. Starting at 7 p.m. Alsfasser and three men were keeping watch behind the Saint-Etienne church. At 8:30 p.m. the police chief was driving alone, followed by the Peugeot 402 of the Morhange group. When he reached the deserted Place du Grand-Rond, the car that was following him was ready to pass and open fire with a submachine gun. At that very moment the chief veered to the left, cutting off the Peugeot, and stepped on the gas. Was it a coincidence? Had he noticed that he was being followed and thought the way the car was behaving was suspicious? In any case the group didn't insist and merely drove on. The operation was cancelled until another date could be set when it would be carried out differently.

In front of the police chief's house there was a small vacant lot with a few thick bushes where one or two men could hide. A car could easily be parked in the street about 360 yards away without being seen by anyone in the house.

On Saturday, October 23, 1943, at 7:45 p.m., Alsfasser and a man from the Morhange group hid in the bushes already darkened by nightfall. They both carried a Thompson submachine gun. The Peugeot 402 that dropped them off was parked in darkness and ready to take off. The police chief's car arrived at 8:15 p.m. and drove into the garage next to the house, and then he appeared with his briefcase. Two bursts of submachine gun fire cut him down. In a few seconds Alsfasser and his partner were driving away in the Peugeot.

The execution had a huge impact on the region. The authorities ordered a curfew from 9 p.m. to 5 a.m. but it was useless: 15,000 people were checked and 1,700 searches made. The feeling that no one could hide from the patriot's revenge was now real to the top administrative echelon, including the police, the Abwehr, and Gestapo leadership. London radio mentioned that execution as a warning to those Frenchmen regarding the consequences of engaging in acts of treason.

The Morhange group was now wound up and ready to continue its retribution. It received a lot of valuable help from other patriots and policemen in particular. In November 1943 Pierre Rous joined the group. His intelligence and connections in the "underworld" allowed even more intensive repression operations in the Toulouse region, spreading to Paris where Taillandier wanted to pursue the gangsters of the Bonny-Lafont gang.

Alsfasser was to pay with his life for his devotion and courage. He was supposed to return to Cap Camarat during the night of November 26-27, 1943 to board the *Casabianca* back to Algiers. At 8 p.m. he was at the Achille Ottou farm at Ramatuelle. That quiet wine grower had been dodging Italian and German patrols for months. His mother, sister, and his friend Olivier gave refuge and comfort to our passengers and made sure they were safe. Ottou also headed the local resistance group.

At the meeting point that evening there was General Giraud's daughter, 16-year-old Monique Giraud, whom we wanted to save from the Gestapo. The enemy had arrested nine members of her family at the residence assigned to them by the Vichy government and they were all deported to German concentration camps. Monique remained alone with her 70-year-old grandmother. I could see her father's anguish since he had already been hit by the deportation of another one of his daughters. Despite his torment and other political problems General Giraud wasn't complaining. He wasn't asking for any favors, but when I told him on October 18, 1943 that I could get his daughter to Algiers I saw his eyes well up with tears. One of Giraud's deputies, Captain Laffitte—who later would also be arrested and deported— picked up Monique and kept watch over her at Achille's farm. She told me about that tragic night:

> Achille and his sister, with all their heartfelt generosity, took care of everyone, feeding us and giving us something to drink. Yet a cloud came over me. I let a glass fall and without being superstitious thought of a bad omen and felt unhappy for a few minutes. Alsfasser reassured me; it was the last thing he would tell me: "But on the contrary, let's celebrate; it's white glass and that's a good omen for us."
>
> At 11 p.m. our team, including the intended passengers of the submarine along with the mail carriers, went out into the night. Two columns of resistance fighters from the maquis were on either side, about 40 yards away. That walk through the shadows and the outlines of other people was hallucinating. We stopped from time to time to listen to the faintest sounds, then we would start walking again, hunkering over. Finally we reached the sea. We thought we were saved, when just 100 feet from the water we heard "Halt!" cried out in the silence mixed with the sound of the waves. Shots rang out. That's when Alsfasser was killed. Laffitte was carrying a mailbag and drew me to the rear to escape the enemy patrols. Tracer bullets crossed the sky while we were hiding in the boulders waiting in anguish to see

how the operation would unfold. Then everything fell silent. We couldn't stay there. General Valette d'Osia had my suitcase and umbrella. My hands were free and I managed to follow Laffitte during that race through the darkness. We had to get as far away from the seashore as we could and back to Ramatuelle. Finally, we found a path. Suddenly a German patrol was in front of us, just 30 feet away. "Surrender, surrender. Halt!" There could be only one way out. To my right was a vineyard and I ran into it. Unfortunately I failed to see the root of a vine and stumbled as bullets whizzed around. I was really frightened!

In a few seconds I imagined my mother, who had been deported, getting the sad news of my adventures and my father, who was expecting me to arrive in Algeria. My legs refused to carry me any further. I heard steps coming closer and was surprised to see Laffitte next to me helping me move forward. They were still shooting. We hadn't seen a very deep ditch, in which we could hide, at the far end of the field full of bramble branches. I don't remember how long I stayed there; I had passed out. When I came to my senses my hair was undone, my head hurt, and my knees were bleeding over my teenage girl's white socks. The Germans had thankfully lost track of us and that ditch had saved us for the time being. We had to leave as soon as possible and find our way back. We were walking around in circles. We made a wise decision to stop in some bushes and wait for daybreak. It was very cold and we were in a hurry to leave those difficult surroundings. Several patrols came very close while we were waiting but fortunately they had no dogs! We walked on the road to Saint-Tropez to get on the train back to Marseille and I was strolling at a leisurely pace to avoid looking suspicious when a car suddenly stopped. Two gendarmes got out. I left my companion with them and kept on walking alone. I found that they were taking a long time and yet they had spoken for less than five minutes. I heard the car starting again but didn't look back. I was then surprised to see the car pull up next to me with Laffitte inside. They said not to worry, but that the way we were walking was giving us away and that we had better be with some true French patriotic gendarmes rather than wander around for miles.

I didn't see the look on my father's face when at Colonel Paillole's request he had to cancel the mission of the *Casabianca* at the very last moment, knowing that his daughter was waiting on the far side of the Mediterranean. He never hesitated to risk the lives of his family to save his men. He was thinking of Fabert's motto, which he had adopted as his own: "If to prevent the loss of one of the King's strongholds to the enemy I had to risk my life, my family, and all my possessions, I wouldn't hesitate an instant in doing so."

At the last moment I stopped the submarine en route to Cap Camarat. An enemy broadcast we intercepted on November 26 at 6 p.m. led me to believe that German listening posts near the Maures were on the alert. It was too late to inform Guiraud in Marseille to stop the mission, but we could still warn our sailors. Monique Giraud (who later became Mrs. Marcel Blanc, wife of the prefect of Montpellier) was saved. My service helped her escape through Spain and she joined her father. Alphonse Alsfasser, the orphan without a family, was adopted in death by the villagers and buried in Ramatuelle near the memorial we had built to honor our 300 dead comrades. We go to visit his grave, which the townspeople tend to and cover with flowers, every year.

We refused to accept such a failure. Cap Camarat was no longer a safe place and the Germans closely watched the Mediterranean coast. Our TR organization (old and jr.) in southeastern France was in danger and under the Gestapo's scrutiny. I decided to transfer our submarine operations in agreement with many officers to the Spanish coast. The TR station in Barcelona, well staffed and working perfectly, was ideally suited to receive the "tube" and move our men and mail between France and North Africa. Trautmann, head of Navy intelligence, named a naval officer to make sure the clandestine naval links were maintained effectively. They were to work from January 1944 to the end of the war under the best conditions.

While it was busy helping Monique Giraud and our mail the Marseille TR informed Taillandier of Alsfasser's tragic death.

"He will be avenged!" was his answer.

The security of the Spanish border had become vitally important to us. We had to respond to the reign of terror the Gestapo wanted to enforce in southwestern France and the Pyrenees region. Our answer was the terror of our reprisals and the implacable punishment imparted on all traitors. The Morhange group was entirely committed to this. The tragedy at Ramatuelle led to one of the most spectacular counterespionage operations that took place during the German occupation. A believer in penetration techniques, Taillandier had placed an infiltrator W inside the Toulouse Gestapo. Saint-Laurens was only twenty-five, but a quiet and mature type; he was also reassuring and nondescript but was also brave to the point of being foolhardy. By displaying pro-Nazi sympathies he became friendly with the head of the team, the SS Wilhelm Messack, who was living at the Hotel Capoul on the Place Wilson in Toulouse with his mistress, Paulette Bordier, a young nurse. On December 13, 1943, he was ordered by Paris HQ to go to Nice to work with Retzek, the former boss in Toulouse, and now head of the RSHA in the Alpes-Maritimes and Var departments since the Italian collapse and the Wehrmacht's occupation of the entire region. Retzek found an alarming situation: the Italians, and the OVRA in particular, had not fulfilled their mission properly. Barranco himself was under suspicion of pro-French sympathies and had been arrested by the Nazis in Nice. Reile had to step in to get him out of jail.

The incident of November 26 at Cap Camarat proved the deep roots of the Resistance in the region and the daring of the submarine operations. An urgent reaction was required. Retzek requested reinforcements and got Knochen and Bömelburg to give him Messack as his deputy plus two counterintelligence specialists of Mediterranean matters, the Spanish Colonel Emilio Alzugaray and an Italian, Bruno Toniutti.

Alzugaray reached Toulouse at the end of December after having taken all the files from the RSHA and the Spanish embassy that could help Retzek in southeastern France. Toniutti was a fanatical fascist with extensive knowledge of the French Côte d'Azur. He took all relevant information from the Toulouse Gestapo files that could be of use in Nice. Both the Spaniard and the Italian recruited their own nationals as agents and informers.

Since mid-December under the seemingly indifferent eyes of Jules Tilens (alias Saint-Laurens), Messack was getting ready to leave on January 1, 1944, taking the national highway via Carcassonne, Montpellier, and Nîmes. Taillandier, once informed on December 23, decided to intercept the convoy and seize the files and the men. He knew from Saint-Laurens that there was to be a Peugeot 12 hp van driven by Toniutti filled with files, preceded by a Peugeot 202 driven by the ever-present Jules Tilens and a Citroën 11 hp carrying Messack, his mistress, and Alzugaray. Just before Christmas the head of the Morhange group went to the Toulouse gendarmerie with some flowers and gifts for Captain Abadie and his family. While Mrs. Abadie went to mix a *pastis*, Taillandier and Abadie went into a huddle.

"Captain, I need three or four gendarme uniforms."

"Are you joking?"

"Not at all. We want to give them as a Christmas present to Mr. Perrier.*"

"You want him to have some gendarmes uniforms?"

"No, we'll give them back to you. You know Mr. Perrier is a glutton for documents and we have a priceless opportunity to get him some files."

Taillandier then explained his plans to intercept the Gestapo convoy.

"That's great!" said Abadie. "You'll have the uniforms in two days. I'll also make sure there are no gendarmerie patrols on January 1 and 2 on the *Route Nationale*** (RN) 113 between Toulouse and Montgiscard."

On December 31, 1943, the cars to be used by the Germans were parked in the Hotel Capoul courtyard on the Place Wilson under the constant watch of the Morhange group. During the day it was a shoeshine boy sitting on his box under the awning or a municipal employee working on the sewer across the street. At night there were uniformed guards pacing up and down the Place Wilson. From time to time those spotters went into the cafés nearby to call in mysterious information in hushed voices. Taillandier was waiting at Montgiscard on the road the convoy was to take. He was preparing the ambush, giving orders for the fateful moment. Combatalade, a liaison agent, was traveling back and forth between Taillandier and the Place Wilson.

On Saturday January 1, 1944 the entire group was on the alert and impatient to see action. At 6 p.m. there were many comings and goings in the hotel's courtyard. Messack, Toniutti, Alzugaray, and Tilens were there. Were they about to leave? Not quite. The New Year celebration had been more fun than usual so they decided to leave the next day, Sunday. It was a generally quiet day following New Year's, and Messack thought it was the ideal time to drive.

At 8 a.m. on January 2, 1944 the Gestapo team loaded its baggage, had breakfast, and quickly and silently got into the cars. It was beautiful cool weather and Paulette Bordier nestled up to her lover in the front seat of the Citroën. The convoy got started with the Peugeot 202 driven by Tilens out in front through the Place Saint-Michel and on past the gendarmerie. You could see Abadie at a window with its light still on. Tilens got on RN 113 outside Toulouse. Twenty kilometers from there the cars were stopped and surrounded by four gendarmes and two civil-

---

* Alias of Major Paillole.
** State highway.

ians, police inspectors no doubt; but they could even have been Gestapo agents.

"Your documents, please?"

Messack was smiling and very self-assured as he got out of the car. Suddenly he noticed Tilens on the side of the road and the strange clothing worn by gendarmes. One of them was wearing beige riding breeches, the other a parka and the third a civilian pair of pants, the fourth was properly dressed but he practically disappeared in a long coat that was too big. He understood then that it was a trap. The SS went for his pistol...a burst of submachine gun fire cut him down. Then there was shooting in every direction...then complete silence.

A few people nearby who heard the shots hadn't made a move because of the "gendarmes." A 9:50 a.m. a driver on RN 113 found the dead bodies of Messack, Alzugaray, Paulette Bordier, and Toniutti, as well as the Citroën. The other two cars had vanished. At 10:15 a.m. he alerted the gendarmerie at Montgiscard. Captain Abadie was told at 10:30 a.m.; he thought for a long, long time about what should be done. At the beginning of the afternoon he told the prefecture, who informed the German police, who in turn didn't start their search until 5 p.m.!

The Morhange group had long disappeared and was taking stock of its inventory in one of its safe houses:

> 200 liters of gasoline, something very precious at the time;
> 10,000 francs and other foreign currencies;
> lists of Abwehr and Gestapo sympathizers to be used in southeastern France;
> files on resistance fighters to be arrested and weapons caches;
> various kinds of files (general, accounting, private correspondence, etc.)

A total of some 100 kilos of documents important to counterespionage, and for the Morhange group a hit list that was to impart justice ninety-three times on the Abwehr, the Gestapo, and the traitors. Out of eighty-two agents of the Morhange group that were part of my TR network, twenty-four died, seven returned from concentration camps, three were seriously wounded and permanently disabled.

Marcel Taillandier was arrested and identified by the Feldgendarmerie at Saint-Martin-du-Touch near Toulouse on July 11, 1944, at 3 p.m. and was executed. He was 27 years old. His traveling companion, Léo Hamard, was to die after horrible torture. His main deputy, Achille Viadieu, with whom he had traveled to Barcelona a few days before to receive my orders and funds, had been shot by the Gestapo in a street in Toulouse. The enemy had just figured out that Viadieu, a member of the RNP and friend of Déat, the Gestapo's V Mann in Toulouse, had been a penetration agent of French counterespionage for the past two years.

29

Merging the Special Services:
Traditional and BCRA

W riting this chapter caused real sadness and some misgivings. The merging of the traditional Special Services, which we represented, with the BCRA, created by de Gaulle in London, could have been a positive chapter in our history had it resulted in a single organization made up of two resistance movements that complemented each other in adapting to a new reality.

That was not to be the case. The fortunes of war as well as the ambitions and weaknesses of the men in charge made these two factions look like rivals, if not outright enemies. Partisan politics was felt on the battlefield inside France, even though we were fighting on the same side and shared the same prison cells. It also affected London and Algiers, starting in November 1942 until it reached its peak between May 1943 and April 1944. The struggle for power and a certain vision of how France was to be liberated with all its political consequences became the underlying reason for some very unfortunate clashes we were involved in.

De Gaulle's position was the following:

The occupation of France and the Vichy regime's collaboration with the enemy require political action as well as military action. This means a unified command for the Special Services within the government.

Giraud's view:

We are in a state of siege. Military authorities are responsible for the struggle against espionage and to maintain public order. We are at war. The High Command must be informed and be able to function securely.

De Gaulle considered the Special Services as a branch of the government and should be merged immediately with that idea in mind. According to Giraud they belonged to the military authorities. A change in their structure, if required, should take place in France once the war was over.

The imperious personalities of the two generals made it even more difficult to blend their opposing views. Wrapped up in military rigor an unavoidable conflict was looming, since both men were to share power equally. The crisis reached the boiling point as de Gaulle's political persona gained momentum at the expense of his partner. Once Giraud began experiencing the growing limitations placed on his authority, including the military field, the clash became dramatic. It could end only with the elimination of one of the two men. Civilian power vested in the cleverest and best political operator won the day over the military man. Vested with full power in April 1944, de Gaulle governed by decree and swept away the obstacle named Giraud. The traditional *Service de Renseignements* (SR) was effectively beheaded. But since there was no other solution possible the *Sécurité Militaire* and *Contre Espionnage* were confirmed in their missions and functions. The entire group, along with the BCRA, was merged into the DGSS (*Direction Générale des Services Spéciaux*), reporting to the head of the government. Jacques Soustelle, a very intelligent, highly educated and courteous man of good will, who was deeply attached to the ideals of Gaullism, was the new head of the DGSS.

This brief overview of an entire year of internal strife to reach a solution that appeared logical fails to describe the innumerable challenges we faced while we were still at war. From May 1943 to April 1944 I had to spend as much time defending my services, their structure, and their secrets, as I had to fulfill my task on the counterespionage front and regarding military security issues. This book would be incomplete if I failed to describe some of the events of that period.

The fundamental ideological antagonism between Giraud and de Gaulle could have been much less bitter than it turned out to be. I don't dare say that it could have been "friendly" if the entourage around each general hadn't such obvious political agendas and ambitions. The Special Services could not be insulated from such an unhealthy atmosphere.

Rivet, much to his credit, did his utmost to shield us from those antagonisms. His position during the difficult merger was to attempt to defend the unity and effectiveness of his services: "We cannot allow inexperienced hands tinkering with our organization which has grown tenfold by the German occupation."

The heads of the BCRA did not think in those terms. I always viewed their goal as eliminating a rival who could eliminate their self-assigned role in London and undermine the very strength of Gaullism. "We feared that the Allies could back a different group"—that was what Passy told me on Saturday, March 18, 1944, in my office at El Biar when we openly discussed our ideas and problems. On that day the Giraud-de Gaulle conflict had reached its critical point. That was the background of what some called "the Special Services war."

The victory and liberation of Tunisia in May 1943 proved that the military situation had now turned in our favor. Our good showing in military operations had encouraged the Allied services to trust our effectiveness; we were preparing the landings in Italy and France together. The distance between London and Algiers softened the disagreement between Giraud and de Gaulle. There were however some negative signs regarding our future agreement with the BCRA: the icy response by de Gaulle to the initiative of Bonnefous; the lack of follow-up by the Gaullists to the first agreements I negotiated with Passy in December 1942 that Rivet had confirmed in February 1943. At the beginning of April 1943 Pélabon, a naval engineer representing the BCRA in Algiers, had expressed a real interest, as we did, in working together. Those talks did not get very far.

De Gaulle arrived in Algiers on May 30, 1943. At that time Giraud had reorganized all the services engaged in clandestine warfare under a *Direction des Services Spéciaux* under Ronin, who had been promoted to the rank of general. As co-president of the *Comité de Libération Nationale* the commander in chief, General Giraud, took charge of military power and first and foremost the Special Services.

General de Gaulle, the other co-president, also had as part of his cabinet a political unit called *Comité d'action en France*, which included de Gaulle, Giraud, and a number of commissioners. The BCRA was becoming an action unit with military and political activities. Therefore, de Gaulle wanted to modify the basic mission of the Special Services in Algiers and adjust them to his views, something that could only happen by bending them to his will. The London team examined the situation and tried different approaches, mentioning with self-satisfaction the idea of an "Intelligence Service" to be created. The meetings took place in an atmosphere of forced courtesy, indicating suspicion on one side and hostility on the other.

On August 16, with Ronin, Rivet, and Henri Frenay, who had just arrived in Algiers, we attempted to formulate an organizational response that could work as a compromise as far as duties and certain egos were concerned. On August 24 I had a private lunch with André Philip, commissioner for the interior, who told me that he had been mandated by the CLN to take the Special Services under his wing. He had met with Rivet the day before but knew nothing about our organization. He was very talkative, seeking to be reassuring and was in favor of a merger even though he didn't have the vaguest idea about the nature of our mission. I took him to the DSM at El-Biar. He walked around the offices and wound up in the archives where about twenty clerks were hard at work on the mail that had arrived from France. It was a revelation to him! He congratulated me and then quickly left; I was never to hear from him again.

On September 4, 1943, as I went with Rivet to welcome one of his sons who had traveled by submarine from Cap Camarat, the boss said, "There's something new! The committee has just appointed General Cochet to coordinate and merge the Special Services in London and Algiers."

I knew Cochet from 1940 when he was already in favor of resisting enemy occupation forces. We all thought highly of him but no one could find any why reason he would be competent to bring about a difficult merger. On September 11 both Passy and Pélabon confirmed that feeling. "You can't merge two organizations that are so different." The Allies were unhappy and worried about the merger that was not happening and turning into rivalry instead.

From September 11-15, 1943, William Donovan, head of the OSS (Office of Strategic Services), came to see us and made some discreet inquiries. He was obviously doubtful about the BCRA. He visited the DSM with Colonel Eddy and Holcomb, saw our working methods and their results, especially those of *Force A*. Donovan was pleased about the efficiency of our liaison with his services that were still very new and noticed the great detail with which we were preparing the security for landing operations in France. He was confident and friendly as he left me, offering us all the material support we required.

By the end of September Giraud's position was further weakened.* Without consulting Giraud a decree was passed creating two categories of armed forces: those for war operations under Giraud and those inside the country under the commissioner of national defense, General Legentilhomme. That decision made my job much more complicated. The military security service was serving two masters! I complained to Giraud, who seemed to be somewhat less combative. He was very worried about the fate of his family. Then the Pucheu matter suddenly took on an unexpectedly dramatic political importance. In May 1943 Giraud ordered the arrest at Ksar es-Souk in Morocco of Vichy's former interior minister, who had landed three days before from Spain.

Giraud had agreed to allow Pucheu to come to North Africa on condition that he not reveal his identity and join a fighting unit. But Pucheu, who had been identified on the ship that arrived on May 6, 1943, made no bones about his personal opinions. He had contacted several French political leaders in Morocco and his arrival had been noticed but hadn't caused any incidents. I was surprised by the internment order and asked Giraud on May 10, 1943 whether it wasn't contradicting the friendly words of the letter he sent Pucheu on February 15, 1943. Pucheu was using that letter to protest to Military Security in Morocco against the internment decision. Giraud was very curt with me and didn't appear to remember what he'd written in that letter. I showed him a photocopy; he became irritated.

"As you can see," he said, "my authorization was predicated on conditions that weren't followed."

---

* Already on June 22, 1943 the Committee created two commanders in chief: Giraud for North Africa and West Africa, de Gaulle for the other territories. Rivet and I threatened to resign in protest against the dual command, which was incompatible with the unity of our services.

"General, it's rather difficult to remain incognito once you've been a Vichy minister and your picture is all over the newspapers."

"Perhaps, but I had to consider the police reports that Couve de Murville, the commissioner of the interior, showed me and agree to have Pucheu interned."

On August 10, 1943 the CLN ordered Pucheu's arrest and that he stand trial. On September 3 the CLN declared Pétain and his government ministers were guilty of treason. On August 30 the CNR (*Conseil National de la Résistance*) at a secret meeting in France condemned Pucheu to death. On October 2 the CFLN set up the military court that was to judge the former Vichy minister. Giraud, who could sense that Pucheu's fate was slipping out of his control, was also being pressured to drop him. The twenty-seven Communist deputies Giraud had freed from internment camps in Algeria began a violent campaign demanding that Pucheu be put to death.

One November morning around 11 a.m., on my way to the Palais d'Eté, I met Communist deputies Billoux and Pourtalet with Henri d'Astier de la Vigerie. We chatted and I asked them:

"Why are you here?"

"It's the Pucheu case. We want General Giraud, whose family tragedy[*] we are well aware of and whose anguish and moral dilemma we can understand, abandon this individual to his fate. We now know that Pucheu was responsible for the lists of the forty-nine hostages of Châteaubriant and Nantes.[**] Pucheu had also created the special sections of the court of appeals that were condemning the patriots summarily."

"The general's very upset by the reprisals the Krauts have taken against his own family and by the Pucheu case," I answered. "Whatever Pucheu may have done in France, it's Giraud who authorized him to come to North Africa. How can you expect him to just walk away and appear as an accomplice to entrapment?"

"True," said Pourtalet, "but there are facts that the general wasn't aware of. If he proves his attachment to the Republic's ideals in this case, we'd agree to support him against de Gaulle. Giraud must not block the decisions of the Resistance Committee[***] in France."

---

[*] Except for his daughter, the general's entire family had been arrested and deported.

[**] On October 22, 1941, those hostages, who were mostly communists and labor union members, had been executed by firing squad.

[***] *Conseil National Résistance.*

Following a pathetic trial Pucheu was sentenced to death on March 11, 1944. The court expressed its wish that the sentence not be carried out. On March 16, 1944 I was, along with Dunoyer de Segonzac,* at the house of Henri Frenay, who, since November 10, 1943, had become commissioner for prisoners, deportees, and refugees.

Segonzac expressed my thoughts best:

"You can't let this execution take place without stepping in. Pucheu is here because the authorities in charge authorized him to come. Perhaps they were wrong. That's a different problem. To execute him under such conditions would be a cowardly act, similar to the methods we reject and are fighting. It reminds me of the way Bonaparte got rid of the Duke of Enghien."

Frenay was upset and hesitant, he gave a cautious and disciplined answer:

"I'm sure de Gaulle will weigh the issues. In the final analysis the reason of state will prevail."

On March 17, 1944 Giraud addressed a letter to de Gaulle as head of the government, asking for a stay of execution due to circumstances that had brought Pucheu to North Africa. On March 19, since there had been no answer, he went to see him to repeat his request. De Gaulle remained silent! On March 20, 1944 at 7:30 a.m. on the rue d'Isly I met the two British officers who had replaced Trevor Wilson: Lieutenant Colonel Jarvis and Major Malcolm Muggeridge, the journalist and author. They were both upset and one of them said:

"Pucheu has just been put to death."

I remained silent and felt I had taken part in something bad. Muggeridge saw that I was troubled.

"Major," he said, "the reason of state is an awful requirement. It has nothing to do with justice and goes against human feelings."

Ten days later General Chadebec de Lavalade, one of judges in the trial, asked to see me. He was very agitated and told me why he'd come.

"You're in charge of military security and I seek your protection. I'm getting letters with death threats. I can't sleep. I get insulted over the phone. Yet I only obeyed orders in this case. Like the other judges I re-

---

* Classmate and friend of Henri Frenay, Segonzac was formerly commander of the Ecole des Cadres d'Uriage, where many resistance fighters were trained in 1941 and 1942.

quested that Pucheu not be executed. He was shot in awful circumstances. He commanded the firing squad himself."

There was nothing I could do to help that man's crisis of conscience and could only feel sorry for him.

Two weeks later, on April 4, 1944, a decree reorganized the High Command giving all power to General de Gaulle, no longer mentioning General Giraud. Two Communists became government commissioners. On April 15 Colonel Rivet was promoted to the rank of general and sent into mandatory retirement. Another page of French history had been turned.

But let's not get ahead of events, but rather go back to the end of 1943 when the Cochet experiment ended. Caught between the BCRA and the Special Services in Algiers the general gave up on his mission. Meantime, Ronin, who was also unable to act, resigned as well. The decree of November 27, 1943 merged all the Secret Services into the DGSS under Jacques Soustelle. Giraud was all the more opposed to that decision since he had also been excluded as co-president of the CFLN and decided to fight every step of the way to keep his authority as commander-in-chief and command of "his" Special Services. The committee reacted brutally and cut off our funds.

No one except Henri Frenay gave any thought to our comrades in France and their needs. On November 30, Frenay, the great negotiator, got us all together at his house in Hussein-Dey. Soustelle was there with Pierre Bloch, who had just been appointed deputy commissioner for the interior under Emmanuel d'Astier de la Vigerie, Passy, Pélabon, Rivet, and myself. From 1 p.m. to 5 p.m. the discussion kept on going around in circles.

Both Soustelle and Passy, in very careful language that was at times laudatory, offered their critique of our service. Their conclusion was that given the reason of state tied to a concept of a new and modern France our services had to become part of the DGSS. Those of us, and we were part of that group, who had anything to do with the Vichy government should temporarily step aside to reassure the men leading the new regime. We answered by defending the unity of our services and the secrecy they required that could not work within odd mixes. We proved the effectiveness of our methods and our obligation to work with the High Command.

I didn't mention anything about our work with *Force A*.

"Let's speak frankly. What is it you want?" Rivet asked.

"Control and direction of all SR, CE, and SM work," answered Passy cynically.

"You'd become my technical adviser," said Soustelle, trying to be accommodating.

"Paillole could return six months hence in an even more important post and with higher rank," added Passy.

Rivet rejected all that bargaining. Frenay and Pierre Bloch were shocked and said nothing.

"Should you remain, would you be ready to sign a declaration of loyalty and disinterest?" Passy asked me.

Things had now become odious and even comical. We parted company.

Frenay, who was driving me back to Algiers, acknowledged that the situation was very serious and begged me to speak to Soustelle alone, telling me what a decent and levelheaded man he was. I agreed. With Bonnefous' help—his situation in London had become fragile because of this conflict—we would attempt to get from the general director some conciliatory measures. But we failed to find a solution.

De Gaulle summoned Rivet on December 28, 1943. The boss told me about it:

"He wanted to hear directly from me what obstacles existed to effecting a simple merger. The general listened to me very calmly. At times he would interrupt to ask for more detail or make a comment laced with suspicion. Once I had finished he asked me about our previous activities. His recollection of the fact that we had remained in France until 1942 didn't sound reassuring to him. He feels staying had corrupted us. I protested against that suspicion, which was being spread by his mean-minded aides. I observed that it was much more difficult to fight inside France than in England and that only by remaining in place could we prevent too many Frenchmen from losing their way by backing a government bent on treason.

"What I found surprising with de Gaulle," Rivet continued, "was the fact that he gave such importance to hearsay and gossip that's relayed back to him many times erroneously or in some biased way. This information appears to dominate his thinking and leads him to the wrong conclusions. In Algiers he was told of some missions that Giraud had given to shady characters! I tried telling him we had nothing to do with any of it but he wasn't convinced.

"We chatted for over an hour. Finally, I repeated to him that the crucial question for us remained the sudden intervention on our path of the Action Committee in France and the BCRA. The November 27 decree was absurd in attempting to mix organizations that had no reason to merge. The general appeared annoyed.

"'We must reach a conclusion,' he repeated several times.

"'Yes, general, it's up to you to conclude.' I proposed two solutions: a temporary status quo while we improved the relationship between the two services or to integrate the military intelligence part of the BCRA into our SR; the CE and SM would remain as they are since they don't exist in the Gaullist intelligence service.

"'That's difficult,' answered de Gaulle. 'Our networks also have a political mission besides the military function. The two go together. But I'll give your proposal some thought.'

"I then took my leave of the general. He was friendly when I left. I can't say things are clear now or that they've moved ahead. I noticed how uncomfortable he was because of hasty and partisan decisions."

Had that meeting really encouraged General de Gaulle to reconsider? Did he want to play for time? Would he back an amicable agreement between the BCRA and the traditional services? For three months the president of the CFLN didn't try to impose his views or create a conflict while new attempts—by Soustelle and Passy on the one hand, and Rivet and myself on the other—were taking place. Perhaps the dispute could have been cut short and been less bitter without some partisan and clumsy posturing. There was also a derogatory whispering campaign aimed at undercutting our old service. Everything was a game: lies, calumnies and malevolent innuendo. Rivet, Blémant, Sérot, whose wife had just been deported to Ravensbrück, and myself were all being investigated. My mail was being opened. It was all done very amateurishly and the "investigators" who had become disgusted themselves came to us for suggestions on how to write up the answers. And what was worse, we had no more funds. To keep some money flowing to our networks that were reduced to a pittance, we donated our salaries and borrowed money from private persons. A generous offer from the Americans was not considered despite their insistence.

The silly battle went on with blackmail over the funding and the questions of the "ministers" who were attempting to understand the situation. Emmanuel d'Astier de la Vigerie asked to meet with me. He disliked Passy and said so immediately:

"He wants to approve everything! Action inside France is my domain. It's going to be him or me! But you're not making my job any easier. You've taken the *Surveillance du Territoire* and the best officials who have arrived from France."

He was alluding to the arrival in Algiers of a whole group of excellent policemen who had recently escaped from France; Blémant, Koenig, Petitjean, Ambrosi, Nart, Niger, and many others. They were counterintelligence specialists whom I asked to come to supervise Military Security along with the police volunteers recruited in North Africa.*

"But my dear commissioner," I said, "we're already in a state of siege. Military Security is a high priority in North Africa and I'm within the limits of the law. You must agree that the services in your office are improvised; they don't have the funds to accommodate the personnel or the files allowing them to do efficient work. The heavy climate of suspicion in North Africa encouraged your officials to join the military where the air is easier to breathe and in the fight against espionage, they can avoid the absurd accusation of being 'Vichyites.' It was the end. My section was the only one functioning and that was inevitable because there was nothing else to replace it."

On May 2, 1944 I had a long meeting with de Gaulle at the Villa des Glycines. He was wearing his trademark uniform, austere, and unassuming. He walked over and shook hands.

"Hello Paillole, happy to see you. Sit down."

He looked at me for a second and noted, "You're wearing civilian clothes?"

"I just got back from Spain without any luggage. My military uniforms are not very orthodox."

"Tell me what's happening in Spain"

"Which operation, general?"

"What are Boyer-Mas and Malaise doing?"

I went into detail and outlined our services in Spain, the submarine link to France and through the Pyrenees, and the vital role played by Monsignor Boyer-Mas in getting escapees out of France.

"That's very good. But Malaise, what does that Malaise do?"

"He works against the enemy in his own way a bit marginally to our service."

---

* I also wanted Osvald and Michel Hacq, but couldn't reach them. Tragically, Michel Hacq was deported for having helped us at Ramatuelle.

"With the Americans?" he asked.

"He's used their help since 1941 and still does."

"We must watch that. Our allies can become our worst enemies. And Dungler,* what's he doing?"

'I don't know. I know that he returned to France for General Giraud's services and with help from the Americans."

"Them again. What are they getting involved for? We must put all this in better shape. Are you satisfied with the new organization of the Special Services?"

I thanked the general for signing the April 24, 1944 decision that confirmed for everyone's information the traditional attributions of my services. One sentence in that decision by the president of the CFLN and head of the army was particularly important because it put an end to the wild proliferation of intelligence services, allowing me to enter into permanent agreements with the Allies for operations to liberate France.

All the special sections that have been created to handle counterespionage matters must immediately be merged into the service of Military security of the DGSS. That service is the only one authorized to handle counterespionage matters with French and Allied authorities.

Signed: Charles de Gaulle

I explained that our preparation for the security of the landings and within the liberated areas in France was very advanced as to documents and personnel specialization.

"We still must settle, in my opinion, a fundamental question with the Allied command as to the responsibility for the struggle against espionage and public order in France in various areas that were or were not occupied by the Allies, in the military area, and behind the lines. I wanted that responsibility given to us on French territory and with full sovereignty."

I had hit upon a true buzzword and de Gaulle used it and went on:

"Ah yes! Our sovereignty. We should remember that! We must take it back and not let the Allies lay down the law in our country. The director

---

* Dungler came to North Africa with Pétain's approval. He had been one of the organizers of resistance in Alsace and later attempted unsuccessfully to make a connection with some anti-Hitler Abwehr services to the French Special Services.

general of the Special Services gave me a very good report on you and the fact that the British and Americans trust you. I am relying on you."

The meeting was over; it had lasted forty-five minutes; de Gaulle stood up and walked me to the door. "Goodbye Paillole. Come back to see me if you feel it's necessary."

One could infer that all roadblocks had been removed. But that was not the case. The new Special Services were to attract some rather old novices, rootless people, and draft dodgers of all kinds, with odd ambitions and eleventh-hour reformers. "A Hottentot bazaar," said Rivet, seeing his SR disappear piecemeal.

"Your SR will not get broken!" said Soustelle, who no doubt was sincere at the time.

Soustelle was also swallowed up, and overtaken by so many loud mouths who said they were part of the Resistance and carried with them miraculous solutions and new networks. He had barely emerged from a painful clash where he tried to avoid any sectarianism to keep what he felt was vitally important but he had trouble resisting partisan pressures and pride. It was not for nothing that for many months ignorant, jealous, and nasty people were spreading a pack of lies. A phalanx of the so-called purest of the pure, faithful among the most faithful, were to introduce a system based on denunciation and simple snitching on others.

Once the old services had been beheaded the hurricane continued in its path of destruction. In Barcelona Epstein, sent by the BCRA to the TR station, was spying on my comrades and denounced their participation in a fabricated monarchist plot. To be sure that these lies did in fact reach Algiers he used a foreign diplomatic pouch. I was told to dismiss Captain d'Hoffelize, the head of station. I refused to take any action. Passy's deputy in London, Vandreuil, who had been sent to Bonnefous to work on counterintelligence, was actually observing him and reporting back to his masters. In Algiers a BCRA agent reported on my contacts in the U.S. with Camille Chautemps. Apparently we were plotting to return France to a government along the lines of the Third Republic.

Who could think up such a perverted joke? I had never met the former prime minister and didn't even know what had happened to him. In Rome Guillaumat, a lieutenant in the reserves, had been sent on a tourist mission by the DGSS to the Special Services of the army. He was refused the right of "inspection" of the Military Security Station by Captain Parisot, who said his rank was inappropriate to such a mission and that he was not competent. I was asked to relieve that officer from his duties, something I did not do in the interest of the service. One month later, no doubt in order to prove his competence, Guillaumat was promoted to the rank of lieutenant colonel. Later on when he became minister of national defense he must have laughed at that sudden promotion!

My friend Chevance promoted to the rank of general, one of the heroes of the *Combat* group whom I had met in Marseille in 1941, came to see me to discuss his upcoming mission in France. I congratulated him for his new stars. He hid his "Képi" and rank behind his back and said as he shrugged his shoulders:

"Don't pull my leg! It's a fake, just window dressing!"

At least he has some reason to deserve respect. There was a chasm between real resistance fighters and the zoo of characters elbowing their way into the waiting rooms of power.

On May 6, 1944 I assembled my staff and personnel at El-Biar to honor General Rivet. The head of the SR, de Villeneuve, and several other SR officers were with him. Simonneau, de Villeneuve's deputy, was the only officer still at an important and delicate post, but limited to the part of the SR within the theaters of operations named SRO (*Service de Renseignements Opérationnels*). Saluting the flag displayed for the last time I told the Boss how grateful we were for his example of courage and loyalty to our commitment to those principles he had taught us and expressed our heartfelt affection.

In his deep voice broken by sadness and emotion he told us, and begged us, to overcome our bitterness, to think only of our mission and of France. I promised, and we kept that promise as we remained impervious to the sordid intrigues aimed at us that were already shaking the newborn DGSS at its roots.

Rivet stepped away modestly, suffering from lack of action and forgotten in Algiers until November 1944. I saw him in Paris when I also decided to resign. Physically, he had been affected by the moral wounds he had received which he overcame by preaching the truth as he saw it; his classic and healthy view of the Special Services defending their work and those who had served under him. He rewarded me with his friendship and confidence. Rivet died on December 12, 1958.

A supreme and late tribute would come from the government through Marshal Juin.

"There wasn't a more loyal and honest soldier. There was no one with more disinterested patriotism in the work he performed as a religious mission. The Homeland and the army will not forget that in desperate times he was a son and a servant who rose to the challenge."

30

The Landings
in France and French Sovereignty

"**M**ajor, I'm pleased to see that the political situation in Algiers has now been cleared up. SHAEF* can now discuss with you the responsibilities and areas of our security services during the decisive phase of operations that's about to begin."

The man speaking on April 24, 1944, was a young, elegant British officer, Colonel Dick White, assigned by MI5—British internal counterespionage—to the headquarters of the commander in chief in Europe. As soon as the Allies were told about the CFLN decisions, the end of the dual command between Giraud and de Gaulle, the merger of the Special Services and the confirmation of the SSM's role, the Allied command requested, on April 15, 1944, the authorization of the president of the CFLN and commander in chief of the army to set up with me the framework for our participation in security and counterespionage missions in operational areas and the territories about to be liberated inside France.

Soustelle was very much aware of the importance of such a request, not only from the standpoint of our security services but above all as the

---

* Supreme Headquarters of Allied Expeditionary Forces—Eisenhower's HQ.

442

recognition of the sovereignty of the GPRF* in France. On April 20, 1944 he approved on behalf of de Gaulle. Allied reaction was swift. Four days later Dick White was in my office with British intelligence representatives Lieutenant Colonel Jarvis and Major Malcolm Muggeridge. All three knew my services and the kind of detail that went into our preparation of landing operations in France and in Africa. They had already seen how our security organization worked in North Africa, Italy, and Corsica.

"General Eisenhower's staff would like me to prepare with you your trip to London and the schedule of your work with G2. I must prepare a report on your capabilities and your plans to use them in the military areas and the liberated territories," Dick White said.

I presented to him and his fellow officers the organization chart of the original SM and the TR inside France and summed up our objectives:

"Since July 1940 we've kept an 'accountability of crime.' Our goal is not simply to neutralize but to effectively annihilate enemy intelligence and their appendages. We intend to use the landing operations to seize a maximum of their capabilities before they evacuate our country."

Two sets of operations were planned for the liberation of France: in the north out of England and to the south out of North Africa, Corsica, and Italy. My services were ready to take part in such operations and be responsible for the security of liberated territories.

There was concern that the two operations could create confusion in southwestern France where French and Allied armies could only go later on. I had a solution for such a situation. Since the end of March 1944 Captain Dumont—former military security chief in Morocco—had been undercover in Spain with SM teams ready to act with the original SM groups in Bordeaux, Toulouse, and Montpellier as soon as the first landings began. To be sure that our repressive action in those regions was well coordinated and as effective as possible I had asked Taillandier-Morhange** to travel to Barcelona to be briefed by d'Hoffelize the head of the TR station.

My visitors had listened very carefully. I concluded:

"My wish is simple: to continue in my country, in full sovereignty, the mission we're handling here."

---

* *Gouvernement Provisoire de la République Française* (Provisional Government of the French Republic) replaced the CFLN on June 3, 1944.

** Taillandier went to Barcelona with Hamard, one of his deputies, carrying a huge quantity of counterintelligence documents. He was given directives and funds to take punitive actions with the Morhange group.

Dick White smiled.

"I'll support your proposal with General Bedell-Smith,*" he said. You'll also have another supporter in Major André Poniatowski.**"

"Does the French cause for sovereignty require so many spokesmen?" I asked.

The British officer was embarrassed and I went on.

"I think it should be a matter of course, unless you impose AMGOT, which would be very serious."

Dick White nodded as he pondered the issue; then he cautiously said:

"The merging of the Special Services, the report I shall submit as soon as I return, and your personal initiatives in London, will bear heavily on General Eisenhower's decision. I hope it'll be in your favor."

"When do you feel I should go to England?" I asked.

"As soon as possible."

"That's a bit short!" I said laughing. "After so many changes in the Special Services I need a few days to get my house in order under its new roof."

"In any case, be in London on May 10 at the latest."

"It's a deal," I answered.

On May 7, 1944 I was at Algiers' Maison-Blanche airport ready to fly to England. I was there a few hours early to be with General de Lattre de Tassigny. We waited for the arrival of his wife and son, Bernard. I had organized their escape out of France through Spain. I was struck by General de Lattre's concern about his family. He had been sentenced on January 9, 1943 by the state court in Lyon to 10 years in prison "for having left his command and attempting to commit treason." The general then escaped from prison at Riom on September 3, 1943 with the help of wife and son and had reached Algiers via London at the end of December. I was meeting with him often after the beginning of 1944. He was all at once charming and absolutely odious, demanding and generous, but always enthralling and passionately involved. We often had lunch or dinner together. In conversation I understood that he was obsessed about potential reprisals against his wife and son. One day I offered to get them out of France, offering the example of Monique Giraud, who had been reunited with her father—naturally I was careful not to mention the tragic incident at Cap Camarat. He grabbed both my hands.

---

* Eisenhower's chief of staff.

** Poniatowski had just been appointed liaison to Eisenhower's command.

"Could you do this?"

"Of course, general. Navarre knows where Mrs. de Lattre is located. I assure you that he can help her. I'll have one of my officers travel with her and get to Spain through a secure network."

Following a brief stay in Toulouse with the gendarmerie captain, Abadie, Mrs. de Lattre and her son crossed the Pyrenees. They were helped by TR 120 in Barcelona in crossing Spain, and reached Gibraltar on May 7 with Gilbert Getten, who had successfully been handling their escape since Paris. I barely had time to greet and congratulate them because the general swept all three escapees away and I was unable to chat with Getten. A few moments later my flight to London took off and Bonnefous welcomed me there the next day.

"It was high time that this conflict between Special Services ended and that you came here," said my friend. "Giraud's instructions to accredit me to Eisenhower are no longer valid. In spite of the fact that they wished to accommodate us, the Allies don't want to deal with us in preparing the landings. They no longer understand the functions of this or that officer: the BCRA; General Koenig's staff,* headed now by Passy; there's General Mathenet, representing Giraud; also Hettier de Boislambert leading a mission to work with 'Civil Affairs,' who are in charge of administrative issues; there's Mr. Viénot, our ambassador, who's negotiating to secure maximum rights as soon as the territories are liberated. He's trying to create French military courts for the landings; and then..."

"And then what?" I asked Bonnefous.

"And then there's us! We're the only ones to have the files and the documents everyone wants. You have a lot of work ahead of you!"

The first V1 rockets were being fired on London. I had a rough night at the Hyde Park Hotel. Air raid sirens got me out of bed several times, and I would always run into André Poniatowski in the lobby. Between two blasts he told me how worried he was.

"Everyone's jockeying for position and getting involved in everything. Koenig's the only one keeping things in perspective and the only one Eisenhower's staff thinks highly of. You should meet him."

"I intend to," I said.

Early in the morning I was able to get some rest back in my room. I took a bath and ignored yet another air raid. Suddenly a terrifying explo-

---

* General Pierre Koenig was de Gaulle's military delegate and commander of the forces of the interior.

sion rocked the building and emptied most of the tub. I was stark naked in front of an Englishman with his pajamas covered in plaster. The bomb had blown open the door to my room. The man came in half groggy from the collapse of the ceiling; he was incoherent, walking about like an automaton while I dried up and got my clothes on. In the lobby I saw Poniatowski once more with a suitcase.

"It's impossible to stay here. I have a room outside London at SHAEF and I'm going there. I'll tell Bedell-Smith you're here. He's expecting you."

General Koenig was warm, unassuming, and direct. I felt as if I'd always known him and I explained my views and why I was in London.

"That's very good, old boy, keep me informed of your talks. Do the best you can!"

I asked about his mission.

"It's not easy," he answered. "I'm caught between the Boss, who's angry, and the Allies, who are suspicious of everything. We can't even write to Algiers freely; everything's shut down and nothing can get out of England. A complete blackout. Good luck!"

There was no way we could enforce a blackout on my services just as we were about to decide our role in the landings and coordinate the paperwork and organization of our services with the Allies. As Menzies told me when we met and I alerted him about the serious problem of communications between London and Algiers:

"Don't worry. The blackout's required by the need to keep the coming operations secret. It doesn't concern you."

The head of British intelligence himself wanted to introduce me to General Bedell-Smith and the heads of section at SHAEF. That was how I met Colonel Scheen, head of G2, a friendly American about my age, who looked tough and open. Bedell-Smith confirmed in front of Menzies and Scheen that we were to draft the agreements between the French and Allied security services. Dick White's report must have been excellent because the atmosphere was decidedly very cordial.

The general told me about operational objectives, indicating the landing locations in Normandy on a map. He asked that we reach specific and effective agreements by the end of May at the latest and then said:

"I can't tell you yet the exact date the operation will begin—certainly between June 1 and June 10."

Outside the office Menzies took me by the arm and whispered in my ear:

"I think that for now you're the only Frenchman to have been told such secrets. It's a sign of trust and I congratulate you for it. Keep everything you've seen and heard strictly to yourself."

The request wasn't necessary. I intuitively as well as professionally knew the value of a secret and the rules required to keep it that way. The authority that designates it a secret is its owner, in effect, and remains the only one to decide if and when it should be divulged. To ignore or forget those rules degrades the value of the secret just as much as its inappropriate and often abusive use. I thanked Menzies for the contacts and the warm welcome that boded well for the future. From May 10 to May 30, 1944 there were daily meetings between Scheen and myself, along with our assistants, leading to a draft agreement that we both signed. It guaranteed the sovereignty of our action in France and set the basis for the mutual responsibilities of our services.

"It's a victory!" said Koenig, when he approved those agreements.

Two articles in the draft revealed the spirit of the entire document:

> Art. 13: Within the liberated areas, French military authorities will bear the responsibility for counterespionage (SSM) that will reconstitute the military security bureaus (BSM). The core of those BSM officers already exists within the original military security offices (SSM) established in France. Allied counterintelligence officers will maintain a liaison to the supreme command (SHAEF) and will be attached to the BSM offices.

I found it especially gratifying to see that the article extended to the Allied services the enforcement of our technical instructions imparted by Giraud and confirmed by de Gaulle on April 24, 1944:

> Art. 15: the rules in Instruction 3333/DSM of May 10, 1943 and the Guide Book of the SM officer in wartime remain in force and effect.

Some parts of my services (SM-TR-SA) were to be integrated to larger Allied units. All of them were to have the documents and information necessary to take action, an alphabetical list of suspects, and a summary report on enemy intelligence services (Abwehr and RSHA). Bonnefous, now attached to SHAEF, was in charge of all those services.

A last minute agreement with the French minister of the interior set up the reconstituted *Surveillance du Territoire* as the liberation progressed. Those who were part of that service would wear a uniform and have temporary military ranks. I integrated them to the SM teams that were to land. We agreed with Achille Peretti, head of the "Ajax" network (created with police officers in the resistance in 1943), to appoint Simon Cottoni and Jean Osvald, both of them very experienced police officers and true patriots, as temporary heads of the new ST service inside France. I was pleased to see Peretti once again at the ministry of the interior in Algiers. There were not very many real policemen there! He told me that Cottoni had been forced to escape into Switzerland to avoid being arrested by the Germans.

Menzies was pleased by the agreement.

"I was afraid you'd get AMGOT," he told me. "I'm happy that you got all this instead."

I could hardly wait for the crucial hour and felt overwhelmed by a growing sense of anxiety. I was now fearful of those landings that we were all expecting and that I couldn't reveal to anyone close to me. The secret was heavy to carry. The cost in human lives, ruins, the uncertainty and suffering it would require for other Frenchmen became an obsession and shrouded with fear all the hopes and joys of the deliverance at hand.

I spoke to Muggeridge about all this since he was helping me in my travels. With the magic SHAEF identity card we left London on Monday, June 5, 1944, to a location near Portsmouth. The big event—D-Day— was set for the next day. A continuous convoy of huge monsters on wheels and on tracks wound its way in the darkness; and planes were taking off throughout the night. There was no way we could sleep. The dawn was cold and wet and we were exhausted trying to listen to a useless radio. Suddenly Scheen's deputy pushed open the door to the shack.

"It's on! They're going!"

We looked at each other; we were speechless. We felt both relief and anxiety. It was 5:05 a.m. and we had to get back to London. In a flash I could see my comrades, in the prisons and the camps, full of hope. Those inside France turned towards us, still hunted by the enemy; those who were pushed forward by this titanic undertaking…will they make it in time? Did I do everything I could?

I was back in Algiers on June 20, 1944. It took me over one month to restore peace and quiet to the DSM, which had been subjected to multiple intrusions during my absence—controls, instructions, orders—coming from a management trying to find its way. Fortunately Soustelle and Pélabon were to quickly settle the situation, faster than many BCRA types; they were both courteous and understanding toward me. And they understood the importance of the SSM and the fact that it would help the DGSS and the government itself exercise its authority among French and Allied military leaders. At times some details were to demonstrate that that authority could be fragile. In May and June the BCRA was forced to use the SSM pouch for its correspondence between London and Algiers—even to send in recommendations for promotions. A member of Soustelle's staff was able to reach England only with the help of the DSM. General Koenig himself had to give me his personal and official correspondence addressed to Algiers.

At the end of July and the beginning of August I traveled to Italy and Corsica to set up in accordance with the London agreements the organizations of my services with the Allies. I met General Juin in Rome. As usual he was calm, collected, and relaxed. I told him of the broad positive reaction in England and North Africa to his Italian campaign.

"Had there been more flexibility in the Allied war machine I could've forged ahead. I'd be at the Brenner Pass or even at Lyon today. It would've meant one less landing in Provence. The Germans had had enough; all they wanted was either to fall back in retreat or surrender. Now they're digging in. I tried explaining all this but I didn't get anywhere. Our friends don't intend to make any changes to their plans. It's a bulldozer," said Juin.

"The operation in Provence is being prepared by General de Lattre in Algiers," I said.

"Yes, I know. I don't know how the command issue will be resolved. I'm expecting de Gaulle tomorrow. One thing's clear: I wouldn't like to give up a command that's been so gratifying to me and that my men should be frustrated from operating in France."

The next day on my way to the Rome airport I ran into Soustelle, who was accompanying de Gaulle.

"Is everything going well for you?" Soustelle, the director general of the Special Services, asked me in his polite way.

"Very well," I answered. "I'd like to know the command structure for the coming operations in southern France. Will the CEF* be merged with the 1st French army? How? Under Juin or de Lattre?"

---

* French expeditionary forces in Italy.

"We're here to solve the problem, said Soustelle. "It won't be easy. Juin must hand things over to de Lattre! What do you think?"

"It'll be neither easy nor pleasant…"

A few days later General Juin became chief of staff of national defense. Near Algiers, in a large room of the "Ecole Normale" of the Bouzarea, I saw a huge relief map of the entire coastal region from the Gulf of Genoa to Port-Vendres. There were even more detailed plans in the other rooms. Dozens of GIs who paid no attention to me reported the news coming in from France, thanks to our networks, to the resistance and air reconnaissance. Everything was recorded down to the smallest detail with extraordinary precision: machinegun nests, artillery battery locations, water access points, shelters, houses, fuel dumps, air strips and emergency landing strips, ports, dikes, barbed wire fences, etc. The reports going to each major unit commander were drawn up and completed daily.

The planning files of my landing units were also well prepared and filled with information. In this second giant landing operation, my services were set up in the same manner as for [Operation] *Overlord* (the Normandy invasion). TR commandos, parachuted in or infiltrated behind enemy lines, were to precede the fighting units in attempting to seize enemy files and agents. Each large unit that was landing was to have specialized personnel with SM documents, allowing immediate action within the area and to complete the work of the original Military Security bureaus.

Our forecasts were accurate in both north and south. The original BSM in Rennes under the command of my Saint-Cyr classmate, Le Bouteiller, and Captain Moinet, surfaced in Brittany a few days before the region was liberated. The same took place in Angers. The original BSM in Paris under Colonel Gérar-Dubot initiated the first repressive actions (arrests and seizure of files) on the evening of August 19, 1944. He worked with some FFI groups (*Forces Françaises de l'Intérieur*), very carefully using excellent documentation allowing for precise action. He had informers inside the Gestapo, the Abwehr, and the collaborationist groups and also the top administration in Paris at the prefecture of the Seine,* the prefecture of Police, the Palais de Justice, the PTT, etc.

---

* M. Perrier de Féral, the secretary general of the Seine prefecture, along with his deputy prefect, Yves Cazeaux, were both HCs working for our service after being drafted into the 5th Bureau SCR in 1939.

Major Tupinier, in charge of SM and TR operations for the south as Bonnefous was doing in the north, reported on his work on August 21, 1944. His account summed up the situation:

"I can't tell you my pleasure and emotional feelings in seeing our operations succeed. We found the forward SM and Captain Boffy* after he completed his excellent work without a hitch. I already have a huge mass of documents we can't analyze. It's imperative that the 1st Echelon of the DSM arrives quickly.**

"An SM unit is ready to jump on Toulon. We're entering Digne and Aix-en-Provence now. The solution to the FFI problem is as follows: (a) after checking the resistance fighters, many of whom are latecomers, organize a 'Special Force'; (b) check the countless arrests they made before we arrived. In each village we're placed before the 'fait accompli.' There's a lot of local, political, and 'southern' revenge; we must be tactful to succeed but what a huge waste of time!"

Tupinier concluded: "In brief, the situation is excellent, morale is magnificent, and how could it be otherwise with the enthusiastic welcome we get from the population?"

---

* Parachuted in on August 15 with U.S. airborne units.
** In order to avoid bottlenecks for SM units, we had planned to ship the seized documents back to London or Marseille for analysis.

31

The Liberation of France: The DGER

Fundamental changes in the enemy intelligence services took place during the first half of 1944 once they all came under the RSHA's control. Actually the German High Command had already started a general reorganization of the Abwehr since October 1943 in view of an expected Allied landing and military operations in France. The rigid territorial networks well suited for long-term occupation gave way to a more flexible and mobile organization that had been tested during the campaigns of Poland and France and resurrected in November 1942 when the Wehrmacht invaded the Free Zone. Except for a few recruitment bureaus the Abwehr stations in France had been shut down and replaced by "Kommandos," or mobile units that were attached to the army groups, following their movements. The Ast stations in Germany—Wiesbaden, Münster, Stuttgart, Hamburg—were returned to their intelligence gathering functions in France. The two organizations were sharing their findings.

By June 6, 1944, the date of the Normandy invasion, we knew that the Kommandos covered practically all of French territory. The role played by the Paris Ast—at the Hotel Lutetia—as headquarters had disappeared and general coordination took place in Berlin at the AMT VI of the

452

RSHA headed by Ernst Kaltenbrunner, who had replaced Reinhard Heydrich.

Each one of the three Abwehr sections—I. Intelligence II. Sabotage III. Security and Counterespionage—had set up its own Kommandos. Those of Abwehr I were ordered to limit themselves exclusively to military intelligence. A special group—MIE. AMT.—had been created to check on them inside the AMT VI.* Those in charge of sabotage were strictly forbidden from recruiting agents in political areas. The SS Sturmbannführer Roland Nosek of AMT VI in Paris was exclusively in charge of political recruitment and was to use that prerogative in July 1944 when he met with Jacques Lemaigre-Dubreuil in Madrid where he had "escaped" from North Africa and was seeking a political solution to eliminate de Gaulle and the GPRF.

Abwehr III had been compelled to turn over to Amt IV (Gestapo) all its duties in occupied territories. A few counterintelligence Kommandos were left to report to the military command in France. The most important of these was under Reile's command and remained located at the Hotel Lutétia in Paris, which he was to evacuate on August 17, 1944. Some recent intelligence announced the appearance of "Abwehroffiziere"—security officers—in military units. They were under the command's orders and in charge of security in the army. Apart from that instance, the name "Abwehr" was to officially disappear.

The new organization was rife with backbiting, dressing down sessions, internal snitches leading to a difficult, even unbearable, atmosphere for most of the older officers. Some of them were to attempt finding a solution by coming to the Allies. Following the failures of the head of Abwehr III in Lyon, Unterberg-Gibhardt and Buchholtz, his deputy, in Nice attempted somewhat oddly to contact Algiers and the Americans through Dungler—one of the resistance leaders in Alsace who was with Giraud in Algiers at the end of 1943—then through Pététin and Gabriel Jeantet. Colonel Dernbach leader of an Abwehr III Kommando in the Lyon region tried unsuccessfully to approach us through Verneuil. Others were to join the plot against Hitler, which would fail on July 20, 1944, leading to a bloody repression and the final demise of the old service. Canaris' successor, Colonel Hansen, was arrested and shot. Colonel Freytag-Loringhoven, who had replaced Lahousen as head of Abwehr III, committed suicide on July 26, 1944 to avoid being arrested by the Gestapo.

---

* Walter Schellenberg was the head of Amt I.

Rudolph, former head of the Paris Ast, was denounced as being hostile to the regime; he was indicted and saved his life because of the administrative slowness of the court.

What was left of the Abwehr was humiliated, beheaded, and filled with SS, a mere toy in Nazi hands. Kommandos in France and Ast in Germany were fearful enough but still continued their work even though their hearts weren't in it anymore. The recruitment of French agents by the Nazis had dried up. Only the fanatics of treason, the PPF first and foremost, were still providing some rather mediocre recruits who were being trained hastily in improvised locations. We identified these in Paris, in Dijon at the castle of Dienay, in Avignon, Toulouse, Bordeaux, Nantes, at the castle of Antoigné near Le Mans, the castle of La Croix near Lille, the castle of Lambeau near Brussels. Near Paris some English-speaking Germans with knowledge of the United States were being trained at the castle of Rocquencourt for sabotage. They were to operate behind Allied lines in American uniforms and actually appeared in December 1944 during von Rundstedt's Ardennes offensive—the Battle of the Bulge.

As the Wehrmacht retreated the Kommandos tried to leave networks in place in radio contact with the various offices in Germany. There were a few enemy agents parachuting behind our lines and in North Africa. Once identified when they didn't turn themselves in, enemy agents were neutralized before they could operate. Between June and October 1944 only a score of rather unimportant cases of sabotage could be attributed to them.

From the first operations towards liberating France on June 6, 1944, to the German surrender on May 8, 1945, the results of counterespionage operations took place according to our expectations: a massive amount of files of enemy intelligence had been captured. The most noteworthy were:

> A portion of Paris Abwehr files, its files on France and German embassy files.
> The files of the German consulate in Marseille and those of the Dijon Ast.
> Various archives of German military courts and RSHA stations in France.
> The files of collaborationist groups—LVF, PPF, Milice, RNP, etc.
> 32 radio agents were "turned," joining our penetration network and reinforcing *Force A*.

4,589 agents or collaborators were arrested for espionage and treason.

756 death sentences and 2,688 forced labor and prison sentences issued by military courts and courts of justice.

104 arms and explosives hidden by the sabotage Kommandos were seized, never having been used.

After the end of hostilities there were to be other arrests and sentencings. In October 1944 I set up a *Bureau Interallié de CE* (BICE) with the mission of permanently annihilating enemy intelligence services in Germany and wrap up the accountability of crime we were keeping for four years. I appointed three of my best officers to lead that unit: Colonel Gérar-Dubot and Captains Dumont and Brunel.

It was high time that France be liberated. The defeated SS and RSHA, Darnand's Milice full of hatred and running amok, were all plunging the country into a reign of terror. On June 7 there were the hangings at Tulle and on the 10th the massacre at Oradour-sur-Glane. On July 7 Jonglez de Ligne, head of the forward SM in Marseille, was arrested with about ten of my fellow officers. On July 11 Taillandier-Morhange was gunned down with several TR jr. teams.

Le Hénaff was to die of asphyxiation in the inhuman convoy taking him to Germany. Mercier, TR head in the Nord, witnessed the death of Captain de Peich, whom I had sent to work with Navarre. On July 6, 1944 Lieutenant Colonel Rémi Robelin, deputy director of the guards at Vichy, was arrested. He was our best HC inside the gendarmerie since 1941. The arrest of Johanès in 1943 drew the Abwehr and the Gestapo's attention to him; the Germans and the Milice were watching him. Captain Rouyer, who replaced Johanès at Vichy, was telling him to be cautious, but to no avail. Robelin was setting up with the ORA the wholesale switch of the guard units into the Resistance and he kept on providing us with information on the Milice, which was then relayed to the maquis and the resistance.

He was summoned to Darnand's office for what turned out to be an ambush. There were two Gestapo agents with the head of the Milice who were waiting and arrested Robelin. His deputy captain, Morand, was caught as he went to the home of Courson de Villeneuve (alias Pyramide), the regional military delegate of the resistance who had already been arrested by the enemy. The Gestapo, with the help of Darnand, arrested ten Vichy guard officers and six were to be deported. My friend Robelin, my closest classmate at Saint-Cyr, was to die after the brutal floggings of the torturer who was to make him talk.* We never found his body.

I offer the reader the account of Robelin's agony from the testimony of M. Fischer, alias Bernard:

July 24, 1944

The door just opened faster than usual. Several of them came in. Then a Gestapo agent said to Courson and me, "You're going to help carry and care for the wounded man but the orders are very strict: there'll be no talking." We walked out in silence. There was a young looking man on a gurney, his face looked dark from the pain. He was on his side. We took his clothes off and he moaned a little. Then we saw something horrible: there was a hole as big as a fist in his right buttocks. You could see some of the small bones that looked like fish bones. His right leg was very much swollen, at least four to five times the usual size. There were other wounds all over his body but not as bad. A German doctor cared for the huge hole and then the other wounds. He poured some liquid on the swollen leg. They brought us some sheets and we made up a bed on the ground with two blankets. Then very carefully we took the wounded man to his cell. The doctor prescribed some milk and gave him a few aspirins to lower the fever. Finally, the doctor left with the Gestapo agents. Our "friendly" guard took us back to our cell.

Once we were alone de Courson told me the secret of the wounded man. He was Lieutenant Colonel Robelin of the guard at Vichy. He wanted to join the maquis with 6,000 other guards. He sent his deputy to de Courson but unfortunately had been followed by the Gestapo. The colonel and ten officers were arrested. Robelin was beaten so hard he could no longer stand up. That awful wound we dressed was inflicted by repeated beatings with a riding crop hitting the same area, tearing off the skin piece by piece to create that horrible hole.

The swelling of his right leg came after being beaten with an empty bottle on the shins. We feared the leg would have to be amputated. They sent me to dress Colonel Robelin's wounds. He was feeling a little better and whispered in my ear:

---

* Following a long investigation we found out that the SS Schlimmer, of Romanian origin, was responsible for Robelin's death.

"Don't worry we'll get them anyway." As a man and a soldier, that man had incredible inner strength. Despite his wounds and his imminent death he was still fighting. I'm ready to bow low in front of that great Frenchman. I turned him around so that he would feel more comfortable. I spoon-fed him soup like a child because he couldn't move. He was only able to use his arms to put his head back so I could slowly pour the soup in his mouth. Once he was finished he bit down on an aspirin tablet because he couldn't swallow it. He had some more water and then I left his cell.

I reached Paris on August 27, 1944. I saw Bonnefous, who got in two days before with the 2nd D.B., and he told me what had been going on since August 11, the day he left London.

"On the 12th near Bayeux I saw Colonel Labadie, head of military security for the 21st British Army Group.[*] His teams were hard at work. On the 13th, passing through Caen and Saint-Lô, I reached Périers, where I found our classmate Jean Haye, head of military security for the 12th U.S. Army Group.[**] The liberation of Paris was only a matter of days and we set up with the Allies a special force to be with the 2nd DB to enter the city. At dawn on August 23 we were with General Leclerc on the grounds of the castle of Rambouillet. We agreed to the details of our action with his staff and Military Security.

We entered Paris on August 25 through Longjumeau and the Porte d'Orléans. The crowds were cheering the Allies and when they saw we were French they went wild. But further on everything fell silent; the streets were deserted; there was sporadic shooting. We reached the Petit-Palais where we took cover. Right away we started taking all the files of the German stations in those areas of Paris that we had assigned to each one of our teams. We found Navarre and Gérar-Dubot at 100 rue Richelieu. They had been in action since August 19."

In the basement of the Petit-Palais Jean Haye was working under intense heat to put some order in the work of the security services of the 12th U.S. Army, the FFI, and our own units. His office was filled with weapons and baggage.

"You'll choke in here," I told him. "Let's go upstairs."

"No way, it's a battlefield up there!"

---

[*] Commanded by Montgomery.
[**] Commanded by Bradley.

I didn't understand, so he explained:

"There are some bastards in the garden across the avenue. I don't know who they are and they're shooting at us from time to time without knowing who *we* are. Since this damn building has more windows than walls the bullets go straight through and hit the Grand-Palais right behind us. So those guys at the Grand-Palais think we're shooting at them from here! They shoot back and the shots go right through, across the avenue, hitting those guys in the garden, who then shoot all over again. It's a big fight. I can tell you it's impossible to be in this Petit-Palais anywhere other than here and you better be a hero to do that!"

Jean Haye was describing a very confused situation. He was happy and jocular. I laughed, after four years pleased to be back in a liberated Paris. The presence in Paris of General de Gaulle, of some government ministers, of Prefect of Police Luizet, whom I was happy to see once again—all this avoided the kind of confused situation that took place south of the Loire River. Faced with improvised administrations, which ignored the laws seeking to bypass them, some of our SM stations were having problems setting themselves up and acting openly. There were illegal courts, summary executions that prevented us from undertaking rational counterespionage investigations, where incompetent groups had seized documents that would have been very useful to us. There was a general fear of spies, and private retributions were taking place everywhere.

A new generation of "specialists" cropped up everywhere: Military Security of the FFI command (Colonel Lizé), Military Security of the FFI in Paris (Dr. Avon-Brunetière); counterintelligence groups of resistance movements and networks, security services of the committees of liberation, etc. All these groups have their "good" intelligence, their "excellent" methods, "legitimate" ambitions, and their "comfortable" leadership groups.

In front of the ministry of war in the rue Saint-Dominique a brigadier general as young as Lazare Hoch in 1792 jumped out of a car, saluted everyone graciously, and darted into the building:

"That young man is Chaban-Delmas, de Gaulle's former military delegate in Paris," said Verneuil, who found it amusing. "He often helped Navarre and me when you couldn't send us any funds."

There were officers chatting or walking around the courtyard, dressed in pre-war uniforms and parade képis. They were waiting perennially to see the minister or "someone of importance." I was used to the simple, relaxed and practical ways of the Allied armies and looked upon them with a shudder. A revolution had to take place in that outdated and miserable army, corseted and wrapped up in its past prestige.

It took over one month in Paris and three months south of the Loire to clean up the anarchy that existed but never really threatened the new government. On October 1, 1944, the DSM was established at 2 Boulevard Suchet in Paris. The territorial BSM stations were in place with their files and all their personnel. The *Surveillance du Territoire* that Peretti and Simon Cottoni were attempting to set up had very little personnel just about everywhere.

On November 6, 1944 the minister of the interior, Adrien Tixier—who had replaced Emmanuel d'Astier de la Vigerie—appointed Captain Warin (*aka* Wybot) to take over the new *Direction de la Surveillance du Territoire* (DST). André Pélabon was director of the *Sûreté Nationale*. On November 16 Wybot made the reappearance of the DST official. Despite territorial conflicts, the military courts and courts of justice handled the repression of crimes against state security. The SM and TR units in the armed forces were functioning normally.

It was time to find solutions to place those resistance members who didn't want to join their units at the front. Furthermore, the integration of the FFI into the army—for example some 137,000 FFI joined the 250,000 men of the 1st French Army—created security problems that bothered the minister of war, André Dïethelm. He quite naturally asked for our help. At the DGSS, the former BCRA leaders were being assailed by their many former agents and personnel in the networks, who had discovered an irresistible calling for intelligence or counterintelligence work. Soustelle saw his unit grow and was unable to stop the flow of new personnel. On October 23, 1944, in order to absorb all these new elements and adapt to the new motto, "rebirth and reorganization." Soustelle decided to rename the DGSS to DGER, or *Direction Générale des Etudes et Recherches*. From then on under any pretense, directors, inspectors, controllers, heads of mission were to crisscross the country with exorbitant funds at their disposal. In a few short weeks they gave the Special Services a reputation similar to mafia gangsters.

Soustelle, a cautious and well-informed man, resigned and handed over that job to Passy. André Pélabon had already resigned. Less than one year later it all came crashing down in a scandal that brought about the demise of Passy and a few BCRA veterans.

A new service was then created: the SDECE *Service de Documentation Extérieure et de Contre Espionnage* under M. Ribière, with Fourcaud as his deputy. I could see from Andre Diethelm's problems that some politicians wanted to break up my unit, which was considered too powerful. What had been tolerable if not desirable in Algiers, was no longer seen the same way in Paris just before the victory over Nazi Germany.

On October 28, 1944, in the presence of Jacques Soustelle, I tried to stand up unsuccessfully to Diethelm and General Layer, army chief of staff. Without having any idea of the responsibilities and mission of my unit, they both demanded that we divide them between the ministry of war and the president of the government—the head of the armed forces.

On November 1, 1944 I reminded the minister that we were still at war. Military authority was responsible for the security of the armed forces and of the country. My service, under the name SSM, could only handle those tasks if it remained one organic undivided unit! The offensive CE (TR) was the engine of counterespionage for prevention and repression. We played a vital part in continuing military operations. I made a proposal to the government to choose between keeping my service as one unit under the commander of the armed forces under the prime minister, or transfer it as one unit to the ministry of war—"The CE is a single, unbreakable unit."*

I had few illusions regarding that final battle. It was true that the reform had political overtones; it was also aimed at me personally. My unit represented a closed bastion within the shapeless DGER, off limits to many sorcerer's apprentices as long as I was leading it. Who knows, my presence might also thwart some other ambitious types. They knew that since May 1944 I had trouble taking the attacks on my comrades and on my own pride. They also knew I did not compromise about respect for the law and keeping the integrity of a service that I had molded to the needs of our national defense. This was an excellent opportunity to show me the exit.

On November 17, 1944 General de Gaulle decided to split the services—the Military Security unit went to the ministry of war and the TR, with its files and archives, would go to the DGER.

On November 20 I resigned, saying, among other things: "This decision breaks the unity of counterespionage as I have always viewed it."

On November 22 at 4 p.m. Jacques Soustelle very courteously thanked me for my work. He told me that I was being promoted to lieutenant colonel and that I would be at the disposal of the minister of war. A few

---

* In the DSM report of October 28, 1944 to General de Gaulle.

moments later Colonel Chrétien was introduced to my department heads; he was to effect the split of my services.

At 5 p.m. one after the other I met with my officers. Verneuil was suddenly frightened to discover a situation that I had been careful to conceal from my men in France:

"We can't stay in this side show. We'll leave with you."

"Don't even think of that!" I said. "Enemy intelligence is still out there and we must complete its destruction. There are 20,000 bad Frenchmen who have followed the German army. They're ready to do anything to save a desperate situation. The TR must remain vigilant, keep its offensive stance, and be the vanguard of our security in the future. And then there are our comrades who will return from the camps in Germany whom no one here is even thinking about. They'll need you and need to see familiar faces."

The next day an officer from Soustelle's cabinet brought me a written order to stop making any appearance at my service[*] "to avoid any incidents." Sérot, Bonnefous, Labadie, and several others among my closest colleagues were to follow my fate. They became the backbone of the new Military Security at the ministry of war. Navarre was lucky to be given a command, as he deserved, in the 1st French Army. De Gaulle refused to honor me with such an appointment when de Lattre and Schlesser were asking for me and expected my transfer.

I decided to leave my military career after sending the following farewell letter to my comrades:

> On November 17, 1944 a decision made by General de Gaulle at the Committee of National Defense transferred a portion of the SSM to the minister of war. The CE itself (essentially the TR) is to remain part of the DGER.
>
> I felt I could not take part in setting up this new formation and the president of the GPRF agreed to place me at the disposal of the minister of war to take on other duties. Detailed instructions will be issued shortly as to the functioning of the service. I know that at every level you will continue to do your duty with as much patriotic fervor and objectivity.

---

[*] The Military Security unit returned to the historical office at 2 *bis* Avenue de Tourville, until it had to move because of the renovation of the Invalides in 1975.

As for me, I am proud to have had you as my working companions and I thank you for bearing the crushing workload and the sacrifices you have made in the sole interest of France.

After I leave my thoughts will be with you and with those above all who, because of their commitment to the service, died or are suffering in German prisons.

I ask my close staff at the DSM to know how anchored I remain in my attachment and how immensely grateful I am for the stubborn work they accomplished at my side in such difficult circumstances.

To my old TR teammates especially I address my gratitude for the magnificent work they undertook and the confidence they always demonstrated to me.

To all I say good luck. Your affectionately devoted,

Paul Paillole

The curtain falls on those final images of my life as a soldier. Ever since that autumn day of 1935 when as a young man I plunged into those dark corridors of the 2nd Bureau (SR-SCR) a revolution has taken place among the special services that has radically altered what I thought I knew.

I saw war break out without being declared; subversion, the insidious product of propaganda, was violating without using violence; sabotage had become a moral attack rather than using plastic explosives; espionage taking place without a spies; politics abetting treason; and nations falling without a fight.

For ten years the Axis and its regimes of terror had absorbed our forces and limited our research. They galvanized our will and enriched us with technology.

Emerging from the narrow concepts of repression, counterespionage demonstrated during this war its true scope and great potential. Faced with situations and regimes that were radically different the French intelligence services could only adapt and fulfill their permanent, unchanged mission by setting forth a pure and national attitude. Three hundred of my comrades died with that ideal in mind. But the tracks they left run straight and deep.

Charts

French Special Services
of National Defense Reporting Chart as of September 1939

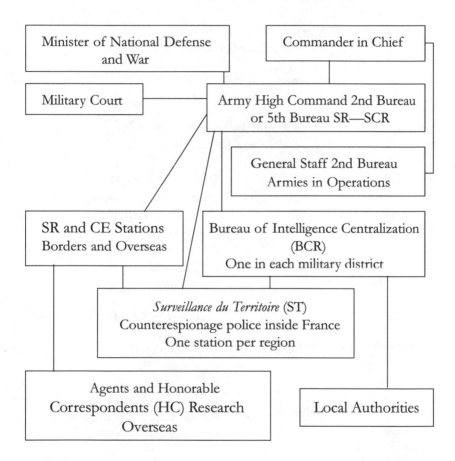

Note: In time of war due to the state of siege the CE reports to military authorities—5th Bureau—they also control the Surveillance du Territoire

Armies in the field have no autonomous CE unit and use the territorial organizations—BCR

During peacetime, the CE operating outside France reports to the Minister of National Defense and War (2nd Bureau SR—SCR the CE inside France reports to the Minister of the Interior (ST).

Organization of the SR (intelligence gathering) and military counterespionage—September 1939

Minister of National Defense and War
Edouard Daladier

Army Chief of Staff
General Colson

Deuxième Bureau SR-SCR
Lt. Col. Rivet/Lt. Col. Malraison

Section A
Administration Finance, Personnel
Major Bergerat
Capt. Marandet

SR—Intelligence Gathering
National Defense and Military
Lt. Col. Perruche
Major Navarre

SR-AV—Air Force Intelligence
Lt. Col. Ronin
Major Pépin

Section Mg: War Supplies
Sabotage
Major Brochu
Capt. Poitou

SCR Intelligence
Centralization Section
Foreign and Army
Counterespionage
Protection of Military Secrecy
Lt. Col. Schlesser
Capt. Paillole

Section D—Codes, Ciphers, and Decryption
Major Bertrand
Capt. Louis

Section Z Wiretaps
Lt. Col. Cazin d'Honincthun
Capt. Lochard

Section T Radio, Photography, Chemicals
Major Arnaud
Lt. Cléry

The navy had its own intelligence gathering service, the *Deuxième Bureau* Marine.

In time of war, the *Deuxième Bureau* (SC-SCR) becomes the 5th Bureau reporting to the High Command and the Commander in Chief—General Gamelin.

466

Organization of the Counter Espionage Service D.S.M.
Algiers, June 1944

Directorate of Military Security -DSM
Director: *Paul Paillole*

Deputy in Algiers: *Col. Serot*
Deputy in London: *Major Bonnefous*

Services
Liaison with Allies
Liaison with Air Force, Navy and Army
Liaison with Civilian Affairs
Mail and information
General Files
War Crimes
Police (*Surveillance du Territoire*)

France Head of TR *Verneuil*	1st Section Administration/ Finance/ Personnel/ Transportation and Supplies
Head of SM *Col. Navarre*	2nd Section CE–Repression/Documents/Reports and Analysis/Repression (police and justice system)/ Counter Sabotage/Inter-Allied Bureau of CE (BICE)
	3rd Section CE-Preventive Action/Protection of Secrets/CE instruction/Surveillance of sensitive areas/ Protection of the Sepcial Services/Security of prisoners and deportees
	4th Section SM Operations/Organization in the Army Units/Documentation/SM vanguard (France) and FFI/ Army Security
	5th Section Offensive CE (TR)/France and French Empire/Foreign/Disinformation—*Force A*/Liaison-Communications/HC Agents technical requirements

Arrests of Axis Agents for Espionage and Treason and endangering the external security of the French State 1935-1945

I.   France and French North Africa 1936-1942

1936: 40   1940: 1,250 (26 death sentences from January to May)
1937: 153   1941: 601*
1938: 274   1942: 1,223* (January to end October)
1939: 494 (18 death sentences)

*   Between January 1, 1941 and November 1, 1942 military courts in
     the so-called Free Zone and French North Africa issued 42 death
     sentences for espionage and treason benefiting the Axis.
     These numbers do not include the D-measures.

II. French North Africa and Colonies (1942-to mid-1944)
     1942: 503 (October to December)
     1943 and first quarter 1944: 759
     Total: 1,262, of which 270 were death sentences

III. France and French Zone of Occupation (June-1944-May-1945)
     4,589 arrests including 756 death sentences

     75% of these arrests were undertaken through the documentation
     seized from enemy intelligence services and the list of suspects estab-
     lished by the CE between 1940 and 1944.

Notes:

1.   In 1939 the counter espionage services of the 2nd Bureau (SR-SCR)
     included 35 officers or adjunct officers (15 of which at the Central
     Offices) and the *Surveillance du Territoire* had 120 policemen.
2.   From 1936 out of 9,886 arrests there had been 1,112 death sentences.
3.   These figures include 90% German agents, 8% Italian agents and 2%
     Spanish agents (who were working with questionnaires identical to
     those of the Abwehr from 1940 to 1943).

German Armed Forces
September 1939

Adolf Hitler
Oberster Befehlshaber der Wehrmacht

General W. Keitel
Chief of the OKW

ABWEHR

OKH Army *General von Brauchitsch*	Abwehr I-Espionage *Col. Pieckenbrock*
OKM Navy *Admiral Raeder*	Abwehr II-Sabotage and Disinformation *Col. Lahousen*
OKL Luftwaffe Forschungsamt *Reichmarshal Göring*	Abwehr III-Counterespionage and Security *Col. Von Bentivegni*
W.Fst Wehrmachtführungsstab Operations Staff *General Jost*	Ausland/Foreign and Military Missions *Admiral Burkner*
Abwehr/Ausland Abwehr *Admiral Canaris*	Zentralabteilung–Z-Organization and Administration *Col. Oster*

AUSLAND-ABWEHR
Organization in 1939-1940

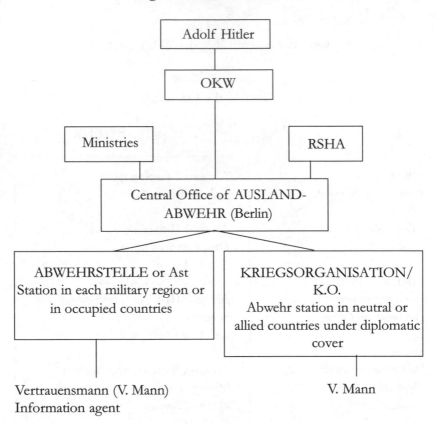

Notes:
1. The Ast offices have the identical organization as the central Service and handle specific geographic areas.
2. Within occupied countries the police action of Section III (counter espionage) is carried out by:

GEHEIMFELDPOLIZEI (GFP): similar to military security
FELDGENDARMERIE
GESTAPO after 1942

AUSLAND-ABWEHR
Organization in September 1939

Admiral Wilhelm Canaris

ABWEHR I Espionage	IZ Command—Centralization-Files IH Intelligence Foreign Armies IM Intelligence Foreign Navies IL Intelligence Foreign Air Forces IG Technical and scientific espionage research (photography, chemicals, radio) Iwi Economic espionage Ip Foreign press for military use Ic Contact intelligence (prisoners, aerial photography, etc.)
ABWEHR II Sabotage	Referat Ia Directorate-Administration—Finance Referat Ib Technical research—Laboratories Group I Action targeting minorities and political groups/Instruction of partisans and guerrillas Group II Organization and preparation of sabotage overseas Battalion and later BRANDENBURG Division: elite corps Specialized in commando-type missions

ABWEHR III
Counterespionage and
Military Security

IIIA   Directorate—Administration—
Finance

IIIw   Counterespionage in the Wehrmacht and POW camps
IIIwi Protection of sensitive areas (factories, fortifications, etc.)
IIIc   Protection of secrets, Surveillance of travel

IIIF	External counterespionage-Penetration of foreign intelligence services – Disinformation materials
IIIS	Espionage assessments – Legal issues
IIIN	Communications surveillance (postal check, wiretaps, cable, radio intercepts)
IIIFest	Counterespionage on the Siegfried Line (fortifications)

AUSLAND
Foreign and military
missions

Ausl.I	Foreign political analysis
Ausl.II	Relations with foreign armies
Ausl.III	Foreign armies organization and plans
Ausl.IV	Navies—Movements—Objectives
Ausl.V	Politics of the foreign press
Ausl.VI	International law
Ausl.VII	Foreign legal issues

Z General
administration

Zo General administration—Mobilization
   —Central file (400,000 names)
ZF Finances – Other
ZR Legal advisors to Abwehr personnel

Organization
of the German Police, Intelligence and Counterespionage
[Following the merger of the Abwehr into the RSHA]
1944

Adolf Hitler

Heinrich Himmler
Reichsführer SS—Head of the German Police

Ernst Kaltenbrunner
SS Gruppenführer—Head of the RSHA Berlin—Reich Security Office

Amt I   Personnel (recruitment—training)
Amt II   Organization, Administration, Technical issues
Amt III   Internal Security of the Reich (SD Inland)
Amt IV   GESTAPO   a.   Political opposition—Communism
                                    b.   Religious and Jewish issues
                                    c.   Files and internments
                                    d.   Foreign workers
                                    e.   Counter espionage
                                    f.   Border police
Amt V   Criminal police (KRIPO)
Amt VI   External Security (SD Ausland) *Walter Schellenberg*
                                    a.   Organization overseas
                                    b.   Western Europe
                                    c.   Eastern Europe – Japan
                                    d.   England – America
                                    e.   Central Europe
                                    f.   Technical office
                                    g.   Wiretaps – Decryptions
                                    h.   Sabotage (Skorzeny)
                                  Wi. Trade and industry
                                  Z   Counter espionage overseas (former Abwehr III)
Amt MIL Military intelligence (former Abwehr I and II)
                                  a.   Organization
                                  b.   West
                                  c.   East
                                  d.   Sabotage
                                  e.   Technical issues
                                  f.   Special operations
Amt VII   Ideological studies
                              Scientific missions
Amt N   Radio broadcasts

RSHA in France—1944

Ordnungspolizei (Berlin) SS Obergruppenführer Kurt Daluege
Ordnungspolizei in France (Paris) rue de la Faisanderie

Karl Oberg
Hoherer SS und Polizeiführer *Frankreich*
Deputy: Herbert Hagen (57 Boulevard Lannes, Paris)
Office for Travel Documents (Hotel d'Orsay) – Passport Office
(rue Huysmans)

Dr. Knochen
RSHA France
72-78, Avenue Foch, Paris

   I. Personnel 85, avenue Foch
  II. Administration 85, av. Foch
 III. Economic issues and Press office 60, av. Foch
 IV. GESTAPO SS Bömelburg and SS Stindt
     80-84, av. Foch and rue des Saussaies
     Communist issues: SS Schlüter
     Jewish issues: SS Rötke
     Counter espionage SS Kieffer
     Counter Resistance SS Wenzel
  V. Criminal Police (KRIPO) 76-78 av. Foch
 VI. Political intelligence: Bickler 76, av. Foch and Blvd. Flandrin
     England, America, Spain, Portugal
     France: SS Roland Nosek, Resistance SS Wentzel

Surveillance of French Police and Camps
85, Blvd. Foch
Special Court for the SS and German Police
7, Blvd. Flandrin

RSHA KOMMANDOS

(Mobile units on the model of the original Abwehr or RSHA)

Paris	SS Hagen later SS Heerd
Bordeaux	SS Nehring and SS Luther
Lyon	SS Knab and SS Barbie
Marseille	SS Senner SS Möhler and SS Dunker
Toulouse	SS Detering
Vichy	SS Marnitz, SS Reiche, SS Geissler later SS Bömelburg
Dijon	SS Muller-Meyer
Rennes	SS Pullmer and SS Grimm
Angers	SS Ernst
Nancy	SS von Krogh
Rouen	SS Muller
Montpellier	SS Hinrich and SS Tanzmann

Military Kommandos in France
(Former Abwehr I, II, III)

Former Abwehr I (Intelligence)	Kommando no. 120 Southern France Kommando no. 130 Northern France
Former Abwehr II (Sabotage)	Kommando no. 210 South and Western France Kommando no. 213 Northern France – Belgium Holland – Luxembourg
Former Abwehr III (Counterespionage)	Kommando no. 306 Paris and Western and Southwestern France Kommando no. 351 Eastern and Southeastern France Kommando no. 314 Franche-Comté and Lorraine

The intelligence service of the PPF (Beugras) was operating in North Africa and in France reporting to Colonels Stephan and Reile of the Abwehr.

This organization chart was established in 1944 with information received by French Counterespionage cross-checked against the interrogations of SS leaders.

Index

A

Abadie, Captain 316–17, 423–25, 445

Abadie, Mrs. 423

Abbas, Ferhat 211

Abetz, Otto 73, 77–8, 98, 104–06, 108, 164, 199, 208, 220, 225–26, 230–31, 244, 264, 284–86, 288–89, 301, 304

Abetz, Mrs. Otto 77, 231

Abrial, Admiral 86, 239

Abtery 273

Abtey, Captain 49, 84, 122, 196–97

Achard-James, Major 200

Achiary, André 125–26, 178–79, 239, 273–75, 299, 302

Adt 251

Agnely 57

Albert, a radio operator 393–96

Albrecht, Bertie 243–44, 248

Alexander, Harold 389, 391

Alexander, king of Serbia 115

Algaron, a newsman 232

Alibert, Raphaël 184, 220

Allard 251

Allemand xiii, 274, 352, 355, 357, 361, 368, 378

Alsfasser, Alphonse 418–20, 422

Alzugaray, Emilio 423–25

Amblard, *alias of* d'Autrevaux

Ambrosi 437

Amin al Husseini, Grand Mufti of Jerusalem 127, 272

Amourelle, a stenographer 108–09, 130

Andlauer 48

Andrieu, Odette 280

Angelo, *alias of* Seubert, Franz

Angevin, code name of an agent 245, 408

Anquetil, Bernard 205–07

Ansot, Captain 205, 264, 281, 368

Archen, Captain 131

Armand, *alias of* Czerniawski, Roman

Arnaud, Major 169, 466

Arnim von 389–90

Arnaud, Major 169, 466

Arsaguet, a Police Inspector 417–18

Asché, *alias of* Schmidt, Hans-Thilo

Aubert, Marc 82, 85–90, 95, 101, 388

Aubin, newsman 108–09, 130

Aubrac, Raymond 333, 335, 374

Auer 212

Avallard 414–15

Avon-Brunetière, Dr. 458

B

Bachelet, Police Superintendent 251

Badin, Colonel 125, 179

Badoglio, Pietro 48, 329, 382–83

Baker, Joséphine 196–97

Balafrej, Ahmed 127, 212, 384

Ballet 292, 299

Balloli 251

Barbaro, Colonel 48, 156

Barbat 413

Barbie, Klaus 337, 409, 475

Bardon, an aeronautical engineer 233–34

Baril, Colonel 185, 214–15, 217–18, 223, 225–28, 237–39, 268–70, 284, 293

Baron, a French politician 77

Baron, Mrs. 77

Barranco, Rosario 96, 100, 222–24, 300, 319, 329, 336, 381–83, 391, 423

Barre, General 353

Barriot, Captain 5

Bartlett, U.S. vice-consul 197

Battet, Admiral 284, 308

Bauer, a German agent 109

Bayonne, Navy officer 49–50, 186

Bazin, Colonel 212